The Critical Theory of Jürgen Habermas

The Critical Theory of Jürgen Habermas

Thomas McCarthy

The MIT Press
Cambridge, Massachusetts, and London, England

Second printing, 1982
First MIT Press paperback edition, 1981
Copyright © 1978 by
The Massachusetts Institute of Technology

All rights reserved. No part of this book may be reproduced in any form or by any means, electronic or mechanical, including photocopying, recording, or by any information storage and retrieval system, without permission in writing from the publisher.

This book was set in VIP Baskerville by Woodland Graphics, printed and bound by Halliday Lithograph Corporation in the United States of America

Library of Congress Cataloging in Publication Data

McCarthy, Thomas A
    The critical theory of Jürgen Habermas.

    Bibliography: p.
    Includes index.
    1. Habermas, Jürgen. 2. Criticism (Philosophy) 3. Theory (Philosophy)
4. Social evolution. 5. Communication—Social aspects. 6. System theory.
I. Title.
B3258.H324M32   193   78–4540
ISBN 0-262-13138-2 (hard)
ISBN 0-262-63073-7 (paper)

For my parents

Contents

Contents

Preface

A book of this length on a contemporary thinker calls for some explanation, especially when its subject is still relatively young and his work has only recently begun to be discussed in the English-speaking world. Jürgen Habermas is the dominant figure on the intellectual scene in Germany today, as he has been for the past decade. There is scarcely an area of the humanities or social sciences that has not felt the influence of his thought; he is master, in breadth and depth alike, of a wide range of specialized literatures. But his contributions to philosophy and psychology, political science and sociology, the history of ideas and social theory are distinguished not only by their scope but by the unity of perspective that informs them. This unity derives from a vision of mankind, our history and our prospects, that is rooted in the tradition of German thought from Kant to Marx, a vision that draws its power as much from the moral-political intention that animates it as from the systematic form in which it is articulated.

With the translation in recent years of a growing number of his books and articles, Habermas's influence has gradually spread to the English-speaking world. He is now widely recognized as a major figure in the postwar renewal of German philosophy and social theory. But his reception by Anglo-American thinkers has by no means been painless. It has been hindered by the usual problems of cultural distance attending the penetration of any work that is deeply rooted in the German tradition. If our appreciation of Kant is considerably developed, that of Hegel is decidedly less so; and Fichte and Schelling are still relegated to the nether world that we reserve for peculiarly German spirits. If Weber and Freud now have a firm place in our pantheon, Dilthey and Gadamer are still largely unknown. Moreover, the tradition of Western Marxism Habermas seeks to renew has remained comparatively underdeveloped here; a number of important works by Lukács, Korsch, Horkheimer, Adorno, and Marx himself were only recently translated. Then there are problems deriving from Habermas's own approach. In our empirically and analytically inclined culture, we are bound to be dismayed by someone who seems to thrive in the rarefied atmosphere of general ideas and who views social theory so broadly as to include virtually the entire range of systematic knowledge about man. And there are problems of style, dense and convoluted formulations that often seem impenetrable, problems exacerbated at times by inept translations that make what is already difficult impossible. Clearly these are formidable obstacles to an intelligent reception of Habermas's work. If one adds to this the fact that his writings assume the reader's familiarity with a wide range of disciplines, authors, and approaches, that he often makes his point by reviewing broad areas of research and steering ongoing discussions in new directions, the obstacles seem insuperable.

And yet the flow of translations continues, the readership constantly grows, and critical discussions proliferate. But in this very process it has become evident that the basic impediment to understanding Habermas is the lack of a systematic and comprehensive view of his thought. As a result, critical discussions, pro and con, are all too often marred by fundamental misunderstandings. This could hardly be otherwise. Only a portion of his work is available in English, and his most recent writings on the theories of communication and social evolution are represented only by a few scattered articles. It is this need that I hope to fill with the present study. My principal aim is to provide a reliable framework for the critical reception of Habermas's work in the English-speaking world. This aim simultaneously sets the limits of the study.

I have concentrated on explicating, interpreting, connecting, systematizing, supplying background, developing arguments, and the like. My critical energies have been directed primarily against opposing positions, in an effort to lend a dialectical form to the reconstruction of Habermas's views. Although my treatment of his position is obviously sympathetic, it is not, I trust, wholly uncritical. But I raise many points of criticism without developing them, and those that I draw out have been selected and shaped largely from considerations relating to the development of Habermas's own thought. (Thus, for example, the lengthy critique of *Knowledge and Human Interests* in section 2.5 of chapter 2 is intended not merely to demonstrate the problems inherent in this first attempt at systematization but also to make clear the very weighty considerations that motivated Habermas subsequently to recast his views.) In short, I have not attempted to say the last word on Habermas, but rather a first word that might open the way to intelligent discussion.

In the same vein, I make no claim to have provided an adequate account of the origins and development of his ideas. I view intellectual antecedents, contemporary influences, and the contributions of close collaborators (among them, Albrecht Wellmer, Claus Offe, Ulrich Oevermann, Rainer Döbert, and Klaus Eder) not from the distanced perspective of the historian but from a standpoint internal to Habermas's thought. I am not unaware of the irony involved in adopting this approach to the work of a man who himself insists that ideas be viewed historically and in their social contexts. But there are limits to what can be done well within the bounds of a single study, and this approach seemed to be the most effective for my purposes.

Finally this is not an intellectual biography. The organization of the book is more systematic than chronological; but developmental considerations do influence the order of presentation. Chapter 1 introduces the problem of the relation of theory to practice in very general terms, clarifies a few basic concepts (above all the distinction between "labor" and "interaction"), and sets the stage for Habermas's theory of cognitive interests. The writings dealt with belong in the main to the period before the publication of *Knowledge and Human Interests* in 1968. Chapter 2 focuses on that work, which in addition to being a historical prolegomenon is also a first attempt at systematization. After sketching the different interests underlying empirical-analytic, historical-hermeneutic, and critical-reflective inquiry, I review the basic argument of the book as a whole. Despite its immense suggestiveness, it is, I argue, seriously flawed; the weaknesses are dealt with in such a way as to point ahead to Habermas's more recent work.

From a systematic point of view, chapters 3 and 4 are the heart of this study. The former deals with methodological issues, tracing the development of Habermas's conception of critical theory from the late 1950s to the present. After critically surveying a number of approaches to the interpretive tasks of social inquiry, I examine in some detail the central points at issue between hermeneutics and critical theory, and between the latter and social systems theory. The final section provides an overview of Habermas's project for a theory of social evolution. In chapter 4 his recent work on communication theory, contained in a number of widely scattered publications, is brought together in a systematic way. Universal pragmatics, or the theory of communicative competence, is above all a concerted effort to rework the normative-theoretical foundations of critical theory. It is here that we find Habermas's account of the "logics" of truth and morality and the argument for their inseparability. The last section links the theory of communication to social inquiry through an examination of Habermas's writings on socialization. Chapter 5 adopts a more concrete perspective on the conceptual apparatus developed in the preceding chapters by examining its application to contemporary society. The analysis centers on legitimation problems originating in the basic structures of organized capitalism. This provides a context for reviewing some fundamental features of Habermas's critical theory in the concluding pages of the study.

I am aware that the question posed at the beginning of this preface—why a full-length study of Habermas's thought is worth the effort—has not been fully answered. For those readers already familiar with his work, further response is perhaps unnecessary; for the others, I can only add my assurance that it represents a rarely equaled combination of erudition and insight, of synthetic power and moral seriousness. At a time when social theory is disintegrating into ever more specializations with rather tenuous connections to the basic problems of our existence, a contribution of this order ought not to be lightly dismissed. Whether one ultimately agrees or disagrees with Habermas, there is no small advantage to be won from following the thread of his argument through the labyrinths of philosophy and the human sciences and contemplating the view of the whole that he proposes. And whatever one's political convictions, there is considerable benefit to be derived from seriously confronting his extended, carefully reasoned argument for a social order based on a public sphere free from domination in all its forms.

These personal assurances can, of course, be redeemed only in the reader's own encounter with Habermas. I have tried to provide an accurate, coherent, and forceful account of his position and of the arguments on which it rests. Many of these arguments presuppose considerable knowledge of specialized areas of research. For that reason neither Habermas's own writings nor this study make easy reading. In the case of the former, any effort is well spent. In the case of this work, I can only hope that my own shortcomings do not seriously detract from the power of the original.

Whenever possible I have cited available English translations of Habermas's works. In some instances I have altered them, without making special note of the fact, for the sake of accuracy, clarity, or consistency of terminology and style. Otherwise the translations from the German are my own. In addition to published works, the materials cited include unpublished papers that Habermas kindly made available to me.

I wish to acknowledge my indebtedness to the Alexander von Humboldt Foundation for a grant that enabled me to spend the 1975–1976 academic year at the Max Planck Institute in Starnberg, Germany; to Karl Ballestrem, Alasdair MacIntyre, and Marx Wartofsky who read the manuscript at various stages and offered valuable suggestions, many of which I adopted; to my students at Boston University who forced me to clarify my ideas in numerous discussions; to my wife Pat, and my teachers, Nikolaus Lobkowicz and Ernan McMullin for their help and encouragement over the years; to Inge Pethran and Linda Richards for typing the manuscript; and to Jürgen Habermas for his unreserved cooperation and unfailing kindness.

For the paperback edition a number of corrections and clarifications have been made, and references have been updated for sources translated and published in English since 1978. The short bibliography of Habermas's work in the original edition has been replaced by a more complete bibliography prepared by René Görtzen and Frederik van Gelder.

Acknowledgments

I would like to thank Suhrkamp Verlag, Frankfurt am Main, Germany, for permission to quote from the following works: *Erkenntnis und Interesse* © 1968, *Technik und Wissenschaft als 'Ideologie'* © 1968, *Zur Logik der Sozialwissenschaften* © 1970, *Hermeneutik und Ideologiekritik* © 1971, *Theorie der Gesellschaft oder Sozialtechnologie—Was leistet dis Systemforschung?* © 1971, *Philosophisch-politische Profile* © 1971, *Legitimationsprobleme im Spätkapitalismus* © 1973, *Kultur und Kritik* © 1973, *Sprachpragmatik und Philosophie* © 1976, *Zur Rekonstruktion des Historischen Materialismus* © 1976, and the introduction to their new edition of *Theorie und Praxis* © 1971; Luchterhand Verlag, Darmstadt and Neuwied, Germany, for permission to quote from *Theorie und Praxis* © 1963; Verlag Kiepenheuer & Witsch, Cologne, Germany, for permission to quote from the introduction to *Die Entwicklung des Ichs* © 1977; Beacon Press of Boston, Massachusetts, and Heinemann Educational Books, Ltd., of London, England, for permission to quote from the following English translations: *Toward a Rational Society* © 1970 by Beacon Press, *Knowledge and Human Interests* © 1971 by Beacon Press, *Theory and Practice* © 1973 by Beacon Press, and *Legitimation Crisis* © 1975 by Beacon Press; *Philosophy of the Social Sciences* for permission to quote from "A Postscript to *Knowledge and Human Interests*," 3 (1973): 157–189; and Jürgen Habermas for permission to quote from "Wahrheitstheorien," which was published in *Wirklichkeit und Reflexion: Walter Schulz zum 60. Geburtstag* (Pfullingen: Neske, 1973), pp. 211–265, as well as from a number of unpublished papers. Citations are credited individually in footnotes. Complete references can be found in the bibliography.

I would also like to thank *Human Studies* and René Görtzen and Frederik van Gelder for permission to include in this edition a modified version of "Jürgen Habermas: The Complete Oeuvre," 2 (1979): 285–300.

The Critical Theory of Jürgen Habermas

Chapter 1
On Theory and Practice
in Our Scientific Civilization

1.1 THE SCIENTIZATION OF POLITICS

Although the classical tradition of politics continued into the nineteenth century, its ultimate demise was prefigured some two centuries earlier. Adopting the ideal of knowledge of his time, Hobbes declared human behavior to be a legitimate object of scientific knowledge and set about constructing a science of politics. The subsequent emergence of specialized social sciences seeking to emulate the methodology of the natural sciences and the gradual decline of the classical view of political theory appear to have vindicated Hobbes's judgment. To be sure, the "scientization of politics" has never met with a universally positive reception. Early in the eighteenth century, Vico already rejected the presumption that "the method of scientific judgment" could be carried over into "the practice of prudence." And if the last traces of opposition seemed about to disappear in the decades after World War II, there has recently been a recrudescence of dissenting views—so much so, in fact, that yet another critique of positivist social science might seem unnecessary.[1] Nevertheless the epistemological, methodological, and moral-political issues surrounding the nature of social theory and its relation to social practice are still very much open. A systematic and theoretically adequate account of the relation of theory to practice, one capable of countering the hegemony of scientism on all fronts, is still outstanding. Meeting this need has been an abiding concern of Habermas's work.[2] His "theory of society conceived with practical intent" emerges from extended reflections on the nature of cognition, the structure of social inquiry, the normative basis of social interaction, and the political, economic, and sociocultural tendencies of the age. Before turning to these in chapters 2 through 5, I shall examine his "reckoning of profits and losses" in the transition from the classical doctrine of politics to the modern science of politics.[3]

For Aristotle politics was continuous with ethics, the doctrine of the good and just life. As such it referred to the sphere of human action, *praxis*, and was directed to achieving and maintaining an order of virtuous conduct among the citizens of the *polis*. The practical intention of politics (the cultivation of virtuous character in a moral-political order that rendered its citizens capable of leading a good and just life), as well as the nature of its subject matter (the changing and contingent conditions of such a life), determined its cognitive status. Politics, and practical philosophy generally, could not achieve the status of a rigorous science, of *episteme*. Because it had to take account of the contingent and variable, it had to rest content with establishing rules of a "more or less" and "in most cases" character. The capacity thereby cultivated, and the keystone of the virtuous character, was *phronesis*, a prudent understanding of variable situations with a view to what was to be done.

The relations of practical philosophy with the other two branches of knowledge—theoretical and productive—were rather distant. *Theoria* was directed to things that happen "always or for the most part," to the unchangeable and eternal, that is, to the divine. It might properly lay claim to apodictic knowledge, *episteme*, of the order and nature of the cosmos. This theoretical knowledge (desirable for its own sake) could supply only the barest presuppositions of practical knowledge (desired for the sake of action)—for example, by establishing a general picture of human nature as composed of rational and nonrational parts. For the rest, the two spheres converged only in the effects of theoretical wisdom on the life of the individual. The highest, divine-like activity open to man was that of his highest part, the rational soul. Through contemplation of the cosmos, the soul of the theoretician was brought mimetically into accord with the harmony and proportion of the cosmic order. But, as Aristotle went on to say, the purely contemplative life was an unattainable ideal for most, if not for all, men. Moreover the extent to which it could be realized depended on the proper ordering of the *polis*. Thus the life proper to men was primarily a life of virtuous action. And for this one could rely on nothing better than the cultivation of virtuous character, most importantly of prudential judgment. *Theoria* and *praxis* referred in the final analysis to different spheres of being.

On the other side, practical knowledge was not to be confused with productive knowledge. The spheres of *praxis* and *poiesis*, of moral-political action and the production of useful or beautiful artifacts, were no less distinct. Whereas the one domain was reserved for practical prudence, the other belonged properly to workmanlike skill or *techne*. The relation of productive knowledge (desired for the sake of making) to theoretical knowledge was just as distant, for theory concerned itself precisely with an order of reality that could neither be "made" nor "done" but only contemplated—the invariant and eternal, divine order of the cosmos. It could contribute nothing directly to the *techne* of the craftsman or artist, which was based on acquired skills and experiences. Like *phronesis*, *techne* was a precondition of the life of the *polis* in which the contemplative ideal could be pursued. But— again like *phronesis*—it could neither be derived from nor justified by theory.[4]

With the rise of modern science the classical constellation of theoretical, practical, and productive knowledge was drastically altered. Theory came to mean the logically integrated systems of quantitatively expressed, lawlike statements characteristic of the most advanced natural sciences. Although the pursuit of science for its own sake (that is, in order to comprehend the true order of nature) was historically at least as important as the Baconian motivation, *scientia propter potentiam,* a potential for predictive and technological application is intrinsic to theoretical knowledge of this sort. Given a description of the relevant initial conditions, scientific laws can be used (within certain limits) to predict future states of a system. Providing that the relevant factors are manipulable, these laws can also be used to produce a desired state of affairs.[5]

Contrary to widespread belief, this technological potential of the new science did not play a significant role in the industrial revolution. The relevant technological knowledge was much more the result of a centuries-old tradition of arts and crafts than the first fruits of the scientific revolution, of *techne* rather than technology. The close connection between pure and applied research which is familiar to us today arose gradually only in the nineteenth century.[6] Since that time the systematic, institutionalized connection between science and technology has undergone constant development, until today technological considerations play a dominant role in determining the direction of progress in many areas of pure science. At the same time craftsmanship, *techne,* has become less and less important for the reproduction of the material conditions of existence. Thus the classical conceptions of contemplative theory and theory-free *techne* have given way to the modern conceptions of scientific theory and theoretically grounded technology.

The classical conception of practical knowledge has undergone a similar, if less unequivocal, transformation. In the middle of the seventeenth century, Hobbes had already outlined a program that took human behavior as the material for a science of man, society, and the state. Given a correct understanding of the laws of human nature, it would be possible to establish once and for all the conditions for a proper ordering of human life. The classical instruction in leading a good and just life, the formation of virtuous character, and the cultivation of practical prudence were to be replaced by the application of a scientifically grounded social theory, by the production of the conditions that would lead to the desired behavior according to the laws of human nature. In this way the sphere of the practical was absorbed into the sphere of the technical. The practical problem of the virtuous life of the citizens of the *polis* was transformed into the technical problem of regulating social intercourse so as to ensure the order and well-being of the citizens of the state.

Subsequent developments in the natural and social sciences and the rise of positivist philosophy to interpret and justify these developments appear to have pushed the classical doctrine of politics into the irretrievable past. In its place we are left with a political science having little more than its name in common with the old politics. Whether this development represents just another episode in the steady march of science or instead involves some basic misconceptions of the foundations, methods, and goals of political inquiry is still a much debated issue. At the heart of the discussion lie conflicting conceptions of the relation of reason to action, of theory to practice.

At least since Max Weber's contribution to the *Werturteilsstreit*—the controversy over the role of value judgments in social inquiry—the claim to the title of social *science* has been taken to imply an exclusion of the normative elements associated with the classical tradition of politics.[7] The investigations into the "logic and methodology of science" carried out by the logical positivists and their successors ratified this separation. With the aid of the familiar distinctions between "is and ought," "facts and values," they argued that the application of *the* scientific method to the study of social phenomena required the rigorous avoidance of normative considerations. Value judgments did not admit of truth or falsity; they were not rationally (scientifically) decidable. Scientific knowledge could, of course, be brought to bear on practical matters—for example, in analyzing the preconditions and consequences of a given course of action, in weighing the economy and efficiency of alternative means to a desired end, or even in criticizing proposed ends from the point of view of their technical feasibility. But the choice of ends itself, the adoption of certain interests to the exclusion of others, was ultimately a question of values and not of facts, a matter for decision and not for demonstration. The failure to recognize and honor this strict separation of knowledge from morality was a principal cause for the retarded development of social *science.* The traditional insinuation of normative considerations into social inquiry could result in dogmatism and ideology but never in that cumulative progress of objective knowledge characteristic of empirical science.

Armed with the newly explicated concept of scientific methodology and the firm distinction between empirical knowledge and value judgments, positivist philosophy set itself the task of combating pseudoscience in all its forms. It unmasked the normative—and thus "noncognitive," "subjective," "irrational"—basis of the global views of man and society that were used to justify particular ethical and political systems. Masquerading as science and often even as a form of knowledge higher than science, these normative world views were actually a barrier to the progress of science and the rationalization of human life. Bringing to light their confusion of facts and values revealed their pseudoscientific, ideological character and robbed them of their power to blind. In this way the "positivist critique of ideology" certified its continuity with the tradition of the Enlightenment, its commitment to the centuries-old battle of reason against all forms of ignorance, superstition and dogmatism. It is, however, not at all clear how this commitment can itself be justified on positivist premises.

In the eighteenth century, reason was emphatically regarded as a guide to practice. Indeed the meaning of enlightenment was in the first instance practical: the liberation of mankind from internal and external compulsions whose power derived in large part from their nontransparency. Reason, as critical, penetrated this opacity and dissolved the appearance of objectivity, necessity, and inalterability.

Reason takes up a partisan position in the controversy between critique and dogmatism, and with each new stage of emancipation it wins a further victory. In this kind of practical reason, insight and the explicit interest in liberation by means of reflection converge. The higher level of reflection coincides with a step forward in the progress toward the autonomy of the individual, with the elimination of suffering and the furthering of concrete happiness. Reason involved in the argument against dogmatism has definitly taken up this interest as its own—it does not define the moment of decision as external to its sphere. Rather, the decisions of the subjects are measured rationally against that one objective decision which is required by the interest of reason itself. Reason has not as yet renounced the will to the rational.[8]

But this inherent relation of critical reason to enlightened practice is transformed in the positivist framework. The relation of theory to practice is conceived instead in terms of the potential for prognosis and technology proper to empirical theory.

For as our civilization has become increasingly scientific, the dimension within which theory was once directed to practice has become correspondingly constructed. The laws of self-reproduction demand of an industrially advanced society that it look after its survival on the escalating scale of a continually expanded technical control over nature and a continually refined administration of human beings and their relations to each other by means of social organization. In this system science, technology, industry and administration interlock in a circular process. In this process the relationship of theory to practice can now only assert itself as the purposive-rational application of techniques assured by empirical science.[9]

The limitation of reason, at the level of theory, to the disinterested employment of the scientific method and, at the level of practice, to the predictive and technological application of the empirical knowledge that results renders positivist philosophy incapable of justifying its own interests. If all values are subjective, if practical orientation in life is ultimately beyond rational justification, then the positivist commitment to science and technology and its opposition to dogmatism and ideology is itself subjective and rationally unjustifiable (that is, dogmatic). If, on the other hand, the interest in enlightenment is itself rational, then reason harbors a practical interest and cannot be exhaustively defined in terms of science and technology.

This dilemma is only one symptom of the peculiar tension between rationality and irrationality that haunts the positivist understanding of the relation of theory to practice in general. A particular form of reason, the scientific, is ascribed exclusive rights in the domain of theory. Understood as value-neutral, its only legitimate relation to practice is technical: the strengthening and refining of means for the purposive-rational (*zweckrational*) pursuit of ends that can themselves neither be derived from nor justified by theory.[10] All practical questions that cannot be posed and solved technically, that go beyond considerations of economy and efficiency of means, feasibility of ends, and the like, cannot be rationally resolved. They must be left to decisions that are, in the final analysis, subjective and irrational. The cost of abandoning a more comprehensive, substantial concept of reason is an irrational decisionism in the domain of practice.

But positivism is value-neutral in appearance only. By ceding a monopoly to a particular type of theory-practice relationship and actively criticizing all competing claims to a rational orientation of practice, "*nolens volens* it takes a partisan position in favor of progressive rationalization."[11] The scientific-technological rationality that it privileges reflects a particular interest, a particular relation to life (*Lebensbezug*):

The economy in the selection of purposive-rational means that are guaranteed by conditional predictions in the form of technical recommendations is the sole admissible "value"; and even it is not seen explicitly as a value because it seems simply to coincide with rationality as such. In fact, we have here the formalization of one sole relation to life, namely the experience of success as feedback control, built into systems of social labor and already realized in every elementary accomplishment of work.[12]

Any theory that relates to practice other than by extending and rationalizing our control over natural and social processes stands convicted of ideology. The social potential of theory is reduced to the power of technical control. Its potential for enlightened action, in the historical meaning of the term, disappears.

Emancipation by means of enlightenment is replaced by instruction in control over objective or objectified processes. Socially effective theory is no longer directed to the consciousness of human beings who live together and discuss matters with each other, but to the behavior of human beings who manipulate. . . . The real difficulty in the relation of theory to practice does not arise from this new function of science as a technological force, but rather from the fact that we are no longer able to distinguish between practical and technical power. Yet even a civilization that has been rendered scientific is not granted dispensation from practical questions; therefore a peculiar danger arises . . . no attempt is made to attain a rational consensus on the part of citizens concerning the practical control of their destiny. Its place is taken by the attempt to attain technical control over history by perfecting the administration of society, an attempt that is just as impractical as it is unhistorical.[13]

Habermas's argument then is that positivism conceals a commitment to technological rationality behind a facade of value-freedom. Through an aggressive critique of all nonscientific forms of theory and all nontechnological conceptions of the relation of theory to practice, it attempts to remove all barriers to the dominance of scientific thought and its technical utilization. But this amounts to partisanship for a particular form of rationalization with far-reaching implications for the organization of society. The implications vary with the level of rationalization envisaged.[14]

At the most elementary level—technological rationality in the strict sense—we employ techniques placed at our disposal by science for the realization of specific goals. Instrumental action is rationalized in this sense to the extent that the organization of means to defined ends is guided by technical rules based on empirical knowledge. The information provided by empirical science in the form of lawlike regularities and scientifically tested predictions replaces traditional criteria of appropriateness, as well as rules of experience developed unsystematically in the arts and crafts. If, however, we are faced with a choice between alternative means that are, technically speaking, equally suitable and functionally equivalent, a rationalization on a second level is required. Decision theory clarifies the relation between alternative techniques and given goals on the one hand, and value systems and maxims for reaching decisions on the other. Purposive-rational action is rationalized in this sense to the extent that the choice between possible alternatives is correctly deduced from preference rules and decision procedures. This type of rationality refers to the form and not the content of decisions. The value system on which a choice is based, and thus the results of a decision, need not be reasonable in the ordinary substantive sense.

If the progressive rationalization of practice is limited to these first two levels, there remains a core of irrationality in the orientation to values, goals, and needs.

On the first two levels the rationality of conduct enforces an isolation of values which are removed from any and every cogent discussion and can only be related to given techniques and concrete goals in the form of hypothetically entertained imperatives. . . . The subjectivistic reduction of the interests which are decisive in the orientation for action to "sentiments" or "perceptions" which cannot be rationalized beyond that is a precise expression for the fact that the value freedom central to the technological concept of rationality functions within the system of social labor, and that all the other interests of life are subordinated for the benefit of the sole interest in efficiency and economy of means. The competing interest perspectives, hypostasized to values, are excluded from discussion. Revealingly enough, according to the criteria of technological rationality agreement on a collective value system can never be achieved by means of enlightened discussion carried on in public politics, thus by way of consensus rationally arrived at, but only by summation or compromise—values are in principle beyond discussion.[15]

This conception of the relation of theory to practice is frequently invoked in support of *decisionistic models* for the organization of society.[16] According to Max Weber, for example, the fact that political practice can never be sufficiently legitimated through reason implies a strict separation of the functions of the expert from those of the politician. Although the politician uses the technical knowledge of the expert, his exercise of power ultimately rests on rationally unjustifiable decisions among competing values and interests and on the will to carry them out. In our own time, the development of the social sciences as applied sciences in the service of administration is nourished by a related tendency to withdraw the ends of political practice from rational reflection and leave them to the outcome of competition among existing interest groups. But decisionistic models of the relation of technical expertise to political practice are increasingly giving way to *technocratic models* in which the objective necessity disclosed by experts seems to predominate over the decisions of leaders.

The dependence of the professional on the politician appears to have reversed itself. The latter becomes a mere agent of a scientific intelligentsia which, in concrete circumstances, elaborates the objective implications and requirements of available techniques and resources as well as of optimal strategies and rules of control. . . . The politician would then be at best something like a stopgap in a still imperfect rationalization of power, in which the initiative has in any case passed to scientific analysis and technical planning.[17]

This development can be related to conceptions of the rationalization of practice that go beyond those previously mentioned. In situations that call for the rational calculation of conduct in the face of opponents who also act rationally in the pursuit of competing interests, the elementary forms of rationalization no longer suffice. Game theory clarifies strategies of control over situations in which information remains incomplete in principle because the opponent also has a choice between alternative plans of action. Strategic action is rationalized in this sense to the extent that decision-making processes are systematically organized so as to maximize the possibilities of self-assertion (or minimize risks and so forth) in such competitive situations. At this level even the formation of values is subject to criteria of rationalization. The value systems that remained external and prior to purposive-rational action at the first two levels are now relativized in terms of the superordinate value of self-assertion. That is, instead of assuming a particular hierarchy of values as given, as an independent variable, the suitability of different value systems is itself measured against a basic formalized value.

At a fourth level of rationalization, this formalized notion of system goals is connected with the notion of feedback mechanisms in the idea of a self-regulating system. Systems theory analyzes the structure and functioning of self-regulating systems with a view to their capacity for self-maintenance in complex environments. Action systems are rationalized in this sense to the extent that their steering mechanisms guarantee the fulfillment of certain formalized system goals (such as stability and adaptability) necessary for self-maintenance. At this stage of rationalization, critical reflection on traditional values as values is rendered superfluous, for now they "enter as liquid mass into the adaptive procedures of a machine which stabilizes its own equilibrium and programs itself."[18]

Habermas regards the idea of a cybernetically self-regulated organization of society as the highest expression of the technocratic consciousness. In this "negative utopia of technical control over history," man appears not only as a homo faber objectifying himself in his achievements and products, but as a homo fabricatus totally integrated into his technical apparatus. The traditional view of society as a system of interaction among human beings who consciously organize their practice through communication is abandoned for an "instinct-like self-stabilization of social systems" in which the political enlightenment of the citizenry becomes superfluous.[19] To the extent, therefore, that the positivist commitment to scientific-technological rationality encompasses these higher forms of rationalization, it implies a substantive philosophy of history.

The substantive rationality suppressed in the innocent partisanship for formal rationality reveals, in the anticipated concept of a cybernetically self-regulated organization of society, a tacit philosophy of history. This is based on the questionable thesis that human beings control their destinies rationally to the degree to which social techniques are applied, and that human destiny is capable of being rationally guided in proportion to the extent of cybernetic control and the application of these techniques. But such a rational administration of the world is not simply identical with the solution of the practical problems posed by history. There is no reason for assuming that a continuum of rationality exists extending from the capacity for technical control over objectified processes to the practical mastery of historical processes. The root of the irrationality of history is that we "make" it without, however, having been able until now to make it consciously. A rationalization of history cannot therefore be furthered by an extended power of control on the part of manipulative human beings, but only by a higher stage of reflection, a consciousness of acting human beings moving forward in the direction of emancipation.[20]

Both decisionistic and technocratic models of political practice reflect the transformation of practical into technical questions and their consequent withdrawal from public discussion. In the former the citizenry serves only to legitimate ruling groups by acclamation through periodic plebiscites. Political decisions themselves remain beyond the authority of rational discussion in the public sphere; decision-making power can be legitimized but not rationalized.[21] In the technocratic models, on the other hand, the exercise of power can be rationalized but once again only at the expense of democracy. The reduction of political power to rational administration—that is, administration guided by theoretical insight into what is objectively necessary (for stability, adaptability, growth, and so forth)—deprives the public sphere of any function save that of legitimating the administrative personnel and judging the professional qualifications of officials. In neither model does the public body of citizens conferring in an unrestricted fashion about matters of the commonweal play an essential role.

The triumph of the technocratic consciousness would accordingly mean the final demise of the liberal model of the public sphere that arose in the eighteenth century and persists, despite marked weakening, in the social welfare democracies of today.[22] It would mean the surrender of the idea of rationalizing power through the medium of public discussion that is both critical in intent and institutionally guaranteed. In its place there would remain at most the need for public relations work to secure for ruling elites the loyalty of a depoliticized public.

In opposition to these conceptions, Habermas proposes a model of "the dialectic of enlightened will and self-conscious potential." Dewey already analyzed the interdependence of values and techniques that can be utilized for the satisfaction of value-oriented needs. He argued that value convictions persist only to the extent that they can be connected to available and imaginable techniques for their realization. Failing this connection, they become functionless for practice and tend to die out as ideologies. On the other hand, the continued development and improvement of techniques does not simply remain bound to traditional values. Increased technological potential can itself give rise to new interest situations from which emerge new values. From this point of view, the decisionistic separation of questions of fact from questions of value appears abstract; there is a critical interaction between practical orientations and available techniques.

Thus, on the one hand the development of new techniques is governed by a horizon of needs and historically determined interpretations of these needs, in other words, by value systems. This horizon has to be made explicit. On the other hand, these social interests, as reflected in the value systems, are regulated by being tested with regard to the technical possibilities and strategic means for their gratification. In this manner they are partly confirmed, partly rejected, articulated and reformulated, or denuded of their ideologically transfigured and compelling character.[23]

Once this interaction is recognized, Habermas goes on, a fundamental problem of our scientific civilization becomes clearer: "How can the relation between technical progress and the social life-world, a relation that is today still clothed in a primitive, traditional and unchosen form, be reflected upon and brought under the control of rational discussion?"[24] In some ways this is a very old problem. It is distinctive of its present form, however, that available techniques are no longer restricted to the fruits of the traditional crafts but have assumed the form of science and technology and that practical orientations are no longer naively defined in traditional terms but are mediated through historical and sociological consciousness. In this situation, Habermas argues, rational discussion cannot be focused exclusively on technical means—for "technology does not release men from action. Just as before, conflicts must be decided, interests realized and interpretations found through action and transaction structured by ordinary language."[25] Nor can it be focused exclusively on the application of traditional norms of behavior—for "historicism has broken the natural-traditional validity of action-orienting value systems."[26] Instead the reflection that is required must bring the social potential constituted by technical knowledge and ability into rational connection with the practical orientations that determine the conduct of life. It is just this type of reflection that the technocratic consciousness blocks, and in doing so it fulfills the ideological function of concealing behind a facade of objective necessity the social interests that actually determine technological development.

The assertion that politically consequential decisions are reduced to carrying out the immanent exigencies of disposable techniques and that therefore they can no longer be made the theme of practical considerations, serves in the end merely to conceal preexisting, unreflected social interests and prescientific decisions. . . . The direction of technical progress is still largely determined today by social interests that arise autochthonously out of the compulsion of the reproduction of social life without being reflected upon and confronted with the declared political self-understanding of social groups. In consequence, new technical capacities erupt without preparation into existing forms of life-activity and conduct. New potentials for expanded power of technical control make obvious the disproportion between the results of the most organized rationality and unreflected goals, rigidified value-systems and obsolete ideologies.[27]

Habermas contends that a reflected "dialectic of potential and will," that is, a rational mediation between technical progress and the conduct of social life, can be realized only through basing political decision-making processes on general and public discussion free from domination. The notion of the enlightenment of political will can be broken down into several analytically distinguishable aspects. To begin with, the historically determined, tradition-bound preunderstanding (*Vorverständnis*) of practical interests and needs can be explicated hermeneutically with a view to articulating previously unreflected social interests. But hermeneutic reflection as such does not call into question the imperative force of traditional norms and interpretations; it merely clarifies them.[28] Validity claims sanctioned by tradition can, however, be analytically dissolved or revised, as well as redeemed, by critical social science. The critique of ideology pushes beyond any historically generated self-understanding to the constellation of economic, political, and social interests that it reflects. In unmasking the ideologically sanctioned suppression of common interests, it contributes to a reinterpretation of practical needs, corresponding goals, and action-orienting norms and values. At the same time, these needs, goals, norms, and values can become specific and determinate only in relation to available and potential techniques for the realization of interests. In this sense self-consciousness about technical potential is an essential aspect of the enlightenment of political will.

This is only one side of the coin. The dialectic of enlightened will and self-conscious potential also has implications for the pace and direction of technological development. The attempt to bring under rational control the traditional, unplanned relations between technical progress and the social life-world requires the self-conscious formulation of research policy. This in turn requires both the articulation of originally vague practical problems to a point where the development of specific technologies and strategies become relevant to their solution, as well as the translation of scientific-technological information into potential answers to practical questions. Moreover proposed technical solutions have to be evaluated in view of the total context in which their practical consequences will be felt—that is, on the basis of interpretations of concrete historical situations, their potentials, institutions, and interests. The whole process moves in a circle.

The attempt at a long-term research and education policy oriented to immanent possibilities and objective consequences . . . must enlighten those who take political action about their tradition-bound self-understanding of their interests and goals in relation to socially potential knowledge and capacity. At the same time it must put them in a position to judge practically, in the light of these articulated and newly interpreted needs, in what direction they want to develop their knowledge and capacity in the future. The discussion necessarily moves within a circle. For only to the extent that knowing the technical potential of our historically determined will, we orient ourselves to the given situation can we know in turn what specifically oriented expansion of our technical potential we want for the future.[29]

In contrast to decisionistic and technocratic models of the relation of technical progress to the conduct of social life, this conception, Habermas argues, is essentially related to democracy, understood as "the institutionally secured forms of general and public communication that deal with the practical question of how men can and want to live under the objective conditions of their ever-expanding power of control."[30] Central to this conception is the idea of a permanent communication between the sciences, considered in terms of their political relevance, and informed public opinion. The public as a political institution, the "public sphere" in which public opinion can be formed through unrestricted discussion of matters of general interest, is assigned a critical and controlling function in relation to the transposition of technology into practice. Thus the enlightenment of political will, self-conscious of its potential, not only *proceeds from* the public sphere—that is, from the hermeneutically and critically reflected interpretation of a concrete historical situation—but *through* it—that is, through the unrestricted discourse of citizens about what the situation calls for—and must *lead back* to it:

The enlightenment of political will can become effective only within the communication of citizens. For the articulation of needs in accordance with technical knowledge can be ratified exclusively *in the consciousness of the political actors themselves*. Experts cannot delegate to themselves this act of confirmation from those who have to account with their life histories for the new interpretation of social needs and for accepted means of mastering problematic situations.[31]

For the rationalization of politics in this sense, the relation of technical progress to political enlightenment is constitutive. It transpires in the thoughts and actions of political agents and not above their heads or behind their backs.

Whatever its attractions, this alternative model is far from being immediately plausible. It has been sketched in strokes too broad for detailed appraisal and there has as yet been little mention of the epistemological, methodological, and empirical presuppositions of its application. Suppose, for instance, that the positivist restrictions on reason and knowledge could be vindicated; then the notion of a rationalization of practice, as practice, on which the model relies would be without foundation (an epistemological "nonstarter"). Again if positivists are correct in claiming that social inquiry, if it is to be scientific, must adopt the empirical-analytic methods of the natural sciences, then the idea of a critical social theory oriented to enlightenment and emancipation would appear to be a (politically dangerous) regression. Furthermore it is painfully clear that the empirical conditions for the application of the model are absent. The "structural change in the bourgeois public realm," its decline as a political institution, has gone hand in hand with a depolitization of the mass of the population and a privatization of needs and interests. Instead of a general and unrestricted discussion of practical questions, there is a seemingly irresistible tendency toward a bureaucratized exercise of power complemented by a public realm confined to spectacles and periodic acclamation. We shall have an opportunity to consider these and other problems in the remainder of this study. Before doing so, however, we shall take a closer look at Habermas's distinction between purposive-rational and communicative action, for this is the key to his notion of two analytically distinct, yet historically interdependent, processes of rationalization: the technical and the practical.

1.2 LABOR AND INTERACTION: THE CRITIQUE OF INSTRUMENTAL REASON

For Marx the difficulties in arriving at an adequate conception of critique arose not from the side of the positive sciences but from the false claims of the philosophy of his time. The Young Hegelians, he argued, saw in the conflicts of the day only the critical confrontation of philosophy with the world, without realizing that philosophy itself belonged to this world as its ideal expression and complement. As a result, their critique remained abstract, capable at best of achieving "a merely theoretical emancipation." Political emancipation actually required the "negation of previous philosophy, of philosophy as philosophy."[1] On the other hand, natural science was a paradigmatic instance of thinking that constantly proved its truth in practice. Accordingly the establishment of an adequate mode of critique required the justification of its scientific character against philosophy.

In the first of his *Theses on Feuerbach,* Marx based the rejection of traditional materialism and idealism on the notion of *praxis.*

The chief defect of all previous materialism (including Feuerbach's) is that the object, actuality, sensuousness is conceived only in the form of the *object* or *perception,* but not as *sensuous human activity, practice,* not subjectively. Hence, in opposition to materialism the *active* side was developed by idealism—but only abstractly since idealism naturally does not know actual, sensuous activity as such.[2]

In distinguishing his own scientific form of critique from the philosophical modes of critique practiced by the Young Hegelians, Marx went on to interpret this "sensuous human activity," this "practice," as labor; material production became the basic paradigm for his analysis of human action. The reduction of *praxis* to *techne,* which this suggests, was offset somewhat by Marx's conception of labor as social labor: the productive activity of man took place in symbolically mediated institutional settings; productive forces were applied to nature only within definite relations of production. Nevertheless material production and social interaction were not viewed as two irreducible dimensions of human practice. Instead the latter was incorporated into the former. For Marx the reproduction of the human species took place primarily in the dimension of the reproduction of the material conditions of life. In capitalist society, in particular, all social phenomena were to be explained in terms of their material (economic) basis. This reductivist line of thought is clearly expressed in the famous preface to *A Contribution to the Critique of Political Economy:*

In the social production of their existence, men inevitably enter into definite relations, which are independent of their will, namely relations of production appropriate to a given stage in the development of their material forces of production. The totality of these relations of production constitutes the economic structure of society, the real foundation, on which arises a legal and political superstructure and to which correspond definite forms of social consciousness. The mode of production of material life conditions the general process of social, political and intellectual life. It is not the consciousness of men that determines their existence, but their social existence that determines their consciousness.[3]

It is precisely this reductivist model—the independence of the "laws" of social life from the consciousness of men—to which Marx frequently appealed in justifying the scientific character of his critique.[4]

On the other hand, Marx's own critique of political economy clearly transcends the narrow categorical framework he articulated. His empirical analyses incorporate in an essential way the structure of symbolic interaction and the role of cultural tradition. To this dimension belong the configurations of consciousness that Marx calls ideology, as well as their reflective critique, the formation of class consciousness and its expression in revolutionary practice. His theory is essentially a "critical" one. It is both an analysis of the crisis-ridden dynamics of the capitalist economy and a critique of ideology, an empirical theory and the critical consciousness of revolutionary practice. It becomes practical only by awakening class consciousness through initiating a process of self-understanding. On this reading, which is essentially that of Habermas, there is a basic unresolved tension in Marx between the reductivism and scientism of his theoretical self-understanding and the dialectical character of his concrete social inquiry.[5]

From the time of the Second International this ambiguity was resolved in official Marxism by an almost exclusive focus on the scientistic side of Marx's work. Dialectical materialism became a general ontology of nature, history, and thought that enabled its adherents to discover the laws behind the phenomena. Knowledge of the laws of motion of society and history made possible the prediction and control of social processes. Thus "DiaMat" could be used to legitimate party politics and technocratic social management. Ideology, as a particular case of the general dependence of thought on matter, forfeited the internal relation to critique and emancipation that it held for Marx. The critique of political economy, viewed as a deterministic science of the "iron laws" of the development and inevitable downfall of capitalism, could be used to legitimate the severance of "revolutionary practice" from the formation of class consciousness—in a variety of forms from "vanguard" activism to opportunistic quietism.

Since the early 1920s, Western Marxists have tended to adopt a quite different point of view. In his analysis of the progressive rationalization of modern life, Max Weber had articulated a problem that was to become their central preoccupation. With the concept of rationalization, he attempted to grasp a whole complex of tendencies related to scientific and technical progress and its effects on the institutional framework of traditional society. These included the extension of the areas of society subject to criteria of rational decision (such as economic activity, private law, and bureaucratic authority), the progress of industrialization and its consequences (such as the urbanization of the mode of life), the bureaucratization of administration and the expansion of bureaucratic control, the radical devaluation of tradition, and the progressive secularization and disenchantment of the world. Whatever the ambiguities in his own feelings toward this process, Weber clearly regarded it as irreversible: modern man was fated to live in a "shell of bondage." A socialist revolution, in particular, could lead only to a further extension of bureaucratic control.

Weber's conclusions presented a clear challenge to Marxist theory, especially in its scientistic form. Lukács responded in the early 1920s by attempting to integrate the analysis of the process of rationalization and bureaucratization into the critique of political economy.[6] He reinterpreted rationalization in terms of the "reification of consciousness" and traced the latter back to the "fetishism of commodities" that Marx had analyzed in the first volume of *Capital*. In this way, rationalization could be regarded as a consequence of the universalization of the commodity form in capitalist society. The internal breakdown of capitalism would then create the objective possibility of overcoming the reification of consciousness. Weber's pessimistic conclusions were unjustified.

Lukács's recognition of the ideological functions that the fetishism of commodities fulfilled in capitalist society was shared by the members of the Frankfurt school in the early 1930s, but there was a noticeable shift in emphasis. Although they presupposed the essential correctness of Marx's critique of political economy, they questioned the assumption that the internal development of capitalism would create not only the objective conditions but also the subjective conditions for a transformation of society. There was a recognized need to supply the missing link between Marx's critique of political economy and his theory of revolution through systematically incorporating the sociocultural dimensions neglected by "mechanical" Marxism. Post–World War I capitalism was no longer liberal capitalism. The growth of the interventionist state, the progressive rationalization and bureaucratization of institutions, the increasing interdependence of science and technology, and the "reification" of consciousness were aspects of a social formation whose analysis required a further development of Marx's thought.[7]

In their major collaborative effort of the postemigration years, the *Dialectic of Enlightenment,* Horkheimer and Adorno clearly articulated the revisions of the categorical framework of historical materialism that had been underway since Lukács.[8] For Marx, the overcoming of philosophy as philosophy was the precondition for establishing critique as scientific. For Horkheimer and Adorno, in contrast, the overcoming of scientism was the precondition for restoring Marxist theory as critique. Philosophical idealism, in which the ideals of reason and freedom were kept alive—albeit in a distorted form—was replaced by positivist materialism as the chief enemy of critical thought. The "critique of instrumental reason" became the principal task of critical theory, for in creating the objective possibility of a truly human society, the progressive mastery of nature through science and technology simultaneously transformed the potential subjects of emancipation. The reification of consciousness was the price paid for the progressive liberation from material necessity. For Horkheimer and Adorno, then, human emancipation could be conceived only as a radical break with merely "formal" rationality and merely "instrumental" thought.

More recently Herbert Marcuse has made the "political content of technical reason" the point of departure for his critique of advanced capitalism. He argues that formal rationality has specific substantive implications. Not only does it remove from reflection the social interests that determine the application of techniques, but it is limited by its very structure to relations of possible technical control. As he puts it:

The very concept of technical reason is perhaps ideological. Not only the application of technology but technology itself is domination (of nature and men)—methodical, scientific, calculated, calculating control. Specific purposes and interests of domination are not foisted upon technology "subsequently" and from the outside; they enter the very construction of the technical apparatus. Technology is always a historical-social *project*: in it is projected what a society and its ruling interests intend to do with men and things. Such a "purpose" of domination is "substantive" and to this extent belongs to the very form of technical reason.[9]

The intrinsic relation of technical reason to domination shows that what Weber called "rationalization" realizes "not rationality as such, but rather, in the name of rationality, a specific form of unacknowledged domination."[10] It remains "unacknowledged" because the institutionalized growth of the forces of production following from scientific and technological progress itself becomes the basis of legitimation for the social system: the existing relations of production present themselves as the technically necessary organizational form of a rationalized society. In Marcuse's words:

In this universe, technology also provides the great rationalization of the unfreedom of man and demonstrates the "technical" impossibility of being autonomous, of determining one's own life. For this unfreedom appears neither as irrational nor as political, but rather as submission to the technical apparatus which enlarges the comforts of life and increases the productivity of labor. Technological rationality thus protects rather than cancels the legitimacy of domination and the instrumentalist horizon of reason opens on a rationally totalitarian society.[11]

Thus reason loses its function as a critical standard against which to measure the existing organization of society; it becomes instead the ideological basis of its legitimation and an instrument for its perfection: "what can still be said is at best that society is 'poorly programmed.'"[12] Marcuse's conclusion, like that of Horkheimer and Adorno, is that human emancipation requires a radical break with "one-dimensional" thought.

Habermas is in general agreement on the need for a critique of instrumental reason to restore the philosophical dimension to critical theory: "the latter occupies its distinctive position between philosophy and positivism in such a manner that a critical self-enlightenment of positivism leads into the same dimension at which Marx arrived, so to speak, from the opposite direction."[13] But he feels that the earlier attempts of the Frankfurt school often verged on a romantic rejection of science and technology as such.

If the phenomenon on which Marcuse bases his social analysis, i.e., the peculiar *fusion of technology and domination*, rationality and oppression, could not be interpreted otherwise than as a world "project," as Marcuse says in the language of Sartre's phenomenology, contained in the material a priori of the logic of science and technology and determined by class interest and historical situation, then social emancipation could not be conceived without a complementary revolutionary transformation of science and technology themselves. In several passages Marcuse is tempted to pursue this idea of a New Science in connection with the promise, familiar in Jewish and Protestant mysticism, of the "resurrection of fallen nature." This theme, well known for having penetrated into Schelling's (and Baader's) philosophy via Schwabian Pietism, returns in Marx's *Paris Manuscripts*, constitutes today the central thought of Bloch's philosophy, and, in reflected forms, also directs the more secret hopes of Walter Benjamin, Max Horkheimer, and Theodor W. Adorno.[14]

Habermas's own view is that while the specific historical forms of science and technology depend on institutional arrangements that are variable, their basic logical structures are grounded in the very nature of purposive-rational action. As long as this does not change, as long as human beings have to seek their own self-preservation and emancipation from material necessity through social labor aided by means that substitute for work, there can be no "more humane" replacement for scientific-technical progress: "technology, if based at all on a project, can only be traced back to a project of the human species *as a whole*, and not to one that could be historically surpassed."[15]

The real problem, Habermas argues, is not technical reason as such but its universalization, the forfeiture of a more comprehensive concept of reason in favor of the exclusive validity of scientific and technological thought, the reduction of *praxis* to *techne*, and the extension of purposive-rational action to all spheres of life. The proper response, then, lies not in a radical break with technical reason but in properly locating it within a comprehensive theory of rationality. As a first step in this direction, Habermas breaks down Marx's concept of "sensuous human activity" into two components, which, though interdependent in social practice, are nevertheless analytically distinguishable and mutually irreducible: labor or purposive-rational action, and social interaction or communicative action. Social systems expand their control over outer nature with the help of forces of production. For this they require technically utilizable knowledge incorporating empirical assumptions with a claim to truth. "Inner nature" is adapted to society with the help of normative structures in which needs are interpreted and actions prohibited, licensed, or enjoined. This transpires in the medium of norms that have need of justification. Only on the basis of a distinction between work according to technical rules and interaction according to valid norms can we reconstruct the development of the human species as a historical process of technological and—interdependently—institutional and cultural development. Political emancipation cannot be identified with technical progress. While rationalization in the dimension of instrumental action signifies the growth of productive forces and extension of technological control, rationalization in the dimension of social interaction signifies the extension of communication free from domination. — *explain*

Habermas develops this distinction at a number of levels. At a "quasi-transcendental" level, the theory of cognitive interests distinguishes the technical interest in prediction and control of objectified processes from the practical interest in maintaining distortion-free communication.[16] At a methodological level, a distinction is drawn between empirical-analytic inquiry and hermeneutic or critical inquiry.[17] At the sociological level, subsystems of purposive-rational action are distinguished from the institutional framework in which they are embedded. And at the level of social evolution, the growth in productive forces and technological capacity is distinguished from the extension of interaction free from domination.[18] For the present I shall be concerned only with elucidating the fundamental difference between purposive-rational and communicative action.

In "Technology and Science as 'Ideology,'" Habermas formulates the distinction at some length:

By "work" or *purposive-rational action* I understand either instrumental action or rational choice or their conjunction. Instrumental action is governed by *technical rules* based on empirical knowledge. In every case they imply empirical predictions about observable events, physical or social. These predictions can prove correct or incorrect. The conduct of rational choice is governed by *strategies* based on analytic knowledge. They imply deductions from preference rules (value systems) and decision procedures; these propositions are either correctly or incorrectly deduced. Purposive-rational action realizes defined goals under given conditions. But while instrumental action organizes means that are appropriate or inappropriate according to criteria of an effective control of reality, strategic action depends only on the correct evaluation of possible alternative choices, which results from calculation supplemented by values and maxims.

By "interaction," on the other hand, I understand *communicative action,* symbolic interaction. It is governed by *binding consensual norms,* which define reciprocal expectations about behavior and which must be understood and recognized by at least two acting subjects. Social norms are enforced through sanctions. Their meaning is objectified in ordinary language communication. While the validity of technical rules and strategies depends on that of empirically true or analytically correct propositions, the validity of social norms is grounded only in the intersubjectivity of the mutual understanding of intentions and secured by the general recognition of obligations. Violation of a rule has a different consequence according to the type. *Incompetent* behavior which violates valid technical rules or strategies, is condemned per se to failure through lack of success; the "punishment" is built, so to speak, into its rebuff by reality. *Deviant* behavior, which violates consensual norms, provokes sanctions that are connected with the rules only externally, that is by convention. Learned rules of purposive-rational action supply us with *skills*, internalized norms with *personality structures*. Skills put us into a position to solve problems; motivations allow us to follow norms.[19]

Because this distinction is so fundamental to Habermas's project as a whole, I shall examine it in some detail.

The distinction within the sphere of purposive-rational action between strategic and instrumental action is an attempt to separate analytically criteria of rational choice from criteria of technical appropriateness. That is, one can—as in decision theory—regard empirical knowledge in the form of technical rules as part of the information basis relevant to a decision. Given the information basis and the preference rules that specify the total objective of an action, it is possible to analyze different decision procedures from the point of view of maximizing expected utilities. (There are a number of different possibilities here; for example, the "maximin" rule directs us to maximize the minimum expected utility, whereas the "maximax" directs us to maximize the maximum expected utility.)[20] Habermas considers the distinction important because it permits us to separate the contribution of technical progress to the rationalization of action from the rationalization effected by improvements in decision-making procedures themselves. But it is misleading to present the distinction, as he does here, as one between two *types* of action. Rational decision and the application of technically appropriate means appear rather to be two *moments* of purposive-rational action. In rationally pursuing certain specified ends, the agent must take account of both the available information (including general laws, empirical regularities, technical possibilities, particular circumstances, alternative means and their different probabilities of success, the side-effects and after-effects of employing the different means, and so forth) and the preference rules and decision maxims that he has adopted. The fact that questions concerning the technical appropriateness of means can be distinguished from questions concerning the correctness of inferences from preference and decision rules is not sufficient grounds for distinguishing different types of action.

The confusion is compounded when Habermas, in other contexts, uses the term strategic action to refer to action that is social in Max Weber's sense ("it takes account of the behavior of others and is thereby oriented in its course")[21] and at the same time purposive-rational in Weber's sense ("determined by expectations as to the behavior of external objects and of other men, and making use of these expectations as 'conditions' or 'means' for the rational, success-oriented pursuit of the agent's own rationally considered ends").[22] This usage predominates in contexts in which Habermas is concerned with the differences between social interaction governed by traditionally valid consensual norms and social interaction in spheres set free (legally and morally) for the strategic maximizing of the individual's own pleasure or advantage (for example, when he is discussing the historical importance of modern natural law and bourgeois formal law).[23] Strategic action in this sense is a type of social action. It differs from other types in that the relevant social norms merely delimit scopes of action in which the individual can pursue his interests privately and autonomously by employing all legally permissible means to attain his particular (legally permissible) ends. While Weber clearly includes this type of action in the classification "purposive-rational," Habermas equivocates according to whether he focuses on its social character or on its means-ends character. When, for instance, he characterizes the process of rationalization in modern society as an extension of subsystems of purposive-rational action, he clearly intends to include the expansion of spheres of social life in which strategic action is set free from traditional constraints.[24] When, on the other hand, he is discussing transformations in the moral and legal basis of social interaction, he just as clearly intends to include the extension of spheres of strategic action.

To avoid unnecessary confusion, in the remainder of this study the term *rational decision* will be used to designate that *moment* of purposive-rational action discussed above; *strategic action* will be confined to that *type* of action that is both social and means-ends oriented. *Purposive-rational action* and *social interaction* will be used in both broader and narrower senses, that is, as including or excluding strategic action. Where the context does not make clear which sense is intended, it will be explicitly noted.

The distinction between purposive-rational action and social interaction cited above appeals to a number of distinguishing characteristics. The former is governed by technical rules that imply conditional predictions, as well as preference rules and decision maxims that imply conditional imperatives; it is directed to the attainment of goals through the evaluation of alternative choices and the organization of appropriate means; it is sanctioned by success or failure in reality. The latter is governed by consensual norms that define reciprocal expectations; it is grounded in the intersubjectivity of mutual understanding and secured by the general recognition of obligations; it is

sanctioned conventionally. One of the more obvious difficulties with this formulation is that purposive-rational action would seem (if the contrast is to have a point) to be not governed by social norms, not grounded in intersubjectivity, not sanctioned by convention, in short, not social. If we consider, however, the phenomena that Habermas intends to illuminate with the aid of this category—the progress of science and technology and the concomitant rationalization of social life—it is clear that this cannot be the case. The activity of scientists and technicians, of producers and planners, is manifestly subject to consensual norms, based on reciprocal expectations, grounded in intersubjectivity, and sanctioned by convention (as Habermas himself repeatedly points out in other contexts). The same point can be made by returning to the structure of purposive-rational action. The total objective of an agent acting rationally in this sense cannot be specified independently of the general constraining principles, moral and legal norms, contractual commitments, social conventions, and the like to which he is subject. That is, the ends of purposive-rational action are defined and pursued in a social context.

Employing a similar line of argument, a number of critics have accused Habermas of falling behind Marx by substituting abstract action types for the concrete notions of social labor, social production, and, more generally, social practice.[25] In these notions the interdependence of the mode of production and the institutional and cultural "superstructure" is preserved, whereas Habermas's scheme seems to leave us with an abstract opposition that ignores both the social nature of work and the decisive influence of the mode of production on the structure of social interaction. In response, Habermas claims that this criticism misses the point of his distinction: "I do not mind at all *calling* both phenomena [work and interaction] praxis. Nor do I deny that normally instrumental action is embedded in communicative action (productive activity is socially organized in general). But I see no reason why we should not adequately *analyze* a complex, i.e. dissect it into its parts."[26] And it is true that Habermas repeatedly adverts to the symbolic mediation that is an essential feature of human labor. In his discussion of Hegel's Jena philosophy, for instance, he writes:

Instrumental action, as soon as it comes under the category of actual spirit, as social labor, is also embedded within a network of interactions, and therefore dependent on the communicative boundary conditions that underlie every possible cooperation. Even disregarding social labor, the solitary act of using tools is also dependent on the employment of symbols, for the immediacy of animalistic drive satisfaction cannot be moderated without the creation of distance from identifiable objects.[27]

But if this is the case, that formulation of the distinction exemplified in the lengthy citation above is highly misleading. It is not a distinction between one type of action that is governed by norms, conventions, and reciprocal expectations and one that is not. Following Habermas's suggestion, the distinction might be reformulated (without damage to his systematic intentions) as follows: first as an attempt "to analyze a complex." Granted that purposive-rational action is typically "embedded within a network of interactions," associated with social roles and the like, it is nevertheless possible to focus on the "task elements" of actions or action systems. Under this *aspect* we thematize the means-ends orientation of the action, the technical knowledge and decision procedures on which it is based, its degree of success "in reality," in short, the economy and efficiency with which means are employed to realize specified ends. On the other hand, granted that social interaction typically involves expectations concerning the performance of tasks, it is nevertheless possible to focus on the intersubjective structure of action or action systems. Under this *aspect* we thematize the consensual norms, reciprocal expectations, mutual understanding in which the intersubjectivity of action is grounded. Second, a distinction between different *types* of action or action systems can be drawn mediately, that is, through an examination of which aspects or components of a complex predominate. Clearly this is a matter of degrees, and the transitions are frequent and fluid.

Nevertheless there are spheres of action in which the aspect of goal attainment typically predominates (that is, the task elements are decisive), and others in which the economic and efficient pursuit of ends is secondary to considerations of interpersonal relations.

As we shall see, Habermas uses the distinction in both of these ways. Unfortunately he does not always make clear which sense he intends, with the confusing result that abstract aspects of action are sometimes designated as concrete action types.[28]

A further complication of the distinction between work and interaction can be brought out by comparing it to Weber's classification of action types (which is apparently the immediate inspiration of Habermas's scheme). Weber distinguishes between "social action" (oriented to the behavior of others) and nonsocial action (oriented solely to the behavior of inanimate objects).[29] He then classifies social action as purposive-rational (*zweckrational*), value-rational (*wertrational*), affectual-emotional, and traditional. He defined purposive-rational action as "determined by expectations as to the behavior of external objects and of other men, and making use of these expectations as 'conditions' or 'means' for the rational success-oriented pursuit of the agent's own rationally considered ends."[30] By an obvious extension, if only "expectations as to the behavior of external objects" are involved, we might speak of nonsocial purposive-rational action. We then have, at first glance, the following parallels with the Habermasian schema: to Weber's nonsocial purposive-rational action corresponds Habermas's purposive-rational action; to Weber's social purposive-rational action corresponds Habermas's strategic action; to Weber's social nonpurposive-rational action corresponds Habermas's social interaction. But the correspondence is imperfect for many reasons. I shall confine myself to noting the following: while Weber's nonsocial purposive-rational action is "oriented solely to the behavior of inanimate objects," Habermas's purposive-rational action (in the narrow sense) apparently includes the application of technical knowledge to the control of human behavior.[31] This seems to be implied, for instance, when he cedes to purely behavioral approaches to human action a certain—albeit extremely limited—domain of applicability.[32] And in some passages he explicitly refers to the possibility of adopting an objectivating attitude to society.[33] If this observation is correct, then work or purposive-rational action in the narrow sense would include not only action oriented to-

ward inanimate objects but also action oriented toward other human
beings, where the orientation is predominantly one of technical control. This would seem to be Habermas's meaning when, for example,
he speaks of the rationalization of administration through the application of empirical knowledge supplied by the behavioral sciences. Although such action is "symbolically mediated" and "embedded in a
network of interactions," it is in a sense "monologic," for the control
that it achieves is a control over "objectified" processes. That is, to the
extent that an agent acts instrumentally toward others, he comprehends their behavior in terms of observable regularities and therefore as effectively controllable. He is involved in a subject-"object" relationship in which the "object's" capacity for a moral relationship,
"its" potential for communicative relations with the agent, recedes
into the background. The norms, values, and standards that are decisive for this relationship are not the consensual norms of a shared
tradition but standards of technical appropriateness, criteria of
efficient organization of means for the realization of values that are
not communicatively validated.[34]

Habermas insists, however, that a subject treated as an object of instrumental action in this way retains a capacity for communicative relations, that is, remains a potential partner or rival in interaction.
(Compare Hegel's master-slave dialectic.) As long as our cultural tradition is not radically altered—more particularly, as long as socialization processes are tied to claims about the truth of statements and the
justifiability of norms—the objectification of human beings cannot be
total.[35] Once again it is a question of degree (human relations can to a
greater or lesser extent be structured as relations of technical control
or as relations based on "complementarity," "reciprocity," and
"mutual recognition") and a question of aspects (we can thematize
both the instrumental and the interactional dimensions of social relations).

Our results to this point can be summarized as follows. Work or
purposive-rational action in the narrow sense refers to actions or systems of action in which elements of rational decision and instrumentally efficient implementation of technical knowledge predominate.
The orientation to technical control over objectified processes, natural
or social, is decisive. Purposive-rational action in the broader sense includes strategic action. This is bounded by consensual norms (the
"rules of the game") and transpires at the level of intersubjectivity (the

"players" are subjects capable of pursuing their own strategies); but the calculated pursuit of individual interests predominates over considerations of reciprocity. Interaction in the narrow sense, or communicative action, refers to actions or systems of action in which the moments of complementarity and consensus predominate. The orientation to reciprocity based on mutual understanding is decisive. In a broader sense, strategic action can be included as a restricted form of social interaction. The distinction is also used to refer to aspects of a complex whole. Under the category "work," Habermas thematizes questions concerning the technical mastery of the natural and social environment. Under the category of "interaction," he thematizes questions concerning social relations among communicating individuals (that is, moral relations).

Rather than continuing to explicate the distinction in the abstract, I shall turn now to two discussions in which it plays a central role: Habermas's discussion of Hegel's Jena philosophy and his discussion of Weber's rationalization thesis. This will not only furnish some content to the work/interaction schema and its different uses but will lead us to the heart of Habermas's philosophical and sociological reflections.

In a provocative essay on Hegel's Jena lectures, Habermas contrasts Kant's "empty identity" of the ego as an original unity of transcendental consciousness with Hegel's "insight that the identity of self-consciousness is not an original one, but can only be conceived as one that has developed."[36] This self-formative process transpires in three equally significant, interrelated but irreducible dimensions: language, labor, and moral relations. For our purposes, it is Habermas's discussion of "the moral relationship" (das sittliche Verhältnis) and the "dialectic of the moral life" that is most revealing. Hegel explains the moral relationship in terms of love, which he understands as "the dialogic relation of recognizing oneself in the other."[37] He does not derive the "dialogic situation" directly from intersubjective relations; instead he presents it as the result of a movement, as the reconciliation of a preceding conflict. The suppression and reconstruction of "social interaction based on reciprocity" or "mutual recognition" is reconstructed as the dialectic of the moral life.

In his earlier fragment on the Spirit of Christianity, Hegel developed this dialectic through the example of the punishment that befalls one who destroys a moral totality. The criminal who revokes the moral basis, "namely the complementarity of unconstrained communication and the mutual satisfaction of interests," by putting himself as an individual in the place of the totality, sets in motion the causality of fate.[38] On Habermas's interpretation, this is the causality of symbols and relations "that have been withdrawn from the context of communication and thus are valid and operate only behind the backs of the subjects."[39] The criminal, faced with lost complementarity and past friendship, experiences "in the repression of the lives of others the deficiency of his own life, and in his turning away from the lives of others his own alienation from himself."[40] The causality of fate, in which "the power of suppressed life is at work," can be brought to rest and the moral relationship restored only when the contending parties "recognize their hardened opposition as the result of detachment and abstraction from their common life context, and experience the common basis of their existence in the dialogic relation of recognizing oneself in the other."[41] The dialectic of the moral life refers then not to "unconstrained intersubjectivity" itself but to the history of its suppression and reestablishment.

In the Jena lectures Hegel developed this idea again in the "struggle for recognition." Although the details are different, he retained the overall schema. The "abstract self-assertion" of individuals who "have inflated their singularity into a totality" is avenged by the causality of fate. The destruction of the "self-assertion which severs itself from the moral totality" makes possible interaction "on the basis of mutual recognition—namely, on the basis of the knowledge that the identity of the 'I' is possible solely through the identity of the other who recognizes me, and who in turn is dependent upon my recognition."[42]

For the Hegel of the Jena period, moral relations represent only one "medium" for the self-formation of the subject; language and labor are equally original media. In contrast to Kant's "abstract" unity of the moral, theoretical, and technical consciousness, he presents the identity of the *I* as the result of "three heterogeneous patterns of formation": the dialectic of the moral life, the dialectic of representation, and the dialectic of labor. In opposition to Kant's notion of the synthetic achievements of a transcendental consciousness conceived apart from all formative processes, the dialectic of representation ties the synthesis of the manifold to the employment of symbols that we ourselves have produced. The identity of the "naming consciousness" cannot then be regarded as prior to the process of knowledge; it is formed in the same process through which the objectivity of the world takes shape in language. Similarly Kant's "cultivated" subject, who is skilled in purposive action according to technical rules (hypothetical imperatives) is conceived by Hegel as a changing result of social labor. The dialectic of labor presents the "cunning consciousness" as developing through the use of tools and instruments that "retain the rules according to which the domination of natural processes can be repeated again at will."[43] In this way Kant's abstract *I*, the unity of moral, theoretical, and technical consciousness, gives way in Hegel to a developmental conception of spirit represented by three heterogeneous patterns of formation.

This heterogeneity raises the question of the unity of the self-formative process, that is, of the relation of the different media. Language, as cultural tradition, is a presupposition of moral interaction, "for only the intersubjectively valid and constant meanings which are drawn from tradition permit orientation toward reciprocity, i.e. complementary expectations of behavior."[44] It is equally a presupposition of social labor, "which is embedded within a network of interactions, and therefore dependent on the communicative boundary conditions that underlie every possible cooperation."[45] Both labor and interaction are symbolically mediated. Hegel establishes an interconnection between labor and interaction by way of "the legal norms, on which social intercourse based on mutual recognition is first formally stabilized."[46] The institutionalization of mutual recognition between legal persons is a matter of "individuals recognizing each other as proprietors in the possessions produced by their labor or acquired by trade."[47] Thus the possessions arising from the labor process function as the substratum of legal recognition. The exchange of equivalents, formally institutionalized in the contract, becomes the model for the reciprocity on which interaction is based. In this way the result of the "struggle for recognition," the legally recognized self-consciousness, incorporates the results of the labor process by which we free ourselves from the immediate dictates of nature. "The dialectic of love and conflict cannot be separated from the successes of instrumental action. . . . The result of emancipation by means of labor enters into the norms under which we act complementarily."[48]

Hegel did not develop this schema of heterogeneous but interconnected patterns of self-formation any further. Under the presupposition of the absolute identity of spirit with nature, it lost its significance; self-reflection became the model for the movement of absolute spirit. According to Habermas, Marx rediscovered the interdependency between labor and interaction, but because of a tendency to reduce the latter to the former, he failed to develop it adequately.

Marx conceives the moral totality as a society in which men produce in order to reproduce their own life through the appropriation of an external nature. Morality is an institutional framework for processes of production. Marx takes the dialectic of the moral life, which operates on the basis of social labor, as the law of motion of a defined conflict between definite parties. The conflict is always about the organization of the appropriation of socially created products, while the conflicting parties are determined by their position in the process of production, that is as classes. As the movement of class antagonism, the dialectic of the moral life is linked to the development of the system of social labor. The overcoming of abstraction, that is the critical-revolutionary reconciliation of the estranged parties, succeeds only relative to the level of development of the forces of production. The institutional framework also incorporates the constraint of external nature, which expresses itself in the degree of mastery of nature, the extent of socially necessary labor, and in the relation of available rewards to socially developed demands. Through the repression of needs and wishes, it translates this constraint into a compulsion of internal nature, in other words into the constraint of social norms. That is why the relative destruction of the moral relation can be measured only by the difference between the *actual* degree of institutionally *demanded* repression and the degree of repression that is *necessary* at a given level of the forces of production. It is those who establish such domination and defend positions of power of this sort who set in motion the causality of fate, divide society into social classes, suppress justified interests, call forth the reactions of suppressed life, and finally experience their just fate in revolution. They are compelled by the revolutionary class to recognize themselves in it and thereby to overcome the alienation of the existence of *both* classes. As long as the constraint of external nature persists in the form of economic scarcity, every revolutionary class is induced, after its victory, to a new "injustice", namely the establishment of a new class rule. Therefore the dialectic of the moral life must repeat itself until the materialist spell that is cast upon the reproduction of social life, the Biblical curse of necessary labor, is broken technologically.[49]

But even then the dialectic of the moral life does not automatically come to rest. Scientific-technical progress does not of itself lead to

human emancipation, to self-conscious control of the social life process. The institutional framework, the organization of social relations,
is not *immediately* "a stage of technological development, but rather a
relation of social force, namely the power of one social class over
another."[50] Thus the growth of productive forces, the substitution of
machinery for men, the emancipation of society from the forces of nature are not immediately a lessening of oppression, a substitution of
communicative relations for relations of domination, an emancipation
of society from social force.

The two developments do not converge. Yet they are interdependent.
Marx tried in vain to capture this in the dialectic of forces of production and relations of production. In vain—for the meaning of this
"dialectic" must remain unclarified as long as the materialist concept
of the synthesis of man and nature is restricted to the categorial
framework of production.[51]

Marx does not actually explicate the interrelationship of interaction
and labor, but instead, under the unspecific title of social praxis, reduces the one to the other, namely communicative action to instrumental action . . . the productive activity which regulates the material
exchange of the human species with its natural environment, becomes
the paradigm for the generation of all the categories; everything is resolved into the self-movement of production. Because of this, Marx's
brilliant insight into the dialectical relationship between the forces of
production and the relations of production could very quickly be mis-
interpreted in a mechanistic manner.[52]

Whatever their exegetical merit, these interpretations of Marx and
Hegel are instructive for an understanding of Habermas's own
schema. Under the title of "work," he wishes to thematize the process
of emancipation from nature, the growth of productive forces as a
function of the development of technically exploitable knowledge and
its application. Under the title of "interaction," he wishes to thematize
social relations among individuals capable of communication. Such relations may be termed moral relations, but then morality is not to be
conceived in individualistic terms. Rather "problems of morality arise
solely in the context of an intervening communication and the
intersubjectivity that emerges among actors on the always precarious
basis of mutual recognition."[53] Here Habermas follows Hegel in rejecting the separation of morality from politics that arose in modern
philosophy.

Politics was understood to be the doctrine of the good and just life; it was the continuation of ethics. Aristotle saw no opposition between the constitution formulated in the *nomoi* and the ethos of civil life; conversely, the ethical character of action was not separable from custom and law. . . . In Kant, in contrast, the ethical conduct of the individual who is free only inwardly is distinguished from the legality of his external actions. And just as morality is separated from legality, so the two in turn are separated from politics, which is accorded a most dubious role as the technical expertise in a utilitarian doctrine of prudence.[54]

Because Hegel did not conceive the constitution of the self as a solitary act of self-reflection but rather in terms of a formative process that transpired in a complex of interactions, he regarded Kant's autonomous will as a

peculiar abstraction from the moral relations of communicating individuals. By presupposing autonomy—and that means the will's property of being a law unto itself . . . Kant expels moral action from the very domain of morality itself. . . . (*He*) defines moral action according to the principle: "act only according to that maxim by which you can at the same time will that it should become a universal law." . . . The moral laws are abstractly universal in the sense that, as they are valid as universal for me, *eo ipso* they must also be considered as valid for all rational beings. Therefore, under such laws interaction is dissolved into the actions of solitary and self-sufficient subjects, each of which must act as though it were the sole existing consciousness; at the same time, each subject can still have the certainty that all its actions under moral laws will necessarily and from the outset be in harmony with the moral actions of all possible other subjects. The intersubjectivity of the recognition of moral laws accounted for *a priori* by practical reason permits the reduction of moral action to the monologic domain. The positive relation of the will to the will of others is withdrawn from possible communication, and a transcendentally necessary correspondence of isolated goal-directed activities under abstract universal laws is substituted.[55]

With Hegel and against Kant, Habermas regards moral action as essentially communicative, a relation between subjects who are "involved in a complex of interactions as their formative process."[56] Since personal identity can be achieved only on the basis of mutual recognition, individuation can be comprehended only as a process of socialization.[57] The moral subject, the subject of *praxis*, is inconceivable in abstraction from communicative relations with others. Conversely social interaction is eo ipso moral interaction; it is, at least potentially, a dialogic relationship "that emerges among actors on the always precarious basis of mutual recognition."[58] The words *potentially* and *precarious* are important here, for while the ideal of unconstrained intersubjectivity is posited in the very structure of human communication, it is obvious that the conditions of actual communication usually fall short of it. Historically the organization of social relations has reflected institutionalized power relations rather than public and general communication free from domination. Thus *interaction*, as a category for comprehending processes of social evolution, does not refer immediately to unconstrained intersubjectivity but to the history of its repression and reconstitution: the dialectic of the moral life. In adopting this perspective, Habermas is not attempting to substitute a "normative" for an "empirical" approach to society. He is, rather, attempting to bring to light the moral dimension of empirical social relations and the empirical (social) dimension of morality.

The point of insisting on the "heterogeneity" or "irreducibility" of work and interaction is to avoid just that conflation of *techne* and *praxis*, of technical progress and the rational conduct of life, that we found to be at the roots of the technocratic ideology. Rationalization is not emancipation. The growth of productive forces and administrative efficiency does not of itself lead to the replacement of institutions based on force by an organization of social relations bound to communication free from domination. The ideals of the technical mastery of history and of liberation from the quasi-natural forces of social and political domination, as well as the means for their realization, are fundamentally different. For this reason it is of decisive importance for a critical theory of society that the different dimensions of social practice be made explicit; only then can we comprehend their interdependence.

The same point, in a more sociological guise, emerges from Habermas's reinterpretation of Weber's concept of rationalization. Having distinguished work from interaction, he goes on to distinguish "*the institutional framework of a society*," which "consists of norms that guide symbolic interaction," from "*subsystems of purposive-rational action* that are 'embedded' in it," that is, subsystems "in which primarily sets of purposive-rational actions are institutionalized."[59] This is then applied to a comparison of "traditional" with "modern" societies. The former

tolerated technical innovation and organizational improvement only with definite limits. . . . For despite considerable progress, these sub-systems, developing out of the system of social labor and its stock of accumulated technically exploitable knowledge, never reached that measure of extension after which their "rationality" would have be-come an open threat to the authority of the cultural traditions that legitimate political power. The expression "traditional society" refers to the circumstance that the institutional framework is grounded in the unquestionable underpinning of legitimation constituted by mythical, religious, or metaphysical interpretations of reality—cosmic as well as social—as a whole. "Traditional" societies exist as long as the development of subsystems of purposive-rational action keeps within the limits of the legitimating efficacy of cultural traditions.[60]

Since the establishment of the capitalist mode of production, how-ever, technical innovation and organizational improvement have themselves been institutionalized: "the capitalist mode of production can be comprehended as a mechanism that guarantees the *permanent* expansion of subsystems or purposive rational action and thereby overturns the traditionalist 'superiority' of the institutional frame-work to the forces of production."[61]

The process that Weber referred to as rationalization can accord-ingly be broken down into two interrelated tendencies: (1) the in-stitutionalization of economic growth and an ensuing extension of means-ends rationality to more and more sectors of life (traditional structures are increasingly subordinated to instrumental or strategic rationality); (2) as a consequence, the traditional forms of the legiti-mation of power break down, "for measured against the new standards of purposive-rationality, the power-legitimating and action-orienting traditions, especially mythological interpretations and religious world-views, lose their cogency."[62] In the early modern period traditional world views, having lost much of their power and validity as unquestionable tradition, were "reshaped into subjective belief systems and ethics which insured the private cogency of modern value-orientations (the 'Protestant ethic')."[63] At about the same time, within the framework of a mechanistic world view, classical natural law was transformed into modern natural law, which pro-vided the principles for a new form of legitimation, a legitimation which is no longer called down from the lofty heights of cultural tradition but instead summoned up from the base of social labor. The institution of the market, in which private property owners exchange commodities—including the market on which propertyless private individuals exchange their labor power as their only commodity—promises that exchange relations will be and are just owing to equivalence. Even this bourgeois ideology of justice, by adopting the category of reciprocity, still employs a relation of communicative action as the basis of legitimation. But the principle of reciprocity is now the organizing principle of the sphere of production and reproduction itself.[64]

With this the traditional legitimation of the property order—mediately, through a legitimation of social and political relations—was reversed. It was now the power structure that was justified in terms of legitimate relations of production; "the institutional framework of society is only mediately political and immediately economic."[65]

Taking this as his point of departure, Marx developed the critique of bourgeois ideology as a critique of political economy. Attacking the illusion of just exchange, he brought to light the relations of social force that underlay the wage-labor relationship. Habermas is convinced that the conditions relevant for the application of Marx's version of critical theory no longer obtain in advanced capitalism. The necessity for permanent regulation of the economic process by means of state intervention amounts to a repoliticization of the institutional framework of society.

It no longer coincides immediately with the relations of production, i.e. with an order of private law that secures capitalist economic activity and the corresponding general guarantees of order provided by the bourgeois state. But this means a change in the relation of the economy to the political system: politics is no longer *only* a phenomenon of the superstructure. . . . Then, however, a critical theory of society can no longer be constructed in the exclusive form of a critique of political economy. A point of view that methodically isolates the economic laws of motion of society can claim to grasp the overall structure of social life in its essential categories only as long as politics depends on the economic base. It becomes inapplicable when the "base" has to be comprehended as in itself a function of governmental activity and political conflicts . . . the power structure can no longer be criticized *immediately* at the level of the relations of production.[66]

This new constellation of politics and economics requires a new, direct legitimation for political power, one that secures sufficient latitude for state intervention (to defend against the dysfunctional tendencies that arise from the private form of capital utilization, to ensure growth and stability, and the like). Habermas wants to argue (on this point in agreement with Marcuse) that this need is met to a considerable extent by a depoliticization of practical issues. They are defined as technical problems whose solution must be left to the appropriate technicians. With the fusion of science, technology, industry, and administration, a perspective arises in which "the development of the social system *seems* to be determined by the logic of technical progress."[67] Politics appears to be increasingly a function of "objective exigencies" that must be obeyed if the needs of society are to be met. From this perspective a democratic form of decision-making tied to general and public discussion could only make more difficult the appropriate solution of technical problems. The public sphere can at best function only as a device for choosing between alternative groups of administrators and technicians.

This discussion of the concept of rationalization has thus led us back to the issues surrounding the scientization of politics. Their importance for a critical theory of society should be evident. Science and technology, in the form of the "technocratic consciousness," fulfill the ideological function of legitimating the exercise of political power over the heads of a depoliticized public. The version of critical theory Marx developed for liberal capitalism no longer suffices in the face of this new ideology.

For with the veiling of practical problems it not only justifies a *particular class'* interest in domination and represses *another class'* partial need for emancipation, but affects the human race's emancipatory interest as such.[68]

Technocratic consciousness reflects not the sundering of an ethical situation but the repression of "ethics" as such as a category of life.[69]

The ideological nucleus of this consciousness is the *elimination of the distinction between the practical and the technical.* . . . The new ideology consequently violates an interest grounded in one of the two fundamental conditions of our cultural existence: in language, or more precisely, in the form of socialization and individuation determined by communication in ordinary language. This interest extends to the maintenance of intersubjectivity of mutual understanding as well as to the creation of communication without domination. Technocratic consciousness makes this interest disappear behind the interest in the expansion of our power of technical control. Thus the reflection that the new ideology calls for must penetrate beyond the level of particular historical class interests to disclose the fundamental interests of mankind as such.[70]

The earlier Frankfurt school was, Habermas feels, too one-sided in its response to this changed situation. What is required is not a critique of science and technology as such but a critique of their totalization, of their identification with the whole of rationality. To this end the different forms of reason and rationalization must be distinguished. In particular the notion of rationality proper to the medium of social interaction must be rescued from the positivist strictures on meaningful discourse. A critique of positivist epistemology and the development of a theory of knowledge accommodating the different interests that knowledge can serve therefore become necessary tasks for the critical theory of contemporary society. We shall turn now to consider Habermas's efforts in this direction.

1.3 POSITIVISM AND PHILOSOPHY

The leitmotif of Habermas's critique of positivist philosophy is formulated tersely in the preface to *Knowledge and Human Interests:* "that we disavow reflection is positivism." This charge obviously requires some qualification if it is to hold up, for the outstanding contribution of positivist philosophy has been a sustained reflection upon the logic and methodology of the empirical sciences. It is, to be more precise, a specific type of reflection that positivism disavows:

Positivism certainly still expresses a philosophical position with regard to science, for the scientistic self-understanding of the sciences that it articulates does not coincide with science itself. But by making a dogma of the sciences' belief in themselves, positivism assumes the prohibitive function of protecting scientific inquiry from epistemological self-reflection. Positivism is philosophical only in so far as is necessary for the immunization of the sciences against philosophy.[1]

The prototype for the epistemological self-reflection in question is Kant's critical philosophy. The central question of modern philosophy since Descartes had been, How is reliable knowledge possible? Although mathematics and physics often served as paradigmatic instances, the rationalists and empiricists generally stopped short of identifying knowledge with science. Philosophical knowledge retained the task of comprehending science, its structure and limits, its legitimate place within the economy of human thought. From Kant's transcendental perspective, philosophy continued to maintain its sovereignty in relation to science; science was to be comprehended epistemologically as one category of possible knowledge. The idea of reason in critical philosophy encompassed not only theoretical reason but also practical reason and reflective judgment, as well as critique itself.

With the ascendancy of positivism in the second half of the nineteenth century, this picture was radically altered. Knowledge was identified with science; the theory of knowledge became the philosophy of science, an explication of scientific method. Habermas refers to this belief in the exclusive validity of empirical science—"that the meaning of knowledge is defined by what the sciences do and can thus be adequately explicated through the methodological analysis of scientific procedure"—as "scientism."[2] Because it excludes any epistemology that transcends the framework of methodology, scientism has led to the obliteration of a dimension of the problem of knowledge that was in the forefront of Kant's transcendental philosophy: the thematization of the knowing subject. With the aid of distinctions such as those between the context of discovery and the context of justification and between questions of genesis and questions of validity, problems relating to the subjective conditions of knowledge are consigned to the psychology and sociology of science, themselves understood as empirical sciences. Oriented exclusively toward the systems of propositions and rules according to which empirically meaningful statements can be formed and tested, epistemology qua methodology renounces *philosophical* inquiry into the knowing subject. The subjects who put forward and criticize these statements, who proceed according to these rules, have no *epistemological* significance. In Kantian terms, the synthetic achievements of the knowing subject, the constitution of the objects of possible experience and of the facts with which science deals, drop from sight. According to Habermas, this blindness fosters a tendency toward "objectivism," the belief in a world of self-subsistent facts whose lawlike connections can be grasped descriptively. It conceals the transcendental basis of the world of facts, the generation of meaning from structures of experience and action.

Although positivism has, in a sense, regressed behind the level of reflection Kant represented, the scientistic and objectivistic "illusions" that it sustains cannot be overcome by simply returning to Kant: "Every discussion of the conditions of possible knowledge *today* . . . must begin from the position worked out by analytic philosophy of science."[3] On the one hand, positivism has to be undercut from within through an "*immanent critique* of important theorems of analytic philosophy, with the aim of pushing the theory of science and linguistic analysis beyond the limits of their present position into an area of transcendental reflection where the preconditions of experience and reasoning reveal themselves as problematic."[4] On the other hand, it is important to understand the historical process of the dissolution of epistemology in favor of the philosophy of science, "to reconstruct the pre-history of modern positivism," "to make one's way over abandoned stages of reflection" in order to comprehend how "philosophy's position with regard to science . . . has been undermined by the movement of philosophical thought itself."[5] In what follows I shall examine briefly one line of development of the "immanent critique," that represented by the work of Popper and Kuhn.[6] Habermas's reconstruction of what happened to philosophy from Kant through Marx that enabled positivism to triumph on the ruins of epistemology will be sketched in the next chapter.

The inquiries of traditional empiricists into the "origin, certainty and extent of human knowledge" were based largely on a recourse to sensory experience. The various notions of the immediately given—ideas, impressions, sensations, and the like—were supposed to provide an empirical basis for our knowledge of "matters of fact," a basis possessing the indubitability of immediate, evident experience. How far this indubitability carried was a question concerning the relation of factual propositions that were not simple reports of present experience to this empirical basis. Of course, within this broad empiricist framework there was room for a variety of outlooks, from the epistemological realism of Locke to the skepticism of Hume.

The early phenomenalist variants of positivism retained this notion of the immediately given, the indubitable basis of scientific knowledge. With it they inherited a number of the problems of traditional empiricism, among them the interrelated problems of accounting for the subject to whom the immediately given is given, and for the intersubjective reliability of scientific knowledge, which was, after all, one of its distinctive features. If the empirical basis was to be the *indubitable* foundation of knowledge, it had to be immediately given in sensory experience and thus in a sense subjective; if, on the other hand, it was to be the foundation of *scientific* knowledge, it had to be intersubjectively valid and in this sense objective. Phenomenalist attempts, such as that of Mach, to get rid of the subject, consciousness, as a distinctive dimension of reality, to regard the ego as just another construction from sensations or "elements" (that is, as a fact among facts) merely displaced the problem. Apart from the question of what sense can be made of sense certainty without consciousness, there arose the question of how to characterize the facticity of the facts that science—as opposed to metaphysics—dealt with. Mach's "ontology of the factual" (Habermas) left him with the problem of justifying his own doctrine of elements.

Its own status is contradictory. By explicating the totality of facts as the object domain of the sciences and delimiting science from metaphysics through its replication of the facts, it cannot justify any reflection that goes beyond science, including itself. The doctrine of elements is the reflected form of science, but one that prohibits any reflection going beyond science. . . . How then, *prior* to all science, can the doctrine of elements make statements about the object domain of science as such, if we only obtain information about this domain *through* science?[7]

Furthermore the phenomenalist reduction of the subject to the level of facts overcame the solipsistic tendencies of subjective empiricism in appearance only. While Mach was no longer left with an explicit image of the world—including other subjects—as his world, a construction from the sensory givens of his conscious life, his doctrine did nevertheless imply a "methodical solipsism": "the tacit assumption that *objective* knowledge should be possible without intersubjective understanding."[8] If subjects can be validly known only as objects of science, that is, if the experience of human intersubjectivity is reducible to the experience of facts on the same plane as other facts, then there is a tacit "presupposition that the knowing subject can, in principle, win objective knowledge of the world without at the same time presupposing knowledge by sign-interpretation or intersubjective understanding, . . . that one solitary subject of knowledge could objectify the whole world, including his fellow men."[9] Mach's phenomenalism is no more able than the traditional subjectivistic forms of empiricism to account systematically for the role of the "community of scientific investigators" in the construction of scientific knowledge. The phenomenalist language is designed for describing and explaining a world of facts; it is not suited to expressing the communication that nevertheless underlies the scientific enterprise. Human beings, so long as they are considered as possible partners in communication, as fellow members of the scientific community, cannot be reduced to objects of phenomenalist description; they have to be dealt with in the context of the communication structures characteristic of the community of scientists, for it is within these structures that scientific theories are put forward and criticized, alternatives are suggested and supported with arguments, rules and standards are proposed and refined and—in spite of Mach—the "facts" are reported, disputed, and revised.

The "myth of the given" and the models of science based on it have been subjected to repeated criticism from philosophers of science. At about the same time as Mach was proposing his doctrine of elements, Charles Sanders Peirce was developing a view of scientific inquiry that explicitly rejected any recourse to original impressions of sensation and focused instead on the intersubjectively acknowledged cognitive progress that was the exemplary feature of natural-scientific knowledge. Viewing inquiry as the process by which we move from doubt to belief, he centered his analysis on the procedures through which an uncompelled and stable consensus among members of the community of investigators (the "fixation of belief") could be achieved. I shall have more to say about Peirce in my discussion of Habermas's conception of the "technical interest" underlying empirical science. For present purposes it will be helpful to consider briefly one of the most influential contemporary critiques of empiricist assumptions in positivist philosophy of science, the work of Karl Popper and his school.[10]

Rejecting all inductivist accounts of science, Popper regards the formation of scientific hypotheses as a creative exercise of the imagination. A hypothesis is to be considered scientific not on the condition that it can be justified by reference to sensory experience—which is, as Hume showed, impossible—but on the condition that it can be empirically falsified by negative observations, that is, that it excludes some observable possibilities. The more falsifiable a hypothesis is, the more empirical content it possesses. The proper method of science, then, is to formulate the most falsifiable hypotheses and to test energetically whether any of the singular observation statements that can be deductively derived from them—the potential falsifiers—turn out to be actually false. Although no hypothesis can be conclusively verified, its continued survival of serious attempts at falsification provides a measure of corroboration and permits its provisional acceptance. The growth of knowledge consists in the progressive elimination of error in favor of better-corroborated theories with more empirical content.

In contradistinction to traditional empiricism, Popper does not regard the empirical basis of science as composed of sense-contents passively received by the knowing subject. The basic observation statements used in testing hypotheses are restricted existential statements referring to publicly observable material objects at a specified time and place. Since such statements employ general terms, they cannot be construed as simple descriptions of particular sense experiences (although they may be motivated by such experiences). They are themselves subject to empirical tests in the light of other basic statements and accepted scientific theories. Furthermore basic observation statements are "theory-impregnated":

In science it is *observation* rather than perception which plays the decisive part. But observation is a process in which we play an intensely *active* part. An observation is a perception but one which is planned and prepared. We do not "have" an observation (as we may "have" a sense experience) but we "make" an observation. . . . An observation is always preceded by a particular interest, a question, or a problem—in short, by something theoretical.[11]

The knowing subject comes to experience with a biologically and culturally conditioned "horizon of expectations":

At every instant of our pre-scientific or scientific development we are living in the center of what I usually call a "horizon of expectations." By this I mean the sum total of our expectations whether these are subconscious or conscious, or perhaps even explicitly stated in some language. Animals and babies have also their various and different horizons of expectations though no doubt on a lower level of consciousness than, say, a scientist whose horizon of expectations consists to a considerable extent of linguistically formulated theories or hypotheses. . . . Yet in all these cases the horizon of expectations plays the part of a frame of reference: only their setting in this frame confers meaning or significance on our experiences, actions and observations.[12]

This account of the theory-ladenness of the observation statements through which theories are tested clearly raises the issue of circularity (to which so much of the current literature in the philosophy of science is devoted). Popper insists that this circularity is not vicious. The circle (or infinite regress) that seems to result from surrendering the myth of the given can be halted at any point by a conventional assignment of truth to basic statements. But these conventions are not dogmatic; they are provisional in the sense that if the basic statements in question are challenged, they can always be subjected to empirical tests (which requires, of course, that other conventional truth assignments be made). In spite of his rejection of traditional empiricist models of experience, Popper wants to hold on to the idea that falsified theories clash with reality and not *merely* with other theories and that the goal of science can still be properly characterized in realistic terms as an approach or approximation to a true description and explanation of reality. I shall return to this idea below; for the present, it is important to note that the conception of a horizon of expectations assigns a central role in science to history and tradition.

Science never starts from scratch; it can never be described as free from assumptions; for at every instant it presupposes a horizon of expectations—yesterday's horizon of expectations, as it were. Today's science is built on yesterday's science; and yesterday's science is built on the science of the day before. And the oldest scientific theories are built on prescientific myths, and these, in their turn, on still older expectations.[13]

The growth of scientific knowledge may be conceived as a "learning process" in which error is eliminated and the "verisimilitude" or truth content of our theories is increased. The mechanism of progress is the disappointment of expectations, of dispositions to react, which are adapted to a stage of the environment yet to come. Learning from experience consists in modifying dispositions, and correcting our horizon of expectations in the light of disappointments. From this point of view, science appears as a systematic "continuation of the prescientific repair work on our horizons of expectations."[14] At the level of science, disappointments take the form of falsifications through basic observation statements; modifications take the form of new theories that repair and rebuild the damaged parts of our horizon in such a manner that the damaging observations are no longer felt as disruptive but are somehow integrated in a consistent whole with those expectations that have not been disappointed.

Although science is continuous in this sense with prescientific attempts to understand, predict, and control events, the scientific method does introduce a new dimension: the critical attitude.

In the place of a dogmatic handing on of the doctrine (in which the whole interest lies in the preservation of the authentic tradition) we find [in ancient Greece] a critical discussion of the doctrine. . . . Doubt and criticism certainly existed before this stage. What is new, however, is that doubt and criticism now become, in their turn, part of the tradition of the school. A tradition of a higher order replaces the traditional preservation of the dogma: in the place of the traditional theory—in place of the myth—we find the tradition of criticizing theories. . . . It is only in the course of this critical discussion that observation is called as a witness. . . . Thus it seems to me that it is the tradition of criticism which constitutes what is new in science, and what is characteristic of science.[15]

Popper's critique of the empiricist presuppositions of positivism relies on a conception of the subject of knowledge as active, biologically and culturally conditioned, and situated in a process of historical development from which the critical tradition constitutive of science emerges. On the one hand, something like transcendental functions are assigned to this subject; only in the setting of the frame of reference constituted by our horizon of expectations is meaning or significance conferred on our experience and action. Sense experience is not the primary experience of a manifest immediacy proposed by empiricism; it is preformed by physiology, previous experience, tradition, by what has been learned and what is anticipated. In this sense, "facts" are not "given" but "constituted." On the other hand, the subject of scientific knowledge is not the pure transcendental ego of Kant. It is the community of investigators, sharing a basic physiological makeup and communicatively interacting within institutional and cultural frameworks that undergo historical evolution. Scientific inquiry is intimately connected with social life processes; it is the systematic continuation of the learning processes through which the species comes to terms with its environment. One might say of Popper, then, what Habermas says of Peirce: that he approaches a conception of "quasi-transcendental" conditions of knowledge that are formed under empirical conditions.

The logic of inquiry is situated as it were between formal and transcendental logic. It goes beyond the realm of the formal conditions of
the validity of propositions, but falls short of the cognitively constitutive determinations of a transcendental consciousness as such. . . . Like
transcendental logic, the logic of inquiry extends to the structure of
the constitution of knowledge. . . . But as a process of inquiry, this
logical structure materializes under empirical conditions. . . . The logical analysis of inquiry, therefore, is concerned not with the attributes
of a transcendental consciousness as such but with those of a subject
that sustains the process of inquiry as a whole, i.e. with the community
of investigators, who endeavor to perform their common task communicatively.[16]

This is, of course, decidedly not Popper's understanding of where
his reflections have taken him. In contrast to the position suggested by
Habermas, Popper formulates his theory of knowledge as an "epistemology without a knowing subject."[17] He regards attempts (such as
those of Thomas Kuhn, for example) to thematize the structure of interaction in the scientific community as sociology of knowledge and
excludes them from the logic of inquiry as such. The grounds for this
apparent reversal include a correspondence theory of truth; a quasi-
Platonic conception of theories, problems, arguments, and the like as
inhabitants of a "third world"; and a decisionistic foundation of critical rationalism itself.[18]   The correspondence theory of truth permits
Popper to maintain the independence of facts and to argue for an objectivistic conception of theories as striving to approximate an
adequate conception of an independent reality. This effectively
short-circuits the transcendental turn implied by his own thesis that
facts are constituted only within frames of reference or horizons of
expectations. Given the independence of facts, Popper can avoid pursuing the consequences of his view that basic observational statements
are established by convention. Conventions, of course, result from
some form of agreement. If they are not arbitrary, there must exist
rules for attaining such agreement, forms of argument that are appropriate to supporting or challenging it, standards and values that
might be appealed to in such argument, and so on. In short the notion
of conventions, no less than that of constitutive frames of reference,
seems to call for a systematic analysis of communication structures
within the community of investigators. The surprising, and inconsistent, retention of an objectivistic notion of facts is at the root of Popper's failure to complete his transcendental turn.

It also contributes to his decisionistic foundation of critical rationalism. Since justification is identified with deduction and rationality is limited to the scientific method of conjecture and refutation (by comparison with the facts), it is, according to Popper, not possible to justify or rationally ground the critical attitude itself. We are faced with a choice between competing traditions, competing models for knowledge and action, and the choice of the critical attitude is just that—a choice that can be neither deductively justified nor scientifically corroborated; hence it is the prerational or, more bluntly, the irrational foundation of rationality. If Popper consistently pursued his insights that scientific discourse includes the critical discussion of alternative techniques of inquiry, competing theories, various definitions of basic predicates, in short, of different frames of reference and their elements; that "it is only in the course of the critical discussion that observation is called in as a witness"; and that even this witness depends on standards and rules, then he could not limit rationality to trial and error in the sense of confrontation with the facts. If science is to serve as the paradigm of rationality, then all of the forms of argumentation involved in this process of critical discussion are rational. But the rational motivation of the acceptance of standards and rules, the criticism and support of attitudes and outlooks, cannot proceed by way of deduction and falsification. This is merely one element in a more comprehensive rationality. (In point of fact, despite his explicit renunciation of a rational justification for the critical attitude, Popper's methodological writings are replete with good reasons for adopting it, reasons based on an understanding of the process of inquiry as a whole in relation to basic structures of human life, that is, to the learning process on which the reproduction of human life depends.)

Of course Popper cannot simply revert to empiricist models of experience, observation, and theory. He introduces a conception of the third world that—although it is a "natural product of the human animal, comparable to a spider's web"—nevertheless retains its objectivity and autonomy vis-à-vis the subjects who produce it.[19] A full discussion of this conception would require a rather detailed look at the theory of meaning and language behind it. These questions will be taken up in discussing the theory of communicative competence. The results of that discussion should make clear that Popper's third world is an untenable reification of language, tradition, and culture. In any event, the "objectivity and autonomy of the third world" enable him to minimize the importance of reflection on the subject of knowledge for his theory of "objective knowledge." But Popper's classification of theories of knowledge into subjectivistic and objectivistic fails to consider that mode of thematizing the subject suggested above. Under subjectivistic approaches, he includes the traditional thematization of the knowing subject as an isolated, individual consciousness, as well as psychological and sociological studies of cognition.[20] The idea that there could be a nonpsychological, nonsociological treatment of the subjective conditions of knowledge, in which the subject is regarded not as a pure ego or consciousness but as the community of investigators, is not systematically pursued, although his own methodological reflections point precisely in that direction.

It does not help matters that contemporary methodologists who conspicuously orient their inquiries in this direction—most prominently Thomas Kuhn and his supporters—themselves lack an adequate conception of the status of their inquiries. Thus they too easily open themselves to charges of substituting the history and sociology of science for the logic and methodology of science and of denying the seemingly undeniable progress of science in favor of an irreducible relativity of theoretical frameworks.[21] Under the pressure of such criticism, however, Kuhn has made it increasingly clear that he regards the "shift of professional commitments" involved in paradigm change as guided in part by a deep-seated commitment to values "constitutive of science."

Probably the most deeply held values concern predictions: they should be accurate; quantitative predictions are preferrable to qualitative ones. . . . There are also, however, values to be used in judging whole theories: they must, first and foremost, permit puzzle-formulation and solution; where possible they should be simple, self-consistent and plausible, compatible, that is, with other theories currently deployed.[22]

As a result of this constitutive commitment, Kuhn goes on to say, the development of science is a unidirectional process.

Imagine an evolutionary tree representing the development of the modern scientific specialties from their common origins in, say, primitive natural philosophy and the crafts. A line drawn up that tree, never doubling back, from the trunk to the tip of some branch would trace a succession of theories related by descent. Considering any two such theories, chosen from points not too near their origin, it would be easy to design a list of criteria that would enable an uncommitted observer to distinguish the earlier from the more recent theory time after time. Among the most useful would be: accuracy of prediction, particularly of quantitative prediction; the balance between esoteric and everyday subject matter; and the number of different problems solved. Less useful for this purpose, though also important determinants of scientific life, would be such values as simplicity, scope, and compatibility with other specialties. Those lists are not yet the ones required, but I have no doubt that they can be completed. If they can, then scientific development is, like biological, a unidirectional and irreversible process. Later scientific theories are better than earlier ones for solving puzzles in the often quite different environments to which they are applied. That is not a relativist's position, and it displays the sense in which I am a convinced believer in scientific progress.[23]

Of course it is not only these transhistorical, constitutive values that are shared by members of a scientific community. The constellation of group commitments, or "disciplinary matrix," which is shared by the members of a particular community of investigators, also includes particular symbolic generalizations, particular models, particular values, particular exemplars of successful scientific practice, and so on. Although these commitments are not constitutive of science as such, they are definitive of the particular tradition of normal science practiced by that community. Shifts in the constellation of these commitments constitute paradigm change. The argumentation that produces them involves, among other things, an appeal to precisely those values that are constitutive of science. (Such appeals do not, Kuhn points out, automatically lead to a new consensus, for shared values can be differently interpreted and applied, and there can be disagreement as to which of a set of values are most important in a particular case.)

It should be clear that Kuhn's theory of science is not so totally at odds with Popper's position as some have thought. For one thing, Popper's "critical attitude" has many points in common with Kuhn's constitutive commitment to predictive and puzzle-solving capability; and Kuhn's paradigms or disciplinary matrices serve many of the same functions as do Popper's frames of reference or horizons of expectations.[24] On the other hand, if the criticisms of Popper sketched above are valid, Kuhn's conception of the theory of science is a step in the right direction. At the very least, it opens up a dimension in which we might begin to make sense of the "conventions," "frames of reference," "dispositions," "traditions," and the like to which Popper constantly refers in explicating the logic of inquiry but which are finally denied a systematic role in his "epistemology without a knowing subject." The investigation of the structure of communication in the scientific community cannot simply be relegated to the sociology of knowledge. Although commitments, values, rules, conventions, attitudes, frames, and so forth clearly do arise and develop under empirical conditions, they are just as clearly conditions of possibility of scientific knowledge. It is in this dimension—combining the empirical and the transcendental—that the logic of inquiry moves. Having taken us to the point where "the conception of a new and transformed transcendental philosophy" (Habermas) becomes necessary, Popper and Kuhn fail in different ways to pursue systematically the questions central to its elucidation—Popper largely because of his (seemingly inconsistent) recourse to the independence of facts and an abstract opposition between the "objective approach" to an autonomous third world and the "subjective approach" to the subject of knowledge, Kuhn largely because of his failure to develop a clear idea of the differences between empirical psychology and sociology of knowledge and the "quasi-transcendental" logic of inquiry. Habermas's theory of cognitive interests is an attempt to formulate the relevant questions and to provide some guideposts on the way to their resolution.

Chapter 2
Knowledge and Human Interests

2.1 A PRELIMINARY SKETCH

Of Habermas's works *Knowledge and Human Interests* is perhaps the most intrinsically difficult for Anglo-American readers to comprehend. Most of the authors discussed, as well as the structure of the argument as a whole, are deeply rooted in the tradition of German philosophy and social theory. Moreover the book represents Habermas's first attempt to present his position systematically; with few exceptions the major theses he advances have been subsequently reformulated or revised. Even this characterization as a first systematic statement is misleading; the book is, as Habermas points out in the preface, a historical prolegomenon, an attempt to understand the "dissolution of epistemology which has left the philosophy of science in its place," "to make one's way over abandoned stages of reflection." Thus it must be read as an effort to open—or rather to reopen—certain avenues of reflection that were blocked by the ascendancy of positivism during the last hundred years.

The "abandoned stages of reflection" to which Habermas refers are historically located in the movement of German thought from Kant to Marx. His concern is with that alteration of the relation between "epistemological self-reflection" and "empirical-analytic science" discussed in chapter 1. In Kant's critical philosophy, science was comprehended as one category of possible knowledge; theoretical reason was located in a comprehensive framework that encompassed practical reason, reflective judgment, and critical reflection itself. But this construction was unable to withstand Hegel's critique of the unacknowledged presuppositions of transcendental philosophy. The intention of "first philosophy" that informs Kant's critique is illusory; transcendental reflection is not an absolute beginning but depends on something prior and given. In particular the knowing subject cannot be construed as an absolute origin, a self-contained unity outside of or above the movement of history. Rather critical consciousness is itself the outcome of self-formative processes (*Bildungsprozesse*) of both the species and the individual. Accordingly "phenomenological reflection" must reconstruct its own genesis from sense certainty, through successive stages of the appearance of consciousness, to the stage of critique; it is reason reflecting on the different forms that it has taken in the course of its own history.

Habermas agrees that the knowing subject must be comprehended in its historical development; but he takes issue with the way in which Hegel himself develops this insight, namely as a philosophy of Absolute Spirit in which epistemology is not radicalized but abolished. I shall have more to say of this. For now it is necessary to note only that Hegel's philosophy of identity led not to a critical comprehension of empirical science as one category of possible knowledge but to its dissolution in a science of absolute knowledge. And this construction proved unable to withstand either the march of science or the rise of its positivistic misinterpretation.

When philosophy asserts itself as authentic science, the relation of philosophy and science completely disappears from discussion. It is with Hegel that a fatal misunderstanding arises: the idea that the claim asserted by philosophical reason against the abstract thought of mere understanding is equivalent to the usurpation of the legitimacy of the individual sciences by a philosophy claiming to retain its position as universal scientific knowledge. But the actual fact of scientific progress had to unmask this claim, however misunderstood, as bare fiction.[1]

Marx represents for Habermas a second missed opportunity to radicalize the epistemological project. In his metacritique of Hegel, he argued that forms of consciousness arise and are transformed not idealistically, through the self-movement of Absolute Spirit, but materialistically, through the development of productive forces and the struggle of social classes. The forms are, as it were, encoded representations of the self-reproduction of the species, a process that takes place under contingent material conditions. The subject of knowledge is neither a transcendental ego nor an absolute spirit but an embodied, laboring subject whose capacities develop historically in the changing forms of the confrontation with nature that is "the perpetual natural necessity of human life." The synthetic activity of the knowing subject Kant disclosed is merely a pale reflection of the "sensuous human activity" through which laboring subjects regulate their material exchange process with nature and in so doing constitute a world. Thus Marx detached the reconstruction of the self-formative process of the species from its idealist assumptions and thereby opened an avenue of reflection on the subject of knowledge that avoided both the individualistic and ahistorical limitations of Kant's transcendental critique, as well as the idealist excesses of Hegel's philosophy of identity. But he too failed to realize the potential for a radicalization of epistemology that his metacritique had created. Instead of comprehending science epistemologically, he claimed for his own work the mantle of a rigorous science; it disclosed the "economic laws of motion of modern society" as "natural laws." In this form it too was unable to sustain radical reflection against the onslaught of positivism later in the century.

These then are "the abandoned stages of reflection" that Habermas hopes to revive. His theory of cognitive interests is an attempt to radicalize epistemology by unearthing the roots of knowledge in life. It is his central thesis that "the specific view points from which we apprehend reality," the "general cognitive strategies" that guide systematic inquiry, have their "basis in the natural history of the human species." They are tied to "imperatives of the socio-cultural form of life." The reproduction of human life is irrevocably bound to the reproduction of the material basis of life. From the most elementary forms of wresting an existence from nature, through the organized crafts and technical professions, to the development of a technologically based industry, the "material exchange process" with nature has transpired in structures of social labor that depend on knowledge that makes a claim to truth. The history of this confrontation with nature has, from the epistemological point of view, the form of a "learning process." Habermas's thesis is that the "general orientation" guiding the sciences of nature is rooted in an "anthropologically deep-seated interest" in predicting and controlling events in the natural environment, which he calls the *technical* interest.

The reproduction of human life is just as irrevocably based on reliable intersubjectivity in ordinary language communication. The transformation of the helpless newborn into a social individual capable of participating in the life of the community marks his entrance into a network of communicative relations from which he is not released until death. Disturbances to communication in the form of the nonagreement of reciprocal expectations is no less a threat to the reproduction of social life than the failure of purposive-rational action on nature. The development of the historical and cultural sciences from professions in which practical knowledge was organized, transmitted, and applied brought with it a systematic refinement and extension of the forms of understanding through which intersubjectivity can be maintained. Habermas's thesis is that the general orientation guiding the "historical-hermeneutic" sciences is rooted in an anthropologically deep-seated interest in securing and expanding possibilities of mutual and self-understanding in the conduct of life. He calls this the *practical* interest.

The third mode of inquiry that he considers—critical reflection—and the interest in which it is grounded—emancipation from pseudonatural constraints whose power resides in their nontransparency—obviously carry less initial plausibility than the aforementioned. Habermas wants to accommodate under this rubric both the tradition of philosophical reflection (to which his own book belongs) and that of critical self-reflection after the manner of Marx and Freud. In fact the argument of the book rests in part on construing the latter as the proper realization of the former. I shall argue below that this construal is less than convincing. My purpose in making this point at some length is not only to demonstrate the problems arising from this first systematic statement but also to make clear the very weighty considerations that motivated Habermas's subsequent recasting of his views. Without this clarification, his most recent work on communication theory and the theory of social evolution might appear to be an abandonment rather than a necessary development of his original project.

Beyond the discussion of the dissolution of epistemology from Kant to Marx, the book includes lengthy examinations of three late nineteenth- and early twentieth-century thinkers who, in Habermas's view, initiated (each in a different one of the three spheres of inquiry) a radicalized self-reflection of the sciences: Peirce, Dilthey, and Freud. But each ultimately succumbed to a "scientistic self-misunderstanding" of his own work. In falling prey to the "spell of positivism," they failed to realize the potential for transcending it that their reflections had created. The aim of Habermas's discussions is to bring out this potential and develop it in the framework of his theory of cognitive interests.

This introductory section will conclude with a brief overview of the theory. In sections 2.2–2.4, I shall sketch the conceptions of the technical, practical, and emancipatory interests of the empirical-analytical, historical-hermeneutic, and critical-reflective "sciences." (*Wissenschaften*). Finally, in section 2.5, I shall review critically the argument of the book as a whole.

In his inaugural lecture at Frankfurt University in 1965, Habermas presented the idea of cognitive interests (*Erkenntnisinteressen*), or interests that guide knowledge (*erkenntnisleitende Interessen*), by way of opposition to an understanding of theory that can be found in both classical philosophy and modern positivism. These seemingly disparate orientations possess certain essential features in common, he argued. In the first place, *theoria, as* contemplation of the *cosmos*, shares with the sciences, as positivistically understood, a commitment to "the theoretical attitude that frees those who take it from dogmatic association with the natural interests of life and their irritating influence."[2] Second, both aim at "describing the universe theoretically in its lawlike order, just as it is."[3] Although they share the theoretical attitude—the severance of knowledge from interest—and the basic ontological assumption of a structured, self-sufficient world, which it is the task of theory to describe, they differ on the question of the practical efficacy of theory. The traditional connection of *theoria* and *cosmos*, of *mimesis* and *bios theoretikos*, has no counterpart in positivistic theories of knowledge. The conception of theory as a process of cultivation of the person—whether in the classical form of its influence on the conduct of life through the soul's likening itself to the order and proportion of the *cosmos*, or in the modern version of the formation among theorists of a thoughtful and enlightened mode of life—has become apocryphal.

In his critique of the classical and positivistic conceptions of theory, Habermas focuses on their common "objectivism"; for both, "the world appears objectively as a universe of facts whose lawlike connection can be grasped descriptively."[4] This "objectivist illusion" conceals the constitution of these facts', "it suppresses the transcendental framework that is the precondition of the meaning of the validity of such [theoretical] propositions"[5] As soon as this illusion is dispelled and theoretical statements are understood in relation to prior frames of reference in the life-world, their connection with interests that guide knowledge becomes apparent.

Habermas classifies processes of inquiry (*Forschungsprozessen*) into three categories: *empirical-analytic sciences*, including the natural sciences and the social sciences insofar as they aim at producing nomological knowledge; *historical-hermeneutic sciences*, including the humanities (*Geisteswissenschaften*) and the historical and social sciences insofar as they aim at interpretive understanding of meaningful configurations; and the *critically oriented sciences*, including psychoanalysis and the critique of ideology (critical social theory), as well as philosophy understood as a reflective and critical discipline. For each category of inquiry he posits a connection with a specific cognitive interest: "the approach of the empirical-analytic sciences incorporates a *technical* cognitive interest; that of the historical-hermeneutic sciences incorporates a *practical* one; and the approach of critically oriented sciences incorporates the *emancipatory* cognitive interest."[6] These connections are to be demonstrated through an analysis of fundamental categories and of the methods of establishing, testing and, applying the systems of propositions proper to the type of inquiry in question. The cognitive interests appear—as Habermas later puts it—as "general orientations" or "general cognitive strategies" that guide the various modes of inquiry. As such they have a "quasi-transcendental" status.

These cognitive interests are of significance neither for the psychology nor for the sociology of knowledge, nor for the critique of ideology in any narrower sense; for they are invariant. . . . [They are not] influences on cognition that have to be eliminated for the sake of the objectivity of knowledge; rather they themselves determine the aspect under which reality can be objectified and thus made accessible to experience in the first place. They are, for all subjects capable of speech and action, the necessary conditions of the possibility of experience that can claim to be objective.[7]

Although the sciences must preserve their objectivity in the face of *particular* interests, the conditions of possibility of the very objectivity that they seek to preserve include *fundamental* cognitive interests. "Orientations toward technical control, toward mutual understanding in the conduct of life and toward emancipation from seemingly 'natural' constraint establish the specific viewpoints from which we can apprehend reality in any way whatsoever."[8]

Although the cognitive interests, considered from the perspective of the different processes of inquiry, have a transcendental status, they have their basis in the natural history of the human species. The subject of inquiry is no transcendental ego but a community of investigators, a subsystem of a larger social system that is itself a product of the sociocultural evolution of the human species. The specific viewpoints from which reality is apprehended

originate in the interest structure of a species that is linked in its roots to definite means of social organization: work, language and power [*Herrschaft*]. The human species secures its existence in systems of social labor and self-assertion through violence, through a tradition-bound social life in ordinary language communication, and with the aid of ego identities that at every level of individuation reconsolidate the consciousness of the individual in relation to the norms of the group. Accordingly the interests constitutive of knowledge are linked to the functions of an ego that adapts itself to its external conditions through learning processes, is initiated into the communications system of a social life-world by means of self-formative processes [*Bildungsprozesse*], and constructs an identity in the conflict between instinctual aims and social constraints.[9]

These then are the basic elements of Habermas's theory of cognitive interests: a rejection of the "objectivist illusion" according to which the world is conceived as a universe of facts independent of the knower, whose task it is to describe them as they are in themselves; a thematization of the frames of reference in which different types of theoretical statements are located; a classification of processes of inquiry into three categories distinguished by their general cognitive strategies; and the connection of these strategies with specific cognitive interests that have their basis in the natural history of the human species. This preliminary and, from most points of view, rather implausible account of the relation of knowledge and interest should be sufficient to suggest the problems the theory raises and the objections it has to meet. What, exactly, are cognitive interests? How, precisely, can their connection with different processes of inquiry be demonstrated? How is their "quasi-transcendental" status to be reconciled with their roots in the natural history of the human species? Doesn't Habermas fall back on a naturalistic reduction of logical and methodological issues, an empirical answer to conceptual problems? Is it conceivable that work, language, and power could play such a fundamental role in the theory of knowledge? Doesn't the connection of empirical science to a technical interest amount to a conceptually and historically erroneous underestimation of its theoretic dimension? Isn't the very classification of processes of inquiry questionable? Are we to take seriously the category of "critically oriented sciences" and the "emancipatory interest" that guides them, to place them on the same footing with the more established sciences? One could go on in this way indefinitely. In the remainder of this chapter I shall take a more detailed look at the elements of Habermas's theory with the aim of answering some of these questions and objections and of motivating a reformulation of others. In doing so, we shall have to keep in mind the programmatic status of the theory: "These argumentations are certainly unsatisfactory as far as their degree of explication and completeness is concerned; I have always been aware of the fragmentary and provisional character of these considerations."[10] But Habermas does feel that his historical and exploratory reflections have been carried far enough to make clear the program of his theory of knowledge. My intention in what follows is to trace the contours of this program in sufficient detail to permit a tentative evaluation.

2.2 THE TECHNICAL INTEREST
OF THE EMPIRICAL-ANALYTIC SCIENCES

Knowledge and Human Interests was published in 1968; its basic theses were already advanced in the inaugural lecture of 1965. The conception of natural-scientific inquiry developed in the book goes back, as Habermas tells us in the preface, to his lectures at Heidelberg University in the 1963–1964 winter semester. These dates provide important clues to the problem situation in which that conception was worked out. In the early 1960s the philosophy of science was still dominated by the writings of the logical empiricists, whom Habermas regarded as presenting a "scientistic misconception" of science. There were, to be sure, oppositional currents flowing into the discussion at that time, but they were, with few exceptions, by no means so extensively developed and forcefully advanced as the ruling orthodoxy (which, as we now know, was already in the process of being seriously undermined). The major exception, Popper's critical rationalism, presented a number of challenges to logical positivism; but Popper stopped short of drawing the radical consequences for the theory of knowledge that his work implied. In the end, critical rationalism served to shore up the scientistic misunderstanding of science on several important fronts.[1]

In this setting, the writings of Charles Sanders Peirce apparently represented for Habermas a more nearly adequate conception of the foundations of scientific inquiry and a convenient vehicle for stating his own ideas on the subject. To date Habermas has not extensively revised this statement (as he has his treatments of historical-hermeneutic and critical-reflective inquiry). Habermas has, it is true, suggested how the "protophysics" of the Erlangen school (Paul Lorenzen and his colleagues) and the cognitive developmental psychology of Piaget and his followers could be used to develop the idea that the basic categorical framework in which we interpret nature is rooted in structures of instrumental action.[2] But he has not yet updated his general statement in the light of the most recent discussions of the development of scientific knowledge (by Kuhn, Popper, Lakatos, Toulmin, Feyerabend and others).[3] One of the aims of the brief discussion in section 1.3 was to suggest that this somewhat altered state-of-the-problem might provide equally fertile ground for developing Habermas's idea of a quasi-transcendental approach to the philosophy of science. The break with inductivist conceptions of theory appraisal, the emphasis on historical development, the focus on the scientific community's definition of problem situations, and the thematization of norms, conventions, values, and standards are certainly not inimical to his point of view. He would, I think, want to defend the directionality of the history of science against relativistic interpretations, and he would probably point for support to the capacity for prediction and technological control, which, despite often discontinuous *conceptual* shifts, has undergone continued expansion.[4] Well-established empirical regularities may be repeatedly refined and reconceptualized, but they are not simply dropped; we do not dismantle bridges or bombs when theories change.

Be this as it may, the terms of the discussion in *Knowledge and Human Interests* are set by the strategy of playing off Peirce against positivism. Habermas holds that on most crucial points the former provides a more adequate conception of scientific inquiry than the latter. Nevertheless he is not always able to avoid formulations that derive from logical-positivist conceptions and are inconsistent with his expressed pragmatist preferences.[5] But it is clear that these formulations have to be read (often "read out") in the light of the official statement of his position in the chapters on Peirce.

Habermas introduces the idea of a technical interest in his discussion of Marx. He compares the "materialist concept of synthesis"—which, he claims, Marx programmatically suggested but did not work out in any detail—with the Kantian notion of synthesis. The materialist concept preserves the distinction between form and matter; only now the forms are not primarily categories of understanding but of "objective activity." Kant's notion of a fixed framework within which the subject forms a substance that it encounters is retained. However, in the materialist version, this framework is not established through the equipment of transcendental consciousness but derives from the invariant relation of the human species to its natural environment: labor processes are the "perpetual natural necessity of human life."[6] The behavioral system of instrumental, feedback-monitored action (*Funktionskreis des instrumentellen/erfolgskontrollierten Handelns*) arose, contingently, in the natural evolution of the human species. It is grounded, contingently, in the action-oriented, bodily organization of man. At the same time, however, this system of action binds, with transcendental necessity, our knowledge of nature to the interest in possible technical control over natural processes.

Habermas elaborates this Kantian component of the materialist concept of synthesis into an instrumentalist theory of knowledge, which he develops by way of an interpretation of Peirce's pragmatism. Peirce distinguished three forms of inference necessary for the logic of inquiry—deduction, induction, and abduction—which, taken together, constitute a procedure that generates intersubjectively recognized beliefs more successfully than any other proposed method. If our criterion of success for a method is its reliability in arriving at beliefs that future events will confirm rather than render problematic, the scientific method has proved itself to be the most successful. And it is precisely in relation to this criterion that the meaning of the validity of scientific statements must be explicated: the three forms of inference are methods for the settlement of opinions, the elimination of uncertainties, and the acquisition of unproblematic beliefs, in short, for the "fixation of beliefs."

They fulfill these functions in a specifiable objective context, the sphere of purposive-rational action. According to Peirce, the definition of a belief is that we orient our behavior according to it. "Belief consists mainly in being deliberately prepared to adopt the formula believed in as the guide to action"; "the essence of belief is the establishment of a habit; and different beliefs are distinguished by the different modes of action to which they give rise."[7] The validity of beliefs is, on this view, intrinsically connected with behavioral certainty. A belief remains unproblematic so long as the modes of behavior that it guides do not fail in reality. When they do and a given behavioral habit is rendered uncertain, the validity of the belief that guides that behavior is subject to doubt. There follows an attempt to discover new beliefs that will restabilize the disturbed behavior. Thus the meaning of the validity of beliefs must be viewed in the context of the purposive-rational, feedback-monitored, habitual behavior that they guide.

The capacity for purposive-rational control of the conditions of existence is acquired and exercised in a cumulative learning process. Any action guided by a belief is at the same time a test of that belief, and any failure of such action is a potential refutation that might require a reorientation of both belief and behavior. The reorientation of behavior so as to take account of the disappointment of expectations is at the same time an extension of a previously exercised power of instrumental control and the result of a learning process. Scientific inquiry is the reflected and systematic form of this prescientific learning process that is already posited with the structure of instrumental action as such. The refinement takes place primarily in three dimensions:

(1) It [the process of inquiry] isolates the learning process from the life process. Therefore the performance of operations is reduced to selective feedback controls. (2) It guarantees precision and intersubjective reliability. Therefore action assumes the abstract form of experiment mediated by measurement procedures. (3) It systematizes the progression of knowledge. Therefore as many universal assumptions as possible are integrated into theoretical connections that are as simple as possible.[8]

As the systematic continuation of the cumulative learning process that proceeds on the prescientific level within the behavioral system of instrumental action, empirical-analytic inquiry aims at the production of technically exploitable knowledge and discloses reality from the viewpoint of possible technical control over objectified processes. The lawlike hypotheses characteristic of this type of science can be interpreted as statements about the covariance of events. Given a set of initial conditions, they make predictions possible. "Empirical-analytic knowledge is thus possible predictive knowledge."[9] The connection of hypotheses to experience is established through controlled observation, typically an experiment. We generate initial conditions and measure the result of operations carried out under these conditions. In reality, then, basic statements do not provide immediate evidence with no admixture of subjectivity. They are "not simple representations of facts in themselves but express the success or failure of our operations."[10] The basic operations are measurement operations, which make possible the univocal correlation of operatively determined events and systematically connected signs: "If the framework of empirical-analytic enquiry were that of a transcendental subject, then *measurement* would be the synthetic activity which genuinely characterizes it. Only a theory of measurement, therefore, can elucidate the conditions of the objectivity of possible knowledge for the nomological sciences."[11]

All of this shows, Habermas argues, that the behavioral system of instrumental action ultimately determines the structure of empirical-analytic inquiry. The methodological commitments constitutive of such inquiry arise from structures of human life, from imperatives of a species that reproduces itself (in part) through purposive-rational action that is intrinsically tied to cumulative learning processes. These processes have to be maintained in the form of methodological inquiry if the self-formation of the species is not to be endangered. The term *technical cognitive interest* is meant to convey the basic orientation of inquiry, the general congnitive strategy, that derives from this fundamental condition of the reproduction of human life.

This view of empirical-analytic science (as guided by an "anthropologically deep-seated" interest in securing and expanding control over objectified processes) raises a number of problems, the most obvious of which is its adequacy as an account of natural science. It should be clear from the preceding exposition that Habermas is not making a psychological claim about the intentions of natural scientists or a historical claim about specific connections between the development of science and the rise of industry. His analysis is directed, rather, to the *meaning* of a certain class of scientific statements and to the type of validity that they can claim. His thesis is that the origins, structure, and application of such statements show them to be intrinsically related to possibilities of action of a certain sort: purposive-rational action. Thus counterarguments would have to come not from the psychology and history of science but from the logic and philosophy of science. No attempt will be made here to establish the adequacy of Habermas's account of natural science or to deliver a final word in the debate concerning scientific instrumentalism vs. realism that is so alive today. But a few brief remarks might be in order to sharpen his position a bit and to avert some possible misunderstandings.

Hans Albert has raised against Habermas the standard objections to instrumentalist views of scientific theory, for instance, that theories cannot be regarded as instruments since the logic of trying out an instrument and finding it suitable or unsuitable differs from the logic of testing a theory and finding it corroborated or falsified; instruments cannot be falsified.[12] But this type of objection misses the mark. Habermas's pragmatic interpretation of empirical-analytic science is not a theories-as-instruments view. Theories are, according to him, systems of statements that can be correct or incorrect, corroborated or falsified. This is not in question. The question is rather; What do such statements, if valid, disclose about reality? Does their meaning bear an intrinsic relation to possibilities of action of a certain sort?

Habermas's response—that empirical-analytic inquiry provides information that is technically utilizable—would be widely agreed to, if somewhat less interesting, were it intended in a realist sense. If science could be conceived as presenting or approximating a true picture of the regular order of a nature-in-itself, it would follow routinely that this information might be put to practical use.[13] The thesis of the technical interest guiding science has a bite only if understood in a quasi-transcendental sense: as making a claim about the conditions of possibility of objectively valid knowledge of nature and thus about the very meaning of scientific statements. But how is one to decide between the realist and transcendental accounts of the technical utility of scientific information? Granted that statements about the regular covariance of observable events make possible prediction and control of these events, why is this not simply a consequence rather than a condition of fruitful inquiry?

One line of argument in support of Habermas's position follows from the discussion of Popper and Kuhn in chapter 1. Scientific inquiry is a human activity. The actions in which members of the scientific community engage—observation and experimentation, measurement and concept formation, theory construction and testing, and so forth—are subject to certain rules, norms, standards, and the like. Although commitments to standards can shift over time and vary among different groups at any one time, certain fundamental commitments are constitutive of scientific inquiry as such—for example, commitments to the testability of hypotheses through controlled observation and/or experimentation and to the predictive accuracy, particularly quantitative accuracy, of proposed laws and theories. If such commitments are constitutive for scientific inquiry, it is clear that the prognostic and technical virtues of the information it produces are not merely an accidental consequence. The very nature of the procedures for constructing and testing scientific theories ensures that successful theories will have predictive and technical potential. Furthermore the realist account of this potential often rests on a conception of truth—truth as a correspondence of statements with reality—which becomes increasingly implausible once the idea of immediate sensory evidence is given up in favor of some sort of "theory-ladenness" of observation statements. We shall have an opportunity to consider Habermas' concept of truth in chapter 4. For the present it is important to note only that his theory of interests does not imply a reduction of scientific truth to technical utilizability, a version of the "if-it-works-it's-true" view. His position is much closer to Peirce's ideal consensus theory of truth.

Another type of objection to the idea of a technical interest might be raised from within the Frankfurt school itself. It appears that this conception limits our knowledge of nature to information that is technically utilizable and our intercourse with nature to instrumental mastery of objectified processes. Horkheimer and Adorno, as well as Marcuse, explicitly rejected any such limitation.[14] They argued, in fact, that the orientation exclusively to the domination of nature was a basic factor in the deformation of subjective capacities for emancipation. As we saw in section 1.2, Habermas rejects their implicit conception of a New Science and a New Technology, arguing that the logical structures of science and technology as we know them represent an objectification of the essential structural elements of the behavioral system of instrumental action.

Realizing this, it is impossible to envisage how, as long as the organization of human nature does not change and as long therefore as we have to achieve self-preservation through social labor and with the aid of means that substitute for work, we could renounce technology, more particularly our technology, in favor of a qualitatively different one.[15]

There is no "more humane" substitute for the achievements of scientific-technical progress. The real problem is not technical reason as such but its expansion "to the proportions of a life form, of the 'historical totality' of a life world"[16] Understood in this way, Habermas argues, the proper response to the deformation of the subject that has resulted from the universalization of technological rationality and the logic of domination is not the replacement of science and technology through some version of the "resurrection of fallen nature" but a cultivation of the reflective understanding of science as one category of knowledge, of technical control as one mode of action. Technological rationality must be assigned its legitimate, if limited, place within a comprehensive theory of rationality. It is for this task that the theory of cognitive interests is designed.

But is this enough? Are we not left in the end with only one legitimate attitude toward nature: technical mastery? And is this not seriously inadequate as an account of the multifaceted relationships with nature, both "outer nature" and the "inner nature" of our own bodies, which are in fact not only possible but necessary for a full realization of our humanity? Habermas does not exclude the possibility of other *attitudes* toward nature—mimetic, poetic, playful, mystical, fraternal. He does not even exclude a priori the possibility of some sort of communicative relation with nature.[17] But his theory does seem to exclude modes of cognizing nature other than the empirical-analytic. Objections to this exclusion might come from several directions. On what grounds could all cognitive content be denied to those modes of consciousness described above as attitudes? The history of mankind, as well as our own experience in the everyday life-world, are replete with alternative ways of viewing nature. Can all of these be plausibly classified either as protoscientific or noncognitive (say, as emotional, appetitive, or expressive)? To maintain that they must would seem to imply a preconception of cognition, at least with respect to nature, that is highly restrictive and in need, at the very least, of some explication and defense.

Although there is some doubt as to how Habermas would respond to these questions, there is less doubt as to what his position would be vis-à-vis objections that might be raised from the standpoint of metaphysics. The notion that beyond the scientific image of nature it might be possible, and even necessary, to seek a "deeper," metaphysical understanding appears to be ruled out by Habermas's theory of interests. Against traditional ontology he employs the "transcendental turn": the separation of Being and Time, which underlies ontology, conceals an "objectivistic illusion," the suppression of the constitutive role of the subject of knowledge. But even if this is granted, there remains the question whether some type of alternative approach to nature might be compatible with, and even required by, Habermas's theory of interests. I shall return to this question in the concluding section of this chapter.

2.3 THE PRACTICAL INTEREST
OF THE HISTORICAL-HERMENEUTIC SCIENCES

Habermas finds a fundamental indecision in Marx's writings. In his material investigations Marx always took account of both the productive activity of societal individuals *and* the organization of their interrelations. He treated social relations as subject to norms that determined, with the force of institutions, how obligations and rewards were distributed. On the other hand, in his theoretical remarks Marx often seemed to regard the development of the human species as transpiring solely in the dimension of social labor, of processes of production. This tendency to reduce the "self-generative act" of the human species to labor, to eliminate in theory, if not in practice, the structure of symbolic interaction and the role of cultural tradition, was, according to Habermas, at the root of the failure of classical Marxism to develop a reflective theory of knowledge, for it is in this very dimension that the critique of knowledge (as well as of ideological consciousness) moves.

According to the theory of cognitive interests, the specific viewpoints from which we apprehend reality originate in the interest structure of a species that is tied to definite means of social organization. Whereas the technical interest arises from imperatives of a form of life bound to work, the practical interest is anchored in an equally deep-seated imperative of sociocultural life: the survival of societal individuals is linked to the existence of a reliable intersubjectivity of understanding in ordinary language communication.

In its very structure hermeneutic understanding is designed to guarantee, within cultural traditions, the possible action-orienting self-understanding of individuals and groups as well as reciprocal understanding between different individuals and groups. It makes possible the form of unconstrained consensus and the type of open intersubjectivity on which communicative action depends. It bans the danger of communication breakdown in both dimensions: the vertical one of one's own individual life history and the collective tradition to which one belongs, and the horizontal one of mediating between the traditions of different individuals, groups and cultures. When these communication flows break off and the intersubjectivity of mutual understanding is either rigidified or falls apart, a condition of survival is disturbed, one that is as elementary as the complementary condition of the success of instrumental action: namely the possibility of unconstrained agreement and non-violent recognition. Because this is the presupposition of practice, *we call the knowledge-constitutive interest of the cultural sciences* [*Geisteswissenschaften*] "practical".[1]

It is precisely this sphere of unconstrained agreement and open intersubjectivity to which Habermas appealed in his critique of the positivist program for a unified science. The communication structures presupposed by the community of natural scientists cannot themselves be grasped within the framework of empirical-analytic science. The dimension in which concepts, methods, theories, and so forth are discussed and agreed upon, in which the framework of shared meanings, norms, values and so on is grounded, is the dimension of symbolic interaction that is neither identical with nor reducible to instrumental action. The rationality of discourse about the appropriateness of conventions or the meaning of concepts is not the rationality of operations on objectified processes; it involves the interpretation of intentions and meanings, goals, values, and reasons. Thus the objective knowledge produced by empirical-analytic inquiry is not possible without knowledge in the form of intersubjective understanding. This availability of an intersubjectively valid pre- and meta-scientific language, of a framework of shared meanings and values, is taken for granted in the natural sciences. The cultural life-context (*Lebenszusammenhang*), of which scientific communication is only one element, belongs instead to the domain of the cultural sciences.

This distinction between domains of inquiry is not an ontological one between different material objects of inquiry. Human beings can be regarded as part of nature and dealt with in the categories of natural science (as, for instance, in biology). Furthermore human behavior can, within limits, also be treated as subject to the categories of objectified processes (as, for instance, in the strictly behavioral sciences). The distinction is, rather, an epistemological or "transcendental-logical" distinction between formal objects of inquiry. It rests on the different modes of "constituting" the objects of inquiry, on "the system of primitive terms which categorize the objects of possible experience . . . and . . . the methods by which action-related primary experiences are selected, extracted from their own system and utilized for the purpose of the discursive examination of claims to validity, and thus transformed into 'data.'"[2] In the one orientation, we encounter bodies in motion, events and processes capable of being causally explained; in the other, we encounter speaking and acting subjects, utterances, and actions capable of being understood.

In *Knowledge and Human Interests* the "self-reflection of the *Geisteswissenschaften*," is developed through a suggestive—if, from a purely exegetical point of view, often debatable—interpretation of Dilthey.[3] In his more narrowly methodological writings, however, Habermas's account of the nature and limitations of historical-hermeneutic knowledge makes little direct use of Dilthey. He draws instead on contemporary phenomenological, hermeneutic, and linguistic approaches. I shall, therefore, restrict the discussion of Habermas's Dilthey interpretation to the presentation of a few central ideas, putting off until the next chapter a more complete discussion of the critical issues associated with interpretive procedures and their claimed irreducibility to the procedures of empirical-analytic inquiry.

Dilthey anchors skilled understanding in prior modes of understanding in everyday life. "Hermeneutic understanding is only a methodically developed form of the dim reflexivity or semitransparency with which the life of pre-scientifically communicating and socially interacting men takes place in any case."[4] The "meanings" that are the object of such "understanding" are constituted in two dimensions. On the one hand, they derive from the role of particular elements in an entire developmental history. The significance that a person or thing acquires for a subject (group) is a function of its place in his (their) life as a whole, the unity of which is constituted through ever changing retrospective interpretations. In this dimension, the life history of an individual is the pattern for the hermeneutic relation of the whole to its parts. "This guarantees that every specific significance is integrated into a meaning structure that represents the inalienably individual (and not merely singular) unity of a world centered around an ego and of a life history held together by ego identity."[5] On the other hand, meanings that are fixed in symbols are never private. They always have intersubjective validity. A symbolically structured element of a life history owes its semantic content as much to its place in a linguistic system valid for other subjects as it does to its place in a biographical context. Even self-understanding always moves in the medium of mutual understanding with other subjects. "I understand myself only in the 'sphere of what is common' in which I simultaneously understand the other in his objectivations. For our two experiences of life are articulated in the same language, which for us has intersubjectively binding validity."[6] Thus ego identity and communication in ordinary language, preservation of nonidentity and reciprocal identification, are complementary concepts designating the conditions of interaction in dialogue.

Dilthey, postulates the "community of life unities" (Gemeinsamkeit der Lebenseinheiten), defined by the dialogue relation and reciprocal recognition on the one hand, and ego-identity and the process of self-formation in life history on the other, as the objective framework of the cultural sciences. It is

characterized by a double dialectic of the whole and its parts. The first is the horizontal level of communication, marked by the relation of the totality of a linguistic community to the individuals who, within it, identify with each other to the same extent that they simultaneously assert their non-identity against each other. The second is the vertical dimension of time, marked by the relation of the totality of a life history to the singular experiences and life relations of which it is constructed.[7]

The ground of the intersubjectivity that makes interaction and mutual understanding between individuals possible is ordinary language. If hermeneutics is to be analyzed as an explicit procedure, the specific characteristics of ordinary language that allow for the communication, no matter how indirectly, of what is ineffably individual must be explicated. Dilthy distinguishes three classes of "life expressions" (Lebensäusserungen): linguistic expressions, actions, and (nonverbal) experiential expressions (gestures, nervous glances, blushing, intonations and the like). The three classes of expressions are integrated and mutually interpret one another. Symbolic interaction is as much a form of representation as is linguistic communication. The convertibility of the meaning of sentences into actions and of actions into sentences makes reciprocal interpretations possible:

Mutual understanding about linguistic symbols is subject to a permanent control through the actual occurrence of the actions expected in a given context, and these in turn can be interpreted through linguistic communication if there is a disturbance of consensus. The meaning of linguistic symbols can be made clear through participation in habitual interactions. Language and action interpret each other reciprocally; this is developed in Wittgenstein's concept of the language game.[8]

Neither in linguistic communication nor in symbolic interaction can the concrete background of the individuated life histories, which determines the specific meanings of particular expressions and actions, be directly expressed. The individual conditions of life in which communication is situated cannot be transposed completely or unaltered into actions that obey general norms or into the general categories of ordinary language.[9] The third class of life expressions helps the interpreter to close this gap. Experiential expressions— primarily psychological, expressive phenomena linked to the responses of the human body—function as signals for unstated intentions and thus provide indications of the role that the subject takes on pretends to take in any given context of its actions and dialogues.

The dialectic of general and individual made possible in the intersubjectivity of talking and acting can also make use of the accompanying flow of bodily movements and gestures and correct itself by them . . . Ordinary language does not obey the syntax of a pure language. It becomes complete only when enmeshed with interactions and corporeal forms of expression. The grammar of language games in the sense of a complete structure of conduct regulates not only the combination of symbols but also the interpretation of linguistic symbols through actions and expressions.[10]

A "pure language," in Habermas's terminology, could be exhaustively defined by metalinguistic rules of construction. A natural language, on the other hand, defies formally rigorous reconstruction because of its "reflexivity "; it incorporates into itself nonverbal forms of expression (actions and experiential expressions) through which it is interpreted. In this sense, ordinary language is its own metalanguage.

This singular integration of language and practice makes comprehensible the function of understanding in the conduct of life. A breakdown in communication threatens the "action-orienting self-understanding" of individuals and groups, as well reciprocal understanding between individuals and groups. The communication flow can be reestablished only by successfully interpreting those life expressions that cannot be understood and that block the reciprocity of behavioral expectations.

The function of understanding in the conduct of life is analogous to that demonstrated by Peirce for empirical-analytic inquiry. Both categories of investigations are embedded in systems of actions. Both are set off by disturbances of routinized intercourse whether with nature or with other persons. Both aim at the elimination of doubt and the reestablishment of unproblematic modes of behavior. The emergence of a problematic situation results from disappointed expectations. But in one case the criterion of disappointment is the failure of a feedback-controlled purposive-rational action, while in the other it is the disturbance of a consensus, that is the non-agreement of reciprocal expectations between at least two acting subjects. Accordingly, the intentions of the two orientations of inquiry differ. The first aims at replacing rules of behavior that have failed in reality with tested technical rules, whereas the second aims at interpreting expressions of life that cannot be understood and that block the mutuality of behavioral expectations. Experiment refines the everyday pragmatic control of rules of instrumental action to a methodical form of corroboration, whereas hermeneutics is the scientific form of the interpretive activities of everyday life.[11]

Like the empirical-analytic sciences, the hermeneutic sciences are anchored in a specific system of action, in this case, the system of interactions mediated by ordinary language. This rootedness in a specific life structure means that hermeneutic inquiry is governed by a specific cognitive interest, in this case, a "practical interest" in maintaining the type of open intersubjectivity and nonviolent recognition on which communicative action depends. It is this interest that underlay the emergence of the cultural sciences from categories of professional knowledge that developed systematized interpretation into a skill. "The cultural disciplines did not develop out of the crafts and other professions in which technical knowledge is required but rather out of the professionalized realms of action that require practical wisdom."[12]

In consequence of the different interest structure of hermeneutic inquiry, the logic of inquiry in the cultural disciplines is, Habermas maintains, fundamentally different from that which obtains in the empirical-analytic sciences. In the present context the difference in question might simply be stated as one between the roles of the transcendental frameworks in the two types of inquiry. Habermas puts it as follows:

Empirical-analytic sciences disclose reality in so far as it appears within the behavioral system of instrumental action . . . nomological statements about this object domain . . . grasp reality with regard to technical control that, under specified conditions, is possible everywhere and at all times. The hermeneutic sciences do not disclose reality under a different transcendental framework. Rather they are directed toward the transcendental structure of various actual forms of life, within each of which reality is interpreted according to a specific grammar of world views and of action . . . They grasp interpretations of reality with regard to an intersubjectivity of action-orienting understanding possible from a given hermeneutic starting point.[13]

The pattern of communicative action does not play a transcendental role for the hermeneutic sciences in the same way that the framework of instrumental action does for the nomological sciences. Although it is true that the rules of every interpretation are determined by the structure of symbolic interaction in general, it is also true that, once the interpreter is socialized in his mother tongue and has been instructed in interpreting as such, "he does not proceed *subject* to transcendental rules, but *at the level* of the transcendental structures themselves."[14] The hermeneutic inquirer can interpret the meaning of his "texts" only in relation to the structure of the world to which he belongs. Here the role of transcendental framework is played by the grammar of ordinary language, which establishes schemata of world interpretation. Interpretations of interpretations of reality proceed at a different level than do interpretations of reality; in semantic terms, sentences about sentences are of a different order than sentences about facts. On the other hand, the traditional semantic contents that are the objects of hermeneutic inquiry are at once symbols and facts.

Thus interpretation is simultaneously empirical and conceptual analysis. It is directed to the elements of a world constituted through ordinary language and at the very "grammatical" rules that constitute this world.

2.4 THE EMANCIPATORY INTEREST OF CRITICAL THEORY

In dealing with the technical and practical interests, Habermas could begin with generally accepted modes of inquiry and go on to present arguments for their intrinsic connection to "anthropologically deep-seated" systems of action. In the case of the emancipatory interest, the situation is palpably different. It is said to be the guiding interest of the "critically oriented sciences" and of philosophy. By the former, Habermas understands a type of social inquiry concerned to go beyond the production of nomological knowledge and

to determine when theoretical statements grasp invariant regularities of social action as such and when they express ideologically frozen relations of dependence that can in principle be transformed . . . [It] takes into account that information about lawlike connections sets off a process of reflection in the consciousness of those whom the laws are about. Thus the unreflected consciousness, which is one of the initial conditions of such laws, can be transformed. Of course, to this end a critically mediated knowledge of laws cannot through reflection alone render a law itself inoperative, but it can render it inapplicable.[1]

Although Marxian critique of ideology and Freudian psychoanalysis are the classical examples of such critically oriented inquiry, they cannot, Habermas argues, simply be adopted as paradigms. As presented by their founders, they were both subject to "scientistic misunderstanding." Thus the construction of an adequate model for critical social theory is still outstanding. Similarly although Kant's transcendental critique of knowledge and Hegel's phenomenological reflection of consciousness in its manifestations provide the point of departure for Habermas's discussion of the theory of knowledge, he regards neither as an adequate conception of philosophy. The development of a mode of philosophical inquiry appropriate to the emancipatory interest is also still outstanding. Consequently in his discussion of the third interest, Habermas cannot simply appeal to reflection on generally accepted modes of inquiry as he did with the first two interests. He is not plumbing the foundations of established disci-

e [commentary or introductory instructor]

plines but engaging in epistemological reflection as a propaedeutic to formulating a new conception of social and philosophical inquiry.

The idea of a critical social theory incorporating an emancipatory interest takes us to the center of Habermas's thought. We shall encounter it in various forms and from various points of view in the remainder of this study. Although the rough outlines of his conception of critical theory are drawn in *Knowledge and Human Interests,* its further development—even at a very general, programmatic level— had to await the construction of a general theory of communication. In this section my treatment will be confined to the historical considerations and preliminary formulations found in that earlier work. In the final section of this chapter, I shall examine more critically a few of its basic concepts and assumptions.

The history of philosophy provides a number of variations on the theme; "the truth shall make you free." In ancient Greece, Socrates's pursuit of the Delphic injunction to "know thyself" is only the most obvious example. The systematic endeavors of Plato and Aristotle were no less informed by an interest in emancipation. The attitude of pure theory, disinterested contemplation, promised purification from the inconstant drives and passions of everyday life.

The release of knowledge from interest was not supposed to purify theory from the obfuscations of subjectivity but inversely to provide the subject with an ecstatic purification from the passions . . . Catharsis is no longer attained through mystery cults but established in the will of individuals themselves by means of theory.[2]

In modern times, the Enlightenment assigned reason a partisan position in the war against dogmatism. Progress of critical insight meant progress toward the autonomy of the individual; the dissolution of dogmatic constraints was the condition of the liberation of society from unnecessary, because self-imposed, suffering. As Holbach put it:

To error we owe the oppressive chains which despots and priests everywhere forge for the people. To error we owe the slavery in which people languish in almost all countries. To error we owe the religious terrors which freeze human beings in fear and make them slaughter each other for the sake of figments of the mind.[3]

Emancipation by enlightenment required the will to be rational. In his reply to the question; What is Enlightenment?, Kant made this its motto:

Enlightenment is man's release from his self-incurred tutelage. Tutelage is man's inability to make use of his understanding without direction from another. Self-incurred is this tutelage when its cause lies not in lack of reason but in the lack of resolution and courage to use it without direction from another. *Sapere aude!* "Have courage to use your own reason!"—that is the motto of enlightenment.[4]

Thus the idea of Reason encompassed the will to be rational, the will to achieve *Mündigkeit,* autonomy, and responsibility in the conduct of life.[5]

Although the concept of an interest of reason appears in Kant's practical philosophy, the notion that reason should include a drive to realize reason is, strictly speaking, inconceivable within his transcendental framework. To allow the will to be determined by anything other than respect for the laws of practical reason, to act from desire or inclination, is for Kant heteronomy of the will, a surrender of one's freedom and rationality. The motive of a free act, a rational act, cannot be a subjective interest in the object of the action; it must be a motive valid for all rational beings as such. On the other hand, moral feeling attests to something like a factual interest in the realization of moral laws, of a realm of freedom. This interest cannot be a sensual one. Thus Kant calls practical pleasure in morality, that is, in actions that are determined by principles of reason, a "pure interest" (in contrast to the "pathological" interest in the object of the action). The concept of a pure interest ascribes to reason a causality opposed to that of the faculty of desire.

In order to will that which reason alone prescribes to the sensuously affected rational being as that which he ought to will, certainly there is required a power of reason to instill a feeling of pleasure or satisfaction in the fulfillment of duty, and hence there must be a causality of reason to determine the sensibility in accordance with its own principles. But it is wholly impossible to discern, i.e. to make a priori conceivable, how a mere thought containing nothing sensuous is to produce a sensation of pleasure or displeasure. For that is a particular kind of causality of which, as of all causality, we cannot determine anything *a priori* but must consult experience only.[6]

Thus to account for the experience of morality Kant must introduce the concept of a pure interest of reason in *Mündigkeit*: reason itself harbors an interest in the achievement of autonomy and responsibility.

If pure reason is to be the cause of an effect that occurs in experience—pleasure in the fulfillment of duty—then a moment of facticity is introduced into reason itself. Thus an answer to the question, How can pure reason be practical? would require the concept of an interest that was neither empirical nor entirely severed from experience. But from Kant's viewpoint, this is inconceivable, as he concedes in the conclusion to the lines quoted above:

But since experience can exemplify the relation of cause to effect only as subsisting between two objects of experience, while here pure reason by mere Ideas (which furnish no object for experience) is to be the cause of an effect which does lie in experience, an explanation of how and why the universality of the maxim as law (and hence morality) interests us is completely impossible for us men.[7]

On the basis of Kant's conception of reason, then, while we can be certain *that* pure reason can be practical, we are entirely incapable of comprehending *how* this is possible.

Fichte provides a framework in which the interested employment of pure reason can be comprehended, but only at the cost of reducing nature to the posit of an absolute ego. He overcomes the Kantian split between theoretical and practical reason by making a principle of the primacy of practical reason. The fundamental form of dogmatism that is to be overcome by enlightenment is the fixation of the immature (*unmündigen*) consciousness on things. A consciousness that comprehends itself as a product of the things around it, as a product of nature, is dogmatically enslaved: "The principle of the dogmatists is belief in things for their own sake, that is, indirect belief in their own self, which is dispersed and supported only by objects."[8] Only from the idealist standpoint is it possible to transcend the dogmatism of natural consciousness and achieve mature autonomy (*Mündigkeit*). But to raise itself to this standpoint, the ego must have an interest in its own autonomy, a will to emancipate itself from its dependence on things. Dogmatism is as much a moral lack as a theoretical incapacity. Correspondingly the intellectual intuition in which the ego apprehends itself as the self- and world-positing subject is an original act of freedom motivated by the interest of reason in emancipation. As Habermas puts it:

In the interest in the independence of the ego, reason realizes itself in the same measure as the act of reason as such produces freedom. Self-reflection is at once intuition and emancipation, comprehension and liberation from dogmatic dependence. The dogmatism that reason undoes both analytically and practically is false consciousness: error and unfree existence.[9]

On Fichtean premises dogmatism—as unreflected, natural consciousness—becomes all-pervasive. It does not first have to establish itself (as with Holbach) as prejudice, private or institutionalized; it is present wherever there is unawareness of one's autonomy. In this setting, enlightenment is idealism, the reduction of nature to indeterminate material for acting subjects. From the standpoint of his idealism, Fichte can conceive of reason as inherently practical, as tied to the practical intention of a subject that seeks its own autonomy. In this sense, "the highest interest and the ground of all other interest is interest in ourselves."[10] This autonomy is attainable only through an act of self-reflection in which the subject apprehends itself as the source of consciousness and of the world. Thus the interest of reason is constitutive both for knowing and for acting. In Habermas's terms, "As an act of freedom interest precedes self-reflection just as it realizes itself in the emancipatory power of self-reflection."[11]

Unlike the absolute self-positing of Fichte's ego, Hegel's phenomenological self-reflection surmounts dogmatism by reflectively reconstructing the self-formative process (*Bildungsprozess*) of mind (*Geist*).[12] Critical reflection is not an absolute origin; it is dependent on something prior, which it takes as its object while simultaneously originating in it. Beginning with the natural consciousness of the everyday life-world in which we already find ourselves, phenomenological reflection traces its own genesis through the successive stages of the manifestation of consciousness. This movement combines reason and interest, since at every stage it overcomes both a world view and a form of life.

For reflection destroys, along with a false view of things, the dogmatic attitudes of a habitual form of life. . . . In false consciousness, knowing and willing are still joined. . . . The reversal of consciousness means the dissolution of identifications, the breaking of fixations, and the destruction of projections.[13]

The experience of reflection proceeds by way of a determinate negation that guards against empty skepticism. The unmasking of a dogmatic attitude contains a positive moment that is incorporated in a new reflected attitude.

A form of life that has become an abstraction cannot be negated without leaving a trace or overthrown without practical consequences. The revolutionized situation contains the one that has been surpassed, because the insight of the new consists precisely in the experience of revolutionary release from the old consciousness.[14]

Critical consciousness, proceeding by way of determinate negation, aims at comprehending the context of its own genesis, the self-formative process of which it itself is the outcome. Through a systematic repetition of the manifestations of consciousness that constitute the history of mankind, it works itself up to its present standpoint through stages of reflection. At every stage a new insight is confirmed in a new attitude. Phenomenological reflection is accordingly a mode of reflection or self-knowledge in which theoretical and practical reason are one.

At the end of the *Phenomenology of Mind*, Hegel asserts that this critical consciousness is absolute knowledge. In Habermas's view, this can only mean that "from the very beginning Hegel presumes as given a knowledge of the Absolute."[15] For phenomenology, as a reflective appropriation of the self-formative process of the human species, would not otherwise confer upon critical consciousness the status of absolute knowledge, would not otherwise eventuate in the absolute unity of subject and object. This indicates that Hegel has a different understanding of phenomenology: "He presumes that phenomenological experience always keeps and has kept within the medium of an absolute movement of the mind."[16] From this standpoint, rather than a radicalized critique of knowledge that unifies theoretical and practical reason, phenomenology becomes a "metaphysical philosophy of mind and nature."[17]

In contrast to Fichte's absolute self- and world-positing ego and Hegel's absolute movement of mind, Marx conceives of the self-formative process of the human species as conditioned: it depends on contingent conditions of nature. Mind is not the absolute ground of nature; it is nature that is the ground of mind in the sense of a natural process that gives rise both to the natural human being and to the na-

ture that surrounds him. In reproducing its life under natural conditions, the human species regulates its material exchange with nature
through processes of social labor. Social labor, "sensuous human activity," is not only a condition of human existence but a transcendental
accomplishment. "The system of objective activities creates the factual
conditions of the possible reproduction of social life and *at the same
time* the transcendental conditions of the possible objectivity of the objects of experience. . . . It regulates material exchange with nature *and*
constitutes a world."[18] The objects of experience share with nature
the property of being-in-itself, but they also bear the character of
produced objectivity resulting from the activity of man. In opposition
to idealism, the subject of world constitution is not transcendental
consciousness in general but the concrete human species reproducing
its life through processes of social labor.

Because of the invariant relationship of the species to its natural
environment—expressed in structures of human sensuous activity
that are rooted in the bodily organization of man—the transcendental
accomplishment of world constitution transpires within a fixed
framework. On the other hand, the specific forms in which nature is
objectified change historically in dependence on the system of social
labor. We have access to nature only through a historically alterable
stock of categories and rules that reflects the organization of our material activities. Alterations in the system of social labor brought about
by the development of the forces of production give rise to alterations
in the societal categories through which anything like a world can be
given. In other words, although the labor process may be considered
independently of every specific social form, it designates not a fixed
human essence but only a fixed mechanism of the evolution of the
species. In the labor process, what changes is not only the nature
worked upon but the nature of the laboring subjects themselves. "History is the true natural history of man."[19]

From this standpoint, Marx can detach the reconstruction of the
self-formative process of the human species from its idealist presuppositions. The stages of the manifestation of consciousness are dependent on the historical stages of development of the forces and relations of production. Since the system of social labor is the result of
the labor of past generations, the present subject comprehends itself
by knowing itself to have been produced as by itself through the production of past subjects. . . . A social subject attains consciousness of

itself in the strict sense only if it becomes aware of itself in its production or labor as the self-generative act of the species in general and knows itself to have been produced by the "labor of the entire previous course of world history."[20]

Human reason and the partisanship of reason against dogmatism develop historically in the process of the confrontation of laboring subjects with nature. In contrast to the subjective form of Fichte's classification of men (into dogmatists and idealists) and of their interests (in things or in themselves), Marx anchors the division of classes and interests in historically specific configurations of alienated labor and suppressed freedom. Dogmatism, in the form of false consciousness and reified social relations, cannot be overcome by a Fichtean withdrawal into the autonomous subject. Rooted as it is in material interests, it must be criticized practically at the level of the objective context of delusion, that is, at the level of the system of social labor itself. Dogmatism assumes the form of ideology, and reason is active as the critique of ideology. The partisanship of reason against dogmatism has the same objectivity as the illusion that it criticizes; the interest in a rational organization of society is no less historically determined, no less embedded in the objective social context.

In Habermas's view, Marx's work contains the principal elements required for an adequate conception of reason and the interest of reason in emancipation. But this promise, he argues, was never realized.

Notwithstanding, the philosophical foundation of his materialism proves itself insufficient to establish an unconditional self-reflection of knowledge and thus prevent the positivist atrophy of epistemology. Considered immanently, I see the reason for this in the *reduction of the self-generative act of the human species to labor.* Alongside the forces of production in which instrumental activity is sedimented, Marx's social theory also incorporates into its approach the institutional framework, the relations of production. It does not eliminate from practice the structure of symbolic interaction and the role of the cultural tradition, which are the only basis on which power [*Herrschaft*] and ideology can be comprehended. But this aspect of practice is not made part of the philosophical frame of reference. It is in this very dimension, however, which does not coincide with that of instrumental action, that phenomenological experience moves. In this dimension appear the configurations of consciousness in its manifestations that Marx calls ideology, and in it reifications are dissolved by the silent force of a mode of reflection to which Marx gives back the Kantian name of critique. Thus in Marx's works a peculiar disproportion arises between the practice of inquiry and the limited philosophical understanding of the inquiry. In his empirical analyses Marx comprehends the history of the species under categories of material activity *and* the critical abolition of ideologies, of instrumental action *and* revolutionary practice, of labor *and* reflection at once. But Marx interprets what he does in the more restricted conception of the species' self-reflection through work alone.[21]

On the one hand, in his material investigations, Marx treats the self-formative process of the human species as mediated not only by the productive acticity of individuals but also by the organization of their interaction, that is, by the institutionalized relations of power and the cultural traditions that regulate men's interactions among themselves. Although it is the development of the forces of production that provides the impetus for overcoming rigidified forms of life and consciousness, this development does not, taken by itself, lead to that reflexive comprehension of the social life process from which self-conscious control could result. Emancipation from relations of social force, from the power of one class over another, requires revolutionary struggle, including the critical reflective activity through which ideological delusions are dispelled. From this perspective, Marx, going beyond Hegel, can regard the reconstruction of the manifestations of consciousness as an encoded representation of the self-reproduction of the species. Forms of consciousness arise and are suspended not idealistically, through the self-movement of an absolute mind, but materialistically, through the development of the forces of production and the struggle of social classes. Critical consciousness, in the form of the critique of ideology, is itself involved in the self-formative process it reflectively appropriates.

On the other hand, at the categorial level, Marx tends to view the self-formative process of the species unidimensionally in terms of progress through productive activity. The institutional framework is regarded as an aspect of the productive process.[22] The form of knowledge adequate to this process is a "human natural science." Invoking the model of physics, Marx claims to represent "the economic laws of motion of modern society" as a "natural law." This shows, according to Habermas, that although the idea of the self-constitution of mankind through labor sufficed to criticize Hegel, it was inadequate to render comprehensible the real significance of the materialist appropriation of Hegel.

This demand for a natural science of man, with its positivist over-tones, is astonishing. For the natural sciences are subject to the tran-scendental conditions of the system of social labor, whose structural change is supposed to be what the critique of political economy, as the science of man, reflects on. Science in the rigorous sense lacks pre-cisely this element of reflection that characterizes a critique investigat-ing the natural-historical process of the self-generation of the social subject and also making the subject conscious of this process.[23]

Marx's failure to develop consistently the idea of a science of man as critique, his understanding of the critique of political economy as a natural science of society, completed the disintegration of philoso-phy's position with regard to science. Neither Hegel's science of abso-lute knowledge nor Marx's scientific materialism could sustain the di-mension of radical reflection against the onslaught of positivism in the second half of the nineteenth century. With positivism the theory of knowledge became the philosophy of science; reason became scientific reason; and the interest of reason was either denied or equated with the technical interest in prediction and control of objectified process-es. To restore the notions of a comprehensive reason and an interest of reason in human emancipation, it is, according to Habermas, necessary to return to the dimension of thought opened (and sub-sequently undermined) by Hegel and Marx: critical reflection. But the nonscientistic, nonreductivist side of Marx's thought has to be drawn out and developed. Habermas attempts to do this in *Knowledge and Human Interests* by incorporating a number of Freud's ideas into a re-vised historical materialism.[24]

In his writings on the theory of civilization (*Kultur*), Freud turns to the "diagnosis of communal neuroses." Whereas the preliminary concep-tions of normality and deviance that the analyst employs in individual therapy are culturally conditioned, the analysis of human society must go beyond the standards of a given sociocultural framework and take account of the cultural evolution of the human species. What elevated men above animals was the development of the family, an agency of socialization capable of transforming instinctual behavior into com-municative action and of canalizing surplus libidinal and aggressive impulses into socially acceptable modes of behavior. The institutional demands placed on the emerging individual are represented by the parents. The reality that confronts the dependent child and forces the denial of instinctual needs is thus not immediately that of external nature; it is instead the reality of society itself making its demands felt through the agency of family structure.

As a system of self-preservation, society must be secured against the constraints of external nature through the collective effort of societal individuals. "The motive of human society is in the last resort an economic one."[25] Economic scarcity, in turn, requires defenses against inner nature in the form of libidinal and aggressive impulses which transcend the system of social labor: "since it [society] does not possess enough provisions to keep its members alive unless they work, it must restrict the number of its members and divert their energies from sexual activity to work."[26] The renunciations imposed by economic scarcity vary historically in dependence on the level of development of productive forces, as well as on the organization of their employment and the distribution of the goods produced. As the pressure of reality decreases with the expansion of the forces of production, it becomes possible to replace institutionalized repression of instincts by their rational mastery. But the extent to which this possibility is realized depends not on technological development alone, for the institutionalized repression of instinctual impulses also serves to sustain a particular system of social labor: "regulations, institutions, and commands . . . aim not only at effecting a certain distribution of wealth but at maintaining that distribution."[27] In addition to the general, socially necessary level of repression demanded by economic scarcity, there are class-specific privations and prohibitions linked to the organization of labor and the distribution of wealth. The difference between the actual degree of institutionally demanded repression and the degree of repression that is necessary at a given level of the forces of production is a measure of objectively superfluous domination. In this context Freud introduces a notion of class struggle:

If . . . a culture has not got beyond a point at which the satisfaction of one portion of its participants depends upon the suppression of another, and perhaps larger, portion—and this is the case in all present day cultures—it is understandable that the suppressed people should develop an intense hostility toward a culture whose existence they make possible by their work, but in whose wealth they have too small a share. . . . It goes without saying that a civilization which leaves so large a number of its participants unsatisfied and drives them into revolt neither has nor deserves the prospect of a lasting existence.[28]

Habermas sees the specific advantage of incorporating Freud's ideas into historical materialism in the possibilities this opens for re-conceptualizing "power" and "ideology" and for clarifying the status of a critical science. Institutionalized power relations, like individual neuroses, bring about a relatively rigid reproduction of behavior that is removed from criticism. Based on social norms, they permit the partial replacement of manifest compulsion through open force by inner compulsion through the affective force of unconscious mechanisms. Repressed motives for action are excluded from com-munication and directed into channels of substitute gratification. These symbolically redirected motives are the forces that dominate consciousness by legitimating existing power relations. In this sense, institutions of power are rooted in distorted communication, in ideologically imprisoned consciousness.

From this perspective, ideology assumes a substantive role in the formation, maintenance, and transformation of society. As Freud puts it:

With the recognition that every civilization rests on a compulsion to work and a renunciation of instinct and therefore inevitably provokes opposition from those affected by these demands, it has become clear that civilization cannot consist principally or solely in wealth itself and the means of acquiring it and the agreements for its distribution; for these things are threatened by the rebelliousness and destructive mania of the participants in civilization. Alongside of wealth we now come upon the means by which civilization can be defended—measures of coercion and other measures that are intended to recon-cile men to it and recompense them for their sacrifices. The latter may be described as the mental assets of civilization.[29]

These "mental assets" —religious world-views, ideals and value sys-tems, art, and so forth—are in Freud's terms "illusions." In providing publicly sanctioned compensations for the renunciations imposed by the existing order, they fashion substitute gratification into legitima-tions of this order. Although they exist at the level of public com-munication, they represent systematic distortions of communication that remove from criticism the interpretations of life and the world on which rationalizations of the existing order are based. But illusions are not simply delusions. Like the latter, they are derived from human wishes; unlike the latter, they are not necessarily false, that is,

unrealizable. Individual wishes incompatible with the institutional reality of established society cannot be realized. But for the species as a
whole, the boundaries of this reality are movable. In Habermas's
words:

> With the development of technology, the institutional framework,
> which regulates the distribution of obligations and rewards and
> stabilizes a power structure that maintains cultural renunciation, can
> be loosened. Increasingly, parts of cultural tradition that at first have
> only projective content can be changed into reality. That is, virtual
> gratification can be transposed into institutionally recognized grat-
> ification. "Illusions" are *not merely* false consciousness. Like what Marx
> called ideology, they too harbor utopia. If technical progress opens up
> the objective possibility of reducing socially necessary repression
> below the level of institutionally demanded repression, this utopian
> content can be freed from its fusion with the delusory, ideological
> components of culture that have been fashioned into legitimations of
> authority and be converted into a critique of power structures that
> have become historically obsolete.[30]

Within the framework of a historical materialism that has incorporated Freud in this way, it is possible, Habermas believes, to clarify the
status of the critical science that reconstructs the self-formative process of the species and to explicate the ideas of reason and of an
emancipatory interest of reason that underlie it. The forms of the
manifestation of consciousness that were, according to Hegel, successively overcome in the absolute movement of mind, can now be
grasped as rigidified forms of life, constellations of power and ideology that have been undermined by the development of the forces of
production. They are overcome through the "critical-revolutionary"
activity of suppressed classes, including the reflective critique of
ideologically frozen forms of consciousness. The movement of reflection in history is thus determined simultaneously by processes of reproduction through labor and by processes of self-formation under
conditions of distorted communication. The development of the
forces of production creates the objective possibility of lessening the
pressure of the institutional framework and—in Freud's terms—of
replacing "the affective basis of [man's] obedience to civilization by a
rational one," of "providing a rational basis for the precepts of civilization."[31] The goal of the transformation of institutional frameworks

and destruction of ideologies is, in Habermas's terms, "an organization of social relations according to the principle that the validity of every norm of political consequence be made dependent on a consensus arrived at in communication free from domination."[32] Informed by this telos, critical revolutionary activity attempts to promote enlightenment by testing the limits, under given conditions, of the realizability of the utopian content of cultural tradition. Since there can be no certainty that a rational organization of society through communication free from domination is realizable in all circumstances, the logic of the movement of reflection is a "logic of trial and error," a "logic of justified hope and controlled experiment."[33]

From this perspective, critical social theory can be seen to belong essentially to the self-formative process on which it reflects. Extending in methodical form the practical self-understanding of social groups, it seeks to raise their self-consciousness to the point where it "has attained the level of critique and freed itself from all ideological delusion."[34] In unmasking the institutionally anchored distortions of communication that prevent the organization of human relations on the basis of unconstrained intersubjectivity, the subject of critical theory does not take up a contemplative or scientistic stance above the historical process of human development. Knowing himself to be involved in this development, to be a result of the "history of consciousness in its manifestations" on which he reflects, he must direct the critique of ideology at himself. In this way critical theory pursues self-reflection out of an interest in self-emancipation.

It is only in comprehending the emancipatory interest behind critical reflective knowledge, Habermas maintains, that the correlation of knowledge and human interest in general can be adequately grasped. The dependence of the natural and cultural sciences on technical and practical interests, their embeddedness in objective structures of human life, might seem to imply the heteronomy of knowledge. It might seem that reason, in itself disinterested, is thereby placed in the service of interests that are themselves irrational, interests linked to the self-preservation of the species. But the elucidation of the category of critical reflective knowledge shows, according to Habermas, that the meaning of reason, and thus the criterion of its autonomy, cannot be accounted for without recourse to an interest of reason that is constitutive of knowledge as such.

In the case of an objectivation whose power is based only on the subject not recognizing itself in it as its other, knowing it in the act of self-reflection is immediately identical with the interest in knowledge, namely in emancipation from that power. The analytic situation makes real the unity of intuition and emancipation, of insight and liberation from dogmatic dependence, and of reason and the interested employment of reason developed by Fichte in the concept of self-reflection. Only self-reflection is no longer the act of an absolute ego. . . . Given materialist presuppositions, the interest of reason therefore can no longer be conceived as an autarchic self-explication of reason. The proposition that interest inheres in reason has an adequate meaning only within idealism, that is only as long as we are convinced that reason can become transparent to itself by providing its own foundation. But if we comprehend the cognitive capacity and critical power of reason as deriving from the self-constitution of the human species under contingent natural conditions, then it is *reason that inheres in interest.*[35]

As a "system of self-preservation," human society, confronted with economic scarcity, must defend itself against libidinal and aggressive impulses that threaten the system of social labor. As long as the pressure of reality is overpowering and ego organization is weak, this defense is achieved affectively through institutionalized repression in the form of power and ideology. Because individual and social pathology assume the form of structural deformations of communication, the interest in their alteration is simultaneously an interest in enlightenment.

This interest aims at reflection on oneself. . . . Self-reflection brings to consciousness those determinants of a self-formative process . . . which ideologically determine a contemporary practice and conception of the world. . . . [It] leads to insight due to the fact that what has previously been unconscious is made conscious in a manner rich in consequences: analytic insights intervene in life.[36]

It is this connection between critical reflection and liberation from "dependence on hypostasized powers," from "seemingly natural constraints," that underlay Habermas's "fourth thesis" in his inaugural lecture at Frankfurt University: "In self-reflection knowledge for the sake of knowledge attains congruence with the interest in autonomy and responsibility. . . . In the power of self-reflection knowledge and interest are one."[37] Since critical reflection undermines the dogmatic character of both a world view and a form of life, the cognitive process coincides with a self-formative process: knowing and acting are fused in a single act.

With this connection in mind, it is possible to dispel the appearance of heteronomy that attaches to the two "lower" interests, where the two moments of acting and knowing do not immediately coincide in this way. It is an error, says Habermas, to regard knowledge guided by the interests in technical control or mutual understanding as if an autonomous reason, free of presuppositions, through which reality was first grasped theoretically, were only subsequently taken into the service of interests alien to it. The meaning of reason and the criteria of its autonomy cannot be grasped without recourse to a connection with cognitive interests. The technical and practical interests are constitutive of knowledge; they determine the conditions of the objectivity and validity of statements. Thus they are themselves rational.

This does not mean that reason can be conceived as if it were merely an organ of adaptation for men just as claws and teeth are for animals.

True, it does serve this function. But the human interests that have emerged in man's natural history . . . derive both from nature and *from the cultural break with nature.* Along with the tendency to realize natural drives they have incorporated the tendency toward release from the constraints of nature. Even the interest in self-preservation, natural as it seems, is represented by a social system that compensates for the lacks in man's organic equipment and secures his historical existence *against* the force of nature threatening from without. . . . The cognitive processes to which social life is indissolubly linked function not only as means to the reproduction of life; for in equal measure they themselves determine the definitions of this life. What may appear as naked survifal is always in its roots a historical phenomenon. For it is subject to the criterion of what a society intends for itself as *the good life.*[38]

The interest in self-preservation cannot be defined independently of the cultural conditions of human life; societal subjects must first interpret what they count as life. These interpretations, in turn, are oriented to ideas of the good life. The notion of the good life is neither a pure convention nor a fixed essence. The ideal of autonomy and responsibility is posited in the very structure of communication, anticipated in every act of communication.[39] But this ideal is not yet real, nor is it attainable in a single act of self-intuition, for the self-formative process of the species is not unconditioned. It depends on conditions of symbolic interaction and material exchange with nature. Consequently the measure of *Mündigkeit* that is attainable at a given stage of historical development is also conditioned.

Reason's interest in emancipation, which is invested in the self-formative process of the species and permeates the movement of reflection, aims at realizing those conditions of symbolic interaction and instrumental action; and, to this extent, it assumes the restricted form of the practical and technical cognitive interests. Indeed, in a certain measure, the concept of the interest of reason introduced by idealism needs to be reinterpreted materialistically: the emancipatory interest is itself dependent on interests in possible intersubjective action-orientation and in possible technical control.[40]

2.5 THE IDEA OF PHILOSOPHY AND ITS RELATION TO SOCIAL THEORY

We are by now well acquainted with the rationale behind the "linguistic turn" in twentieth-century philosophy. *Knowledge and Human Interests* makes a case for the necessity of taking an additional turn, a "social turn," on the way to an adequate theory of knowledge. If the traditional analysis of the isolated consciousness, its acts and ideas, represented a peculiar abstraction from the intersubjectively valid "grammars" of (ordinary or ideal) languages, the recent analysis of language represents a no less peculiar abstraction from the structures of social action. On this view, further radicalization of the critique of knowledge calls for reflection on the function of knowledge in the reproduction of social life and on the objective conditions under which the subject of knowledge is historically formed.

In addressing himself to this task, Habermas attempts to open up and chart a territory lying between the realms of the empirical and the transcendental. On the one hand, the theory of cognitive interests, "like the transcendental logic of an earlier period, seeks a solution to the problem of the a priori conditions of possible knowledge."[1] On the other hand, it is concerned not with attributes of transcendental consciousness but with "logical structures that materialize under empirical conditions"; not with a transcendental ego but with a "naturally generated and socially formed subject," the "community of investigators who endeavor to perform their common task communicatively."[2] Considered from the point of view of the organization of inquiry, the "basic orientations" (or "interests") revealed by this type of analysis "have a transcendental function"; but they are rooted in "actual structures of human life," in "specific fundamental conditions of the possible reproduction and self-constitution of the human species, namely work and interaction."[3]

In *Knowledge and Human Interests* Habermas introduces this theory by way of a "history of philosophy written with a systematic intent." Although this mode of presentation is undeniably suggestive, it certainly leaves much to be desired in regard to the clarity and precision of basic concepts and the detailed articulation of central arguments. Nevertheless the general outlines of the theory are sufficiently clear to have sparked an extensive critical literature. Some of the issues raised—concerning, for instance, the distinctions drawn between empirical-analytic, historico-hermeneutic, and critical-reflective modes of inquiry, the a priori character of the interest in *Mündigkeit* that is said to be inherent in the structure of communication, the authoritarian or resignative implications for practice of a theory modeled after psychoanalysis—will be taken up in later chapters. In this section, I shall focus on a set of problems relating to Habermas's notion of reflection and to its implications for the nature of philosophy, and I shall do so in such a way as to point ahead to subsequent developments of his thought, especially those issuing in the theory of communicative competence.

Self-reflection is clearly one of the most important concepts in the theory of cognitive interests; it is also one of the most problematic. To begin with, there is some ambiguity concerning its anthropological status. At times the objective structures of human life that give rise to the different cognitive orientations are specified as work, language, and power.[4] This construction seems to place the orientation toward "emancipation from seemingly natural constraints" on the same anthropological footing as the orientations toward technical control and toward mutual understanding in the conduct of life. Self-reflection as a mode of experience and action appears to be on a par with instrumental action and symbolic interaction. This is not very plausible, even if one accepts the general approach of the theory of interests. Experiences of systematically distorted communication and attempts to remove such distortions through critical self-reflection do not, on the face of it, possess the same anthropological primordiality as the mastery of nature and the achievement of understanding in ordinary language communication.

Usually, however, Habermas reserves the designation "fundamental condition of our cultural existence" for work and interaction.[5] In this construction, power and ideology are located *within the sphere of interaction* as distortions of "the moral relationship." The interest of self-reflection in emancipation is viewed then as an interest in social relations organized on the basis of communication free from domination. From this perspective power, ideology, and critical self-reflection do not have the same anthropological status as work and interaction.

In subsequent clarifications of his theory, Habermas has explicitly favored this second version. In the introduction to *Theory and Practice*, for example, he links the "two 'lower' interests" to "imperatives of a sociocultural form of life dependent on labor and language."[6] He treats the emancipatory interest differently: "This interest can only develop to the degree to which repressive force, in the form of the normative exercise of power, presents itself permanently in structures of distorted communication—that is, to the extent that domination is institutionalized."[7] In the postscript to *Knowledge and Human Interests*, this difference is made yet more explicit.

Compared with the technical and practical interests in knowledge, which are both grounded in deeply-rooted (invariant?) structures of action and experience—that is in the constituent elements of social systems—the *emancipatory interest in knowledge* has a derivative status. It guarantees the connection between theoretical knowledge and an "object domain" of practical life which comes into existence as a result of systematically distorted communication and thinly legitimated repression. The type of action and experience corresponding to this object domain is, therefore, also derivative.[8]

This characterization of the third interest as derivative should not, of course, be taken to mean that it is less important than the other two. The point of the comparison is not the relative importance but the relative invariance of the different conditions of human life. Whereas work and interaction are for Habermas invariant constituents of our sociocultural form of life, systematically distorted communication is not (or rather, one may adopt the "practical hypothesis" that it is not).

To be sure, there is a sense in which the interest in emancipation is itself invariant. As Habermas stated in his inaugural lecture at

Frankfurt University (and as he attempts to prove in his theory of communication), the human interest in autonomy and responsibility (*Mündigkeit*) is "posited" in the very structure of human communication; in the language of German Idealism, "reason also means the will to reason."[9] But although this telos itself is invariant, the actual pursuit of emancipation through critical self-reflection develops only in connection with historically variable conditions of work and interaction. In contrast then to the structures of purposive-rational and communicative action, "the structure of distorted communication is not ultimate; it has its basis in the logic of undistorted communication in language."[10]

There are other, more fundamental ambiguities in the concept of self-reflection as it is used in *Knowledge and Human Interests*. On the one hand, taking Kant as his point of departure, Habermas attempts to revive and radicalize the idea of a *critique of knowledge*. In this context "self-reflection" means reflection on the subjective conditions of knowledge, on the "a priori constitution" of the facts with which the objectifying sciences deal, on the "synthetic achievements of the knowing subject." It is primarily in this sense that Peirce advanced the "self-reflection of the natural sciences" and Dilthey the "self-reflection of the cultural sciences." On the other hand, taking Marx and Freud as points of departure, Habermas attempts to develop the idea of a *critique of ideology* that aims at freeing the subject from his dependence on "hypostasized powers" concealed in the structures of speech and action. In this context "self-reflection" refers to a "dialectic that takes the historical traces of suppressed dialogue and reconstructs what has been suppressed,"[11] that brings to consciousness "those determinants of a self-formative process which ideologically determine a contemporary praxis and world view."[12] It is in this sense that Marx reconstructed the history of the species as a self-formative process mediated by social labor and class struggle and lifted the ideological veil from the relations of production in capitalist society. And it is in this sense that Freudian psychoanalysis "reveals the genetically important phases of life history to a memory that was previously blocked, and brings to consciousness the person's own self-formative process."[13]

These two notions of self-reflection are not identical. In the one case, we are dealing with philosophical reflection on the *general* presuppositions and conditions of valid knowledge and action. From Socrates, through the Enlightenment, to Kant and beyond, this type of reflection has frequently been characterized as the highest court of reason, as reason in its purest form. When Habermas opposes this conception of reflection to the positivist identification of reason with science, he is standing on familiar ground. The other case concerns reflection on the specific formative history of a *particular* (individual or group) subject; its goal is a restructuring of the subject's own action-orienting self-understanding through liberation from self-deception. When Habermas speaks of the "identity of reason with the will to reason" and opposes the "unity of reason and the interested employment of reason" to contemplative models, he is positing an inherent connection of reason with self-reflection in this latter sense as well. This is abundantly clear in passages in which he characterized the "experience of reflection" as follows:

I mean the experience of the emancipatory power of reflection, which the subject experiences in itself to the extent that it becomes transparent to itself in the history of its genesis. The experience of reflection articulates itself substantially in the concept of a self-formative process. Methodically it leads to a standpoint from which the identity of reason with the will to reason freely arises. In self-reflection, knowledge for the sake of knowledge comes to coincide with the interest in autonomy and responsibility. For the pursuit of reflection knows itself as a movement of emancipation. Reason is at the same time subject to the interest in reason. We can say that it obeys an *emancipatory cognitive interest,* which aims at the pursuit of reflection.[14]

In such passages the overtones of German Idealism are unmistakable. And in *Knowledge and Human Interests* it is indeed Fichte and Hegel that provide the bridge from Kant's transcendental critique of reason to the Marxian and Freudian critiques of false-consciousness.[15] Fichte supplies the notion of a practical interest in autonomy operative within reason itself, an interest that both precedes self-reflection and realizes itself therein: "Self-reflection is at once intuition and emancipation, comprehension and liberation from dogmatic dependence."[16] Hegel replaces the absolute self-positing of Fichte's ego with a phenomenological self-reflection of the self-formative process of the individual and the species. But phenomenological self-reflection retains the combination of reason and interest: "Since at every stage it strikes at the dogmatic character of both a world view and a form of life, the cognitive process coincides with a self-formative process."[17] It is then both a reflection on the conditions of knowledge and a critical-reflective dissolution of dogmatic forms of life.

The argument of *Knowledge and Human Interests* clearly relies on this twofold meaning of reflection. But it is not at all clear that the latter is consistent with Habermas's rejection of idealism:

> The conditions under which the human species constitutes itself are not just those posited by reflection. Unlike the absolute self-positing of Fichte's ego or the absolute movement of mind, the self-formative process is not unconditioned. It depends on the contingent conditions of both subjective and objective nature: conditions of the individuating socialization of interacting individuals on the one hand, and on the other, those of the "material exchange" of communicatively acting persons with an environment that is to be made technically controllable. Reason's interest in emancipation, which is invested in the self-formative process of the species and permeates the movement of reflection, aims at realizing these conditions of symbolic interaction and instrumental action.[18]

On materialist presuppositions, the interest in emancipation extends to the practical change of established socioeconomic conditions. It is obvious that this sort of "revolutionary praxis" cannot be reduced to "self-reflection." The implications for theory are also problematic; the identification of reason with critical self-reflection jeopardizes its claim to universality. In an idealist framework the convergence of reason and freedom does not necessarily entail a particularizing of reason. In a materialist framework, however, the identification of reason with reflection on "those determinants of a self-formative process which ideologically determine a contemporary praxis and world view" seems to entail a specification of reason in terms of a particular content and particular goals. In short Habermas's materialist appropriation of the idealist identification of reason with the will to reason appears to do justice neither to theory nor to practice.

This has been argued by several critics. While sharing Habermas's reading of the emancipatory intention of enlightenment, Karl-Otto Apel criticizes his "simple identification of reflection and practical engagement."[19] Reflection, in the sense of a relentless discursive examination of the presuppositions and grounds of any claim to cognitive or normative validity, may be said to pursue an interest in emancipation—from dogmatism in all its forms, from the sway of unjustified and unjustifiable opinions and norms. It is an interest that is realized in theoretical reflection in general but it is not to be confused with that interest to which Marx appealed when he proclaimed against philosophy that the world was not to be interpreted but changed. This interest is realized only through practical engagement in the sense of a "risky, politically effective 'taking sides.'" To identify the two interests is to succumb to "an idealist illusion."[20]

Similarly Dietrich Böhler criticizes Habermas for confusing the "formal interest" in freedom and autonomy that is presupposed by theoretical enlightenment with the interest behind "situationally engaged enlightenment through self-reflection on unreflected or repressed connections to interests and motives."[21] This amounts, he argues, to placing all epistemic subjects as such under an obligation to practical-critical engagement; it amounts to claiming that a "general transcendental reflection on the highest cognitive interest reveals an obligation to that specific historical engagement that 'critical theory' pursues."[22] For Böhler, this "effusiveness" (*Überschwenglichkeit*) of the Habermasian construction can be traced back to an undigested Fichtean moment: the interest in ourselves as the ground of all other interests and the interest that ultimately guides all our thinking. Statements like "the emancipatory cognitive interest aims at the pursuit of reflection as such" make sense, he argues, only if reflection is understood as the critical examination of the presuppositions and grounds of all validity claims and emancipation is understood as the overcoming of dogmatism, especially in the form of an objectivistic blindness to the subjective conditions of knowledge. From this perspective, the "will to reason" that is inherent in reason is the formal interest in theoretical enlightenment, in a rigorous pursuit of the ultimate conditions of knowledge and action. It does not, Böhler continues, include a "concrete orientation of social and private-existential life, and even less a concrete partisan engagement to guarantee the progress of practical humanity."[23] But this, he feels, is what is implied by the Marxian moment of Habermas's understanding of reflection and emancipation: "reason's interest in emancipation . . . aims at realizing [the necessary] conditions of symbolic interaction and instrumental action." The implication is that the emancipatory interest aims not simply at the pursuit of knowledge and reflection as such but at a practical change of established conditions, a partisanship guided by a critical insight into specific structures of power and ideology.

The failure to make this distinction spares Habermas the disillusion-ment with his own effusiveness. *Formal* and universally valid *reflection* is the business of transcendental philosophy: knowledge at the abstract level of "consciousness in general." . . . Reflection poses the question as to the conditions of possibility of knowledge (e.g. as to the "interests" of knowledge). It can do so only by abstracting from the material content [of knowledge]. . . . This distancing from the un-reflected, the uncomprehended, is as a matter of fact also one of the *conditions of possibility of critique and practical emancipation;* but it is not emancipation itself. . . . If such *distancing* is to make possible a *concrete* turning away from (and transformation of) *determinate* relations and modes of life, whose meaning is not understood and whose possible effects are not comprehended, then there must be added a partisan *identification* with an anticipated state of affairs in which one sees one-self. . . . Practical emancipation, as *a historical self-reflection,* does not aim at the pursuit of universal knowledge or reflection as such. Rather it aims at the *practical transposition* of the situational knowledge that particular individuals and groups can gain through clarifying their personal life history or their social situation. Thus historical self-reflection is not a matter of formal-emancipatory knowledge *for the sake of knowing* and in general, but of practical-emancipatory knowl-edge *for the sake of action* and in a concrete situation. . . . *That* is the emancipatory (cognitive) interest of "critical sciences" of the same type as that "critique of ideology" which Marx inaugurated and the Frankfurt School developed further: "critique" with the *practical claim* to rationally reorient social practice.[24]

Habermas's critique of systematically distorted communication, concludes Böhler, can make no such claim to guide a *praxis* aimed at the transformation of social conditions. In its generality it avoids that "moment of decision and partisanship" that is inherent in the "en-gaged projection of new social formations *and* of strategies of action for their realization."[25] The attempt to ground practice in the tran-scendental conditions of theory does justice to neither.

These criticisms, which obviously go to the very heart of Haber-mas's efforts to restructure the foundations of critical theory, cannot be easily dismissed. The crucial distinctions to which they refer are indeed blurred in *Knowledge and Human Interests.* Habermas would deny, no doubt, that he ever intended to equate critical reflection with practical engagement or critical insight with practical emancipation. Yet he often seems to be doing just that. The Fichtean conception of the emancipatory interest—according to which it aims at the pursuit of reflection as such—glides too easily over into the materialistic conception—according to which it aims at realizing certain conditions of symbolic interaction and instrumental action—without sufficient attention being paid to the crucial differences between them.[26]

Granting that this distinction is not sufficiently elaborated in *Knowledge and Human Interests* and that this failure impairs the formulation of a number of its central theses, there remains the systematic question of whether the distinction is intrinsically incompatible with Habermas's reconceptualization of the foundations of critical theory. It does dilute the bonds between theory and practice; even when understood as critical self-reflection, theory does not of itself amount to practical emancipation. But one could still argue that this type of theory is a necessary moment in any genuinely emancipatory practice, that a practice which aims at overcoming relations of domination and realizing conditions of autonomy must be informed by this kind of "action-orienting self-understanding."

This would not, I think, be denied by the critics cited above. Their basic point turns rather on another distinction: that between critical self-reflection and transcendental reflection on the general conditions of knowledge and action. This distinction too is blurred in *Knowledge and Human Interests* and in this case the blurring is important to the argument because it helps to bridge the gap between Kant and Marx. Even if one grants the relation (not identity) between critical self-reflection and practical emancipation, the claimed interest of reason in emancipation further requires that the two senses of self-reflection be somehow unified. And the point of the criticisms cited above is precisely that "theoretical enlightenment" through transcendental reflection on universal conditions is not at all the same as "situationally engaged enlightenment" through critical reflection on a particular formative process. This point must be granted in general. However Habermas might still attempt to defend his original line of argument by singling out one formative process as crucial to the theory of knowledge: the self-formative process of the human species. He might differentiate, that is, between reflection on specific determinants in the formative processes of particular subjects and reflection on the self-formative process of the species as a whole, and claim that the latter is indeed the proper framework for the theory of knowledge. In fact, the insufficient clarity on this point notwithstanding, this seems to be precisely what is intended by the idea of a materialistically transformed phenomenology. Of course this interpretation leaves us with the problems of making plausible the notion of a species-subject of history (in the singular)[27] and of articulating the precise connection between its development and the conditions of possibility of valid knowledge. But even this would not suffice to bridge the gap between universal and situational reflection, for the reconstruction of the history of the species is itself quite distinct from critical self-reflection in the interest of clarifying concrete situations and practical possibilities. (Compare the distinction between the theory of historical materialism and the critique of political economy.) This is not to deny that universal reflection, whether transcendental or phenomenological, has a relation to practice; but whatever that relation is, it cannot be so direct as the argument of *Knowledge and Human Interests* seems to suggest.

I shall not pursue this matter any further, since Habermas himself has tended to respond to critics rather in terms of subsequent developments of his position.[28] The reliance on adapting themes from classical German thought, which is characteristic of his earlier work, gives way to the construction of general theories of communication and social evolution, which sometimes involve more than a mere reformulation of his earlier position. To conclude the present discussion, we might note only that these later developments include an acknowledgment of the importance of distinguishing critical self-reflection from transcendental reflection (or, as he now refers to it, "rational reconstruction"):

The studies I published in *Knowledge and Human Interests* suffer from the lack of a precise distinction . . . between reconstruction and "self-reflection" in a critical sense. It occurred to me only after completing the book that the traditional use of the term "reflection", which goes back to German Idealism, covers (and confuses) two things: on the one hand, it denotes reflection upon the conditions of the capacities of a knowing, speaking and acting subject as such; on the other hand, it denotes reflection upon unconsciously produced constraints to which a determinate subject (or a determinate group of subjects, or a determinate species subject) succumbs in its process of self-formation. In Kant and his successors, the first type of reflection took the form of a search for the transcendental ground of possible theoretical knowledge (and moral conduct). . . . In the meantime, this mode of reflection has also taken the shape of a rational reconstruction of generative rules and cognitive schemata. Particularly the paradigm of language has led to a reframing of the transcendental model.[29]

Whereas critique is brought to bear on something particular, reconstructions deal with anonymous rule systems that any subject may follow insofar as he has acquired the requisite competence. Whereas critical self-reflection makes unconscious factors conscious in a way that has practical consequences, reconstructions render explicit a know-how (that is, the intuitive knowledge acquired with a competence) without involving practical consequences of this sort.[30] And critique remains bound to "the system of action and experience" in a way that reconstruction does not. Since it embraces the particulars of a self-formative process and aims at transforming the specific determinants of an ideologically distorted practice and world view, it is historically situated reflection. By contrast, reconstructions of the universal conditions of speech and action are not context bound in this way. They represent the "purest" form of theoretical knowledge, for they issue neither from a technical interest in control of objectified processes nor from a pratical interest in securing action-oriented mutual understanding nor directly from an interest in emancipation. Rather they are "first generated within a reflexive attitude," that is, from a concern to render explicit what is always implicitly presupposed.[31]

In one sense this development meets the objections considered above: the missing distinctions have now been drawn. But this is, of course, not the real issue. The important question is whether this more differentiated restatement still permits Habermas to maintain that relation of reason to emancipation on which he wished to base critical theory. In trying to do justice to the theoretical character of theory (rational reconstructions as "pure" knowledge) and the practical character of practice (critique as bound to the system of action and experience), he seems to have reintroduced the gap between theory and practice, between reason and emancipation that *Knowledge and Human Interests* tried to close. More specifically, if it is only reflection in the sense of critique that pursues a direct interest in liberation from the self-deception embedded in systematically distorted communication; and if the identification of reason (in its purest form) with reflection makes sense only if reflection is understood as the reconstruction of the universal presuppositions of speech and action, then it seems to follow that the interest in emancipation is not proper to reason as such but only to a particular employment of reason: critical self-reflection. "Transcendental" reflection appears to be an exception to the "interest-ladenness" of cognition; it pursues neither the technical, the practical, nor the emancipatory interest.[32] It is, in this sense, "interest free" —and we are back to something like the traditional notion of disinterested reason. Or, at most, it pursues an interest in the completion of transcendental reflection itself—and we are back to something like a "pure" interest in explicating the implicit presuppositions of reason. In either case the radical claims of the theory of cognitive interests would have to be considerably trimmed. The thesis of the inherent relation of the other forms of inquiry to different systems of action and experience remains, it is true, untouched by this argument. But if we recall that a central concern of the theory was to demonstrate an inherent connection of reason as such to an enlightened form of life, it is clear that this exception, if allowed to stand, would constitute a serious retreat from the original position. As our discussion of the theory of communication in chapter 4 will make clear, Habermas has not surrendered the claim that such a connection exists, but he has shifted the grounds on which he is prepared to defend it.[33]

The distinction between two senses of enlightenment has other problematic implications for the argument of *Knowledge and Human Interests*. As long as reflection included both moments, Habermas could maintain that philosophy "passes over" (*geht . . . über*) into the critique of ideology.

If Marx had reflected on the methodological presuppositions of social theory as he sketched it out, and not overlaid it with a philosophical self-understanding restricted to the categorial framework of production, the difference between rigorous science and critique would not have been concealed. . . . Rather, this idea [of a science of man] would have taken up Hegel's critique of the subjectivism of Kant's epistemology and surpassed it materialistically. It would have made clear that ultimately a radical critique of knowledge can be carried out only in the form of a reconstruction of the history of the species. . . . On this foundation philosophy's position with regard to science could have been explicitly clarified. Philosophy is preserved in science as critique. A social theory that puts forth the claim to be a self-reflection of the history of the species cannot simply negate philosophy. Rather, the heritage of philosophy issues in [*geht . . . über*] the critique of ideology, as a mode of thought that determines the method of scientific analysis itself. Outside of critique, however, philosophy retains no rights. To the degree that the science of man is a material critique of knowledge, philosophy, which as pure epistemology robbed itself of all content, indirectly gains its access to material problems. As philosophy, however, the universal scientific knowledge that philosophy wanted to be succumbs to the annihilating judgment of critique.[34]

The historical background to this conception is provided by Habermas's reading of the development of philosophy from Kant to Marx in terms of a "radicalization of the critique of knowledge." Once Hegel had called into question Kant's "empty identity" of the ego as an original unity of transcendental consciousness, philosophical reflection on the subjective conditions of knowledge took the form of a phenomenological self-reflection on the genesis of the knowing and willing subject. In working through the self-formative processes of the individual and the species, "phenomenological experience moves in a dimension in which transcendental determinations themselves take form;"[35] it is reason reflecting on the different forms it has taken in the course of its development to the stage of critique. Marx followed Hegel in rejecting Kant's conception of the knowing subject as a self-contained unity outside of history; but he criticized the idealist presuppositions under which the formative process of the species became the self-movement of absolute spirit. The Hegelian model of the "dialectic of consciousness in its manifestations" is inadequate for reconstructing the history of a species whose formation is conditioned by developments in the system of social labor. Under materialist presuppositions, the forms of the manifestation of consciousness must be comprehended as constellations of power and ideology that are undermined by the expansion of the forces of production and overcome through "critical-revolutionary activity."

At this point Habermas introduced his distinction between the reductionistic and nonreductionistic sides of Marx's thought. From the former point of view, the self-reflection of the knowing subject would amount to a reconstruction of the history of the species in terms of changing modes of production. From the latter point of view, however, the formation and transformation of modes of thought and action is linked not only to developments in the sphere of production but simultaneously (and interdependently) to developments in the organization of social relations. The institutional framework of society does not *immediately* represent a stage of development of productive forces "but rather a relation of social force, namely the power of one social class over another."[36] This relation is anchored in institutionalized norms and values that regulate social interaction; it is legitimated by world views that conceal the true (repressive) nature of the organization of society. The transformation of the institutional framework does not occur *directly* through productive activity but rather through the revolutionary activity of struggling classes, including the critical activity of unmasking ideologically concealed relations of force. Thus social practice "does not only accumulate the successes of instrumental action, but also, through class antagonism, produces and reflects upon objective illusion."[37]

A materialistically transformed phenomenology attempts to capture this "dialectic of class consciousness in its manifestations"[38] to reconstruct the formation and transformation of world views and forms of life in connection with changes in the systems of labor and interaction. Extending in methodical form the practical self-understanding of social groups, it seeks to raise the self-consciousness of the species to the point where it "has attained the level of critique and freed itself from all ideological delusion."[39] Under materialist presuppositions epistemological reflection on the subjective conditions of knowledge takes the form of a critique of ideology.

Once again we encounter the conflation of transcendental reflection and critical self-reflection that is essential to the argument of *Knowledge and Human Interests.* Its implications for philosophy are no less problematic than they proved to be for theory and practice, for the arguments advanced to justify the "passing over" of philosophy into the critique of ideology can be used to question the very possibility of critique, at least insofar as it involves claims to validity. Before making this case it will be helpful to consider Habermas's understanding of traditional philosophy, especially the reasons why he considers it to be no longer possible.

In his remarks on the role of philosophy in Marxism, Habermas recalls the ambiguity of the young Marx (and of the Marxist tradition in general) toward philosophy.[40] On the one hand, the rational *content* of Hegel's system was evident to the Young Hegelian; on the other, he regarded the philosophical *form* of consciousness itself as ideological. While its essential insights could be preserved within a materialist framework, the absolutism of a theory seemingly independent of practice had to be abandoned. More specifically, what had to be abandoned was the idea of a "philosophy of origins" (or "first philosophy": *Ursprungsphilosophie*), which claimed to provide the ultimate grounds of reality as a whole.

According to Habermas, it is this claim to totality and finality that characterized the great systems of philosophy.[41] They were attempts to comprehend rationally the totality of what is, the natural and the human world, and to formulate the ultimate principles of being, thought, and action. With the rise of the modern empirical sciences, philosophy did not abandon its claim to provide ultimate grounds; it maintained it in an epistemological guise. Since Hegel, Habermas argues, this claim has no longer been defensible.[42] Philosophy has become self-critical, critical of its own historical pretensions to provide an "affirmative exegesis of the whole of things in being," which could serve as the foundation of both science and practice. The question arises whether philosophy is anything more than an "empty exercise in self-reflection," a critique whose only object is the excesses of its own tradition. "And if this is so, why should philosophy continue?"[43] Why should it not fade away along with the "spirit [*Geist*] that can no longer know and maintain itself as absolute?"[44]

Similar reflections have motivated others to confine philosophy to the logic of science, or to the therapeutic dissolution of the bewitching powers of language, or to the construction of formal languages devoid of such charms. For reasons that should now be obvious, Habermas finds these responses to the situation to be not only theoretically inadequate but practically dangerous. If the sphere of practical life is to be preserved from the irrationalities of decisionism and technocratism, reason must be granted some measure of its traditional comprehensive powers. This is the tension with which contemporary philosophy must live. In the words of Theodor Adorno (whom Habermas frequently cites when discussing these issues):

The only philosophy we might responsibly engage in, after all that has happened, would no longer be free to credit itself with power over the absolute. It would indeed have to forbid itself to think the absolute, lest it betray the thought—and yet it must not allow itself to be gulled out of the emphatic concept of truth. This contradiction is its element.[45]

Philosophy was the tradtional guardian of the "emphatic concept of truth," the ideas of reason and freedom, goodness and justice. But while it kept these ideas alive, it also betrayed them. In its traditional form as *Ursprungsphilosophie*, it fostered the illusion that these ideals, which it could really only anticipate, were actually realized. And they were realized through the power of reason alone to think the absolute. The *Seinsgebundenheit* of thought, its rootedness in the material conditions and historical forms of social life, was neglected. Reason, whether in the form of Socratic dialogue, metaphysical theory, or transcendental reflection, was assumed to be possible independently of the actual conditions of existence. The ideas of truth and freedom and justice were thought in separation from the structures of social life in which they could alone be realized.

The ontological illusion of pure theory . . . promotes the fiction that Socratic dialogue is possible everywhere and at any time. From the beginning philosophy has presumed that the *Mündigkeit* posited with the structure of language is not only anticipated but real. It is pure theory, wanting to derive everything from itself, that succumbs to unacknowledged external conditions and becomes ideological. Only when philosophy discovers in the dialectical course of history the traces of violence that deform repeated attempts at dialogue and recurrently close off the path to unconstrained communication does it further the process whose suspension it otherwise legitimated: mankind's evolution toward *Mündigkeit*.[46]

The idea of reason is the idea of a form of life. It can be fully actualized only in an emancipated society and on the basis of communication free from domination. The philosophic form of reason as pure theory, self-sufficient and divorced from practice, is ideological. It sets itself above the historical reality of systematically distorted communication and thus discourages that critical practice through which alone its ideals could be realized. "Philosophy remains true to its classic tradition by renouncing it," that is, by assuming the form of a critique of ideology.[47]

If, however, philosophy is "no longer free to credit itself with power over the absolute," we have to inquire about the normative-theoretical basis of the critique of ideology. The identification and criticism of distorted thought seems to presuppose what Alasdair MacIntyre has called an "epistemological self-righteousness" on the part of the critic.

Claims about hallucination, illusion, distortion of thought, and the like can in general be made only from the standpoint of claims that the contrast can clearly be drawn between the hallucinatory, illusory, or distorted mode of perception or thought, on the one hand, and genuine perceptions of reality or rigorous and undistorted reflection and deliberation on the other. Hence, to identify ideological distortion one must not be a victim of it oneself. The claim to a privileged exemption from such distortions seems to be presupposed when such distortion is identified in others.[48]

This is a familiar problem and one that has been especially troublesome for neo-Marxists. Once critique could no longer be identified with rigorous science (as in Marx and "official" Marxism) or grounded in the privileged historical position of the proletariat (as in Lukács), it became incumbent upon them to provide another justification for the standpoint of the critic. And indeed one can find in the early writings of the Frankfurt School repeated attempts to do so, to distinguish the critique of ideology from a relativistic sociology of knowledge. The charge of universal distortion inexorably turns back on critique itself, as Horkheimer and Adorno realized.

We underestimated the difficulty of the exposition because we still trusted too much in contemporary consciousness. . . . The fragments that we have collected here show, however, that we had to abandon that trust. . . . The complete self-destruction of the Enlightenment forces thought to forbid itself to be in the least unsuspicious toward the habits and directions of the spirit of the times. When the public sphere has reached a state in which thought inescapably becomes a commodity which speech inevitably promotes, then the attempt to get behind such depravity must refuse allegiance to the established requirements of speech and thought.[49]

This can be done only if critique remains negative and forbids itself any positive theory. "If it willingly leaves its critical element . . . then it unwillingly propels the transformation of the positive it has chosen into something negative, destructive."[50]

Adorno himself consistently avoided "the metamorphosis of critique into affirmation" by confining himself to a "negative dialectic," which not only strictly refused to construct any positive system but even renounced the "concrete negation" (*bestimmte Negation*) of the Hegelian dialectic. The positive movement of reflection that is presupposed by this notion is already a form of affirmation. As Habermas points out, this ascetic renunciation of any form of affirmative systematic thought cannot avoid "the question as to the privileged status which the authors [of the *Dialectic of Enlightenment*] must claim for their experience vis-à-vis the stunted contemporary subjectivity."[51] In other words, the question, How is critical thought itself to be justified? cannot be answered merely negatively, by pointing to distortion. It demands that we specify positively the "legitimating grounds" (*Rechtsgründe*) of critique. But under the presupposition of universal distortion, any such positive specification would itself be suspect. The radical critic, like the radical skeptic, appears to be condemned to silence.

The conception of critical theory developed in *Knowledge and Human Interests* seems to be beset by a similar dilemma. On the one hand, Habermas shares with the Marxist tradition the thesis that thought is rooted in the material conditions and historical forms of social life, the thesis that the capitalist organization of social relations represents an institutionalization of social force, and the conclusion that the modes of thought rooted in capitalist social reality are ideologically distorted. Further he shares with Horkheimer and Adorno their refusal to justify critique either as rigorous science or as a privileged insight of proletarian consciousness. On the other hand, he evidently does not share their asceticism in regard to systematic thought: phenomenological self-reflection is to reconstruct the history of the species as a "dialectic of the moral life" under material conditions.[52] The question is; To what standard does this materialist phenomenology appeal in unmasking ideological world views and forms of life? To what perception or theory of reality does it appeal in characterizing other perceptions and theories as distorted? To what theory of history does it appeal in distinguishing progressive from regressive modes of thought and practice? In short, to what "emphatic concepts of truth," normative and theoretical, can Habermas appeal to justify his critical enterprise?

Hegel's phenomenological self-reflection of the "dialectic of consciousness in its manifestations" proceeded under the presupposition of a notion of absolute truth. The truth claim of any stage of consciousness short of the absolute could be measured against this implicit standard and revealed in its limitedness. Habermas's phenomenological self-reflection of the "dialectic of class consciousness in its manifestations" proceeds under materialist presuppositions. The standards it applies in assessing the validity claims of historical forms of life are said to be implicit in the very structure of communication.

It is no accident that the standards of self-reflection are exempted from the singular state of suspension in which those of all other cognitive processes require critical evaluation. They possess theoretical certainty. The human interest in autonomy and responsibility is not mere fancy, for it can be apprehended a priori. What raises us out of nature is the only thing whose nature we can know: *language*. Through its structure autonomy and responsibility are posited for us.[53]

But this is unsatisfactory, and for several reasons. In the first place, on what grounds can we be certain that the interest in *Mündigkeit* is no mere fancy, that it—or at least our perception of it—is not just a particular and historically relative interest, an impulse of the discontented? The appeal to apriori insight, reminiscent of idealism, seems to disregard the possibility that the insight into and anticipation of ideals is itself subject to distortion. There is no obvious reason why the suspicion of ideology should come to a halt here. Furthermore, the appeal to self-reflection as the unimpeachable court of last appeal is implausible if self-reflection means the reconstruction of the history of a species whose self-formative process is conditioned by changing modes of production and organizations of social relations (and not the reconstruction of the movement of absolute spirit). The collection, interpretation, and classification of data on the historical forms of labor and interaction, the articulation and testing of hypotheses concerning the causes of their formation and transformation, the examination of the contents of cultural tradition with a view to the power relations concealed in the symbolic structures of speech and action, and the like, can be characterized as self-reflection only in a wildly metaphorical sense. To reduce the standards of adequacy for these tasks to the privileged "standards of self-reflection" can politely be described as "overburdening the concepts of the philosophy of reflection," against which Habermas himself warns.[54] The construction of a theory of social evolution, no less than the justification of the normative basis of critique, requires positive theoretical affirmations, which must somehow be exempt from the suspicion of ideology if critique is not to be self-defeating.[55]

Finally the problematic implications of the thesis that philosophy issues in the critique of ideology can be brought to bear against the theory of cognitive interests itself, for this theory seems to be an attempt to provide "ultimate grounds," at least in the sense of limits "beyond which one cannot go" (*unüberschreitbar*).[56] The fundamental interests are "conditions of possible objectivity"; they "establish the viewpoints from which we can apprehend reality as such in any way whatsoever."[57] Although we "can become aware of this natural basis" through reflection, "the latter cannot cancel out interest."[58] Clearly this is a type of claim reminiscent of *Ursprungsphilosophie*, at least in its epistemological guise. The fact that Habermas, in opposition to Kant, locates the transcendental conditions of reason in the natural history of the species is not of itself sufficient grounds for his disclaimer regarding its philosophical status. And the fact that the theory constitutes a critique of positivism is of itself no reason for classifying it with Marx's critique of political economy rather than Kant's critique of empiricism or Husserl's critique of objectivism.

This is not simply a terminological issue; it concerns the nature of the foundations of critical theory. If under present historical conditions philosophy is not possible as "pure theory" or "Socratic dialogue" but only as critique of ideology, it becomes very difficult to see how critique can be grounded, epistemologically or otherwise. Habermas himself has admitted as much. In his later writings, the theory of cognitive interests and the theory of communicative competence are characterized as "transformed transcendental philosophy" and attributed to a mode of reflection that is distinct from critical self-reflection.[59] In many respects this constitutes a shift in models from a materialistically transformed "phenomenological self-reflection" to a materialistically transformed "transcendental reflection." The Kantian moment of *Knowledge and Human Interests* moves into the foreground. The Hegelian moment is displaced into a theory of social evolution, which, although it is based on the theory of communication and is constructed in a reflective attitude, clearly involves empirical hypotheses. It is less a "phenomenological self-reflection" than a "reconstruction of historical materialism."

Knowledge and Human Interests, a history of ideas with systematic intent, does not "claim more than the role of a prolegomenon."[60] For this reason, it has seemed advisable to confine the discussion here to pointing out some of the problems that it poses for the subsequent development of Habermas's program. Before closing this section, however, we should take a closer look at the very idea of a "quasi-transcendental" theory of knowledge, for in attempting to combine a "transcendental" with a "naturalistic" approach to the subjective conditions of knowledge, Habermas appears to be caught in a dilemma: either nature has the transcendental status of a constituted objectivity and cannot, therefore, be the ground of the constituting subject; or nature is the ground of subjectivity and cannot, therefore, be simply a constituted objectivity.

Habermas wants, paradoxically, to hold on to both horns. He maintains, *on the one hand,* that the conditions of instrumental action "bind our knowledge of nature with transcendental necessity to the interest of possible technical control over natural processes. The objectivity of experience is constituted within a conceptual-perceptual scheme determined by deep-seated structures of human action; this scheme is equally binding on all subjects that keep alive through labor."[61] This "Kantian component" of the materialist conception of synthesis is elaborated in an instrumental theory of knowledge that elucidates "the transcendental structure of labor processes within which, and only within which, the organization of experience and the objectivity of knowledge become possible from the standpoint of the technical controllability of nature."[62] The "non-Kantian component" of the concept of synthesis is developed in the idea that a "particular 'objective nature' is given to each social system" (that is, to social subjects at each particular stage of historical development).[63] Although "the transcendental framework within which nature appears objectively to these subjects does not change,"[64] the specific "categories of man's manipulation . . . belong to the historically alterable inventory of societies."[65] According to this line of argument, then, nature is an objectivation of the knowing subject; it is constituted subject to the general conditions of purposive-rational action ("fixed framework"), as well as to the specific conditions of historically variable systems of social labor. It seems to follow that nature cannot be consistently appealed to as the ground of subjectivity. To do so would amount, in Kantian terms, to grounding transcendental consciousness in a phenomenal realm, which exists only in relation to it. In Habermas's terms, the categories and methods of empirical-analytic science would both be explained (transcendentally) by reference to structures of human action and be employed to explain (empirically?) these structures.

On the other hand, however, Habermas ascribes to the subject of knowledge not only the "intelligible character of a community that constitutes the world from a transcendental perspective" but also "the empirical character of a species having emerged in natural history."[66] From this latter point of view, the emergence of the "objective structures of human life that give rise to the orientations of inquiry" (work and interaction) is to be explained by a theory of evolution. It seems to follow that nature is the ground of subjectivity. And this is, on the face of it, flatly incompatible with its status as a constituted objectivity.

In the view of Michael Theunissen, the roots of this dilemma lie in the very idea of a critical theory.[67] As Horkheimer's programmatic statement made clear, critical theory distinguishes itself from traditional theory in its conception of the relation of nature to history.

Theoria immerses itself in the divine, i.e. in the natural universe or cosmos regarded as divine because of the unchangeable nature of its eternally recurring movements. Critical theory, in contrast, occupies itself with the historically moved human world which, because of its changeable character, was for the Greeks precisely not a worthy object of theoretical science. . . . While classical theory recognizes the eternal circuit of the natural cosmos as the whole, critical theory reverses this, seeing in history the outermost horizon into which the knowledge of nature also has to enter.[68]

The contrast, then, is between an approach that grants priority to nature—in which, as the whole, history is to be included — and one that gives priority to the historical, human world—in which, as the whole, interpretations of nature appear as human constructions. As we saw above, Habermas rejects the former approach because of the "objectivism" of the natural ontology that it presupposes.[69] But he fails, according to Theunissen, to abide by this rejection consistently. His theory of cognitive interests exhibits a tendency "to fall back to that stage which it proposed to overcome: to the stage of an unquestionably objectivistic nature-ontology, or at least to that of a mode of thought that grants nature priority over history and raises it to the status of the absolute origin."[70] And the roots of this relapse are to be found in an "overburdening" of the empirical subject:

Looked at from the point of view of the history of philosophy, all the representatives of critical theory once again repeat for themselves the post-Hegelian repetition of Kant—attempted above all by the left Hegelians—on the basis of history prepared by Hegel. Viewed systematically, the overburdening of empirical subjects arises from transferring the powers with which Kant outfitted "consciousness in general" to the human species (whose real unity is as yet only anticipated).[71]

With this the nature that appears in history becomes simultaneously and paradoxically the ground of history.

Habermas is not unaware of this paradox. On the contrary, he locates it in the rejection of previous idealism and materialism that Marx took as his point of departure.[72] Whereas Hegel regarded mind as the absolute ground of nature, for Marx nature was the ground of mind. But as the first thesis of Feuerbach made clear, he was not opposing to Hegel an ordinary materialism or naturalism. The "active side" developed by idealism in opposition to materialism was preserved and transformed in the notion of "sensuous human activity," "social practice." Because of the productive activity of concrete laboring subjects, objective nature bore the character of a produced objectivity. Thus Habermas's dilemma is inherited—not only from Marx but from a situation confronting all serious attempts at a radical critique of knowledge, "a situation created by Kant and Darwin": "Firstly, by being the act of a subject, every 'objective' cognitive insight exists only as a result of certain 'subjective' conditions. Secondly, we must ask what we can know about the subject of cognition when we consider that it lives in the world of objects, being one of its parts."[73]

Habermas's efforts to extricate himself from this "dilemma arising from the simultaneous inevitability and unfeasibility of transcendental reflection" turn upon several distinctions. To begin with, he reconstructs the Marxian differentiation of "subjective nature," "objective nature," and "nature-in-itself."[74] In opposition to Hegel, Marx conceives of nature as a "substratum on which the mind contingently depends. Here the mind presupposes nature but in the sense of a natural process that, from within itself, gives rise likewise to the natural being man and the nature that surrounds him."[75] Thus he assumes "something like a nature-in-itself" that "has priority over the human world," "a nature preceding human history."[76] Nature in this sense "is at the root of laboring subjects as natural beings,"[77] for social labor "presupposes the evolution of nature to the human stage"; it is "founded in a history of nature that brings about the toolmaking animal as its result."[78]

At the human level, nature "separates out into the *subjective nature* of man and the *objective nature* of his environment. At the same time nature mediates itself through the reproductive process of social labor."[79] "Subjective bodily nature," a result of natural history, refers not only to the "bodily attributes of an organism dependent on its environment (sensuous receptivity, need, emotionality, vulnerability)" but also to "the adaptive modes of behavior and active expressions of life of an 'active natural being.'"[80] More specifically, and most importantly, it refers to "sensuous human activity," to social labor, which creates "not only the factual conditions of the possible reproduction of social life" but, at the same time, "the transcendental conditions of the possible objectivity of the objects of experience."[81] It is simultaneously a natural process regulating our material exchange with nature and more than a natural process, a "transcendental accomplishment" that constitutes a world. Thus, although we must presuppose nature as existing in itself, "we ourselves have access to nature only within the historical dimension disclosed by labor processes."[82] Accordingly "objective environmental nature" refers not to nature-in-itself but to a nature that is "constituted as *objective nature for us* only in being mediated by the subjective nature of man through processes of social labor."[83]

Nevertheless it retains both its externality and contingency; it is not *merely* a constituted correlate of laboring subjects.

The unity of the social subject and nature that comes into being "in industry" cannot eradicate the autonomy of nature and the remainder of complete otherness that is lodged in its facticity. As the correlate of social labor, objectified nature retains both *independence* and *externality* in relation to the subject that controls it. Its independence manifests itself in our ability to learn to master natural processes only to the extent that we subject ourselves to them. . . . The externality of nature manifests itself in the contingency of its ultimate constants. . . . The process of production regulated in systems of social labor is a form of synthesis of man and nature that binds the objectivity of nature to the objective activity of subjects on the one hand, but does not eliminate the independence of its existence on the other.[84]

Thus the objects of experience have a twofold character: as natural objects they "share with nature the property of being in itself"; at the same time, they "bear the character of produced objectivity owing to the activity of man."[85]

Habermas's reconstruction of Marx's implicit epistemology makes it possible to identify more precisely the different dimensions of the problem stated above in general terms. To begin with, it should be evident from our brief summary that the term *nature-in-itself* is used equivocally to refer both epistemologically to something like a Kantian thing-in-itself that "appears" subject to the conditions of possible knowledge and natural-historically to a nature preceding human history that gave rise to the natural being man and the nature that surrounds him. Not only are these conceptions—of an (unknowable?) thing-in-itself and of a natural-historical explanation of transcendental subjectivity—individually problematic; their relation raises a further problem. Habermas appears to regard the two referents—if not the two senses—as identical: "Kant's 'thing-in-itself' reappears under the name of a nature preceding human history."[86] But the epistemological functions of the thing-in-itself seem to make it unsuitable for natural-historical purposes: an unknowable thing-in-itself cannot be a reconstructible natural process. On the other hand, nature-as-known, objective nature, seems equally ill suited for explaining the emergence of a transcendental subject: as a *constitutum*, it cannot be used to explain the *constituens*. Furthermore the notion of "subjective nature" raises similar problems. On the one hand, it seems to possess the priority of nature-in-itself: "the action-oriented bodily organization of man" in which objectivity is grounded must be "prior" in some sense to the world that is constituted, for the transcendental framework that makes synthesis possible is "posited with the behavioral system of instrumental action" and "grounded in the species-specific bodily organization of man as such."[87] On the other hand, since we can identify and delineate the structures of human life in which cognition is rooted, subjective nature cannot be an unknowable thing-in-itself.

Habermas is aware of the problematic aspects of this reconstructed Marxian epistemology, and he offers some suggestions as to how the principal difficulties might be overcome. These can be conveniently organized around the three senses—epistemological, subjective, and natural-historical—in which nature is said to be prior to the human world.

1. The epistemological arguments for the necessity of something like a thing-in-itself are advanced in the context of his analysis of Peirce's pragmatism. Peirce rejected as meaningless the notion of a thing-in-itself in the sense of transcendental philosophy: "a reality that *affects* our senses while yet merely *appearing* under the transcendental conditions of possible objectivity and thus unknowable as such."[88] He advanced a concept of reality corresponding to his methodological concept of truth: reality is the sum of those states of fact about which we

can obtain final opinions. The predicate "real" has no explicable meaning apart from states of fact about which we can make true statements. Accordingly we cannot meaningfully conceive of a reality that is in principle beyond knowledge. On the other hand, Peirce recognized that the facts cannot be exhaustively reduced to our interpretations. The process of inquiry (which, at the limit, leads to final opinions and thus knowledge of reality) depends on "information inputs"; it incorporates "impulses deriving from experience"; it is prompted by "independent original stimuli, which attest to reality's resistance to false interpretations.[89] The problem for Peirce, then, was how to conceive the independence of experiential inputs. As symbolically unmediated constraints on symbolic mediation, they could not, on his understanding of the term, be "real." But as constraints, marked by their facticity and particular qualities, they could not be just nothing.

With regard to methodical progression to a universe of valid, that is general and permanently recognized beliefs, the power of affecting the senses present in actual experiences obviously functions to render prevailing opinions problematic and stimulate efforts to obtain unproblematic beliefs. . . . The constraint of reality, embodied in the qualitative immediacy of singular sensations and feelings, is the occasion for constituting reality in the form of true statements. Yet it does not itself belong to reality. But how, then, can we say anything at all about it? By explicating the meaning of something that is not part of reality and thus cannot be the object of a true belief, we are insinuating once again the concept of a thing-in-itself.[90]

Habermas finds several different attempts by Peirce to resolve this problem: first, a resort to the logic of language ("for if reality is defined by the totality of possible true statements . . . then why should the structure of reality not be elucidated in relation to the structure of language?");[91] second, a resort to ontology (Peirce's doctrine of categories);[92] and third a return to the system of reference of the logic of inquiry ("non-intentional contents of experience are converted into symbolic representations owing to a synthesis that a consistent pragmatism can develop only in the framework of a logic of the process of inquiry").[93] He criticizes the first two on grounds that I shall not consider here and proceeds to draw out the implications of the third. His conclusion, in regard to the problem at hand, is that "we do reckon with the existence of a reality that is independent of men who can act instrumentally and arrive at a consensus about statements. But what the predication of properties catches 'of' this reality is *constituted only* in the perspective of possible technical control."[94] Applied to Peirce's well-known example of the hardness of a diamond, this means that

> the class of all conditional predictions that can be used to explicate the concept of hardness says about an object that satisfies the initial conditions of these predictions that its "hardness" *exists in itself,* even independently of whether or not we perform even a single test. But this universal matter of fact is real only in relation to possible operations of this sort in general. The object called diamond *is* hard only in so far as it is constituted as an object of possible technical control and is *capable* of entering the behavioral system of instrumental action.[95]

This proposed resolution amounts to a further explication of the twofold character of natural objects that was introduced in the discussion of Marx: "natural objects . . . share with nature the property of being in itself but bear the character of produced objectivity owing to the activity of man."[96] The *meaning* of true statements about reality, and thus of the properties ascribed to reality, must be understood in relation to the structure of instrumental action. In this sense reality is *constituted.* But our experience of reality also attests to its "independence," "externality," and "facticity," its "resistance to false interpretations," "the constraint" it places on inquiry. The *existence* ascribed to things and events, properties and relations, in true statements about reality, is an existence-in-itself, independent of any actual thought or action. In this sense reality is *disclosed.*[97] (Diamonds are hard in themselves; that is, they are capable of entering the system of instrumental action in a certain way.)

This construction makes it possible to avoid some of the problematic features of Kant's thing-in-itself. For one thing, nature-in-itself is not unknowable; it is knowable but only subject to the conditions of possible objectivity. It "appears" only in relation to possibilities of instrumental action; what we "catch 'of'" it is its technical controllability. But we still seem to be caught in the familiar circle of applying to nature-in-itself categories that properly have a meaning only in relation to appearances, for example, the power to affect our senses causally. Although Habermas does not specifically address these problems, it is clear from his general approach that his response would be as follows. From one point of view, the power of things to affect our senses is a relation constituted within the realm of objective nature, that is, subject to the causal categories of empirical-analytic science. From the point of view of the process of inquiry, however, "the affecting power of things . . . is nothing other than the constraint of reality which motivates us to revise false statements and generate new ones."[98] In this transcendental perspective, nature-in-itself does not refer to unknowable but causally effective things-in-themselves; it refers instead to that moment of knowable nature designated by the terms *independence, externality, facticity,* and the like. That is, it refers to the "resistance" and "constraint" manifested by nature in the experience of inquiry. The constraint of reality is "a complementary concept to the idea of the process of inquiry."[99] To comprehend this process, we must take account of the way in which it incorporates the resistance of reality to false interpretations. Conversely the resistance of reality can be comprehended only in relation to this process. In this sense,

nature-in-itself is an abstraction which is a requisite for our thought. . . . This conception has the important epistemological function of pointing to the contingency of nature as a whole; in opposition to the idealist attempt to reduce nature to a mere externalization of mind, it preserves nature's immovable facticity despite its historical embeddedness in the universal structures of mediation constituted by laboring subjects.[100]

Whatever the merits of this proposal in mitigating the paradoxes inherent in the epistemological conception of a nature-in-itself, it apparently intensifies the problem of its relation to the subjective and natural-historical conceptions. How can an "abstraction" of this sort be at the same time a "natural process that gives rise to the natural being man?"

2. For Marx "subjective bodily nature" referred primarily to "the physical organization specific to the human species under the category of possible labor: the tool-making animal."[101] For Freud, in contrast, subjective nature referred primarily to "the physical organization specific to the human species under the category of surplus impulses and their canalization: the drive inhibited and fantasizing animal."[102] As we have seen, Habermas attempts to combine the two perspectives. The (subjective) natural basis of history includes both "life structures," work and interaction. These are not only fundamental structures of human existence but transcendental conditions of objectivity, natural processes and world-constituting processes. In this context our dilemma takes the following form: If nature is knowable

only under the conditions of instrumental action, then subjective bodily nature, as known, would have the status of an objectivity constituted under these conditions. But as a prior condition of constitutive activity, subjective bodily nature cannot be a constituted objectivity. Therefore either subjective bodily nature is not a prior condition of possibility of cognition, or it is and we cannot know it. In either case the theory of interests would be untenable.

Habermas escapes this dilemma by distinguishing the ways in which we know subjective and objective nature. Objective nature is known subject to the conditions of instrumental action. (This includes, of course, empirical-analytical knowledge of the "bodily attributes" and "physical constitution" of the human organism in biology.) Subjective nature—in the sense in which this is epistemologically relevant—is, however, known not in an objectivating perspective but in a reflection on the conditions of objectivity. As epistemological categories, work and interaction are not construed biologically or behavioristically but precisely as structures of action.

The concept of "interest" is not meant to imply a naturalistic reduction of transcendental-logical properties to empirical ones. Indeed, it is meant to prevent just such a reduction. Knowledge-constitutive interests mediate the natural history of the human species with the logic of its self-formative process. . . . But they cannot be used to reduce this logic to any sort of natural basis. . . . Work and interaction by nature include processes of learning and arriving at mutual understanding. . . . That is why the knowledge-constitutive interests rooted in the conditions of work and interaction cannot be comprehended in the biological frame of reference of reproduction and preservation of the species. The reproduction of social life absolutely cannot be characterized adequately without recourse to the cultural conditions of reproduction, that is to a self-formative process that *already* implies knowledge in both forms.[103]

The specific conditions of subjective nature on which the self-formative process of the species depends cannot be comprehended in an objectivating frame of reference, that is, in abstraction from the specific connection of knowledge and action, for labor and interaction already "include the pertinent categories of knowledge"; they cannot be defined independently of them.[104] This apparent circle is broken only by the power of reflection. Although we cannot take up a position "beneath" or "outside of" the structures of thought and action, we can grasp them reflectively "from the inside;" "the mind can reflect back on the interest structure that has previously joined subject and object. . . . If [self-reflection] cannot cancel out [*aufheben*] interest, it can to a certain extent catch up with [*einholen*] it."[105]

In an epistemological context, then, subjective nature refers neither to an unknowable nature-in-itself nor to an objectively constituted nature. It refers rather to structures of human life that are grasped reflectively in an attempt to elucidate the nature, conditons, and limitations of human knowledge. But if this is the case, why are these conditions referred to as "natural"? This designation seems to imply a positive relation to nature in the other senses. What is the proposed relation, and on what grounds is it advanced? We might distinguish three sorts of consideration. At the most abstract level, there is a transcendental consideration. The structures of life from which the cognitive interests derive are simply "encountered" in the attempt to elucidate reflectively the subjective conditions of knowledge.[106] That is, they are simply "facts" beyond which we cannot go. This "facticity" and "contingency" certify their priority to the historically changeable forms of will and consciousness and mark them as "facts of nature": "it is evidently a fact of nature that the human species, confined to its sociocultural form of life, can only reproduce itself through the medium of that most unnatural idea, truth."[107]

As we have seen, it is necessary for Habermas, under pain of circularity, to separate rigorously the ways in which we know subjective and objective nature. On the other hand, it seems obvious that at least part of the force and motivation behind the designation of the subjective conditions of knowledge as "natural" derives from what we know empirically about "the concrete human species." According to Habermas, the interest structures (which cannot be defined independently of forms of action and the pertinent categories of knowledge) are grounded in the "physical constitution of this natural being and some constants of its natural environment,"[108] "in the species-specific bodily organization of man as such."[109] Now the "bodily attributes of the human organism" and "its adaptive mode of behavior" are evidently also objects of empirical science. What is the relation between the results of empirical inquiry into human nature and the life structures uncovered by transcendental reflection? Are they completely unconnected? And if not, what is the nature and status of the empirical framework in which they are to be connected? Habermas clearly grants priority to a nonobjectivating science of man: "a reconstruction of the history of the species that does not depart from the basis of critique must remain heedful of the basis of its experience. It must comprehend the species, from the 'moment' when it can reproduce its life only under cultural conditions, as a *subject*."[110] The logic of such a nonobjectivating science of man (a science, however, that does incorporate the results of objectivating inquiry) will be the topic of the next chapter.

The third sort of consideration that motivates Habermas to designate the subjective conditions of knowledge as natural is the conviction that they "arose contingently in the natural evolution of the human species."[111] This brings us to an examination of the third sense, the natural-historical, in which nature is prior to history.

3. In this context, our dilemma takes the following form: how can the subject that transcendentally constitutes nature be at the same time the result of a natural process? Habermas is keenly aware of this paradox and very tentative regarding the possibility of resolving it. He writes that although Marx conceives of the subject of social production as "founded in a history of nature that brings about the tool-making animal as its result . . . he does not say *how* we can comprehend history as a continuation of natural history. . . . It is still an open question . . . how it [natural history] can be comprehended as the pre-history of transcendental consciousness."[112] At the close of the Peirce discussion the question is left open, but both strictly transcendental and strictly empirical resolutions are ruled out.

The transcendental framework of the process of inquiry establishes the necessary conditions for the possible extension of technically exploitable knowledge. Since it is posited with the behavioral system of instrumental action, this framework cannot be conceived as the determination of a transcendental consciousness as such. Rather it is dependent on the organic constitution of a species that is compelled to reproduce its life through purposive-rational action. Hence the framework that establishes a priori the meaning of the validity of empirical statements is contingent *as such*. Just as little as it can be elevated to the transempirical plane of pure noumenal determinations, however, can it be conceived as having originated under empirical conditions—at least not as long as its origins have to be conceived under the very categoies that it itself first defines.[113]

The same problem is posed once again toward the end of the Freud discussion. Although it remains unresolved, Habermas does offer a positive, if rather vague, suggestion as to how natural history can be conceived as the prehistory of transcendental consciousness. The theory in question must somehow take the form of a reflection on the prehistory of culture, which is dependent on a prior understanding of the sociocultural form of life.

Freud . . . introduced an energy model of instinctual dynamics with an objectivist turn. Thus he sees even the species' process of civilization as linked to a dynamic of the instincts. The libidinal and aggressive instinctual forces, the prehistorical forces of evolution, permeate the species subject and determine its history. But the biological scheme of the philosophy of history is only the silhouette of a theological model; the two are equally precritical. The conception of the instincts as the prime mover of history and of civilization as the result of their struggle forgets that we have only *derived* the concept of impulse privatively from language deformation and behavioral pathology. At the human level we never encounter any needs that are not already interpreted linguistically and symbolically affixed to potential actions. The heritage of natural history, consisting of unspecialized impulse potentials, determines the initial conditions of the reproduction of the human species. But, from the very beginning, the means of this social reproduction give the preservation of the species the quality of self-preservation. We must immediately add, however, that the experience of collective self-preservation establishes the pre-understanding in terms of which we privatively infer something like preservation of the species for the animal prehistory of the human species.[114]

The implicit suggestion is that at least some of the categories fundamental to a theory of human evolution will have to be derived from our prior understanding of social life and read back "privatively" (by taking account of the relevant differences and limitations) into the animal prehistory of the species.

In the introduction to *Theory and Practice* he advances this hypothesis explicitly:

As long as these interests of knowledge are identified and analyzed by way of a reflection on the logic of inquiry that structures the natural and the human sciences, they can claim a "transcendental" status; however, as soon as they are understood in terms of an anthropology of knowledge, as results of natural history, they have an "empirical" status. I place "empirical" within quotation marks because a theory of evolution which is expected to explain emergent properties characteristic of the socio-cultural form of life—in other words to explain the constituents of social systems as part of natural history—cannot, for its part, be developed within the transcendental framework of objectifying sciences. If the theory of evolution is to assume these tasks, it cannot wholly divest itself of the form of a reflection on the prehistory of culture that is dependent on a prior understanding of the sociocultural form of life. For the time being these are speculations which can only be confirmed by a scientific clarification of the status enjoyed by the contemporary theory of evolution and research in ethology. Till then, at most, they designate a perspective for the formulation of problems.[115]

Rather than attempting to assess the value of these speculations on the form that a theory of human evolution will finally take, let us pause briefly to consider whether and how the different senses of the priority of nature over history fit together. Are we talking about the same "nature" in each instance; and if so, is its priority consistent with a transcendental approach?

Habermas would apparently answer both questions in the affirmative. "Objective nature for us" is constituted, the result of a "synthesis" subject to an interest in technical control. As such it obviously cannot be prior to the human world. The notion of a nature that is such is "an abstraction which is a requisite for our thought." We construct this notion to take account of the moment of "facticity" or "contingency" in our experience. This has two sides. On the one side, the structure of inquiry attests to the independence of reality, its resistance to arbitrary interpretation. On the other side, reflection on the conditions of knowledge leads us back to certain "facts" about the subject of knowledge that define the initial conditions of its constitutive activity. Thus cognition appears to be bounded on both sides by contingent conditions. For this reason, according to Habermas, we cannot conceive of synthesis as absolute or as the activity of a pure transcendental consciousness. The contingent conditions of synthesis "point to a nature-in-itself that has been disclosed." More precisely we have to construct such a notion to make sense of our experience: "Nature-in-itself is a construction." It is a notion of something independent of and prior to human constitutive activity that accounts for the contingent conditions of this activity. Habermas immediately goes on to say that it "designates a *natura naturans* that has created both subjective nature and what confronts it as objective nature."[116] That is, he joins the epistemological priority of the contingent conditions of synthesis with the (temporal) priority of a nature preceding human history that gives rise to the cognitive subject. Only because of this conjunction does the theory of evolution acquire the status of a "prehistory of transcendental consciousness." But how is this move to be justified? Isn't it a "precritical" reversion to an ontology of nature? And if so, doesn't Habermas find himself back in the realm of "metaphysics" (and thus in competition with other metaphysical attempts to discover "ultimate origins")? In his own defense, he might point out that nature-in-itself, even in its epistemological setting, does not designate an unknowable thing-in-itself. As a construction based on that moment of externality and independence that characterizes nature-as-known, it designates an independent reality that "appears," albeit subject to certain conditions. Thus into the very construction is built a relation of "appearance" or "disclosure," between nature-in-itself and nature-as-known. But objective nature can be adequately known, apparently, only in a developmental framework (that is, as an evolving nature). And this evolution includes the evolution of the human species to the sociocultural form of life. Thus, it might be argued, the very function of the construction—nature-in-itself, as that which is disclosed in nature-as-known-leads to its identification with a nature preceding human history.

There are obvious problems with this line of argument. If what we "catch 'of'" nature-in-itself is always bound to the conditions of instrumental action, why should developmental theories be exempted? As results of empirical-analytic inquiry they would seem to disclose nature only from the point of view of its technical controllability. The hypothesis of a nonobjectivistic, reflectively cast theory of human evolution avoids this particular problem, but it raises others of its own. In the first place, it pushes the "break" in science back from the nature/man boundary to the point at which nature begins to exhibit the character of subjectivity. Does this point fall within the sphere of ethology? Or does it come with the emergence of life? And what becomes of the thesis that nature can be known only within the framework of instrumental action? Perhaps there is hovering in the background the idea of a unified science of nature and history without any such break.[117] But according to the theory of interests, such a theory would have to combine several different, and apparently incompatible, cognitive strategies.

In any event, the dilemma with which we begin this discussion does not seem to have been resolved. No matter what form it takes, nature-in-itself remains, within a transcendental framework, "an abstraction required by our thought." That such an abstraction should simultaneously be the ground of thought is incomprehensible. Perhaps this is what Habermas means when he writes:

The unavoidable (for the time being?) circle in which we have to move as soon as we tackle problems that are equivalent to the traditional problem of ultimate foundations—although this can very well be explained—may be a sign that, among other things, the concepts "contingency-necessity" are no longer sharply separable at this level of argumentation. Presumably, assertions about the contingency or necessity of cognitive interests, just as those about the contingency or necessity of the human race or the world as a whole, are meaningless.[118]

Chapter 3

Toward a Methodology of Critical Theory

3.1 EMPIRICAL PHILOSOPHY OF HISTORY WITH A PRACTICAL INTENT

From his early (1957) "Literaturbericht zur philosophischen Diskussion um Marx und den Marxismus" to his recent (1976) *Zur Rekonstruktion des Historischen Materialismus,* Habermas's conception of critical theory has undergone significant development.[1] His exchange with representatives of analytic philosophy of science forced restatements, as did his debate with exponents of philosophical hermeneutics.[2] More recently the preliminary sketch of a theory of communication, the assimilation of contemporary systems theory, and the programmatic delineation of a theory of social evolution have signaled important developments in his methodological views.[3] Nevertheless certain general features of the original conception are still recognizable in the latest statements: critical social theory is empirical without being reducible to empirical-analytic science; it is philosophical but in the sense of critique and not of first philosophy; it is historical without being historicist; and it is practical, not in the sense of possessing a technological potential but in the sense of being oriented to enlightenment and emancipation.[4]

These features could be discerned in the discussion of the relations of theory to practice in chapter 1 and of knowledge to interest in chapter 2. The principal loss incurred in the transition from the classical doctrine of politics to modern political science was said to be the replacement of a direct access to practice with a technological understanding of the theory-practice relationship. The principal gain was the introduction of scientific rigor into the study of society. Accordingly the outstanding task for a postpositivist methodology of social inquiry was somehow to combine the access to practice of classical theory with the methodological rigor "which is the irreversible achievement of modern science."[5] In other words, what was called for was a marriage of the scientific and empirical with the practical and critical. The nature of this connection was suggested in the subsequent analysis of the emancipatory interest behind critical social theory. The discussion of Kant and Hegel, Marx and Freud issued in the conception of a "materialistically transformed phenomenology," which was to reconstruct the self-formative process of the species in an attempt to achieve a self-understanding freed from ideological delusion. This reconstruction was to serve as the framework for a critique of knowledge and, simultaneously, for a critical theory of society. Although the general outlines of Habermas's conception could be glimpsed in these discussions, the details remained decidedly hazy. And what was visible was highly problematic.

In this chapter I shall examine the details and consider some of the problems. Although the discussion follows a roughly chronological order from the earliest treatments of "empirical philosophy of history with a practical intent" to the most recent outlines of a "theory of social evolution," I shall be concerned only incidentally with questions of development. The principal aim is to gain a systematic overview of Habermas's conception of critical theory and to suggest some of its strengths and weaknesses.

In the light of the previous discussion of his views on philosophy, it might seem surprising that Habermas first appealed to the idea of a philosophy of history to characterize critical theory, for surely this is among the most speculative of philosophic endeavors. It is all the more surprising if one considers that his earliest discussions of the matter already express a basic agreement with Marx's dictum that the demands and results of philosophy could be preserved only through "the negation of previous philosophy, of philosophy as philosophy," that philosophy could be realized only through its sublation.[6] But this endorsement is precisely an indication that Habermas does not use the term *philosophy* in its traditional sense as a "philosophy of origins" or "first philosophy." It does not designate a presuppositionless mode of thought that provides its own foundations; nor can the ideals inherent in philosophy—truth and reason, freedom and justice—be realized by means of philosophy itself. Philosophy belongs to the world on which it reflects and must return to it. From its mythological origins to its philosophic culmination in Hegel, the philosophy of history was marred by a failure to realize this.[7] Pretending to a contemplative view of the whole of history, prospective as well as retrospective, it claimed to reveal its meaning. "The meaning" of world history was typically rendered through a construction of necessary progress toward some metaphysically guaranteed goal, and it was ascribed to a fictive "subject of history": God or Nature, Reason or Spirit, or a self-constituting human species.

As Habermas interprets him, the early (if not the later) Marx rejected this construction.

Knowledge of the "necessity" of revolution grants no dispensation from the scientific investigation of the conditions of its possibility, or from the scientific demonstration that, when and where these conditions are historically existent. The reliance of critique on science—on empirical, historical, sociological and economic analyses—is so essential that it [critique] can be refuted scientifically and, at the level of theory, only scientifically. But this doesn't mean that it could also be adequately proved by science. Given the scientifically ascertained conditions of possibility of revolution, the revolution itself requires in addition that this possibility be decisively grasped; it requires a practice that is aroused (not determined) by insight into the practical necessity of revolution. Marx distinguishes between practical and theoretical necessity. The latter marks those categories of social changes that happen over the heads of men, "objectively" (and thus that can be calculated and pre-calculated "with the accuracy of modern science"). The former, on the other hand, marks that very different category of social changes that take place with the will and consciousness of men, not "objectively" (and thus that can be calculated and precalculated only as regards their objective conditions of possibility, but not as such).[8]

For the young Marx, the movement of history is not at all a matter of metaphysical necessity; it is contingent in regard to both the empirical conditions of change and the practical engagement of social actors. The meaning of history, its goal, is not a subject for metaphysical hypostatization but for practical projection; it is a meaning that men, in the knowledge of "objective" conditions, can seek to give it with will and consciousness. The exaggerated epistemic claims of traditional philosophy of history derived in part from its failure to appreciate the essentially practical nature of its prospective dimension. The projected future, which confers meaning on the past, is not a matter of contemplation or scientific prediction but of practice. Kant's dictum that we can prophesy the future only to the extent that we bring it about is shared by Marx. But the practical reason in which he grounds the meaning of history is not Kant's pure practical reason in general (the source of regulative ideas for moral action, in particular of the idea of a kingdom of ends); it is rather a situationally bound practical reason that is decisive for theory as well.

The meaning of the actual historical process is revealed to the extent that we grasp a meaning (derived from "practical reason") of what should be and what should be otherwise (measured against the contradictions of the social situation and its history) and theoretically test the presuppositions of its practical realization. This has nothing to do with blind decisionism. For in the theoretical-empirical testing we must interpret the actual course of history and the social forces of the present from the point of view of the realization of that meaning.[9]

Thus Habermas already finds in the young Marx many of the necessary correctives to the excesses of traditional philosophy of history. But in his desire to distance himself from the "merely philosophic" critique of the left Hegelians, Marx increasingly ascribed to his own theory the features of a purely empirical theory of society. Thus the mature Marx fell into many of the same errors as did previous philosophers of history. Especially in the hands of his "orthodox" followers, Marxism seemed to provide a purely theoretical guarantee of the outcome of history; the importance of critical self-reflection and enlightened practice receded behind the solid, objective necessity of inexorable laws of history. The spectacle of this retrogression is one of the reasons behind Habermas's stress on the philosophical dimension of Marxism. A second is the advance in our understanding of the possibilities and limitations of science in the strict sense—the philosophy of science has made us aware not only of the advantages of pursuing a rigorously scientific methodology but of its costs as well. The price that social inquiry has paid for the mantle of science is a methodological blindness to the historical character of society and a renunciation of direct access to practice. From the standpoint of strictly nomological science, history is reduced to a source of data for the formulation and testing of general (timeless) social laws and to a field of application for causal explanations using such laws. There are no historical laws as such; nor is history a proper subject for theory in the strict sense.[10] Historical research is primarily concerned with ascertaining initial and boundary conditions that might figure in nomological explanations based on sociological (that is, nonhistorical) laws. Sociology as a generalizing science itself has a technical relation to practice; it produces knowledge that can be used to administer society.

This was, to be sure, not the understanding that sociology had of itself as it finally became detached from the traditional corpus of practical philosophy.[11] The great Scottish moralists of the second half of the eighteenth century—Smith, Ferguson, Millar—located socioeconomic inquiry in the framework of a "natural history of civil society." Society was to be conceived in developmental, evolutionary terms; its history was to be rationally reconstructed as a progress in the civilization of mankind. As theoretical history, sociology provided the knowledge needed for a practical—political and pedagogical— furtherance of this process. Although the shock waves from the French Revolution later unsettled the belief in continuous progress, the social theorists of the early nineteenth century retained the historical and practical view of their enterprise. Sociology became a science of society in crisis; in both its progressive and conservative forms (advocated, for example, by St. Simon and de Bonald, respectively) it aimed at grasping the historical roots of the contemporary crisis in order to bring it to a successful resolution. The distance that separates the self-understanding of contemporary social science from that of its modern founders is striking. Today the idea of comprehending society as a historically developing whole for the sake of enlightening practical consciousness, building a collective political will, and rationally guiding practice appears to be an anachronism.

On the other hand, even in our scientific civilization, this figure of thought does not seem out of place at the level of individual practice. When an individual attempts in reflection to make sense of his own not-yet-completed life, he does so prospectively as well as retrospectively. How he interprets the events and actions of his past life will not be independent of what he projects for the future. And these projections, if they are to be realizable, will not be independent of what he discovers about his past life and present situation. The meaning to him of his life as a whole, then, is not merely a theoretical or empirical question; it has an inexpungable practical dimension. It depends on what he wants to be as well as what he has become, on where he wants to go as well as where he has been and is. This type of action-orienting self-understanding is essentially beyond the grasp of strictly empirical science. A detailed knowledge of the facts of one's past life and a secure grasp of the results of the behavioral sciences do not exempt one

from having to act in the future; and the structure of action—
involving motives and intentions, principles and values, choices and
goals—is not that of a mere happening. As an actor, the individual
subject cannot regard his own future simply as a matter for objective
determination and he cannot therefore regard the meaning of the
past that opens onto this future or of the life that includes both, as
simply a theoretical-empirical question.

While this interlacing of the empirical and the practical, the retrospective and the prospective, seems plausible enough in the case of individual subjects, its application to society or to the human species
raises a number of questions. How is "the" subject of history to be defined? In what sense does it have a unitary past, and how is this past
accessible? In what sense does it act? And to what extent can its future
be a matter for self-determination? Philosophy of history traditionally
assumed or hypostatized a unitary subject of world history that somehow, in the course of history, makes itself to be what in another way it
already is. Marx himself adopted the notion of history as the self-
formative process of a self-producing species subject; and (as is evident from the discussion of his theory of interests in chapter 2),
Habermas did the same. In his more recent writings, he admits to having previously made "uncritical use of the idea of a human species
which constitutes itself as the subject of world history," explaining that
it was not until he began work on his communication theory of society
that "the import and implications of the hypostatizing generation of
subjectivity on higher levels" became clear to him.[12] There can be no
simple transference from the level of individual consciousness to that
of a collective. Terms such as *class consciousness* and *class interest*, for
example, are "designations for something that can only be arrived at
intersubjectively, in the consulation or cooperation of individuals living together."[13] The self-constituting species-subject was and is a "fiction"; but the intention that was (inadequately) conveyed by this notion is not meaningless: "to tie the development of social systems to
control through self-reflection, in the sense of a politically effective
institutionalization of discourse."[14] The goal of establishing communication structures free of domination, through which the formation of a collective political will could take place, is not itself a
fiction but a "practical hypothesis." Nevertheless "even if social evolution should point in the direction of united individuals consciously
influencing the course of their own evolution," this would in no way

create "large scale subjects, but (only) self-produced, higher-level, intersubjectively shared structures [*intersubjektive Gemeinsamkeiten*]."[15]

If the transposition of the idea of the unity of nature to the "unity of history," and the imputation to the latter of a unitary subject, were fictions, they were fictions from which the philosophy of history lived. Does their surrender imply the dissolution of "the history of the species" into a multiplicity of only partly interconnected histories of individuals, societies, and cultures? And does this imply the end of the philosophy of history, at least in its traditional sense? In Habermas's view, this situation calls not for the renunciation but for the radicalization of this mode of thought.[16] It must itself become more historically self-conscious, for the presuppositions of the philosophy of history are themselves the result of historical development. The consciousness of the unity of mankind, for example, arose in the eighteenth century in the wake of the period of colonization.[17] About the same time, the process of modernization—the institutionalization of the growth of forces of production in capitalism and the acceleration of social change that accompanied it—gave rise to the consciousness of progress and the idea of exercising rational control over history. But the breakdown of feudal relations, the erosion of cultural traditions, and the uncontrolled consequences of capitalist expansion were also experienced as a crisis of society that called for a self-conscious resolution. The experiences that gave rise to the philosophies of history of the eighteenth century and to the theories of social evolution of the nineteenth century have not become obsolete. On the contrary,

the tendencies described here have grown stronger. On the basis of industrial society and its technically mediated commerce, the interdependence of political events and the integration of social relations have progressed so far beyond what was even conceivable two centuries ago that within this overall complex of communication particular histories have coalesced into the history of *one* world. Yet at the same time, mankind has never before been confronted so sharply by the irony of being capable of making its own history, yet still deprived of control over it. . . . Thus the immanent presuppositions of the philosophy of history have by no means become invalid; on the contrary, it is only today that they have become true. . . . On the other hand . . . the framework which philosophy has taken over from theology, of history as a totality, becomes questionable. If the loose threads of historical development are tied together in a network of world-historical interconnections only at a relatively late stage, this network cannot then be retrospectively made to cover history as a whole. . . . If, in addition, social conditions become accessible to rational planning on the part of human beings only at a relatively late stage of their development, then the possibility of its being made can also not be asserted for history as a whole. . . . Especially the materialist philosophy of history should comprehend its presuppositions in terms of the context of the epoch in which it emerged historically.[18]

Thus a radicalized philosophy of history has to be critically self-conscious that some of its basic presuppositions—for example, global unity and the capacity for rational social planning—have themselves become true only at a specific phase of historical development. On the other hand, it must be aware that the notion of mankind making itself with will and consciousness is a fiction that merely anticipates a possible outcome of that development: the self-conscious control of social relations through the institutionalization of political discourse free from domination. But this anticipated end state is not merely a regulative ideal projected by practical reason in general; it has become the sole hope of human survival. The demands that Kant located in pure practical reason have

in the meantime been objectivated in a conflict arising from the historical situation in such a way that . . . Kant's sketch of a cosmopolitan order no longer concretizes moral-philosophical postulates for improving the world; under present conditions it defines, rather, theoretically ascertainable chances of survival for the world as a whole. It can today be extracted from historical reality itself as the concrete negation of palpable risks. It is another question, whether in addition to these objective needs the objective possibilities of their satisfaction can be theoretically ascertained in an adequate manner. In any case, for the first time a situation has come to pass which . . . . has made the fate of the entire world a theme of political decisions. "All or nothing" is today not a problem for the philosophy of history, but in the first instance for history itself.[19]

Marx's interpretive framework, the preunderstanding that guided his concept and theory formation, has not lost its actuality; "nature," the process of the material reproduction of society, dominates the system of social life, but this domination can be historically overcome.[20] Of course these are empirical claims, and the subsequent development of capitalist society—especially the changed relationship between politics and economics and the expanded role of science and technology in the reproduction process—has made revisions necessary. Nevertheless the basic disproportion between the expansion of powers of technical control and our limited capacity to guide social development rationally, between the "makeability" (*Machbarkeit*) of history and the "maturity" (*Mündigkeit*) of historical subjects, remains. And this disproportion—the impotence of historical subjects who are not yet really the subjects of history—is behind the undiminished poignancy and legitimacy of the philosophy of history. Human progress is to be measured not solely against advances in productive capacity but against the advancement of enlightenment and self-determination as well: *Machbarkeit* and *Mündigkeit*.

I shall close this introductory section with a few remarks on Habermas's early conception of the peculiar combination of the empirical and the philosophical that characterizes critical theory. Under the empirical aspects of critical social theory, he usually includes the determination of the objective conditions of possibility for social transformations and the specification of objective structures and tendencies that assert themselves "over the heads" of social subjects. More generally the historical (sociological, physchological, political, economic) material that informs critical theory must be worked up empirically. And this material provides a check on its claims—the assertions of critical theory are empirically falsifiable. But the precise meaning of "empirical" is left unclear in Habermas's early writings. In particular he does not provide a detailed analysis of the differences between data that are gained through the objectifying procedures of empirical-analytic inquiry and data that can be ascertained only through the interpretive procedures of hermeneutic inquiry. He does, to be sure, use the distinction from the beginning (for example, in discussing the nature of ideology critique); but it becomes thematic only after his entrance into the *Positivimusstreit*,[21] and is fully developed only in the course of his debate with Gadamer.

The indefiniteness in his understanding of "empirical" can also be seen in Habermas's discussion of the empirical checks on critical theory. We are told that

even a dialectical theory may not clash with experience, however restricted. On the other hand, it is not obliged to renounce any idea that escapes this experience [the controlled observation of empirical-analytic inquiry]. Not all of its theses can be translated into the formal language of a hypothetico-deductive framework; not all of its theses, least of all the central ones, can be smoothly validated by empirical findings.[22]

But it is not clear which types of assertions are beyond empirical control and in what sense, or how and why, this is the case. Some indication can be found in his explication of the senses in which critical theory is philosophical (as well as scientific) and practical (as well as theoretical).

In one passage Habermas locates the philosophical dimension of Marxism in the concern to derive "from the contradiction of the existing society the concept of that very society as well as the standard for its critique and the idea of critical practical activity."[23] The notion of bringing an object (the existing society) to its concept has unmistakable Hegelian overtones. And in a later defense (qua restatement) of Adorno's methodological views, certain Hegelian themes do indeed come to the fore: "Adorno conceives of society in categories that undeniably have their source in Hegel's logic. He conceives of society as a totality in the strictly dialectical sense."[24] Habermas's restatement consists mainly in an elucidation of the concepts of "totality" and "dialectic." The former is delimited negatively, by way of denying its identity with the functionalist concept of a social system; the relation between a totality and its moments is not the same as that between a system and its elements. But it is difficult to discover what exactly the positive content of this concept is. In any case it plays a much less prominent role in his later writings, whereas the concept of a social system (as developed, for example, by Parsons and Luhmann) plays an increasingly important role. I shall therefore pursue this line of argument no further.

The concept of dialectic is explicated in a number of ways. The unifying thread seems to be "the insight that the research process organized by subjects belongs—through the very act of knowing itself—to the objective complex that is supposed to be known." This is a reference to the fact that the critical theorist is himself part of the social reality that he wishes to analyze, that his problems and his interests, as well as his concepts and judgments, issue from and belong to the very traditions and institutions under investigation. Critical theory is doubly reflective: it is self-conscious of its origins in the historical development of society, and it is self-conscious of its role in the further development of society.[25] This double reflexivity distinguishes it not only from the objectivism of the exact sciences but from the self-sufficiency of traditional philosophy. In the strict sense of the term, critical theory is no longer philosophical; it raises no claims to self-grounding or to self-realization: "where the logic of history . . . is without metaphysical guarantee, philosophy of history is no longer philosophical. It becomes instead the critical prologue to practice."[26] In another sense, however, critical theory is philosophical, and the key to this sense is its relation to practice.

Regarded from this point of view, the difference between philosophy and science is determined by their respective relations to practice. The rationality of science is technical . . . particular. . . . The rationality of philosophy is by contrast universal. It transcends the means-ends relation because it sets and discovers purposes itself. . . . Practice is not external to philosophy as it is to science; it is rather always the force behind its inherent movement. It cannot therefore develop its theses purely contemplatively and subsequently translate them into practice. . . . Philosophy lives from the uncertainty that is constantly renewed in the unresolved tension between theory and practice, a tension that can disappear only through the sublation of philosophy as philosophy. As is the case with science, philosophy, too, is particular; but its universal rationality anticipates the totality which it already (as philosophy) is, without (as philosophy) wholly being able to be.[27]

This characterization should be seen in the light of our previous discussion of the thesis: "philosophy is preserved in science as critique." Once we are aware that philosophy is part of the reality to be criticized, that radical critique must also direct itself to its own presuppositions, pure philosophy appears as an "abstract totality," abstract because the ideals that it claims to ground and to realize are viewed in isolation from the historical reality in which they originate and in which alone they can be realized. From this standpoint, philosophy can be pursued only as dialectical critique: "the attempt to comprehend the analysis [of the social world as a historically developed whole] at every moment as part of the analyzed social process, and as its possible critical consciousness,"[28] "a theory that is at every step guided and permeated by the self-consciousness of its own relationship to practice."[29]

In Habermas's later writings, this rather vague conception of critical theory gradually takes on the shape of a relatively differentiated research program—though not without significant revisions. The principal vehicle for this development is his critical appropriation of the main strands of contemporary sociology.

3.2 UNDERSTANDING AND SOCIAL INQUIRY

The original members of the Frankfurt school were acutely aware of the growing hegemony of positivism and the challenge that it presented to their own ideas. They felt called upon to develop their position in a continuing debate with "instrumental thought" and to support it with a critique of the positivist theory of science. At the time of Habermas's appearance, this hegemony had been firmly established and the debate had blossomed into the *Positivismusstreit in der deutschen Soziologie*. Habermas was aware from the beginning that the dominant intellectual climate was unfavorable, even hostile, to the idea of a philosophy of history with a practical intent (and with a rather ambiguous relationship to the canons of empirical science). The strategy he chose to pursue in this situation might be loosely characterized as the path of "concrete negation," a wide-ranging examination of the leading contemporary approaches to social inquiry, with the aim of criticizing their claims to self-sufficiency while appropriating their positive insights. This is the strategy that Marx had pursued with respect to the philosophic, socioeconomic, and political thought of his day. And its adoption lends to Habermas's work, as it did to Marx's, the character of a critical guide through the maze of contemporary social research. It will be convenient to open our discussion with a consideration of his views on the relationship between "positivist" and *"verstehenden"* sociology.

The term *positivism* now functions more as a polemical epithet than as a designation for a distinct philosophical movement. Even leaving aside the positive philosophy of Saint-Simon and Comte, the evolutionary positivism of Spencer and Haeckel, and the phenomenalism of Mach and Avenarius and concentrating on the "logical positivism" of the Vienna circle and its descendants, it is difficult to specify a common "positivist" perspective. The subsequent development of the more or less unified program of the original members of the circle has led to its disintegration as a distinct philosophical movement. This is not to say that logical positivism has disappeared without a trace; on the contrary, it has been absorbed into such influential traditions as empiricism, pragmatism, and linguistic analysis. The net result is that the "legacy of logical positivism"—a legacy of convictions and attitudes, problems and techniques, concepts, and theories—pervades contemporary thought. Methodological positions are most easily identified, because they so identify themselves, with respect to this legacy, pro or con. For our purposes it will be sufficient to indicate a few of the central positivist tenets regarding the nature of social inquiry.

The striking developments in the systematic study of the human world — from historiography and philology to sociology and anthropology—that took place in the course of the nineteenth century were generally viewed against the background of the established natural sciences. One or the other of these was usually taken as a paradigm of scientificity and a standard against which progress in the human sciences was to be measured. This perspective is also characteristic of the logical positivism of the twentieth century. The original members of the Vienna circle were, for the most part, neither social scientists nor pure philosophers but "had devoted a large part of their academic studies, often including their doctoral work, to logic and mathematics, to physics, or to a combination of these subjects."[1] It was then quite natural that their attention was focused for the most part on logic, the foundations of mathematics, and the methodology of the physical sciences and that they paid comparatively little attention to the social sciences. While the focus of neopositivism gradually expanded to include the latter, the original commitment to the paradigmatic status of the "exact" sciences remained firm. The characteristic tenets of its approach to social inquiry derive from this commitment.[2] These include:

1. The unity of scientific method: despite differences in the specific concepts and techniques proper to diverse domains of inquiry, the methodological procedures of natural science are applicable to the sciences of man; the logic of inquiry is in both cases the same.

2. More particularly the goals of inquiry—explanation and prediction—are identical, as is the form in which they are realized: the subsumption of individual cases under hypothetically proposed general laws. Scientific investigation, whether of social or nonsocial phenomena, aims at the discovery of lawlike generalizations that can function as premises in deductive explanations and predictions. An event is explained by showing that it occurred in accordance with certain laws of nature as a result of certain particular circumstances. If the laws and circumstances are known, an event can be predicted by employing the same deductive form of argument.

3. The relation of theory to practice is primarily technical. If the appropriate general laws are known and the relevant inital conditions are manipulable, we can produce a desired state of affairs, natural or social. But the question of which states of affairs are to be produced cannot be scientifically resolved. It is ultimately a matter of decision, for no "ought" can be derived from an "is," no "value" from a "fact." Scientific inquiry is itself "value-free"; it strives only for objective (intersubjectively testable) value-neutral results.

4. The hallmark of scientific knowledge is precisely its testability (in principle). To test a hypothesis, we apply deductive logic to derive singular observation statements whose falsehood would refute it. Thus the empirical basis of science is composed of observation statements (that is, statements referring to publicly observable objects or events) that can be said either to report perceptual experiences or, at least, to be motivated by them.

In recent years, the applicability of these tenets to social inquiry has once again become a subject of controversy. And questions concerning the nature and role of interpretive understanding have proved to be of fundamental importance at every point in these epistemological and methodological debates. Those who argue for the distinctiveness of the social from the natural sciences—whether in respect to the existence of general laws, the nature of explanation, the relation to values, the access to data—typically base their arguments on the necessity in social inquiry of procedures designed to grasp the meaning of social phenomena. Conversely those defending the methodological unity of the sciences typically give a rather low estimate of the importance of *Verstehen* for the logic of the social sciences. It is either rejected as unscientific or prescientific or analyzed as a "heuristic device," which, although useful, belongs in the anteroom of science proper, that is, to the "context of discovery," not to the "context of validation."

The unity of science program rests on a tacit division of labor between the "sciences" and the "humanities." Methodologists, it seems, are not required to analyze the distinctive research procedures and forms of argumentation that obtain in the latter, for these are, after all, not "sciences" but "arts." Apart from periodic reminders of the undesirable consequences likely to result from the mutual isolation of the "two cultures," philosophers of science have been contented by and large with their peaceful coexistence. But this tenuous arrangement can endure only so long as there are no fundamental disagreements about respective spheres of influence. Precisely this sort of territorial dispute has entered contemporary discussions of the logic of social analysis. Across a broad front—ranging from the phenomenological and ethnomethodological approaches that stem from the work of Husserl and Schutz, through the linguistic approaches inspired by the later philosophy of Wittgenstein, to the hermeneutic approaches deriving from the work of Heidegger—the positivist program has been attacked for its systematic neglect of the meaning that is constitutive of social reality.[3] In different ways, and from different points of view, it has been argued that access to a symbolically structured object domain calls for procedures similar in important respects to those developed in the humanities.

Habermas takes this territorial dispute as his point of departure.

While the natural sciences and the humanities [*Geisteswissenschaften*] are able to live side by side, in mutual indifference if not in mutual admiration, the social sciences most resolve the tension between the two approaches and bring them under one roof. Here the research practice itself forces us to reflect on the relationship between analytic and hermeneutic procedures.[4]

It is important to note that Habermas sees the problem as one of bringing the two approaches "under one roof," and not as one of replacing the methods of causal analysis by those of interpretive understanding, or conversely. It is not a matter of choosing between the two but of criticizing any pretension to universal and exclusive validity on the part of either, and of finding some sort of higher synthesis in which both have a place.[5] Habermas is surely not the first to pose the problem in this way. Early in this century Max Weber followed a similar course in his attempt to resolve the *Methodenstreit* that preoccupied the social scientists of his time.

It is no accident that contemporary methodologists so frequently refer back to Weber. Taking up the discussion of the differences between the natural and the cultural sciences where the neo-Kantians (above all, Rickert) left off, Weber's reflections on his own research practice are exemplary in their attempt to unify principles and procedures previously assigned to different realms of inquiry. But they are also decidedly ambivalent. If one compares, for example, his reflections on "Objectivity in Social Science and Social Policy" with the methodological remarks in the opening sections of *Economy and Society*, one is struck by the differences in orientation and emphasis. Talcott Parsons, who has had a decisive influence on the reception of Weber's work in the English-speaking world, has interpreted this as a shift away from the "fallacy of historicism" toward a more rigorously empirical-scientific conception of social inquiry. In the introduction to his own translation of parts of *Economy and Society*, Parsons explained the development and the ambivalence of Weber's thought from this point of view.

What Weber did was to take an enormous step in the direction of bridging the gap between the two types of science, and to make possible the treatment of social material in a systematic scientific manner rather than as an art. But he failed to complete the process, and the nature of the half-way point at which he stopped helps to account for many of the difficulties of his position.[6]

Habermas, on the other hand, regards precisely the tensions in Weber's thought as the most productive starting point for methodological reflection, for these tensions point to fundamental and still unresolved problems in the logic of social science. He distinguishes three aspects of Weber's methodological ambivalence: as it relates to the procedures, to the goals and to the presuppositions of social research.[7]

1. In the opening lines of *Economy and Society*, Weber defines sociology as a "science which attempts the interpretive understanding of social action in order thereby to arrive at a causal explanation of its course and effects."[8] The causal explanation of social action, like that of natural phenomena, requires the subsumption of statements describing the events to be explained under general statements of empirical regularities. But in contrast to the uniformities characterizing natural processes, those exhibited by social action have the distinctive property of being understandable. Social action is "human behavior when and in so far as the acting individual attaches a subjective meaning to it."[9] It is thus intentional action. As such it is accessible to motivational understanding. Although the ability to "put one's self in the place of the actor and thus sympathetically participate in his ex-

periences" can be of great help in achieving this understanding, it is "not a necessary prerequisite."[10] Furthermore "no matter how clear an interpretation as such appears to be from the point of view of meaning, it cannot on this account alone claim to be the causally valid interpretation. . . . More generally, verification of subjective interpretation by comparison with the concrete course of events is, as in the case of all hypotheses, indispensable."[11]

What Weber calls "explanatory understanding" consists in placing a particular act in an understandable sequence of motivation that corresponds to an empirically verifiable regularity of behavior. It's correctness is a function of both "adequacy at the level of meaning" and "causal adequacy." Thus the stress that neopositivists place on the need to corroborate empirically hypotheses suggested by motivational understanding is in agreement with one aspect of Weber's doctrine. On the other hand, he would not have subscribed to their relegation of *Verstehen*, as a heuristic device, to the anteroom of science proper. It was his view that "if adequacy in respect of meaning is lacking, then no matter how high the degree of uniformity and how precisely its probability can be numerically determined, it is still an incomprehensible statistical probability. . . . Statistical uniformities . . . constitute 'sociological generalizations' only when they can be regarded as manifestations of the understandable subjective meaning of a course of social action."[12] Even if future research should discover nonunderstandable uniformities, this would "not in the least alter the specific task of sociological analysis or of that of the other sciences of action, which is the interpretation of action in terms of its subjective meaning."[13]

2. With respect to the goals of social inquiry, Weber's position is somewhat more ambivalent. In some contexts he emphasizes the empirical-analytic side. Accordingly the primary task of sociological analysis is said to be the discovery of empirically reliable regularities of social action with a view to their employment in causal explanations and conditional predictions. From this point of view, the need for understanding the meaning of social actions is of secondary importance. In other contexts, however, the order of priority is reversed. In his policy statement upon assuming editorial responsibility for the *Archiv für Sozialwissenschaft und Sozialpolitik* in 1904, for example, Weber explicitly subordinated the discovery of causal laws and factors to the articulation of the "significance" of cultural phenomena.

The determination of those (hypothetical) "laws" and "factors" would in any case only be the first of many operations which would lead us to the desired type of knowledge. The analysis of the historically given individual configuration of those "factors" and their *significant* concrete interaction, conditioned by their historical context, and especially the *rendering intelligible* of the basis and type of this significance would be the next task to be achieved. This task must be achieved, it is true, by the utilization of the preliminary analysis, but it is nonetheless an entirely new and *distinct* task. . . . For all these purposes, clear concepts and the knowledge of those (hypothetical) "laws" are obviously of great value as heuristic means—but only as such.[14]

In such passages the *hermeneutic* goal of cultural science—the analysis of the "phenomena of life in terms of their cultural significance"—is viewed as primary. It is the discovery of causal laws that is of secondary importance.

3. Neopositivists have been quite willing to allow that the investigator's values play a role in the selection of problems. Their thesis of value-freedom is meant only to exclude (extrascientific) value judgments from the process of theory formation and testing. Here too Weber's position is much less clear-cut. Although he explicitly excludes value judgments (*Werturteile*) from the domain of science proper, he frequently attaches a "transcendental" sense to the category of value relations (*Wertbeziehungen*).

The concept of culture is a *value-concept.* Empirical reality becomes "culture" to us because and insofar as we relate it to value ideas. It includes those segments and those segments of reality which have become significant to us because of this value-relevance. Only a small portion of existing concrete reality is colored by our value-conditions interest and it alone is significant to us. . . . We cannot discover what is meaningful to us by means of a "presuppositionless" investigation of empirical data. Rather, perception of its meaningfulness to us is the presupposition of its becoming an *object* of investigation.[15]

This value-relevance is decisive not only for the constitution of the object of inquiry but for the process of concept formation as well.

In other words, the choice of the object of investigation and the extent or depth to which this investigation attempts to penetrate into the infinite causal web, are determined by the evaluative ideas which dominate the investigator and his age. In the *method* of investigation, the guiding "point of view" is of great importance for the *construction* of the conceptual scheme which will be used in the investigation."[16]

Of course the historical situation of the investigator and the point of view that guides his inquiry are not fixed.

For none of those systems of ideas which are indispensable in the understanding of those segments of reality that are meaningful at a particular moment can exhaust its infinite richness. They are all attempts, on the basis of the present state of our knowledge and the available conceptual patterns, to bring order into the chaos of those facts which we have drawn into the field circumscribed by our *interest*. . . . This process shows that in the cultural sciences concept-construction depends on the setting of the problem, and the latter varies with the content of culture itself. The relationship between concept and reality in the cultural sciences involves the transitoriness of all such syntheses. . . . The greatest advances in the sphere of the social sciences are substantively tied up with the shift in practical cultural problems and take the guise of a critique of concept construction.[17]

Weber minimized the logical consequences of this state of affairs by appeal to the notion of *Werturteilsfreiheit*, freedom from value judgments. Ultimate value perspectives are, on this account, incapable of being rationally grounded. But this irrationality remains extrascientific. Once a subjective point of view is adopted, social analysis may and must proceed free from value judgments. In this way it can achieve "objective" results, that is, results that are intersubjectively valid for all competent investigators. As W. G. Runciman has pointed out, Weber's solution is of doubtful validity.

We have seen that Weber believes, against the extreme positivist view, that the social sciences differ in kind from the natural. Even leaving aside the problem of the arbitrariness of basic points of view, the uniqueness of historical sequences and the meaningfulness of human behavior mean that there is a latitude of interpretation always confronting the social scientist which the natural scientist is luckily denied. Weber's procedure in the face of this situation breaks down not because he fails to concede that a sociological inquiry cannot be framed in value-neutral terms, but because this concession doesn't buy as much immunity from the remaining problems as he thinks. The arbitrariness of standpoints cannot be merely conceded in the original choice of terms, after which, with this sole limitation, the inquiry conducted can be kept value-free. The infection of values cannot all be passed off on to the questions asked and thereby kept away altogether from the answers given. The evaluative terms will have to be used in inquiries within which—and this is my point—no matter how rigorous the techniques of validation applied there will still be some interpretive latitude.[18]

These brief remarks on Weber should serve to indicate the nature and the importance of the *Verstehen* problematic in the logic of the social sciences. The issues he raised have been subsequently and repeatedly subjected to analysis. Habermas uses these more recent discussions as a foil for developing his own views. My presentation will follow the line of argument in *Zur Logik der Sozialwissenschaften,* beginning with the positivist minimal interpretation of *Verstehen* and closing with the hermeneutic arguments for its universality.

The ambiguities in Weber's position disappear in the neopositivist treatment of the relation of understanding to explanation. Although the notion of *Verstehen* and the problems associated with it are usually attributed to Weber, references to his work are typically limited to the discussion in *Economy and Society.* Accordingly the issue is formulated as one concerned exclusively with the understanding of individual or group actions in terms of their motives. And ignoring Weber's own disclaimers in this regard, this is in turn interpreted as a problem concerning the role of empathy or sympathetic imagination in the explanation of human action. Thus in his now classic article of 1948, which set the terms for much of the later discussion, Theodor Abel characterized "The Operation Called Verstehen" as a process "based on the application of personal experience to observed behavior. We 'understand' an observed or assumed connection if we are able to parallel either one with something we know through self-observation does happen."[19] His analysis of this process yields the following results. (1) *Verstehen* is directed to understanding action. Faced with an observed sequence of behavior, the social scientist imputes to the agent certain "psychological states" (for example, motives, beliefs, values, emotions) that might account for it. This is basically a matter of postulating an "intervening process 'located' inside the human organism" in order to make the observed behavior comprehensible. (2) The operation itself relies on "introspective capacity" and can be broken down into three steps: internalizing the stimulus, internalizing the response, and applying a behavior maxim. Each step is based on the "application of personal experience to observed behavior." (3) So defined, *Verstehen* could not be a "method of verification," Abel argues, but at best a heuristic "aid in preliminary explorations of a subject," with perhaps the additional capacity "to relieve us of a sense of apprehension in connection with behavior that is unfamiliar or unexpected." In the last analysis, "the probability of a connection" can be established "only by means of objective, experimental and statistical tests."[20] The result of this analysis is that the employment of *Verstehen* does not affect the *logic* of inquiry. It is merely a heuristic device that is sometimes useful for pursuing the familiar tasks of constructing, testing, and employing statistical laws referring to sequences of observable behavior.

Abel illustrates his analysis with several examples. One case involves a neighbor chopping wood and building a fire after there has been a drop in temperature. Sympathetic imagination enables us to connect low temperatures with feeling cold and the observed behavior with seeking warmth. Another case connects a drop in the annual rate of crop production in a farming community with a drop in the marriage rate by internalizing the former into "feelings of anxiety" and the latter into "fear of new commitments." In each case the establishment of a connection between the two feeling states draws on a "behavior maxim" generalized from personal experience—for example, "A person feeling cold will seek warmth," or "People who experience anxiety will fear new commitments." As Habermas points out, this process of internalizing stimulus and response and applying behavior maxims is by no means unproblematic.

There is no need for marriage to be judged primarily from the point of view of the economic burdens it occasions; in situations of insecurity [the establishing of] one's own family might just as well appear to be a security-enhancing formation of an intimacy group. How farmers will behave, in cases of crop failure, with respect to familial matters obviously depends on inherited values and institutionalized roles. Such cultural patterns and social norms, however . . . do not belong to the class of behavior maxims that are seemingly introspected with certainty. Rather, they require a controlled appropriation through the hermeneutic understanding of their meaning. . . . Only if the symbolic content of the norms in force is disclosed through the understanding of meaning [*Sinnverständnis*] can motivational understanding [*Motivverstehen*] comprehend observed behavior as subjectively meaningful action in relation to those norms.[21]

The point of this criticism is clear. As social scientists have long noted, behavior in society depends on the agent's "definition of the situation"; social actors themselves have an interpretation of their behavior, ideas about what they are doing and why they are doing it. But this definition of the situation, through which the agent's behavioral reactions are mediated, is not simply a matter of subjective motivation, of "an intervening process 'located' inside the human organism." The "meanings" to which social action is oriented are primarily intersubjective meanings constitutive of the social matrix in which individuals find themselves and act: inherited values and world views, institutionalized roles and social norms, and so forth.

In the normal case social action is oriented to a communicable meaning . . . [which] has its source in the transmitted semantic contents [*tradierten Sinngehalten*] of a cultural tradition, and which has—to the extent that it motivates social action—entered into the definition of socially binding norms. . . . The orienting meaning has the form of a binding group expectation of situation-specific modes of behavior. Social action follows norms. The norms that determine action are collective behavioral expectations. These expectations are segments of a cultural tradition relevant for institutionalized action. The cultural tradition is a complex of symbols that fixes the world view—articulated in ordinary language—of a social group, and thus the framework for communication within this group. Consequently, social action is given only in relation to the system of transmitted cultural patterns in which the self-understanding of social groups is articulated. The methodology of the sciences of action cannot avoid the problematic of understanding meaning [*Sinnverständnis*] through which the cultural tradition is hermeneutically appropriated.[22]

Thus Abel's reflections on *Verstehen* (and the essentially identical analyses of Hempel, Nagel, Rudner and others) do not cut deeply enough. Empathetic *Motivverständnis* presupposes a *Sinnverständnis* of the cultural and institutional setting, which gives the behavior to be explained its significance. And the latter cannot be reduced to a "construction of psychological models." It involves a *Symbolverstehen* that is similar in important respects to the hermeneutic appropriation of traditional meanings. Thus the experiential basis of social inquiry, the mode of access to social reality, is neither the controlled observation and experimentation of the natural sciences nor an empathetic identification based on introspection and imagination. It is rather a type of linguistically based "communicative experience" proper to any inquiry that accepts "meaning" as a basic category.[23]

By selecting as examples rather unproblematic actions in his own cultural vicinity, Abel could pass over, in presupposing, the work of interpretive analysis. Had he dealt, as the anthropologist must, with behavior in a foreign culture or as the historian must, with epochs far removed in time from his own, it would have become obvious that the work of *Verstehen* begins at a much more fundamental level than his schema implies.[24] The critical problems of understanding already arise at the level of observation and description, for the identification or description of a sequence of movements as an action of a certain sort already presupposes an interpretation of the behavior as having a certain point, as situated within a cultural and institutional framework, as obeying or infringing relevant norms, rules, or expectations, and so on. In another social setting, for example, the gathering of and setting fire to wood might have to be understood, say, as the preparation for a ritual sacrifice or as a signal before it could properly be explained in terms of motives. Which designation is applicable to the "response"—lighting a fire, lighting a ritual fire, lighting a signal fire,—determines in turn what the relevant "stimulus" and motives might be. In Wittgensteinian terms, the proper identification of an action depends on knowing the stock of action descriptions available in a given language game, as well as the criteria for their application. An interpretive understanding of the form of life in which it is located is a prerequisite not only for the proper identification of an action but for the identification of relevant "stimuli" and motives as well.

Seen in this light, the problems that the understanding of meaning raises for the program of a unified science are much more wide-ranging and fundamental than neopositivists have supposed. In fact Habermas considers this to be the Achilles heel of the positivist theory of science. "It is the gate through which methodology must pass if positivistically paralyzed reflection is to be brought to life once again."[25] However, the analysis of *Verstehen* as a heuristic device based on empathy is not the only strategy for justifying the thesis of the methodological unity of science. A more radical justification might be based on the rejection of "meaning" as a fundamental category of social inquiry. This is the strategy pursued by strictly behavioral science (the first results of which can be seen in the fields of psychology and social psychology—learning theory, theories of cognitive dissonance, small group research, and so forth). A less radical approach might accept the meaningfulness of social action but standardize the procedures for interpreting it in such a way that empirical, transcultural, and transhistorical laws are not excluded. This is the strategy adopted by those who employ various models of rational action as a general interpretive framework for social inquiry. Its most extensive employment is to be found in the mathematical models of neoclassical economics. Short of rejecting meaning as a basic category or of construing it in terms of rational action and deviations therefrom, it is possible to regard the object domain of social science as symbolically structured in the full sense of the term and yet as being no less accessible to general theories of the empirical and causal type. This is the strategy pursued by functionalists and systems theorists who locate meaningful action in social systems that are governed by objective laws of self-maintenance. Its results can be viewed in functionalist social anthropology, the structural-functional theory of action (Parsons) and contemporary systems theory. At the opposite extreme from behaviorism, one might accept *Sinnverstehen* not only as the experiential basis of social research but as its sole methodological procedure. This approach is represented, in different ways, by various phenomenological, linguistic, and hermeneutic currents of social analysis.

In his methodological writing Habermas analyzes all of these approaches, and his strategy is always that of "concrete negation." He measures each against its own claim to be an adequate framework for a general theory of society. None is simply dismissed as a confusion; instead each is shown to possess a certain "right." At the same time, the right of one is relative to the rights of the others. Thus it is essential to bring out the limitations of the different approaches as well, to specify in which situations, in what ways, and to what ends they might properly be employed. The goal of this procedure is to construct a unified framework that is adequate for general social theory and in which the positive elements of other approaches are somehow preserved. It will not be possible to review here all that Habermas has to say about each position. The remainder of this section will be confined to a brief discussion of his views on behavioristic, decision-theoretic, and phenomenological programs. In the following sections language analysis, hermeneutics, functionalism, and systems theory will be examined at somewhat greater length, for it is upon these that Habermas draws most heavily in the formulation of his own ideas.

The behaviorist program requires that both animal and human behavior be studied according to the same methodological rules that obtain in the natural sciences. The problems associated with a *sinnverstehenden* access to social reality are obviated by the denial of its necessity—the experiential basis of behavioral research is restricted to intersubjectively observable and physically describable behavior. Habermas's critique of this program is basically a recapitulation of some of the familiar criticisms to be found in the extensive literature on behaviorism.[26]

1. At the logical level, the various attempts to transform statements about intentions and actions into statements about observable behavior or to translate them into an empiricist (extensional and truth-functional) language have met with apparently insuperable obstacles. This is not surprising, for statements about intentional action refer to a domain that is already linguistically structured. They belong therefore to another level or type than first-order statements about physical objects and their behavior.

2. The attempts to overcome these difficulties by constructing behaviorist theories of language have proved no less problematic. The reduction of linguistic communication to "verbal behavior," construed as a particular dimension of the generally adaptive behavior of the organism (for example, by Morris), involves explicating the "sameness of meaning" that is constitutive for linguistic symbols in terms of the uniformity of reactions to these symbols. In this schema communicative interaction is less fundamental than the external coordination of different but similar response sequences. But this construction conflicts with the situation of the investigator himself; as a member of the community of investigators, he can pursue behavioristic research only within a framework of intersubjectively shared meanings. That is, the experience of intersubjectively valid rules and norms, of shared intentions and obligations, of the sameness of meaning, and so forth is a presupposition of the activities of identifying, describing, correlating, and so forth that comprise his research. As such it can consistently neither be explained away by the results of that research nor subordinated to the constructions that emerge from it.

3. One might attempt to avoid the difficulties that arise from this "reflexive relation of theory and object levels" by constructing a general theory of language acquisition in such a way that the "verbal behavior" of the investigator could (in principle) also be causally explained and predicted. Habermas's critique of Skinner's attempt to accomplish this through an application of learning theory to language

is basically a synopsis of that developed by Chomsky. I shall not repeat it here.[27]

4. The fundamental difficulty with all such attempts to reduce meaning to behavior is that they fail to appreciate the internal connection to ideas that is constitutive of behavior at the human level. Action and ideas are not independent variables; actions express intentions that cannot be comprehended independently of language. To disregard this connection methodologically is to pretend that there is no basic difference between animal and human behavior.

At the level of animal behavior the element of intentionality is not yet disconnected from behavioral modes and transformed in symbolic systems. Action is first made possible when intentional contents have been rendered independent in language. A more or less stringent system of drives, which defines species-specific significations (from behind, as it were) and attaches them to selected environmental conditions, is released from univocal correlations with the environment only at the cultural level. Only then can it [the system of drives] be itself subjected to new definitions through a linguistic system with variable significations. Whereas significations in the form of signals depend on need dispositions and merely announce pre-selected instinctual objects, the symbolic significations rendered independent in linguistic systems have acquired power to react back on the interpretation of the needs themselves. Action theory relies on this state of affairs in presupposing that a course of action must be grasped through the interpretation of the actor himself—the motive for action shifts from the level of the drive system to that of linguistic communication. In contrast, behavioral research—even when concerned with social action—requires an orientation in which linguistic symbols are once again conceived as signals, motivation through symbolized meaning as drive motivation, and intentional actions as modes of stimulated behavior.[28]

If the attempted reduction of action to behavior rests on (logical and empirical) misunderstandings, then we are obliged to explain the successes of behavioral research on other grounds. Ethological investigations of animal behavior present no grave difficulties since the element of "intentionality" in goal-directed, adaptive, animal behavior has not yet been transformed in culturally variable symbolic systems. But this does not mean, Habermas argues, that the methodological basis of ethology is identical with that of the strictly empirical-analytic sciences. The categorial framework is, rather, rooted in a preunderstanding of intentional action at the human level.

A preconception of intentional complexes has surreptitiously in-sinuated itself into the theoretical approach. Behavior itself is defined as understandable behavior; it is only apparently "objective." Be-havior is constantly interpreted in the framework of a situation which we interpret from our own experiences. The class of observable events that we call "modes of behavior" is distinguished from the class of remaining events through a reference system . . . that established a functional connection between the internal state of an organism, its environment (including conditions of existence and stimuli) and an end-state of the organism. . . . The connection is functional from the point of view of a need satisfaction that is not directly observable—we have already understood what it means to satisfy a need. . . . This in-terpretation from our own experience is not merely superimposed. It provides the prior criterion for delimiting the class of events that can be comprehended as behavior. In addition, it first makes possible theoretical assumptions about the constant significance of different classes of events for a given organism. Thus behavioral research in biology relies on triggering stimuli that "signify" enemy, prey, brood or sex.[29]

The argument, then, is that the categorial framework and proce-dures of ethology rely on preconceptions derived from our under-standing of human behavior and applied—privatively—to animal be-havior. By comparison, learning-theoretical approaches to animal behavior employ a conceptually "thinner" apparatus (for example, as regards innate drives and instincts). Nevertheless the categorial framework is not completely purified of intentional components. The delimitation of a certain class of events as "behavior" and the distinction between "rewards" and "punishments," for example, rely no less on preconceptions derived from the experience of human action.

Although the "privative" employment of quasi-intentional models has proved quite effective in studying animal behavior, its successes at the human level have been rather modest. The radical restriction of intentional elements that results from systematically ignoring the spe-cific characteristics of the sociocultural form of life severely limits the significance of behaviorist social research. A general theory of action cannot simply abstract from the symbolic dimension of human social life; it must somehow integrate it into its basic categories, assump-tions, and procedures.[30]

Acceptance of the irreducible meaningfulness of human action does not itself entail a renunciation of general social theory in favor of cultural hermeneutics. There have been various attempts to combine interpretive understanding with empirical hypotheses about social uniformities. One of the most influential, especially in connection with the development of economic theory, has been the employment of various models of rational action. Weber too recommended this method of combining explanation with understanding. On the one hand, lawlike statements of social regularities are empirically testable and can function in causal explanations and conditional predictions. On the other hand, because of the intentional character of social action, they differ from natural laws in being understandable. We can interpolate understandable motives into observable regular sequences of behavior. The connection between interpretive and causal analysis is especially strong in the case of purposive-rational action. Here understanding the motive makes it possible to derive empirically testable hypotheses about uniformities of behavior under specifiable conditions. In the light of this connection we can appreciate

why Max Weber assigns a methodologically privileged position to purposive-rational action. The *sinnverstehend* interpolated end, the assumed intention, will as a rule lead to an empirically correct explanation only if the end furnishes in fact a sufficient motive for the action. But this is the case when the action is guided by the intention of achieving success through the employment of purposive-rationally chosen means . . . when it is oriented to the choice of adequate means for a subjectively clear end.[31]

In cases of irrational action, the derivation of assumptions about uniformities of overt behavior from knowledge of subjective motives becomes problematic. For this reason Weber proposes construing irrational behavior as a deviation from the "ideal type" of purposive-rationality.

In a similar vein, neoclassical economists employ models of rational choice to develop axiomatic deductive systems of microeconomical laws (for example, those relating supply, demand, and price fluctuations). In these models it is assumed that economic subjects act according to various maxims (normally of the optimization type) and on the basis of specifiable preferences, in choosing among alternative ways of employing available means. Given the relevant initial and boundary conditions, the maxims and preference rules permit a deductive inference of the appropriate course of action. The term *appropriate* points up the well-known limitations of this approach. The theoretical assumptions built into such models are not, in the first instance, statements of empirical regularities but normative rules of rational action. And rules may or may not be actually adopted by social actors. Thus the rationality models represent only abstract possibilities of action. If they are to serve as empirical theories, we require the further assumption that social subjects actually do act in this way. Even within the sphere of economic behavior, this latter assumption has proved to be largely counterfactual.

Nevertheless the employment of models of rational action in the construction of empirical social theories has been defended on various grounds. It has been argued, for instance, that the idealizing procedures of neoclassical economics are typical of scientific theory in general.[32] The laws of natural science (such as Galileo's law of free fall or Boyle's law for gases) are also typically formulated in such a way that they obtain only under ideal conditions (sufficiently "near" the surface of the earth; when the temperature is not too low or the pressure too great). But an analysis of the use of rationality assumptions in pure economics makes clear that they are not treated as empirical hypotheses that can be falsified. The abstraction from noneconomic dimensions of the social milieu and from extraeconomic patterns of motivation is such that the empirical correctness of the rationality assumptions can be maintained only through an in principle indeterminate employment of the *ceteris paribus* clause. And this amounts to an immunization from experience that renders the assumptions tautological.[33]

This critique, Habermas points out, is directed against a false understanding of the status of models of rational choice and not against their use as such. The problem arises from misinterpreting normative-analytic constructions as empirical-analytic theories. If we cease to regard the principal task of models of rational choice as being the delivery of information about empirical regularities and view such models in the framework of decision theory instead, the difficulties disappear. Then, however, the main point of such constructions lies not in their (rather weak) empirical content but in the normative aids to decision making that they provide.

A science that incorporates in its theories fundamental assumptions about idealized action is normative-analytic. The assumptions about actions under pure maxims obtain only for limited segments of social reality, and even there only approximately. More importantly, the rationality assumptions are not treated as conditional, i.e. empirically testable hypotheses. They are hypothetically assigned an unconditional validity; and this determines in turn the meaning of the possible validity of normative-analytic knowledge. The latter does not so much convey information about empirical uniformities—first-order technical knowledge—as information about the purposive-rational choice of strategies that presuppose if necessary the employment of first-order technical knowledge. We can consider such information as second-order technical knowledge.[34]

From this point of view, pure microeconomics is a specialized decision theory for situations of economic choice. Whereas empirical-analytic knowledge can be transformed into technical recommendations, normative-analytic knowledge can be transformed into strategic recommendations regarding the choice among alternative ways of employing available means for the realization of subjectively preferred ends.

Neither the wholesale renunciation of interpretive understanding nor its predefinition in terms of strategic action provides an adequate methodological basis for social theory. If we are to capture the characteristically symbolic dimension of social action and do so without abstracting from the specific cultural and institutional settings in which it is located, there seems to be no way of avoiding a *sinnverstehenden* access to the data. Since the "meanings" that have to be grasped have at the same time the status of "facts," of something empirically encountered, the experiential basis of social inquiry must somehow combine both understanding and observation.

The object domain of the sciences of actions consists of symbols and modes of behavior that can't be grasped [as] actions independently of symbols. Access to the data includes here not only the observation of events but simultaneously the understanding of meaning complexes. In this sense we can distinguish sensory from communicative experience. Of course, all sensory experiences are interpreted; to this extent they are not independent of previous communication. Conversely, understanding is not possible without the observation of signs. But communicative experience is not directed to states of affairs in the same way as observation; it is directed to pre-interpreted states of affairs. It is not the perception of facts that is symbolically structured, but the facts as such.[35]

Behavior in society is mediated through the interpretive schemata of the actors themselves. Consequently the attempt to grasp social reality independently of the participant's own "definition of the situation," to pursue the tasks of concept and theory formation in abstraction from the prior categorial formation of the object domain, is condemned to failure. On the other hand, the methodological incorporation of this dimension itself raises considerable problems. The difficulties appear already at the level of measurement.

Speaking generally, measurement procedures serve to transform experiences into data that satisfy the demands of intersubjective reliability. In testing the validity of truth claims, data of this kind have the advantage of permitting controversies to be settled through an appeal to mutually recognized standards. Because measurement makes possible a more precise differentiation and description of data, it is also of fundamental importance for the formation of categories and the construction of theories. For these reasons measurement operations have been regarded as a sine qua non of systematic science. In particular the development of reliable procedures for measuring social phenomena seems to be a condition of possibility for a "science of society." But if social phenomena are meaningfully structured, the question arises whether and how they can be measured at all. It is in part to avoid this difficulty that behaviorists choose to abstract methodically from the dimension of meaning. In normative-analytic approaches the problem is resolved by schematizing social action as rational choice along dimensions (such as wealth or power) for which there already exist prescientifically institutionalized modes of quantification (such as prices or votes). In formulating measurement procedures, the social scientist can then take up, refine, and idealize preexisting standards. An empirical social theory that neither disregards meaning nor predefines it in terms of strategic rationality has to face squarely the problem of developing reliable measurement procedures for the full range of sybolically structured phenomena accessible to interpretive understanding. But can the intersubjectivity of communicative experience (understanding) be guaranteed in the same way as that of sensory experience (observation)—through the introduction of standardized rules of measurement?

Social scientists have developed numerous research techniques—content analysis, interviews, surveys, questionnaires—that seem to do just this. By means of such techniques the preinterpreted phenomena of everyday life are reorganized and transformed into measured data.

The latter apparently function in the normal way in regard to the formulation and testing of empirical hypotheses about lawlike regularities. If this is indeed the case, it seems that the meaningfulness of social phenomena has consequences only for the particular techniques, not for the fundamental logic of inquiry. But this appearance is misleading; the application of such measurement procedures is fraught with notorious difficulties. At every crucial point—for example, the formation of categories in terms of which the phenomena are to be classified, the segmentation of classificatory concepts into a number of different areas, the specification of indicators for each area, the recombination of segmented judgments into a quantitative index, and so on—there arises a type of problem foreign to the natural sciences.[36] To put it rather abstractly, the successful application of such procedures demands that the social scientist always keep one eye on the participant's understanding of the phenomena being measured. One cannot measure in this way without understanding; and if the understanding is a misunderstanding, then the measurements that rely on it are likely to be of little value.

These difficulties are not merely technical; they point to a basic feature of concept and theory formation in the social sciences. Sociological concepts are "second-level constructs" (Schutz); the "first-level constructs" are those through which social actors have already prestructured social reality prior to its scientific investigation. And since social action is mediated through the interpretive schemata of the actors and cannot be grasped independently of them, the first-level constructs are the necessary point of departure for the formation of second-level constructs. The adequacy of measurement procedures depends on somehow bridging the gap between the two levels (a gap that is all too frequently manifest when we compare the prescientifically articulated problems of social life with their quantified "solutions"). The difficulties are particularly pressing when the relevant features of everyday life are themselves constructed independently of quantitative considerations, for then the "abstract demand to measure social facts" finds no obvious point of contact in the first-level constructs. The measurement procedures must be developed after the fact, from case to case, and in a more or less ad hoc manner.[37]

In the sciences of action there does exist a prior correspondence between the experiential basis and the analytic framework; but this is established . . . independently of possible measurement operations through the interpretations of everyday practice inculcated in ordinary language. The formulation of sociological concepts takes as its immediate starting point pre-scientifically structured communicative experiences. Measurement procedures must be subsequently adjusted to a transcendental agreement that has taken shape in the cultural self-understanding of social life-worlds entirely without regard to measurement practices, i.e. to technical mastery. For this reason there can be no protophysics of the sciences of action. Strictly speaking its place would be taken by an analysis of the rules that transcendentally determine the construction of social life-worlds. Since these rules do not coincide with ideal measurement requirements, the disparity between theories and data is not accidental and not simply a matter to be referred to theoretical progress.[38]

Such reflections have led a number of thinkers to regard the analysis of the "rules governing the construction of social-life worlds" as a necessary propaedeutic to social theory (or even as the proper form of its realization). Without recourse to some prior understanding of the everyday world, the social scientist cannot know what he is supposed to be capturing with his measurement operations. Social theory thus requires a prior reflection on the nature and conditions of communicative experience, on the relation between preexisting meanings, measured data, and theoretical concepts. In a tradition extending from Husserl's transcendental phenomenology, through Schutz's "phenomenology of the social world," to contemporary phenomenological sociology and ethnomethodology, the foundations of *verstehenden* sociology have been developed in the form of a theory of the life-world (*Lebenswelt*).[39] Habermas has reviewed the high points of this tradition in several of his writings. My remarks will be confined to a brief summary of its limitations as he sees them.

Speaking very generally, the point of departure for phenomenological sociology is a conception of the social life-world as a product of human activity. The fundamental task of sociological analysis becomes the reconstruction of the processes through which this meaningfully structured social reality is produced. In this sense phenomenological sociology is committed to a "constitution theory" of society or, more precisely, of the everyday world of lived experiences.[40] As such it is obliged to provide an account of the constituting subject(s), of the basic modes of their constitutive activity and of the rules by which the latter is governed. It is Habermas's contention that the phenomenological approach is unable to discharge these obligations satisfactorily. From the time of Husserl's later writings, it has been troubled by a perceptible tension between the "egological" and "transcendental" presuppositions of phenomenological categories and procedures on the one hand, and the sociological and empirical nature of its tasks on the other.

When Husserl first recognized as fundamental the practical realm of everyday beliefs and activities (which had been regarded as the sphere of non-being in the philosophical tradition) and incorporated the natural life-world into transcendental genesis, the unity-versus-plurality of the meaning-constituting transcendental ego(s) became a problem. His own attempt (in the *Cartesian Meditations*) to derive intersubjective relation—among subjects who apprehend themselves in the reciprocal interlacing of their perspectives and shape a common world horizon—from the monological activities of the ego was doomed to failure.[41]

The "monological" approach of Husserl's transcendental phenomenology made it impossible to explain satisfactorily the foundations of intersubjectivity. The "other," the intersubjectively shared life-world, and the objective world founded in it could consistently be construed only as *constituta* of the individual monad in its "unique philosophical loneliness."

Although Alfred Schutz, the principal architect of phenomenological sociology, progressively moved away from Husserl's transcendental concerns and toward a "mundane" phenomenology of the life-world, he retained even in his later writings the characteristic emphasis on subjective intentionality. On the one hand, he stresses the fact that we experience the world we live in not as a private world but as an intersubjective one—a world common to all of us. On the other hand, he often writes as if this shared world originates in the subjective intentions of individual actors:

It is the insight of the actor into the dependencies of the motives and goals of his actions upon his biographically determined situation which social scientists have in mind when speaking of the subjective meaning which the actor "bestows upon" or "connects with" his action. . . . The postulate of subjective interpretation has to be understood in the sense that all scientific explanations of the social *can*, and for certain purposes *must*, reflect the subjective meaning of the actions of human beings from which social reality originates.[42]

Schutz's emphasis on the "biographical situation" behind everyday meanings signals the continuing influence of Husserl's subjectivistic and individualistic perspective; and his description of the "scientific situation" in which the neutral scientific observer formulates his "second-level constructs" indicates that the perspective of the transcendental spectator, however modified, is still operative in his phenomenology of the life-world. In Habermas's view, it is precisely the retention of these Husserlian elements that accounts for the limits of Schutz's approach. The focus on subjective intentionality and the tendency to treat social life as a derivative of individual activity exposes even "mundane phenomenology" to the pitfalls of subjective idealism. It is not possible, Habermas argues, to understand action solely through the explication of subjectively intended meanings. The empirical interconnections among actions governed by social norms go beyond what is subjectively intended. And the effective determinants of the actions themselves need not coincide with manifest motives. An approach that remains within the confines of an analysis of structures of consciousness is methodologically incapable of grasping the objective context of social action. It is in a sense a sociology without society.[43]

Garfinkel's ethnomethodology decidedly shifts the focus away from intuitable structures of individual consciousness. The domain of ethnomethodological inquiry consists rather of "members' situated practices," which produce for themselves and for observers the sense of objective social structures. Large-scale sociological theory, in concentrating on these "objective structures" and neglecting the practices that human beings employ in constructing their social orders, inevitably involves misunderstandings and reifications. By switching our attention to "extremely small-scale studies of formal structures of practical, everyday activities," to the "rational properties of indexical expressions, the modalities of use and comprehension of natural languages, and the artful conduct of routine affairs," we can actually study (rather than deny, ignore, or simply presuppose) "members' methods of solving the methodological problems of practical sociological reasoning."[44] The ethnomethodological program thus represents a decisive turn away from the superiority claims of scientific sociology vis-à-vis common-sense descriptions of society. At the same time, it avoids many of the pitfalls of earlier phenomenological approaches by referring the construction of everyday orders to "situated practices" rather than to activities of consciousness. Nevertheless the exclusive focus on the interpretive procedures of "members" themselves raises the familiar problems of subjectivism; it implies that social processes and structures can be understood only from the point of view of those engaged in them.[45]

Generally the phenomenological perspective subordinates the analysis of specifically social structures (such as roles and institutions, social norms and values, systems and traditions) to the analysis of perceptions of, interpretations of, and orientations to these structures (such as "role taking" and "role performance," translating social norms into motives for action). The key to the latter is found in the biographical situation of the actor and the perspectives it opens. Habermas regards this accent on the individual interpretation of social structures as a necessary corrective to sociological "objectivism." But it is only one side of the coin; the significance of social norms transcends the subjectively intended meanings of individuals acting according to norms.

The rules of interpretation [for transforming social norms into individual motives] are not part of the invariant life-equipment of individuals or groups. They constantly change with the structure of the life-world, sometimes in unnoticeable, continuous shifts, sometimes in a disconnected and revolutionary manner. . . . They are not ultimates, but products of social processes that have to be understood. Apparently the empirical conditions under which transcendental rules take shape and determine the constitutive order of a life-world are themselves the result of socialization processes. I cannot see how these processes can be comprehended without reference to social norms. If this is the case, those rules of interpretation cannot in principle be separated from the rules of social action. Without recourse to social norms, we could explain neither how the "constitutive order" of a life-world arises, nor how it changes. And yet this order is in turn the basis for the individual transformation of norms into actions from which we "read off" what counts as a norm. The analytic separation of rules of interpretation and social norms certainly makes good sense. But neither category of rules can be analyzed independently of the other; both are moments of the complex of social life.[46]

That is, the investigation of individual interpretations of and orientations to intersubjective social structures gives us a one-sided picture of social life. It must somehow be integrated with analyses of the "objective" structures themselves and of the empirical conditions under which both dimensions of the social life-world develop and change.

But this integration cannot be achieved so long as we hold fast to models derived from a theory of consciousness. As the work of Husserl and Schutz make evident, such models inevitably involve us in the predicament of deriving intersubjective relations from monological premises. Both authors start from consciousness and experience and work outward to language and communication, and both fail to make this transition plausible. The attempt to ground language in primary experiences of "appresentation" tacitly presupposes the idea of representation of meaning by signs. As Husserl's own analyses in *Experience and Judgment* show, every intention, no matter how "originary," includes categorial determinations. The structure of consciousness cannot be conceived independently of the structure of language. (As Wittgenstein asked, how would we know that a translation of wordless thoughts into words was correct?) And linguistic structures are not the properties of isolated monads; they presuppose communicative relations.

For this reason Habermas favors the reverse procedure: taking intersubjectivity as the starting point and construing subjectivity in relation to it. This is the procedure represented in Mead's model of a role that establishes reciprocal expectations about behavior and in Wittgenstein's model of a rule that at least two subjects must be able to follow. Concepts such as "role" or "rule" must be defined from the outset in intersubjective terms. Thus the priority of the solitary private consciousness is replaced by that of communicative relations. Furthermore the underlying systems of rules are no longer attributed to individual subjects; they account rather for the generation of intersubjective relations in which subjects themselves are formed.[47] Accordingly Habermas next considers approaches that take language, and not consciousness, as their point of departure: Wittgenstein's theory of language games and Gadamer's hermeneutics.

3.3 LANGUAGE, HERMENEUTICS, AND THE CRITIQUE OF IDEOLOGY

In the English-speaking world, a powerful challenge to the neopositivist logic of unified science has emerged from one of the nerve centers of analytic philosophy itself: the later philosophy of Ludwig Wittgenstein. Wittgenstein's early work, the *Tractatus*, was—along with Russel's logical atomism and the ideas of the Vienna circle—itself a principal source of logical positivism. In it he attempted to fix the limits of language (and of thought and of the world) by disclosing its uniform logical structure: the universal structure of language, its "essence," was located in the logical form concealed beneath the surface of everyday discourse; and this form mirrored the structure of the world. As a number of interpreters have noted, this early conception had a distinctively Kantian ring.[1] The idea that logic covers everything that can be said in advance of experience (a priori), and that in disclosing the structure of factual discourse it discloses the structure of reality, bore strong analogies to Kant's transcendental critique of pure reason. At the same time it provided a valuable propaedeutic to the unified science program: the logical syntax of language fixed the boundaries within which meaningful factual propositions were possible. It determined in advance the logical form of such propositions and the structure of reality that they reflected. It was, in this sense, the logical syntax of a universal language of science. What could not be said in such a language—for example, the propositions of religion, ethics and aesthetics—could not be meaningfully said at all.

In Wittgenstein's later work, most importantly in the *Philosophical Investigations*, this "transcendental" analysis of language is explicitly rejected in favor of a more or less "sociolinguistic" analysis of concrete "language games" as "forms of life."[2] Language is no longer represented as a logically rigid essence. Rather, expressions have meaning only within diverse language games, which are complexes of speech and action. These polymorphous arrays of language and practice are not, however, without their own structures of "grammars." The activities that comprise a language game proceed according to rules (although they are not everywhere circumscribed by rules). In learning a natural language, we come to engage in agreed common practices and to share agreed common criteria for their performance. "Understanding a language" and "being able to speak" refer, then, to skills that one has acquired, to activities that one has learned to carry out in common with others. This internal connection of language with practice, with knowing how to do certain things, is evident in the learning situation itself.

It disperses the fog to study the phenomena of language in primitive kinds of application in which one can command a clear view of the aim and functioning of the words. A child uses such primitive forms of language when it learns to talk. Here the teaching of language is not explanation, but training. . . . The children are brought up to perform *these* actions, to use *these* words as they do so, and to react in *this* way to the words of others.[3]

One has mastered a language when one has learned to do these things in the common agreed upon way.

From the perspective of Wittgenstein's later philosophy, the relation of language to the world is not in the first instance theoretical but practical. The unique, ontologically grounded "picturing" relation of the *Tractatus* gives way to the conception of a plurality of reference systems or life-worlds in which reality is interpreted. The task of analysis is no longer the transformation of unanalyzed everyday expressions into expressions of a universal language; it is directed rather to exhibiting the orders or grammars of natural languages themselves. Although Wittgenstein did not himself focus on problems of sociological understanding and although his own analyses of human action sometimes tended in a more or less behavioristic direction, the importance of these later ideas for a logic of *Verstehen* is evident. As Habermas puts it:

At this stage, language analysis loses the significance for the logic of science claimed by the *Tractatus;* it no longer delimits the contestable domain of the natural sciences. Instead it gains a special significance for the social sciences; it not only delimits the domain of social action, but makes it accessible. . . . In disclosing the grammars of forms of life, the logical analysis of ordinary language touches the very object domain of the social sciences.[4]

These ideas seem to point philosophy in the direction of a sort of anthropology of conceptual systems. But Wittgenstein himself was inspired by more ascetic ideals. Philosophers are not called upon to propound theories or even systematic descriptions and comparisons of language. Their task is, rather, therapeutic: to exhibit, indirectly, facts about language that are already familiar, to make us conscious of the functioning of our language games in order to break the hold upon our minds of philosophical confusions and paradoxes. For this task there is no need to appeal to any alleged "metalanguage"; the grammars of language games can be elucidated "from within" by a reflective application of the grammars themselves. The apparent circularity is rendered harmless precisely by the inner connection of language and practice.

Following a rule is analogous to obeying an order. We are trained to do so; we react to an order in a particular way. But what if one person reacts in one way and another in another to the order and the training? Which one is right? Suppose you came as an explorer into an unknown country with a language quite strange to you. In what circumstances would you say that the people there gave orders, understood them, obeyed them, rebelled against them, and so on? The common behavior of mankind is the system of reference by means of which we interpret an unknown language.[5]

The basic test of whether one has learned a rule is the attempt to participate in the language game in question, to do things in the "same" way. Successful participation is a sign that one has it right; disturbance in communication, on the other hand, indicates that one has not yet grasped the rule correctly. In this sense, the adequacy of our mastery of rules—rules that pertain now not merely to the formation and transformation of propositions, but to an interplay of symbols and activities—can be corroborated only in interaction, by a kind of consensus among those acting together. "'So you are saying that human agreement decides what is true and what is false?'—it is what human beings *say* that is true and false; and they agree in the *language* they use. This is not agreement in opinions but in forms of life."[6]

In virtually anticipating this agreement, the analyst does not merely invent situations in which an expression might be used. His imagination must draw on his experience and memory of how the expression actually is used. Finally he is brought back to the learning situation itself, to the training and exercises in which the expression was (or could be) learned (or taught). "In such a difficulty always ask yourself: How did we *learn* the meaning of this word ("good" for instance)? From what sort of examples? In what language games?"[7]

In Habermas's view, Wittgenstein's approach implies an inner relation between understanding language (*Sprachverstehen*) and the virtual repetition of socialization processes.

Grammatical rules . . . are not metalinguistic rules for connecting symbols, but didactic rules for language instruction. Strictly speaking, the grammars of language games contain the rules according to which children are trained in an existing culture. Because ordinary language is the last metalanguage, it contains the dimension in which it can be learned; thus it is not "only" language, but also practice.[8]

In 1958 Peter Winch took this theory of language as the starting point for his development of the foundations of *verstehenden* sociology. His book, *The Idea of a Social Science and Its Relation to Philosophy,* has ever since been the subject of controversy, for Winch not only spells out the challenge of Wittgenstein's ideas to the neopositivist logic of unified science; he uses them to withdraw social inquiry from the realm of science and to locate it in the immediate vicinity of philosophy:

To elucidate the concept of a "form of life" has been shown to be precisely the aim of epistemology. It is true that the epistemologist's starting point is rather different from that of the sociologist but, if Wittgenstein's arguments are sound, that is what he must sooner or later concern himself with. That means that the relations between sociology and epistemology must be very different from, and very much closer than, what is usually imagined to be the case. . . . The philosophical problems which arise there [in sociology,] are not tiresome foreign bodies which must be removed before sociology can advance on its own independent scientific lines. On the contrary, the central problem of sociology, that of giving an account of the nature of social phenomena in general, itself belongs to philosophy. In fact, not to put too fine a point on it, this part of sociology is really misbegotten epistemology.[9]

In many ways Winch's methodological ideas are similar to those advanced by phenomenologists. He too stresses the meaningfulness of human behavior and the necessity of grasping the structures of the everyday world prior to formulating theoretical concepts. But these structures are now viewed as structures of language games and not of consciousness; thus their explication calls for a peculiar type of empirically oriented language analysis. And the key to this type of analysis is the notion of "following a rule."

In the second chapter of his book, Winch characterizes meaningful behavior as behavior that is "ipso facto rule governed."[10] This is not to say that it is simply a putting into effect of preexisting principles. Rather principles and rules "arise in the course of conduct and are intelligible only in relation to the conduct out of which they arise." On the other hand, "the nature of the conduct out of which they arise can only be understood as an embodiment of these principles."[11] Thus the sociologist cannot arrive at a "more reflective understanding" of social phenomena without first grasping "the participant's unreflective understanding."

Mill's view is that understanding a social institution consists in observing regularities in the behavior of its participants and expressing these regularities in the form of generalizations. Now if the position of the social investigator (in the broad sense) can be regarded as comparable, in its main logical outlines, with that of the natural scientist, the following must be the case. The concepts and criteria according to which the sociologist judges that, in two situations, the same thing has happened, or the same action performed, must be understood *in relation to the rules governing sociological investigation.* But here we run against a difficulty; for whereas in the case of the natural scientist we have to deal with only one set of rules, namely those governing the scientist's investigation itself, here *what the sociologist is studying,* as well as his study of it, is a human activity and therefore carried on according to rules. And it is these rules, rather than those which govern the sociologist's investigation, which specify what is to count as "doing the same kind of thing" in relation to that kind of activity.[12]

Thus although Winch does not conceive of *Verstehen* as empathetic identification, he does insist that the fundamental criteria for identifying actions are taken from the rules according to which the activity under investigation is itself carried out. To mention one of his own examples, the criteria according to which the social investigator must decide whether two utterances belong to the same class of religious activity (say, prayer) are not taken from sociology but from religion itself. Hence, Winch goes on, the relation of the sociologist to performers of religious activity "cannot be that of the observer to the observed." It is, rather, analogous to the participation of a member of a social group in the activities of that group.[13]

Contrary to what Winch's critics frequently allege, he does not deny the possibility of developing and employing sociological categories other than those of the participant.[14] His claim is rather that the social scientist's access to his data, as well as his formulation and application of "more reflective" or "technical" concepts, must be mediated through "those other concepts which belong to the activity under investigation";—he must understand the "language game" that is being "played." And this, Winch maintains, is much more akin to "tracing the internal relations" of a system of ideas than to the "application of generalizations and theories to particular instances."[15] "Social relations between men and the ideas which men's actions embody are really the same thing considered from different points of view."[16]

Habermas has serious reservations about Winch's conception of social inquiry. For one thing, the replacement of the empathy model with a participation analogy raises a number of problems. What language game is the sociologist playing? What is the relationship of his language game to that under investigation? The reference to the participant's unreflective understanding may or may not suffice for Wittgenstein's therapeutic purposes; it certainly does not suffice as an explication of sociological understanding. Winch's sociological investigator is not simply "assembling reminders" in and about the language in question; he is offering an account of one language game or form of life in terms of another language game, his own. How is this possible and what are the logical issues involved? By holding to the participation analogy, Winch avoids these questions and seems to end up with a linguistic version of the historicist idea of *Verstehen* as a self-transposition into other forms of life.

Winch seems to have in mind a linguistic version of Dilthey. From a free-floating position the language analyst can recreatively slip into the grammars of any given language game—without himself being bound to the dogmatics of a language game of his own that is binding for the analysis. Winch relies, as naively as Schutz, on the possibility of pure theory. . . . If we pursue language analysis with a descriptive intention and cease to limit ourselves to therapy, we must break through the monadic structure of language games and reflect on the context in which the pluralism of language games is first constituted. In this case, the language of the analyst cannot simply coincide with that of the given object language. There must be a translation between the two linguistic systems, just as there is among the analyzed language games themselves. . . . The interpreter mediates between different patterns of socialization; at the same time his translation depends on the patterns of his own socialization. Reflexive linguistic analysis actually achieves a communication between different language games. The example of the anthropologist in a land with an alien culture is not chosen accidently. Wittgenstein does not analyze it satisfactorily when he highlights only the virtual recovery of socialization into other forms of life. Finding one's way into an alien culture is possible only to the extent that one successfully translates between it and one's own.[17]

The "sociolinguistic" stage of reflection on the nature and conditions of interpretive understanding does not go far enough; it leaves a number of crucial issues unresolved. There are, Habermas argues, at least two ways to proceed from here. If it were possible to develop a universal theory of language, the "grammars" of different language games could be given standard descriptions in a theoretical language. "Translations" of different object languages into the language of the analyst, and thus the intertranslation of analyzed languages among themselves, could then take place according to general transformation rules. In this case language analysis would no longer be tied to the "dogmatics" of the analyst's particular, socioculturally transmitted patterns of linguistic socialization; it could be undertaken "in a theoretical attitude." Taking the work of Chomsky and others as his point of departure, Habermas investigates this line of thought in his later writings on "universal pragmatics."

In *Zur Logik der Sozialwissenschaften* he examines the other basic strategy: a further radicalization of reflection on the conditions of interpretive understanding, one that thematizes precisely what is taken for granted in Winch's linguistic version. This more radical stage of reflection has been attained in Gadamer's hermeneutics. As we shall see, the interpretation and critique of hermeneutics provide Habermas with the opportunity to reformulate and refine a number of fundamental ideas that were left rather vague in his earlier treatment of "the dialectical character" of an empirical philosophy of history with practical intent.

Hermeneutics, the art of textual interpretation, developed in intimate connection with theology and jurisprudence.[18] The gradual disintegration of the medieval world fostered a growing awareness of the problems involved in correctly interpreting canonical texts. Biblical exegesis in particular was forced to become more self-conscious in response to the palpable distance from the original. A similar consciousness of distance, and the problems it implies for correct understanding, exercised the Renaissance humanists in their encounter with classical texts. From its beginnings as an auxiliary to theology and jurisprudence, hermeneutics eventually expanded to include the whole range of text-interpreting philologies. With the awakening of historical consciousness in late eighteenth- and early nineteenth-century Germany (Herder, Romanticism, Hegel), the importance of interpretive procedures for deciphering the meaning and significance of historical phenomena became apparent. At the very latest, Dilthey's investigation of the conditions of possibility and validity of *Verstehen* marked the generalization of hermeneutic procedures to the whole of the human world.

But in the process of expansion, the original self-understanding of hermeneutics became problematic. In the interpretation of canonical texts (religious or legal), the text's claim to meaning and truth provided the standard of adequate understanding. Interpretation was "normative-dogmatic" in the sense that it took its orientation from the authority of the text and inquired after its normative meaning for the present. Its aim was the transmission—not the criticism, not the disinterested presentation—of traditional beliefs and norms; they were to be mediated with or applied to present circumstances. This respect for the normative validity of tradition was also an element of the humanists' orientation to the classical texts of "the golden age of man." Although there were certainly instances of critical hermeneutics before the nineteenth century (for example, Spinoza's interpretation of the Bible), the connection of hermeneutics with normatively binding tradition was seriously undermined only with the rise of historicism. The view that cultural phenomena could be understood and assessed only in relation to the historical context in which they were rooted tended to lead to moral and intellectual skepticism vis-à-vis tradition. Dilthey's psychologistic approach to *Verstehen*—as a self-transposition into the life of the author or agent—eliminated its practical relation to life in favor of a contemplative model of scientific objectivity. Rather than a source of transhistorically valid truths and values, history became a repository of the wealth and variety of human life. Historical consciousness was no longer the shepherd of tradition but the "musée imaginaire" of the past.

More recently Heidegger's existential ontology has provided the point of departure for a hermeneutics of language that attempts to steer between the dogmatic traditional views of interpretation on the one hand and the relativistic historicist views on the other. The most differentiated presentation of this approach is to be found in the writings of Hans-Georg Gadamer. In his main work, *Wahrheit und Methode*, Gadamer was not concerned with working out methodological procedures for the social sciences or with elucidating their theoretical foundations; he wanted instead to disclose "linguisticality" (*Sprachlichkeit*) as the basic mode of human existence.[19] This he did in exploring the structures of understanding in the traditional hermeneutic domains of aesthetics, philology, and history. Largely through the efforts of Habermas and Karl-Otto Apel, his work has since been introduced into contemporary German discussions of the foundations of social inquity.

In *Zur Logik der Sozialwisschaften* Gadamer's hermeneutic reflections are situated methodologically by way of a confrontation with the ideas of Wittgenstein and Winch. The principal points of contrast might be organized as follows: (1) the intertranslatability of natural languages versus the "monadology of language games"; (2) the paradigm of translation between two languages versus the paradigm of socialization into a primary language; (3) the emphasis on history and tradition versus the ahistorical, "unbroken" reproduction of forms of life; and (4) the theoretical attitude of language analysis versus the practical attitude of hermeneutic appropriation.[20]

1. Wittgenstein and Winch both tend to describe language games and forms of life as if each were an individual linguistic totality, a "windowless monad" closed off from all others. Gadamer insists on the "unity of reason" in the plurality of natural languages. In Habermas's words,

We are never locked within a single grammar. Rather, the first grammar that we learn to master already puts us in a position to step out of it and to interpret what is foreign, to make comprehensible what is incomprehensible, to assimilate in our own words what at first escapes them. The relativism of linguistic world views and the monadology of language games are equally illusory."[21]

2. The paradigm behind Wittgenstein's remarks on understanding language is usually the learning of a primary language, that is, the "training" or process of socialization through which one comes to be able to use language in the first place. In his book, Winch seems to rely on this paradigm: the relation of the sociologist to his subjects is not that of observer to observed but is analogous to the participation of a member of a group in the activities of that group. Grasping the "participant's unreflective understanding"—which is a presupposition of social theory—seems to require something analogous to socialization into the language community in question. In contrast Gadamer starts with the situation in which the interpreter and his subject have already mastered their respective languages and sets the problem in

terms of achieving an understanding between them. He expressly rejects the primary socialization process as a paradigm for *Verstehen*.

> The understanding of a language is itself not yet really *Verstehen*, but an accomplishment of life [*Lebensvollzug*]. For one understands a language in that one lives in it. . . . The hermeneutic problem is not therefore a problem of the correct mastery of a language. . . . Such mastery . . . is [rather] a precondition for understanding in dialogue.[22]

The proper level, then, at which to pursue the analysis of interpretive understanding is not the learning of "language in general" but the achieving of understanding in dialogue.

Difficulties in understanding and the need for interpretation constantly arises even within the ambit of one's own language. However the problems involved and the ways of overcoming them emerge more clearly when we consider situations in which understanding is particularly difficult to achieve, for instance, when two different languages are involved and some form of translation is needed. In such situations the conditions of successful understanding are more likely to become explicit. For this reason Gadamer turns to translation as the paradigm from which to develop his analysis of the logic of *Verstehen*. This orientation excludes from the start an explication in psychological terms (for example, empathy) or in terms of a virtual repetition of the training through which native speakers are socialized into their languages. Understanding is for Gadamer inextricably bound up with interpretation, with an articulation in the interpreter's language of meanings constituted in another universe of discourse. The interpreter does not approach his subject as a tabula rasa, as an ideally neutral observer with a direct access to the "given." Rather he brings with him a certain horizon of expectations—of beliefs and practices, concepts and norms—that belong to his own life-world. He sees the subject from the perspectives opened by this horizon.

The process of interpretation itself has a hypothetical and circular character. From the perspectives available to him, the interpreter makes a preliminary projection (*Vorentwurf*) of the sense of the text as a whole. With further penetration into the details of his material, the preliminary projection is revised, alternative proposals are considered, and new projections are tested. This hypothetico-circular process of understanding the parts in terms of a projected sense of the whole, and revising the latter in the light of a closer investigation of the parts, has as its goal the achieving of a unity of sense: an interpretation of the whole into which our detailed knowledge of the parts can be integrated without violence. The standards of objectivity governing such a process cannot, according to Gadamer, be specified or applied independently of the corroboration or certification of a projected interpretation in the light of the material at hand. Arbitrary preconceptions deriving from the interpreter's own cultural context show themselves to be arbitrary only in collision with the material. The unsuitability of carrying over certain conceptions and beliefs into contexts culturally removed from one's own becomes evident in and through further penetration of the material, a penetration that must be guided by a trained openness for cultural differences. But such openness cannot be a matter of the interpreter's ridding himself of all preconceptions and prejudgments. This is a logical impossibility—the idea of an interpreter without a language. All interpretive understanding is necessarily bound to preconceptions and prejudgments. The problem for interpretation is not simply the having of a structure of prejudices or prejudgments (*Vorurteilsstruktur*) but the unselfconscious imposition of this structure, and the violence to an adequate interpretation which that entails.[23] Openness can only help the interpreter gradually to become aware of his own structure of prejudices in the course of his interpretive activity. There is, of course, no possibility of raising to consciousness all-at-once and once-and-for-all one's preconceptions and prejudgments. It is rather in the interpretive process itself that one's own structure of prejudices gradually becomes clearer.

The interpreter, like the translator, must capture the sense of his material in and through articulating it in a symbolic framework different from that in which it was originally constituted as meaningful. And as the translator must find a common language that preserves the rights of his mother tongue and at the same time respects the foreignness of his text, so too must the interpreter conceptualize his material in such a way that while its foreignness is preserved, it is nevertheless brought into intelligible relation with his own life-world. In Gadamer's terms, a successful interpretation entails a fusion of horizons (*Horizontverschmelzung*). But this means that there is no such thing as *the* correct interpretation, in itself as it were. If interpretation is always a hermeneutic mediation between different life-worlds and if the hermeneutic "initial situation" is itself caught up in the movement of history, the notion of a final valid interpretation makes no sense. "Each time will have to understand the written tradition in its way . . . one understands otherwise if one understands at all."[24] Unless there is an end to history, there can be no end to the interpretive process.

3. It has often been remarked that Wittgenstein's account of language is basically ahistorical, and Winch has been accused of carrying this over into his theory of social science.[25] In any case, it is clear that historical perspective plays no great role in their reflections. Gadamer, on the other hand, moves the historical dimension of understanding into the foreground. Language and tradition are inseparable; tradition is the medium in which language is transmitted and developed. Habermas describes the difference as follows:

The process of socialization through which the individual grows into his language is the smallest unity of the process of tradition. Against this background we can see the foreshortening of perspective to which Wittgenstein succumbed; the language games of the young do not simply reproduce the practice of their elders. With the first fundamental rules of language the child learns not only the conditions of possible consensus, but at the same time the conditions of possible interpretations of these rules. . . . Actually spheres of language are not monadically closed off, but inwardly as well as outwardly porous. The grammar of a language cannot contain a rigid design for its application. Whoever has learned to apply its rules has not only learned to express himself but to interpret expressions in this language. Both translation (outwardly) and tradition (inwardly) must be possible in principle. Along with their possible application, grammatical rules simultaneously imply the necessity of interpretation. . . . With Gadamer language gains a third dimension—grammar governs an application of rules which in turn further develops the system of rules historically. . . . Language exists only as transmitted. For tradition reflects on a large scale the life-long socialization of individuals in their language.[26]

Because Gadamer does—whereas phenomenologists and language analysts typically do not—explicitly thematize the historical dimension of language, his analysis of *Verstehen* includes a number of features that relate directly to the nature of historical understanding. He argues, for example, that the usual description of the hermeneutic circle in terms of wholes and parts is merely formal and, as such, inadequate to historical understanding. The interpretive appropriation of one's own tradition has, to be sure, a circular structure; but it is of a material or substantive nature. The anticipation or projection of meaning that guides the interpreter's work is in this case itself a product of the tradition he is trying to understand. That is, the interpretive understanding of one's own tradition starts with a "structure of prejudices," with preconceptions and prejudgments, which have themselves been shaped by this tradition. This is especially true of the study of classical cultures and their products, since these, by definition, have had a particularly important historical influence or *Wirkungsgeschichte*; their interpretive appropriation has played a significant role in the development of the tradition to which the interpreter belongs. And his interpretation is itself a reappropriation, a further development of the very tradition to which both he and his object belong. In Gadamer's view, this substantive circle has a positive significance, for it ensures that there is some common ground between the interpreter's horizon of expectations and the material that he is studying, that his points of reference for understanding the tradition have a basis in that tradition itself.

Thus the circle is not a formal circle. It is neither subjective nor objective, but describes understanding as the interplay between the movement of tradition and that of the interpreter. The anticipation of meaning which guides our understanding of a text is not an action of subjectivity; it is determined instead by what is common to us and the tradition and binds us to it. What is common, however, is constantly being developed in our relationship to tradition.[27]

From this perspective it becomes clear that any conception of hermeneutic understanding as a reproduction of an original meaning is mistaken.

The actual meaning of a text, as it speaks to the interpreter, is not dependent on the occasion represented by the author and his original public. At least it is not exhausted by it; for the meaning is also determined by the historical situation of the interpreter, and thus by the whole of the objective course of history. . . . The meaning of a text goes beyond its author, not only occasionally but always. Understanding is therefore not merely reproductive, but also productive.[28]

The meaning of transmitted documents is not independent of the events and interpretations that follow. It is, rather, "an aggregate of sedimented significations that continuously emerge from new retrospectives."[29] The meaning of a text is in principle incomplete, open for interpretations from future perspectives. The movement of history and the changing situation of the interpreter bring out new aspects and cast former elements in a new light. This is the basis of the philologist's experience of the "inexhaustibility" of the meaning of transmitted texts; each age attempts to provide a better interpretation, and it does so from perspectives that were unavailable to previous ages.

This openness to reinterpretation applies not only to transmitted texts but to historical events as well. Historical events are reconstructed within narrative frameworks, and such reconstruction involves relating them to other, later events. Thus as Danto has argued, narrative statements represent an event in terms of categories under which it could not have been observed (for example, "The Thirty Years War began in 1618").[30] Consequently the historical description of events becomes in the course of time richer than empirical observation at the moment of their happening permits, for the historical meaning of events is a meaning that accrues to them partly in the light of what happens later and from the point of view of those who were born later. As long as new points of view arise, the same events can enter into other narratives and acquire new significations (for example, the Thirty Years War: a military happening that extended through three decades; the political collapse of the German empire; the postponement of capitalist development; the end of the Counter-reformation). We could give a definitive and complete account of a historical event only if we could anticipate the future course of events, the point of view of the last historian. As a result, Danto argues, a complete account of the past presupposes a complete account of the future, a philosophy of history that fixes the meaning of history as a whole. This he takes to be impossible.

Any account of the past is essentially incomplete. It is essentially incomplete, that is, if its completion would require the fulfillment of a condition which simply cannot be fulfilled. And my thesis will be that a complete account of the past would presuppose a complete account of the future, so that one could not achieve a complete historical account without also achieving a philosophy of history. So that if there cannot be a legitimate philosophy of history, there cannot be a legitimate and complete historical account.[31]

Danto draws the further conclusion that the essential incompleteness of historical descriptions implies that they are in principle arbitrary.

Completely to describe an event is to locate it in all the right stories, and this we cannot do. We cannot because we are temporally provincial with regard to the future. We cannot for the same reasons that we cannot achieve a speculative philosophy of history. The complete description then presupposes a narrative organization, and narrative organization is something that we do. Not merely that, but the imposition of a narrative organization logically involves us with an inexpungable subjective factor. There is an element of sheer arbitrariness in it. We organize events relative to some events which we find significant in a sense not touched upon here. It is a sense of significance common, however, to all narratives and is determined by the topical interests of this human being or that.[32]

It should now be evident why the discussion of hermeneutics plays such an important role in Habermas's methodological deliberations; it leads back to a set of ideas that were central to his earlier formulations of critical social theory without being satisfactorily developed in them. Gadamer explicitly takes into account what Schutz and Winch either took for granted or failed to appreciate: the essentially historical dimension of *Sinn* and *Sinnverstehen*. By drawing out the dependence of interpretive understanding on the sociocultural "initial situation" of the interpreter and disclosing the essentially historical nature of the latter, hermeneutics forces us to reflect on the relations of theory to history and, more particularly, to the philosophy of history.

Historicism created the illusion that the development of historical consciousness had once and for all broken the quasinatural power of tradition. The advent of industrial society seemed to confirm this: the future needed no longer be an unreflected product of the past; it could now be planned and technically mastered. Society, no less than nature, seemed accessible to purposive-rational control on the basis of scientific knowledge. This attitude is reflected in neopositivist accounts of the relation of sociology to history. Whereas sociology, as a nomological science, is concerned with the formulating and testing of general laws, history is concerned with the causal explanation of particular events by appeal to these laws. From this perspective, the historical past ceases to function as a tradition that operates within social inquiry itself; it is a "cosmos of facts" that must be approached objectivistically, in a theoretical attitude.

Today the predominant view is that the social sciences have broken away from the jurisdiction of the *Geisteswissenschaften* and have found an unproblematic relation to history. The general theories of social action lie, so to speak, perpendicular to the historical complex of tradition. Sociology . . . proceeds in indifference to history. It works up its data without considering the specific context; the historical position of the data is neutralized from the start. For sociology all history has become present. . . . [It] is projected onto a plane of simultaneity and thus robbed of its real spirit.[33]

For Habermas, as for Gadamer, the ideas of a society freed from history and for a technical mastery of its future, of a history that has been disempowered as *Wirkungsgeschichte,* and of a posthistorical social science freed from the context-bound interpretation of its historical situation are equally illusory. They themselves have to be hermeneutically comprehended in their relation to the sociocultural development of modern society. In reality, the allegedly universal theories of social action remain rooted in, and reflect, this very development. This is already evident in the formulation of basic categories.

Status and contract, *Gemeinschaft* and *Gesellschaft,* mechanical and organic solidarity, informal and formal groups, culture and civilization, traditional and bureaucratic authority, sacral and secular associations, military and industrial society, status group and class, etc. . . . [are] "historically rooted concepts" which, not by accident, arose in connection with the analysis of the unique historical transformation of European society from feudalism to modern capitalism. They emerged in the attempt to grasp specific tendencies in this development: urbanization, bureaucratization, industrialization, etc. . . . In the same way, categories like "role" and "reference group" are dependent on the self-understanding of industrially advanced society. None of these concepts lose their situation-bound, specific content through formalization. This can be seen precisely when a theoretical framework constituted of historically substantive concepts is supposed to be employed in the analysis of culturally foreign and removed contexts. In such transpositions the instrument becomes peculiarly blunt. This experience leads to the suspicion that there exists in sociology a tacit connection between the categorial framework of general theories and a guiding pre-understanding of the contemporary situation as a whole. The further such theories are removed from their domain of application, the less they contribute to interpretation, the less they "signify" or "make understandable."[34]

It is precisely this tacit connection that hermeneutic reflection brings to consciousness. If the social scientist is not to proceed with his head in the sand, he must reflectively take into account the dependence of his conceptual apparatus on a prior understanding that is rooted in his own sociocultural situation. He must become hermeneutically and historically self-conscious.

4. In Habermas's view, the most provocative feature of Gadamer's hermeneutics is the claim—against historicism and, by implication, against phenomenology and linguistic analysis—that *Sinnverstehen* has an irreducibly practical dimension, "that it is linked with transcendental necessity to the articulation of an action-orienting self-understanding."[35] In a certain sense this is a rehabilitation of the prehistoricist view of interpretation as being realized only in the application of a normatively binding meaning (for example, a religious, legal, or classical text) to present circumstances. But Gadamer does not want to restrict this connection to the interpretation of canonical or institutionally sanctioned texts, nor does he wish to base it simply upon a dogmatic attitude toward tradition. He attempts instead to show that the applicative moment of *Verstehen* is universal and necessary: "there always takes place something like an application of the text to be understood to the situation of the interpreter."[36] Once we have given up the view that understanding amounts to a self-transposition into the situation of the author or agent (which enables us "to see things exactly as he saw them") and have accepted the view that understanding beliefs and practices involves making them intelligible in one's own frame of reference, it follows, according to Gadamer, that the interpreter must somehow relate the text to his situation if he wants to understand properly.[37]

The hermeneuticist cannot assume a purely subject-object relation to his own cultural heritage; he is not an absolute ego for whom everything else—including his language and culture—are just so many cogitata; nor is he a transcendental consciousness originally outfitted only with a definite and invariant set of forms of intuition and categories of understanding. He is rather a concrete historical subject. And his concepts, beliefs, ideals, standards, and norms issue from the very tradition that he wishes to interpret. In this sense, the relation to his cultural heritage is constitutive of the hermeneuticist's situation; in a way, he himself belongs to the object domain under investigation.

There can then be no question of theoretically dominating our past with the usual objective techniques of science. As Ricoeur has put it:

A human being discovers his finitude in the fact that, first of all, he finds himself within a tradition or traditions. Because history precedes me and my reflection, because I belong to history before I belong to myself, pre-judgment also precedes judgment, and submission to traditions precedes their examination. The regime of historical consciousness is that of a consciousness exposed to the effects of history. If therefore we cannot extract ourselves from historical becoming or place ourselves at a distance from it in such a way that the past becomes an object for us, then we must confess that we are always situated within history in such a fashion that our consciousness never has the freedom to bring itself face to face with the past by an act of sovereign independence. It is rather a question of becoming conscious of the action which affects us and of accepting that the past which is a part of our experience keeps us from taking it totally in charge, of accepting in some way its truth.[38]

In this sense hermeneutics subordinates the critical aspects of interpretive understanding to participation in "the profound movement of human existence." It is an essential aspect of our finite condition that we become subjects by participating in a world already structured by beliefs and values. In attempting to understand this world, we are at the same time engaged in the process of self-understanding; we are reflectively becoming aware of elements that have been become internalized in the development of our subjectivity. In this way, hermeneutic understanding is the continuation of a self-formative process. As such it has a practical significance for the "articulation of an action-orienting self-understanding."

Gadamer's notion of the "applicative moment" of *Verstehen* can be exhibited from another perspective: we understand a text to the extent that we can make sense of it. Making sense of a text involves rearticulating its meaning in terms that make sense to us as well, that is, finding a common language in which the beliefs and values expressed in the text become intelligible to us. And this involves finding points of reference in our own situation from which those beliefs and practices can be said to have a point from our own point of view. This does not mean that we have to accept all the validity claims raised by the text; but it does mean that we have to see them as possible responses to questions and concerns that we ourselves share, that is, as "worthy of dialogue."[39]

In Gadamer's view the dismissal of beliefs and values as mistakes pure and simple is an admission of a failure to understand. In the strong (hermeneutic) sense, to understand is to explicate to a point at which the belief or value in question appears worthy of consideration from a common point of view of humanity. It is only when we fail in this attempt that we have to appeal to error, self-delusion, and so forth to explain something that we are not able to understand. The interest behind hermeneutics is an interest in dialogue (with others, with the past, with alien cultures) about the common concerns of human life. The hermeneutic orientation is not that of the neutral observer but that of the partner in dialogue. Since we have no monopoly on truth and goodness, we must maintain an openness to the beliefs and values of others; we must be prepared to learn from them. As Winch once put it, "Seriously to study another way of life is necessarily to seek to extend our own."[40]

Habermas accepts, at least in its general outlines, the argument that the interpreter necessarily relates what is to be understood to his own concrete hermeneutic situation, and the consequent significance of interpretive understanding for self-understanding. But he has serious reservations about Gadamer's account of that relation and the conservative implications that he draws from it.

In Gadamer's view, on-going tradition and hermeneutic inquiry merge to a single point. Opposed to this is the insight that the reflected appropriation of tradition breaks down the nature-like (*naturwüchsige*) substance of tradition and alters the position of the subject in it. . . . The hermeneutic insight is certainly correct, viz. the insight that understanding—no matter how controlled it may be—cannot simply leap over the interpreter's relationship to tradition. But from the fact that understanding is structurally a part of the traditions that it further develops through appropriation, it does not follow that the medium of tradition is not profoundly altered by scientific reflection. . . . Gadamer fails to appreciate the power of reflection that is developed in understanding. This type of reflection is no longer blinded by the appearance of an absolute that can only be self-grounded; it does not detach itself from the soil of contingency on which it finds itself. But in grasping the genesis of the tradition from which it proceeds and on which it turns back, reflection shakes the dogmatism of life practice.[41]

The fact that "the moment of historical influence is and remains effective in all understanding of tradition" is itself no justification of the legitimacy and authority of tradition. To identify hermeneutic inquiry simply with the continuation of tradition is to place a one-sided stress on participation and dialogue over distantiation and critique. In critical reflection we reject as well as accept traditional validity claims. In either case "the element of authority that was simply domination" is replaced by the "less violent force of insight and rational decision."

The substantiality of what is historically pre-given does not remain unaffected when it is taken up in reflection. A structure of prejudices that has been rendered transparent can no longer function as a prejudice. But this is precisely what Gadamer seems to imply. . . . Gadamer's prejudice for the rights of prejudices certified by tradition denies the power of reflection. The latter proves itself however in being able to reject the claim of tradition. . . . Authority and knowledge do not converge. To be sure, knowledge is rooted in actual tradition; it remains bound to contingent conditions. But reflection does not exhaust itself on the facticity of transmitted norms without leaving a trace. It is condemned to be after the fact; but in glancing back it develops retroactive power. We can turn back on internalized norms only after we have first learned, under externally imposed force, to follow them blindly. Reflection recalls that path of authority along which the grammars of language games were dogmatically inculcated as rules for interpreting the world and for action. In this process the element of authority that was simply domination can be stripped away and dissolved in the less violent force of insight and rational decision.[42]

The root of the difficulty, as Habermas sees it, lies in the absolutizing of language and tradition. In an explicit countermove to Hegel, Gadamer wishes to demonstrate the finite, historically situated character of reflection. "Hegel's experience of reflection shrinks to the consciousness that we are delivered up to a happening [of tradition] in which the conditions of rationality change irrationally, according to time and place, epoch and culture."[43] Reflection can no longer be conceived of as absolute; it is always rooted in the contingent complex of tradition. Although he accepts Gadamer's point about the finitude and context-boundedness of human understanding, Habermas rejects his relativistic and idealistic conclusions regarding the logic of *Verstehen*. In the *first* place, hermeneutic interpretation must be conjoined with the *critique of ideology*.

The objectivity of a "happening of tradition" [*Überlieferungsgeschehen*] that is made up of symbolic meaning is not objective enough. Hermeneutics comes up against walls of the traditional framework from the inside, as it were. As soon as these boundaries have been experienced and recognized, cultural traditions can no longer be posed as absolute. It makes good sense to conceive of language as a kind of metainstitution on which all social institutions are dependent; for social action is constituted only in ordinary language communication. But this metainstitution of language as tradition is evidently dependent in turn on social processes that are not exhausted in normative relationships. Language is *also* a medium of domination and social power. It serves to legitimate relations of organized force. In so far as the legitimations do not articulate the relations of force that they make possible, in so far as these relations are merely expressed in the legitimations, language is also ideological. Here it is not a question of deceptions within a language, but of deception with language as such. Hermeneutic experience that encounters this dependency of the symbolic framework on actual conditions changes into the critique of ideology.[44]

Like the phenomenological and linguistic approaches, hermeneutics tends to reduce social inquiry to the explication of meaning. Although it does not limit meaning to subjectively intended meaning, it hypostatizes cultural tradition to "the all-encompassing." As a result there is a tendency to sublimate social processes entirely into cultural tradition and to reduce sociology to the interpretation of transmitted meanings. If, however, culture is viewed in relation to the social, political, and economic conditions of life, it loses the appearance of self-sufficiency. It becomes evident that traditional meanings can conceal and distort, as well as reveal and express these conditions.

Of course the critique of ideology requires a system of reference that goes beyond tradition, one that deabsolutizes tradition by systematically taking into account the empirical conditions under which it develops and changes. Hermeneutic understanding must, *second*, be conjoined with the *analysis of social systems*.

The objective framework within which social action can be comprehended without surrendering its intentionality is not merely a web of transmitted meanings and linguistically articulated tradition. The dimensions of labor and domination cannot be suppressed in favor of subjectively intended symbolic contents. A functionalistic framework can also give non-normative conditions their due. Cultural tradition then loses the appearance of an absolute that a self sufficient hermeneutics falsely lends to it. Tradition *as a whole* can be assigned its place; it can be conceived in its relation to the systems of social labor and political domination. It thus becomes possible to grasp functions that the cultural tradition assumes within the system as a whole, functions that are not made explicit *as such* in tradition—i.e. ideological relations. . . . In a word, functionalism permits the analysis of action complexes from the double perspective of the subjectively determining and the objective meaning.[45]

Developments in the spheres of social labor and political domination can themselves bring about a restructuring of world views. To be sure, these developments are themselves linguistically mediated; but they are not, as a rule, simply the results of a new way of looking at things. Rather changes in the mode of production or the system of power relations can themselves overturn accepted patterns of interpretation. A reduction of social inquiry to *Sinnverstehen* could be justified only on the idealist assumption that linguistically articulated consciousness determined the material conditions of life. But the objective framework of social action is not exhausted by the dimension of intersubjectively intended and symbolically transmitted meaning. The latter is rather a moment of a complex that, however symbolically mediated, is also constituted by the constraints of reality, "by the constraint of outer nature that enters into procedures for technical mastery, and by the constraint of inner nature that is reflected in the repression of relations of social force."[46] Sociology cannot then be reduced to *verstehenden* sociology. "Social action can only be comprehended in an objective framework that is constituted conjointly by language, labor and power [or domination—*Herrschaft*]."[47]

If social theory is to investigate the conditions under which patterns of interpretation and of action develop and change, it will, Habermas maintains, have to be historically oriented. Hermeneutic inquiry must, *third*, be conjoined with a *philosophy of history*. At first sight this demand seems inconsistent with Habermas's acceptance of Gadamer's point about the situation-dependency of historical understanding— thought is always rooted in actual history; there is no point outside of history from which to view the whole, as if it were given to consciousness as a completed totality. It also seems inconsistent with his renunciation of the theologically motivated belief that progress (whatever it might consist in) is somehow guaranteed—if the movement of history depends instead on the decisions and actions of historical subjects, there appears to be no way of theoretically anticipating the future course of mankind's development. We can recall the skeptical conclusions that Danto drew from this state of affairs: any account of the past involves the imposition of a narrative organization; narrative organization is always relative to some judgment of significance; if we are unable to anticipate the future course of events, there can be no philosophy of history; in the absence of a philosophy of history, judgments of significance involve an "inexpungable subjective factor," an element of "sheer arbitrariness"; thus any account of the past is not only essentially incomplete but relative to "the topical interests of this human being or that."

Habermas's response to this line of argument is, roughly, to accept it while inverting it: if any account of the past implicitly presupposes a philosophy of history (to the extent, at least, that narrative organization involves judgments of significance), then every historian is, at least implicitly, a philosopher of history.

Every historian is in the role of the last historian. Hermeneutic deliberations about the inexhaustibility of the horizon of meaning and the new interpretations of future generations remain empty; they have no consequences for *what the historian has to do*. For he does not at all organize his knowledge according to standards of pure theory. He cannot grasp anything that he can know historically independently of the framework of his own life-practice [*Lebenspraxis*]. In this context the future exists only in a horizon of expectations. And these expectations fill out hypothetically the fragments of previous tradition to a universal-historical totality, in the light of which—as a prior understanding—every relevant event can in principle be described as completely as possible for the practically effective self-understanding of a social life-world. Implicitly every historian proceeds in the way Danto wishes to forbid to the philosopher of history. From the viewpoint of practice he anticipates end-states from which the multiciplicity of events is structured without force into action-orienting histories. Precisely the openness of history, that is, the situation of the actor, permits the hypothetical anticipation of history as a whole without which the retrospective significance of the parts would not emerge.[48]

Danto's arguments lead to skepticism only if we accept the idea of complete description as a meaningful historiographic ideal; we conceive of philosophy of history as a purely theoretical undertaking with no internal relation to practice; and we conceive of the viewpoints of practice as essentially irrational (that is, beyond rational discussion). Against this Habermas argues that complete description is an illegitimate ideal. As has repeatedly been pointed out, even in connection with the natural sciences, the notion of a complete description is fraught with logical difficulties; and even if it could be consistently thought, it would not be relevant to science, which explains phenomena only under certain descriptions. He goes on to argue that while philosophy of history is impossible as a contemplative enterprise (that is, as a closed theory of an open future), it is possible as a practical enterprise. As an actor I can project or anticipate a future, which I can also work to bring about. The closure that is impossible in theory, is not only possible but necessary in practice. Finally he argues that practical projections of the future need not be arbitrary. They can be made on the basis of an examination of the real determinants of social processes and in the light of an analysis of the real possibilities of development in the present. What Danto declares to be impossible, we do everyday in our practical lives: project the future on the basis of our understanding of the past and present, which in turn is not independent of our goal settings. What he declares to be impossible is what every historian must do: reconstruct the past from the point of view of judgments of significance based on some (usually tacit) anticipation of the future. His skeptical conclusions are unavoidable only if we share his contemplative ideal of history. If however we cease to think of history in terms of pure theory and view it instead in relation to practice, we can progress from skeptical resignation to an examination of conditions of possibility.

Historical representations that have the form of narrative statements can appear in principle incomplete and arbitrary only if they are measured against a mistaken ideal of description. . . . If we examine the validity of hermeneutic statements in the framework proper to them, the framework of knowledge that has consequences for practice, then what Danto has to regard as a defect proves to be a transcendental condition of possible knowledge. Only because we project the provisional closure of a system of reference out of the horizon of life-practice, can interpretations of events (which can be organized into a history from the point of view of the projected end) as well as interpretations of parts (which can be described as fragments from the point of view of the anticipated totality) have any information content at all for that life-practice.[49]

This presentation of Habermas's views on social theory in terms of a threefold supplementation of *Sinnverstehen* (with critique of ideology, systems theory, and philosophy of history) is misleading. In fact what he is after is not simply an aggregate of several useful approaches but

an integrated framework for social theory. Nevertheless it will be convenient to organize the remaining sections of this chapter around
these three themes: psychoanalysis as an example of critical theory,
Habermas's appraisal of functionalism and systems theory, and his
program for reconstructing historical materialism as a theory of social
evolution. In each section, however, the discussion will make evident
that he is pursuing an integrated methodology for critical social
theory. Before passing on to these topics, I will add a few words on the
continuation of the debate between Gadamer and Habermas.[50]

At first glance, their exchange might appear to be no more than a re-
sumption of the Enlightenment versus Romanticism controversy of
the late eighteenth and early nineteenth centuries. The Enlightenment had regarded tradition as a fetter upon man's freedom and defined reason by its power to uproot tradition. Romanticism reversed
the priorities, celebrating *mythos* over *logos*, and pleading for the old at
the expense of the new. But the contemporary debate between hermeneutics and critical theory has managed to avoid some of the steril-
ity of the earlier controversy because it has been carried out at a "transcendental," or, if you prefer, "logical" level. Gadamer does not simply plead the advantages of tradition; he argues that participation in a
cultural heritage is a condition of possibility of all thought, including
critical reflection. Thus in his reply to Habermas, he accuses him of
employing an oversimplified concept of critique and of setting up an
abstract opposition between tradition and reflection: "Reflection on a
given pre-understanding makes me aware of something that otherwise happens behind my back. Something—not everything. For historically effective consciousness [*wirkungsgeschichtliches Bewusstsein*] is
ineradicably more being [*Sein*] than consciousness [*Bewusstsein*].[51]
    The reflecting subject inevitably takes for granted a host of con-
cepts, judgments, principles, and standards that are not themselves
made thematic; he cannot call everything into question all at once.
Thus critique is necessarily partial and from a particular point of
view. If the critical point of view is itself subjected to reflection, this is
inevitably done from another point of view and on the basis of other
taken-for-granted presuppositions. Seen in this light, Gadamer concludes, Habermas's concept of critique is "dogmatic"; he ascribes to
reflection a power that it could have only on idealistic premises. It is
true, Gadamer grants, that the appeal to tradition is itself no argu-

ment, "at least not there where reflection demands an argument. But that is the point: where does it demand an argument? Everywhere? To this notion I have opposed the finitude of human existence and the essential particularity of reflection."[52] Reflection is no less historically situated, context-dependent, than other modes of thought. In challenging a cultural heritage one presupposes and continues it.

Gadamer also rejects the view that language is one dimension of social life among others, one that has to be relativized in a more comprehensive framework that includes the system of social labor and relations of power. The claim of hermeneutics to universality is grounded in the view that

understanding and coming to an understanding do not refer primarily or originally to a methodically trained behavior toward texts; rather they are the form in which the social life of men is carried out, a social life which—rendered formally—is a community in dialogue [Gesprächsgemeinschaft]. Nothing is excepted from this community, no experience of the world whatever. Neither the specialization of the modern sciences and their increasingly esoteric management, not material labor and its form of organization, nor the political institutions of rule and administration which hold the society together, are located outside of this universal medium of practical reason (and unreason).[53]

What Habermas designates as "real determinants of social processes" (such as economic and political factors) and sets against language and culture are themselves linguistically mediated and accessible to interpretive understanding, for hermeneutic Sinnverstehen is not limited to subjectively intended meanings, to motivational understanding. It is rather concerned with "understanding everything that can be understood"; and this includes the ideological distortions that Habermas reserves to the critique of ideology: "As if it were not the case that every ideology—as linguistically articulated, false consciousness—not only presents itself as understandable meaning, but can also be understood in its 'true' meaning, e.g. in connection with an interest in domination."[54] The preconceptions and prejudgments that hermeneutic reflection brings to light—both the interpreter's and the author's or agent's—include those that are rooted in economic and political interests. "What else are the prejudices which hermeneutics strives to grasp in reflection? From where else are they supposed to come? From cultural tradition? Certainly, from there as well. But of what is this composed?"[55] Thus concludes Gadamer, there is no need to go beyond hermeneutic analysis to get at "real" factors. It is, rather, only in attempting to understand that such sources of prejudice are brought to consciousness.

Gadamer denies that hermeneutics can be simply opposed to critical reflection as the renewal of traditional authority is opposed to its dissolution.

What is at issue is merely whether reflection always dissolves substantial relations or whether it can also *consciously* accept them. . . . That tradition as such should be and remain the only ground of validity of pre-judgments—a view that Habermas attributes to me—flies directly in the face of my thesis that authority rests on knowledge. Having attained maturity, one can—but need not!—accept from insight what he adhered to out of obedience.[56]

Hermeneutics does not imply a blind subjection to tradition; we also understand when we see through prejudices that distort reality. "In fact this is when we understand most of all"[57] But this does not mean that we understand only when we unmask pretense or false consciousness. For Gadamer, then, the point at issue is not whether we accept or reject a given validity claim. The question is rather how we become conscious of and evaluate preconceptions and prejudgments. This is not, he argues, something that can be done all at once in a supreme act of reflection. It is rather precisely in trying to understand other points of view, in trying to come to an understanding with others, that my own, as well as their, "structure of prejudices" becomes perceptible. Reflection is not something opposed to understanding; it is an integral moment of the attempt to understand. To separate them as Habermas does is a "dogmatic confusion."

Finally there is no alternative to dialogue as a medium for clarifying and evaluating opposing validity claims. The critic of ideology assumes a superiority for his point of view that he cannot in reality justify. He pretends to anticipate the outcome of rational dialogue before it has taken place. Like the critique of ideology, hermeneutics is guided by the anticipation of a just life. But "this very ideal of reason forbids anyone to claim for himself the correct insight into another's delusion."[58] The specification of the ideals of reason and justice cannot be achieved independently of the attempt to come to an understanding in dialogue, that is, of hermeneutic understanding. "The good for man is something that is encountered in human practice, and it cannot be specified in isolation from the concrete situation in which something is preferred to something else. . . . As a general idea, the idea of the just life is empty.[59]

These counterarguments might be summarized as follows:

1. Habermas attributes a false power to reflection. As historically situated, reflection is always limited, partial, and based on taken-for-granted preconceptions and prejudgments.

2. Habermas wants to "get behind" language to the "real" conditions under which it historically develops. But language is not simply one aspect of society among others; it is the "universal medium" of social life. In particular labor and power are not located "outside of" language but mediated through it.

3. According to Habermas, the existence of systematically distorted communication requires that we go beyond hermeneutic *Sinnverstehen* to the critique of ideology. But ideology is not inaccessible to hermeneutic understanding. It appears to be such only if we set up a false opposition between understanding qua affirmation of traditional prejudice and reflection qua dissolution of traditional prejudice. In reality understanding involves the rejection of unjustifiable prejudices as well as the recognition of justifiable authority.

4. The claims that Habermas raises on behalf of critical reflection are excessive. The critic cannot pretend to be in sole possession of the truth. His ideas of the just life are not exempt from revision and rejection in dialogue with others. Thus critical self-reflection, as well as the critique of ideological distortion, cannot be pursued in isolation from the attempt to come to an understanding with others. The ideals of reason are inherently bound up with an openness to dialogue—both actual dialogue with contemporaries and virtual dialogue with the past.

These arguments go to the the heart of Habermas's position because they issue from a perspective that has much in common with his own, including recognition of communication as a "universal medium" of social life, awareness of the historicity of human existence, and the ideal of a dialogic resolution of practical questions. His response to Gadamer points ahead to developments of his own program that we shall be considering in due course. At this point, a brief indication of its general thrust will have to suffice. One can, Habermas argues, recognize communication and understanding, dialogue and historicity, as fundamental to social life without accepting Gadamer's methodological conclusions. From a methodological point of view, the principal issue is whether hermeneutic *Sinnverstehen* is or can be the sole and adequate basis of social inquiry. And this question, Habermas feels, has to be answered in the negative. Accordingly in his reply to Gadamer he stresses the limitations of an approach based solely upon the normal competence of a speaker of a natural language to understand symbolically structured objects and events.[60] The absolutizing—by way of ontologizing—of hermeneutics results in an aprioristic devaluation of methods of social analysis with a theoretical basis that goes beyond normal linguistic competence. In stressing the possibility of theoretically grounded analyses of meaningful phenomena, Habermas has in mind theories of natural language that attempt to reconstruct linguistic competence (for example, Chomsky) or communicative competence (see chapter 4); genetic theories that attempt to explain the acquisition of cognitive (for example, Piaget), moral (for example, Kohlberg), and interactive (for example, Mead) competences; theories of distorted communication (for example, Freud) that combine both hermeneutic and causal modes of analysis; theories about the structure and functioning of systems of action (for example, Parsons); theories of social evolution (for example, Marx). He admits that the current state of development of such theories is unsatisfactory (and much of his recent work is an attempt to rework, develop, and integrate them into a coherent framework for social analysis). But this is not the point here. The point is rather that Gadamer's insights, viewed methodologically and not ontologically, are not incompatible with such theoretical approaches. And these approaches are based on more than normal competence; they draw on systematically generalized empirical knowledge beyond that available to the competent speaker as such. This knowledge frequently makes quasi-causal explanations of social phenomena possible. It also reduces the context-dependency of understanding; that is, the preunderstanding that functions in any attempt to grasp meanings can be theoretically grounded and methodologically secured. It need not be simply a reflection of the particular sociocultural situation of the interpreter.

If these methodological issues are overlooked, it might appear that the different emphases of Gadamer and Habermas—on historicity, participation, and dialogue with the past versus enlightenment, critical distance, and anticipation of the future—spring only from their different attitudes toward tradition. Whereas Gadamer speaks of tradition primarily as a source of insights and values that have to be constantly reactualized in ever new situations, Habermas stresses the elements of domination, repression, and distortion, which are also incorporated in our heritage and from which we must continually strive to emancipate ourselves. Whereas Gadamer speaks of "the dialogue that we are," Habermas speaks of the dialogue that is not yet but ought to be. Whereas Gadamer is moved by respect for the superiority (*Überlegenheit*) of tradition,[61] Habermas is motivated by the anticipation of a future state of freedom. As others have pointed out, there is no need to remain at this kind of impasse. Hermeneutic understanding can be pursued critically, with an interest in enlightenment and emancipation. And critique would remain empty without concrete input from our cultural heritage. As Ricoeur puts it:

None of us finds himself placed in the radical position of creating the ethical world *ex nihilo*. It is an inescapable aspect of our finite condition that we are born into a world already qualified in an ethical manner. . . . We can perhaps "transvaluate" values, but we can never create them beginning from zero. The passage through tradition has no other justification than this antecedence of the ethical world with regard to every ethical subject. But, on the other hand, we never receive values as we find things. . . . Our interest in emancipation introduces what I call "ethical distance" into our relation to any heritage. . . . Nothing survives from the past except through a reinterpretation in the present. . . . Ethical distance thus becomes a productive distance, a positive factor in reinterpretation. . . . There are no other paths, in effect, for carrying out our interest in emancipation than by incarnating it within cultural acquisitions. Freedom only posits itself by transvaluating what has already been evaluated. The ethical life is a perpetual transaction between the project of freedom and its ethical situation outlined by the given world of institutions. . . . However, on its side, a hermeneutic which would cut itself off from the regulative idea of emancipation would be no more than a hermeneutic of traditions and in these terms a form of philosophical restoration. . . . the relation between the project of freedom and the memory of its past conquests constitutes a vicious circle only for analytic understanding, not for practical reason.[62]

Habermas does not deny the intimate connection of critical reflection to hermeneutic understanding.[63] But he does deny that the differences between himself and Gadamer are no more than differences concerning the proper approach to tradition—in a spirit of acceptance of its superior authority, or in a spirit of critique of any validity claims that cannot be grounded in rational discourse. Gadamer's universalization of hermeneutics rests on a logical argument against the possibility of methodologically transcending the hermeneutic point of view: any attempt to do so is inconsistent with the very conditions of possibility of understanding: the linguisticality and historicity of human existence. Habermas's counterposition is an attempt to mitigate the radically situational character of understanding through the introduction of theoretical elements; the theories of communication and social evolution are meant to reduce the context-dependency of the basic categories and assumptions of critical theory. How he goes about this and to what extent he has been successful will occupy the remainder of this study.

3.4 PSYCHOANALYSIS AND SOCIAL THEORY

It is difficult for us to imagine today that Freudian psychoanalysis and Marxist social theory were once regarded as irreconcilably opposed. That they are no longer so regarded is due in large part to the work of the earlier Frankfurt school. Where Reich had failed to gain recognition for his ideas within either movement, the attempts by Horkheimer, Adorno, Fromm, and Marcuse to reconcile Freud and Marx succeeded in firmly establishing this topos within the ambit of critical theory.[1] In the first issue of the *Zeitschrift für Sozialforschung* Horkheimer already stressed the necessity of integrating individual psychology into Marxist social theory.[2] In the same issue Fromm laid the groundwork for this integration in an essay, "Über Methode und Aufgabe einer analytischen Sozialpsychologie." He argued there that psychoanalysis could provide the missing link between ideological "superstructure" and socioeconomic "base." To this end, however, the "biological" and ahistorical elements of Freud's thought, in particular his theory of instincts, had to be overhauled. In the years following the Frankfurt school's emigration, its interest in Freud continued, but there was a noticeable shift in accent. A number of fundamental differences developed between Fromm and the other members of the institute, culminating in the 1940s with Horkheimer's and especially Adorno's critique of the "revisionist" attack on Freud's instinct theory. In *Eros and Civilization* (1955), Marcuse went even further in emphasizing the critical import of this aspect of Freud's thought.

Habermas's approach to Freud can be located with respect to these earlier discussions. As is evident from the discussion of the "emancipatory interest" in chapter 2, he continues to use psychoanalytic concepts to establish a link between the institutional framework of society and individual paychology. This is especially evident in his discussion of the interrelations between power and ideology. On the other hand there is comparatively little use made of the instinct theory as such; and even this is rather general and qualified. Thus although Habermas grants the necessity of incorporating "into the natural basis of history the heritage of natural history, however flexible, consisting in an impulse potential that is both libidinal and aggressive," he regects as objectivistic any attempt to view history as determined by a "dynamic of the instincts":

The conception of the instincts as the prime mover of history, and of civilization as the result of their struggle, forgets that we have only derived the concept of impulse privatively from language deformation and behavioral pathology. At the human level we never encounter needs that are not already interpreted linguistically and symbolically affixed to potential actions. The heritage of natural history, consisting of unspecified impulse potentials, determines the initial conditions of the reproduction of the human species. But from the very beginning, the means of this social reproduction gives the preservation of the species the quality of self-preservation.[3]

Such reconstructed impulse potentials may be regarded as defining the initial situation of the "conflict-ridden formative process of the species," but "the forms in which the conflict is carried out—namely work, language and power—depend on the cultural conditions of our existence."[4] Methodologically this means that the basic categories of social theory cannot be reduced to those of individual psychology; they must be suited to grasping economic, political, and sociocultural structures in their historical development.

On this point Habermas is essentially in agreement with the original position of the Frankfurt school. However in developing the psychological dimension of social analysis, he ranges freely over the fields of contemporary individual and social psychology. Thus he draws heavily on different forms of identity theory, role theory, symbolic interactionism, and theories of cognitive development. As a result Freudian psychoanalysis plays a more limited role in Habermas's treatment of the "links" between individual psychology and institutional framework than it did for earlier critical theorists.[5] Further-more his orientation to Freud's own work is more strongly methodo-logical than was theirs. Thus in *Knowledge and Human Interests* he in-troduces his discussion of Freud by explaining that "psychoanalysis is relevant to us as the only tangible example of a science incorporating methodical self-reflection.[6] Taking Alfred Lorenzer's work as a point of departure, he then goes on to recontruct psychoanalysis as a theory of distorted communication.[7] The lessons he derives from this recon-struction are largely methological; it furnishes us with a more pre-cise conception of the logic of a reflective science and thus provides us with guidelines for the construction of a critical social theory. Having already discussed the use Habermas makes of Freud's theory of civili-zation, I shall confine the analysis in this section to his reconstruction of psychoanalytic methodology. The more general problem of the place of psychology in critical theory will be dealt with later in this chapter and in section 4.4.

Freud never doubted that psychology was a natural science; he even considered it possible in principle that psychoanalytic therapy might be someday replaced by psychopharmachology. Having worked in physiology for a number of years at the start of his career, he first at-tempted to develop psychology as a branch of neurophysiology. Al-though he soon abandoned this program, he retained much of the neurophysiological terminology (energy quanta, energy tension and discharge)—and presented his own psychoanalytic findings in an energy-distribution model. In short he regarded his metapsychology as the framework for a strictly empirical science. As Habermas points out, this physicalistic self-understanding was clearly a misunder-standing:

Freud erred in not realizing that psychology, insofar as it understands itself as a strict empirical science, cannot content itself with a model that keeps to a physicalistic use of language without seriously leading to operationalizable assumptions. The energy-distribution model only creates the semblance that psychoanalytic statements are about measurable transformations of energy. Not a single statement about quantitative relations derived from the conception of instinctual eco-nomices has ever been tested experimentally. The model of the psychic apparatus is so constructed that metapsychological statements imply the observability of the events they are about. But these events are never observed—nor can they be observed.[8]

The error becomes obvious if one examines more closely the evidential basis of psychoanalysis, namely, the clinical experience to which Freud himself constantly referred in defending the scientific status of his work. The analytic dialogue between patient and therapist was the sole empirical basis for the development and quasi-experimental testing of psychoanalytic theory; thus the meaning of its concepts and hypotheses must be explicated in connection with the analytic situation and not in terms of an empirically unjustifiable energy-distribution model.

The basic categories of the new discipline, the conceptual constructions, the assumptions about the functional structures of the psychic apparatus and about mechanisms for both the genesis of symptoms and the dissolution of pathological compulsions—this metapsychological framework was first derived from experiences of the analytic situation and the interpretation of dreams. The meaning of this observation bears on the methodology and not only on the psychology of research. For these metapsychological categories and connections were not only *discovered* under determinate conditions of specifically sheltered communication, they cannot even be *explicated* independently of this context. The conditions of this communication are thus the conditions of possibility of analytic knowledge for both partners, doctor and patient likewise.[9]

Accordingly Habermas sets about reconstructing Freudian psychoanalysis as a theory of systematically distorted communication.

To begin with, psychoanalysis might be approached as a special form of interpretation. Freud himself consciously patterned the interpretation of dreams after the hermeneutic model of philological research, occasionally comparing it to the translation of a foreign author. But the interpretive efforts of the analyst require a hermeneutics that is expanded to take account of special dimension: the latent content of symbolic expressions, a content that is inaccessible to the author himself. Freud coined the phrase *internal foreign territory* to capture the dual character of this new domain; it refers to the alienation of something that is still the subject's very own. In contrast to normal hermeneutices, then, psychoanalytic interpretation deals with "texts" that both express and conceal their "author's" self-deceptions.

The flaws eliminated by its critical labor are not accidental. The omissions and distortions that it rectifies have a systematic role and function. . . . The meaning of a corrupt text of this sort can be comprehended only after it has been possible to illuminate the meaning of the corruption itself. This distinguishes the peculiar task of a hermeneutics that cannot be confined to the procedures of philology, but rather *unites linguistic analysis with the psychological investigation of causal connections.*[10]

As Wittgenstein stressed in his account of "language games," the "grammar" of ordinary language governs not only the connection of linguistic symbols but also the interweaving of speech, action, and bodily expression. In a normally functioning language game, these different classes of expressions are complementary. In pathological cases, however, they no longer fit one another; actions and nonverbal expressions belie what is expressly stated. The acting subject either does not observe the discrepancy or is not able to understand it. Nevertheless the symptomatic expressions (such as obsessive thoughts, repetition compulsions, hysterical body symptoms) are expressions of the subject. They cannot be dismissed as accidents: "their symbolic character, which identifies them as split-off parts of a symbolic structure, cannot be permanently denied. They are the scars of a corrupt text that confronts the author as incomprehensible."[11]

The "depth hermeneutics" that Freud developed to deal with such "texts" relies on theoretical perspectives and technical rules that go beyond the normal competences of a speaker of a natural language.

The fundamental rule of analysis introduced by Freud secures a communication between the analyst and the patient which satisfies, as it were, experimental conditions. The virtualization of the serious situation [*Ernstsituation*] and free association on the part of the patient, as well as the purposely reserved reaction and reflected participation on the part of the analyst, make possible the occurrence of a transference situation that can serve as a foil for translation. Secondly, the pre-understanding of the analyst is directed to a small sector of possible meanings—to early object relations disturbed by conflict. The linguistic material that emerges from conversations with the patient is arranged in a narrowly circumscribed context of possible double meanings. This context consists of a general interpretation of early-childhood patterns of interaction which are coordinated with a phase-specific model of personality formation. These two features make it evident that scenic understanding—in contrast to hermeneutic understanding—connot be conceived as a theory-free employment of communicative competence that first makes theories possible. The theoretical assumptions on which the depth-hermeneutic analysis of language tacitly rests can be developed from three points of view.

1) The psychoanalyst has a preconception of the structure of nondistorted communication in ordinary language; 2) he traces the systematic distortion of communication back to the confusion of two developmentally separate stages of symbol organization, the prelinguistic and the linguistic; 3) he explains the origin of the deformation with the aid of a theory of deviant socialization processes that covers the connection of early childhood interaction patterns with the formation of personality structures.[12]

Habermas's thesis is that a full and consistent development of the theoretical basis of psychoanalysis would require a general theory of communicative competence. Such a theory would not only have to explicate the structural conditions of "normal" (undistorted) communication; it would also have to provide a developmental account of the acquisition of communicative competence, as well as of the conditions under which systematic distortions in communication arise. Freud himself did not construct an explicit theory of normal communication. (This is still today an outstanding task, one to which Habermas has devoted much of his energy in recent years.) But Freud's metapsychology, purged of its neurophysiological trappings, can be reconstructed as a theory of systematically distorted communication.

The agency model [of ego, id and super-ego] tacitly rests on a model of the deformation of ordinary language intersubjectivity. The dimensions of personality structure defined by id and super-ego clearly correspond to the dimensions of deformation of the structure of intersubjectivity given in unconstrained communication. The structural model that Freud introduced as the categorical framework of metapsychology can thus be traced back to a theory of deviations of communicative competence.[13]

Habermas grounds the legitimacy of his communications-theoretic reinterpretation of Freudian metapsychology through an examination of the evidence basis that Freud actually relied upon in its construction and testing: the analytic dialogue between physician and patient. The model of the ego, id, and superego is in the first instance an interpretation of the analyst's experience of the patient's resistance. The notions of the conscious and the preconscious refer to what is "public" or communicable. In contrast the "unconscious" refers to what is "suppressed" or removed from public communication. Freud emphasized that psychoanalytic theory is based on the perception of the resistance offered by the patient when the analyst attempts to make his unconscious conscious to him. This resistance is construed as the manifestation of a defensive agency and the material defended against or repressed. This constellation of consciousness, repressed material (that nevertheless "urges" toward consciousness and creeps into the public domain), and defensive agency is repeatedly encountered by the analyst in communicating with his patients. It is this constellation that Freud tried to capture in his structural model. The "ego" (that is, *Ich* or *I*) is the agency responsible for testing reality and censoring drives[14] Excessive libidinal and aggressive instinctual demands are dysfunctional for the individual as for the species; they clash with reality. The reality-testing capacity of the ego makes these clashes foreseeable. Instinctual impulses that would result in dangerous situations if permitted to motivate actions become sources of anxiety. The ego reacts defensively; where neither intervention in reality nor flight is possible, it directs itself against the instinctual demands themselves. In this sense the intrapsychic defensive process is analogous to a flight from danger: the ego "flees" by "hiding from itself." The text in which the ego understands itself in its situation is thus purged of representatives of the undesired instinctual demands; in other words, it is censored. The self's identity with this defended-against part of the psyche is denied; the latter is reified for the ego into a neuter, an id. [15] Thus the id (the *es* or *it*) is the name for the parts of the self that have been isolated from the "ego" (or I). It is represented mediately in observable symptoms and immediately in pathological, "paleo-symbolic" elements that creep into language.

The same clinical experience on which the constructions of the ego and the id are based shows that the activity of the defensive agency is itself mostly unconscious. This motivated Freud to introduce the category of the superego (the *Über-Ich:* "above" or "over the I"), a special agency that represents demands of a restrictive and rejecting character. The superego is the intrapsychic extension of social authority.

Intelligent adaptation to external reality, which enables the ego to test reality, has its counterpart in the appropriation of social roles through identification with other subjects who confront the child with socially sanctioned expectations. The super-ego is formed through the internalization of these expectations on the basis of introjection, the establishment of abandoned love objects in the ego. The residues of abandoned object-choices give rise to the agency of conscience, which anchors in the personality structure itself the repressive demands of society against "surplus" instinctual aims. . . . The ego then exercises the function of censoring the instincts under the supervision of the super-ego. As long as it acts as the executive organ of the super-ego, the defensive process remains unconscious. It is in this way that it is distinguished from the conscious mastery of instincts. The dependent child is obviously too weak to carry out defensive operations from moment to moment in an effective way based on its own powers. Thus is established in the self that agency which compels the ego to flee from itself with the same objective force that lets the offshoots of the id confront the ego objectively as the result of repression.[16]

The experiential basis of Freud's metapsychology does not fit well with his basic mechanistic view of the structure of psychic life. The very names of the three agencies betray an intrinsic connection to a form of communication into which physician and patient enter with the aim of setting in motion a process of enlightenment and bringing the patient to self-reflection. Following Lorenzer, Habermas interprets this as a process of "resymbolization" aimed at reversing a previous "desymbolization." He conceives of repression—the defensive reaction through which the ego "hides from itself"—as the banishment of symbols representing undesirable instinctual demands from public communication. The suppression of undesired needs and motives by "excommunicating" or "splitting off" the corresponding symbolic representations results in a privatization of semantic content, that is, in "deviant symbol formations" that do not obey the grammatical rules of everyday language. The starting point of psychoanalytic theory is the resistance that blocks the free and public communication of repressed contents. The path of analysis is precisely the reverse of that of repression—split-off symbolic contents must be "translated" from a mode of expression deformed as a private language into the mode of expression of public communication; "desymbolized motives" must be "resymbolized," that is, reintegrated into the realm of normal intercourse with oneself and others.

The "translation" of what is unconscious into what is conscious is at the same time a process of reflection, a reappropriation of a lost portion of the self. In contrast to ordinary philological hermeneutics, such a translation requires a peculiar combination of interpretive understanding and causal explanation.

It reveals the meaning of specifically incomprehensible life experiences only to the extent that it succeeds in reconstructing the original scene and clarifying the genetic conditions of the un-meaning [*Unsinn*]. We cannot "understand" the "what"—the semantic content of the systematically distorted expression—without at the same time "explaining" the "why"—the origin of the symptomatic distortion itself.[17]

The fact that psychoanalytic constructions are themselves interpretations demonstrates a certain kinship with the hermeneutic method. On the other hand, the fact that these constructions can function as explanatory hypotheses with regard to symptoms indicates an affinity with causal-analytic methods. But the "causality" in this case refers to the workings of repressed motives and split-off symbols. Borrowing a phrase from Hegel, Habermas designates this as a "causality of fate" in contrast to the causalty of nature, for the causal connections do not represent an invariance of natural laws but an invariance of life history that can be dissolved by the power of reflection. They refer to the sphere of "second nature," the unconscious, which is both an empirical structure and a structure of meaning.

Like conscious motives, unconscious motives have the form of interpreted needs; thus they are given in symbolic contents and can be hermeneutically understood. The analysis of dreams, or the interpretation of hysterical symptoms and compulsive actions do employ hermeneutic procedures. On the other hand, unconscious motives are precisely not accessible to the acting subject himself; they are excluded from consciousness by repression. . . . Because they assert themselves behind the subject's back, they have the status of causes.[18]

Thus hypotheses referring to unconscious motives assert a type of connection that can be interpreted as causal. Repressed motives, although excluded from public communication, nevertheless continue to affect behavior. Functioning like external causes, they subject communicative action to the "causality of nature-like relations." But they are still motives, action-orienting meanings, and their causality operates "through the symbolic means of the mind; this is why it can be overcome through the power of reflection."[19]

These brief remarks should serve to indicate the general thrust of Habermas's reconstruction of Freudian metapsychology. Let us turn now to his suggestion that the "example" of psychoanalysis, properly understood, can furnish us with guidelines for the logic of critical science in general.

Habermas distinguishes three levels of psychoanalytic thought: (1) the *metapsychology* (in the narrow sense), consisting of fundamental assumptions concerning the connection between language deformation and behavioral pathology; (2) *a general interpretation of psychodynamic development,* in the form of a systematically generalized narrative; and (3) the application of the interpretive framework to the *reconstruction of individual life histories.*

1. I have already sketched Habermas's interpretation of the metapsychology and noted his claim that it presupposes a theory of ordinary language communication. It should be added that he does not view the metapsychology as an empirical theory in the ordinary sense of the term. Although it possesses a certain "material content," it is properly speaking a "metatheory" or "metahermeneutic," for it is primarily an explication of "the logic of interpretation in the analytic dialogue."[20] On the one hand, the basic metahermeneutical assumptions are derived from reflection on the structure of communication between physician and patient, that is, on the very conditions of psychoanalytic knowledge. On the other, they are not directly accessible to empirical corroboration: "They can be confirmed or rejected only indirectly, with regard to the outcome, so to speak, of an entire category of processes of inquiry."[21]

2. In contrast general interpretations can be subjected to empirical tests. This is the level of psychoanalytic thought that most closely corresponds to empirical theory. But there are important differences, for general interpretations are systematically generalized histories.

Metahermeneutical statements . . . elucidate the methodological framework in which empirically substantive interpretations of self-formative processes can be developed. These general interpretations, however, must be distinguished from the metapsychological framework. They are interpretations of early childhood development (the origins of basic motivational patterns and the parallel formation of ego functions) and serve as narrative forms that must be used in each case as an interpretive scheme for an individual's life history in order to find the original scene of his unmastered conflict. The learning mechanisms described by Freud (object choice, identification with an ideal, introjection of abandoned love objects) make understandable the dynamics of the genesis of ego structures at the level of symbolic interaction. The defense mechanisms intervene in this process when and where social norms, incorporated in the expectations of primary reference persons, confront the infantile ego with an unbearable force, requiring it to take flight from itself and objectivate itself in the id. The child's development is defined by problems whose solution determines whether and to what extent further socialization is burdened with the weight of unsolved conflicts and restricted ego functions, creating the predisposition to an accumulation of disillu-sionments, compulsions and denials (as well as failure)—or whether the socialization process makes possible a relative development of ego identity.[22]

Thus what corresponds to general theory in psychoanalysis is a sys-tematically generalized history of psychodynamic development that serves as a "narrative foil" for the reconstruction of individual life histories. It contains assumptions about interaction patterns of the child and his primary reference persons, about corresponding conflicts and forms of conflict mastery, and about the personality structures that result from early childhood socialization. It is the metapsychological fromework that makes this systematic generaliza-tion possible by permitting, for example, the representation of conflicts in terms of defense mechanisms, and of personality struc-tures in terms of the relations between ego, id, and superego. The general interpretations developed in this framework are themselves the result of numerous and repeated clinical experiences. In contrast to the hermeneutic preunderstanding of the philologist, a general in-terpretation is "fixed" to the extent that it, like a general theory, con-tinues to prove itself in practice, that is, to the extent that hypothetical predictions derived from it are empirically corroborated.

3. But general interpretations also exhibit important logical differ-ences from empirical theories of the usual sort. With a generalized narrative schema as background, the physician attempts to combine the fragmentary information obtained in analytic dialogue and to offer suggestions for a story that the patient himself cannot tell. The physician's hypothetical reconstruction anticipates the patient's reflec-tive appropriation of elements of his own life history. And it proves itself only to the extent that the patient adopts it and tells his own story.

Analytic insights possess validity for the analyst only after they have been accepted as knowledge by the analysand himself. For the empiri-cal accuracy of general interpretations depends not on controlled ob-servation and subsequent communication among investigators, but rather on the accomplishment of self-reflection and subsequent communication between the investigator and his "object," . . . In the case of testing theories through observation . . . the application of the assumptions to reality is a matter for the inquiring subject. In the case of testing general interpretations through self-reflection . . . this application becomes *self-application* by the object of inquiry. . . . The subject cannot obtain knowledge of the object unless it becomes knowledge for the object—and unless the latter thereby emancipates himself by becoming a subject.[23]

This peculiarity of psychoanalytic inquiry has implications for the logics of application, corroboration, and explanation. First, the *application* of a general interpretation is a form of *translation* into the ordinary language or life-world of the patient. General theories are applied with the aid of semioperationalized, more or less standardized criteria (usually involving measurement procedures) for identifying instances that fall under their general concepts. But a general interpretation is applied by constructing histories in which subjects can recognize and understand themselves and their world. Its concepts are schematic or type concepts that have to be translated into individuated situations.

What characterizes systematic generalization, therefore, is that . . . the abstraction from many typical histories with regard to many individual cases has already taken place. A general interpretation contains no names of individuals, but only anonymous roles. It contains no contingent circumstances, but recurring configurations and patterns of action. It contains no idiomatic use of language, but only a standardized vocabulary. It does not represent a typical process, but describes in type-concepts the scheme of an action with conditional variants. . . . All attempts to provide metapsychology with a more rigorous form have failed, because the conditions of the application of general interpretations exclude the formalization of ordinary language. For the terms used in it serve the structuring of narratives. It is their presence in the patient's ordinary language which the analyst and the patient make use of in completing an analytic narrative scheme by making it into a history. By putting individual names in the place of anonymous roles and filling out interaction patterns as experienced scenes, they develop ad hoc a new language, in which the language of the general interpretation is brought into accord with the patient's own language.[24]

Because the material to which interpretive schemata are applied is structured symbolically within particular language games or lifeworlds, the application has an inescapable hermeneutic dimension.

The *corroboration* of general interpretations is based on *the successful continuation of self-formative processes.* Neither the rejection nor the acceptance of a construction by the patient is decisive. His "no" might indicate that a correctly diagnosed resistance is too strong, or that the interpretation, though correct, is still incomplete in important ways. And a plain "yes" might be merely a convenient defensive strategy. Not even the patient's behavior is an unmistakable indicator of success; symptoms that disappear might be replaced by other symptoms which are initially inperceptible. In short "only the context of the self-formative process as a whole has confirming and falsifying power."[25] Reflective or critical science cannot rely exclusively either on the controlled observation of empirical-analytic inquiry or the experience of understanding of hermeneutical inquiry.

Finally, as I pointed out above, the *explanations* achieved with the aid of general interpretations *combine hermeneutic understanding with causal explanation.*

Habermas regards the methodological features of psychoanalysis as a clue to the methodology of critical theory in general. As we shall see in the following section, at this stage in the development of his thought he takes the goal of critical sociology to be the construction of a "general interpretive framework" in the form of a "systematically" or "theoretically generalized history," which can be applied to a "historically oriented analysis of present society with practical intent." Before concluding this section, I would like to take a closer look at one apsect of this analogizing approach: the suitability of psychoanalysis as a model for the critique of ideology. I shall focus on a set of problems arising from prima facie disanalogies between analytic therapy and political enlightenment.

In a reply to Habermas, Gadamer argues that the legitimacy of psychoanalytic therapy accrues to it on the basis of consensual recognition within a given social order. But this social agreement also sets limits to its practice—in the form of codes of professional conduct, legal sanctions, shared expectations as to the conditions under which the therapeutic relationship is appropriate, and so forth. Habermas's attempt to extend analytic techniques to a critique of the consensual basis of society as a whole, and to a political practice aimed at transforming an existing social order, neglects these limits and forfeits this legitimacy.[26] The generalization of the physician-patient model to the political practice of large groups thus runs the risk of encouraging an uncontrolled exercise of force on the part of self-appointed elites who dogmatically claim a privileged insight into the truth.

But then the analogy between psychoanalytic and sociological theory becomes problematic. For where is the latter supposed to find its limits? Where does the patient stop and social partnership come to its unprofessional rights? With respect to which self-interpretation of social consciousness—and all morals is such—is or is not this "getting behind things" in place (in the form, say, of a revolutionary will for change)? These questions appear to be unanswerable. The inescapable consequence seems to be that the dissolution of all constraints of authority is what the (on principle) emancipatory consciousness intends—and this means that its ultimate guiding image is an anarchistic utopia. This certainly appears to me to be a hermeneutically false consciousness.[27]

Gadamer locates the roots of this "hermeneutically false consciousness" precisely in that concept of critical reflection to which Habermas appealed in his critique of hermeneutics. As we saw above, Gadamer opposes to this the hermeneutical insight into the dialogical basis of all truth, practical as well as theoretical. Differences of opinion based on differences in experience and in social situations cannot simply be written off as delusions, for this involves a presumption—itself illusory—that one knows in advance of any practical confrontation where the truth lies. In reality the truth can emerge only from an openness to other points of view and a willingness to seek agreement in dialogue. Politics is no exception: "all social and political manifestations of will are dependent on building up common convictions through rhetoric. This implies—and I think that this belongs to the concept of reason—that one must always reckon with the possibility that opposing convictions, whether in the individual or the social sphere, could be right."[28]

Coming from the opposite direction, Hans Joachim Giegel has pointed out certain features of psychoanalytic therapy that seem to make it unsuitable as a model for revolutionary political practice. He agrees with Habermas, against Gadamer, that where the conditions of dialogue are lacking, where there are systematic barriers to communication, "we have to turn to other forms of social relation, and indeed forms that suspend communication, at least temporarily, not in order to suppress dialogue in general, but rather in order to create the *presuppositions* for agreement-bringing dialogue in the first place."[29] Under certain conditions psychoanalytic therapy can achieve just this; but these are not the conditions under which class struggle takes place.

The revolutionary struggle is by no means a psychoanalytic treatment on a large scale. The difference between these two forms of emancipatory practice is a result of the fact that the patient is helped to free himself from *compulsions to which he is subjected*. The attempt to release the ruling class from the compulsions of the social order could only appear to them as a threat to the *domination which they exercise* over other classes. The opposition presents itself in a much sharper form here than in the case of psychoanlysis. The oppressed class not only doubts the ruling class' capacity for dialogue, but also has good reason to assume that every attempt on its part to enter into dialogue with the ruling class could only serve as an opportunity for the latter to secure its domination. For this reason, the oppressed class may not, on pain of a set-back to their emancipatory efforts, follow the psychoanalytic path.[30]

In his introduction to *Theory and Practice,* Habermas takes these criticisms as an opportunity to clarify his own views on "the organization of political enlightenment." The issues involved here are not identical with those that arose in our theoretical—epistemological and methodological—discussions of the relation of theory to practice. They are more directly practical issues connected with the political application of a theory conceived with practical intent. Habermas's remarks nevertheless, remain, rather general and, if you will, theoretical. But they do suffice to set off his position from those attributed to him by Gadamer and Giegel, as well as from other "theories of practice" familiar within the Marxist tradition.[31] At the heart of his position is a distinction between three aspects of the problem.

The mediation of theory and practice can be clarified only if we begin by distinguishing three functions which are measured in terms of different criteria: the formation and extension of critical theorems which can stand up to scientific discourse; the organization of processes of enlightenment in which such theorems are applied and can be tested in a unique manner by the initiation of processes of reflection in particular target groups; and finally the selection of appropriate strategies, the solution of tactical questions, and the conduct of the political struggle. On the first level, the aim is true statements; on the second, authentic insights; and on the third, prudent decisions. Because in the tradition of the European working-class movement all three at once were assigned to the party organization, specific differences have become obscured.[32]

To each of these functions corresponds a distinctive model of interaction and distinctive criteria of evaluation. *At the level of theory*, the appropriate model of interaction is that of scientific discourse, the advancing and argumentative testing of hypotheses. Viewed ideally this requires a symmetrical relationship among the partners in discussion to ensure that the outcome is determined not by external or internal constraints on communication but solely by "the force of the better argument." The process of theory formation within politically organized groups who consider themselves as the bearers of enlightenment is thus subject to the usual standards of scientific discourse. A theory that does not survive discursive examination must be rejected. But a critical theory can never be confirmed in this way; as in the case of psychoanalysis, the final test of critical theorems is their successful application to processes of enlightenment, that is, their self-application by the "objects" of enlightenment. Thus in the case of critical theory, the first—theoretical—function intrinsically refers to the second—political—function.

At the level of the organization of processes of enlightenment, the appropriate model of interaction is that of therapeutic discourse. Here the position of the partners is asymmetrical, for the inability of the "patient" to meet the conditions of genuine dialogue is the presupposition of this kind of communication. Viewed ideally the aim of enlightenment is precisely to remove these barriers and to make a symmetrical relationship possible. The position of the bearers of enlightenment vis-à-vis their "target groups" is thus, normatively speaking, subject to a fundamental safeguard against exploitative deception: the appropriateness of the critic's interpretation requires confirmation in successful self-reflection; the "patient" himself is the final authority.

The theory serves primarily to enlighten those to whom it is addressed about the position they occupy in an antagonistic social system, and about the interests of which they could become conscious— as objectively their own—in this situation. Only to the extent that organized enlightenment and counsel lead to the target group's recognizing itself in the interpretations offered does the analytically proposed interpretation become an actual consciousness, and the objectively attributed interest situation become the real interest of a group capable of action.[33]

Of course although critical theory is developed with the aim of initiating and guiding processes of reflection and self-emancipation, it does not bear the names of its specific addresses within itself.[34] Which groups are actually accessible to enlightenment in a particular historical situation is largely an empirical question. Critical social theory is even less capable of providing a priori answers to the strategic and tactical questions that arise within the course of political struggle itself.

At the level of the conduct of political struggle, there is no single model, appropriate in all situations, for the interaction between political groups struggling for emancipation and political groups whose vested interests in the existing order lead them to oppose any fundamental change. There are situations in which radical reformism is more effective than revolutionary struggle, as well as situations in which the reverse is true; there are situations in which, as Marx put it, the weapon of critique is more effective than the critique of weapons, as well as situations in which even the groups whose "objective" interests lie with radical change are subjectively and profoundly opposed to such change; and there are situations "in the face of which such considerations are either scurrilous or simply ridiculous—in such situations we must act as best we can, but then without appealing to a theory whose capacity for justification does not extend that far."[35] Such questions cannot be decided a priori. But there is, in Habermas's view, a model for the manner in which they are to be decided.

The organization of action must be distinguished from the process of enlightenment. While the theory legitimizes the work of enlightenment and can itself be refuted or corrected if communication fails, it can, a fortiori, by no means legitimize the risky decisions of strategic action under concrete conditions. Decisions for the political struggle cannot be first justified theoretically and then carried out organizationally. The sole possible justification at this level is a consensus attained in practical discourse among the participants, who, in the consciousness of their common interests and in the knowledge of the circumstances, predictable consequences and side-effects, are the only ones who can know what risks they are willing to take and with what expectations. There can be no theory which assures from the outset a world-historical mission in return for potential sacrifices. The only advantage of which Marx might have assured a proletariat acting in solidarity would be that a class, which constitutes itself as a class with the aid of true critique, is only then in a position to make clear in practical discourse how it is to act politically in a rational manner . . . a political struggle can be legitimately conducted only under the condition that all decisions of consequence depend on the practical discussion of the participants. Here too, and especially here, there is no privileged access to truth.[36]

The model of "practical discourse," like that of "theoretical discourse," requires a symmetrical relation between participants—a democratic organization within political groups struggling for emancipation. Attempts at emancipation are, "practical hypotheses," the "testing" of which involves the "experimenter" as well as his "subjects." No theory and no enlightenment can do away with the risks of taking a partisan position or with the unintended consequences of action. Since all participants are equally involved in the "design of the experiment," all must have the opportunity to know what they are doing, that is to act on the basis of a consciously formed common will.

Failure to respect the proper autonomy of the different functions (theory construction, organization of enlightenment, and political action) typically leads to a betrayal of the emancipatory intention. "An organization which tries to master all three of these tasks according to the same principle will not be able to perform any of them correctly. And even if this organization is successful according to the usual criteria of merciless history—as Lenin's party was—it exacts the same price for its success that ambivalent victories have always exacted in the heretofore unbroken continuity of a history subject to nature-like causality."[37]

Habermas's reply to the objections of Gadamer and Giegel is based on this distinction of tasks. Therapeutic interaction is not intended as a model for the strategic confrontation between opposed political groups but only for the organization of enlightenment itself. On the other hand, the dialogic resolution of theoretical and practical issues stressed by Gadamer functions as a normative model for discourse within the group seeking emancipation. But its force as a regulative ideal extends even to interaction with opposed groups, for although particular situations may call for purely strategic action against opponents, the final confirmation of a critical social theory can lie only in its self-application by all those to whom it refers. It must then be counterfactually presupposed that an opponent who is presently incapable of dialogue would, under suitable conditions, accept the interpretation offered. In the light of his present incapacity, there is no alternative to an "objectivating application" of theory—for example, in interpreting the constellation of forces in the struggle and in ensuring that the victories sought do not lead merely to the assertion of particular interests but toward the intended goal of emancipation for everyone involved. In the context of such objectivating applications, strategic action against an opponent is viewed as a moment of a collective formative process that is not yet concluded. It is interpreted from the point of view of an end-state that can only be anticipated. In this sense its final justification lies in the future.

That the strategic action of those who have decided to engage in struggle—and that means to take risks—can be interpreted hypothetically in a retrospection which is possible only in anticipation, but that it cannot at the same time be *compellingly justified* at this level with the aid of a reflexive theory, has its good reason: the claimed superiority of the enlighteners over those to be enlightened is theoretically unavoidable, but it is at the same time fictive and in need of self-correction—in a process of enlightenment there can be only participants.[38]

Although this separation of different functions might serve as an initial response to the specific objections of Gadamer and Giegel, it clearly leaves a number of important questions unanswered. There are, for instance, questions relating to the normative conceptions of theoretical and practical discourse upon which Habermas's argument relies. And there is certainly the question of their suitability as a model for the internal organization of groups involved in political struggle. At present, however, I shall confine myself to his conception of the therapeutic relation between the bearers and subjects of enlightenment, for it is at this level that the psychoanalytic model is specifically invoked.

The claim is that the interaction between analyst and patient can be used for normatively structuring the relationship between the social critic and the oppressed groups that are to be enlightened about their true situation and interests. There are a number of prima facie weaknesses in this analogy. As Habermas himself points out, a precondition of the success of psychoanalytic therapy is the patient's experience of suffering and desperation and his desire to be released from this condition. Does this mean that social groups who do not experience profound dissatisfaction with their situation are incapable of political enlightenment? The success of psychoanalytic therapy requires that the physician not allow the patient's suffering to come to a premature end. If the symptoms disappear before therapy is completed, the suffering must somehow be reinstated through privation. How does the critical theorist manage this in relation to social groups over which he has no institutionally sanctioned control? The key to psychoanalytic therapy is the resistance of the patient; in fact this resistance is intensified in the course of treatment. Informing the patient of his true situation regularly exacerbates the conflict within him. What forms would the intensification of resistance and the exacerbation of conflict take at the social level? And how could the critic deal with them in the absence of an institutionally secured definition of his relationship to the oppressed groups?

The difficulties (and dangers) multiply when we consider that a patient's resistance is not overcome simply through the analyst's communication of information to him. The gap between communication and enlightenment is closed by the process of "working through." This "struggle between the doctor and the patient" (Freud) is carried out in the situation of "transference." The patient is subject to the compulsion to repeat his original conflict in the analytic situation. The physician "assumes the role of interaction partner, converting the neurotic repetition compulsion into a transference identification, preserving ambivalent transferences while suspending them and, at the right moment, dissolving the patient's attachment to him."[39] What would correspond to "working through" and "transference" at the political level? If the critical theorist has not only to inform oppressed groups of their ideological self-deception but has also to overcome their "resistance," and if he has to do this not only outisde of but in opposition to sustaining institutional authority, what are his chances of success? Of survival? One could go on at length enumerating prima facie disanalogies—to the reliance of therapy on an artificial suspension of the pressures of life, to the connection of success with the patient's ability to remember a lost portion of his life history, and so forth. Perhaps it is possible to construct plausible translations for much of this into the sphere of political practice. Perhaps we have taken the model too literally, and there is no need to find a correlate for every feature of the psychoanalytic situation. In any case it is evident that the model of psychoanlaytic therapy is a rather broad

metaphor when applied to the organization of political enlightenment. It serves primarily to highlight the normative goals of
enlightenment—self-emancipation through self-understanding, the
overcoming of systematically distorted communication, and the
strengthening of the capacity for self-determination through rational
discourse—as well as the standards of validation for critical social
theory—ultimately the successful continuation of self-formative processes on the part of the addressees.

3.5 ON THE SCOPE AND LIMITS OF
FUNCTIONALIST THEORY

In *Zur Logik der Socialwissenschaften* Habermas criticized purely hermeneutic approaches to social inquiry on several grounds. He pointed
to the type of meaning expressed in systematically distorted communication, claiming that it was explicable only through a special kind
of "explanatory" or "quasi-causal" understanding. He also argued for
the necessity of constructing an interpretive framework within which
cultural tradition could be grasped "in its relation to other moments
of the complex of social life, in order that we might designate the
conditions outside of tradition under which transcendental rules of
world-comprehension and of action empirically change."[1] If social research is not to be restricted to the analysis of language or to the history of ideas, the investigator must somehow grasp the "objective
framework" of social action. In part, this is a question of grasping the
unintended consequences of intentional action, the "meanings" that
actions have beyond those intended by actors and those articulated in
the cultural tradition. A number of models suggest themselves here.
For example, philosophers of history have proposed various schemata
in which history is represented as moving toward a certain goal. The
latter is not intended by historical agents but is realized "over their
heads," through the unintended consequences of their action. This
"plan of history" is variously assigned to a subject "outside" of history
(such as God) or "beneath" history (such as Nature), or to a "collective
subject" of history (such as the species). In some versions it is the teleological model of the craftsman, employing certain means to the attainment of a desired end, that is operative. Other versions are based
on a dialectical model of the play, in which the actors, by playing out
their roles, make transparent a certain meaning related to the human

condition. But there is no need to turn to the philosophy of history for a framework that encompasses "objective" as well as "subjective meaning". Within the tradition of empirical social science there has emerged a functionalist model of the self-regulating system.

Stemming from biology, and already perceptible in the work of some of the pioneers of modern social research (among them Durkheim), the functionalist approach was explicitly adopted by English cultural anthropologists in the 1920s and 1930s (for example Malinowski and Radcliffe-Brown). More recently, after having been developed into a general framework for sociological analysis (by Parsons, Merton and others), it has exerted a dominant influence on contemporary social thought. Finally with the incorporation of various cybernetic concepts and assumptions, modern systems theory claims to have at last discovered the true path to a science of society.

In his article on anthropology for the 1926 edition of the *Encyclopaedia Britannica*, Malinowski characterized functional analysis as the

explanation of . . . facts . . . by the part they play within the integral system of culture, by the manner in which they are related to each other within the system, and by the manner in which this system is related to the physical surroundings. . . . The functionalist view . . . insists therefore upon the principle that in every type of civilization, every custom, material object, idea and belief fulfills some vital function, has some task to accomplish, represents an indispensable part within a working whole.[2]

Radcliffe-Brown linked the notion of function with that of structure by focusing on the contributions to the totality of social life made by persistent forms or patterns of social relations (such as marriage arrangements). In doing so, he made explicit the organic, biological analogies behind his approach.

If we consider any recurrent part of the life-process (of an organism), such as respiration, digestion, etc., its function is the part it plays in, the contribution it makes to, the life of the organism as a whole. . . . We may note that the function of a recurrent physiological process is thus a correspondence between it and the needs (i.e. necessary conditions of existence) of the organism. . . . To turn from organic life to social life, if we examine such a community as an African or Australian tribe we can recognize the existence of a social structure. Individual human beings, the essential units in this instance, are connected by a definite set of social relations into an integrated whole. The continuity of the social structure, like that of an organic structure, is not destroyed by changes in the units. . . . The continuity of structure is maintained by the process of social life, which consists of the activities and interactions of the individual human beings and of the organized groups into which they are united. The social life of the community is here defined as the functioning of the social structure. The function of any recurrent activity . . . is the part it plays in the social life as a whole and therefore the contribution it makes to the maintenance of structural continuity.[3]

The small-scale, "primitive" societies with which cultural anthropologists were primarily concerned offered a number of advantages for the functionalist approach: the "boundaries" of the social systems in question were more readily identifiable; their "structures" were relatively stable; social life exhibited a high degree of "integration"; and the "survival" of such societies in their traditional form could reasonably be construed as the overall goal of the social system. These assumptions became much less plausible when applied to larger, less isolated, and rapidly changing societies, comprising a number of subgroups often hostile to one another.

Merton and Parsons subsequently expanded and refined the functionalist framework to a more suitable instrument for sociological analysis. Merton argued, for example, that functionalist theory need not be conservative; the interpretation of particular elements in terms of their consequences for larger units in which they are implicated need not take "society as a whole" as the unit in question, nor need the "consequences" discovered contribute to the perpetuation of the existing social system. An institutional practice may, for instance, be functional with respect to the radical interests of a particular subgroup. Merton also distinguished between "manifest" and "latent" functions: the consequences of a cultural element or institutional practice may be functional within a specific context without being intended as such. In fact the primary aim of functional analysis is to disclose such unintended, latent functions.[4]

In his "structural-functionalism," Parsons claims to have finally developed an adequate general framework for social inquiry.[5] On the one hand, he does not ignore the meaningfulness of social action but incorporates it into the basic concepts and assumptions of the theory. On the other hand, he does not restrict the significance of social action to the manifest meanings to which social actors are oriented. The integration of the two perspectives is achieved through a concept of the social system as a functional complex of institutions within which cultural values are made binding for action. Sociological analysis is concerned with cultural tradition to the extent that it has been incorporated in binding social norms or institutionalized values, that is, to the extent that it has attained normative force for orienting action. The type of theory appropriate to such an object domain must include assumptions about empirical connections between social norms, connections that go beyond the subjective intentions of those acting under the norms. The significance for social life of the objective connections within the system of social roles is latent. Its disclosure requires the discovery of the functions that specific elements fulfill in maintaining the continuity of the social system. As Habermas puts it:

Only if social norms, which institutionalize cultural patterns or values, are comprehended as structures within self-regulating systems, can social processes be analyzed on the basis of assumptions about the understandable empirical interconnections among organized behavioral expectatations. The functions which they always have in maintaining or altering a defined state of the system are an expression of the latently meaningful, empirical interconnection of the manifestly, i.e. subjectively, meaningful actions of individuals and groups.[6]

In his later writings, Parsons employs the terminology of cybernetics to characterize the basic features of social systems. The "goal state" is the preferred state that a self-regulating system tends to achieve and, once achieved, to maintain, across a wide range of environmental and internal variations. A state description of such a system involves a determination of the values of its constituent variables. Parsons offers the following schema for state descriptions:

The four exigencies to which a system of action is subject are those of "goal attainment," "adaptation," "integration" and "pattern maintenance." These are dimensions of a space in the sense that a state of the system or of its units' relations to each other may be described relative to satisfactory points of reference, as "farther along" or less far along on each of these dimensions; a change of state may be described in terms of increases or decreases in the values of each of these variables.[7]

The goal state or state of equilibrium of a self-regulating system can then be described in terms of those values of the state variables that the system tends to achieve and maintain. Habermas calls these the "control values" (*Kontrollwerte*) or "goal values" (*Sollwerte*) of the system.

Parsons's framework has been subjected to repeated criticism. On the sociological side it has been argued, for instance, that social conflicts and social change cannot be adequately analyzed within it, that it has a built-in conservative bias and thus functions as an ideology rather than as an empirical theory. Habermas centers his critique around logical considerations developed by Hempel and Nagel who have argued that the validity of functional explanations presupposes the fulfillment of certain conditions.[8] Most importantly it must be possible to give a reliable empirical delimitation of the *boundaries* of the system in question, to identify and specify precisely the *state* in which the system tends to maintain itself, to determine empirically the *functional requirements* of the system, and to designate the *alternative processes* through which these requirements can be met. Only if these conditions are satisfied is it possible to offer a cogent explanation of an element by reference to the necessity of the functions it performs for the self-maintenance of the system in which it is located. An examination of the functional explanations provided by social scientists discloses that these conditions are rarely met. Nagel draws the critical conclusion:

It follows that proposed explanations aiming to exhibit the functions of various items in a social system in either maintaining or altering the system have no substantive content, unless the state that is allegedly maintained or altered is formulated more precisely than has been customary. . . For in the absence of descriptions precise enough to identify unambiguously the states which are supposed to be maintained in a social system, those claims cannot be subjected to empirical control, since they are compatible with every conceivable matter of fact and with every outcome of empirical inquiries into actual societies.[9]

For Hempel and Nagel functional explanations, if valid (that is, if they meet the above-mentioned and other relevant conditions), are at bottom a species of causal explanation. Their distinctness is a matter of formulation and point of view, not one of logic. They focus attention on the consequences or products of specific processes, in particular, upon the contributions of various parts of a system to the maintenance of its global properties or modes of behavior. But the connections they assert can also be formulated in terms of the conditions under which various processes are initiated or persist, and of the factors on which the continued manifestation of certain system traits is contingent. The difference is one of emphasis and perspective in formulation. Whereas teleological explanations view things from the perspective of certain selected "wholes," their nonteleological translations view the same things from the perspective of the more elementary factors that make up the wholes. Thus understood, the functionalist approach presents no challenge to the unity of science program; it is rather a particular research strategy within it. This strategy recommends itself when the domain of investigation comprises organized systems for which the necessary conditions of explanation can be satisfied. This is above all the case in biology. In the social sciences, on the other hand, the fruitfulness of the functionalist perspective is dubious; and the situation can be improved only to the extent that our causal-analytic knowledge of social processes itself expands.

For Habermas, by contrast, the inadequacies of functionalist social theory are in principle insuperable so long as it is understood as a form of empirical-analytic inquiry. An organism is easily demarcated from its environment, and the state in which it maintains itself can be characterized in terms of a series of processes, with empirically specifiable tolerances, necessary for life. The same cannot be said for social systems. Even if they could be precisely demarcated in some complicated way (spatial and temporal boundaries will not do), it appears impossible to determine the goal states of such systems in an empirically reliable manner.

Unlike the reproduction of organic life, the reproduction of social life is not fixed by values that can be grasped descriptvely. Physical survival is a necessary, but by no means a sufficient condition for the maintenance of social systems. . . . The difficulty is obvious—the standards of historical life and survival are dependent on the interpretations that obtain in given social systems.[10]

In the course of history, not only the elements but the boundaries and goal states of societies undergo change; consequently their identity becomes blurred. A given modification might be regarded either as a learning process and regeneration of the original system or as a process of dissolution and transformation into a new system. There is apparently no objective way to determine which description is correct. To a certain extent we are forced to rely on the interpretations of the members of the system, to their experience of the modifications as a continuity or rupture of tradition.[11]

Given the difficulties in objectively determining the goal states and goal values of social systems, the presuppositions of functional analysis might be satisfied by turning it into a form of normative-analytic inquiry. If the investigator were to stipulate the goals of a system, the functionalist perspective could be used to analyze the conditions necessary for realizing these goals (as is often done, for example, in economices and in organization theory). But this would mean that the empirical-analytic claims of functional analysis would have to be renounced in favor of a systems research based on pragmatically determined goals and purposes. Such research would provide "second-level technical knowledge."

Parsons would not, of course, accept this reorientation of structural-functionalism. He wishes to preserve its status as an empirical-analytic science. But he can do this only by presupposing as given what is actually a matter of political controversy and ideally a matter for rational consensus.

Parsons supposes that the control values of a system are "given" in the same way as the cultural values that determine social norms. . . . In reality, parameters for the goal state of a social system cannot be ascertained in the same way as for the parametrically determined equilibrium state of an organism. That is, the empirical values that can be ascertained for a given system along the dimensions designated [by Parsons] cannot be related to an optimal value [as a point of reference]. Such control values are not "given"; at best they can be "found" by way of a political formation of will. But this would be possible only under the presupposition of a general and public discussion among members of the society, based on available information about the given conditions of reproduction of the system. In this case they could come to a relative agreement on a value system that included the objective goal values previously withdrawn from the knowledge and will of citizens. In such a communication, previously recognized cultural values could not function only as standards; cultural values would themselves be drawn into the discussion. In confrontation with available techniques and strategies, in deliberation on given and alterable circumstances, they would be examined pragmatically and cleansed of their ideological components.[12]

If functionalism is to serve as a framework for empirical analysis (rather than as a normative-analytic technique), it will, Habermas argues, have to be transformed into a historically oriented theory with practical intent, that is, into a critical social theory. This involves a number of fundamental changes. For one thing, properly hermeneutic procedures would have to be reintroduced: "The analysis of role systems presupposes a correct understanding of so-called cultural value systems. For the action-orienting meaning of social norms stems from an accompanying cultural tradition. . . . If they are to be grasped descriptively and not constructed as pure behavior maxims, value systems pose the same methodological problems for the social scientist as does the meaning of documents for the historian or the significance of texts for the philologist.[13] Parsons disposes of this problem with the simplifying assumption of a universal value schema: all value systems are built up from the same set of basic value orientations ("pattern variables") fundamental to all social action.[14] As a number of critics have pointed out, neither the universality nor the completeness of his table of categories is apparent. Upon closer analysis, "the four pairs of alternative value orientations, which are supposed to take into account all possible fundamental decisions, are tailored to an analysis of *one* historical process," that is, the transformation from traditional to modern society.[15] In other words, there is a preunderstanding of the historical situation incorporated into Parsons's formulation of his fundamental concepts. If the historically situated character of functional analysis is taken systematically into account, the problem and methods of hermeneutics become unavoidable.

Parsons short-circuits not only the hermeneutic dimension of social inquiry but its critical dimension as well. The categorial framework he proposed does not permit a systematic separation of the utopian, purposive-rational, and ideological contents of value systems. In institutions cultural values are made binding for social action; they become institutionalized values, social norms, and roles. The normative validity of social roles is secured by an adequate integration of the drives, which, together with personality traits, enter the social system "from below." In Parsons's terminology, institutions integrate "value orientations" and "motivational forces" or "potency." Habermas finds this construction overly harmonistic.

In the framework of action theory, motives for action are harmonized with institutional values, i.e. with the intersubjectively valid meaning of normatively binding behavioral expectations. Non-integrated motive forces which find no licensed opportunity for satisfaction in the role system are not analytically grasped. We may assume, however, that these repressed needs, which are not absorbed in social roles, transformed into motivations and sanctioned, nevertheless have their interpretations. Either these interpretations "overshoot" the existing order and, as utopian anticipations, signify a not yet successful group identity; or, transformed into ideologies, they serve projective substitute gratification as well as the justification of the repressing authorities. . . . In relation to such criteria, a state of equilibrium would be determined according to whether the system of domination in a society realized the utopian elements and dissolved the ideological content to the extent that the level of productive forces and of technical progress make objectively possible. Of course, society can then no longer be conceived exclusively as a system of self-preservation. . . . Rather, the meaning in relation to which the functionality of social processes is measured is now linked to the idea of communication free from domination.[16]

A functionalist approach that incorporated the historico-hermeneutic and critical moments would have the advantage of retaining the dimension of meaningfulness without succumbing to the hermeneutic absolutization of cultural tradition. Tradition could be comprehended in its relation to the systems of social labor and political domination, thus making it possible to uncover latent functions that it fulfills without expressing. But a functionalism of this sort could no longer be understood on the model of biology, that is, in the sense of the strict empirical sciences. It would be a "general interpretation," analogous in important respects to the "theoretically generalized history" that we examined in the context of psychoanalysis.

The classical theories of society from Marx to Comte to Oppenheimer and Max Weber pursued this intention more or less without avowing it. These older social theories, which reflectively grasped the formative process of society as a whole and reconstructed the respective contemporary situation of collective action from past complexes of interaction, were thoughtlessly identified with empirical sciences, even by their authors. If one applies this standard, then Popper's critique of them [in the *Poverty of Historicism*], hits the mark. But these social theories . . . need not be compared with strict empirical sciences. . . . For historically oriented functionalism does not at all aim at technically useful information; it is guided by an emancipatory cognitive interest that aims only at reflection and calls for enlightenment about one's own formative processes which are deposited in the structural change of social systems, and which can be reflectively grasped, i.e. systematically narrated, from an anticipated point of view. A story has a beginning and an end. . . . The end can only be anticipated in a historically situated experience of reflection. Thus the general interpretive framework, however saturated with previous hermeneutic experiences and however corroborated in particular interpretations, retains a hypothetical moment—the truth of an historically oriented functionalism is confirmed not technically, but only practically, in the successful continuation and completion of a self-formative process.[17]

The "objective meaning" that such a framework enables us to grasp is not functionalist in the usual sense of latent, purposive-rational or adaptive, unintended consequences of action. It is more akin to the type of meaning represented in the model of the play; elementary processes appear as parts of a complex of interaction through which a meaning for life history is disclosed. But in a formative process, "we are actors and critics at once. In the end, we who are caught up in the drama of life history must ourselves become critically conscious of the meaning of that process."[18] The critique of functionalism thus leads us back to the notion of an empirical philosphy of history with a practical intent; but the emphasis now is on a *theoretically or systematically generalized history*.

Four years after the appearance of his critique of Parsons, Habermas refined his views on the nature and limits of functional analysis in the context of a debate with Niklas Luhmann, the leading German (social) systems theorist.[19] Luhmann's attempt to adapt the categorical framework of cybernetics to social analysis is particularly interesting since he neither ignores the problem of meaning nor short-circuits it by adopting behaviorist assumptions. Instead he accepts "meaning" as a fundamental category of systems analysis at the sociocultural level, while construing it in such a way that it is compatible with a thoroughly functionalist approach to society. Thus his theory is not sociocybernetics in the strict (reductionist) sense. It involves rather a generalization and reformulation of cybernetic concepts and assumptions that is intended to extend their applicability beyond the domains of information-processing machines and biological systems for which they were developed. Using this framework, Luhmann radicalizes the functionalist approach in several ways. (1) In place of Parsons's structural-functionalism, he offers a functional-structuralist systems theory. Thus instead of treating system structures and boundaries as the givens of functional explanation, he regards the formation and change of structures and boundaries as themselves amenable to functional analysis. (2) With admirable consequence, Luhmann applies the functionalist perspective to systems theory itself. Science is a subsystem of society; its problems and solutions are those of the social system to which it belongs. Accordingly systems theory is an organ of self-maintenance; it is one with practice. (3) Luhmann criticizes Parsons for neglecting to analyze "meaning" itself in functionalist terms. He attempts to go behind meaning to the functions it fulfills for social reproduction. (4) Even the notions of truth and value are explicated functionalistically, that is, in connection with their contributions to the fulfillment of systemic imperatives.

There are other distinctive features of Luhmann's functional-structuralism, but these should suffice to indicate its radical thrust. Habermas discusses Luhmann at greater length and in more detail than he did Parsons. Nevertheless I shall confine my remarks here to a few general lines of criticism that suggest some of the limitations of a radically and exclusively functionalist approach to social systems. The four points mentioned in the preceding paragraph will serve as a framework for these remarks.[20]

1. Functionalist explanations have traditionally suffered from the inability to specify clearly the boundaries and goal states of social systems. As a result explanations of inner-systemic processes in terms of their contributions to structural continuity have tended to lose their force at the level of society. Luhmann, who recognizes the difficulty, attempts to overcome it by treating the differentiation of structure and process as itself functional from the point of view of a more fundamental systems problem: "reduction of complexity." Generalizing the categories of cybernetices, he views systems as relatively invariant structural units that maintain themselves in a complex and changing environment by stabilizing an inner-outer difference. The relation of a system to its environment can be formally specified in terms of its complexity, that is the number of different states that are compatible with its structure. The environment of a system is always more complex than the system itself; the structure of the system excludes more states than the environment can assume (for example, body temperature, temperature of the environment).

According to this usage, complexity is a measure of the number of events and states of a system (self-complexity). With their stabilized boundaries, systems form and maintain islands of lesser complexity; the order of a system is less probable than that of its environment. It is a condition of self-maintenance of a system that it can assume sufficiently many states to enable it to adapt to the changing events in the environment. Its self-complexity must suffice to permit system-maintaining reactions to changes in the environment that affect the system. (This is an informal expression of Ashby's "law of requisite variety".) The portion of world complexity—i.e. the class of system-relevant events in the world—that the system can "register" [*erfassen*] and to which it can react with appropriate alterations is "reduced." This is then the operatively mastered environment of the system. A system can solve its problem of self-maintenance so long as the selection achievements suffice to register and operatively to master the portion of the world that is actually relevant to the persistence of the system.[21]

In Luhmann's view, this schema can be used not only to analyze the functioning of systems whose structure is given (for example, organisms) but also to analyze changes in system structures themselves. The formation of structures is as much a "selective accomplishment" through which "complexity is reduced" as are processes within the system. System structures are, so to speak, congealed reduction of world complexity. From this point of view, structural development and inner-systemic processes are functionally equivalent alternatives for reducing complexity. A systems theory that takes this "double selectivity" into account can, Luhmann argues, analyze the function of structural change without presupposing a more general system structure as a point of reference. The ultimate systems problem is not structural continuity but the reduction of world complexity and the heightening of self-complexity.

Habermas argues that this attempt to circumvent the structural presuppositions of functional analysis results in a paradoxical overextension of the systems-theoretic framework.

If reduction of world complexity is supposed to be the "ultimate," structure-independent point of reference for the analysis, then world complexity must be introduced as a problem that is objectively posed *prior* to any formation of structures. "The world" must then be thought of as a problem "in itself," so that the formation of structures (and indeed of "first" structures) can appear as a solution to that original problem. . . . World complexity is problematic only for the maintenance of systems. The task of reducing world complexity cannot therefore (in this frame of reference) be determined independently of possible system structures. . . . . For without reference to a system whose existence is threatened, Luhmann cannot identify a problem in the first place.[22]

These paradoxical implications suggest that functional analysis must indeed be based on a reliable determination of structures and boundaries, as well as on the specification of a goal-state whose attainment or maintenance constitutes the "problem" that serves as a point of reference. Although these conditions can often be satisfied in biocybernetics, the central concepts become "imprecise" at the sociocultural level. "The 'clearly defined' problem of death and a corresponding criterion of survival are lacking, because societies never reproduce 'naked' life, but always a culturally defined life."[23] In the absence of "operationally satisfactory" procedures for objectively determining the goal values and goal states of social systems, we are forced, Habermas argues, to fall back upon hermeneutic and critical procedures.

. . . at the socio-cultural level of development the problem of survival becomes imprecise. The definition of life . . . is *no longer pre-given* with the specific equipment of the species. Instead, continued attempts to define cultural life are a necessary component of the very life process of socially related individuals. . . . If the definitions of existence depend on the structural change of interpretive systems, this change cannot in turn be analyzed within the framework of a systems theory of society, which, as we seen, must start with the basic problem of securing the continued existence of social systems, and thus must take this existence as an independent datum. Of course, we should not suppose that all the objective problems of existence and all the operative goals are also declared in the cultural definitions of life as they are met with in the self-understanding of a society. The theory of interpretive systems has the task of a theory of ideologies. The latter can grasp the latent functions of interpretive patterns only if it can compare the *de facto* states of social systems with counterfactually introduced, idealized goal states.[24]

In this way, functionalist social analysis necessarily involves an explication and critique of the historically variable interpretive systems in which social subjects understand themselves and their worlds, secure their identities, and determine what counts as human life.

2. Luhmann grants the necessity of including the dimension of

meaning in social analysis, but he poses the problem in such a way that it is set within, rather than setting a limit upon, the systems-theoretic perspective: "meaning" is construed as a mode of reducing complexity that is peculiar to social systems. It is the form in which we process experience so as to integrate the momentarily given with other unactualized but virtually retained possibilities. This distinctive "mode of selection" heightens the self-complexity of systems and expands their capacity to register world complexity. But in doing so, it creates a new source of pressure for selection: there are always more possibilities of experience and action than can actually be realized. That is, systems in which the reduction of world complexity is mediated through meaning have themselves a form of self-complexity—in the form of unactualized but meaningful possibilities—that presents a problem for selection. There arises the possibility of a discrepancy between what is merely registered (*erfasst*) and what is operatively mastered, of a disproportional growth in information relative to the ability to translate it into action.

Naturally, the complexity which affects action systems in this way is not the complexity of reality, but that of the meaningfully structured "world" which social systems produce as their environment [*Umwelt*] through the symbolically mediated registering of world complexity. At the level of meaningful selectivity, then, the immediate task is not the reduction of world complexity, but the reduction of self-produced, so to speak, surplus self-complexity.[25]

In the case of organic systems, it is the world—as the totality of real events and states—that is the immediate source of problems of survival. In the case of social systems, it is on the contrary the symbolically structured "world"—in which world complexity is already registered through meaningful selection—that is the immediate source of the pressure for selection; for action involves a choice among a multiplicity of meaningfully preselected possibilities. Reduction of world complexity is furthered by the creation of new possibilities for reaction to changes in the world, that is, by the heightening of "world" complexity. By contrast the reduction of "world" complexity is the reduction of superfluous self-complexity. Thus an increase in self-complexity through the projection of new possibilities is at the same time a reduction of world complexity *and* a heightening of "world" complexity. It represents both a problem solution and a new problem.

This is another indication, Habermas argues, that the basic con-

cepts of information and systems theory become imprecise when
(over)extended to social systems. Luhmann does, it is true, attempt to
give both types of reduction their due. The persistence of social systems requires both projecting new possibilities for choice and rendering choice sufficiently unproblematic through "structurification"
(*Strukturifizierung*). To avoid inundating their capacity for action with
too many alternative possibilities, social systems must structurally
predetermine (in institutions, for example) the outcome of choices to
the extent necessary for survival. Thus social stability requires an immunization against conscious decisions, in Luhmann's terms: "the
necessary latency of many structures and functions"; in Habermas's
terms: "counter-enlightenment." Whatever one's political preferences, the logical shortcomings of Luhmann's framework remain.

Under Luhmann's own assumptions of a mode of selection mediated
through meaning, there are two possibilities: either the projection of
possibilities of action heightens the self-complexity of the action system and thereby serves to reduce world complexity; or this production of alternative possibilities of action registers world complexity in
the peculiar manner that additional problems for selection are
created (in the form of surplus "world" or self-complexity). In the latter case, the additional possibilities do not contribute to the solution of
the problem of reducing complexity, but sharpen it. My objection is
that under the assumption of a mode of selection mediated through
meaning the basic categorial framework of systems theory . . . does
not suffice to formulate that alternative cogently. . . . There is no satisfactory criterion for deciding. Luhmann cannot state when an expansion of alternative possibilities of action at the cost of de-structuring
(processes of enlightenment) is functional, and when the structurification of certain decisions at the cost of a restriction of the horizon of
possibilities that is held present (as in the case of dogmatization) is
functional—just that is arbitrary.[26]

3. As we saw in the discussion of Parsons, one could remedy some of
the methodological shortcomings of functional analysis by simply
stipulating the goal values and goal states that will guide the analysis
of a given system. But this amounts to surrendering the claim to
empirical-analytic theory in favor of a normative-analytic approach
that produces second-order technical knowledge (as in the cybernetically modeled sociology of organizations, for example). Luhmann attempts to undercut this alternative by applying the systems-theoretic perspective reflexively by functionally analyzing functionalist theory itself.

General systems theory, insofar as it contributes to the reduction of complexity, is itself a moment of the evolutionary social process that it analyzes. It is "the organ which, in view of the developing functional primacy of the system of science, is preparing itself to take over the lead in the process of social self-production; as such, theory is immediately practical."[27] With the growing complexity of society, functional analysis has become, in Luhmann's view, the only reliable way of rationalizing social decisions. Given the indeterminacy of problems relating to the self-maintenance of the social system as a whole, objectively given social problems are to serve as its point of departure. Concrete crisis situations, or recognizable dangers to social stability provide the reference points from which the systems theorist analyzes functions and functional alternatives. In discovering functional equivalents for problematic processes and structures, systems research extends the range of possibilities from which society may choose. It thus becomes the principal instrument for stabilizing the social order and dealing with conflicts and crises.

Systems research is so deeply implicated in the life process of society that it is always called upon and directed in a compelling way by objectively posed systems problems. In the face of the power of the reproduction of life in the great systems, science—which is integrated in them as a subsystem—cannot win critical autonomy. The problems and solutions of theory are always also the problems and solutions of the society to which it belongs. . . . Behind the attempt to justify the reduction of world complexity as the ultimate point of reference for social-scientific functionalism is concealed an unadmitted obligation of theory to pose problems in a way that conforms to domination, to serve as an apologetic for what exists in order to maintain its existence.[28]

The political implications of Luhmann's approach emerge most clearly in his discussion of complexity and democracy. He regards Habermas's attempt to link the validity of normative claims to public and general discussion as "out of step with social reality." The enormous selection pressure of world complexity, and especially of self-complexity, on highly developed social systems requires instead a high degree of autonomy for the administrative system. "To demand an intensive, engaged participation of all [those affected by decisions] would be to make a principle of frustration. Anyone who understands democracy in this way has, in fact, to come to the conclusion that it is incompatible with rationality."[29] Rational social policy requires comprehensive, nonparticipatory social planning by an administration shielded from party politics and the public realm. It thus requires the withdrawal of normative validity claims from problematization and critique. Rather than democratic enlightenment, political survival calls for an increasing latency of functions, safeguarded by a mode of legitimation that refers only to the correctness of decision-making procedures. The question of legitimacy must shrink to the question of legality, and this requires in turn a positivization of law. "The law of a society is positivized when the legitimacy of pure legality is recognized, that is, when law is respected because it is made by responsible decision, and in accordance with definite rules. Thus in a central question of human co-existence, arbitrariness becomes an institution."[30]

Habermas denies that the belief in legitimacy can be reduced to a belief in legality.

The unobjectionable manner in which a norm comes into being, that is, the legal form of a procedure, guarantees as such only that the authorities which the political system provides for, and which are furnished with certain competencies and recognized as competent within that system, bear the responsibility for valid law. But these authorities are part of a system of authority which must be legitimized as a whole if pure legality is to be able to count as an indication of legitimacy. In a fascist regime, for example, the legal form of administrative acts can have at best a masking function. This means that the technical legal form alone, pure legality, will not be able to guarantee recognition in the long run if the system of authority cannot be legitimized independently of the legal form of exercising authority. . . . The naive validity claims of norms of action refer in each case (at least implicitly) to the possibility of discursive foundation. If binding decisions are legitimate, that is, if they can be made independently of the concrete exercise of force and of the manifest threat of sanctions, and can be regularly implemented even against the interests of those affected, then they must be considered as the fulfillment of recognized norms. This unconstrained normative validity is based on the supposition that norms could, if necessary, be justified and defended against critique. And this supposition itself is not automatic. It is the consequence of an interpretation which admits of consensus and which has a justificatory function, in other words, of a world view which legitimizes authority.[31]

Thus Habermas's critique is based on a particular view of the validity claims implicit in norms of action, and of their inherent reference to the possibility of discursive justification. (I shall examine this view and its political implications in chapters 4 and 5.) For his part, Luhmann, once again with admirable consistency, supports his position with a countertheory, a functionalist theory, of cognitive and normative validity claims.

4. From a radically functionalist perspective, truth is not a matter of correspondence with an allegedly independent reality or of rational consensus but of stabilizing certainty under the pressure for decision. To the question, What are the achievements of "truth" in regard to systems maintenance? Luhmann responds that it is a medium of communication with a function similar to that of other media (for example, power, money, influence): to secure the intersubjective transferability of selection performances among individuals and groups. Through these media an already achieved reduction of complexity can be passed on without loss. The problem of truth, then, is equivalent to the problem of stabilizing intersubjectively shared certainty, of guaranteeing a de facto consensus.

Once again Habermas's basic criticism of Luhmann's approach points ahead to the theory of communication that we shall be considering in the next chapter.[32] For the present, it will be sufficient to point out a few inconsistencies in Luhmann's position. The functionalist reduction of truth to a mode of stabilizing certainty without resort to force fits well with Luhmann's conception of theory as practice. But both are incompatible with the truth claims he himself makes, and inevitably must make, for his own general systems theory. Critical theory does, it is true, follow a similar line of argument insofar as it locates cognitive processes in the very object domain under investigation and sees itself as a catalytic moment within the historical complex it analyzes. But the differences are crucial. Since critical theory regards the social life process as a self-formative process and construes the reflexive application of the theory as an enlightenment of the subject about elements of his own formation, it can consistently attach a truth claim to its insights: self-*knowledge* sets one free. For systems theory, on the other hand, the social life process is a matter of self-maintenance of social systems. The aim of the theory is not, then, reflective enlightenment but the securing of continued existence. In fact, according to its most basic assumptions, the stabilization of social order requires that a sufficient quantity of selective achievements be immunized from reflective critique through "structurification." There must always be a disproportion between consciously grasped (manifest) and objectively posed and resolved problems. In other words, the latency of basic functions is a necessary condition for the satisfactory functioning of the system and thus for its continued existence. But this means that the goal of a universalized systems theory such as Luhmann's (complete self-transparence) is incompatible with its own assumptions. Since science is a subsystem of society, its proper functioning must also rest on the latency of its functions; full transparence would be dysfunctional. In Habermas's view, this dilemma results from the overextension of a meaningful (but limited) research strategy to a general theory of society.

In line with his immediate (unmediated) identification of theory with practice, Luhmann understands functionalism as a technique for expanding possibilities of action. It provides systems that are under the pressure of selection in situations of uncertainty with functionally equivalent possibilities of self-stabilization. But this, Habermas argues, presupposes a knowledge of the different causes that can produce a desired state of affairs; it presupposes, that is, nomological knowledge, which makes a claim to theoretical validity. "For nomological statements . . . can be translated into recommendations for instrumental action only because they correctly 'describe' reality (to be sure, exclusively from the view-point of possible technical mastery). . . . Nomological statements have a function for possible complexes of interaction because they are true; they are not true because they have such a function."[33]

The other major component of the means-ends schema of action that Luhmann regards as basic—the value orientations that determine the selection of ends,—is also interpreted functionalistically. Goals and purposes are not rationally justifiable, but the arbitrariness that this implies is limited by institutionalized value systems that serve as boundary conditions for purposive-rational action. The validity claims on which the acceptance of values rests are not matter for critical examination but for functional analysis. They are neither true nor false, justifiable nor unjustifiable. They are rather functional or dysfunctional. Thus the proper question is not, Are the validity claims valid? but, What functions do value systems fulfill, and which are the possible functional equivalents? The same applies to the ideological world views that allegedly justify recognized systems of norms. Norms, values, and world views are at bottom only so many ways of stabilizing action orientations that are basic to the continued existence of social systems. From this point of view, the task of systems theory is restricted to the analysis of functionally equivalent means, and of the expected consequences and side-effects of these alternatives. Since the value systems that establish the relevant preference orderings are themselves irrational, they can in turn be analyzed only with reference to the power of selection they furnish to the system in question, as more or less functional in comparison to possible alternatives.

This approach, Habermas argues, systematically underestimates the problems connected with the claim to validity inherent in norms of action and the need for the justification of authority.

The functionalist concept of ideology misses the connection between legitimation and the restriction of communication. To the extent that they fulfill the function of legitimizing domination, world views are always ideological. That is, they provide a solution to the paradoxical problem posed by the obligation of taking into consideration the claim to justifiability inherent in social norms without, however, being able to permit that unconstrained discourse which would, if allowed, convict existing institutions of a false claim. World views that legitimize domination produce the objective appearance of justifying norms that . . . are precisely not capable of being justified.[34]

This objection can be substantiated, and its force appreciated, only after we have considered Habermas's theory of communication. What is at issue here is the possibility of completely integrating the social subject into a society that functions as a self-regulating system. The limits to Luhmann's vision of a homo fabricatus, if there are any, would have to be rooted in the fundamental structures of thought and action.

3.6 TOWARD A RECONSTRUCTION OF HISTORICAL MATERIALISM

In recent years Habermas has attempted to integrate the various positive elements that emerged from his analyses of existing approaches into a unified conception of critical theory.[1] It is important to keep in mind that this is a research program that is still being developed. Habermas constantly reminds his readers of its tentative, exploratory character and warns against construing as a finished product what is at present an ongoing attempt to clarify basic categories and assumptions. As a consequence of their programmatic status, these recent methodological writings still draw heavily on other established research traditions: "the appearance of eclecticism will be unavoidable so long as a complex and explanatorily powerful theory is still *in statu nascendi*."[2] Nevertheless the general contours of Habermas's own program for a critical theory of society are by now relatively definite.

As our previous methodological discussions would lead us to expect, this program represents an attempt to integrate basic categories and assumptions of action theory (meaning and intentionality, roles and norms, beliefs and values, and so forth) with elements of functionalist systems theory (structure and function, system and process, differentiation and adaptation, and so forth). The framework in which this is accomplished has the form of a theory of social evolution inspired by Marx's version of historical materialism. There is, however, a new element that plays an increasingly important role in Habermas's recent writings: structuralism. Although he acknowledges having learned something from the French structuralist Marxists (especially Godelier), he feels that their approach involves too radical an exclusion of essential elements of the action frame of reference. By contrast, the genetic structuralism of the Piaget school provides a suggestive combination of structuralist, action theoretic, and developmental perspectives. "The stimulus that encouraged me to investigate normative structures from the point of view of developmental logic also came from Piaget's *genetic* structuralism, that is, from a conception which has overcome the traditional structuralist front against evolutionism and has assimilated motifs of the theory of knowledge from Kant to Peirce."[3]

Habermas's reworking of the foundations of action theory in terms of a theory of communication will be considered in chapter 4. In this section, I shall examine his program for a theory of social evolution. It should be kept in mind, however, that this theory essentially presupposes the results of his analysis of communication.

Habermas describes his theory of social evolution as a "reconstruction of historical materialism." In this connection "*reconstruction* means that one takes a theory apart and puts it back together in a new form, in order better to achieve that goal which it set for itself. This is the normal (in my opinion, normal also for Marxists) way of dealing with a theory that requires revision in many respects, but whose potential for stimulation has not yet been exhausted."[4] These "many respects" include the inadequacy of its philosophical and methodological foundations, especially in view of the objectivistic turn these have been given in orthodox Marxism; the unclarity of the normative foundations of critical theory, especially since "bourgeois consciousness has become cynical," and we can no longer—as Marx still could—"take literally and criticize immanently the normative content of reigning bourgeois theories, of modern natural law, and of political economy"[5]; as well as analytic and empirical difficulties with the specific concepts, assumptions, and explanatory models of historical materialism: "Whereas Marx localized the learning processes that release epochal developments . . . in the *forces of production,* there are in the meantime good reasons for assuming that learning processes also take place in the dimension of moral insight, practical knowledge, communicative action and the consensual regulation of conflicts—processes which are precipitated in maturer forms of social integration, in new *relations of production,* and which in turn first make possible the introduction of new forces of production."[6] It is primarily this last set of difficulties that will concern us here.

Before turning to consider them, however, we should consider why Habermas even bothers with revising historical materialism. What is it that makes a theory of social evolution important for critical theory? Why not confine ourselves to an analysis of capitalism? For one thing, the Marxist theory of capitalism is a crisis theory; it attempts to identify structurally inherent contradictions within the capitalist organization of society. As our discussion of systems theory suggested, however, the identification of such contradictions has an element of arbitrariness so long as we are unable to specify structures essential to the continued existence of this system and to distinguish them from other elements that can change without the system's losing its identity. This can be done, Habermas claims, only within the framework of a general theory of social evolution.

. . . what is demanded is a level of analysis at which the *connection* between normative structures and steering problems becomes palpable. I find this level in a historically oriented analysis of social systems, which permits us to ascertain for a given case the range of tolerance within which the goal values of the system might vary without its continued existence being critically endangered. . . . Ranges of variation for structural change obviously can be introduced only within the framework of a theory of social evolution.[7]

In the introduction to *Zur Rekonstruktion des Historischen Materialismus*, he illustrates his point with questions that are central to the analysis of contemporary society but that cannot be unequivocally answered in the absence of such a theory. One question concerns the proper conceptualization of advanced capitalism. Some theorists argue that the organizational principle of capitalist society has gradually shifted from the economic to the political; others maintain that the changes in question are properly conceived as a gradual realization of the same principle of organization in ever-expanding spheres of life, that capitalism has been and still is in the process of establishing itself vis-à-vis traditional forms of social organization. The same phenomena are interpreted from one point of view as the replacement of market functions by state regulation and from the other as the administrative establishment of the commodity form in spheres previously governed by "nature-like" traditional relations. Deciding between these (and other) competing interpretations is a prerequisite for determining the significance of specific changes for the development of capitalist society in general and for identifying crisis tendencies in particular.[8] If this decision is not to be arbitrary, it must, Habermas argues, be based on a theory of social evolution.

If we had at our disposal a theory of social evolution which explained the transition to modern society as the emergence of a new—and well defined—social organizational principle, it would be possible to examine which of the two competing approaches is more compatible with the rise of capitalism. For each interpretation specifies a different organizational principle for capitalist development. According to the first version, the organizational principle consists in a complementary relation between a non-productive state and a depoliticized economic system; the latter is organized through markets as a sphere of decentralized decisions by strategically acting private subjects, while the state guarantees the prerequisites for the continued existence of an economy disengaged from its sphere of sovereignty; it thereby both excludes itself from the production process and—as a state based on taxation—renders itself dependent on it. According to the other version, the organizational principle consists in the relation between capital and wage labor, where the state—somewhat *ex machina*—has to function as the agent for establishing this principle in an originally hostile environment.[9]

It is true, Habermas grants, that the anatomy of capitalist society provides important clues to the constitutive features of earlier social formations and that it serves as a point of departure for the theory of social evolution: "With Marx, I see in the anatomy of man a key to the anatomy of the ape, i.e. in the categories of the most developed formation of society at a given time a pattern of structures whose developmental logic can be traced back through past social formations."[10] But this does not mean that the "logic of capital" is a key to the logic of social evolution in general; the types of systems problems that arise within the capitalist process of reproduction cannot be read back into all previous social formations. Moreover, since the analysis of contemporary society is fraught with the familiar problems of historical perspective, it is important to test our assumptions against the broad range of available anthropological and historical material. This is the only way in which we can mitigate our temporal provinciality.

Assumptions about the organizational principle of a society, about learning capacities and ranges of possible structural variation, cannot be clearly and empirically tested until historical developments have put the critical limits to the test. Evolutionarily oriented analyses of the present are always under a handicap because they cannot observe their object retrospectively. For this reason, theories of this type—whether Marxist or non-Marxist—have to monitor their assumptions (which already underlie the delimitation and description of the object) against an instructive theory of social development. Characterizations of contemporary society as industrial, post-industrial, technological, scientized, capitalist, late-capitalist, state-monopolistic, state-capitalist, modern, post-modern, etc. spring from just as many developmental models that connect the present social formation with earlier ones. In this respect, historical materialism can take on the task of determining the organizational principle of contemporary society from the perspective of the emergence of this social formation, e.g. with statements about the systems problems which traditional societies failed to resolve, and about the innovations with which modern bourgeois society met the evolutionary challenges.[11]

On this view, "the theory of capitalist development is integrated into historical materialism as a sub-theory [*Teiltheorie*]."[12]

The reconstruction of historical materialism aims at a general theory of social evolution capable of explaining particular evolutionary developments—above all, the transition from primitive societies organized around kinship relations to civilizations organized as class societies with a differentiated political system and the transition from developed premodern civilizations to liberal capitalist society, as well as the evolution of the latter to the stage of advanced capitalism. As we shall see below, the type of theory (and of explanation) that Habermas has in mind is not modeled after the natural sciences; his paradigms are taken instead from the reconstructive theories that have been developed primarily in linguistics and cognitive developmental psychology.

Habermas organizes his discussion of historical materialism around two basic concepts—"social labor" and the "history of the species,"—and two basic assumptions—the theory of "base and superstructure" and the "dialectic of forces and relations of production."[13]

1. Marx designated socially organized labor as the specific way in which humans as distinguished from animals reproduce their life. Habermas explicates this notion in terms of three types of rules. The basic aspect is the purposeful reshaping of material according to rules of instrumental action. The instrumental activity of different individuals must be organized for the purposes of production; thus the rules of strategic action that guide this coordination are an essential element of the labor process. Finally means of subsistence are produced in order to be consumed; the distribution of the products of labor is socially organized through "the systematic connection of reciprocal expectations or interests," that is, through social norms or rules of communicative action.[14] A system that socially regulates labor and the distribution of its products in this way is called an *economy*. For Marx the economic form of reproducing life is that characteristic of the human stage of development.

Drawing on recent anthropological findings concerning the development from primates to humans, Habermas argues that this now appears inadequate as a characterization of the specifically human form of reproduction—"it reaches too deeply into the evolutionary scale."

Not only humans but hominids too were distinguished from the anthopoid apes in that they converted to reproduction through social labor and developed an economy. The adult males formed hunting bands, which a) made use of weapons and tools (technology), b) cooperated through a division of labor (cooperative organization), and c) distributed the prey within the collective (rules of distribution). . . . Thus the Marxian concept of social labor is suitable for delimiting the mode of life of the hominids from that of the primates; but it does not capture the specifically human reproduction of life.[15]

It appears now that the evolutionary novelty that distinguishes homo sapiens is not the economy but the family; only with humans did the social structure that had arisen among the vertebrates break up—that one-dimensional rank-ordering in which each animal has a single (transitive) status in the hierarchy. In contrast the family system made it possible for the adult male to combine a status in the male system of the hunting band with a status in the female and child system, via the role of the father, which is the structural core of the family. In this way functions of social labor were integrated with those relating to the nurture of the young, and functions of male hunting were coordinated with those of female gathering (division of labor based on sex). The organization of society along kinship lines means the replacement of the animal status system with a system of social roles and norms. And this, Habermas argues, presupposes the development of language.

The implications of all this for the basic concepts and assumptions of historical materialism seem to be the following:

—the concept of social labor is fundamental, since the social organization of labor and distribution evidently precedes the emergence of developed linguistic communication; and this in turn precedes the formation of social role systems;

—but the specifically human mode of life can be adequately characterized only if we join the concept of social labor to that of organization along kinship lines;

—the structures of role behavior mark a new evolutionary threshold vis-à-vis those of social labor; the rules of communicative action—that is, intersubjectively valid and ritually secured norms of action—cannot be reduced to rules either of instrumental or of strategic action;

—production and socialization, social labor and care of the young, are of equal importance for the reproduction of the species; therefore, the kinship structure, which governs the integration of *both* external and internal nature, is fundamental.[16]

2. For Marx, the key to the reconstruction of the history of the species (*Gattungsgeschiechte*) was the notion of a "mode of production." Habermas analyzes this notion in terms of the forces and relations of production. Productive forces consist in the labor power of producers, technical knowledge insofar as it is converted into means and techniques that heighten productivity, and organizational knowledge

insofar as it is employed for the mobilization, qualification, and organization of labor power. The relations of production, on the other hand, are the institutions and social mechanisms that determine how labor power can be combined with the available means of production at a given level of productive forces. Moreover, "the regulation of access to the means of production . . . indirectly determines the distribution of social wealth. The relations of production are an expression of the distribution of power—they determine the distributional pattern of socially recognized opportunities to satisfy needs, and thus the interest structure which exists in a society."[17]

Historical materialism proceeds from the assumption that forces and relations of production do not vary independently but exhibit a structural correspondence to one another in such a way that there results a finite number of structurally analogous stages that reveal a developmental-logical order. Thus in the orthodox version, five modes of production are differentiated: the primitive communal, the ancient, the feudal, the capitalist, and the socialist, to which an asiatic mode was later added. These six modes of production are supposed to designate universal stages of social evolution in terms of which any particular economic structure can be analyzed from an evolutionary point of view.

There is a "dogmatic" version of this approach to *Gattungsgeschichte*, which shares many of the objectionable features of eighteenth- and nineteenth-century philosophy of history. According to this version, the previous course of world history—viewed as a sequence of these five or six modes of production—exhibits the unilinear, necessary, continuous, and irreversible development of a macro- or species-subject. As we saw above, Habermas feels that Marx's own version—at least as presented in his earlier writings—did not share these weaknesses (with the exception of the "species-subject"). His own version of a theory of social evolution—relying as it does on a distinction among structural patterns, empirical learning mechanisms, and contingent boundary conditions—requires neither unilinearity, nor necessity, nor continuity, nor irreversibility in history. But there is one feature of traditional philosophic conceptions of history that was undeniably shared by Marx and is retained in Habermas's theory of social evolution: teleology. The very term *evolution* implies a conception of cumulative processes in which a direction can be perceived. Even if one does not subscribe to the necessity and irreversibility of evolutionary processes, any talk of directionality or hierarchical ordering seems to presuppose criteria of historical progress. Marx located these in two dimensions: the development of productive forces and the maturation of forms of social intercourse. As we might expect, Habermas wishes to defend a revised version of this view for these are precisely the two dimensions of rationalization (cognitive-technical and moral-practical) that he distinguished in his earlier writings.

But even if it is reformulated to meet the well-known objections against the idea of a necessary and irreversible evolution of a species subject, the notion of *Gattungsgeschichte* as a developmental sequence of modes of production is problematic. It has, to be sure, distinct advantages over a number of competing approaches for ordering historical material developmentally, such as, for example, periodizations in terms of primary materials (from stone, bronze, and iron to artificial materials) or the most important energy sources (from fire, water, and wind to atomic and solar energy), for these present us sooner or later with the problem of finding a developmental pattern for the techniques of getting at and working natural resources. And even this is inadequate as a key to social evolution since "the great technical inventions have not produced, but only accompanied new epochs."[18] By comparison Marx's concept of a mode of production takes into account that not only productive forces but also productive relations are crucial to any attempt at periodization. Because of this bidimensionality, it is also more informative than approaches that focus solely on forms of organizing cooperative labor (from family and cottage industry through the factory system to national and multinational concerns), or on market structures (from household, city, and national economies to the world economy), or on the social division of labor (hunting and gathering, cultivation of the soil and animal husbandry, urban crafts and rural farming, industry and agriculture, and so forth). None of these developments in societal complexity tells us of themselves about developments in the forces of production.

Nevertheless the application of the Marxist schema of five or six modes of production to available anthropological and historical material has encountered a number of difficulties. In addition to problems connected with mixed and transitional forms (rarely is the economic structure of a particular society a pure form of a single mode of production; usually it is a question of complex structures that have to be analyzed as a combination of several modes), there are problems that arise in applying the schema to the transition from Paleolithic to Neolithic societies (both supposedly primitive communal modes but exhibiting marked differences in both productive forces and organizational forms); to the "asiatic" mode of production (the last stage of the primitive communal order or the first form of class society? a universal developmental stage or a specific line of development of class societies alongside of the ancient?); to feudalism (a single mode or a concatenation of several? a universal developmental stage or a unique appearance in medieval Europe?); to the differences between archaic and developed civilizations (within the framework of the same political form of class organization, there took place a remarkable change in the structure of dominant world views in China, India, Palestine and Greece); to advanced capitalism (is state-regulated capitalism the last phase of an old mode of production or the first of a new one?); and to bureaucratic socialism (a variant of the same stage as organized capitalism or a higher stage?).[19]

These (and other) difficulties suggest that the concept of a mode of production is an inadequate key to the analysis of social development. Basically it allows for two levels of comparison: the regulation of access to the means of production and the structural compatibility of these rules with a given level of development of productive forces. But these are not a sufficient basis for the differentiations that appear to be required by the historical material. The usual strategy for meeting this problem is to introduce further differentiations (for example, degrees to which private property has been established or forms of exploitation).[20] But Habermas feels that this strategy, in an attempt to do justice to the empirical material, runs the danger of surrendering the very concept of a Gattungsgeschichte.

These general sociological perspectives certainly permit a concrete description of a given economic structure, but they lead to a broader range rather than a deeper analysis. The result of this procedure would be a pluralistic compartmentalization of modes of production and a weakening of their developmental logic. At the end of this inductive path lies the surrender of the concept of the history of the species—and thus of historical materialism. We cannot exclude a priori that anthropological-historical research might one day make this necessary. But in the meantime, it seems to me that the opposite direction has not yet been sufficiently explored.[21]

The opposite direction is that of even stronger generalization and even greater abstraction—the idea being that the universals of social evolution and the ordering principles of a developmental logic must be formulated at a level abstract enough to avoid social and historical specificity. Within such a general framework, it might then be possible to take account of this specificity in terms of particular empirical mechanisms, initial and boundary conditions, and so forth. In other words Habermas is proposing the combination of a genetic-structural level of analysis with an empirical-historical level of analysis in order to meet both developmental-logical and empirical conditions of adequacy. Just how he intends to do this will be discussed below. For the present we shall note that he introduces his program in terms of the Marxian concept of a social formation (*Gesellschaftsformation*) and the hypothesis that the formation of a society at any given time is determined by a fundamental principle of organization (*Organisationsprinzip*).

By principle of organization I understand those innovations which become possible through learning processes that can be reconstructed in a developmental logic, and which institutionalize a new societal level of learning. The organizational principle of a society circumscribes ranges of possibility; in particular, it determines within which structures changes in the system of institutions are possible; to what extent the available productive capacities can be socially utilized or the development of new productive forces can be stimulated; and thereby also to what degrees system complexity and steering performances can be heightened. A principle of organization consists of such abstract regulations that within the social formation determined by it several functionally equivalent modes of production are permitted. Accordingly, the economic structure of a particular society would have to be examined at two levels: firstly in terms of the modes of production which have entered into a concrete connection within it; and then in terms of that formation of society to which the dominant mode of production belongs. Such a postulate is easier to put forward than to realize; I can only attempt to explain the research program and to make it plausible.[22]

In *Legitimation Crisis* (1973) Habermas attempted to discover organizational principles inductively and to elaborate them with reference to the "institutional nucleus" (for example, kinship system, political system, economic system) that determined the dominant form of social integration at a given stage of development. In *Zur Rekonstruktion des Historischen Materialismus* (1976), he takes the first steps toward a theoretical classification of forms of social integration in terms of fundamental evolutionary characteristics that is, in terms of a developmental logic.[23]

3. According to the theory of "base" and "superstructure," the forces and relations of production of a society form an economic structure by which all other subsystems are determined. There are a number of different versions of this theory, involving (among other things) different readings of the term *determined*. In orthodox Marxism, various ontological or "economistic" versions have predominated, according to which processes in any "higher" subsystem are causally dependent upon, or structurally limited by, those in the "lower"—in the final analysis the economic—subsystems. In Hegelian Marxism, the model of societal strata is replaced by an essence-appearance model in which the economic structure is construed dialectically as the essence that appears in the observable social phenomena. Habermas proposes another interpretation:

The context in which Marx propounds his theory makes it clear that the dependence of the superstructure on the base was meant in the first instance only for the critical phase in which a society is passing over to a new developmental level. What is meant is not some ontological constitution of society, but rather the leading role which the economic structure assumes in social evolution.[24]

The priority in question relates to the explanation of evolutionary innovations; Marx's thesis is that innovations are to be explained as issuing from problems that arise in the basic sphere of society.

Seen in this light, the identification of "base" and "economic *structure*", can be misleading; it can lead to the view that the basic sphere of society (in which evolutionarily significant problems arise) is always equivalent to the economic *subsystem*. But this is true only of capitalist societies; if relations of production are defined functionally (in terms of regulating access to the means of production and thereby indirectly regulating the distribution of social wealth), then the "relations of production" are fixed in primitive societies by the kinship system and in premodern civilizations by the political system. Only with the rise of capitalism did productive relations take on a purely economic form. The conclusion of this line of argument is that

the relations of production can draw upon different institutions. The institutional nucleus around which productive relations crystallize determines a particular *form of social integration*—understood in the Durkheimian sense of securing the unity of a social life-world through values and norms. If systems problems cannot be resolved in accord with the dominant form of social integration, if this must itself be revolutionized in order to create latitude for new problem solutions, the identity of the society is in danger.[25]

On this interpretation, the basic sphere of society, the institutional nucleus around which the relations of production are organized, need not belong to the economic subsystem in the narrow sense. Whatever the particular form of these relations—kinship, political, economic—they embody the form of social integration. A challenge to this institutional nucleus is thus a challenge to social identity—a crisis.

4. Marx saw the mechanism of crisis in a dialectic of forces and relations of production. This has often been understood in the "technologistic" sense (by Plechanov and Stalin, for example) that productive techniques themselves determine a certain organization of labor and thereby particular relations of production. A more differentiated structuralist interpretation runs as follows: there exists an endogeneous learning mechanism that provides for spontaneous growth of technical knowledge and its conversion into productive forces; a mode of production is in a state of equilibrium only if there exists a structural correspondence between the developmental stages of the forces and relations of production; the endogeneous development of productive forces generates structural incompatibilities between these two orders; these in turn evoke imbalances in the existing mode of production and thereby lead to a revolution in the relations of production. Even this version, Habermas argues, is inadequate.

In this formulation it still remains unclear wherein the developmental mechanism consists, with the aid of which evolutionary innovations are to be explained. The postulated learning mechanism explains the growth of a cognitive potential and perhaps also its conversion into technologies and strategies that heighten the productivity of labor. It can explain the emergence of systems problems which, if the structural dissimilarities between forces and relations of production become too great, threaten the continued existence of the mode of production. But this learning mechanism does not explain how these problems can be resolved. The introduction of new forms of social integration—e.g. the replacement of the kinship system with the state—requires knowledge of a moral-practical kind, not technically useful knowledge . . . not an expansion of our control over outer nature, but a knowledge that can be incorporated in structures of interaction. . . . Thus, the development of forces of production can be understood as a problem-generating mechanism that *triggers, but does not bring about* the revolution of relations of production and an evolutionary renewal of the mode of production.[26]

But even with this emendation the thesis does not stand up to the empirical evidence. There are some cases (in Polynesia and South Africa for example), where the primitive communal order seems to have broken down as a result of an increase in productive forces; but the great developments that led to the rise of the first civilizations, or those that led to the rise of capitalism, did not have any noteworthy development of productive forces as a condition but only as a consequence. In the latter cases, the cognitive potential produced by the postulated learning mechanism (but not yet, or only marginally implemented) could be exploited for developing productive forces only when a new institutional framework and a new form of social integration had emerged.

The endogeneous growth of knowledge is thus a necessary condition of social evolution. But only when a new institutional framework has emerged can previously unsolved system problems be worked on with the aid of stored up cognitive potential—out of which there *results* an increase in productive forces. Only in *this* sense can the proposition be defended: that a social formation does not perish, and new, higher relations of production do not replace it, "before their material conditions of existence have been hatched in the womb of the old society itself."[27]

The fundamental question is now, How does the evolutionary step to a new form of social integration come about? How is it possible? The descriptive answer of historical materialism is through social conflicts, political struggle, and social movements (which, if they take place within a class society, can be analyzed as class struggles). But a theory of social evolution requires, in Habermas's view, an analytic response.

Only an analytic answer can explain *why* a society accomplishes an evolutionary step and how social struggles lead under certain conditions to a new form of social integration and to a new developmental level of society. The answer I would like to suggest is this: the species learns not only in the dimension of technically utilizable knowledge (which is decisive for the development of productive forces), but also in the development of moral-practical consciousness (which is decisive for structures of interaction). The rules of communicative action develop in reaction to changes in the sphere of instrumental and strategic action; but in doing so they are governed by a logic of their own.[28]

Although it is still in the process of being developed, the research program designed to carry through on this suggestion is sufficiently articulated to permit a sketch of its main outlines. The leading idea is that social evolution can be comprehended as a *learning process,* not in the sense of behavioristic psychology—which, Habermas feels, is not complex enough to grasp more than peripheral learning mechanisms—but in the sense of cognitive developmental psychology. Central to this approach is the notion of a *developmental logic* that incorporates a distinction between formally characterized levels of learning and the learning processes that are possible at each level. Drawing on these ideas, Habermas construes organizational principles of society as sociostructural innovations that institutionalize developmental-logical levels of learning; they establish the structural conditions for technical and practical learning processes at particular stages of development. Principles of organization circumscribe ranges of possibility within which institutional systems can vary, productive forces can be developed and utilized, and system complexity and steering capacity can be increased. The concrete embodiments of these abstract principles are the "institutional nuclei" that function as relations of production and determine the dominant form of social integration (for example, kinship relations in primitive societies, the political order in traditional societies, the economic system in liberal capitalist societies). Social evolution can then be thought of as a bidimensional learning process (cognitive/technical and moral/practical), the stages of which can be described structurally and ordered according to a developmental logic. "Collectively shared structures of consciousness are understood as levels of learning, i.e. as structural conditions of possible learning processes. Evolutionary learning consists then in the constructive acquisition of new levels of learnings. It is reflexive learning, i.e. learning applied to the structural conditions of learning.[29]

Habermas's explication of the key notions of a developmental logic and of levels or stages of learning are adapted from the Piaget tradition in cognitive psychology.[30] The idea underlying ontogenetic studies of this type is that the various abilities of the adult subject result from an integration of maturational and learning processes. These run through an irreversible sequence of discrete and increasingly complex developmental stages, whereby no stage can be passed over and each higher stage implies or presupposes the previous stages. (This does not exclude regressions, overlaps, arrested developments, and the like.) Stages are constructed wholes that differ qualitatively from one another; phase-specific schemata can be ordered in an invariant and hierarchically structured sequence; no later phase can be attained before earlier ones have been passed through, and elements of earlier phases are preserved, transformed, and reintegrated in the later. In short, the developmental-logical approach requires the specification of a hierarchy of structured wholes in which the later, more complex, and more encompassing developmental stages presuppose and build upon the earlier.[31]

Of course, ontogenetic models of developmental processes cannot be transposed without further ado to the domain of social evolution. There are numerous restrictions that have to be taken into account— for example, the fact that not all individuals are equally representative of the state of development of their society, or the fact that (since we are dealing with structures of adult thought and action) the ontogenetically earliest stages have no correlates in the interaction structures of even the earliest societies.[32] But the basic source of difficulty is clearly the notion that not only individuals but societies learn. Habermas provides at least an initial clarification.

Naturally we cannot draw any precipitous conclusions for the developmental levels of societies from ontogenesis. Social-evolutionary learning processes cannot be ascribed exclusively either to society or to the individual. Of course, the personality system carries the ontogenetic learning process; and in a certain way it is only socialized subjects that learn. But social systems can, by exploiting the learning capacities of socialized subjects, form new structures in order to solve critical steering problems. To this extent, the evolutionary learning process of societies is dependent on the competences of the individuals that belong to them. The latter, in turn, do not acquire their competences as isolated monads, but by growing into the symbolic structures of their life-world.[33]

The suggestion, then, is that the learning ability of individuals is the basis of "societal learning"; ontogenetic learning processes provide a "resource" that can be drawn upon in the formation of new social structures. At the same time, these processes are themselves conditioned by the developmental level of society. This is then a model of mutual interdependence.

Since the cognitive development of the individual takes place under social boundary conditions, there is a circular process between social and individual learning processes. One can, to be sure, ground a primacy of social over individual structures of consciousness in the fact that the rationality structures embodied in the parents/family must first be retrieved by the child (as he overcomes the preconventional stage) in the development of his interactive competence. On the other hand, the initial stage of archaic societies . . . could have been changed only through the constructive learning of socialized individuals themselves. It is only in a transposed sense that societies "learn."[34]

Under "society" Habermas understands "all systems which—through linguistically coordinated (instrumental and social) actions —appropriate outer nature in production processes and inner nature in socialization processes."[35] Since social systems are systems of action, the basic concepts of a genetic theory of action can be regarded in two ways: either as a conceptualization of the competences acquired in stages by subjects capable of speech and action as they grow into a life-world or as a conceptualization of the "infrastructure" of social action systems themselves. The development of this societal infrastructure can be traced in two dimensions: technical and practical.

Learning processes take place not only in the dimension of objectivating thought, but also in the dimension of moral-practical insight; accordingly, the realization of action is precipitated not only in productive forces but—mediated through the dynamic of social movements—also in forms of social integration. Rationality structures are incorporated not only in what strengthens purposive-rational action in technologies, strategies, organizations and qualifications, but also in the mediation of communicative action—in mechanisms for settling conflicts, in world views and in identity formations. I would even like to defend the thesis that the development of these normative structures is the pace-maker [Schrittmacher] of social evolution, because new organizational principles of society mean new forms of social integration; and these in turn first make possible the implementation of available, or the development of new productive forces, as well as the heightening of societal complexity.[36]

Accordingly a theory of social evolution of the type Habermas envisages would have to construct a developmental logic for both dimensions: productive forces and forms of social integration. For reasons mentioned above, he has until now focused his attention on the latter dimension. As to the former—productive forces—he has suggested a few possible points of departure for research: Gehlen's attempt to interpret technical development as if the human species had projected the elementary components of the behavioral system of purposive-rational action onto the level of technology, thereby successively relieving itself from and enhancing the corresponding functions, first of movement (hands and legs), then of energy production, finally of the sense apparatus and of the brain;[37] Moscovici's interpretation of the successive "models of nature";[38] and most importantly, Piaget's ontogenetic model for cognitive development generally (from preoperational through concrete-operational to formal-operational thought) and for the development of logical structures, hypothetical thinking, concepts of space, time, causality, substance, and so forth, in particular.[39]

But the development of productive forces cannot be grasped independently of developments in the forms of social integration (relations of production) and in the world views connected with them: "It is possible to depict the history of technics in the ontogenetically analyzed stages of cognitive development, so that the logic of the development of productive forces becomes visible. But the historical series of modes of production can be analyzed in terms of abstract principles of social organization only if we can specify which structures of world views correspond to particular forms of social integration and how these structures limit the development of profane knowledge."[40] Accordingly Habermas's recent efforts have been directed to working out a plausible research program for the development of forms of social integration.

Needless to say, this is an immense undertaking, which will require considerable time even to formulate the central problems and to delineate promising research strategies. For one thing, an integrated model of individual development has not yet been constructed. To do so would require a consolidation of several different—and heretofore largely disconnected—research traditions, and of the developmental models that have issued from them, models of cognitive, linguistic, moral, interactive, motivational, and psychosexual development.[41] Furthermore, there are a number of different aspects to the evolution of forms of social integration that would have to be analytically distinguished and investigated before a unified account of their interrelations could be worked out. Habermas suggests beginning with a distinction among the structures of world views, of social identities, and of legal and moral systems.[42] His own work has been concerned primarily with the development of legal and moral systems, and I shall confine my remarks to that dimension. It will serve as an illustration of the type of investigation he is proposing.

One reason for beginning with this aspect of social evolution is the considerable amount of work that has been done on moral development within the Piaget tradition, especially by Lawrence Kohlberg and his associates. Kohlberg's schema of the stages of moral consciousness can be summarized as follows.

I. *Preconventional level*—At this level the child is responsive to cultural rules and labels of good and bad, right and wrong, but interprets these labels in terms of either the physical or the hedonistic consequences of action (punishment, reward, exchange of favor), or in terms of the physical power of those who enunciate the rules and labels. This level is divided into the following two stages:

Stage 1: *the punishment and obedience orientation.* The physical consequences of action determine its goodness or badness regardless of the human meaning or value of these consequences. Avoidance of punishment and unquestioning deference to power are valued in their own right, not in terms of respect for an underlying moral order supported by punishment and authority (the latter being stage 4).

Stage 2: *the instrumental relativist orientation.* Right action consists of that which instrumentally satisfies one's own needs and occasionally the needs of others. Human relations are viewed in terms like those of the market place. Elements of fairness, of reciprocity, and of equal sharing are present, but they are always interpreted in a physical pragmatic way. Reciprocity is a matter of "you scratch my back and I'll scratch yours," not of loyalty, gratitude or justice.

II. *Conventional level*—At this level, maintaining the expectations of one's family group or nation is perceived as valuable in its own right, regardless of immediate and obvious consequences. The attitude is not only one of conformity to personal expectations and social order, but of loyalty to it, of actively maintaining, supporting and justifying the order, and of identifying with the persons or groups involved in it. At this level, there are the following two stages:

Stage 3: *the interpersonal concordance or "good-boy-nice-girl" orientation.* Good behavior is that which pleases or helps others and is approved by them. There is much conformity to stereotypical images of what is majority or "natural" behavior. Behavior is frequently judged by intention—"he means well" becomes important for the first time. One earns approval by being "nice."

Stage 4: the "law and order" orientation. There is orientation toward authority, fixed rules, and the maintenance of the social order. Right behavior consists in doing one's duty, showing respect for authority, and maintaining the social order for its own sake.

III. Postconventional, autonomous or principled level—At this level there is a clear effort to define moral values and principles which have validity and application apart from the authority of the groups or persons holding these principles, and apart from the individual's own identification with these groups. This again has two stages:

Stage 5: the social-contract legalistic orientation, generally with utilitarian overtones. Right action tends to be defined in terms of general individual rights, and standards which have been critically examined and agreed upon by the whole society. There is a clear awareness of the relativism of personal values and opinions and a corresponding emphasis upon procedural rules for reaching consensus. Aside from what is constitutionally and democratically agreed upon, the right is a matter of personal "values" and "opinion." The result is an emphasis upon the legal point of view," but with an emphasis upon the possibility of changing law in terms of rational considerations of social utility (rather than of freezing it in terms of stage 4 "law and order"). Outside the legal realm, free agreement and contract is the binding element of obligation. This is the "official" morality of the American government and constitution.

Stage 6: the universal ethical principle orientation. Right is defined by the decision of conscience in accord with self-chosen ethical principles appealing to logical comprehensiveness, universality and consistency. These principles are abstract and ethical (the Golden Rule, the categorical imperative); they are not concrete moral rules like the Ten Commandments. At heart these are universal principles of justice, of the reciprocity and equality of human rights, and of respect for the dignity of human beings as individual persons.[43]

Habermas wants to use this schema for the development of moral consciousness (or, more precisely, of its cognitive side, the ability to make moral judgments) as a clue to the development of moral and legal systems, for these represent attempts to resolve morally relevant conflicts on a consensual basis and without resort to manifest violence: "To the extent that action conflicts are regulated not with force or strategic means, but on a consensual basis, there come into play structures which stamp the moral consciousness of individuals and the moral and legal systems of societies. They comprise the core area of the aforementioned general structures of action."[44] The special institutions that maintain or reestablish an intersubjectivity threatened by conflict are to be distinguished from the institutions and norms that govern normal interaction (within the family for example). Furthermore it is necessary to distinguish the expression of structures of moral consciousness in the simple judgment of conflicts from that in the active resolution of conflicts. As in the case of individuals, different structural levels may be involved in the way a society operates in these different spheres. Thus, for example, in Neolithic societies the moral and legal systems relevant to conflict resolution operate at the level of preconventional morality (law of arbitration and feuds), while normal interaction is structured within the framework of kinship relations (at a conventional level); and although the world views of such societies often contain narratively articulated models of conflicts and their resolution that correspond to the conventional level of moral consciousness, these are not incorporated in legal institutions. On the basis of this distinction of the general structures of normal interaction from (morally relevant) structures of world views and of both from structures of institutionalized law and binding moral codes, Habermas sketches a "very tentative" schema for the development of forms of social integration.[45]

1. In Neolithic societies normal interaction is conventionally structured; mythical world views, which are still directly interlaced with the action system, contain conventional patterns of conflict resolution; the legally institutionalized regulation of conflicts is, however, tied to preconventional points of view (such as assessment of the consequences of action, compensation for damages, restoration of the status quo ante).

2. In archaic civilizations normal interaction is conventionally structured; mythical world views, set off now from the system of action, take on the function of providing legitimation for the occupants of dominant positions; conflicts are regulated from the standpoint of a conventional morality tied to the dominant figure who administers the law or represents justice (evaluation according to intentions, transition from retaliation to punishment, from group to individual liability).

3. In developed civilizations normal interaction is conventionally structured; there is a break with mythical thought and the formation

of rationalized (cosmological and monotheistic) world views containing postconventional moral representations; conflicts are regulated from the point of view of a conventional morality disengaged from the person of the ruler (expanded system of legal administration, law dependent on tradition but systematized).

4. In early modern societies certain spheres of interaction are structured postconventionally—spheres of strategic action (such as capitalist enterprise) are regulated universalistically, and there are the beginnings of political will-formation grounded on principles (formal democracy); legitimating doctrines are developed along universalistic lines (rational natural law, for example); conflicts are regulated from the point of view of a strict separation of legality and morality (general, formal, and rationalized law; private morality guided by principles).[46]

Even if this tentative sketch could be worked out in satisfactory detail and in accord with available empirical evidence and even if it were possible to show that it represented a developmental logic, (that is, to demonstrate the relevant hierarchical relations of dependence and interdependence among the different stages of morality and legality), it would clearly not yet be a theory of social evolution (or of one aspect thereof). Hierarchical structural patterns do not of themselves supply an account of how and why developments actually come about.

The systematically reconstructible patterns of development of normative structures . . . describe a *developmental logic* inherent in cultural traditions and institutional change. This tells us nothing about developmental mechanisms; it only says something about the range of variation within which cultural values, moral ideas, norms, etc. can be altered at a given organizational level of society and can find different historical expression. In its developmental dynamic this change of normative structures remains dependent on the evolutionary challenges of unsolved, economically conditioned system problems and on learning processes that are a response to them.[47]

The *explanation* of a transition from one social formation or principle of social organization to another (such as the rise of state-regulated class societies or of capitalism) requires—in addition to a structural description of the relevant *levels of learning*—recourse to *system problems* (which overburden the capacities of the old social formation), to societal *learning processes* (in which the "surplus" learning capacities of individuals are exploited and institutionalized in a new form of social organization), and to *contingent initial and boundary conditions* (which stimulate or prevent, support or hinder, further or limit these processes).

Societal learning is based on individual learning. Habermas suggests that the relevant learning mechanisms belong to the basic equipment of the human organism (whether and to what extent actual learning takes place, however, is dependent on contingent, in part phase-specific, empirical conditions). In the theory of social evolution, learning mechanisms play a role vaguely analogous to that played by mutation in the theory of biological evolution: they produce an evolutionarily relevant variety. Whereas individual learning processes—since they do not affect the genetic constitution of the organism—are unimportant for biological evolution, the results of learning at the socio-cultural level can be passed on as part of tradition. In this sense, cultural tradition serves as a medium for preserving and handing on variety-producing innovations. There are, of course, numerous disanalogies between genetic mutations and social learning; whether the comparison is anything more than a loose heuristic device can be decided only by the outcome of future research.

Whereas biochemistry has succeeded in recent years in analyzing mutation processes, the learning mechanism that underlies such a complex phenomenon as cultural tradition is almost unknown. Cognitive and analytic developmental psychology have made promising attempts in this regard, the former taking accommodation and assimilation as mechanisms for acquiring new cognitive structures, the latter taking identification and projection as mechanisms for building up a motivational basis. As long as these mechanisms are not sufficiently analyzed, however, we cannot judge whether the comparison between mutation and tradition is simply metaphorical, or whether the basic social learning mechanism exhibits a certain functional equivalence to the process of mutation. *One* difference ought to arouse our suspicion—mutation produces chance variations, whereas the ontogenesis of structures of consciousness is a highly selective and directional process.[48]

Whatever the outcome of ontogenetic research, a theory of social evolution is still left with the problem of explaining how what is learned by individuals or marginal social groups could eventually become the basis for a new principle or organization of society as a whole. Habermas's suggestion is that the results of evolutionarily relevant learning processes find their way into the *cultural tradition,* the world views and interpretive systems of society; in the form of empirical knowledge and moral-practical insights, they comprise a kind of cognitive potential that can be drawn upon by *social movements* when irresolvable systems problems require a transformation of the basic form of social integration.

Functionalism explains evolutionary advances by coordinating functionally equivalent solutions to system problems. It thus directs attention from the evolutionary learning processes which alone could have explanatory force . . . This [gap] can be filled with a theory of social movements . . . Of course, the action orientations that attain dominance in social movements are in turn structured through cultural traditions. If one conceives of social movements as learning processes through which latently available rationality structures are transposed into social practice, so that they eventually find an institutional embodiment, there follows the further task of identifying the rationalizing potential of traditions.[49]

In additon to available but not yet institutionalized levels of learning, Habermas's model points to unresolved *system problems,* which disturb the process of social reproduction, as an important initial condition of evolutionary advance. Whether and how problems that overburden the structurally limited steering capacity of a society arise is contingent. And whether and how this challenge is (or is not) successfully met by a change in the established form of social integration also depends on contingent conditions (while the question of how such evolutionary advances are at all possible requires recourse to developmental-logical considerations, learning is thus a necessary condition). For the analysis of systems problems themselves and of the specific forms of resolutions (among those which are structurally possible at a given organizational level), Habermas appeals to the concepts and assumptions of functionalist systems theory.

Social evolution proceeds at two levels insofar as it takes place both in processes of learning and adaptation *at each given* level of learning (to the point at which its structural possibilities are exhausted) and in those improbable evolutionary thrusts that lead to new learning levels. A society can learn in a constructivist sense, in that it takes up the evolutionary challenges before which the available steering capacity fails, and meets them by drawing upon and *institutionalizing* surplus individual innovative potentials (which are already latently available in world views). The first step in this process is the establishment of a

new form of social integration (via kinship, state forms of organization, universalized exchange and legal relations—with corresponding
collective identities such as tribe, empire, nation, etc.). Only this new
form of social integration makes possible a further increase in system
complexity—e.g. the social utilization of productive forces, the shaping of new organizational forms, new media, etc. It is here that
functionalist analysis becomes useful in explaining why individual
societies at a given level of development select different developmental variants—why, for example, the same principle of organization
(kinship) takes on the different forms of matrilinear, patrilinear or
bilinear kinship systems.[50]

It is obvious that this proposal for a theory of social evolution requires considerable clarification and development before it can be effectively "tested" against the available anthropological and historical
evidence. Habermas and his associates—especially Klaus Eder and
Rainer Döbert—have been attempting to refine the fundamental concepts and assumptions by applying them to particular problem areas.
Following is a brief summary of an explanation sketch that has been
developed to explain the transition from Neolithic societies to class
societies organized around a state. It serves as an illustration of their
approach.

a) *The phenomenon to be explained* is the emergence of a political order
which organizes a society so that its members can belong to different
lineages. The function of social integration passes from kinship to
political relations. Collective identity is no longer represented in the
figure of a common ancestor, but in that of a common ruler.

b) *Theoretical explication of the phenomenon:* A ruling position gives the
right to the exercise of legitimate power. The legitimacy of the power
cannot be based solely on authorization through kinship status; for
claims based on family position, or on legitimate kinship relations in
general, are limited precisely by the political power of the ruler.
Legitimate power crystallizes around the function of administering
justice and around the position of the judge, after the law is reorganized in such a way that it possesses the characteristics of a conventional morality. This is the case when the judge, instead of being
bound as a mere referee to the contingent constellations of power of
the involved parties, can judge according to intersubjectively recognized legal norms sanctified by tradition; when he takes the intention
of the agent into account as well as the concrete consequences of action; when he is no longer guided by the ideas of reprisal for damages
caused and of the restoration of a *status quo ante,* but punishes the
guilty party's infringement of a rule. Legitimate power has in the first

instance the form of a power to dispose of the means of sanction in a conventional administration of justice. At the same time, mythical world views also take on—in addition to their explanatory functions—justificatory functions, in the sense of legitimating domination.

c) *The goal of explanation* follows from this: The differentiation of ruling positions presupposes that the presumptive ruler shapes legitimate power by virtue of a conventional administration of justice. Thus the emergence of the state should be explained through the successful stabilization of a judicial position, which permits a consensual regulation of action conflicts at the level of conventional morality.

The explanation sketch runs as follows:

d) *The initial state:* I consider those neolithic societies in which the complexity of the kinship system has already led to a more strongly hierarchical organization to be the evolutionarily promising societies. They already institutionalize temporally limited political roles. Of course, the chieftains, kings or leaders are judged by their concrete actions; their actions are not legitimate *per se.* Such roles are only temporarily institutionalized (e.g. for warfare) or limited to special tasks (e.g. to provide for rain and a good harvest). Viewed socio-structurally, these roles have not yet moved to the center of social organization.

e) *Particular systems problems:* In the evolutionarily promising Neolithic societies systems problems arise which cannot be mastered with an adaptive capacity limited by the kinship principle of organization. This may be a matter of, e.g. ecologically conditioned problems of land scarcity and population density, or problems having to do with an unequal distribution of social wealth. These problems, irresolvable within the given framework, become more and more visible the more frequently they lead to conflicts that overburden the archaic legal institutions (courts or arbitration, feuding law).

f) *The testing of new structures:* A few societies which are under the pressure of evolutionary challenges from such problems make use of the cognitive potential in their world views, and institutionalize—at first on a trial basis—an administration of justice at a conventional level. Thus, for example, the war chief is empowered to adjudicate cases of conflict, no longer only according to the concrete distribution of power, but according to socially recognized norms grounded in tradition. Law is no longer only that on which the parties can agree.

g) *Stabilization through the formation of systems:* These judicial positions can become the pacemakers of social evolution. However, as the example of the African Barotse empire shows, not all promising experiments lead via such judicial functions to the permanent institutionalization of a ruling position, that is, to evolutionary success. Only under suitable conditions—such as, for example, the military victory of a tribe or the construction of an irrigation project—can such roles be permanently differentiated, i.e. stabilized, in such a way that they become the core of a political subsystem. This marks off the evolutionarily successful from the merely promising social systems.

h) *The emergence of class structures:* "On the basis of political authority the material process of production can then be uncoupled from the limiting conditions of the kinship system and reorganized via relations of domination " [*Eder*]. The ruler secures the loyalty of his officials, priest and warrior families by assuring them privileged access to the means of production (palace and temple economy).

i) *Development of productive forces:* "The forces of production which were already discovered in the Neolithic revolution can only now be utilized on a large scale: the intensification of agriculture and stock farming, and the expansion of the crafts are the results of the enlarged organizational capacity of class society. Thus emerge new forms of cooperation (e.g. in irrigational farming) or of exchange (e.g. in the market exchange between town and country)" [*Eder*][51]

The research program he is proposing has, Habermas contends, distinct advantages over competing evolutionary approaches. For one thing, it does not restrict attention to the synchronic analysis of existing structures as purely structuralist approaches tend to do but requires an investigation of structure-forming processes as well. For another, it focuses attention—as functionalist neoevolutionism (espoused by Parsons, Lenski, and Luhmann for example) does not—on variety-producing learning mechanisms at both the individual and societal levels. A specification of systems problems and of functionally equivalent possible solutions does not of itself *explain how* a social system actually acquires the capacity to solve these problems. The recourse to learning processes is meant precisely to explain why some systems expand their problem-solving capacity, while others fail in the face of similiar problems. Furthermore the directional criteria of progress typically invoked by neoevolutionists (for example, increase in system complexity or steering capacity through differentiation, functional specification, integration, and so on) are inadequate. Even at the level of biological evolution, an increase in the complexity of bodily organization or mode of living may be an evolutionary dead-end. What is needed here is a determination of the "inner logic" of a series of morphological changes or of an expansion of reaction potential. (Compare, for example, the role of the structure and development of the central nervous system in phylogenetic comparisons.) Similarly a developmental ordering of social systems requires a knowledge of the general structures and inner logic of social learning processes. ("The fundamental cognitive structures in which technical and moral-practical knowledge is produced corresponds to the central nervous system.")[52]

The interpretation of history as a directional process of cumulative learning might easily give rise to misunderstandings. It could, for instance, be read as implying that there is a corresponding and proportional increase in well-being, or decrease in suffering, at each stage. While Marx ascribed linear progress only to the development of productive forces (but conceived the development of productive relations dialectically), this evolutionary schema asserts learning and development for both productive forces and forms of social integration. Habermas warns us, however, that

the amount of exploitation and repression by no means stands in inverse relation to these developmental levels. Social integration that is achieved through kinship relations and secured (in cases of conflict) through preconventional legal institutions belongs, from a developmental-logical perspective, to a lower stage than social integration that is achieved through relations of domination and secured (in cases of conflict) through conventional legal institutions. At the same time, despite this progress, the exploitation and repression that is *necessarily practiced* in political class societies must be regarded as a regression in comparison to the less considerable social inequalities that are *allowed* in kinship systems. Because this is so, class societies are structurally unable to satisfy the need for legitimation which they themselves produce. Indeed, this is the key to the social dynamic of class struggle.[53]

Habermas's analysis of the "dialectic of progress" proceeds from the observation that new levels of learning not only expand the range of options but also introduce a new problem situation. Although a higher stage of development releases a society from problems specific to the previous social formation, it also creates new problems that— insofar as they can at all be compared to the old ones—may increase in intensity. In bringing certain diseases under control, for instance, medical progress creates the consciousness of contingency with respect to sickness in general, and this in turn means new "needs" and new forms of suffering.

The dialectic of progress manifests itself in the fact that with the acquisition of new problem-solving capacities new problem situations come to consciousness. . . . Suffering from unmastered contingencies takes on a new quality to the extent that we believe ourselves competent to deal with them rationally. This suffering is then the negative side of a new need. Thus we can attempt to interpret social evolution around those problems that are first called forth by evolutionary achievements.[54]

The prominent place assigned to the notion of a cumulative learning process that follows a developmental logic could give rise to other misunderstandings as well, for example, to the view that Habermas wishes to explain the history of the species through an internal "history of mind [*Geist*]," that he has simply dropped the materialist assumptions concerning the motor of historical development in favor of logical patterns—in short, that he has substituted "philosophical mystifications" for empirical, historical analysis. To forestall such misunderstandings, Habermas emphasizes that the rationally reconstructible, hierarchical patterns of increasingly comprehensive structures of rationality describe only the "logical space" within which structural formation takes place. Whether and when new structures are formed, however, depends on contingent circumstances. If this distinction is made, there is no need to impute necessity and irreversibility to the course of history; neither regressions nor arrested developments can be excluded a priori. With this in view, Habermas insists that the above-mentioned suspicions are groundless.

The analysis of the dynamics of development is "materialist" insofar as it refers to crisis-producing systems problems in the sphere of production and reproduction. It remains "historically" oriented insofar as it must look for the causes of evolutionary changes in the whole breadth of the contingent circumstances under which a) new structures are acquired in individual consciousness and transposed into world views; under which b) systems problems that overburden the steering capacity of society arise; under which c) the institutional embodiment of new rationality structures can be tried and stablized; and under which d) the new ranges of possiblility for mobilizing resources are utilized. Only after rationalization processes (which require a historical and materialist explanation) have taken place, can developmental patterns for the normative structures of society be given. These developmental logics betoken the obstinacy, and to this extent the internal history, of the mind. The procedures of rational reconstruction have their place here. My guess is that cognitive and interactive developments merely exhaust the logical range of possible structural formations that already emerged with the natural-historical innovation of linguistically established intersubjectivity at the thresh-hold to the socio-cultural form of life.[55]

The critical queries to which Habermas's conception of social evolution gives rise are legion. They begin with questions concerning the status of the ontogenetic theories upon which he draws, for the work of Piaget, Kohlberg, and the others is itself fraught with difficulties relating to fundamental concepts (for example, "stage"), to fundamental assumptions (for example, that ontogenesis follows a developmental logic), and to methodological procedures (for example, the extent to which these approaches incorporate a substantive, culturally rooted bias);[56] and they extend to questions concerning the applicability of ontogenetic models to social systems—the characterization of the infrastructure of society as a network of actions certainly does not suffice to justify this transposition. For various reasons (not the least of which are my own limitations), I shall leave the formulation and substantiation of these problems to others. In the concluding pages of this chapter, my remarks will be limited to a few general observations on the direction in which Habermas has taken critical theory.

There have been several significant shifts in his position on methodology. The original conception of "an empirical philosophy of history with practical intent" (section 3.1) stressed the inexpungable practical dimension of critical theory. Its theses were not first put forward theoretically and only subsequently translated into practice; rather the theory was guided at every step by its relation to practice. Thus the course of previous history, as well as the nature of the present situation were to be interpreted from the standpoint of the possible realization of a practical meaning. This meaning issued not from pure practical reason in general but from a historically situated practical reason, a reason rooted in the very social reality that was to be comprehended.

In *Zur Logik der Sozialwissenschaften,* the characteristics that distinguished critical theory from pure theory were retained but qualified (section 3.3). *On the one hand,* its historico-practical dimension was explicated in connection with the logic of hermeneutic *Sinnverstehen:* access to a linguistically structured social reality required the employment of interpretive procedures; and the interpretive process involved a mediation of what was to be understood with the interpreter's own life-world. Thus social inquiry was unavoidably rooted in the investigator's historical situation; it was "tacitly connected to his action-related pre-understanding" of that situation. As the discussion of Danto made evident, this connection extended to the work of the historian. Temporally provincial with regard to the future, he could interpret the past only from the horizon of his own life practice.

On the other hand, the hermeneutic, situation-dependent character of social inquiry was not absolute. The guiding preunderstanding of the investigator could be freed, at least partly, from the "dogmatics" of his own socialization process by building into it a theory of distorted communication, a functionalist analysis of the nonintentional, "objective" meaning of social life processes, and an investigation of the universal-historical context in which the transcendental conditions of theory and practice were constituted. Taken together these elements issued in the conception of a "historically oriented functional analysis," guided by an emancipatory interest and proceeding within the framework of a "general interpretation" of self-formative processes (section 3.5). The construction of a general interpretive framework made it possible to pursue a "theoretically" or "systematically generalized history" and thus to mitigate the radically situational character of a purely hermeneutic approach. Nevertheless the intrinsic relation of critical theory to practice remained: while the past could be systematically narrated, the future could be only practically anticipated. And since the confirmation of an interpretive framework depended finally on the successful continuation of self-formative processes (in the future), it was a practical as well as theoretical matter.

For historically oriented functionalism does not aim at technically useful information; it is guided by an emancipatory cognitive interest that aims only at reflection and demands enlightenment about one's own formative process. . . . The species too constitutes itself in formative processes that are precipitated in the structural change of social systems, and that can be reflected—i. e. systematically narrated—from an anticipated point of view . . . The end [of history] can only be anticipated, in a situation-bound way, in the experience of reflection. Thus the general interpretive framework, however saturated with previous hermeneutic experiences and however corroborated in individual interpretations, retains a hypothetical moment. The truth of historically oriented functionalism is not confirmed technically, but only practically, in the successful continuation and completion of formative process.[57]

Thus, despite the incorporation of an expanded theoretical framework, critical theory retained its distinctive practical and historico-hermeneutic features; it was still a mode of thought intrinsically related to the historical situation of the critic, to the "framework of his own life practice."

Although the problematic and frame of reference of *Knowledge and Human Interests* were new, the notion of a "materialistically transformed phenomenology" retained essentially the same combination of empirical and philosophical, systematic and historical, theoretical and practical elements (Sections 2.4, 2.5, and 3.4). Critical theory aimed at a reconstruction of the history of the species, a reflective appropriation of its self-formative process. And this reconstruction was not purely theoretical; it was also practical, interested, and historically rooted. In Habermas's terms, phenomenological self-reflection on the genesis of the knowing and willing subject extended the action-orienting self-understanding of social groups. As critique of ideology, it viewed the development of the forms of the manifestation of conscious—understood as constellations of power and ideology—from the anticipated standpoint of a form of social organization based on universal, undistorted communication. On the other hand, it was a systematically generalized and methodologically anchored self-reflection," it was based on a metatheory of communication and proceeded within an empirically supported general interpretive framework fashioned from elements of Marx and Freud.

Thus although Habermas retained the basic features of the original conception of an empirical philosophy of history with practical intent in the writings of the late 1960s, he shifted toward a more strongly theoretical program. His critical theory was still essentially historical but it aimed at a theoretically generalized history. It was still bound to the hermeneutic situation, but the construction of a general interpretive framework permitted a theoretically based and methodologically secured mode of interpretation. It was still practical and critical but the viewpoints of practice, the anticipated end-state of history, could be at least formally circumscribed in a theory of undistorted communication.

Methodology of Critical Theory

This shift toward a more strongly theoretical program became more pronounced in the course of the debate with Gadamer (section 3.3). After having embraced a number of fundamental hermeneutic insights, Habermas could distance himself from what he took to be the inherently situational and relativistic character of a purely hermeneutic approach only by further developing the theoretical side of critical theory. As my discussion of *Knowledge and Human Interests* indicated, this theoretical shift was also required in order to avoid the difficulties that beset the notion of self-reflection. The problematic conflation of critical self-reflection (on the particulars of a self-formative process) and transcendental reflection (on the universal and necessary conditions of speech and action), as well as the apparent need for a normative-theoretical basis of critique (itself free from the suspicion of ideology), led Habermas to introduce the notion of rational reconstruction as a form of pure theory. I argued there that this represented a certain break with his previous epistemological conception of the inseparability of knowledge and interest. In the present (methodological) context, we shall have to ask whether it also represents a break with his previous conception of the unity of theory and practice, for it is this notion of rational reconstruction that is employed to characterize the methodological status of a theory of social evolution.

In *Zur Rekonstruktion des Historischen Materialismus,* Habermas apparently understands the hypotheses he advances as theoretical statements in the strict sense. They are, to be sure, elements of an "empirical-reconstructive" and not of an "empirical-analytic" theory. Nevertheless they are not "practical hypotheses" but assertions that are to be tested in theoretical discourse. "The name 'theory of social evolution' already signals the claim that general hypotheses about an object domain are put forward and tested in a discursive attitude."[58] This is at first sight a decidedly different claim from that originally associated with the theses of an empirical philosophy of history with practical intent or that later raised in connection with a materialistically transformed phenomenology. The theoretical nature of the claim seems to exclude precisely the practical and hermeneutic dimension that made critical theory methodologically distinct from traditional theory.

That there has been a fundamental shift in Habermas's conception of critical theory is undeniable. For one thing, the hermeneutically situation-bound character of evolutionary theory is restricted to a *general* dependency of reconstructive theories on the *general* state of development of mankind.

Developmental sequences can be reconstructed only for those competences which are objectively accessible to us at the contemporary level of development of our society. In a similiar methodological context, Marx advances the idea that "labor" first became recognizable as a universal determination of social systems to the extent that, with the development of capitalism, it was established in the form of abstract labor and determined the social process as a whole. We cannot dismiss *a priori* the possibility that in the future structures other than the cognitive-instrumental and moral-practical structures of consciousness familiar today will be accessible to reconstruction—structures of which we presently have only an intuitive mastery. This circumstance restricts the validity claim of evolutionary theory to statements about learning processes that can be retrospectively known.[59]

Nevertheless within these limits, reconstructive hypotheses make claims to universal validity, that is, to a validity independent of a historico-hermeneutic standpoint: "For the development of a competence . . . there is only one correct theory; whether a presently accepted theory is replaced by a better one does not depend on the progress of events and on changed retrospectives."[60] It depends on theoretical and empirical considerations.

To this point, it indeed seems as if the theory of social evolution marks the abandonment of the originally asserted unity of theory and practice. That this is not entirely the case can be seen if we turn our attention from the retrospective reconstruction of past developments to the prospectively oriented analysis of contemporary society. Critical social theory does not exhaust itself in the construction of a theory of social evolution (the reconstruction of historical materialism); its primary aim remains a historically oriented analysis of contemporary society with practical intent (a reconstruction of the critique of capitalist society). And for this analysis the hermeneutic, critical, and practical dimensions are, as before, methodologically constitutive.

Evolution-theoretic statements about contemporary social formations have an immediately practical reference insofar as they serve to diagnose developmental problems. The requisite restriction to retrospective explanations of historical material is thereby surrendered in favor of a *retrospective projected from the perspectives of action;* the diagnostician of the present assumes the fictive standpoint of an evolution-theoretic explanation of a future past . . . . As a rule, Marxist explanations of developed capitalism also share this asymmetric postion of the theoretician who analyzes developmental problems of the contemporary social system with a view to structural possibilities that are not yet institutionalized (and perhaps never will find an institutional embodiment). From this can be seen that the application of evolutionary theories to a diagnosis of the present makes sense only in the framework of a discursive formation of the will, i.e. in a practical argumentation dealing with reasons why particular actors, in particular situations, ought to choose particular strategies of action over others.[61]

Habermas seems to have the following distinction in mind: *on the one hand,* the explanation of a past evolutionary development (one already completed) is an empirical-theoretical task. First, the description of the phenomena to be explained, of the initial and end-states of the transformation, is undertaken in a theoretical attitude; the respective principles of organization are characterized in structural terms and within the framework of a developmental logic. Second, the designation of unsolvable systems problems in the reproductive process of the old society is also undertaken in a theoretical-empirical attitude, that is, within the framework of a (transformed) theory of social systems. Third, since the development to be explained actually took place, the designation of the social groups that were the agent of transformation, as well as of the contingent circumstances in which they acted, can be approached as an empirical question. Of course it is not necessary (or usually even plausible) to regard the institutionalization of the new form of social organization as the fully anticipated and intended goal of social struggle. But the mediations between conscious goals and contingent circumstances, between intended and unintended consequences, between projected transformations and functional constraints, can also be empirically investigated. In short the construction of a satisfactory evolutionary explanation is, in all fundamental respects, a theoretical-empirical task.[62]

On the other hand, the analysis of contemporary society has an inescapable practical dimension. The developmental-logical specification of the present level of social organization, as well as the designation of problems (economic, political, sociopsychological, and so forth) inherent in the existing form of reproduction can perhaps be construed as theoretical-empirical tasks. But since we cannot know in advance the course of future development—whether these problems will lead to a regression, disintegration, or self-annihilation of contemporary society or whether they will be successfully resolved in a new social formation, and which particular institutional form this will take—we can only project the future practically, engage ourselves for it politically, and analyze the present in a prospective retrospective from the vantage points opened by practice. Thus, for example, the analysis of existing constellations of power and interest involves a hypothetico-practical moment.

A social theory critical of ideology can, therefore, identify the normative power built into the institutional system of a society only if it starts from the *model of the suppression of generalizable interests* and compares normative structures existing at a given time with the hypothetical state of a system of norms formed, *ceteris paribus*, discursively. Such a counterfactually projected reconstruction . . . can be guided by the question (justified, in my opinion, by considerations from universal pragmatics): how would the members of a social system, at a given stage in the development of productive forces, have collectively and bindingly interpreted their needs (and which norms would they have accepted as justified) if they could and would have decided on the organization of social intercourse through discursive will-formation, with adequate knowledge of the limiting conditions and functional imperatives of their society . . . The social scientist can only hypothetically project this ascription of interest; indeed a direct confirmation of this hypothesis would be possible only in the form of a practical discourse among the very individuals or groups involved. An indirect confirmation on the basis of observable conflicts is possible to the extent that the ascribed interest positions can be connected with predictions about conflict motivations.[63]

Our "provinciality with respect to the future" means that we cannot adopt a purely theoretical attitude toward it; We are forced to anticipate it practically. This places the critical theorist in the role of an advocate for a more human society, with all the situation-dependency, uncertainty and risks that this implies. The theory of social evolution does not alter the fact that "in a process of enlightenment there can only be participants."

Notwithstanding the retention of this hermeneutico-practical moment in the analysis of contemporary society, Habermas stresses what is new in his conception of critical theory. Thus, in "Geschichte und Evolution" he explicitly distinguishes his theory of social evolution not only from a philosophy of history but also from a universal (world) history; while universal history—itself a problematic notion—remains bound to a narrative framework (and thus to a particular hermeneutic standpoint), the reconstruction of social evolution is a theoretical undertaking. More revealing he also distinguishes it from a systematically generalized history: historical materialism is no longer regarded as a general interpretive framework, "which helps to structure a narrative presentation of history with systematic intent." The reasoning behind this reversal seems to be the following: Habermas continues to regard history, even systematically generalized history, as inevitably ("transcendentally") bound to a hermeneutical-practical standpoint; but he now understands historical materialism as a theoretical (reconstructive) enterprise; he can reconcile these two views only by introducing a separation of powers between the writing of history (as narrative) and the reconstruction of social evolution (as theory).

Historical research has an irreplaceable heuristic function in the *construction* of evolutionary theorems; and in the testing of these theorems, it has the equally irreplaceable function of gathering and evaluating data. But to these functions of historical *research* in a theory of social evolution, there correspond no tasks that the theory of social evolution could take on, conversely, for the *writing* of history. For evolution-theoretic explanations, let us say, of the transition to archaic civilizations (rise of the state) or of the transition to modern society (the differentiation of a market system and the complementary rise of the modern state based on taxation) not only do not *need* to be further transformed into a narrative, they *cannot* be brought into narrative form. In the framework of developmental theory, these transitions have to be thought of as abstract transitions to new levels of learning (which can be intuitively grasped, perhaps, as developmental stages in the formative process of the species).[64]

A narratively applied theory of evolution would . . . burst the reference system of historical writing and lead to a "theoretization of history." But "history" is a cognitive form in which theoretical knowledge is not organized, but only applied. Historical expositions are action-related knowledge; they lie at the same level as the contemporary historical consciousness. There exists between the historian and his audience no such gap as that between the participants in a discourse and actors.[65]

This separation does not seem to be entirely plausible. If one looks at the essential elements of an evolutionary explanation—structural descriptions of the "before" and "after," the specification of systems problems and relevant contingent boundary conditions, the designation of social movements that are the agents of change, an account of the testing and stabilization of new organizational structures, and so forth—it is not at all obvious that they could not figure in a "theoretically generalized history."[66] In any case it is clear that a successful evolutionary explanation of, say, the transition from feudalism to capitalism would not simply take its place alongside of existing historical explanations; it would have to claim, over against them, to be the correct explanation. If the theorist designates these problems, these conditions, these social groups, these features of traditional world views, and so forth as decisive for the transition, that cannot be a matter of indifference to the historian, who is after all concerned with the same factors of change.

I think that the relation of the theory of social evolution to narrative history (and thus of Habermas's recent ideas to his earlier views) can be clarified only if we carefully distinguish several different aspects of critical social theory. There is, first, a *developmental-logical schema* of the different stages of rationality. This is a hierarchical pattern of abstract structures that exhibit various internal relations (such as presupposition, generalization) to one another. Such a schema is not itself a narrative and its construction might properly be regarded as a theoretical task. But it is also not yet a *theory of social evolution*. The construction of such a theory requires that one employ the developmental schema, together with hypotheses about learning mechanisms, systems problems, social movements, and so forth, to explain the history of the species as a learning process. The focus here is on historical changes that can be regarded as "epochal innovations" resulting in new levels of learning. That is, the theory is designed to grasp transitions from one developmental-logical level of social organization to another.[67] Within the framework of evolution theory, such transitions are "thought of as abstract transitions to new levels of learning," as developmental stages in the formative process of the species. Thus Habermas is correct in stressing that the construction of such a theory is not identical with the writing of narrative history. The level of generality and abstractness, as well as the exclusive focus on profound structural transformations, indicate the theoretical nature of the task. Nevertheless as I have argued, even this very general reconstruction of human development has a narrative component: it is, after all, a developmental logical reconstruction of the *history* of the species.

It should be evident that the aims of a *critical* social theory are not exhausted in the construction of a theory of social evolution. Primary among these aims is the analysis of contemporary society; and this analysis requires both a practical and a historical orientation. It requires, that is, a critical, historical account of how we came to be what we are, a reflection on the particulars of our self-formative process.

In introducing the notion of rational reconstruction, Habermas stresses both its differences from and its relation to critical self-reflection; reconstructive sciences provide the theoretical basis for critical self-reflection. In the present context this means that the theory of social evolution supplies the theoretical framework for a critical historical account of the genesis of contemporary society and its pathologies. This account is itself not a matter for pure theory (whether reconstructive or empirical-analytical); it is rather a systematic history with a practical intent. In the language of *Knowledge and Human Interests,* it has the structure of a "dialectic of the moral life writ large," of a critique of ideology that "takes the historical traces of suppressed dialogue and reconstructs what has been suppressed."[68]

My point here is that the theory of social evolution does not replace the earlier conceptions of critical social theory as historically situated, practically interested reflection on a formative process. Rather it represents a further enrichment of its theoretical basis. In addition to a horizontal account of the structure of nondistorted communicative interaction, critical self-reflection can also draw on a vertical account of the development of structures of interaction. Despite this enrichment, however, critical theory—insofar as it is a theory of contemporary society—retains its essentially historical and practical nature.

The theory of social evolution contributes in other ways as well. For one thing, it locates historical changes in an evolutionary framework: history, with all its diversity and contingency, takes on the shape of a learning process. While we are accustomed to this perspective in relation to the development of technical knowledge and productive capacity, the history of morals and politics, of social organization in general, tends to be regarded as mere change. Habermas wants to insist that the *Gattungsgeschichte* exhibits learning in this dimension as well, that the history of the species is a formative process with an identifiable direction and a specifiable telos. Moreover this perspective becomes all important in the analysis of contemporary society. As we shall see in chapter 5, it permits Habermas to conceive of the crisis tendencies in organized capitalism in terms of a developmental logic and with reference to the possibility of overcoming them through learning.[69]

In short the theory of social evolution grounds a teleological reading of past history and provides the normative-theoretical basis for a historically oriented analysis of the present with an interest in the future.

Chapter 4

Foundations: A Theory of Communication

4.1 THE IDEA OF A UNIVERSAL PRAGMATICS

Time and again, at critical junctures in this discussion, it has been necessary to issue "promissory notes" referring to Habermas's theory of communicative competence. Thus in the concluding section of chapter 2, after analyzing the strain placed on the notion of self-reflection in *Knowledge and Human Interests*, I pointed ahead to the subsequent distinction between "critical self-reflection" and "transcendental reflection" or "rational reconstruction" of the conditions of speech and action. And after raising the issue of the normative basis of a critical theory that denies to philosophy its traditional status of a presuppositionless mode of thought, I indicated that the whole question of foundations was to be recast in communications-theoretic terms. Again, the controversy between Gadamer and Habermas turned on the question of whether it was possible to "go behind" dialogue in ordinary language to a theory of communication that might simultaneously provide a normative basis for critique. And the discussion of psychoanalysis as a model for critical theory pointed in precisely the same direction. In short Habermas's entire project, from the critique of contemporary scientism to the reconstruction of historical materialism, rests on the possibility of providing an account of communication that is both theoretical and normative, that goes beyond a pure hermeneutics without being reducible to a strictly empirical-analytic science.

In a way this is not surprising. The theory of communicative competence is a new approach to a familiar task: to articulate and ground an expanded conception of rationality. In this century the idea of critical theory was developed in opposition to the tendency to define reason solely in objectivistic and instrumental terms. The earlier members of the Frankfurt school were already concerned to overcome the empiricist split between "is" and "ought" and the separation of theory from practice that followed from it. I suggested in section 2.5 that they were not entirely successful. In his inaugural lecture of June 1965 at Frankfurt University, Habermas expressed his own concern with this problem, proclaiming that his theory of knowledge remained faithful to the "insight that the truth of statements is linked in the last analysis to the intention of the good and true life."[1] If it was not already clear at that time that his own attempt to establish this linkage would focus on language and communication, it became so shortly thereafter: "Today the problem of language has replaced the traditional problem of consciousness; the transcendental critique of language supersedes that of consciousness."[2] Regarded in this light, the theory of communicative competence is decidedly not a theoretical luxury in the context of critical social theory; it is a concerted effort to rethink the foundations of the theory-practice problematic. The success or failure of such an effort cannot be a matter of indifference to a social theory designed with a practical intent. As we shall see, Habermas's argument is, simply, that the goal of critical theory—a form of life free from unnecessary domination in all its forms—is inherent in the notion of truth; it is anticipated in every act of communication.

In this chapter, after sketching Habermas's theory of communication in a predominantly linguistic setting, I shall examine its implications for the theory of truth, for the foundations of ethics and politics, and for the theory of socialization.

Approaches to the "logical analysis of language" stemming from Carnap have tended to restrict their focus of interest to syntactic and semantic features of language in abstraction from its pragmatic dimension; the latter might be brought in subsequently by way of empirical (for example, psychological) rather than "logical" analysis. Similarly mainstream linguistics has delimited its object domain in terms of phonetics, syntax, and semantics, relegating the pragmatic dimension to the domain of such empirical investigations as psycholinguistics and sociolinguistics. According to Habermas, there is a kind of "abstractive fallacy" at work here:

The pragmatic dimension is brought in subsequently in such a way that the constitutive connection between the generative accomplishments of speaking and acting subjects on the one hand, and the universal structures of speech on the other, cannot come into view. . . . This abstraction of "language" from the use of language in "speech" [*langue-vs. parole*] . . . is meaningful. But this methodological step does not warrant the view that the pragmatic dimension of language from which one abstracts is inaccessible to a logical or linguistic analysis. . . . The separation of the two analytical levels: "language" and "speech," cannot be made in such a way that the pragmatic dimension of language is left to an exclusively empirical analysis.[3]

In his *Aspects of the Theory of Syntax* Chomsky draws a distinction between linguistic competence and linguistic performance. The concern of generative grammar is with the former to the exclusion of the latter:

Linguistic theory is concerned primarily with an ideal speaker-listener . . . unaffected by such gramatically irrelevant conditions as memory limitations, distractions, shifts of attention and interest, and errors (random or characteristic) in applying his knowledge of the language in actual performance. . . . To study actual linguistic performance, we must consider the interaction of a variety of factors of which the underlying competence of the speaker-hearer is only one.[4]

The justification for this separation of tasks is that "the actual use of language in concrete situations" (performance) is not susceptible to the same type of theoretical reconstruction as "the ideal speaker-hearer's knowledge of his language" (competence). More particularly what the ideal speaker-hearer knows about his language that enables him to use and to understand it—so far as this is restricted to phonetic, syntactic, and semantic components—can be reconstructed in a theory of (formal and substantive) linguistic universals, whereas the study of performance necessarily involves us with the extralinguistic, empirical, and contingent limiting conditions of actual speech.

Habermas's conception of a universal pragmatics rests on the contention that not only phonetic, syntactic, and semantic features of *sentences* but also certain pragmatic features of *utterances*—that is, not only language but speech, not only linguistic competence but "communicative competence"—admit of rational reconstruction in universal terms.

[Universal pragmatics] thematizes the elementary units of speech (utterances) in the same attitude as linguistics does the elementary units of language (sentences). The aim of reconstructive linguistic analysis is the explicit description of the rules that a competent speaker must master in order to form grammatical sentences *and to utter them in an acceptable way.* . . . The assumption is that communicative competence has just as universal a core as linguistic competence. A general theory of speech acts would thus describe exactly that system of rules that adult speakers master insofar as they can satisfy the *conditions for a happy employment of sentences in utterances*—no matter to which particular language the sentences belong and in which accidental contexts the utterances are embedded.[5]

In recent times there have been numerous and various initiatives in the direction of pragmatics: empiricist approaches, stemming from the work of Charles Morris, with both behavioristic and information-theoretic bents; Bar Hillel's pragmatic extension of the logical analysis of language; the examination in linguistics of presuppositions, conversational postulates, speech acts, dialogues, and texts; investigations of the logic of referring expressions by analytic philosophers; and the use theory of meaning stemming from Wittgenstein, among others.[6] In Habermas's view the most promising approach is the theory of speech acts based on the work of Austin and Searle; and it is this that he takes as the point of departure for his own theory of communicative competence. Following Searle he designates the speech act as the elementary unit of linguistic communication. A speech act is not a symbol, word, or sentence, or even the token of a symbol, word, or sentence; it is the "production or issuance of a sentence token under certain conditions," the employment of a sentence in an utterance.[7] Utterances can in general be analyzed into a "propositional content" and an "illocutionary force." For example, in the utterances: "I assert that *p*," "I promise that *p*," "I command that *p*," the same propositional content, *p*, appears with varying illocutionary force. Put another way, each speech act consists (in the "deep structure," not necesarily in the "surface structure") of two sentences: a dominating sentence—(such as "I promise (you)," "I assert (to you)," "I command (you)")—and a sentence of propositional content.[8] The dominating (or "performative") sentence establishes the illocutionary force of the utterance, the mode of communication between speaker and hearer, and thus the pragmatic situation of the dependent sentence. The dependent sentence, consisting in general of an identifying (referring) phrase and a predicate phrase, establishes the connection of the communication with the world of objects and events. The competence

Competence

of the ideal speaker, Habermas argues, must be regarded as including not only the ability to produce and understand grammatical sentences but also the ability to establish and understand those modes of communication and connections with the external world through which speech in ordinary language becomes possible. In contrast to empirical pragmatics (such as psycholinguistics and sociolinguistics), which investigates the extralinguistic, empirical, and contingent limiting conditions of actual communication, universal pragmatics undertakes the systematic reconstruction of general structures that appear in every possible speech situation, that are themselves produced through the performance of specific types of linguistic utterances, and that serve to situate pragmatically the expressions generated by the linguistically competent speaker.[9]

Before proceeding any further with the details of Habermas's reflections on communication, I should say a few words about the methodological status of "reconstructive sciences." Habermas uses this term to designate any undertaking aimed at the explicit, systematic reconstruction of implicit, "pretheoretical" knowledge. Familiar examples would be "the explication of a concept" as construed by Carnap, the logical analysis of propositions and arguments, and the logic and methodology of science, as well as Chomsky's conception of generative grammar. Roughly and in a general way, the task of disciplines of this type can be characterized in terms of Ryle's distinction between "knowing how" and "knowing that." The underlying idea is that acting and speaking subjects know how to achieve, accomplish, perform, and produce a variety of things without explicitly adverting to, or being able to give an explicit account of the concepts, rules, criteria, and schemata on which their performances are based. Thus one might produce meaningful statements, sound arguments, good theories, or grammatical sentences simply by drawing on one's implicit knowledge and abilities—that is, without knowing that one is thereby employing certain operations, applying certain standards, following certain rules. The aim of rational reconstruction is precisely to render explicit, in "categorial" terms, the structure and elements of such "practically mastered, pretheoretical" know-how.

There are a number of important points to be made concerning this type of undertaking.

1. The object doman of a reconstructive science is of a different order than those of the physical sciences; it belongs to the "symboli-

cally structured reality" of the social world (discussed in chapter 3).

2. Although all disciplines with a hermeneutic dimension investigate this order of reality, it is distinctive of the reconstructive sciences that they seek to disclose its "deep structure." That is, whereas many forms of meaning explication are concerned primarily with the semantic relations that can be read off the "surface structure" of a language (culture, form of life, and so on), rational reconstruction aims at revealing the system of rules underlying the production of meaningful symbolic configurations. Its goal is not a paraphrase or a translation of an originally unclear meaning but an explicit knowledge of rules and structures, the mastery of which underlies the competence of a subject to generate meaningful expressions.[10]

3. "If the pre-theoretical knowledge that is to be reconstructed expresses a universal know-how, a universal cognitive, linguistic or interactive competence (or sub-competence) . . . reconstruction is aimed at species-competences. Such reconstructions can be compared with general theories in their range and status."[11] Thus, for example, the linguist's concern with generative grammar, the logician's concern with relations of exclusion, implication, and consistency among propositions, the developmental psychologist's concern with cognitive schemata are not directed merely to special competences of particular groups or individuals but to universal competences of the species.

4. Although reconstructive sciences of the type of theoretical linguistics are empirical sciences, they differ in important respects from the sciences of nature. The data relevant to the formation and testing of reconstructive hypotheses are supplied primarily by the actual performances and introspective reports of competent subjects. As Chomsky puts it, the requisite information is "neither presented for direct observation nor extractable by inductive procedures of any known sort." Any proposal "must be tested for adequacy by measuring it against the standard provided by the tacit knowledge that it attempts to specify and describe;" it must "meet the empirical conditions of conforming, in a mass of crucial and clear cases, to the linguistic intuition of the native speaker." There is, in his words, "no way to avoid the traditional assumption that the speaker-hearer's linguistic intuition is the ultimate standard" for determining the accuracy of the linguists' proposals.[12] This is not to say, however, that the relevant tacit knowledge is always immediately available to the competent subject. It has to be drawn out by what Habermas calls a "maeutic" proce-

dure of questioning the subject with the aid of systematically arranged examples (through the use of suitable examples and counterexamples, of contrast and similarity relations, of paraphrases, and the like).[13] Thus the relation of reconstructive theories to everyday knowledge differs from that of the empirical-analytic sciences. The latter normally refute and replace our pre-theoretical knowledge of their object domains with a (provisionally) correct theoretical account. (*Eppur si muove!*) By contrast reconstructive hypotheses make explicit (rather than falsify) pretheoretical knowledge; their relation to their object domain resembles in this respect that of explicans to explicandum rather than that of explanans to explanandum. Finally while the relations of empirical-analytic theories to their object domains allow various interpretations—realist, instrumentalist, conventionalist—rational reconstructions necessarily make an "essentialist" claim: "If they are true they must correspond to precisely those rules that are operative in the object domain, i.e. that actually determine the production of surface structures."[14]

5. Although it is true, as Chomsky claims, that the reconstruction of a competence is a necessary preliminary to the study of its acquisition, his own maturational hypothesis (generative grammar represents an innate "language acquisition device") appears to Habermas to be too strong: "Within the reconstructive strategy a more plausible assumption is sufficient, viz. that grammatical theory represents the linguistic competence of adult speakers. This in turn is the result of a learning process that perhaps even follows a rationally reconstructible pattern in a way similar to cognitive development or the development of moral consciousness."[15] Thus, Habermas views the task of reconstructive sciences in two dimensions: the "horizontal" reconstruction of a few fundamental competences and the "vertical" reconstruction of the (genetic) logic of development of these competences. The two tasks are related but distinct; although the latter presupposes the results of the former, it involves—as we saw in Section 3.6—problems and methods peculiar to genetic-structural investigations.

6. In discussing *Knowledge and Human Interests*, I indicated that Habermas's recent work on foundations tended in the direction of a "transformed transcendental philosophy;" this phrase can now be read as "rational reconstruction of universal competences." Like Kant's transcendental philosophy, universal pragmatics aims at disclosing conditions of possibility, but the focus shifts from the possibil-

ity of experiencing objects to the possibility of reaching understanding in ordinary language communication. Moreover the strong apriorism of the Kantian project (the transcendental deduction) is surrendered in favor of a "relativized a priori," one that recognizes empirical boundary conditions, the phylogenetic and ontogenetic development of universal structures, and the structural interconnection of experience and action.[16] Kant drew a sharp distinction between transcendental and empirical analysis. Rational reconstruction, by contrast, is dependent on a posteriori knowledge:

On the one hand, the rule-consciousness of competent speakers is for them an a priori knowledge; on the other hand, the reconstruction of this knowledge requires that inquiry be made of empirical speakers— the linguist procures an a posteriori knowledge. . . . [He] cannot rely on reflection on his own linguistic intuitions. The procedures that are employed in constructing and testing hypotheses, in evaluating competing reconstructive proposals, in procuring and selecting data, are in many respects similar to the usual procedures of the nomological sciences.[17]

In short reconstructive sciences must be classified as empricial (although not empirical-analytic or nomological) sciences. This is particularly obvious in the case of genetic-reconstructive sciences (such as cognitive developmental psychology) in which assumptions about causal mechanisms and empirical boundary conditions have to be brought in to explain the development of various competences. For these reasons Habermas now prefers to drop the potentially misleading "transcendental" terminology in favor of that of "rational reconstruction."

In locating universal pragmatics on the semiotic map, the key distinction is that between "rules for the generation of sentences in any language" (grammatical theory) and "rules for situating sentences in any speech act" (universal pragmatics), "for the production of sentences according to rules of grammar is something different from an employment of sentences according to pragmatic rules that form the infrastructure of speech situations in general."[18] Briefly and as a first approximation, what Habermas understands by this infrastructure can be glimpsed through considering the "relations to reality" (*Realitätsbezüge*) that accrue to a grammatically well-formed sentence through its being uttered in a particular situation. The act of utterance, he maintains, situates the sentence in relation to external reality ("the" world of objects and events about which one can make true or false statements), inner reality (the speaker's "own" world of intentional experiences that can be expressed truthfully or untruthfully) and the normative reality of society ("our" social life-world of shared values and norms, roles and rules that an act can "fit" or "misfit" and that themselves are either "right"—legitimate, justifiable —or "wrong"). From this point of view, a speaker in uttering a sentence necessarily (but usually only implicitly) makes "validity claims" (*Geltungsansprüche*) of different types.[19] In addition to the claim that what he utters is comprehensible (grammatical in the linguistic sense), the speaker also claims that what he states is true (or, if no statement is made, that the existential presuppositions of his utterance's propositional content are fulfilled);[20] that his manifest expression of intentions is truthful (or veracious: *wahrhaftig*); and that his utterance (his speect *act*) itself is right or appropriate (*richtig/angemessen*) in relation to a recognized normative context (or that the normative context it satisfies is itself legitimate). The claim to comprehensibility is the only one of these claims that is "language-immanent"; the others place the speaker's utterance in relation to extralinguistic orders of reality.[21] Thus the pragmatic infrastructure of speech situations consists of general rules for arranging the elements of speech situations within a coordinate system formed by "the" world, one's "own" world, and "our" shared life-world. Accordingly the analysis of communicative (as opposed to merely linguistic) competence requires an account of the speaker's ability not only to produce grammatical sentences but

—to select propositional content in such a way that he represents . . . an experience or fact (so that the hearer can share the knowledge of the speaker);

—to express his intentions in such a way that the linguistic expression accurately renders what is meant (so that the hearer can trust the speaker); and

—to carry out a speech act in such a way that it satisfies recognized norms or accepted self-images (so that the hearer can agree with the speaker in these values).[22]

This conception of universal pragmatics, introduced here rather abruptly and without considering the grounds for its plausibility, will be elaborated in the remainder of this chapter. At present it might be helpful to have an overview of the principal lines of research it encompasses. These reflect the classification of the "pragmatic functions" of speech (which in turn reflect the different "relations to reality" sketched above) into the representative, the expressive, and the interactive.

Corresponding to the first function (and thus to the truth claim implicit in speech) would be an analysis of the universal and necessary (that is, not context-specific and variable) conditions for making statements about "the" world. This domain of research is already established within analytic philosophy as the theory of the elementary sentence, that is, of reference and predication. A pragmatics of the representative function of language would have to include an account of such pragmatic universals as deictic expressions of place and time, articles, and demonstrative pronouns, which form the reference system of possible denotations.[23] The competence to use language representatively is a precondition of the ability to make a distinction fundamental to the definition of any speech situation: the distinction between a public world (*Sein:* being, that which really is) and a private world (*Schein:* illusion, that which merely seems to be).

Corresponding to the second function (and thus to the claim to truthfulness or veracity) would be an analysis of the universal and necessary conditions for expressing the intentional experiences of one's "own" world, of transparently representing one's own subjectivity. This domain of research is today still theoretically underdeveloped. A pragmatics of the expressive function of language would have to include an account of such pragmatic universals as intentional verbs and certain modal verbs used to express intentional content. The competence to use language expressively is a precondition of the ability to make a second distinction that is fundamental to the definition of any speech situation: the distinction between the individuated self (*Wesen:* essence) and the various utterances, expressions and actions in which it appears (*Erscheinung:* appearance).

Corresponding to the third function (and thus to the claim to rightness or appropriateness) would be an analysis of the universal and necessary condition for linguistically establishing the interpersonal relations that constitute "our" world, a shared life-world based on the reciprocity of expectations. For this line of research the theory of speech acts provides a convenient point of departure. A pragmatics of the interactive function of language would have to include an account of such pragmatic universals as performative verbs and personal pronouns.[24] The competence to use language interactively is a precondition of the ability to mark a third distinction fundamental to the definition of any speech situation: the distinction between what is (*Sein*) and what out to be (*Sollen*).

It should be clear from this brief sketch that a complete universal pragmatics would have to integrate many of the concerns heretofore assigned to disparate and only occasionally related disciplines. A theory of communicative competence, (the ability to "embed" language in a network of relations to the different orders of reality) would thus provide a unifying framework for a variety of theoretical endeavors, ranging from the theories of knowledge and action to the theories of socialization and ideology. To put it rather roughly, since speech is the distinctive and pervasive medium of life at the human level, the theory of communication is the foundational study for the human sciences; it discloses the universal infrastructure of sociocultural life. Habermas's particular concern is with the theory of social action; for this the third aspect of communication (the establishment of interpersonal relations) is central. Thus his own work in universal pragmatics has been focused on a development of the theory of speech acts.

A striking feature of communication in ordinary language is its characteristic "double structure." If speaker and hearer are to reach an understanding, they must communicate simultaneously at two levels: "a) the level of inter-subjectivity on which speaker and hearer, through illocutionary acts, establish the relations that permit them to come to an understanding *with one another;* and b) the level of *experiences and states-of-affairs* about which they want to reach an understanding in the communicative function determined by (a)."[25] If we focus our attention on explicit speech acts in standard form, this double structure can be read off their surface structure, which consists of an illocutionary and a propositional component.[26] The illocutionary component consists in general of a personal pronoun in the first person, a performative verb, and a personal pronoun in the second person—for example, "I (hereby) promise you . . .," "I (hereby) command you . . .," "I (hereby) assert to you . . ." The appropriateness of the expression *hereby* is an indicator of the fact that performative utterances establish (*herstellen*) the very relation that they linguistically represent (*darstellen*) (Austin's "doing things in saying something").

From the point of view of a theory of communicative action, the keystone of the theory of speech acts is an explanation of the illocutionary force proper to performative utterances, that is, of their power to generate the interpersonal relations intended by the speaker. Following Austin and Searle, Habermas's analysis takes the form of an investigation of the necessary conditions for the success of a speech act. He understands these as the conditions under which its illocutionary force results in the coming to be of that interpersonal relation intended by the speaker. Success or failure in this respect is a question not merely of comprehensibility (in the linguistic sense) but of acceptability: "With an illocutionary act a speaker makes an offer that can be accepted or rejected.²⁷ Of course the concern of universal pragmatics is not with the variety of contingent reasons for which such an offer may in fact be rejected but with the general conditions that have to be met before a speaker can be said to have made an acceptable offer.

Austin's analysis of the "infelicities" that lead to "misfires" (misinvocations, misexecutions, misapplications, and the like) is developed primarily from cases of "institutional" (in Habermas's terms, "institutionally bound") speech acts (for example, baptizing, marrying, appointing, sentencing). In such cases the acceptability of speech acts is based on rules or norms that are a presupposition of the type of act in question. Habermas's concern, however, is with "institutionally unbound" speech acts, speech acts that do not presuppose *particular* institutions but can fit into a variety of institutional settings.²⁸ For these Searle's analysis of the types of conditions that must be met for a speaker to perform a given speech act "successfully and nondefectively" provides a more promising point of departure.²⁹ He groups these into "propositional content," "preparatory," "essential," and "sincerity" rules. Confining ourselves to the last three and speaking roughly, the preparatory rules determine the general context restrictions typical for a given type of speech act—for example, the "*sine quibus non* of happy promising" are that a promise is to be uttered only if the hearer *H* would prefer *S*'s doing *A* to his not doing *A*, and only if it is not obvious to both *S* and *H* that *S* will do *A* in the normal course of events. If conventional presuppositions of this sort are not met, the speech act in question is pointless.

The sincerity rules place certain restrictions, typical for a given type of speech act, on the psychological state of the speaker—for example, a promise is to be uttered only if S intends to do A. When a speaker lacks the psychological state expressed in his speech act—for example, belief in asserting, wish or desire in entreating, intention in promising, gratitude in thanking—the speech act in question is insincere.

The essential rules seem to be simply a paraphrase of the meaning of the corresponding performative verbs—for example the utterance of a promise counts as the undertaking of an obligation to do A; the utterance of a question counts as an attempt to elicit information from H; the utterance of a request counts as an attempt to get H to do A. But they are alike in containing the phrase *counts as*, and this, Habermas feels, is as it should be.

The essential presupposition for the success of a speech act is that the speaker enter into a specific *engagement*, so that the hearer can rely on him. An utterance can "count" as a promise, assertion, request or question if and only if the speaker makes an offer which, insofar as the hearer accepts it, he is ready "to make good"—the speaker has to "engage himself, that is to indicate that in certain situations he will draw the consequences for action. The kind of obligation constitutes the *content* of the engagement. This is to be distinguished from the sincerity of the engagement . . . hereafter I shall take speaker-engagement to include both a specific content and the sincerity with which the speaker is willing to enter into the engagement.[30]

In the case of institutionally bound speech acts, illocutionary force—the power to bring about the type of relation intended by the speaker—can be traced back directly to the binding force of established norms. In the case of institutionally unbound speech acts, illocutionary force derives instead from the "recognizable and sincere willingness of the speaker" to enter into the indicated relation, to accept its obligations, and to draw the consequences for action (for example, to regard a question as settled when a satisfactory answer has been given; to let an assertion drop when it turns out to be false; to follow a piece of advice oneself if one should find oneself in the same situation as the hearer). But how can the speaker's apparent engagement move the hearer to place his trust in the typical obligations undertaken by the former in the utterance of his speech act? What is the source of the illocutionary force connected with speech acts? At this point Habermas's reflections take a decisive turn. He argues that the hearer's confidence in or reliance on the seriousness of the engagement indicated by the speaker need not be merely a result of the power of suggestion; it can have a rational basis.

With their illocutionary acts, speaker and hearer raise validity claims and solicit their recognition. But this recognition need not follow irrationally, because the validity claims have a cognitive character and can be tested. I would like therefore to defend the following thesis: in the final analysis, the speaker can have an illocutionary effect on the hearer (and vice versa) because the speech-act-typical obligations are tied to cognitively testable validity claims that is, because the reciprocal bonds have a rational basis. The engaged speaker normally connects the specific sense in which he wants to take up an interpersonal relation with a thematically stressed validity claim.[31]

Thus "constative" speech acts (such as asserting, reporting, narrating, explaining, predicting, denying, contesting), through which we mark the distinction between being and illusion, thematically stress the claim to truth. "In the cognitive use of language the speaker proffers a speech-act-immanent *obligation to provide grounds.* Constative speech acts contain the offer to recur if necessary to the *experiental source* from which the speaker draws the *certainty* that his statement is true. If this immediate grounding does not dispel an ad hoc doubt, the persistently problematic truth claim can become the subject of a theoretical discourse."[32]

"Regulative" speech acts (such as commands, requests, warnings, excuses, recommendations, advice), through which we mark the distinction between what is and what ought to be, thematically stress the claim to rightness or appropriateness. "In the interactive use of language the speaker proffers a speech-act-immanent *obligation to provide justification.* Of course, regulative speech acts contain only the offer to indicate if necessary the *normative context* which gives the speaker the *conviction* that his utterance is right. Again, if his immediate justification does not dispel an ad hoc doubt, we can pass over to the level of discourse, in this case a practical discourse. In such a discourse, however, the subject of discursive examination is not the rightness claim directly connected with the speech act, but the *validity claim of the underlying norm.*"[33]

"Representative" speech acts (such as to reveal, expose, admit, conceal, pretend, deceive, express), through which—in conjunction with intentional verbs (think, believe, hope, fear, love, hate, want, desire, and the like)—we mark the distinction between the "real" self and the expressions in which it appears, thematically stress the claim to truthfulness or veracity.

In the expressive use of language the speaker also enters into a speech-act-immanent obligation, namely the *obligation to prove trustworthy [Bewährungsverpflichtung]*, to show in the consequences of his action that he has expressed just that intention which actually guides his behavior. In case the immediate *assurance* expressing what is *evident* to the speaker himself cannot dispel ad hoc doubts, the truthfulness of the utterance can only be checked against the consistency of his subsequent behavior.[34]

Thus the obligations immanent to speech acts can be met at two levels: immediately in the context of interaction—through recourse to experiential certainty, through indicating the relevant normative background, or through the assurance of what is evident to onself—or mediately—either in theoretical or practical discourse, or in a sequence of consistent actions.

Habermas sums up the "provisional" results of his investigation of illocutionary force as follows:

1. A speech act succeeds, i.e. it brings about the interpersonal relation that S intends with it, if it is
—comprehensive and acceptable, and
—accepted by the hearer.

2. The acceptability of a speech act depends on (among other things) the satisfaction of two pragmatic presuppositions:
—the existence of speech-act-typically restricted contexts (prepatory rule);
—a recognizable engagement of the speaker to enter into certain speech-act-typical obligations (essential rule, sincerity rule).

3. The illocutionary force of a speech act consists in its capacity to move a hearer to act under the premise that the engagement signalled by the speaker is seriously meant;
—in the case of institutionally bound speech acts the speaker can borrow this force from the binding force of existing norms;
—in the case of institutionally unbound speech acts the speaker can develop this force by inducing the recognition of validity claims.

4. Speaker and hearer can reciprocally move one another to recognize validity claims because the content of the speaker's engagement is determined by a specific reference to a thematically stressed validity claim, whereby the speaker, in a cognitively testable way, assumes

—with a truth claim obligations to provide grounds
—with a rightness claim obligations to provide justification
—with a truthfulness claim obligations to prove trustworthy.[35]

As early as 1965, in his inaugural lecture at Frankfurt University, Habermas had proclaimed that "the human interest in autonomy and responsibility [*Mündigkeit*] is not mere fancy, for it can be apprehended a priori. What raises us out of nature is the only thing whose nature we can know: *language*. Through its structure autonomy and responsibility are posited for us. Our first sentence expresses unequivocally the intention of universal and unconstrained consensus."[36] The theory of communicative competence is an attempt to make good this claim by reconstructing the normative basis of speech as a system of "universal and necessary" validity claims. As a first approximation, it can be said that the fundamental task of the theory is "to identify and reconstruct the universal conditions of possible understanding [*Verständigung*]."[37] The rationale behind this approach is that language cannot be comprehended apart from the understanding that is achieved in it. To put it roughly, understanding is the immanent telos or function of speech. This does not, of course, mean that every actual instance of speech is oriented to reaching understanding. But Habermas regards "strategic" forms of communication (such as lying, misleading, deceiving, manipulating, and the like) as derivative; since they involve the suspension of certain validity claims (especially truthfulness), they are parasitic on speech oriented to genuine understanding.

There is a further distinction to be drawn within the sphere of nonstrategic communication, one between speech that aims at bringing about an understanding and speech that takes place within the framework of an already achieved consensus. Although the former is more usual in normal intercourse, the latter—which Habermas calls a "limit case of social action"—has a priority for the purposes of analysis, since communication oriented to understanding (*verständigungsorientiert*) has as its goal precisely the attainment of consensus or agreement.

The motivation for my special attention to consensual action is that the constituents of action oriented to understanding can be more easily grasped in this limit case. I also believe that in action oriented to understanding, language finds the use for which it is fundamentally designed. In the end, the non-communicative [strategic,] use of speech in action oriented to success presupposes the communicative use of language.[38]

Thus the initial task of universal pragmatics is the reconstruction of "the general presuppositions of consensual speech actions [*Sprechhandlungen*].[39]

Summing up, Habermas appears to adopt the following research strategy: he uses the analysis of consensual speech as a basis for his analysis of speech that is oriented to achieving understanding and moves from there to the analysis of derivative (strategic) and defective (deformed) modes of speech. He uses the results of his analysis of speech actions to work out a general notion of "communicative action" (one that includes nonverbal action) with the aim of providing a suitable basis for social inquiry.

Confining ourselves now to consensual speech actions, Habermas's central thesis is that they rest on a background consensus formed from the reciprocal raising and mutual recognition of four different types of validity claims: the claims that the speaker's utterances are *comprehensible* and that their propositional contents (or existential presuppositions) are *true*, and the claims that the speaker is *truthful* or veracious in uttering them and that it is right or appropriate for him to be doing so.

The speaker has to select a *comprehensible* expression in order that the speaker and hearer can *understand one another;* the speaker has to have the intention of communicating a *true* propositional content in order that the hearer can *share the knowledge* of the speaker; the speaker has to want to express his intentions *truthfully* in order that the hearer can *believe in* the speaker's utterance (can trust him); finally, the speaker has to select an utterance that is *right* in the light of existing norms and values in order that the hearer can accept the utterance, so that both speaker and hearer can *agree with one another* in the utterance concerning a recognized normative background.[40]

It might be helpful to think of these validity claims as four different dimensions in which communicative interaction can break down or suffer disturbances. At the most basic level, if the very comprehensibility of one's utterances is questioned, communication can continue only if the misunderstanding is cleared up in the course of interaction (such as through explication, elucidation, paraphrase, translation, semantic stipulation). Assuming mutual comprehensibility, consensus is endangered if the truth of what one says is challenged. This kind of disturbance can be overcome within the context of interaction by pointing to relevant experiences, supplying information, citing recognized authorities, and the like. But it is possible for situations to arise in which the truth of what one says is challenged in so fundamental a way that communication either breaks off (and the involved parties go their separate ways, resort to force or enter into strategic competition) or is continued at a different level, that of theoretical discourse in which problematic truth claims, regarded now as hypothetical, are subjected to the force of argument and counterargument. Consensus is no less endangered if one of the interacting parties questions the intentions of the other (for example, by accusing him of lying, deceiving, misleading, pretending). If communication is to continue on a consensual basis, mutual trust must be restored in the course of further interaction as the good faith of each party becomes apparent through assurances, consistency of action, readiness to draw, accept and act on consequences, willingness to assume implied responsibilities and obligations, and so forth. Finally the consensual basis of communication is disrupted if one party's right to perform the speech acts he performs is called into question, on the grounds, for example, that his role or status does not entitle him to do so, or that his acts contravene accepted norms or conventions, fall outside established relational patterns, are inconsistent with recognized values. This type of disturbance can be removed within the context of interaction by appeal to recognized norms (that were, say, overlooked or misunderstood by the challenging party), accepted values, established authorities, and so on. But it is possible for situations to arise in which the rightness or appropriateness of one's speech actions are challenged in so fundamental a way that communication either breaks off (and there is a resort to force, strategy, or the like) or it is continued at a different level, that of practical discourse in which problematic norms, regarded now hypothetically, are subjected to the force of argument and counterargument. As we shall see in the following section, it is important for Habermas's argument that while all four types of validity claims can be redeemed (*eingelöst:* vindicated) within the context of interaction, the claims to truth and rightness are such that their vindication may call for "stepping out" of a given action context and "into" a discursive situation.

Consensual action takes place against an unproblematic background consensus. Speaker and hearer implicitly know that each raises and indeed must raise claims of these types; they suppose that these claims are rightly made, and they naively accept their validity. To say this, however, is not to underwrite a static model of social interaction. The typical case is that in which a common definition of the situation has to be worked out or "negotiated" by the parties involved; and this is a dynamic process.

The goal of reaching understanding [*Verständigung*] is the bringing about of an agreement [*Einverständnis*] that terminates in the intersubjective communality of mutual comprehension, shared knowledge, reciprocal trust and accord with one another. Agreement rests on the basis of the recognition of the four corresponding validity claims: comprehensibility, truth, truthfulness and rightness. . . . If full agreement, containing all four of these components, were a normal state of linguistic communication, it would not be necessary to analyze the process of reaching understanding under the dynamic aspect of *bringing about* an agreement. [But] the typical states are those in the grey area.[41]

Both forms of "communicative action"—consensual and understanding-oriented—must be grasped in relation to implicitly raised validity claims. In the former case interaction takes place on the basis of an already achieved common definition of the situation; it presupposes a background consensus that includes a "common recognition" of the validity claims raised by the involved parties; there is a supposition that they have been rightfully raised and have been or could be redeemed. In the case of the latter, the common definition of the situation is in the process of being worked out; interaction is aimed at achieving an agreement based on a common recognition of validity claims; the presupposition is that this can be done within the context of interaction and without a breakdown in communication. If the presupposition at the basis of both forms of communicative action—that the implicit validity claims are rightfully raised and can be redeemed—is suspended, the involved parties are faced with the alternative of breaking off communication altogether, switching over to strategic forms of interaction (such as conflict or competition), or raising communication to the level of argumentative discourse for the purpose of examining the problematic (hypothetical) claims. For ob-

vious reasons, this last choice occupies a preeminent position in
Habermas's scheme of things.

Inasmuch as normal interaction involves regarding the other as a
subject, it involves supposing that he knows what he is doing and why
he is doing it, that he intentionally holds the beliefs and pursues the
ends that he does, and that he is capable of supporting them with reasons if necessary. Although this "supposition of responsibility" is frequently (perhaps even usually) counterfactual, it is of fundamental
significance for the structure of human relations that we proceed as if
it were the case: "on this unavoidable fiction rests the humanity of intercourse among men who are still men."[42] When fundamental differences in beliefs and values block the initiation or continuation of
communicative relations, the possibility of discursively resolving these
differences takes on a particular significance. It represents the possibility of instituting or reinstituting a consensual basis for interaction
without resort to force in any of its forms from open violence to latent
manipulation; it represents the possibility of reaching agreement
through the use of reason and thus by recourse to, rather than violation of, the humanity of those involved.

4.2 ON THE LOGIC OF THEORETICAL DISCOURSE: TRUTH

In its many different forms the distinction between the attitude of
everyday life (*doxa*, opinion, common sense, the unreflected, uncritical, natural standpoints) and the theoretical attitude (*episteme*, knowledge, science, the reflected, critical, phenomenological standpoints)
has played a central role in the development of Western thought.
Habermas draws a related distinction between two different forms of
communication: communicative action (interaction) and discourse.
Whereas the validity claims that are unavoidably (even if only implicitly) raised with every speech act are more or less naively accepted
in ordinary interaction, their validity is regarded as hypothetical and
explicitly thematized in discourse. Thus discourse represents a certain
break with the normal context of interaction. Ideally it requires a
"virtualization of the constraints of action"—a putting out of play of
all motives except that of a willingness to come to a rationally
grounded agreement—and a "virtualization of validity claims"—a
willingness to suspend judgment as to the existence of certain states of

affairs (they may or may not be the case) or as to the rightness of certain norms (they may or may not be justified). In Habermas's terms, discourse is that "peculiarly unreal" form of communication in which the participants subject themselves to the "unforced force of the better argument," with the aim of coming to an agreement about the validity or invalidity of problematic claims. The supposition that attaches to such an agreement is that it represents a "rational consensus," that is, that it is the result not of the peculiarities of the participants or of their situation but simply of their subjecting themselves to the weight of evidence and the force of argument. The agreement is regarded as valid not merely "for us" (the actual participants) but as "objectively" valid, valid for all rational subjects (as potential participants). In this sense discourse is, as Habermas puts it, "the condition for the unconditioned."

This description of argumentative discourse is admittedly idealized; but it represents an ideal that has been operative in our tradition, not only in the lives of exemplary individuals but in the historical attempts to institutionalize discursive modes of examining certain types of validity claims.

It is only late in history that discourses have lost their sporadic character. Only when discourses are *institutionalized* for certain domains, to the extent that under specifiable conditions there exists a general expectation that discursive interchanges will be initiated, can they become a systematically relevant learning mechanism for a given society. In the course of social evolution, such institutionalizations of partial discourses specific to certain domains signify innovative achievements, rich in consequences, that would have to be explained in connection with the development of productive forces and the expansion of steering capacities. Dramatic examples are, firstly, the institutionalization of discourse in which the validity claims of mythical and religious world-views could be systematically questioned and tested; we understand this as the beginnings of philosophy in the Athens of the classical period. Secondly, the institutionalization of discourses in which the validity claims of the technically exploitable profane knowledge transmitted in the professions could be systematically questioned and tested; we understand this as the beginnings of modern empirical science, with precursors of course in antiquity and towards the close of the Middle Ages. Finally, the institutionalization of discourses in which the validity claims connected with practical questions and political decisions *were supposed to be* continually questioned and tested; in 17th century England, then on the Continent and in the United States, with precursors in the Italian cities of the Renaissance, there arose the bourgeois public sphere, and in connection with it representative forms of government—bourgeois democracy.[1]

It should be obvious that it is the institutionalization of this last type of discourse (practico-political) that is the guiding ideal of Habermas's critical social theory. Nevertheless he has devoted considerable attention to the elucidation of the structure of theoretical discourse, and with good reason; not only is an account of theoretical discourse itself a sine qua non of an adequate theory of truth, but it provides important clues to the structure of practical discourse. Although the types of questions dealt with in the two cases are importantly different, and although (as a consequence) the specific logics of argumentation exhibit crucial differences, at a very general level the structures and assumptions of theoretical discourse are also operative in practical discourse.

In his introduction to *Theory and Practice* Habermas situates the action/discourse distinction in the context of a response to certain objections raised against *Knowledge and Human Interests*. He is particularly concerned with the criticism that the theory of cognitive interests, by tying all forms of knowledge to "deep-seated imperatives" of human life, undercuts the notions of objectivity and truth. Anchoring cognitive schemata to action schemata in this way seems to amount to a new form of naturalistic reductionism (in the case of the technical interests) or sociohistorical reductionism (in the case of the others). What then becomes of the unconditional character usually associated with claims to truth? How can Habermas claim anything more than an interest-relative truth for his own theories? Doesn't his position involve him in the same type of difficulty that plagued, say, the radical pragmatism of William James? As a matter of fact, Habermas's way of avoiding these difficulties is not unlike that of another pragmatist, C. S. Peirce, who differentiated the action-related organization of experience (his pragmatist theory of meaning) from the argumentative process of settling truth claims (his consensus theory of truth). Briefly Habermas wants to draw an explicit distinction between problems concerning the "constitution" of different spheres of reality and those concerning the "redemption" of truth claims about these different spheres. His thesis is that although the structure of a given object doman—the basic categories and principles through which it is organized—and thus the fundamental truth claims referring to it, do indeed reflect an underlying cognitive interest, the testing of these claims in argumentative discourse warrants attaching to those that emerge unscathed the honorifics: "true," "objective," "valid," and so forth.

In previous investigations I have brought out the connection between knowledge and interest without making clear the critical threshold between communication which remains tied to the context of action and discourses which transcend the constraints of action. To be sure, the constitution of scientific object domains can be construed as a continuation of the objectivations that we undertake in the social lifeworld prior to all science. But the claim to objectivity genuinely raised by science is based on a suspension of the pressure of experience and decision, and it is only this that permits a discursive testing of *hypothetical* validity claims and thus the generation of *grounded* knowledge. Against the objectivistic self-understanding of the sciences, which refers naively to the facts, an indirect relation to action can be shown for theoretical knowledge, but nothing like a direct derivation from imperatives of life-practice (which I never asserted in any case). . . . The interests which guide knowledge preserve the unity of the respective system of action and experience vis-à-vis discourse; they retain a latent nexus of theoretical knowledge to action throughout the transformation of opinions into theoretical sentences and their translation back into action-orienting knowledge. But in no way . . . do they affect the difference between validity claims which are recognized as a matter of fact and those which are rationally grounded [*begründet*].[2]

To put this point another way, Habermas wants to distinguish two "transcendental" problematics: "the constitution of the objects of possible experience" and "the argumentative vindication of validity claims."[3] This can be understood as a twofold revision of the Kantian enterprise. *In the first place,* the overthrow of Newtonian physics and the fallibilistic-melioristic view of the nature of science that has resulted means that an account of the "a priori of experience" can no longer be regarded as being at the same time an account of the conditions for the truth of theoretical statements. In Kant's scheme this entailment followed from "the highest principle of all synthetic judgments": "that the conditions of the possibility of experience in general are likewise conditions of the possibility of objects of experience, and that for this reason they have objective validity in a synthetic a priori judgment."[4] But this can no longer be maintained, since

the objectivity of experience could only be a sufficient condition of truth . . . if we did not have to understand theoretical progress as a critical development of theory languages which interpret the scientific object domain more and more "adequately." The "adequacy" of a theory language is a function of the truth of those theorems (theoretical statements) that can be formulated in that language. If we did not redeem these truth claims through argumentative reasoning, relying instead on verification through experience alone, then theoretical progress would have to be conceived as the production of *new* experience, and not as a reinterpretation of the *same* experience. It is therefore more plausible to assume that the objectivity of experience guarantees not the *truth* of a corresponding statement, but the *identity* of experience in the various statements interpreting that experience.[5]

In the second place, even the analysis of the necessary conditions for experiencing something objectively cannot be carried through on Kantian presuppositions. The subject of experience is not a transcendental ego outfitted from the start with a priori forms of intuition and categories of understanding. It is an empirical subject that develops only by acting on the world and interacting with other subjects. Consequently the constitution of a world of objects of possible experience has to be viewed as the result of a "systematic interplay of sense reception, action and linguistic representation."

Descriptive statements with empirical content belong to a language with a specific grammar: either to a thing-event language or to an intentional language which, in addition to expressions for things and events, also permits expressions for persons and their utterances. In analyzing the syntax of the languages, we encounter the categories that give a priori structure to the object domain of possible experience. . . . We impute to our sensory experiences an object domain of bodies-in-motion and to our communicative experiences an object domain of speaking and acting subjects (which is always coordinated with the domain of perceptible objects). Object domains represent systems of fundamental concepts in which possible experiences must be capable of being organized and formulated as opinions. In the case of the organization of experiences with objects, we can view the fundamental concepts as cognitive schemata; in the case of the formulation of opinions about objects of experience, we can view them as semantic categories. The connection between these two levels of experience and language is apparently established through action, that is through instrumental or through communicative action.[6]

With regard to these two "transcendental" problematics (which, although analytically distinguishable, obviously have to be integrated in a theory of knowledge), Habermas has concentrated his energies almost exclusively on the development of an account of truth in terms of the logic of theoretical discourse. Concerning the "constitution theory of experience" he has merely supplied a number of programmatic suggestions. But they are sufficiently interesting to warrant brief mention here.

1. He agrees with the analytic Kant reception (for example by Strawson) that the notion of the "transcendental" can be retained only in a reduced sense, that is (roughly speaking) without the claims attached to the transcendental deduction. Every coherent experience is organized in a network of categories; insofar as we discover the same system of fundamental concepts behind every experience, we can regard them as "quasi-transcendental." But he does not agree that this entails a restriction to logico-semantic analysis (that is, a renunciation of the concept of "constitution"). The universal-pragmatic analysis of the employment of these concepts may be regarded as a transformed "constitution theory of experience."[7]

2. The keystone of this theory is an account of the conditions of possibility of employing propositional contents in speech acts, more particularly of successfully referring to objects in the world and making predications of them (that is, a pragmatics of the elementary sentence). Here Habermas suggests that successful reference—the use of deietic expressions, demonstrative pronouns, denotative expressions in general—presupposes a mastery of the concepts of space, time, substance, and causality:

When we identify objects about which we state something (on the basis of experience we have had), we do so either ostensively or by means of names and characterizations. It is true, predicative determinations are not used predicatively in the context of denotative expressions. But a properly functioning system of reference has to have a certain propositional content. This minimum content of properties which objects as such have is the categorial framework for objectivating experience-able happenings as happenings. In this respect, Piaget's cognitive developmental psychology has confirmed Kant's analyses; the basic notions of substance, space, time and causality are the minimum conditions for determining a system of reference for objects of possible experience.[8]

3. Although this reference system functions for both the object domain of "bodies-in-motion" and that of "acting and speaking persons," the categories are—to use a Kantian term—"schematized" differently in the two cases; the underlying rules for identifying things and events are different but coordinated with those for identifying persons and their utterances (or cultural objects).

The sense of substance and causality, of space and time, is differentiated according to whether these categories are applied to objects within a world or to the linguistically constituted world of speaking subjects itself. The interpretive schema "substance" has a different meaning for the identity of objects that can be clearly categorized analytically than it does for speaking and acting subjects whose ego-identity cannot be grasped with clear-cut analytic operations. The interpretive schema "causality," when applied to observable events, leads to the concept of "cause"; when applied to a nexus of intentional actions, it leads to the concept of "motive." Analogously, space and time are schematized differently in regard to the physically measurable properties of objects and events than they are in regard to the intersubjective experience of contexts of symbolically mediated interactions. In the first case the categories serve as a coordinate system for observation controlled by the success of instrumental action; in the latter case they serve as a frame of reference for the subjective experience of social space and historical time.[9]

In the one case we have a reference system for empirical *descriptions*, in the other a reference system for *narratives*.

4. It seems likely that this basic conceptual structure of possible experience developed phylogenetically and that it arises anew in every normal ontogenesis. Thus developmental studies of the type pursued by Piaget will have to be integrated into any adequate analysis of the "a priori of experience." We require not only a reconstruction of the competence to refer to and predicate successfully but an account of the acquisition of this competence.

5. Piaget's studies of cognitive development underline the relation between cognitive schemata and action systems that is stressed by Habermas. "The universality of the reference systems within which we objectify reality arises from the development of cognitive operations related to the manipulation of physical objects (things and events). The child learns the logic of using denotative expressions through concrete operations . . . and not immediately with grammati-

cal functions."[10] Similarly the mastery of the reference system for persons and their utterances—including the ability to employ personal pronouns and performative verbs—has to be viewed in relation to communicative experience and the development of interactive competence.

The use of categories like "bodies-in-motion" or "acting and speaking individuals" implies an a priori relation to action such that "observable bodies" are simultaneously "instrumentally manipulable" bodies; whereas "understandable persons" are simultaneously "participants in linguistically mediated interaction," hence something which can be both an object of instrumental action and a counterpart in interactions. We create the two fundamental object domains by "schematizing" the same set of categories (or cognitive schemata) either in the realms of instrumental or of communicative action. A conceptual analysis of the objects of sensory and communicative experience on the one hand, and of the objects of instrumental and communicative action on the other, would have to confirm the existence of such a *transcendental* link between experience and action.[11]

6. The differences in the "categorial meaning" of statements referring to the different object domains of "action-related experience" carry over into the logics of inquiry. They are reflected in the different procedures for acquiring data and forming concepts, for constructing and testing theories, as well as in the different types of application appropriate to the theoretical knowledge gained. Nevertheless despite these categorial and methodological differences, the "unity of reason" is preserved at the level of discourse.

The a priori of experience (the structure of objects of possible experience) is independent of the a priori of argumentative reason (the conditions of possible discourse). However *both* serve to define the boundaries of empirical scientific theories. . . . Theories can only be constructed and developed under the *conditions* of argumentation and at the same time within the *limits* of the prior objectivation of experienciable happenings . . . [that is] in the form of discursively examined systems of propositions [and] in a theoretical language whose fundamental predicates remain tied to independently constituted objects of possible experience. The theory languages, which undergo a discontinuous development in the course of scientific progress, can *interpret* and in a certain sense even reformulate the structures of prescientific object domains; but so long as we are neither angels nor animals these languages cannot *transform* the structures into the conditions of another object domain . . . The *unity of argumentative reason-*

ing is compatible with this *differential meaning-constitution of object domains.* In all sciences argumentation is subject to the same conditions for the discursive redemption of truth claims. These conditions of a rationality that is not scientistically restricted can be elucidated within the framework of a logic of theoretical discourse.[12]

I shall turn now to an examination of this logic.

What Habermas calls "the cognitive use of language" occupies a special place in communication. In constative speech acts we explicitly thematize the propositional content of utterances while the interpersonal relations established through them remain in the background. (Thus the usual form of an assertion is p and not the more explicit, "I assert to you that p.") In the other modes of communication the propositional content is merely "mentioned"; but such "unasserted propositions" can be transformed into the explicit propositional content of assertions. And this transformation brings to the fore the most unmistakable and most universally recognized of the validity claims underlying communicative action: the truth claim. The logic of theoretical discourse is an analysis of the structure and conditions of that form of communication in which (hypothetical) truth claims are argumentatively examined and rejected, revised, or accepted. As such it is a "logic of truth," an examination of how claims about the world can be rationally settled.

Habermas's theory of truth is a much revised version of Peirce's consensus theory: "The opinion which is fated to be agreed upon by all who investigate is what we mean by the truth."[13] Habermas's version is:

I may ascribe a predicate to an object if and only if every other person who *could* enter into a dialogue with me *would* ascribe the same predicate to the same object. In order to distinguish true from false statements. I make reference to the judgment of others—in fact to the judgment of all others with whom I could ever hold a dialogue (among whom I counterfactually include all the dialogue partners I could find if my life history were coextensive with the history of mankind). The condition of the truth of statements is the potential agreement of all others.[14]

The point of departure for his reflections is, however, not Peirce but the more recent Austin-Strawson debate.[15] He agrees with their common rejection of semantic theories of truth, which regard sentences, rather than statements or assertions, as properly true or false. He then goes on to argue with Strawson and against Austin that truth and falsity are properly predicated of statements not in the sense of particular "historic events" or "speech episodes" (utterances) but in the sense of what is said in constative speech acts. As Strawson puts it: " 'My statement' may be either what I say or my saying of it. My saying something is certainly an episode. What I say is not. It is the latter, not the former we declare to be true."[16] But for Habermas this asserted propositional content is only one side of the story; the other is precisely the "declaring to be true," the performative moment of constative utterances—statements derive their assertive force through being asserted. Thus, he argues, truth must be viewed in a pragmatic context as a validity claim that we connect with statements by asserting them; we claim that the asserted statements are true. What has to be clarified, then, is the "meaning of truth implied in the pragmatics of assertions."[17] And for this task it is necessary to examine not only the conditions under which statements are true but the conditions under which we are justified in claiming statements to be true. Although the two questions are obviously closely related, they appear at first sight to be distinct. A statement that I assert may be true without my being able to provide any rational grounds for holding it to be true. In this case I am making a claim that I cannot make good; I am unable to show that it deserves recognition from others. In this sense my claim is unjustified, ungrounded, or unwarranted. Now although this distinction between "p is true" and S's assertion that p is justified" clearly makes sense in the individual case, it is a far more difficult—and for the theory of truth, decisive—matter to decide whether it makes sense universally, whether we can ultimately separate the criteria for truth from the criteria for the warranted assertion, or "argumentative vindication," of truth claims.

On some views of truth this separation could be maintained. For example, if the criterion of truth were some kind of experience of certainty, it would make sense to say that p is true (evidently given in some sense) even if it were impossible to bring about an intersubjective recognition of its truth through appeal to supporting arguments. But this view of the matter is implausible for a number of reasons. In the first place, there is a privacy to experiences of certainty that contrasts with the intersubjectivity of claims to truth.

Validity claims are distinguised from experiences of certainty by virtue of their intersubjectivity; one cannot meaningfully assert that a statement is true only for a certain individual. . . . By contrast, the certainty of perception, the paradigm for certainties generally, always holds only for the perceiving subject and for no one else. Of course several subjects can share the certainty that they have a certain perception; but in that case they must say so, i.e. make the same assertion. I register a validity claim as something intersubjectively testable; a certainty I can utter as something subjective, even though it might give occasion to place dissonant validity claims in question. I *make* a validity claim; I *have* a certainty.[18]

If I report an experience by making a statement—say, a singular empirical statement of the form "S is p"—then the success of my assertion is ipso facto conditioned by rules of reference and predication that are not private. I enter a claim in the public sphere, and thereby subject myself to standards and rules that are not my private property. Put another way, even singular empirical statements contain general terms whose meanings cannot be exhausted by particular experiences. This is not to deny that "in the case of elementary empirical statements such as 'this ball is red' there exists a close affinity between the objectivity of experience and the proposition expressed in a corresponding assertion. One can perhaps say that the (discursively testable) fact that the ball is red can be founded in corresponding experiences (claming objectivity) with the red ball; or conversely that in the objective experience which I had with a red ball, the fact that the ball is red shows itself."[19] But it is to deny that there is no gap between sense certainty and warranted assertability: "Experience supports the truth claim of assertions. . . . But a truth claim can be made good only through argumentation. A claim founded [*fundiert*] in experience is by no means a grounded [or warranted: *begründet*] claim."[20]

As the history of science has shown, there is no direct route from perceptual experiences to theoretical constructions that would obviate all dangers of going astray. Even the most elementary components of the "evidence basis" are categorically interpreted ("theory-laden") and thus themselves subject to scrutiny, revision, rejection. This is not, of course, meant as a denial of the empirical basis of science but rather of the view that truth claims can be settled by direct appeal to sense certainty. "In asserting a state of affairs, I precisely do not assert an experience. . . . I can only draw upon structurally analogous experiences as data in an attempt to ground the truth claim embodied in my statement."[21] Or as Popper has put it: "It is only in the course of critical discussion that observation is called in as a witness."[22]

The separation of truth from argumentative discourse might also be maintained on the basis of one or another version of the correspondence theory of truth. In this case, it would make sense to say that p is true (it "corresponds" to reality) even if it were impossible to bring about an intersubjective recognition of its truth in critical discussion. But, Habermas argues, correspondence theories of truth are fraught with insuperable difficulties; they "attempt in vain to break out of the sphere of language."[23] The facts with which true statements "correspond" are not—as Strawson points out—"things or happenings on the face of the globe, witnessed or heard or seen"; they are "what statements (when true) state" and as such are "wedded to 'that'-clauses."[24] That is, the "correspondence" of statements with facts is not a correspondence between linguistically structured statements and a linguistically naked reality-in-itself. A statement p is true if it is indeed the case that (or a fact that) p. Both terms of the relation belong to "the sphere of language" — "the fact that p," has the same categorial structure as p. This is not to say that statements are (or rather need be) *about* language. What a statement is about is determined by its denotative component. Thus statements are about (or may be about) "things or happenings on the face of the globe." But what they state is "that" the thing or event referred to possesses the properties, features, and relations predicatively ascribed to it. And operations of predication, no less than those of denotation, are operations in language. They are successful at one level if the governing conventions of the language in question are properly observed. They are successful at another level if the language itself is appropriate or adequate to the object domain under consideration. As our theory languages change and develop, so too does our stock of available statements *and facts*. Correspondence theories of truth are not only unable to supply a criterion of truth (which statements correspond to reality?) independent of critical discussion; they are incapable of giving a coherent account either of the "reality-in-itself" to which true statements are said to correspond or of the relation of "correspondence" that is said to obtain.[25] (This history of philosophy is replete with discarded attempts to characterize the latter in terms of picturing, mirroring, correlation, congruity, likeness, and so forth; but "how can an idea be like anything that is not an idea?")

The conclusion to be drawn from this line of argument is that ultimately there can be no separation of the criteria for truth from the criteria for the argumentative settlement of truth claims. The question, Under what conditions is a statement true? is in the last analysis inseparable from the question, Under what conditions is the assertion of that statement justified? "The idea of truth can be unpacked only in relation to the discursive redemption of validity claims."[26] Accordingly Habermas's "logic of truth" takes the form of a "logic of theoretical discourse," that is, of an examination of the (pragmatic) conditions of possibility of achieving rational consensus through argumentation.

Consensus theories of truth are themselves open to a number of objections.[27] For one thing, they appear to rest on a "category mistake," a confusion of the meaning of "truth" with the methods for arriving at true statements. The meaning of "is true" when predicated of a statement is not on the face of it identical with the meaning of "there is (or can be) a rational (i.e. argumentatively grounded) consensus to the effect that the statement is true." Habermas opens himself to this type of objection by asserting at times that the *meaning* of the claim to truth is "the promise of attaining a rational consensus";[28] or that "it belongs to the nature of validity claims that they can be made good, and that through which they can be made good constitutes their meaning."[29] He defends himself by pointing out that he is not tying the meaning of truth to particular methods or strategies for gaining truth but to the "universal pragmatic conditions" of discourse in general. But it is not at all obvious how this move from specific strategies to universal conditions closes the prima facie gap in meaning between "true" and "capable of rational consensus." To defend his meaning-thesis Habermas would, I think, argue as follows. From a pragmatic viewpoint, the object of analysis is "true" not as a predicate of statements but as the claim that I raise when I assert statements. What is at issue, then, is not the semantic meaning of a word but the pragmatic meaning of an act, claiming to be true. And the meaning of a claim has to be analyzed in terms of the mode of its redemption, the way in which it can be made good.[30]

This may be somewhat more plausible, but it is certainly not obvious. Part of the problem of course is with the meaning of "meaning" itself. There is too much controversy in regard to the meaning of words and sentences to expect that its application to validity claims would be an easy matter. But I shall not pursue this issue here, since it does not seem to me that Habermas's "discourse theory of truth" stands or falls with this meaning-thesis. The formulation that he most frequently employs is that rational consensus is the ultimate criterion of truth, that is, that the settlement of truth claims depends on argumentative reasoning (and not on experiences of certainty or correspondence with a linguistically naked reality). One might grant that truth claims have to be justified discursively without granting that discursive justification is what is meant in claiming a statement to be true. And this seems to be sufficient for Habermas's point: that truth claims inherently point to the possibility of rational consensus.

A second objection frequently raised against consensus theories of truth is that "truth" is a normative concept and thus cannot be tied to the de facto achievement of consensus: not just any agreement that comes to pass can serve as a warrant for truth. This objection has to be taken especially seriously by Habermas in the light of his theory of systematically distorted communication. How can a discursively realized, "rational" agreement be distinguished from the mere appearance of rationality? Which are the criteria of a "true" as opposed to a "false" consensus? If there are no reliable criteria for deciding this question, then Habermas's discourse theory would simply have relocated the problem of truth without contributing substantially to its clarification. Furthermore if the criteria that serve to distinguish a "grounded" from an illusory consensus themselves require discursive justification, we are moving in a circle; if not, we have transcended the consensus framework in establishing it. The only way out of this dilemma, according to Habermas, is through a characterization of a "rationally motivated" consensus—one achieved solely through the "force of the better argument"—entirely in terms of the "formal properties of discourse." The term *formal* is not meant here in the usual, formal-logical sense. From the point of view of pragmatics an argument consists not of sentences but of speech acts, and the move from one stage to the next cannot be explicated in purely formal logical terms. The fundamental modality is not logical necessity or impossibility (contradiction) but the pragmatic modality of cogency (*Triftigkeit*). The guiding idea is that a consensus is "rationally motivated" or "grounded" if brought about solely through the cogency of the arguments employed (and not, say, through external constraints on discourses or through "internal" constraints built into the structure of discourse).

This proposal is fleshed out in two ways: first, through an examination of the levels of discourse, and, second, through an analysis of the "ideal speech situation" that is implicitly presupposed in discourse.

Borrowing from Toulmin, Habermas analyzes the structure of an argument into the conclusion that is to be grounded, that data that is put forward for this purpose, the warrant that establishes the connection between the data, and the conclusion (for example, a general law or principle) and the backing for the warrant itself (for example, observational and experimental backing for a hypothesis).[31] On the basis of this analysis he attempts a very general characterization of the conditions under which argumentation can lead to a rationally motivated or grounded consensus. His central thesis is that these conditions must permit a progressive radicalization of the argument; there must be the freedom to move from a given level of discourse to increasingly reflected levels. More particularly there must be the freedom not only to enter into a critical discussion, to seek discursive justification of problematic claims, and to offer and evaluate various arguments and explanations but also to call into question and (if necessary) to modify an originally accepted conceptual framework ("metatheoretical discourse"). That this is a necessary condition for the rationality of an eventual consensus becomes obvious once one recognizes that the cogency of an argument depends on the linguistic system in which it is formulated, in which data are selected and described, warrants are put forward and backed. As the history of science has shown, it is at this level that the most profound cognitive developments transpire.[32] An assertion that is warranted within one frame of reference may nevertheless prove to be unjustifiable because the frame itself is inadequate. Accordingly the ideal of a perfectly rational consensus must include the possibility of reflectively weighing the relative adequacy of competing frameworks. Failing this, whatever agreement is attained is susceptible to the charge of being merely contingent—contingent, that is, on the linguistic system in which it was achieved. At the most radical level of argumentation—the critique of knowledge—the boundaries between theoretical and practical discourse are no longer sharp. For here we must consider the question, What should count as knowledge? And this requires in turn a consideration of the role of knowledge in life, that is, of the basic interests that knowledge can incorporate. Only to the degree that there is the freedom to move from level to level of discourse is there a justification for regarding an eventual consensus as "rationally motivated." To the extent that these conditions are not met, that actual discourse diverges from the ideal, the agreement to which it leads is open to the suspicion of being merely contingent and thus unwarranted.

The very act of participating in a discourse involves the supposition that genuine consensus is possible and that it can be distinguished from false consensus. If we did not suppose this, then the very meaning of discourse would be called into question. In attempting to come to a rational decision about truth claims, we must suppose that the outcome of our discussion will be (or at least can be) the result simply of the force of the better argument and not of accidental or systematic constraints on communication. This absence of constraint—both external (such as force or the threat of force) and internal (such as neurotic or ideological distortions)—can, Habermas argues, be characterized formally in terms of the pragmatic structure of communication. His thesis is that the structure is free from constraint only when for all participants there is a symmetrical distribution of chances to select and employ speech acts, when there is an effective equality of opportunity for the assumption of dialogue roles.

From this "general symmetry requirement" there follow particular requirements for each of the basic modes of communication. In addition to having the same chance to speak at all (to initiate and perpetuate communication), participants must have the same chance to employ constative speech acts, that is, to put forward or call into question, to ground or refute statements, explanations, and so on, so that in the long run no assertion is exempted from critical examination. But the conditions under which rational consensus is possible—what Habermas calls the "ideal speech situation"—must ensure not only unlimited discussion but discussion that is free from distorting influences, whether their source be open domination, conscious strategic behavior, or the more subtle barriers to communication deriving from self-deception. Thus the symmetry requirements concerning the expressive and the interactive use of speech refer only indirectly to discourse and directly to the organization of interaction: to discourse are admitted only speakers who have, as actors, the same chance to employ representative speech acts, to express their attitudes, feelings, intentions, and so on so that the participants can be truthful in their relations to themselves and can make their "inner natures" transparent to others; to discourse are admitted only speakers who have, as actors, the same chance to employ regulative speech acts, to command, to oppose, to permit, to forbid, and so on, so that privileges in the sense of one-sidedly binding norms are excluded and the formal equality of chances to initiate and pursue communication can in fact be practiced. With these requirements the conditions for ideal discourse are connected with conditions for an ideal form of life; the notion of "pure" discourse (and thus the notion of rational consensus and thus the notion of truth) cannot be conceived apart from the conditions of "pure" communicative interaction. In this sense, the requirements of the ideal speech situation, in which discourse can lead to genuine consensus, include communication-theoretic conceptualizations of the traditional ideas of freedom and justice: "the truth of statements is linked in the last analysis to the intention of the good and true life."

This notion of an "ideal speech situation" presupposed in discourse is central to Habermas's efforts to provide moral-practical foundations for critical theory. I would like therefore to review the steps of his argument for the sake of rendering it somewhat more plausible than it might seem at first sight.

He begins by arguing that truth claims can ultimately be decided only through critical discussion and not through a direct appeal to sense certainty: "truth belongs categorically to the world of thoughts (*Gedanken* in Frege's sense) and not to that of perceptions."[33] This is a familiar and well-argued position in the literature on the theory of knowledge and the philosophy of science, and I shall say no more about it.

He then goes on to point out that if the agreement achieved in critical discussion is to provide a warrant for truth claims, there must be some way of distinguishing a rational consensus from a merely de facto consensus, for the claim to truth requires a stronger justification than our matter-of-fact agreement; it requires that we attach to our agreement the normative sense of being well grounded. We are claiming, in other words, that the evidence and arguments are such that any rational, competent judge would come to the same conclusion; that if anyone should disagree, we could—if only he would let himself be guided by the force of the better argument—bring him to agree with us. The criterion of truth is "not the fact that some consensus has been reached, but rather that at all times and all places, if only we enter into a discourse, a consensus can be arrived at under conditions which show the consensus to be grounded."[34]

This amounts to saying that the consensus that warrants the truth claim is "rationally motivated," due solely to the force of argumentation and not to contingent, extraneous factors. And this implies, Habermas argues, that none of the constitutive elements of the argument were systematically excepted from critical examination. If, for example, the discussion was such that the conceptual framework within which it transpired was simply taken for granted, the consensus arrived at would be open to the charge of being an insufficient warrant of truth—something that occurs regularly in the historical and anthropological examination of cognitive systems. Ideally this means that for a consensus to be regarded as perfectly rational—and thus as a sufficient warrant for truth—it must be able to withstand metatheoretical and epistemological scrutiny. The supporting discourse must be structured in such a way as to allow for freedom of movement to and from even the most reflected levels of argument.

If agreement is to be the product of a "rational will" (Kant), then the only permissible force is the "peculiarly unforced force of the better argument," and the only permissible motive is the cooperative search for truth. Thus the situation of discourse must be such as to exclude structurally constraints on argumentative reasoning— whether these be open or latent, conscious or unconscious. It must, in Habermas's words, be an "ideal speech situation."[35] This freedom from internal and external constraint can be given a universal-pragmatic characterization; there must be for all participants a symmetrical distribution of chances to select and employ speech acts, that is an effective equality of chances to assume dialogue roles. If this is not the case, the resultant agreement is open to the charge of being less than rational, of being the result not of the force of the better argument but, for example, of open or latent relations of domination, of conscious or unconscious strategic motivations. Thus the idea of truth points ultimately to a form of interaction that is free from all distorting influences. The "good and true life" that is the goal of critical theory is inherent in the notion of truth; it is anticipated in every act of speech.[36]

At first glance, this talk of an ideal speech situation appears to be wildly unrealistic. It seems clear that actual situations of theoretical discourse rarely, if ever, even approximate this purity. Hence it is important to be clear about the status Habermas assigns to it. In the first place, his argument is to the effect that this is an unavoidable supposition (*Unterstellung*) of discourse. He is ready to admit that this supposition is usually (and perhaps even always) counterfactual. Nevertheless it is made, and must be made, whenever we enter into discourse with the intention of arriving at rational agreement about truth claims; it is intrinsic to the very sense of doing so. That this is indeed the case is suggested by the fact that calling into question any of the components of this supposition ipso facto casts doubt on the rationality of the consensus arrived at and hence on the justification for the truth claim it supports. The charges, for example, that the outcome of a critical discussion was in some way determined by force or threats of force from the outside, or by a differential distribution of privilege or authority within, or by consciously or unconsciously strategic motivations on the part of any of the participants, or by the inability of any of them to know or to speak their mind or to "listen to reason," would normally be regarded as a challenge to that outcome. If any such charge could be substantiated, the consensus would no longer count as rationally motivated; it would not have been brought about solely by the force of argumentation but would bear the influence of extra-argumentative constraints. To that extent it would forfeit its right to be regarded as a warrant for truth. To state this in another way, in entering into discourse with the intention of settling a truth claim "on its merits," we suppose that we are capable of doing so, that the situation of discourse is such that only these merits will have force—that is, that we are in an ideal speech situation.

But even if we grant that this supposition is constitutive of the meaning of discourse, we know in retrospect that it is counterfactual, that the conditions of actual speech are rarely, if ever, those of the ideal speech situation. Indeed the space-time limitations, the psychological and other limitations of actual discourse seem to preclude a perfect realization of these conditions. Nonetheless this does not of itself render the ideal illegitimate, an ideal that can be more or less adequately approximated in reality, that can serve as a guide for the institutionalization of discourse and as a critical standard against which every actually achieved consensus can be measured. Our history is replete with ideals—religious, ethical, political, cognitive, artistic—that we know to be incapable of complete realization but that are no less effective in shaping social life. Habermas insists, however, that the ideal speech situation is not just an idea spun from thought and placed critically over against a deficient reality, for it is a supposition that must be made if argumentation is not to lose its sense.

The ideal speech situation is neither an empirical phenomenon nor a mere construct, but rather an unavoidable supposition reciprocally made in discourse. This supposition can, but need not be, counterfactual; but even if it is made counterfactually, it is a fiction that is operatively effective in the process of communication. Therefore I prefer to speak of an anticipation of an ideal speech situation. . . . The normative foundation of agreement in language is thus both anticipated and—as an anticipated foundation—also effective. . . . To this extent the concept of the ideal speech situation is not merely a regulative principle in Kant's sense; with the first step toward agreement in language we must always in fact make this supposition. On the other hand, neither is it an existing concept in Hegel's sense; for no historical reality matches the form of life that we can in principle characterize by reference to the ideal speech situation. The ideal speech situation would best be compared with a transcendental illusion were it not for the fact that . . . [in contrast to] the application of the categories of the understanding beyond experience, this illusion is also the constitutive condition of rational speech. The anticipation of the ideal speech situation has . . . the significance of a constitutive illusion which is at the same time the appearance of a form of life. Of course, we cannot know a priori whether that appearance [*Vorschein*] is a mere delusion [*Vorspiegelung*]—however unavoidable the suppositions from which it springs—or whether the empirical conditions for the realization (if only approximate) of the supposed form of life can practically be brought about. Viewed in this way, the fundamental norms of rational speech built into universal pragmatics contain a practical hypothesis.[37]

From this practical hypothesis critical theory takes its start.

4.3 ON THE LOGIC OF PRACTICAL DISCOURSE: MORALITY

It is not difficult to anticipate the general tenor of Habermas's treatment of the foundations of morality after following his discussion of truth to the point at which the fundamental norms of rational discourse became visible. He is concerned above all to argue (against noncognitivists) that practical questions can be decided rationally and yet to avoid the pitfalls connected with traditional ontologistic and naturalistic attempts to assimilate or reduce rightness claims to truth claims. His position is that the undeniable differences between the logics of theoretical and practical argumentation are not such as to banish the latter from the realm of rationality; that moral-political questions can be decided "with reason," through the force of the better argument; that the outcome of practical discourse can be "rationally motivated," the expression of a "rational will," a justified, warranted, or grounded consensus; and thus that practical questions admit of "truth" in an expanded sense of that term.

If rightness as well as truth can qualify as a discursively redeemable validity claim, it follows that right norms must be capable of being grounded in a way similar to true statements. In the philosophical tradition two views (among others) stand opposed. One was developed in classical natural law theory and says that normative statements admit of truth *in the same sense* as descriptive statements; the other has with nominalism and empiricism become the dominant view of today and says that normative statements do not admit of truth at all. In my view, the assumptions underlying both views are false. I suspect that the justification of the validity claims contained in the recommendation of norms of action and of evaluation can be just as discursively tested as the justification of the validity claims implied in assertions. Of course the grounding of right commands and evaluations differs in the structure of argumentation from the grounding of true statements; the logical conditions under which a rationally motivated consensus can be attained in practical discourse are different than in theoretical discourse.[1]

As the universal pragmatic analysis of the conditions of consensual speech revealed, claims to rightness are implicit in all of the different modes of communication. As an action, a speech act takes place against a background of recognized values and norms, roles and institutions, rules and conventions. The relationship established (or "offered") by the performative component of a given speech act can either "fit" this normative background by actualizing an established pattern of relations or clash with it. Thus it is possible for any speech act to fail or to be challenged on the grounds that it is "wrong" or "inappropriate" when measured against accepted norms. In the "interactive" use of speech, the proposed relationship and its normative setting come to the fore; "regulative" speech acts (such as commanding, ordering, refusing, prescribing, proscribing, permitting, recommending, advising, warning, appraising, evaluating) explicitly "invoke" the normative background in a way that, say, assertions do not. In the context of interaction, challenges to the rightness or appropriateness of a given speech act can be met by indicating the relevant norms, by clarifying misunderstandings in respect to accepted conventions, in short, by providing a justification for one's actions within an established normative framework. If the disturbance persists, if the legitimacy of the norms invoked is itself called into question, we are faced with the familiar alternative of breaking off communication, switching over to various forms of strategic interaction, or attempting to continue interaction on a consensual basis by entering into a critical discussion for the purpose of arriving at a rational agreement. Adopting this last option involves—as in the case of theoretical discourse—a willingness to put out of play all forces except the force of the better argument and all motives except the cooperative search for the "right" solution. The aim of practical discourse is to come to a rationally motivated agreement about problematic rightness claims, an agreement that is not a product of external or internal constraints on discussion but solely of the weight of evidence and argument.

As in the case of theoretical discourse, the absence of constraints built into the very structure of communication—and thus of factors that would render the outcome "contingent" on extra-argumentative influences—can be characterized formally in terms of a freedom to move from level to level of discourse. The conditions of practical discourse must allow for a progressive radicalization of the argument. In this case the problematic claim is the claim that a certain action—paradigmatically a command or evaluation—is right or appropriate: "In commands actions are required or forbidden with a claim to rightness. The opponent contests the rightness and asserts the wrongness of the action commanded. In evaluations, objects (events, performances, rules, etc.) are classified as good or bad with a claim to appropriateness. The opponent contests the appropriateness and asserts the inappropriateness of the classification."[2] What is called for is a justification of the contested claim. At a first (prediscursive) level, this can be provided by indicating the relevant data, the features of the situation that make this the "right" or "appropriate" thing to do or say, that is, the reasons for doing or judging things in this way in this situation. The warrant that establishes the connection between the proffered reasons and the problematic action or evaluation is in this case not a general law but a general norm or principle of action, or a general norm or standard of evaluation. In the context of ordinary interaction, the norms and standards appealed to are "existing" norms and standards, those accepted as legitimate, binding, or "in force." It is when such factually recognized norms are called into question that discourse proper begins. De facto validity is no longer a sufficient warrant of rightness for this "validity" itself is now regarded as hypothetical; the norms are regarded as "recommended" and therefore as "replaceable." Whether their claim to validity is justified is precisely the matter at issue.[3]

In practical discourse proper we advance and criticize "theoretical justifications" for problematic norms. The backing that is required here is not (or is not merely) that type of observational and experimental evidence used (inductively) to support hypothetical general laws. The relevant evidence is first and foremost the consequences and side-effects that the application of a proposed norm can be expected to have in regard to the satisfaction or nonsatisfaction of generally accepted needs and wants. As intersubjectively binding reciprocal expectations of behavior, "norms regulate legitimate chances for the satisfaction of needs."[4] Thus what has to be agreed upon in practical discourse is the justifiability of a recommended regulation of such chances. Of course the relation between descriptive statements about consequences for the satisfaction of needs and wants and the normative statements they are intended to back is not, and cannot be, a deductive relation. But as centuries of debate have shown, neither is the relation between observational-experimental evidence and general laws deductive. In both cases we have to do with "casuistic" evidence that renders a statement more or less plausible. We are dealing here with the pragmatic modality of cogency and not with the logical modality of necessity: casuistic evidence, in the form of cogent arguments, provides good reasons or grounds for accepting a proposed explanation or justification. In theoretical discourse the logical gap between evidence and hypothesis is bridged by various canons of induction. The corresponding function in practical discourse is filled by the principle of universalizability: "only those norms are permitted which can find general recognition in their domain of application. The principle serves to exclude, as not admitting of consensus, all norms whose content and range of validity are particular."[5]

The well-known differences between theoretical and practical argumentation stem from the fact that norms and values, roles and institutions, principles and conventions "exist" through being intersubjectively recognized as binding or valid. As long as this is the case they are "in force"; they possess "normative validity" vis-à-vis social actors. When challenged, however, the validity of norms, and thus their very existence, is placed in a state of suspension. Since factually existing norms can prove unjustifiable, and justifiable norms need not factually exist (actually be in force), the relation of practical discourse to social reality can be critical in a way that the relation of theoretical discourse to natural reality cannot. In one way, this makes the discourse model of rightness easier to establish than the discourse model of truth. Since we are not dealing here with an objectively existing external nature but with a mode of existence (normative validity) dependent on intersubjective recognition, the connection between consensus and rightness is initially more plausible than was that between consensus and truth. The principle of universalization gives expression to this connection: if there is to be a rationally motivated agreement concerning the "worthiness to be recognized" (*Anerkennungswüdigkeit*) of a recommended norm or standard, then the pattern of legitimate chances for need satisfaction that it represents must be something that all those potentially affected by it could want. In fact argumentatively achieved consensus is nothing other than a procedural realization of universalizability.

One might grant this inherent relation of normative validity to intersubjective recognition and ideally to consensus while denying that the sobriquet "rational" has a proper place here. If, for example, all needs and interests are irremediably subjective, it seems that any agreement concerning them could be at best a contingent compromise among competing, ultimately irreconcilable self-interests. Habermas is naturally concerned to meet this type of objection. He argues that there are not only particular interests but common or "generalizable" interests; and it is precisely the function of practical discourse to test which interests are capable of being "communicatively shared," (admit of consensus) and which are not (admit at best of a negotiated compromise). In the former case, if the consensus is based on an adequate knowledge of conditions und consequences and on a "truthful" perception by the participants of their "real" interests (and not on deception or self-deception), then it is a rationally motivated consensus. If the motivating force behind the agreement is a nondeceptive recognition of common needs and interests in the light of an adequate knowledge of existing (and effectible) conditions, likely consequences, and so forth, what grounds could there be for denying that the agreement was rational? Just these sorts of considerations are what we mean by saying that there are good or cogent reasons for adopting a recommended principle of action or standard of evaluation. The suspicion of irrationality seems to spring from a conception of needs and interests as themselves prerational or irrational, as irremediably subjective. But this conception either ignores or fails to appreciate the fact that at the sociocultural level "inner nature" is integrated into intersubjective structures of communication.

Language functions as a kind of transformer. When psychic processes like sensations, needs and feelings are integrated into the structures of linguistic intersubjectivity, they are transformed from inner episodes or states into intentional contents; and intentions can only be stabilized over time if they become reflexive, i.e. if they become reciprocally expected intentions. In this way sensations, needs and feelings (pleasure/pain) are transformed into perceptions, desires and gratifications/afflictions; the latter can remain merely subjective, but they can also come forth with a claim to objectivity. Perceptions of objects of experience are always expressed as objective, i.e. as *assertions*. Desires *can* be expressed as objective; in this case they claim to express generalizable interests justified by norms of action; they are expressed, that is, as *commands (or precepts: Gebote).* Similarly, to the extent that they can be objectified, gratifications are justified by standards of evaluation; they are expressed, that is, as *evaluations.* Assertions (declarative judgments), commands (normative judgments) and evaluations (evaluative judgments) all express an objective "content of experience." The objectivity of perception is secured by the intersubjectively shared structure of the objects of possible experience, whereas the objectivity of commands and evaluations is secured by the intersubjectively binding force of norms of action or standards of evaluation, respectively.[6]

Thus although interests and values can be merely subjective (as particular desires or private gratifications), they can also be generalizable (as shared desires or common gratifications). In the latter case, the normative or evaluative judgments that give expression to "reciprocally expected intentions" can claim a kind of objectivity; it is precisely this claim that is embedded in socially binding norms and standards. Given the nature of the claim, it can be made good only by unforced agreement on the part of those whose desires and gratifications are at stake.

This connection between "inner nature" and "linguistic intersubjectivity" makes it clear that a rationally motivated consensus can be achieved in practical discourse only if it is possible to call into question and, if necessary, modify an originally accepted conceptual framework (metaethical, metapolitical discourse). Here too the adequacy of the language system in which phenomena are described, data selected, and arguments formulated and criticized is a condition of the rationality of the consensus. The needs and feelings summoned to bear witness in practical discourse are interpreted needs and feelings; the range and character of the desires and gratifications that can be brought to bear on a moral-political argument are dependent on available interpretations.

The consensus-producing power of argument rests on the supposition that the language system in which the recommendations requiring justification, the norms, and the generally accepted needs cited for support are interpreted, is *adequate*. . . . We call adequate that language of morals which permits determinate persons and groups, in given circumstances, a truthful interpretation both of their own particular needs and more importantly of their common needs capable of consensus. The chosen language system must permit those and only those interpretations of needs in which the participants in the discourse can make their inner-natures transparent and know what they really want. . . . By virtue of its formal properties, practical discourse must guarantee that the participants can at any time alter the level of discourse and become aware of the inappropriateness of traditional need interpretations; they must be in a position to develop that language system which permits them to say what they want under given conditions with a view to the possibility of changing conditions, and to say—on the basis of a universal consensus—what they ought to want.[7]

The importance of conceptual frameworks for moral discourse, and the awareness that there are alternative frameworks, have been sufficiently emphasized by historical and anthropological research. And critical studies at both the psychological and social levels have impressed us with the possibility of systematic self-deception and the difficulty of "knowing what we really want." That all this is relevant for evaluating the rationality of a consensus about norms should be obvious; a discursively achieved agreement concerning the regulation of chances for legitimate need satisfaction can be "rationally motivated" only if the participants to the agreement can know and say what they really want. Deception and self-deception, conscious strategic behavior and unconscious distortion of communication are prima facie grounds for denying that a consensus is warranted, that it is the outcome solely of the force of argumentation.

Finally at the most radical level of practical discourse (corresponding to the critique of knowledge in theoretical discourse), it must be possible to reflect on "the dependency of our need-structures on the state of our knowledge and power—we agree on interpretations of our needs in the light of available information about the scope of what can be made and what can be achieved. Which classes of information will be preferentially pursued in the future is in turn a practical question, e.g. of the priorities in underwriting scientific research (political will-formation regarding knowledge)."[8] At this level the boundaries between theoretical and practical discourse tend once again to become indistinct. Whereas the critique of knowledge required a thematization of the interests underlying different forms of inquiry, the critique of moral-practical consciousness requires asking what we should want to know, and this depends in turn on what we can know. Theoretical and practical reason are inextricably linked; they are moments of a comprehensive rationality whose coherent development signifies the development of a rational will.

From the point of view of moral theory, this discussion of practical discourse is very general and rather thin; it clearly requires considerable development. Just as clearly, there are a host of objections that would have to be met along the way. I shall leave to others their formulation and evaluation. What I would like to do in the remaining pages of this section is suggest several angles of vision from which some of the strengths and weaknesses of Habermas's approach appear in sharper relief.

In section 3.2. I discussed Winch's version of the logic of social inquiry. He argued that the social scientist's access to his data, as well as his formulation and application of "more reflective categories," necessarily led through the participant's own way of viewing his world. Understanding the form of life in which an action was located proved, consequently, to be the fundamental level of social inquiry. And such understanding, Winch claimed, was much more akin to "tracing the internal relations of a system of ideas" than to "the application of generalizations and theories to particular instances." For "social relations between men and the ideas which men's actions embody are really the same thing considered from different points of view." In assessing Winch's argument, I emphasized that the problem of the relation of the social investigator's language to that of the group under investigation was left largely undiscussed in his book. However, in a later article; "Understanding a Primitive Society," Winch takes up this issue. He focuses on "the strain inherent in the situation of the anthropologist" who has to present an account of magical beliefs and practices that is intelligible by the standards of the culture to which he and his readers belong, "a culture whose conception of rationality is deeply influenced by the achievements and methods of the sciences, and one which treats such things as belief in magic or the practice of consulting oracles almost as a paradigm of the irrational."[9] This strain and the problems it raises regarding the universality of criteria of rationality has received a considerable amount of attention from philosophers and anthropologists.[10]

Winch defends what some have called the principle of charity or tolerance in interpretation and others a relativism that undermines all hope of discovering transcultural and transhistorical standards of rationality. In explicit opposition to the "intellectualism" of earlier generations of anthropologists, he argues that the investigator may not simply assume that he and his culture are paradigms of rationality; this inevitably leads to equating cultural difference with cultural inferiority, that is, to misunderstanding other ways of life as merely prescientific or protoscientific. He proposes instead that the anthropologist seek contextually given criteria according to which the alien beliefs and practices appear rational. This requires a sort of dialectical process in which, by somehow bringing the alien conception of intelligible behavior into relation with our own, we forge a new unity for the concept of intelligibility: "Seriously to study another way of life is necessarily to seek to extend our own—not simply to bring the other way of life within the existing boundaries of our own."[11]

This reaction to the practice of anthropologists who understood primitive societies in terms of the opposition between rationality and irrationality—or more precisely between "our" scientific rationality" and "primitive irrationality"—has seemed to many an overreaction. Winch has been accused (especially by critical rationalists of the Popperian persuasion) of defending a relativism that undermines any chance of developing forms of social inquiry deserving of the title "scientific," of placing different conceptions of reality and rationality on a par and thus beyond criticism. I have argued elsewhere that Winch's critics are partially correct but that they fail in the end to make their case against him.[12] They are right in arguing that certain basic elements of scientific thought—such as the fundamental principles of logic, some elementary mathematical concepts and inductive procedures, certain general structures of sensory experience—are historically and culturally universal. But they fail to make their case because it has to be shown that this "protoscience" must, on pain of irrationality, be stressed, developed, and expanded as it has been in our culture. And this involves in the end practical considerations. The question as to how far certain principles of thought are to be pressed, what place they should assume in our lives, which areas of life should be dealt with in which ways, cannot itself be decided by appeal to principles of scientific reasoning. It is, as Winch argues, ultimately a practical issue: how best to deal with the problems of human existence. The underlying weakness of most of the arguments against the relativity of standards of rationality is that they proceed from a notion of rationality restricted to the recognized canons of scientific reasoning. The case against relativism requires a more comprehensive notion of rationality, one that both incorporates a conception of practical reason and expands the conception of theoretical reason so that it is not reduced to "the" scientific method.

It is precisely this comprehensive notion of rationality that the theory of communicative competence attempts to develop. The claims to comprehensibility, truthfulness, rightness, and truth are universal presuppositions of communicative interaction. These claims and the modes for redeeming them, taken together and in their coherence, form the core of a more adequate conception of rationality, one that might plausibly be argued to be universal. On this view, the purest forms of theoretical and practical reason are those depicted in the models of theoretical and practical discourse. It is instructive to ask just how far the discourse model can go toward resolving the relativity debate surrounding cultural anthropology.

In "African Traditional Cultures and Western Science," Robin Horton presents a stimulating account of the ways in which magicoreligious thought is similar to scientific thought. He then goes on to point out the dissimilarities. These revolve around the fact that in traditional African societies there is no developed awareness of alternatives to established bodies of belief. Instead the dominant modes of thought are marked by a protective attitude toward received systems of categories and beliefs. "Particular passages of thought are bound to the particular occasions that evoke them . . . theoretical statements are very much matters of occasion, not likely to be heard out of context or as part of a general discussion of 'what we believe.' . . . Traditional thought has tended to get on with the work of explanation without pausing for reflection on the nature or rules of this work. . . . Second-order intellectual activities [are] virtually absent. . . . There is a noted reluctance to register repeated failures of prediction and to act by attacking the beliefs involved. Instead other current beliefs are utilized to 'excuse' each failure as it occurs ('secondary elaboration'). . . . So too the main classificatory distinctions of the system are defended by taboo avoidance reactions against any event that defies them."[13] In short African traditional cultures largely lack what Popper calls a *critical tradition* and what Habermas terms *institutionalized discourse*. In fact critical discussion is systematically hampered by such devices as secondary elaboration and taboo avoidance reactions. To the extent that this description is accurate, and to the extent that it fits other "primitive" cultures, one might argue that their procedures for settling beliefs and evaluating practices are in some ways less rational than our own (at least sometimes) are, and thus that the critical dimension of anthropological interpretations is not simply a form of cultural imperialism that leads inevitably to misunderstanding.

I suspect that Winch would resist this move as just a more sophisticated version of the intellectualist bias. Why, he might ask, is it more rational to settle validity claims discursively? To what standards could one appeal in justifying this claim? In one sense the answer seems clear. By *rationality* we mean, at least in part, a willingness to press things discursively in this way. But I am sure that Winch would point out that Zande standards of rationality do not require, and in fact do not countenance, that this be done. And he might add that since our standards and attitudes are incompatible with a traditional way of life, the real issue is rather more practical than theoretical. It concerns different forms of life as different ways of filling in the "ethical space" marked out by such universals of human existences as birth, death, and sexual relations.[14]

Is there any answer to this? Karl-Otto Apel, who defends a position similar to Habermas's, advances the following argument: to raise the question of the universality of standards of rationality in this way is already and unavoidably to adopt the discursive attitude.[15] The participants in the relativity debate, including Winch, accept as conditions of their participation the universal and unavoidable presuppositions of argumentative reasoning. Thus they cannot consistently argue that nondiscursive standards of rationality are just as good as, or superior to, their own. At most Winch could silently join the Azande and try to become as they are. This "transcendental tu quoque" argument, as Habermas calls it, undeniably has a certain force. The arguments that relativists put forward on behalf of "primitive" cultures not only appeal to standards of argumentation absent from the cultures they defend but make use of modes of reflective reasoning (metatheoretical, metaethical, epistemological, historical, and anthropological) that are largely unavailable in those cultures. There is an inescapable touch of condescension to the case for the defense; it is a case that the clients themselves could not make without ceasing to be clients.

Despite its appeal, this representation of the theoretician's dilemma is, I think, inconclusive, for it can be read as saying that *if* one views the matter discursively, one is committed—at least while doing so—to recognizing certain standards of rationality. But it does not show that the discursive attitude itself has universal significance. There is, as Habermas points out, a residual decisionistic element in the argument.[16] The entrance into critical discussion is represented as a decision for rationality; any attempt to rationally (argumentatively) justify this decision inevitably involves a vicious circle. Habermas claims to be able to fill this decisionistic gap. He advances two different arguments for the objectivity and universality of discursive standards of rationality: one "empirical" and the other "systematic." The empirical argument is basically an appeal to the developmental logic underlying the acquisition of communicative competence. If the case could be made that the mastery of the ability to reason argumentatively and reflectively about truth and rightness claims represents a developmental-logically advanced stage of species-wide cognitive and moral competences, then it seems that the social investigator would be justified in applying standards of critical rationality in interpreting any system of beliefs and practices. Of course to make this case with sufficient cogency, it would be necessary to provide a more adequate account of such key concepts as *developmental logic* and *stage* than is currently available. It would also be necessary to defuse the lingering suspicion of ethnocentrism that sometimes attaches to developmental studies. The starting points for such studies are typically the cognitive, linguistic, and moral competences of adults in our society. Looking backward, so to speak, we reconstruct the stages of development up to the point at which we, the competent adults, have arrived. A relativist might argue that the concepts of adulthood and competence (or *Mündigkeit*) that underlie these studies are culture-specific; they are decidedly not, at least as far as the "higher" stages are concerned, those of the "primitive" cultures studied by anthropologists. To what extent, then, and on what grounds, is the application of the structures rooted in "our" concepts to "their" culture legitimate?

Apparently we have here a version of the "for us"/"for them" relationship reminiscent of Hegel's phenomenology. And the way around the relativist's objection might very well be another variation on a Hegelian theme; it has to be shown, above all, that the "higher stages" of thought and action really are higher, that their relation to "lower stages" is not merely one of difference and opposition but one of unfolding and development. What is at issue is not simply the empirical question of what comes later but the systematic question of the relation of the later to the earlier. It is clear that this is precisely what is intended by developmentalists. Piaget's studies of the development of logical reasoning, for instance, make an explicit case for the comparative superiority of the logical systems mastered at each subsequent stage; a later system is not merely different from but an extension of earlier systems, which it in turn presupposes. Empirical and systematic arguments thus are really two dimensions of the same argument for growth and development as opposed to mere change.

Applying this now to Habermas's discourse model, it would have to be shown that the settlement of truth and rightness claims through argumentative reasoning (subject to the conditions he describes) represents the realization and completion of competences that are universal to mankind. He clearly believes this to be the case. The ability to communicate, he argues, already places at one's disposal the *formal* means for "constructing" a discursive speech situation.

A speech situation determined by pure intersubjectivity is an idealization. The mastery of the dialogue-constitutive universals does not itself amount to a capacity actually to establish the ideal speech situation. But communicative competence does mean the mastery of the means of construction necessary for its establishment. No matter how the intersubjectivity of mutual understanding may be deformed, the *design* of an ideal speech situation is necessarily implied in the structure of potential speech, since all speech, even of intentional deception, is oriented toward the idea of truth. This idea can only be analyzed with regard to a consensus achieved in unrestrained and universal discourse. . . . On the strength of communicative competence alone, however, and independent of the empirical structures of the social system to which we belong, we are quite unable to realize the ideal speech situation; we can only anticipate it.[17]

The crucial step in this argument is obviously that from the universality of truth (and rightness) claims to discourse as the proper mode of their redemption. In one sense, the discourse models of truth and rightness are meant to establish just this. But the arguments for these models derived their plausibility from our understanding of those claims. For the purposes of the present discussion, what has to be shown is that any form of communicative action involves claims that call for, or at least allow, discursive redemption. In other words, the universality of the standards of rationality built into the discourse model can be demonstrated only if the validity claims implicitly raised in nondiscursive contexts—including interaction contexts in cultures lacking a critical tradition—themselves intrinsically point to the possibility of discursive redemption. In fact, it is on this that Habermas rests the distinction between his position and those that involve some form of "first decision" for critical discussion.

The transcendental tu quoque argument attempts to convince anyone who inquires after the grounds for an argumentatively conceived principle of rationality that the intention behind his question, properly understood, is already based on this principle. . . . This argument can, I believe, be applied not only to someone who has (at least once) entered into argumentation, but to any subject capable of speech and action . . . by appealing to the intuitive knowledge which he, as a competent speaker, "already" has at his disposal. The idea of rational speech, if I may so express myself, is first found not in the general structures of discourse, but in the fundamental structures of linguistic action. . . . Anyone who acts with an orientation toward reaching understanding, since he unavoidably raises truth and rightness claims, must have implicitly recognized that this action points to argumentation as the only way of *continuing* consensual action in case naively raised and factually recognized validity claims become problematic. As soon as we make explicit the meaning of discursively redeemable validity claims, we become aware that we presuppose the possibility of argumentation already in consensual *action*.[18]

Sometimes this argument has a psychological ring to it, and then it is clearly implausible. That all communicative action, even in cultures lacking a tradition of discourse, involves an "implicit recognition" or an "expectation" that validity claims can be discursively redeemed is unlikely on any psychological reading of these terms. As Habermas himself points out, there are in different contexts of action numerous ways of dealing with problematic validity claims—for example, by indicating the experiences on which they are based, or by appeal to accepted authorities or recognized values and norms. In particular the members of "primitive" cultures often disagree about matters relating to oracles, witchcraft, magic, and the like and are able to resolve their differences successfully without recourse to discursive argumentation in the sense at issue. In fact Habermas explicitly considers the institutionalization of discourse to be a relatively late evolutionary development, one of "the most difficult and endangered innovations of human history."[19] And it is only to the extent, and in the spheres, that such institutionalization is developed that we can talk of the general expectation of argumentative justification.

His argument must then be read as some form of conceptual argument; and indeed Habermas usually formulates the case for the implicit reference of validity claims to argumentation with phrases like *ihrem Sinne nach* (according to their meaning or sense).[20] To establish this sort of connection, it is not sufficient to show that truth and rightness claims as we sometimes understand them can ultimately be justified discursively and only discursively. It must be shown that this holds for these validity claims no matter what the context of interaction in which they are raised (provided only that it is oriented to reaching understanding). To this our relativist could object that the meaning or sense of truth and rightness claims has to be understood in connection with the way they actually function in a given language group. If the members of a particular group raise and make good such claims without reference to discursive argumentation, on what grounds could one maintain that these claims, *ihrem Sinne nach*, implicitly point to the possibility of discursive redemption? Where is this *Sinn*, which is not that of the group in question, to be located?

I shall end this discussion with one brief observation. The type of claim Habermas is making is not at all unfamiliar. It has been raised repeatedly by philosophy and other "reflective" disciplines—the claim that the "full" meaning or sense of a given mode of thinking or acting is not always (or even usually) apparent to those engaged in it, that the systematic explication or reconstruction of what is involved in it can lead us to see presuppositions and implications of which the participants were unaware. We find nothing implausible about the claim, say, that elementary operations in arithmetic or elementary steps in reasoning are (*ihrem Sinne nach*) related in certain ways to systems of mathematical and logical principles that were fully developed only at a later historical stage. Nor is there anything inherently implausible in Habermas's contention that nondiscursive modes of settling validity claims point (*ihrem Sinne nach*) to the possibility in principle of critical examination; it is on this possibility that our very conception of the Socratic enterprise is based.

What Habermas calls "communicative ethics" is grounded in the "fundamental norms of rational speech." Communication that is oriented toward reaching understanding inevitably involves the reciprocal raising and recognition of validity claims. Claims to truth and rightness, if radically challenged, can be redeemed only through argumentative discourse leading to rationally motivated consensus. Universal-pragmatic analysis of the conditions of discourse and rational consensus show these to rest on the supposition of an "ideal speech situation" characterized by an effective equality of chances to assume dialogue roles. This unavoidable (but usually counterfactual) imputation is an "illusion" constitutive of the very meaning of rational argumentation; in making it we anticipate a form of life characterized by "pure" (unconstrained and undistorted) intersubjectivity. Thus the universal pragmatic conditions of possibility of rationally justifying norms of action or evaluation have themselves a normative character. The search for the fundamental principles of morals properly begins with a reflective turn, for these principles are built into the very structure of practical discourse.[21]

This is admittedly a highly abstract characterization of ethical foundations. In fact it seems to move at the same level as Kant's "Foundations of the Metaphysics of Morals," focusing as that work did only on "the supreme principle of morality." There are indeed a number of parallels between the two, and in a sense communicative ethics can be viewed as a reconstruction of Kantian ethics. This is not the place to pursue that suggestion in any detail, but it might be in order to indicate that some of the classical objections to Kant's "formalism" do not apply to Habermas's discourse model. The principal revision, and the one on which all others depend, is the shift of the frame of reference from the solitary, reflecting moral consciousness to the community of subjects in dialogue. In the discussion of labor and interaction in section 1.2, I mentioned Habermas's critique of the "monological" presuppositions of Kantian ethics. He argued that Kant's autonomous will represents a peculiar abstraction from the moral relationships of communicating individuals; that Kant's moral solipsism is reconciled with the universality of ethical principles only through a kind of preestablished synchronization of the reflections of all rational beings.

Kant defines moral action with the principle: "Act only according to that maxim by which you can at the same time will that it should become a universal law." . . . Every single subject, in examining his maxims of action for their suitability as principles of a universal legislation, must *attribute* these maxims to every other subject as equally binding. . . . The moral laws are abstractly universal in the sense that, as they hold as universal for me, they must *eo ipso* be thought of as holding for all rational beings. As a result, interaction under such laws dissolves into the actions of solitary and self-sufficient subjects, each of whom must act as though he were the sole existing consciousness; and yet each subject can at the same time be certain that all his actions under moral laws are necessarily and from the outset in harmony with the moral actions of all possible other subjects."[22]

The point of this criticism is evidently that the rationality and universality of maxims of action cannot be decided monologically—within the horizon of the solitary, reflecting moral consciousness. Whether a norm is universalizable, capable of rational consensus, can be ascertained only dialogically in unrestricted and unconstrained discourse. From this point of view Habermas's discourse model represents a procedural reinterpretation of Kant's categorical imperative: rather than ascribing as valid to all others any maxim that I can will to be a universal law, I must submit my maxim to all others for purposes of discursively testing its claim to universality. The emphasis shifts from what each can will without contradiction to be a general law, to what all can will in agreement to be a universal norm.[23] A rational will is not something that can be certified and secured privatim; it is inextricably bound to communication processes in which a common will is both "discovered" and "formed". "Discursively redeemable norms and generalizable interests have a non-conventional core; they are neither merely empirically found already to exist nor simply posited; rather they are, in a non-contingent way, both *formed* and *discovered*. This must be so if there can at all be anything like a *rational* will."[24]

This reference to the formation of a common will regarding generalizable interests indicates another basic difference between communicative ethics and Kantian ethics. For Kant the autonomy of the will requires the exclusion of all "pathological" interests from the choice of maxims for action. To be sure, any action and therefore any maxim has a matter or content as well as a form. But the particular ends of action (which may be summed up as "happiness"), as well as the desires and inclinations urging us toward them, must be excluded as such (not, however, as figuring in the essential characterization of the action and its maxim) from the determining grounds if an action is to be moral.[25] Kant's rationale for this is well known: any maxim that is determined by contingent factors is ipso facto unsuitable for universal legislation; if a maxim is to be universalizable, valid for all rational beings, then it must be independent of my particular inclinations. Put positively, only to the extent that my choice (*Willkür*) is determined solely by the rational will (*Wille*) or pure practical reason does it qualify as a possible content of all other rational wills. This way of attacking the problem of universalizability sets the rational will in opposition to particular inclinations and desires, needs and interests. They must be suppressed qua determining factors in moral choice. The antagonism is an unavoidable consequence of combining an individualistic (monological) frame of reference with the demand for universality—what is really individual must be excluded.

This constellation alters perceptibly when we shift to Habermas's intersubjective (dialogical) framework. The aim of discourse is to come to a consensus about which interests are generalizable. In this construction, individual wants, needs, desires, and interests need not—indeed cannot—be excluded, for it is precisely concerning them that agreement is sought. Of course, in this model, too, an interest that proves to be merely individual is unsuitable as a basis for universal legislation. However, this unsuitability does not attach to it qua interest, from the outset, but only qua nongeneralizable. As a result the meaning and conditions of autonomy are markedly different. It is no longer defined by way of opposition to interest per se, but rather in terms of the rationalization of interests themselves.

The limits of formalistic ethics can be seen in the fact that inclinations incompatible with duties must be excluded from the domain of the morally relevant, and they must be suppressed. The interpretations of needs that are current at any contingent stage of socialization must therefore be accepted as given. They cannot be made in turn the object of a discursive will-formation. Only communicative ethics guarantees the generality of admissible norms and the autonomy of acting subjects solely through the discursive redeemability of the validity claims with which norms appear. That is, generality is guaranteed in that the only norms that may claim generality are those on which everyone affected agrees (or would agree) without constraint if they enter into (or were to enter into) a process of discursive will-formation. . . . Communicative ethics guarantees autonomy in that it carries on the process of the insertion of drive potentials into a communicative structure of action, i.e. the socialization process, "with will and consciousness."[26]

As we saw above, one of the levels of discourse that is a precondition of rational consensus is the thematization of available need interpretations themselves; interests are neither empirically found nor simply posited—they are shaped and discovered in processes of communication. Autonomy requires, then, not the suppression of inclinations but their "insertion" into, or "formation" through, nondistorted communication.

From this hastily sketched comparison it can be seen that Habermas's "formalism" is a formalism with a difference. The objection to Kant, current since Hegel, that concrete norms of action cannot be generated from the pure form of rationality, does not have the same force when directed to the discourse model. It is true that this specifies no particular norms of action but only a "principle of the justification of principles." Since, however, the generalizability of interests is what is at issue in practical discourse, rational consensus means agreement about the norms regulating opportunities for need satisfaction; the content belongs to the very situation of discourse. What this content is, concretely, depends on the historical contours of that situation, on the conditions and potentials of social existence at that time and place. The principle that those affected by proposed norms should seek rational agreement among themselves precludes the possibility of legislating once and for all and for everyone.[27] But it does indicate, admittedly at a very general level, the procedure to be followed in any rationally justifiable legislation at any time.

The changed relation between form and content can be brought out in another way. Kant insists that moral maxims have not only a form (universality) but a matter or end. However, since all particular ends have to be excluded as determining grounds of action, the categorical imperative, when specified with respect to ends, takes the form of a restriction on the admissible contents of volition: "A rational being, as by its nature an end and thus an end in itself, must serve in every maxim as the condition restricting all merely relative and arbitrary ends."[28] The rationale behind this negative formulation is clear: "Since in the idea of an absolutely good will without any limiting condition of the attainment of this or that end, every end to be effected must be completely abstracted (as any particular end would make each will only relatively good), the end here is not conceived as one to be effected but as an independent end, and thus merely negatively. It is that which must never be acted against."[29] All material "ends to be effected" are "without exception only relative, for only their relation to a particularly constituted faculty of desire in the subject gives them worth." Thus "they cannot give rise to any practical laws" but are "grounds for hypothetical imperatives only."[30] The only specifically moral end, humanity, is not an end to be effected but an "independent end"—a negative limiting condition that does not itself specify any particular positive content of volition.

This construction is at the root of Kant's conception of politics and law. They are concerned primarily with securing man's negative freedom (that is, his freedom from external constraint), which is a necessary condition for positive freedom (that is, autonomy and morality). More specifically whereas morality is a question of internal motives (a good will), legality has to do exclusively with external actions. The problem of a good organization of the state is a question of arranging.

the powers of each selfish inclination in opposition . . . [so that] one moderates or destroys the ruinous effect of the other. The consequence for reason is the same as if none of them existed, and man is forced to be a good citizen even if not a morally good person. The problem of organizing a state, however hard it may seem, can be solved even for a race of devils if only they are intelligent. The problem is: "Given a multitude of rational beings requiring universal laws for their preservation, but each of whom is secretly inclined to exempt himself from them, to establish a constitution in such a way that, although their private intentions conflict, they check each other, with the result that their public conduct is the same as if they had no such intentions."[31]

This problem is solved with the establishment of a republican government (which is compatible with a hereditary monarchy if the monarchy is constitutionally limited) in a commonwealth of nations maintaining peace. But the establishment of a civil society under formal laws is not identical with the realization of a genuine moral commonwealth (although it is a necessary condition); for morality, as opposed to legality, requires in addition that the laws be obeyed from duty—and this is the work of freedom; it cannot be accomplished through external legislation.

Because the discourse model requires that the "ends to be effected" themselves be rationalized (communicatively generalized insofar as this is possible) and that valid social norms incorporate these generalizable interests, the gap between legality and morality is narrowed. The criterion of rational consensus under conditions of symmetry retains the restriction specified in Kant's formula of the end in itself: that humanity be treated as an end and never as a means only, that it serve as "the condition restricting all merely relative and arbitrary ends." But this criterion goes beyond specifying an "independent end in itself"; it further specifies the "ends to be effected" in terms of their capacity for being communicatively shared in rational dialogue. Consequently norms established in this way as legally binding are not merely formal; they do not merely delimit compatible scopes of action in which each individual can pursue his "selfish inclinations" in such a way that "one moderates or destroys the ruinous effect of the other." Rather these norms enjoin certain positive ends as being in the common interest. In the discourse model for morality and politics,

the opposition between morally and legally regulated areas is relativized, and the validity of *all* norms is tied to discursive will-formation. This does not exclude the necessity for compelling norms, since no one can know (today) the degree to which aggressiveness can be curtailed and the voluntary recognition of discursive principles attained. Only at that stage, at present a mere construct, would morality become strictly universal. It would also cease to be "merely" moral in terms of the distinction made between law and morality. Internalization too would only be complete when the principle of the justification of possible principles (that is, the readiness to engage in discursive clarification of practical questions) was alone internalized, but in other respects the continuous interpretation of needs was given over to communication processes.[32]

Of course not all interests are generalizable. In any political order, there will be need for compromise and for spheres of action in which individuals may pursue their particular interests freely. But "the question of which sectors should, if necessary, be regulated through compromise or formal norms of action can also be made subject to discussion."[33] That is, compromise between, or the pursuit of, particular interests are themselves rationally justifiable only if the interests in question are really particular (nongeneralizable). And this in turn can be rationally decided only in discourse. Thus "democratic formation of the will" takes precedence as a principle of political order.

The word "principle" is important here. In Habermas's view, democracy cannot be equated with a specific organization of society, a single form of government, or a particular method for choosing rulers. The failure to appreciate this—that is, to separate clearly questions concerning the organizational *principle* and legitimating *grounds* of a political order from those concerning its institutionalization under given conditions—has plagued the discussion of democracy from Rousseau to the current debates between its *empirical* and *normative* theorists.

Rousseau mixed the introduction of a new principle of legitimation with proposals for instituting a just political rule. . . . If one calls democracies precisely those political orders that satisfy the procedural type of legitimation, then questions of democratization can be treated as what they are, i.e. as organizational questions. Which types of organization and which mechanisms are better suited to produce procedurally legitimate decisions depends on the concrete social situation. . . . One must think here in process categories. I can imagine the attempt to order a society democratically only as a self-controlled learning process.[34]

We cannot set a priori limits to this process. The extent to which discursive will-formation can be made an organizational principle of society without overloading the personality system or coming into irresolvable conflict with competing functional imperatives is an open question.[35] And the same can be said for the *ways* in which it might be institutionalized, for the correct answer to this question varies with the historical situation and the restrictions it places on democratization.

Because they are empirical processes, all discourses are subject to restrictions of space and time, psychological and social limitations contingent discrepancies in information, personal influence, etc. . . . These make regulations necessary . . . [as does] the need to organize a discussion, to secure and limit the flow of information, to separate themes and contributions, to order them, etc. . . . All regulations of this kind have a pragmatic, but by no means contemptible status; they are meant to make practical discourse possible under given empirical restrictions. . . . This is almost always difficult and sometimes actually unattainable; but it is not impossible in principle.[36]

Thus democracy, as a principle of political order, does not single out a priori one specific type of organization (for example, a system of soviets) as *the* correct one. Nor does it exclude a priori every arrangement involving representation, delegation, and the like. The point is, rather, to find in each set of concrete circumstances institutional arrangements that justify the presumption that basic political decisions would meet with the agreement of all those affected by them if they were able to participate without restriction in discursive will-formation.

This principle also serves as the standard for critical social theory.

A social theory critical of ideology can, therefore, identify the normative power built into the institutional system of a society only if it starts from the *model of the suppression of generalizable interests* and compares normative structures existing at a given time with the hypothetical state of a system of norms formed, *ceteris paribus,* discursively. Such a counterfactually projected reconstruction . . . can be guided by the question (justified, in my opinion, by considerations from universal pragmatics): How would the members of a social system, at a given stage in the development of productive forces, have collectively and bindingly interpreted their needs (and which norms would they have accepted as justified) if they could and would have decided on the organization of social intercourse through discursive will-formation, with adequate knowledge of the limiting conditions and functional imperatives of their society?[37]

Critical theory thus becomes a theoretically grounded form of advocacy in situations of social conflict; it seeks to ascertain and to articulate "generalizable, though nevertheless suppressed, interests in a representatively simulated discussion between groups that are differentiated (or could be non-arbitrarily differentiated) from one another by articulated, or at least virtual, oppositon of interests."[38]

We shall see how Habermas applies this model to contemporary society in the final chapter. But before doing so I shall complete my sketch of his theory of communication with an examination of its implications for the theory of socialization.

4.4 COMMUNICATION AND SOCIALIZATION

Habermas's basic intention in developing the theory of communicative competence was to provide normative-theoretical foundations for social inquiry. It should be obvious, however, that the universal-pragmatic considerations sketched above move at much too abstract a level to fulfill this task in and of themselves. The main bridge between the general theory of communication and the methodology of social research is the theory of socialization.

From its beginnings, the neo-Marxism of the Frankfurt school was characterized by its emphasis on sociocultural concerns in general and on social-psychological questions in particular. The basic conceptual framework for dealing with the latter was adapted from Freud, and with good reason:

If one considers the normative implications of notions like ego-strength, dismantling the ego-distant parts of the super-ego and reducing the domain in which unconscious defense mechanisms function, it becomes clear that psychoanalysis singles out certain personality structures as ideal. . . . In the social-psychological work of the Institutue for Social Research, it can be shown that the basic concepts of psychoanalysis could enter into description, hypothesis-formation and measuring instruments precisely because of their normative content. The early studies by Fromm of the sado-masochistic character and by Horkheimer of authority and the family, Adorno's investigation of the mechanisms of prejudice-formation in authoritarian personalities and Marcuse's theoretical work on instinct structure and society, all follow the same conceptual strategy: the basic psychological and sociological concepts can be interlaced because the perspective projected in them of an autonomous ego and an emancipated society reciprocally require one another.[1]

In this way critical social theory was linked to a concept of the autonomous self that was, on the one hand, inherited from German

Idealism, but on the other hand, detached from idealist presuppositions in the framework of psychoanalysis. Adorno and Marcuse ultimately despaired of this strategy, proclaiming the "end of the individual" and the "obsolescence of psychoanalysis" in the emergent "total society" that undercut the family and directly imprinted collective ego-ideals on the child.[2] Habermas attributes their pessimism to "an overly sensitive perception and overly simplified interpretation" of certain admittedly real tendencies.[3] In his view it is still possible to develop the normative content of the basic concepts of critical theory in a social-psychological framework; but the framework he envisions involves much more than a readaptation of psychoanalysis. It is, in a way, a reconstruction of Hegel's logic in the form of an integrated model of ego (or self-) development. I shall be examining this model below; before doing so, it will be helpful to preface a few introductory remarks.

1. For Habermas, sociology is always at the same time social psychology:

A sociology that accepts meaning as a basic concept cannot abstract the social system from structures of personality; it is always also social psychology. The system of institutions must be grasped in terms of the imposed repression of needs and of the scope for possible individualization, just as personality structures must be grasped in determinations of the institutional framework and of role qualifications.[4]

In short the reproduction of society is based on the reproduction of competent members of society; and the forms of individual identity are intimately connected with the forms of social integration.

2. The theory of socialization has for some time been dominated by Parsonian role theory. As a number of critics have pointed out, however, the conventional role model—in which the acting subject appears only as a bearer of roles, that is, a function of processes determined by social structures, and in which socialization is conceived as the integration of the organism into existing role systems—rests on overly "sociologistic" assumptions. Thus, for example, Gouldner, Wrong, and others have criticized the assumption of a congruence between individual need dispositions and the value orientations institutionalized in systems of social roles; social interactionists, phenomenologists, and ethnomethodologists have criticized the assumption of a congruence between role definitions and role interpre-

tations, emphasizing instead the activity of the subject in interpreting roles, the dialectic of role taking and role making; and Goffman and others have criticized the assumption of a congruence between binding norms or institutionalized value orientations (roles) and actual motivations, emphasizing instead the importance of role-distance.[5] Habermas shares the suspicion that conventional role theory "surreptitiously stylizes the limit case of total institutions into the normal case": "Role theory has been satisfied with the overly simplified basic assumption that personality structures, especially value orientations and need dispositions, are a mirror image of institutionalized values. There resulted an objectivistic picture of the acting subject, a static picture of the action system, and a harmonistic picture of the social structure."[6]

3. But Habermas's disagreements with the conventional variants of role theory go beyond this to the methodological self-conception that underlies them. Sociological action theory has been understood as a kind of metatheory in which such fundamental concepts as actor, action, situation, role, norm, and value, are clarified in the attempt to establish a categorial framework for empirical-analytic theories. Habermas wants instead to conceive of action theory as a reconstructive science concerned with the rational reconstruction of universal competences.

Concept formation in sociology is obviously linked up with the everyday concepts in which members of social groups construct the normative reality of their social environment. This suggests developing sociological action theory as a theory that attempts to reconstruct the universal components of the relevant pre-theoretical knowledge of sociological laymen. Sociology would . . . no longer choose its basic concepts conventionally, but develop them with the aim of characterizing the general formal properties of the socialized subject's capability for action, as well as those of action systems. To be sure, the phenomenological research program aims in a similar way to grasp general structures of possible social life-worlds; but the development of the program was burdened from the start with the weaknesses of a method that is modelled after the introspective procedures of the philosophy of consciousness. Only the competence-theoretic approaches in linguistics and developmental psychology have created a paradigm that connects the formal analysis of known structures with the causal analysis of observable processes. The expression "interactive competence" stands for the assumption that the abilities of socially acting subjects can be investigated from the perspective of a universal—i.e.

independent of specific cultures—competence, just as are language and cognition.[7]

Adopting this perspective has the added advantage of highlighting a problem dimension that has, ironically enough, been largely ignored in conventional socialization theory: the ontogenesis of the basic qualifications for social interaction (or role behavior). From the perspective of role theory, questions of ontogenesis have been treated primarily in terms of the acquisition of cultural *contents* and not in terms of the development of universal *competences*. Thus the question of the different developmental levels to which the elements it singled out belong was not systematically pursued (Mead's distinctions between play and game, other and generalized other notwithstanding). With the rise of competence-development models in cognitive psychology, the centrality of this problematic for the theory of social action has become evident.

4. Habermas's thoughts on individual development, like those on universal pragmatics and social evolution, have an explicitly programmatic status. (And considering the scope of the problems involved in each of these areas, it could hardly be otherwise.) Moreover in formulating them he relies heavily on already established lines of research; his points are typically made with reference to existing paradigms and have the form of proposals for revision, reorientation, interconnection, and the like. To the extent that he has articulated a unified framework, it derives from his work in the theory of communication. The discussion of communicative competence should have made clear that it cannot be identified with linguistic competence. It is in fact so broad a notion as to include cognitive, interactive, and egological moments as well. To put it briefly, the acquisition of communicative competence involves development in all of these dimensions. Thus it is not completed with the mastery of phonetic and syntactic structures in early childhood but develops in stages at least through adolescence.

Developmental studies are well underway in a number of different areas—psycholinguistics, cognitive psychology (including studies of moral consciousness), psychoanalysis (including analytic ego psychology), and social interactionism, among others. The task, as Habermas sees it, is to work out an integrated framework in which the different dimensions of development are not only analytically distinguished but their interconnections systematically taken into account. Beyond this, empirical mechanisms and boundary conditions of development have to be specified. This is clearly an immense undertaking. Habermas's proposals as to how it might best be approached are based on his theory of communication, more specifically on the distinction drawn among the different dimensions in which an utterance can succeed or fail: comprehensibility, truth, rightness, and truthfulness. Each of these specifies not only a dimension of communicative action, and thus of rationality, but a "region" of reality—language, outer nature, society, inner nature—in relation to which the subject can attain varying degrees of autonomy.

By "external nature" I mean the objectivated sector of reality which the adult subject can (directly or indirectly) perceive and treat manipulatively. Naturally, there can be an objectivating attitude not only in relation to inorganic nature, but in relation to all objects and states of affairs that are directly or indirectly accessible to sense experience. "Society" is meant to designate that symbolically prestructured sector of reality which the adult subject can understand in a non-objectivating attitude, i.e. as a communicative actor. . . . This performative attitude can be replaced by an objectivating attitude toward society. . . . As belonging to "internal nature" I reckon all intentions that an "I" can express as its experiences. Precisely in this expressive attitude, the "I" knows itself not only as subjectivity, but as something that has at the same time already transcended the limits of mere subjectivity in cognition, language and interaction. . . . Finally, I have introduced the medium of our utterances, "language," as a region in its own right . . . that does not exclude our adopting vis-à-vis linguistic utterances or systems of symbols either an objectivating attitude directed to the material substratum or a performative attitude directed to the semantic content.[8]

Using this universal-pragmatic classification of validity claims and corresponding regions of reality as a guide, Habermas has advanced some tentative suggestions for unifying developmental studies. Their main lines might be sketched as follows.

1. Ontogenesis can be construed as a development toward increasing autonomy and responsibility in the dimensions distinguished above, that is as an interdependent process of linguistic, cognitive, interactive, and ego (or self: *Ich*) development.

2. These do not, however, all lie at the same level. Only the first

three can be regarded as separable (but interdependent) lines of development.

I would like to propose a systematically warranted division into cognitive, linguistic and interactive development; corresponding to these dimensions I shall distinguish cognitive, linguistic and interactive competences. This proposal signifies that for each of these dimensions, and indeed only for these dimensions, a specific developmental-logically ordered universal sequence of structures can be given. Following Piaget, I suppose that these general structures of cognitive, linguistic and interactive ability are formed in a simultaneously constructive and adaptive confrontation of the subject with his environment, whereby the environment is differentiated into outer nature, language and society. The structure-forming learning process is also a process of self-production, insofar as in it the subject first forms himself into a subject capable of cognition, speech and interaction.[9]

3. As the last line suggests, the ontogenesis of the ego or self does not represent a line of development separable from the other three but rather a process that runs complementary to them; the ego develops in and through the integration of "inner nature" into the universal structures of language, thought, and action.

Ego or identity development cannot be conceptualized as an analytically independent developmental dimension that has a place alongside the other three. Rather, the ego is constituted in the course of integrating into universal structures the nature that is at first—with the organism of the neonate—still wholly "external" to itself. Thus in the subjectivity of the ego is reflected inner nature, i.e. a nature that attains the capability for cognition, speech and action, that is incorporated in universal structures and becomes internal to the same extent. . . . The universality of the structures secures for the ego the abstract universality of an ego in general (*Ich-überhaupt*), which knows itself to be one with all other subjects that can say "I" to themselves; the accidental nature of the organic substratum at the start of the formative process secures for the embodied ego its equally abstract particularity, which physically separates it from all other subjects; finally, the circumstances that the constitution of the ego takes place under concrete conditions of life through the socializatory medium of language—a medium that establishes intersubjectivity—secures for the ego its individuality.[10]

4. The representation of ego development as transpiring in and through the integration of inner nature into universal structures of

cognition, speech, and interaction is one-sided; it highlights only the structural or—in a broader sense of the term—"cognitive" side of identity formation, that is the acquisition of universal competences. There is, however, another side to the process: affect and motive formation. Unless the subject is able to interpret his needs adequately in these universal structures, development may be pathologically deformed. A general theory of ego development would have to integrate an account of the interdependent development of cognitive, linguistic, and interactive development with an account of affective and motivational development. For this latter task, psychoanalytic studies in general and studies of superego formation and the formation of defense mechanisms in particular provide valuable clues.

These reflections on ego development are not only highly programmatic but in a state of flux as well.[11] I will merely sketch in very broad strokes the principal stages of ego and identity development that Habermas has distinguished. I shall then examine more closely one aspect—but from the perspective of social theory, the central aspect—of ego development: the development of interactive competence.

Taking his clues from psychoanalysis and cognitive-developmental psychology, Habermas "very tentatively" distinguishes four main stages of ego development: the "symbiotic," the "egocentric," the "sociocentric-objectivistic," and the "universalistic."

1. During the first phase of life, there are no clear indications of a subjective separation between subject and object; "the symboisis between child, reference person and physical environment is so tight and we cannot meaningfully speak of a demarcation of subjectivity in the strict sense."[12]

2. During the next period, which covers Piaget's sensory-motor and preoperational phases, the child succeeds in differentiating between self and environment.

It learns to perceive permanent objects in its environment, but without yet clearly differentiating the environment into physical and social domains. Moreover, the demarcation [of the self] in relation to the environment is not yet objective. This is shown by the manifestations of cognitive and moral egocentrism. The child cannot perceive, understand and judge situations independently of its own standpoint—it thinks and acts from a body-bound perspective.[13]

3. The decisive step in demarcating the ego comes with the beginning of the stage of concrete operations and postoedipal latency. The child now "differentiates between perceptible and manipulable things on the one hand, and intelligible subjects and their utterances on the other; and it no longer confuses linguistic signs and their references and meanings." It becomes aware of the perspectival nature of its own standpoint and learns to "demarcate its subjectivity in relation to outer nature and society"; and it acquires the ability "to distinguish between fantasy and perception, between impulse and obligation." At the close of this phase, "cognitive development has led to an objectivation of outer nature, linguistic-communicative development to the mastery of a system of speech acts, and interactive development to the complementary connection of generalized behavioral expectations."[14]

4. With the arrival of adolescence and the ability to think hypothetically, the youth *can* free himself from the "dogmatism of the given and the existing." (Whether he actually does so, depends on a multiplicity of factors, not the least of which are the existing structures of social integration.)

Until then, the epistemic ego, bound to concrete operations, confronted an objectivated nature; and the practical ego, immersed in group perspectives, was dissolved in quasi-natural systems of norms. But as soon as the youth no longer naively accepts the validity claims contained in assertions and norms, he can transcend the objectivism of a given nature and explain the given from contingent boundary conditions in the light of hypotheses; and he can burst the sociocentrism of a traditional order and can understand (and if necessary criticize) existing norms as mere conventions in the light of principles.[15]

In this way, the prescientific object domains in relation to which the ego demarcates itself are "relativized." Theories of nature are related to the achievements of scientific subjects, and systems of norms are traced back to processes of will-formation among subjects living together. The demarcation of the self from the different "regions" of reality becomes "reflexive."

The development of the ego can also be looked at from the more emphatically social-psychological perspective of identity formation.

The concept of identity is the sociological equivalent of the ego concept. We call "identity" the symbolic structure that permits a personality system to secure continuity and consistency in the changes of biographical circumstances and through the different positions in social space. A person asserts his identity for himself and at the same time vis-à-vis others—self-identification, distinguishing oneself from others, must also be recognized by these others. The reflexive relation of the individual who identifies himself with himself depends on the intersubjective relations into which he enters with other persons by whom he is identified. Throughout he is supposed to sustain his identity in the vertical dimension of life history—namely in the passage through different, often contrary stages of life—as well as in the horizontal dimension—that is, in the simultaneous reaction to different, often competing structures of expectation.[16]

Habermas suggests a "provisional" division into three main stages of identity formation: natural identity, role or conventional identity, and ego identity.

1. When the small child first succeeds in differentiating itself from its environment (at stage 1 of ego development), it acquires an identity that may be called natural in the light of its dependence on the temporal continuity and boundary-maintaining properties of the child's body.

2. The child acquires a personal identity as it learns to locate itself in a social life-world:

The unity of the person . . . rests on membership in, and demarcation from, the symbolic reality of a group and on the possibility of localization within it. The unity of the person is formed through the internalization of roles that are tied in the beginning to concrete reference persons and later detached from them—primarily sex and generation roles that determine the structure of the family. This role identity, centered around sex and age and integrated with one's own bodily image, becomes more abstract and simultaneously more individual to the extent that the growing child appropriates extra-familial systems of roles.[17]

Whereas the continuity secured by natural identity is anchored in the persistence of the organism, that secured by role identity is based on intersubjectively recognized, temporally stable expectations (norms and roles), which are also established in the person through ego ideals.

3. Conditional on a number of factors, this conventional or role identity can give way during the adolescent phase to an ego identity:

During this time the youth learns the important distinction between norms, on the one hand, and principles according to which we can generate norms, on the other. Such principles can serve as standards for criticizing and justifying existing norms; to one who judges on principle, all binding norms must appear as mere conventions . . . the ego can no longer identify with itself through particular roles and existing norms . . . it must retract its identity, so to speak, behind the line of all *particular* roles and norms, and stabilize it only through the abstract ability to present itself in all situations as the one who can satisfy the requirements of consistency even in the face of incompatible role expectations and in the passage through a life-historical sequence of contradictory role systems. The ego identity of the adult confirms itself in the ability to construct new identities and simultaneously to integrate them with those overcome, so as to organize oneself and one's interactions in an unmistakable life history.[18]

This should not be taken to mean that a successful resolution of the adolescent crisis demands the formation of an ego-identity behind all conventional roles. The reconstruction of a role identity bound to the family can take place at the same level. In this case identity based on family membership (and bound up with sex and generation roles) is replaced by an identity based on membership in more abstract groups, for example, in vocational or status groups, in communities, nations, political orders, or linguistic-cultural groups. The youth emerges from the family and assumes active roles (vocational, civic, sexual, parental) and in this way fulfills the expectations connected with adult status. Furthermore the acquisition of such a more abstract role identity is normally a presupposition of attaining ego identity. In this case, the second-stage conventional identity breaks down again, and in the process the individual learns how "to generalize and carry over to other situations the ability to overcome old identities and construct new ones. The particular cores of surrendered identities are then only the biographical traces of a learning process through which identity formation has become reflexive; and in every critical situation, this process is brought anew into motion."[19]

From this perspective, the socialization process appears to be comprised of two central movements: the child first becomes a person by growing into the symbolic universe of the family and later becomes an adult by growing out of it. Thus two developmental transitions are of particular importance: the first (leading to what is regarded in our culture as "school age") has been conceived psychodynamically as the "oedipal crisis" and from the point of view of cognitive development as the transition from "preoperational" to "concrete-operational" thought; the other (leading to what in our culture is regarded as "youth") has been conceived psychodynamically as the "adolescent crisis" and from the point of view of cognitive development as the transition from "concrete-operational" to "formal-operational" thought. For each of these critical passages it is possible to specify—broadly and in sociological terms—functional problems confronting the subject and requiring the consolidation of its identity at a new level.

With the resolution of the oedipal crisis and the acquisition of sex and generation roles, the child assimilates the social structure of the family. It thereby learns to distinguish particular relations to specific reference persons from generalized behavioral expectations. It constructs internal behavior controls, acquires a role-bound identity, demarcates the family system from its social environments, etc. In adolescence the problem of release from the concretistic bond to early-childhood love objects is repeated at a higher level. The youth must no longer only relativize his membership in the family in relation to peers, but must step out of the family unit and assume active roles related to the system as a whole.[20]

From the point of view of the continuity and stability of social systems, adolescence in particular is a "danger zone." The dissolution of a role identity bound to the parental family and the construction of an identity appropriate to an adult member of society is fraught with risks. It is this transition that determines whether, and the extent to which, the accession of a new generation undermines or reinforces the existing order. The outcome of the adolescent's efforts to fashion a new self-interpretation and orientation to life from elements of the cultural tradition is dependent on a number of factors—among them the available and utilized access to that tradition, as well as the actual contents and structures offered by it. In this last respect, "cultural traditions contain different potentials for stimulation according to their formal [developmental-logical] levels; they can, for instance, offer and stimulate the transition to a post-conventional identity, or hold the restructuring of role identity at the conventional level."[21] (As we shall see in chapter 5, this line of reasoning is basic to Habermas's analysis of contemporary society.) Another factor, and one more immediately connected with the psychodynamic aspects of identity formation, is the structure of communication in the family. Research carried out in recent decades has established a clear link between pathological outcomes of the adolescent crisis and distorted patterns of interaction within the family. Habermas has reviewed and summarized several strands of this research, but I shall not recapitulate it here.[22] Nor will I be considering the structural "homologies" he has suggested between the development of individual identity and the evolution of "social" or "collective" identity.[23] Instead I shall turn to that aspect of ego development around which most of his own work has centered: the acquisition of interactive competence.

Habermas considers the acquisition of interactive competence, the ability to take part in increasingly complex interactions, to be "the core of identity formation." It is moreover the dimension of ego development most directly relevant to the theory of social action; and it is the basis of the development of moral consciousness.[24]

Table 1

Levels of interaction	Actions	Motivations	Actors
1	Concrete actions and consequences of action	Generalized pleasure-pain	Natural identity
2	Roles	Culturally interpreted needs	Role identity
	Systems of norms	(Concrete duties)	
3	Principles	Universalized pleasure-pain (utility)	Ego identity
		Universalized duties	
		Universalized need interpretations	

The fundamental assumptions underlying Habermas's approach are, first, that the ability to participate in social interaction can, despite cultural differences, be traced back to a universal (species-wide) competence; and second, that the acquisition of this competence runs through an irreversible series of distinct and increasingly complex stages that can be hierarchically ordered in a developmental logic. He articulates these ideas in a framework based in part on Mead's theory of social interaction and on the ensuing studies of socialization in terms of stages in role taking: play, game, and universal discourse. This is reflected in the left side of table 1, which depicts the basic structures of social interaction in the order in which the child "grows into" them.

Level 1: For the young child (cognitively still at the preoperational level and psychosexually still in the preoedipal phase), the segment of

Reciprocity requirement	Stages of moral consciousness	Idea of the good and just life	Domain of validity
Incomplete	1 Punishment-obedience orientation	Maximization of pleasure-avoidance of pain through obedience	Natural and social environment (undifferentiated)
Complete	2 Instrumental hedonism	Maximization of pleasure-avoidance of pain through exchange of equivalents	
Incomplete	3 Good-boy-nice-girl orientation	Concrete morality of primary groups	Group of primary reference persons
	4 Law and order orientation	Concrete morality of secondary groups	Members of the political community
Complete	5 Social-contractual legalism	Civil liberties, public welfare	All fellow citizens
	6 Universal ethical principle orientation	Moral freedom	All humans as private persons
	7 Communicative ethics	Moral and political freedom	All as members of a fictive world society

the symbolic universe relevant to interaction consists of individual concrete expectations and actions, as well as consequences of action that can be understood as gratifications or sanctions. The child becomes aware that different actors "see" the same situation from different perspectives (positions, interpretations, intentions, desires, feelings) and gradually learns to coordinate these perspectives by reciprocally relating them to one another. It learns to see its own behavior and intentions from the perspective of an "other" and knows that its actions can fulfill or disappoint the expectations of the other, as conversely the other's actions can fulfill or disappoint its own expectations. The motivating orientation to action is an egocentric tie to one's own balance of gratification (pleasure/pain). To interact at this level, then, the child must be capable of perceiving concrete actors and their concrete actions, of understanding and fulfilling individual expectations, of expressing and fulfilling individual intentions.

Level 2: With the advent (cognitively) of concrete-operational thought and (psychosexually) of the oedipal phase of development, the child learns to play social roles, at first within the family and later within expanded groups. The segment of the symbolic universe relevant to interaction alters; action can be understood as the fulfillment or disappointment not only of concrete individual expectations but of temporally generalized expectations that are reciprocally linked (that is, of roles and norms). The simple expectations of the first level become reflexive: expectations are now expectable. The perception of actors and actions also undergoes a change: the child learns to distinguish particular actions from general norms and particular actors from anonymous role bearers. Similarly the motives of action are no longer perceived only as concrete wishes; a distinction is made between what is required (duty) and what is desired (inclination), between the validity of a norm and the facticity of wants. Thus the child's ability to comprehend action situations and their elements is marked at this stage by increased reflexivity, generalization, abstraction, and differentiation. The egocentrism of early childhood has been transcended. This is true not only cognitively, but affectively as well; the motivations for action are no longer integrated solely in the dimension of pleasure/pain but take on the form of culturally interpreted needs whose satisfaction is dependent on fulfilling socially recognized expectations.

There is no place here to consider the psychodynamics of this transition. It can be characterized structurally in terms of the introduction of the perspective of the observer into the domain of interaction. At level 2,

the reciprocity of perspectives that is bound to the communication roles of "I" and "thou," can itself be made an object. Each of the participants in interaction can not only take up the role of the other, but can also know from the standpoint of a third person how his own perspective is reciprocally connected with that of the other. The concept of a norm of action that entitles all members of a social group to certain expectations of behavior is first formed when interactive egocentrism has been dismantled to such an extent that the child objectivates reciprocal structures of expectation from the standpoint of a group member not actually involved. The communication role of "alter" is split into the role of the "alter ego"—a participating counterpart—and that of the "neuter" who is involved in the interaction only as an observer.[25]

Thus the key structural element in the transition seems to be the differentiation and integration of two attitudes: the performative attitude of the participant and the neutral attitude of the observer. Habermas conjectures that it is based on the introduction into the domain of interaction of a central feature of concrete-operational thought: a decentered perception of reality. With the ability to assume an "objectivating" attitude toward social as well as physical reality, the child acquires not only the competence for role behavior but for strategic action in the strict sense; the system of reciprocally connected perspectives that underlies the perception of action situations at this level can be specified either normatively or strategically.[26] In the latter case, the actor is oriented to his own interests rather than to that which is expected of him; and he regards social norms and values as boundary conditions for the pursuit of these interests. Nevertheless the same cognitive structures are involved in his action; he must orient himself to the interpretations he supposes others to have of his intentions, and thus he must be able to view a system of interlaced perspectives from the neutral standpoint of the observer.

Level 3: With the appearance of adolescence and the capacity for formal-operational thought, the youth can acquire a certain distance from inherited roles, norms, and values; he can learn to place validity claims in question, to suspend recognition of them, and to treat them as hypothetical. The segment of the symbolic universe relevant to interaction expands then to include principles that can serve to generate, justify, or criticize norms. The reflexive expectations of the second level become reflexive once again: norms can now be normed. At the same time the perception of actors and their actions becomes yet more general: actors are viewed not merely as the sum of their role attributes but as individuals who, in applying principles, can organize their lives consistently throughout changes in situations and roles. Not only can particular actions be distinguished from general norms (as at level 2), but norms themselves, regarded now as particular, can be examined from the point of view of their generalizability. Correspondingly the perception of action motives is marked by increased abstraction and differentiation: the distinction between inclination and duty is supplemented by that between heteronomy and autonomy, between following merely traditional or imposed norms and acting in accord with norms that are justified in principle. Thus the youth's ability to perceive and understand the elements of action situations has released him not only from the egocentrism of early childhood but from the sociocentrism of tradition-bound role behavior as well. And this is true not only cognitively but affectively; the quasinatural process of need interpretation dependent on cultural tradition and institutional change can now be made the object of a discursive formation of the will. At this stage, interactive competence has developed to the point at which rational autonomy is possible.

Again, I shall not consider the psychodynamics of this transition. It can be characterized structurally in terms of the introduction of hypothetical thought into the domain of interaction. At level 3 we encounter,

on the one hand, a complex form of strategic action in which the actor is guided by hypotheses . . . and on the other hand, argumentative speech in which validity claims that have become problematic are thematized. . . . As long as the social system has so low a degree of complexity that conflicts [between norms], appear only by accident, or if structurally conditioned they appear only in a transitory and phase-specific way, then special norms of passage (e.g. rites of adolescence, of marriage, etc.) suffice to intercept them. On the other hand, as soon as domains of action arise that are no longer regulated exclusively by tradition—as is regularly the case in modern societies—there results a material for conflict that cannot be mastered within the framework of normal role behavior. Apparently one can leave this framework to engage in strategic action (in the sense of behavior based on rational choice) or to attempt to clarify problematic validity claims argumentatively, if once again a fundamentally new attitude is introduced into the domain of interaction, viz. that tentative attitude we adopt toward hypotheses, in which validity claims are suspended.[27]

On this view then, the second major transformation of the structure of interaction is also based on the introduction into this domain of a cognitive ability first acquired in dealing with the physical world: in this case, that capacity for a hypothetical attitude toward validity claims that is characteristic of formal-operational thought. And again, the structures underlying the perception of action situations at this level can be specified normatively or strategically.[28] In both cases, the normative reality of society is no longer taken for granted. But while normative claims are merely put to one side in strategic action, they are subjected to argumentative examination in discourse; thus the consensual orientation of role behavior is retained at a reflective level. But both "reflective-strategic action" and "discourse" are "limit cases" of social action. What form of action occupies then the central place at level 3 that consensual role behavior occupied at level 2? Habermas's response is "communicative action": that type of action oriented to reaching understanding from which his universal pragmatics takes its start. The distinctive element here is the interpretive activity of the subject: "in role behavior the interacting parties can rely on an understanding that has been previously secured through normative integration; to the extent that this understanding is no longer unproblematic at the next level, it has to be replaced by the interpretive accomplishments of those involved."[29] And to this end—that is, for the purpose of "negotiating" situation definitions or bringing about implicit agreement regarding the "presuppositions of communication"—the limited use of strategic and argumentative means is indispensable.

Especially in complex changeable societies, a fundamentally recognized normative context can be defined so abstractly or so loosely and imprecisely that the normative consensus which interacting parties can presuppose is very diffuse. Then the burden of finding common situation definitions falls entirely on the interpretive accomplishments of those involved. But these processes of interpretation and agreement cannot always be pushed to the level of explicit communication if the flow of interaction is not to be repeatedly interrupted. The interactive expenditure for explicit metacommunication is relatively high; moreover, these forms of communication are often not permitted or in fact not possible. . . . Agents resolve this problem by incorporating strategic elements into action that is oriented to reaching understanding. Because action is here dependent in a special way on the interpretive accomplishments of those involved, that is, by way of employing means of indirect communication, we can contrast it—as communicative action—with norm-guided role behavior. Communicative action occupies the whole spectrum of action possibilities that is bounded on one side by the case of socially integrated role behavior and on the other side by the two pure cases of indirect understanding: strategic action and discourse.[30]

The idea here is evidently that interaction at level 3 presupposes reflective-strategic and argumentative capabilities, not because strategic action or discourse as such are the normal forms of interaction but because communicative action involves the "context-dependent employment, in doses, of means of indirect understanding, an employment that is stylized to strategic action or to argumentative speech only in extreme cases."[31]

Turning now to the right side of table 1, the connecting link is Habermas's thesis that "moral consciousness" is at bottom only the ability to employ interactive competence for a conscious resolution of morally relevant conflicts. On this assumption, the developmental stages of the former can be derived as a special case from those of the latter. The actual connection is established through the concept of reciprocity.

For the consensual resolution of an action conflict, there is required naturally a point of view that can be agreed upon and with the help of which a transitive ordering of the contested interests can be established. But competent subjects will agree about such a fundamental viewpoint—independently of accidental commonalities of social origin, tradition, basic attitude, etc.—only if it arises from the very structures of possible interaction. The reciprocity between acting subjects is such a point of view. In communicative action a relationship of at least incomplete reciprocity is established with the interpersonal relation between the involved parties. Two persons stand in an incompletely reciprocal relationship when one may do or expect x only in so far as the other may do or expect y (e.g. teacher/pupil, parent/child). Their relationship is completely reciprocal if both may do or expect the same thing (x = y) in comparable situations (e.g. the norms of civil law).[32]

The claim here is not that reciprocity per se is a fundamental norm of all interaction but that all subjects capable of speech and action have an intuitive grasp of reciprocity since it belongs to the very structure of interaction. And this *intuitive* knowledge can be drawn upon for the *conscious* resolution of moral conflicts.

Kohlberg's stages of moral consciousness can be derived now by applying the demand for reciprocity (complete and incomplete) to the structures of interaction successively mastered by the developing subject. At the first level these comprise concrete actions and action consequences organized in the dimension pleasure/pain; the demand for incomplete reciprocity here yields Kohlberg's stage 1 (punishment and obedience orientation), and for complete reciprocity his stage 2 (instrumental hedonism). At the second level interaction structures are perceived in terms of reciprocally related, generalized expectations (roles, norms); when the requirement of incomplete reciprocity is applied to the expectations of reference persons or groups, we get Kohlberg's stage 3 (interpersonal concordance or good boy–nice girl orientation); applied to the normative system underpinning the social order it yields stage 4 (law and order orientation). The structure distinctive of the third level is the universal principle, which is consistent only with a demand for complete reciprocity. To generate Kohlberg's stages 5 and 6 (and his own stage 7), Habermas turns to "the degree to which the motives for action are symbolically structured":

If the needs relevant to action are allowed to remain outside of the symbolic universe, then the permissible universalistic norms of action have the character of rules that maximize utility and general legal norms that provides scope for the strategic pursuit of private interests under the condition that the egoistic freedom of one is compatible with that of all. The egocentrism of the second stage is thereby literally raised to a principle. This corresponds to Kohlberg's stage 5 (contractual-legalistic orientation). If the needs are understood as culturally interpreted, but attributed to individuals as natural properties, the permissible universalistic norms of action have the character of moral norms. Each individual is supposed to test the generalizability of the norm in question. This corresponds to Kohlberg's stage 6 (conscience orientation). Only at the level of a universal ethics of language can the need interpretations themselves—that is, what each individual believes he ought to understand and to represent as his "true" interests—also be the object of practical discourse. Kohlberg does not differentiate this stage from stage 6, although this is a qualitative difference: the principle of justification of norms is no longer the monologically applicable *principle* of generalizability, but the communally followed *procedure* of discursive redemption of normative validity claims.[33]

The importance of this distinction should be evident from the brief comparison of Kant and Habermas in the preceding section. If need interpretations are no longer regarded as given but are drawn into the very process of discursive will-formation, the relationship of inner nature to rational autonomy alters signficantly. Viewed exclusively from the perspective of a formalistic ethics, autonomy requires the vigilant separation of inclination from duty and the exclusion of the former from the motives for action; it requires that inner nature, in the form of culturally interpreted needs, be rigorously subordinated to the claims of the rational will in the form of a monologically applied principle of universalizability. Viewed now from the perspective of ego development and identity formation, autonomy requires instead the communicative rationalization of need interpretations themselves; inner nature is not excluded as nature from the realm of freedom but is given "access to the interpretive possibilities of cultural tradition" and made increasingly transparent in the "medium of value-forming and norm-forming communications that incorporate aesthetic experiences."[34]

This discussion has focused almost exclusively on the cognitive rather than the motivational side of development—that is, on the communication structures that the child successively masters rather than on the psychodynamics of the formative process. This reflects the focus of Habermas's own writings on ego development, which is not to say that he considers the motivational side unimportant. On the contrary, he insists that the process of growing into progressively more complex structures of interaction requires, if it is not to result in pathological developments, that the subject's needs find adequate interpretations in these structures. But we do not have to turn to pathology to document the importance of this aspect of the formative process; the frequent discrepancies between the capacity for moral judgment (which Kohlberg tests) and actual moral practice give evidence of the same.

Someone who has acquired the interactive competence of a certain level will form a moral consciousness of the same level to the extent that his motivatonal structure does not hinder him from holding to the structures of everyday action under stress as well, in the consensual resolution of action conflicts. But in many cases the general qualifications for role behavior that suffice for dealing with normal situations cannot be stabilized under the stress of open conflict. The person in question will then fall back below the threshold of his interactive competence in his moral actions, or even in both his actions and judgments; there is thus a shifting between the level of his normal role behavior and the level at which he processes moral conflicts. Because it places the acting subject under the imperative of a *conscious* process-ing of conflicts, moral consciousness is an indicator of the degree of stability of general interactive competence. . . . This throws some light on the meaning of moral action in general: we qualify those persons as morally "good" who hold to the interactive competence acquired for normal conflict-poor situations even under stress, i.e. in morally relevant conflicts of action . . . instead of unconsciously avoiding them.[35]

In the presystematic, critical phase of his development, Habermas's approach to established lines of social research was typically two-sided; he identified both strengths and weaknesses and suggested ways of preserving the former while avoiding the latter. In his more recent systematic, constructive work on communication and socializa-tion, his attitude toward at least one line of research seems more uni-formly positive: competence-development approaches to language, thought, and action. In a way, this is to be expected, since his own methodological reflections led him to single these out; they represent the scientific counterparts to the transcendental and developmental-logical perspectives of classical German philosophy. And in this pro-grammatic stage of development, it is perhaps understandable that Habermas's theoretical endeavors should rely heavily on existing paradigms. On the other hand, there are very real methodological and substantive problems confronting them, and these Habermas has largely ignored. One wonders, for example, how well Kohlberg's claims would stand up to that type of historical-hermeneutic critique that Habermas earlier directed at other allegedly universal interpre-tive frameworks. Do competence-development approaches really provide a way of "reaching behind" the profound historicity of human thought and action? Or is this just the most recent "objectivist illusion," one that could be unmasked by exhibiting the context boundedness of basic categories and assumptions? The shadow of the hermeneutic circle (in its Gadamerian, neo-Wittgensteinian, Kuhnian forms) has by no means been finally dispelled. But I shall have to leave this issue to the general discussion that is already underway and merely note a few of the methodological implications of the theory of communicative competence.

1. As we saw above, Habermas's reconstructed historical materialism is an attempt to integrate systems-theoretic and action-theoretic perspectives; but the latter point of view remains "superordinate":

Societies are *also* systems, but their mode of development does not follow solely the logic of the expansion of system autonomy (power); social evolution transpires rather within the bounds of a logic of the life-world, the structures of which are determined by linguistically produced intersubjectivity and are based on criticizable validity claims.[36]

The reproduction of the social system and the socialization of its members are two aspects of the same process, and they are dependent on the same structures. The exchange between social systems and "outer nature" takes place through the medium of purposive-rational action governed by technical rules that are based on empirical assumptions with a claim to truth. The integration of "inner nature" takes place through the medium of communicative interaction within normative structures implying claims to rightness. Developments in both dimensions exhibit "rationally reconstructible patterns"; they have the form of "directional learning processes that work through discursively redeemable validity claims. The development of productive forces and the alteration of normative structures follow, respectively, logics of growing theoretical and practical insight."[37]

2. Given this view of the basic "constituents of social systems," the approach to action theory is decisive for social inquiry. And here we come to a great parting of the ways between "subjectivistic" approaches that acknowledge and exploit social actors' "foreknowledge" (*Vorwissen*) of their symbolically structured life-worlds, and "objectivistic" approaches that attempt to neutralize this foreknowledge as pre-scientific, culture-bound, and often misleading. Both positions rest on plausible grounds:

On the one hand: if and insofar as the pre-theoretical knowledge of members is constitutive for the social life context, basic categories and research techniques must be chosen in such a way that a reconstruction of this foreknowledge is possible. . . . On the other hand: if and insofar as the pre-theoretical knowledge of members expresses illusions concerning a social reality that can be grasped only counterintuitively, then basic concepts and research techniques must be chosen in such a way that the foreknowledge rooted in the interests of the life-world remains harmless.[38]

As we saw in chapter 3, Habermas's response to this dilemma was to underwrite the necessity for a *sinnverstehenden* approach to social reality, while attempting at the same time to overcome the particularistic, situation-bound character of traditional hermeneutics. Indeed this was a fundamental motive for developing a general theory of communication. On the basis of what has been accomplished in this area, he wants now to distinguish between the universal and the particular components in the foreknowledge of adult members of society. To the former belong the universal structures of cognitive, linquisitc, and interactive competence acquired in socialization processes in general (*überhaupt*); to the latter belong the everyday views and standards of rationality particular to given life-worlds.[39] Social inquiry involves the explicit reconstruction of both components; this reconstructed foreknowledge can be used (together with assumptions concerning empirical mechanisms) in the explanation of social processes.

3. Even if it could be successfully carried out, however, this program would not obviate the need for hermeneutic procedures; for the universal components in question are formal structures that can be filled in in an indefinite variety of ways. The structural characteristics of a given level of communicative competence do not of themselves specify a particular cultural tradition, world view, or institutional system. Gaining access to a particular life-world for purposes of systematic reconstruction would, it seems, still require the "performative" (at least virtually participatory and thus situation-bound) attitude of the hermeneutic interpreter.

Of course an adequate theory of communication would add a number of important theoretical refinements to the interpretive process. For one thing, it would specify the different dimensions along which an understanding has to be achieved—apart from the intelligibility of the symbolic expressions involved, there are questions of truth in relation to "the world," of truthfulness in relation to "each's own world," and of rightness in relation to "our world" (a shared social life-world). And in each of these dimensions it would fix the underlying universal-pragmatic structures not only "horizontally" but "vertically" (that is, developmental-logically). To this extent, the "initial situation" to which hermeneutic interpretation is bound would be theoretically grounded and thus less radically context-dependent. The interpreter could draw on an account of the universal, culturally invariant features of communication—in addition to phonetic and syntactic structures, an elementary reference system (that makes it possible to classify, serialize, localize, and temporalize the objects of experience), an elementary system of personal pronouns and speech acts (with the aid of which interpersonal relations can be established), a system of intentional expressions (for the self-presentation of subjectivity), and so forth. And he could locate different cultural expressions (such as world views and moral and legal systems), at one or another structurally defined level of development.

Now all of this would undeniably reduce the situational character of *Sinnverstehen,* but it would by no means remove it. The obvious interpretive gap between such a universal-pragmatic framework and the concrete expressions of sociocultural life would have to be filled, as always, by the artful employment of hermeneutic procedures.

We understand the meaning of a text only to the extent to which we know why the author felt himself entitled to put forward (as true) certain assertions, to express (as truthful) certain intentions, to recognize (as valid) certain values and norms. Thus the interpreter must ascertain the context which must have been commonly presupposed by the author and the contemporaneous public if those difficulties with which the text today presents us did not arise at the time . . . and the interpreter cannot even identify these presuppositions without taking a position on the validity claims implicitly tied to them. . . . Because a traditional text is understandable only to the extent that it can at the same time be justified with reference to its context, the interpreter will not understand the meaning-content of a text if he is not in a position to imagine to himself the reasons that the author might adduce under suitable conditions. And because reasons (whether for asserting facts, expressing intentions or recommending norms and values) always claim to be valid, the interpreter cannot imagine reasons to himself without judging them. . . . If he would suspend taking a position on the reasons that the author could have adduced for his text, he would not be able to treat reasons as that which they are intended to be. . . . In other words, the interpreter is obliged to retain the performative attitude that he assumes as a communicative actor even and precisely when he inquires about the presuppositions under which the text stands. This step in the analysis of presuppositions leads either to relativizing the world of the author, or to a learning process on the part of the interpreter in which he expands his own world, or to both. . . . In each of these three cases, the interpreter cannot believe that he has understood the text if he does not at the same time suppose that his interpretation fundamentally offers a basis for reaching an understanding with the author himself. . . . A successful interpretation warrants the hope that the author could agree with us on a common understanding of the context of his utterance if he could bridge the temporal distance through a learning process complementary to our interpretive process.[40]

Thus a theory of communication would not extricate social theory from the hermeneutic circle in the sense that critique could now take the form of applied theory. Even when it is theoretically grounded in a universal-pragmatic, developmental-logical account of speech and action, the critical interpretation of concrete social phenomena has an irreducibly "practical" moment. The interpreter cannot assume a purely subject-object relation to the *interpretandum* but must retain the performative attitude of a participant in communication. He must take seriously the validity claims raised by the "text" and at the same time critically examine them. His position is not unlike that of a reflective partner in dialogue: "In thematizing what the participants presuppose, in questioning the naive recognition of reciprocally raised validity claims . . . he does not place himself outside the communication context under investigation. He deepens and radicalizes it in a way that is in principle open to all participants when problems of understanding arise."[41]

It seems then that the theory of communicative competence, while introducing theoretical elements into the interpretive process and thus mitigating its radically situational character, does not entail replacing the hermeneutic orientation of the partner in dialogue with a purely theoretical or observational attitude. Even armed with this theory, the critical theorist can claim no monopoly on truth; critique cannot be pursued in isolation from the attempt to come to an understanding with others. In short it remains the case that "in a process of enlightenment there can be only participants." In this respect, the long journey through communication theory does not seem to have fundamentally altered the relation of critical theory to hermeneutics that I discussed in section 3.3.

Chapter 5

Legitimation Problems in Advanced Capitalism

Habermas's reflections on the "contradictions" and "crisis tendencies" endemic to "advanced" or "organized" capitalism are based on concepts and principles developed in chapters 1 to 4. Briefly he argues that the basic contradiction of the capitalist order remains the private appropriation of public wealth—in terms of the discourse model of practical reason: the suppression of generalizable interests through treating them as particular. As a consequence, political decisions that reflect the existing organizational principle of society ipso facto do not admit of rational consensus. They could not be justified in a general and unrestricted discussion of what, in the light of present and possible circumstances, is in the best interests of all affected by them. Hence the stability of the capitalist social formation depends on the continued effectiveness of legitimations that could not withstand discursive examination. The problem, in short, is how to distribute socially produced wealth inequitably and yet legitimately.

Stated in this way, Habermas's critique appears to be essentially moral; social reality is measured against an abstract standard of reason and found wanting. However if we recall his views on the nature of critical social theory—from the "empirical philosophy of history with a practical intent" to the "reconstruction of historical materialism"—we might expect that he would not leave off with a moral condemnation. And in fact the burden of his argument in *Legitimation Crisis* is to the effect that the basic contradiction of contemporary capitalism issues in crisis tendencies that can empirically ascertained. The critique as a whole, then, assumes a Marxist form: what is morally required is being empirically prepared; the seeds of the new society are being formed in the womb of the old But it is a Marxist critique with important differences. In the first place, the crisis tendencies pregnant with the future are no longer located immediately in the economic sphere but in the sociocultural sphere; they do not directly concern the reproduction of the material conditions of life but the reproduction of reliable structures of intersubjectivity. Habermas thus attempts to make a case for the likelihood of a legitimation crisis, not an economic crisis. (And this, of course, is what we might expect. As we saw earlier, the core of his disagreement with orthodox Marxism was precisely its overemphasis on economic factors to the exclusion of "superstructural" considerations. This was the point of his distinction between labor and interaction and the dominant motif in his reconstruction of historical materialism.)

Other important differences concern the structure and status of the crisis argument itself. Habermas distinguishes four types of "*possible crisis tendencies*" in advanced capitalism, tendencies rooted in the functioning of the economy and the administration, and in the needs for legitimation and motivation.[1] Any one of these tendencies, or more probably some combination of them, *could,* he holds, erupt into an actual crisis.[2] But to say that a crisis could occur is not to say that it *will* occur. And it is the latter claim that is characteristic of Marxist critique. Accordingly the question to which Habermas addresses himself is, Can a crisis of advanced capitalism be systematically predicted today? His response is neither a clear "yes" nor a clear "no" but a qualified conditional thesis.

In the first place, he does not think it possible at the moment to decide cogently the "question about the chances for a self-transformation (*Selbstaufhebung*) of advanced capitalism," that is, for an evolutionary self-transcendence of the capitalist principle of organization.[3]

Assuming that this does not happen, it is possible, he maintains, to construct a systematic argument for a crisis, but not an economic crisis: "I do not exclude the possibility that economic crisis can be permanently averted, although only in such a way that the contradictory steering imperatives that assert themselves in the pressure for capital realization would produce a series of other crisis tendencies. The continuing tendency toward disturbance of capitalist growth can be administratively processed and transferred by stages through the political and into the socio-cultural system."[4] "Administrative processing" of cyclical economic crises gives rise to "a bundle of crisis tendencies that, from a genetic point of view, represent a hierarchy of crisis phenomena shifted upwards from below."[5] The end result of this displacement process is, Habermas argues, a tendency toward a legitimation crisis.

But even the force of this argument is held to be conditional on the continued existence of a truth-dependent mode of socialization, one still "bound to reason." Habermas is thinking here of the chances for a "brave new world" in which the pressure for legitimation would be removed by "uncoupling" the socialization process from norms that require justification. In part 3 of *Legitimation Crisis* he critically reviews the thesis of "the end of the individual" in general and Luhmann's systems-theoretic version of it in particular. His conclusion is that this too is an open question.[6] Thus the argument for a legitimation crisis is twice conditioned; neither the possibility of a self-transformation of capitalism nor that of an "uncoupling" of motive formation from reason can be empirically excluded at present.

Even with this double conditional, the legitimation crisis argument claims no more than a "certain plausibility."[7] From the start Habermas warns against confusing "the clarification of very general structures of hypotheses" with "empirical results."[8] And he ends by acknowledging that his "argumentation sketch" falls short of providing theoretical certainty.[9] In short one has to distinguish between the predictive form of the argument and its hypothetical status.

These qualifications notwithstanding, *Legitimation Crisis* offers an insightful analysis of contemporary society, of its endemic problems and prospective fate. In these last few pages I shall examine the "argumentation sketch" advanced there.

The basic elements of the concept of crisis were already worked out in the aesthetics of the classical tragedy.

In classical aesthetics, from Aristotle to Hegel, crisis signifies the turning point in a fateful process that, despite all objectivity, does not simply impose itself from outside and does not remain external to the identity of the persons caught up in it. The contradiction expressed in the catastrophic culmination of conflict, is inherent in the structure of the action system and in the personality systems of the principal characters. Fate is fulfilled in the revelation of the conflicting norms against which the identities of the participants shatter, unless they are able to summon up the strength to win back their freedom by shattering the mythical power of fate through the formation of new identities.[10]

Through the traditions of *Heilsgeschichte,* eighteenth-century philosophy of history and nineteenth-century evolutionary social theory, this constellation of objectivity and identity, conflict and catastrophe, entered into the formative process of modern social theory. In his "historical materialism" and "critique of political economy," Marx claimed to have finally placed it on a scientific footing.

These same elements figure in Habermas's concept of crisis, but they are interpreted in the light of his theory of social evolution. On his understanding, the "objectivity of the fateful process" is to be construed in terms of systems theory—as "structurally inherent system-imperatives that are incompatible and cannot be hierarchically integrated."[11] This occurs when the "organizational principle" of a society does not permit the resolution of problems that are critical for its continued existence. But problems of "system integration" lead to crises only when they pose a threat to "social integration," that is, when they undermine the consensual foundations of social interaction. In such cases unresolved system problems lead to the disintegration of social institutions: the "identity of the persons caught up in the fateful process" is at stake: "Crisis occurrences owe their objectivity to the fact that they issue from unresolved steering problems. Although the subjects are not generally conscious of them, these steering problems create secondary problems that do affect consciousness in a specific way—precisely in such a way as to endanger social integration. The question is, when do such steering problems arise?"[12]

Marx's answer to this question apropos liberal capitalism is wellknown.[13] The organizational principle in question is the relationship of wage labor to capital anchored in the system of bourgeois law. The institutional nucleus of this system is not the state—which merely secures the structural prerequisites of the capitalist process of reproduction (civil law and its enforcement, labor legislation, education, transportation, communication, tax, banking, and business law and so on)—but the market mechanism: economic exchange is the dominant steering medium. That is, system integration (in Parsons's terms, adaptation and goal attainment) is left to the semiautonomous workings of labor, commodity, and capital markets. On Marx's analysis, this mode of organization regularly leads to structurally insoluble problems in the form, above all, of tendencies to a falling rate of profit (crises of capital accumulation) and to reduced powers of consumption and incentives to invest (crises of capital realization). Consequently the cycle of prosperity, crisis, and depression is typical of liberal capitalism. The underlying systems problems reside directly in the economic sphere; they assume crisis proportions because this same sphere has also taken on basic functions of social integration.

Bourgeois ideologies can assume a universalistic structure and appeal to generalizable interests because the property order has shed its political form and been converted into a relation of production that, it seems, can legitimate itself. The institution of the market can be founded on the justice inherent in the exchange of equivalents; and for this reason the bourgeois constitutional state finds its justification in the legitimate relations of production. This is the message of rational natural law since Locke.[14]

In contrast to traditional societies, the conflict potential of class opposition is transposed from the political into the economic sphere; legitimation no longer comes primarily "from above" (from traditional world views) but "from below" (from the inherent "justice" of the market). Whereas the traditional form of appropriating a socially produced surplus product according to privilege is incompatible with universalistic modes of intercourse, the new form is compatible with universalistic value systems, in the guise, for example, of natural law theories and utilitarian ethics. In short the class relationship is institutionalized through the labor market and therefore "depoliticized."

Because the *social power* of the capitalist is institutionalized as an exchange relation in the form of the private labor contract, and the siphoning off of privately available surplus value has replaced *political dependency*, the market assumes, together with its cybernetic function, an ideological function. The class relationship can assume the anonymous, unpolitical form of wage dependency. In Marx, therefore, theoretical analysis of the value form has the double task of uncovering both the steering principle of commerce in a market economy and the basic ideology of bourgeois class society. The theory of value serves at the same time the functional analysis of the economic system and the critique of ideology of a class domination that can be unmasked, even for the bourgeois consciousness, through the proof that in the labor market equivalents are not exchanged.[15]

The type of crisis endemic to the liberal capitalist order is a function of this transposition of the conflict of class interests into the economic steering system: dangers to system integration (in the form of periodically recurring accumulation crises) are direct threats to social integration. "Economic crisis is immediately transformed into social crisis; for in unmasking the opposition of social classes, it provides a practical critique of ideology of the market's pretension to be free of power."[16] The displacement of conflicts of interest from the political to the economic sphere results in structurally insoluble problems (accumulation crises) that themselves bring to light the latent class antagonism. Thus Marx's critique of political economy could take the form of a systems analysis of the capitalist reproduction process that itself yielded action-theoretic assumptions for the theory of class conflict. His analysis of economic processes can be translated directly into an analysis of social processes. The liberal capitalist process of production is at the same time a "dialectic of the moral life."

Whatever its merits as an analysis of liberal capitalism—and Habermas holds them to be considerable—Marx's critique of political economy can no longer be applied to organized capitalism. There are a number of reasons for this, the primary among them being the changed relationship between the state and the economy; the latter no longer has the degree of autonomy that justified the exclusivity of Marx's focus. By means of global planning, the state regulates the economic cycle as a whole, and it creates and improves conditions for utilizing excess accumulated capital. Habermas is referring here to such phenomena as government credits, price guarantees, subsidies, loans, contracts, income redistribution, and labor policy through which adjustments are made between competing imperatives of steady growth, stability of the currency, full employment, and the balance of foreign trade; and to such phenomena as government organization of supranational economic blocks, unproductive consumption (in armaments and space, for instance), improvement of the material and immaterial infrastructures (such as transportation, communication, health, housing, city planning, science, and research and development), improvement of the productivity of labor (through general education, vocational schools, training programs and the like), and relief from the social costs of private production (by unemployment compensation, welfare, and ecological repair, for example) through which opportunities for capital investment are opened and improved and the productivity of labor is increased. As a result of this altered configuration of the economic and political-administrative subsystems, a number of the presuppositions underlying the classical Marxian crisis arguments no longer hold true. I shall mention two of the most important: (1) Governmental activity has altered the form of the production of surplus value; by filling functional gaps in the market, the state intervenes in the process of capital accumulation. It heightens the productivity of labor through the production of "collective commodities" (material and immaterial infrastructure) and through organizing the educational system in general, and scientific-technical progress in particular. The state

now expends capital to purchase the *indirectly productive* labor power of scientists, engineers, teachers, etc. and to transform the products of their labor into cost-cutting commodities of the category referred to. If one holds fast to a dogmatic conceptual strategy and conceives of reflexive labor as unproductive labor (in the Marxian sense), the specific function of this labor for the realization process is overlooked. Reflexive labor is not productive in the sense of the direct production of surplus value . . . But it is also not unproductive; for then it would have no net effect on the production of surplus value. . . . This reflection shows that the classical fundamental categories of the (Marxian) theory of value are insufficient for the analysis of governmental policy in education, technology and science. It also shows that it is an empirical question whether the new form of production of surplus value can compensate for the tendential fall in the rate of profit, that is, whether it can work against economic crisis.[17]

(2) In certain large sectors of the economy the mechanism of the market has been replaced by "quasi-political compromise" between business and unions in determining the cost of labor power. Since the cost of labor power is the unit of measure in the Marxian calculation of value, this introduces a political dimension into the very foundations of value theory.

Through the system of "political" wages, negotiated on the basis of wage scales, it has been possible—above all in the capital- and growth-intensive sectors of the economy—to mitigate the opposition between wage labor and capital and to bring about a partial class compromise. . . . Of course, one can again hold fast to a dogmatic conceptual strategy and equate by definition the average wage with the costs of the reproduction of labor power. But in so doing one prejudices at the analytical level the (no doubt) empirically substantial question of whether the class struggle, organized politically and through unionization, has perhaps had a stabilizing effect only becuase it has been successful in an economic sense and has visibly altered the rate of exploitation to the advantage of the best organized parts of the working class.[18]

The relations of production have been repoliticized. Price setting, which replaces competition in oligopolistic markets, has its counterpart in the "political price" that the commodity called labor receives. In Marxist terms, "class compromise" of a sort has become part of the structure of advanced capitalism; the real income of the dependent workers depends not only on exchange relations in the market but on relations of political power as well.

The point of this line of argument is that the organizational principle of capitalism has changed. The "unpolitical" relationship between wage labor and capital and the autonomy of the economic sphere vis-à-vis the political, have given way to a "quasi-political" distribution of the social product and to the assumption by the state of market-complementing and market-replacing functions. Thus the Marxian theory of value and the crisis arguments formulated in terms of it are inadequate. This is not to say that economic crises cannot or will not occur. Rather the arguments for their inevitability have lost their cogency. In the present state of knowledge, there are no decisive arguments of a purely economic nature for the necessity of crisis. To the extent that what happens in the economy is a function of government activity, the examination of crisis tendencies in contemporary society has to take into account the nature and limits of administrative intervention.

In making good the functional weaknesses of the market and compensating for its politically intolerable consequences, the state apparatus is faced simultaneously with two tasks.

On the one hand, it is supposed to raise the requisite amount of taxes by skimming off profits and income and to use the available taxes so rationally that crisis-ridden disturbances of growth can be avoided. On the other hand, the selective raising of taxes, the discernible pattern of priorities in their use, and the administrative performances themselves must be so constituted that the need for legitimation can be satisfied as it arises. If the state fails in the former task, there is a deficit in administrative rationality. If it fails in the latter task, a deficit in legitimation results.[19]

Accordingly Habermas moves next to an assessment of arguments for the inevitability of a "rationality crisis" in advanced capitalism. This concept is modeled after that of the economic crisis; it is a form of system crisis in which a breakdown in steering performances (system integration) leads to a breakdown in social integration. However, the steering mechanism in question is no longer a self-regulating market but a state apparatus that has taken on market-replacing and market-complementing functions. A deficit in administrative rationality occurs when the state is unable to reconcile and fulfill imperatives issuing from the economic system. But although rationality crises are in this sense displaced economic crises, the terms of their development and possible resolution are markedly different: administrative planning and the exercise of political power do not have the same "logic" as the market.

Habermas reviews several different arguments for this type of crisis, arguments based on the incompatibility of collective planning with the "anarchistic" interests of private capital and other organized groups; arguments based on the permanent inflation and crisis in public finances that result from the government's assumption of the costs of a more and more socialized production (such as armaments, transportation, communication, research and development, housing, health care, social security, and so on) and the costs of its dysfunctional side-effects (among them, welfare, unemployment, ecological repair, and so forth); arguments based on the tension between the state's responsibility as a global planning authority and its need for immunization against demands for compensation from the capitalist victims of capitalist growth, demands that cripple the process of growth; and arguments based on the systematic propagation of elements incompatible with the economic system that results from government activity (for example politically oriented private investment policies, the proliferation of occupational spheres—planning bureaucracies, public service sectors, science and education—increasingly detached from the market mechanism and oriented to concrete goals, and the growth of the inactive proportion of the population that does not reproduce itself through the labor market).

Although these arguments do point out very real problems inherent in the present organization of society, they do not, Habermas argues, suffice to demonstrate the inevitability of a rationality crisis. The limits of administrative capacity to process such problems are unclear. It is difficult to specify, for example, the critical threshold of tolerance for disorganization and the extent to which it can be adapted to an increasingly disorganized environment. Nor are the limits of administrative negotiation and compromise with various interest groups and sectors of society by any means so clear as the controlling principles of the free market.

Thus there exists no *logically necessary* incompatibility between interests in global capitalist planning and freedom of investment, need for
planning and renunciation of intervention, and independence of the
state apparatus and dependency on individual interests. The possibility that the administrative system might open a compromise path between competing claims that would allow a sufficient amount of organizational rationality, cannot be excluded from the start on logical
grounds.[20]

Again this is not to say that an administrative system crisis cannot or
will not occur. Rather the arguments for the inevitability of a rationality crisis are not decisive. Their cogency rests on the assumption of
limits to planning capacity that cannot be reliably determined in the
present state of knowledge.

There is, however, another side to the capacity of the political system to discharge the necessary planning functions: the need to secure
legitimation for governmental activity. If the adequate level of mass
loyalty and compliance cannot be maintained while the steering imperatives taken over from the economic system are carried through,
there is the danger of a legitimation crisis. Although both rationality
crises and legitimation crises arise in the political system, they are importantly different. The former are "output" crises; they occur when
the state apparatus cannot, under given boundary conditions,
adequately steer the economic system. In this sense, a rationality crisis
is a displaced economic crisis; the threat to system integration, in the
form of a disorganization of steering performances, leads to a withdrawal of legitimation, a threat to social integration. By contrast, the
legitimation crisis is not directly a system crisis, but an "identity crisis,"
that is, a direct threat to social integration.

One would initially suppose that crisis arguments directed to the
sphere of legitimation would be even more tenuous than those focusing on the political-administrative system. If the logic of government
planning is such that hard and fast limits are difficult to determine,
the logic of procuring and maintaining legitimation is, it seems, even
less amenable to the drawing of precise boundaries. Nevertheless it is
here that Habermas takes his stand. He deploys a two-sided argument, focusing first (and inconclusively) on the type of legitimations
needed in organized capitalist society and then on the limits set them
by certain aspects of sociocultural development.

With the repoliticization of the relations of production, the ideology of fair exchange has lost its force. There is a general awareness that the distribution of social wealth depends in no small measure on governmental policies and the quasi-political negotiation of rewards and obligations. At the same time, if the capitalist principle of organization is to be maintained, economic growth has to be achieved in accord with priorities shaped by private goals of profit maximization. Since these priorities have lost the appearance of being "natural," there is a need for legitimation. In this sense, the basis contradiction of organized capitalism remains the private appropriation of public wealth, and the class structure, although latent, is still behind the basic legitimation problem: how to distribute the social product inequitably and yet legitimately. Since the appeal to the inherent "justice" of the market no longer suffices, there is need for some "substitute program."

Recoupling the economic system to the political . . . creates an increased need for legitimation. The state apparatus no longer, as in liberal capitalism, merely secures the general conditions of production . . . but is now actively engaged in it. It must therefore . . . like the pre-capitalist state . . . be legitimated, although it can no longer rely on the residues of tradition that have been undermined and worn out during the development of capitalism. Moreover, through the universalistic value system of bourgeois ideology, civil rights— including the right to participate in political elections—have become established; and legitimation can be dissociated from the mechanism of elections only temporarily and under extraordinary conditions. The problem is resolved through a system of formal democracy. Genuine participation of citizens in processes of political will-formation, that is, substantive democracy, would bring to consciousness the contradiction between administratively socialized production and the continued private appropriation and use of surplus value. In order to keep this contradiction from being thematized, the administrative system must be sufficiently independent of legitimating will-formation.[21]

"Formally democratic" institutions and procedures ensure both a diffuse, generalized mass loyalty and the requisite independence of administrative decision-making from the specific interests of the citizens. They are democratic in form but not in substance. The public realm, whose functions have been reduced largely to periodic plebiscites in which acclamation can be granted or withheld, is "structurally depoliticized."

Essential to this system is a widespread *civil privatism*—"political abstinence combined with an orientation to career, leisure, and consumption"— which "promotes the expectation of suitable rewards within the system (money, leisure, time, and security)."[22] This involves a "high output—low input" orientation of the citizenry vis à-vis the government, an orientation that is reciprocated in the welfare state program of the latter, and a "familial-vocational privatism" that consists in a "family orientation with developed interests in consumption and leisure on the one hand, and in a career orientation suitable to status competition on the other," an orientation that corresponds to the competitive structures of the educational and occupational systems.[23] Furthermore the structural depoliticization of the public sphere is itself justified by democratic elite theories or by technocratic systems theories, which—like the classical doctrine of political economy—suggest the "naturalness" of the existing organization of society.

According to Habermas, legitimation deficits arise in this system when civil privatism is undermined by the spread of administrative rationality itself:

A legitimation deficit means that is it not possible by administrative means to maintain effective normative structures to the extent required. During the course of capitalist development, the political system shifts its boundaries not only into the economic system, but also into the socio-cultural system. While organizational rationality spreads, cultural traditions are undermined and weakened. The residue of tradition, howver, must escape the administrative grasp, for traditions important for legitimation cannot be regenerated administratively. Furthermore, administrative manipulation of cultural matters has the unintended side effect of causing meanings and norms previously fixed by tradition and belonging to the boundary conditions of the political system to be publicly thematized. In this way, the scope of discursive will-formation expands—a process that shakes the structures of the depoliticized public realm so important for the continued existence of the system.[24]

The expanded activity of the state produces an increase in the need for legitimation, for justification of government intervention into new areas of life. At the same time, the very process of subjecting sectors of social life to administrative planning produces the unintended side-effect of undermining traditional legitimations. "Rationalization" destroys the unquestionable character of validity claims that were pre-

viously taken for granted; it stirs up matters that were previously settled by the cultural tradition in an unproblematic way; and thus it
furthers the politicization of areas of life previously assigned to the
private sphere. For example, educational (especially curriculum)
planning, the planning of the health system, and family planning
have the effect of publicizing and thematizing matters that were once
culturally taken for granted. "The end effect is a consciousness of the
contingency, not only of the contents of tradition, but also of the
techniques of tradition." [25] And this development endangers the civil
privatism essential to the depoliticized public realm. "Efforts at participation and the plethora of alternative models . . . are indications of
this danger, as is the increasing number of citizen's initiatives."[26]

Attempts to compensate for ensuing legitimation deficits through
conscious manipulation are faced with systematic limits, for the cultural system is "peculiarly resistant" to administrative control. "There
is no administrative production of meaning. The commercial production and administrative planning of symbols exhausts the normative
force of counterfactual validity claims. The procurement of legitimation is self-defeating as soon as the mode of procurement is seen
through."[27] Thus the effect of the administrative processing of economically conditioned crisis tendencies (that is, of the introduction of
"legitimate power" into the reproduction process) is an increased
pressure for legitimation. This pressure issues not only from the need
to secure acceptance of increased activity in new spheres but from the
unavoidable side-effects of that activity as well; and it cannot be relieved by the "administrative production of meaning." If it cannot be
otherwise relieved, legitimation deficits occur. "The scope for action
contracts precisely at those moments in which it needs to be drastically
expanded." [28]

These arguments, if valid, support the thesis that advanced
capitalist societies encounter legitimation problems. But they are not
sufficient to establish the insolubility of these problems and the necessity of crisis. For one thing, it is not at all certain that some acceptable
trade-off between the ever scarcer resource "meaning" and the more
available resource "value" cannot be managed. If the missing legitimation can be offset by rewards conforming to the system—money, success, leisure, security, and the like— then there is no reason why a
legitimation crisis need occur. The welfare state is, after all, a relatively comfortable and secure abode; by historical standards it might

appear to be palatial. Habermas acknowledges this point and passes accordingly to the last stage of his argument.

This reflection supports my thesis that only a rigid socio-cultural system, incapable of being randomly functionalized for the needs of the administrative system, could explain a sharpening of legitimation difficulties into a legitimation crisis. A legitimation crisis can be predicted only if expectations that cannot be fulfilled either with the available quantity of value or, generally, with rewards conforming to the system, are systematically produced. A legitimation crisis must be based on a motivation crisis—that is, a discrepancy between the need for motives declared by the state, the educational and the occupational systems on the one hand, and the motivation supplied by the socio-cultural system on the other.[29]

Since he does not think it possible to predict shortages of the fiscally available quantity of value, he focuses now on the limits to procuring legitimation set by "normative structures that no longer provide the economic-political system with ideological resources, but instead confront it with exorbitant demands." [30]

It is evident that the arguments for a legitimation crisis and those for a motivation crisis are tightly intertwined. Both are concerned with sociocultural rather than with economic or administrative crisis tendencies, with disturbances in the delicate complementarity between the requirements of the state apparatus and the occupational system on the one hand, and the interpreted needs and legitimate expectations of the members of society on the other. In fact the distinction between them is basically one of orientation: the former focuses on the increased need for legitimation that arises from changes in the political system (expanded state activity), the latter on changes in the sociocultural system itself, changes that tendentially undermine the complementarity referred to above. The two can be regarded as different sides of a single argument for "a legitimation crisis based on a motivation crisis." The core of the second (motivational) strand of the argument is a demonstration that "the socio-cultural system is changing in such a way that its output becomes dysfunctional for the state and the system of social labor." Since the most important motivational patterns required for the continued stability of advanced capitalist society are the "syndromes of civil and familial-vocational privatism" that sustain a formally democratic political order and an economy based on the private appropriation of socially produced wealth, the heart of this demonstration lies in showing that these "syndromes" are being undermined.

Habermas's argument involves both systematic and historical considerations. The systematic considerations concern limitations arising from the form of socialization in which motivations for action are produced.

I doubt whether it is possible to identify any psychological constants of human nature that limit the socializing process from within. I do, however, see a limitation in the kind of socialization through which social systems have until now produced their motivations for action. The process of socialization takes place within structures of linguistic intersubjectivity; it determines an organization of behavior tied to norms requiring justification and to interpretive systems that secure identity. This communicative organization of behavior can become an obstacle to complex decision-making systems. . . . As long as we have to do with a form of socialization that binds inner nature in a communicative organization of behavior, it is inconceivable that there should be a legitimation of any action norm that guarantees, even approximately, an acceptance of decisions without reasons. The motive for readiness to conform to a decision-making power still indeterminate in content is the expectation that this power will be exercised in accord with legitimate norms of action. . . . These limits . . . could be broken through only if . . . the identity of socio-cultural systems [changed]. Only if motives for action no longer operated through norms requiring justification, and if personality systems no longer had to find their unity in identity-securing interpretive systems, could the acceptance of decisions without reasons become routine, that is, could the readiness to conform absolutely be produced to any desired degree.[31]

I shall return to this argument below. The historical considerations concern the erosion of traditions in which motivational patterns essential to capitalist society—especially civil and familial-vocational privatism—were produced and the concomitant spread of dysfunctional motivational structures.

Although Habermas stresses the importance of the ideology of fair exchange in liberal capitalism, he by no means considers it to have been the sole source of sociocultural support for that system. "Bourgeois culture as a whole . . . was always dependent on motivationally effective supplementation by traditional world views" (for example, religion, a traditionalistic civil ethic, the vocational ethos of the middle class, the fatalism of the lower class) and on such "specifically bourgeois value orientations" as possessive individualism and Benthamite utilitarianism.[32] But the process of capitalist development has itself undermined the "remains of prebourgeois traditions" on which liberal capitalism "parasitically fed." Traditional world views proved to be sociostructurally incompatible with the expansion of the sphere of "strategic-utilitarian action," that is, with the "rationalization" (Weber) of areas of life once regulated by tradition; at the same time they proved to be cognitively incompatible with the growth of science and technology and the spread of scientific-technical modes of thought through universalized formal schooling. As a result, the remains of prebourgeois traditions, which fostered civil and familial-vocational privatism, are being "non-renewably dismantled."

On the other hand, core components of bourgeois ideology, such as possessive individualism and orientations to achievement and exchange value, are also being undermined by social change. The *achievement ideology*—the idea that social rewards should be distributed on the basis of individual achievement— becomes problematic to the extent that the market loses its credibility as a "fair" mechanism for allocating these rewards; the educational system fails as a replacement mechanism, either because of intrinsic inequities or because of the increasingly problematic connection between formal education and occupational success; increasingly fragmented and monotonous labor processes undermine intrinsic motivation to achieve; and extrinsic motivation to achieve (such as income) is undermined by the noncompetitive structure of the labor market in organized sectors of the economy and the tendency toward equalization of the standards of living of lower income groups and those on welfare or unemployment. *Possessive individualism* becomes problematic to the extent that capitalist societies attain a level of social wealth at which the avoidance of basic risks and the satisfaction of basic needs are no longer the principal determinants of individual preference systems. The constant interpretation and reinterpretation of needs can—despite massive manipulation—lead to preference systems that are dysfunctional for the political-economic system. Moreover the "quality of life" is increasingly dependent on "collective commodities" (transportation, health care, education, and the like) that are less susceptible to differential demands and private appropriation. Finally *orientation to exchange value* is weakened by the growth of those segments of the population who do not reproduce their lives through the labor market and the proliferation of occupational spheres increasingly detached from the market mechanism and oriented to concrete goals. In addition, as leisure pursuits acquire increased importance, needs that cannot be satisfied monetarily expand.

These arguments, while suggestive, are clearly less than decisive. Whereas the erosion of traditional world views is a well-documented development, the erosion of the "specifically bourgeois value elements" that foster civil privatism (political abstinence) and familial-vocational privatism (crystallized around the achievement motive) is a more recent and more ambiguous phenomenon. It is not at all clear that the motivational patterns associated with welfare-statism, the competitive structures of the educational and occupational spheres, and the orientation to consumption and leisure have been weakened to the extent that we could speak of a tendency to a motivation *crisis*. Moreover even if we grant that normative structures and motivational patterns are undergoing profound change, the question remains as to where these changes will lead. Might they not, for instance, issue in some altered constellation of passivity, privatism, and consumerism no less functional for the formally democratic welfare state?

This question brings us to the next step in Habermas's argument. He maintains that the elements of bourgeois culture that are still relevant for motive formation are dysfunctional; they prevent the formation of functional equivalents for civil and familial-vocational privatism. He is thinking here of scientism, modern art, and universal morality. (1) The "authority of science" is ambiguous. We have seen that scientism, technocracy theories, and the like can fulfill ideological functions. But it is important also to see that this authority encompasses a broadly effective demand for discursive justification and critique of arbitrary structures of prejudice. Traditional attitudes of belief cannot withstand this kind of scrutiny. (2) The relationship of modern art to capitalist society is less ambiguous. Once it shed the aura of classical bourgeois art and proclaimed its radical autonomy from bourgeois society, modern art "expresses not the promise, but the irretrievable sacrifice of bourgeois rationalization, the plainly incompatible experiences and not the esoteric fulfillment of withheld, but merely deferred, gratification."[33] This development has produced a counterculture that strengthens the divergence between the values fostered by the cultural system and those required by the political and economic systems. Clearly neither of these reflections possesses the force that Habermas requires for his crisis argument. And in fact, it is on (3), the development of universal morality, that he places the burden of proof. This brings us back to the systematic considerations concerning socialization and social evolution that were introduced above. It is here that the conceptual apparatus Habermas has developed is brought directly to bear.

His argument can be broken down into the following theses:

[1] The components of world-views that secure identity and are efficacious for social integration—that is, moral systems and their accompanying interpretations—follow with increasing complexity a pattern that has a parallel at the ontogenetic level in the logic of the development of moral consciousness. A collectively attained stage of moral consciousness can, as long as the continuity of tradition endures, just as little be forgotten as can collectively gained knowledge (which does not exclude regression).[34]

This thesis was discussed in section 3.6; in the present state of knowledge it can claim the status only of a working hypothesis.

[2] There is a "conspicuous asymmetry in the form of reproduction of social life. . . . Because the mechanisms which cause develpmental advances in normative structures are independent of the *logic* of their development, their exists *a fortiori* no guarantee that a development of the forces of production and an increase of steering capacity will release exactly those normative alterations that correspond to the steering imperatives of the social system. . . . We cannot exclude the possibility that a strengthening of productive forces, which heightens the power of the system, can lead to changes in normative structures that simultaneously restrict the autonomy of the system because they bring forth new legitimacy claims and thereby constrict the range of variation of goal values.[35]

Although this thesis is formulated in terms of the theory of social evolution, it claims no more than the possibility of disproportionate political-economic and sociocultural developments.

[3] Precisely this is happening in advanced capitalism: normative structures are changing in such a way that the complementarity between the requirements of the political-economic system and the legitimate expectations of society's members is breaking down. This of course is the heart of the argument. Restricted to the critical sphere of moral development it asserts:

1. "As long as we have to do with a form of socialization that binds inner nature in a communicative organization of behavior, it is inconceivable that there should be a legitimation of any action norm that guarantees, even approximately, an acceptance of decisions without reasons."[36]

2. Since liberal capitalism, the need for legitimation of norms can be met only through appeal to universalistic value systems.

3. Today, the only form of universal morality capable of withstanding the destruction of tradition is a communicative ethics in which all politically significant decisions are tied to the formation of rational consensus in unrestricted discourse.

4. The basic elements of a communicative ethics are today already influencing typical socialization processes in several social strata, that is, they have achieved "motive-forming power."

5. As a result, the privatistic motivational patterns essential to formal democracy are threatened with disintegration, a threat that can be documented in the spread of withdrawal and protest syndromes.

Each of these assertions is certainly debatable, both on theoretical and on empirical grounds. Even if we grant the systematic points that moral systems follow a developmental logic and that communicative ethics represents the highest stage of this development, we are left with the demonstration that empirical mechanisms are today actually producing this structural alteration in patterns of motive and identity formation. This is clearly an immense undertaking, and Habermas's suggestions do little more than point the way. To mention only two—but two central—considerations: (1) the sociopsychological studies to which he specifically refers in developing the thesis that communicative ethics today has "motive-forming power" are recent and limited in scope.[37] That they have the long-term and far-reaching implications that he wishes to draw from them is surely not yet established. He does argue more generally that a "conventional" outcome of the adolescent crisis is becoming increasingly improbable because the expansion of the educational system makes possible an extended "psychosocial moratorium" for a larger segment of the population, because improved formal schooling increases the probability of dissonance between proffered patterns of interpretation and perceived social reality, and because the spread of nonauthoritarian childrearing techniques, the loosening of sexual prohibitions, and the temporary liberation (for many) from directly economic pressures are transforming socialization processes. [38] But it is clearly too early to predict that these developments will lead to increased withdrawal and protest rather than to some more or less hedonistic accommodation with the system or to other equally functional motivational patterns. In short they seem to be much too ambiguous at present to carry the weight of Habermas's argument.[39]

(2) More generally the alternative posed in *Legitimation Crisis* between acceptance of decisions without reasons and acceptance of decisions as the expression of a rational consensus may well be too broad to capture actually effective motivations. One face of the growing "cynicism of the bourgeois consciousness" to which Habermas frequently refers might be described as the willingness to accede to a political order *because* it provides an acceptable flow of system-conforming rewards. This too is a reason that can and does serve to legitimate political systems. The point here is not to side with the "brave new world" theorists against Habermas but to introduce a middle ground: acceptance of decisions *for the reason* that nothing better seems practically possible in the given circumstances. Even supposing the stage of universal morality to be widespread and granting that natural law and utilitarian interpretations have lost their force, it is difficult to see why the justification of a political order on the grounds that it provides an acceptable (in an imperfect world) distribution of "primary goods" (Rawls) could not be widely effective in sustaining that order. Appeals to the evident imperfections of the human condition, to the importance of the "bird in the hand" as opposed to the "two in the bush," to the advantages of a reformist as opposed to a revolutionary program, and the like, do not seem to be ruled out either by Habermas's systematic considerations (they have, or could easily be given, a universalistic form) or by his empirical arguments (they seem at present to have at least as much "motive-forming power" as communicative ethics and countercultural motifs).

There are other objections that might be raised against Habermas's case for a motivation crisis; but these brief considerations should suffice to show that it is inconclusive as a predictive argument. Indeed Habermas himself openly acknowledges the inadequacy of his "argumentation sketch" to engender anything more than "a certain plausibility." What is surprising, however, is that he should have given the argument a predictive form in the first place. In his earliest writings he faulted both the traditional philosophy of history and "scientific" Marxism for ignoring the practical dimension of social theory. The movement of history, he argued, is not simply a matter of theoretical necessity but of "practical necessity" as well. Its "meaning" is a meaning that social actors, in the knowledge of objective conditions, can seek to give it. In his writings of the late 1960s the theoretical side of critical theory was further developed in the notion of a "systematically generalized history," but it remained a theory "with a practical intent": to enlighten its addressees about their actual situation, real interests, and practical possibilities. And it remained a theory that could be confirmed only in practice—through self-emancipation and the successful continuation of self-formative processes. Even in his more recent writings on the theory of social evolution—which stress the theoretical and universal at the expense of the hermeneutic and situational—Habermas maintains that at least the analysis of contemporary society has an irreducible practical dimension: if the past can be systematically reconstructed, the future can only be practically projected.

Thus at no point in the development of his conception of critical theory does Habermas recommend, or even recognize, a purely theoretical-predictive approach to the analysis of contemporary society. And yet the argument of *Legitimation Crisis* seems to embody just such a perspective. The crisis tendencies singled out as "pregnant with the future" are, it is true, of a sociocultural nature—changes in normative structures and motivational patterns that are undermining the complementarity between the requirements of the political-economic system and the expectations of social subjects. Nevertheless the structure of the argument is such that no appeal to the practical self-consciousness of any identifiable social group is made, or it seems, need be made. The discrepancies in question appear to issue from the very structure and functioning of the "sociocultural subsystem" in the context of advanced capitalist society as a whole. Although they are in a sense "subjective," they arise, it seems, with something like an "objective necessity."

I do not think that Habermas intends his argument to be read in this way.[40] But the fact remains that his analysis does not exhibit the type of theory-practice relationship delineated in his methodological writings. And this is, I believe, no mere oversight; it has its roots in certain features of his thought. I shall mention only the following:

CRITIQUE

1. Although Habermas has been quite clear about the inadequacies of systems theory and the necessity for unifying systems-theoretic and action-theoretic perspectives, he has not (and does not claim to have) already constructed a suitably integrated framework. He has to be sure suggested a number of guidelines (based on his view of social systems as reproducing themselves through actions incorporating validity claims); but for most purposes, the two different frameworks remain incongruous, alternately employed rather than genuinely integrated. The crisis argument advanced in *Legitimation Crisis* is a case in point. It relies to a certain extent on the use of unreconstructed systems-theoretic concepts and assumptions; as a result, the practical-political activity of social agents tends to recede into the background.

2. More generally the shift in Habermas's conception of social theory, the deemphasis of hermeneutic motifs in favor of a more strongly theoretical program, has fostered the same tendency. As the universalistic elements in the theories of communication and social evolution have come to the fore, the situational and practical aspects of social inquiry have declined in systematic importance. This makes itself felt in a number of ways, some of which (primarily methodological) we have already noted. Here we shall be concerned with its implications for the relationship of theory to practice.

In his early *Literaturbericht* on Marxism, Habermas contrasted Kant's derivation of regulative ideas for social theory and political practice from pure practical reason in general with Marx's appeal to a situationally bound practical reason. For Marx the meaning of a historical process, "if it is not to remain hopelessly external to that process, can no longer be derived from 'consciousness in general' as an idea of practical reason." It must be derived from the "structure of the historical-social situation itself." "Alienated labor," for example, is not "a general structure of human consciousness" but "a part of this specific historical situation." And the idea of its *Aufhebung* arises correspondingly from a reason that is situationally bound and practically engaged.[41] Similar arguments can be found a decade later in the *Literaturbericht* on the logic of the social sciences, especially in the discussions of Gadamer and Danto.[42] But in his more recent writing Habermas appears to have reversed himself. His "reconstructive" derivation of the ideal speech situation from the structure of communication resembles nothing so much as Kant's "metaphysical" derivation of regulative ideas (for example, the kingdom of ends, a cosmopolitan order) from the structure of pure practical reason. And his use of the notions of rational discourse and consensus to interpret the interests that are suppressed in late capitalism again strikes one as more Kantian than Marxian—a reworking of Kant's notion of "publicity" rather than an identification of "class interests."[43] This too renders his argument less emphatically "practical" than one would have expected from the methodological writings.

Even the model for social critique proposed in *Legitimation Crisis* itself—the model of the suppression of generalizable interests—would lead one to expect a different type of argument from that which is actually advanced in the book. The interest in undistorted communication is grounded in the very structure of rational speech; it is in that sense "quasi-transcendental." By contrast generalizable interests are "historical" ones that can be communicatively shared (or agreed upon) in rational discourse. It is to the latter and not to the former that the critique of ideology is immediately directed: "A social theory critical of ideology can, therefore, identify the normative power built into the institutionalized system of a society only if it starts from the *model of the suppression of generalizable interests*," and asks, "How would the members of a social system, at a given stage in the development of productive forces, have collectively and bindingly interpreted their needs (and which norms would they have accepted as justified) if they could and would have decided on an organization of social intercourse through discursive will-formation and with adequate knowledge of the limiting conditions and functional imperatives of their society?"[44] Subjected to this kind of scrutiny, the de facto consensus underlying the institutionalized distribution of opportunities for legitimately satisfying needs may be revealed as unwarranted, illusory, ideological. The point of this type of critique is to make its addressees aware of the "domination" or "injustice" built into prevailing normative structures and their interpretations, and to motivate them to replace "value-oriented action with interest-guided action . . . in politically relevant domains."[45] The assumptions involved in this procedure are similar to ones made by Marx:

I make the methodological assumption that it is meaningful and possible to reconstruct (even for the normal case of norms recognized without conflict) the hidden interest positions of involved individuals or groups by counterfactually imagining the limit case of a conflict between the involved parties in which they would be forced to consciously perceive their interests and strategically assert them, instead of satisfying basic interests simply by actualizing institutional values as is normally the case. Marx too had to make these or equivalent assumptions in the analysis of class struggles. He had: a) to draw a general distinction between particular and general interests; b) to understand the consciousness of justified and at the same time suppressed interests as a sufficient motive for conflict; and c) to attribute, with reason, interest positions to social groups.[46]

According to this model, the "quasi-transcendental" interest in constraint-free communication is not the *immediate* basis of sociopolitical critique; it is rather its *mediate,* normative-theoretical basis, the procedural criterion for assessing the rationality or legitimacy of concrete interests. But *Legitimation Crisis* itself—and this is true, by and large, of Habermas's other critical writings as well—clearly does not move at the level of identifying the "interest positions" of specific social groups. In part this is because he has been primarily concerned with reworking the foundations of critical theory. (Thus, for example, in *Legitimation Crisis* he directs his efforts as much to grounding as to applying his model of critique.) But the focus of his attention is only part of the explanation; the rather diffuse practical import of his analysis of contemporary society results as well from the nature and conclusions of that analysis.

3. From the time of his *Habilitationsschrift* on the *Strukturwandel der Öffentlichkeit*, the political accent of Habermas's writings has been on the deformation and disintegration of the public sphere in capitalist society. In that early work he poignantly contrasted the promise conveyed at the time of the bourgeois revolutions through such notions as "public opinion," "public sphere," and "publicity" (in the sense of the "publicness" of decision-making processes) with the contemporary reality that is expressed in the ideas of "public opinion research," "public relations," and "publicity" (in its current sense). The liberal model of the public sphere was directed against the arcane practices of the absolutist state; it envisioned the replacement of the rule of authority with that of reason: *veritas non auctoritas facit legem.* The public sphere, as a political public of private persons reasoning publicly, was to exercise a critical function in mediating the relations between the essentially separate realms of civil society and the state. Although participation was generally restricted to adult male individuals of

property and education, the public sphere was understood to represent not a particular class, but mankind as such—the *bourgeois* was the *homme*. But the social basis of this model contained the seeds of its disintegration. Recognizing the anarchistic and antagonistic character of civil society, Hegel rejected the liberal fictions on the basis of which the public sphere could be connected, even tendentially, with the universal; it was rather the sphere of the particular, the subjective, the accidental. By the time of Mill and Marx, it was clear that behind the facade of the general interest represented by the bourgeoisie there was in reality a conflict of social interests; and this conflict extended into the political realm—civil society infected the state with its own antagonism.

The later development of capitalism significantly altered the relation between state and society, resulting in a structural transformation of the public sphere.

Group needs that can expect no satisfaction from a self-regulating market tend to be regulated through the state. The public sphere that must now mediate these demands becomes a field for the competition of interests. . . . Laws correspond in a more or less accidental manner to the compromise of conflicting private interests. In the political public sphere today, social organizations act in relation to the state, whether through the agency of political parties or directly in cooperation with the public administration. With the interweaving of the public and private realms, not only do political authorities assume a certain function in the sphere of commodity exchange and social labor, but conversely social powers now assume political functions. This leads to a kind of "refeudalization" of the public sphere. Large organizations strive for a kind of political compromise with the state and with one another, excluding the public whenever possible. But at the same time they must secure at least a plebiscitary support among the mass of the population through the development of demonstrative publicity.[47]

The critical thrust of this early study has a familiar ring: capitalist society is measured against its own legitimating ideals and is found wanting. But the accent here is directly on the political rather than the economic, that is, on the structures and preconditions of a politically functioning public sphere and on the ideal of rational self-determination that it embodies.

As we saw in chapter 1, it is precisely the desiccation of the public sphere, the surrender of the idea of rationalizing power through the medium of public discussion, that was the point of departure for

Habermas's critique of technology and science as ideology. The transformation of practical into technical questions legitimizes their withdrawal from public discussion and deprives the public sphere of its critical function. "Technocratic consciousness," he argued, "not only justifies a particular class' interest in domination and suppresses another class' partial need for emancipation, but affects the human race's emancipatory interest as such."[48] In eliminating the distinction between the practical and the technical, it "violates an interest grounded in one of the two fundamental conditions of our own existence: in language."[49] Faced with this "substitute ideology," critical theory must now "penetrate beyond the level of particular historical class interests to disclose the fundamental interests of mankind as such."[50] That is, since a depoliticized public sphere is essential to the stability of state-regulated capitalism and since this depoliticization is legitimated and sustained by the technocratic ideology, the critique of contemporary society must go beyond the analysis of particular interest positions to reveal the basic human interest in communication free from domination. Thus we find ourselves in a historical situation in which the politically relevant "suppressed generalizable interest" is at the same time a "quasi-transcendental interest."

The significance of this argument for the conception and exercise of critical theory is obvious. For one thing, its potential addressees seem now to be "mankind as such" rather than a particular class, and the interest whose disclosure is to motivate political action appears to be the rather diffuse human interest in rational self-determination through constraint-free communication. It is not at all clear how this level of self-understanding could serve to orient an effective political practice. The effectiveness of the bourgeois appeal to liberty, equality, and justice derived from its function as the ideology of an emerging class; these ideals were interpreted in such a way as to incorporate the particular interests of that class. The Marxian critique and reformulation of them still maintained the politically important connection to the interests of a specifiable class, and thus the connection to political practice. Extending this line of reasoning, one would expect from Habermas that after "penetrating beyond" particular class interests to a fundamental interest of mankind as such, he would return to an analysis of the former. The two levels of critique do not seem to be mutually exclusive. Why then has he not done so?

In part the answer lies once again in his views on the nature of advanced capitalism. He argues in several of his writings that the Marxian concept of class struggle can no longer be applied to this system.

State-regulated capitalism, which emerged from a reaction against the dangers to the system produced by open class antagonism, suspends class conflict. The system of advanced capitalism is so defined by a policy of securing the loyalty of the wage earning masses through rewards, that is, by avoiding conflict, that the conflict still built into the structure of society in virtue of the private mode of capital utilization is the very area of conflict which has the greatest probability of remaining latent. It recedes behind others, which, while conditioned by the mode of production, can no longer assume the form of class conflicts. . . . This means not that class antagonisms have been abolished but that they have become latent. . . . The political system has incorporated an interest—which transcends latent class boundaries—in preserving the compensatory distribution facade.[51]

This is not to deny the potential for conflict, even open and violent conflict, that arises from antagonistic social interests, disparities in the satisfaction of needs, disproportionate developments, and the like; but it is to deny that it can assume the form of class conflict.

. . . so many consequences of disparity can accumulate in certain areas and groups that explosions resembling civil war can occur. But unless they are connected with protest potential from other sectors of society no conflicts arising from such underprivilege can really overturn the system—they can only provoke it to sharp reactions incompatible with formal democracy. For underprivileged groups are not social classes, nor do they even potentially represent the mass of the population. Their disfranchisement and pauperization no longer coincide with the exploitation, because the system does not live off their labor. . . .[They] can in extreme situations react with desperate destruction and self-destruction. But as long as no coalitions are made with the privileged groups, such a civil war lacks the chance of revolutionary success that class struggle possesses.[52]

In this situation there is no clearly defined "target group" to whom—as the potential "agent of social transformation"—critical theory might be addressed. Habermas has, it is true, frequently pointed to the protest potential of youth in an expectant, if hesitant, way. But this does not mean, as some critics have supposed, that he regards students (or other youth groups) as a political force disposed to and capable of overthrowing the existing order. The argument is more subtle than that.

As the review of *Legitimation Crisis* made clear, Habermas regards the repoliticization of the public sphere as the potentially most crisis-laden tendency in contemporary capitalist society. The "syndrome of civil and familial-vocational privacy" is being undermined by (among other things) certain changes in the dominant mode of socialization, changes producing motivational patterns and value orientations that are incompatible with the requirements of the economic and political systems. Youth becomes politically relevant in this situation not as a social class but as a critical phase in the socialization process in which it is decided whether the adolescent crisis has a conventional outcome. Thus the focus is on the passage to adult status in contemporary society and on the factors promoting the formation of postconventional identities,which are, from a systemic point of view, dysfunctional. But the politically important questions remain open:

Can the new potentials for conflict and apathy, characterized by withdrawal of motivation and inclination toward protest, and supported by subcultures, lead to a refusal to perform assigned functions on such a scale as to endanger the system as a whole? Are the groups that place in question, possibly passively, the fulfillment of important system functions identical with the groups capable of conscious political action in a crisis situation? Is the process of erosion that can lead to the crumbling of functionally necessary legitimations of domination and motivations to achieve at the same time a process of politicization that creates potentials for action? . . . We have not yet developed sufficiently precise and testable hypotheses to be able to answer these questions empirically.[53]

If the repoliticization of the public sphere is the "new conflict zone" in organized capitalism; if neither "the old class antagonism" nor "the new type of underprivilege" has the potential to "activate this conflict zone"; and if "the only protest potential that gravitates toward it" arises among groups whose capacity for conscious political action remains doubtful, critical theory finds itself in a familiar embarrassment; there is no organized social movement whose interests it might seek to articulate.[54] It is this, I believe, that is ultimately behind the generality of Habermas's crisis argument. In the absence of an identifiable "agent of social transformation," he is forced to remain at the level of pointing out broad crisis tendencies intrinsic to the structure of advanced capitalism. His critique retains an anonymous character, addressed to "mankind as such" and thus to no group in particular.

In this respect the initial situation of critical theory today is not unlike that in which the earlier members of the Frankfurt school found themselves after the emigration. Habermas's response to it, however, is less pessimistic than was theirs. He has concentrated his considerable energies on developing the positive side of critique and has found reason to believe that the "total society" is not so "seamless" after all. In support of this contention he has met the contemporary sciences of man on their own fields and shaped them into a critical consciousness of the age. No better example could be found for Bloch's dictum: "reason cannot flourish without hope, hope cannot speak without reason."

Notes

NOTES TO CHAPTER 1

Section 1.1

1. Cf. Alvin Gouldner; *The Coming Crisis of Western Sociology* (New York, 1970).

2. Compare the introduction to *Theory and Practice* (Boston, 1973), where Habermas surveys his work from this perspective.

3. See "The Classical Doctrine of Politics in Relation to Social Philosophy" in ibid., pp. 41–81, for his interpretation of this transition.

4. Ibid., passim. Compare Hannah Arendt; *The Human Condition* (Garden City, N.Y., 1958), and Nikolaus Lobkowicz; *Theory and Practice: The History of a Concept* (Notre Dame, 1967). Habermas cites Arendt's work for having brought to his attention the fundamental significance of the Aristotelian distinction between *techne* and *praxis* in *Theory and Practice*, p. 286, n. 4.

5. See, for example, Carl Hempel; *Aspects of Scientific Explanation* (New York, 1965).

6. This is not to deny that the Baconian ideal exerted considerable influence before that time—for instance, on the work of Hobbes—nor that the mechanistic world view that accompanied the rise of modern science was an important factor in the social transformations that followed.

7. See, for example, the essays translated in *The Methodology of the Social Sciences* (New York, 1949) and "Science as a Vocation" in *From Max Weber*, ed. H. H. Gerth and C.W. Mills (Oxford, 1946). Weber's position on this matter was by no means as unequivocal as his interpreters have often made it out to be (See section 3.2).

8. "Dogmatism, Reason, and Decision: On Theory and Practice in Our Scientific Civilization," in *Theory and Practice*, p. 254.

9. Ibid., p. 254.

10. Habermas adopts the term *zweckrational* from Weber to designate means-end rationality. His understanding of the concept will be discussed in section 1.2. For Weber's definition, see *Economy and Society*, ed. G. Roth and C. Wittich (New York, 1968), pp. 24ff.

11. "Dogmatism, Reason, and Decision," p. 268.

12. Ibid., p. 264.

13. Ibid., pp. 254–255.

14. Four levels of rationalization are distinguished in ibid., pp. 270ff.

15. Ibid., p. 271.

16. These different models are sketched in "The Scientization of Politics and Public Opinion," *Toward a Rational Society* (Boston, 1970), pp. 62–80. Habermas does not explicitly connect them with his distinction of levels of rationalization. Neither the classification of models nor that of rationalization levels (nor their interrelation) is meant here to be more than suggestive.

17. Ibid., pp. 63–64.

18. "Dogmatism, Reason, and Decision," p. 274.

19. "Technology and Science as 'Ideology,'" in *Toward a Rational Society*, p. 106.

20. "Dogmatism, Reason, and Decision," pp. 275–276.

21. Habermas refers here to Weber and Schumpeter, and to elite theories in contemporary political sociology; "Scientization of Politics," p. 68. Compare his remarks in *Legitimation Crisis* (Boston, 1975), pp. 123ff.

22. Habermas considers the principle behind the "bourgeois public sphere" to be indispensable, but not its historical forms, which "always included ideological components." For an extensive examination of the notion of a public sphere, the historical situation in which it arose, and the socio-economic developments that have led to its transformation and imminent disintegration, see Habermas's *Strukturwandel der Öffentlichkeit* (Neuwied, 1962). A brief discussion based on this book appeared in the *Fischer Lexikon, Staat und Politik* (Frankfurt, 1964), pp. 220–226. An English translation of the latter with an introduction by Peter Hohendahl appeared in *New German Critique*, no. 3 (Fall 1974,): 45–55.

23. "Scientization of Politics," p. 67.

24. "Technical Progress and the Social Life-World," in *Toward a Rational Society*, p. 53.

25. Ibid., p. 56.

26. Ibid., p. 53.

27. Ibid., pp. 59–60.

28. Compare the discussion of hermeneutics in *Zur Logik der Sozialwissenschaften* (Frankfurt, 1970), pp. 251–290; an English translation appeared in *Understanding and Social Inquiry*, ed. F. R. Dallmayr and T. A. McCarthy (Notre Dame, 1977), pp. 335–363. This topic will be taken up in section 3.3.

29. "Scientization of Politics," p. 74.

30. "Technical Progress and the Social Life-World," p. 57.

31. "Scientization of Politics," p. 75.

Section 1.2

1. "Introduction to the Critique of Hegel's Philosophy of Right," in *Writings of*

the Young Marx on Philosophy and Society, ed. Lloyd D. Easton and Kurt H. Guddat (Garden City, N.Y., 1967). On this point, as well as on the historical remarks that follow, compare Habermas; "Literaturbericht zur philosophischen Diskussion um Marx und den Marxismus" in *Theorie und Praxis* (Frankfurt, 1971), pp. 387–463, and "Between Philosophy and Science: Marxism as Critique" in *Theory and Practice,* pp. 195–252. See also Albrecht Wellmer; *Critical Theory of Society* (New York, 1971), and "Communication and Emancipation: Reflections on the 'Linguistic Turn' in Critical Theory" in *On Critical Theory*, ed. John O'Neill (New York, 1976), pp. 231–263.

2. *Writings of the Young Marx,* ed. Easton and Guddat, p. 400.

3. *A Contribution to the Critique of Political Economy,* ed. Maurice Dobb (New York, 1970), pp. 20–21.

4. See, for example, Marx's preface to the second edition of *Capital.*

5. Compare *Knowledge and Human Interests* (Boston, 1971), chaps. 2 and 3.

6. G. Lukács; *History and Class Consciousness: Studies in Marxist Dialectics* (Cambridge, Mass., 1971).

7. See Martin Jay's informative history of the early Frankfurt school in *The Dialectical Imagination* (Boston, 1973).

8. Max Horkheimer and Theodor Adorno; *Dialectic of Enlightenment* (New York, 1972).

9. Herbert Marcuse, "Industrialization and Capitalism in the Work of Max Weber," in *Negations: Essays in Critical Theory* (Boston, 1968), pp. 223–224. The interpretation that follows is developed by Habermas in " Technology and Science as 'Ideology,'" pp. 81ff.

10. Habermas; "Technology and Science as 'Ideology,'" p. 82.

11. H. Marcuse, *One Dimensional Man* (Boston, 1964), cited by Habermas in ibid., p. 85.

12. "Technology and Science as 'Ideology,'" p. 84.

13. "Between Philosophy and Science," p. 212.

14. "Technology and Science as 'Ideology,'" pp. 85ff. For a more sympathetic account of Marcuse, see W. Leiss; *The Domination of Nature* (Boston, 1974.)

15. "Technology and Science as 'Ideology,'" p. 87. Habermas's criticism is directed only against the radical version of Marcuse's thesis; if the latter's claim that particular interests enter into the very construction of the technical apparatus is understood as referring not to basic logical structures but to specific historical forms of technology (which Marcuse also wants to maintain), then it is clearly correct. Thus Habermas's criticism does not—as some critics have supposed—amount to a denial of the "political content" of technology in every sense. The point is rather to distinguish between the "species-specific" (or as Habermas says, the "quasi-transcendental") interests underlying technological development and the particular interests that flow into concrete historical constellations of technology. Habermas does not deny the validity of the second

line of inquiry, but he does not pursue it in any detail. On this point, see
"Praktische Folgen des wissenschaftlichtechnishcen Fortschritts," *Theorie und Praxis,* pp. 336ff.

16. See chapter 2.

17. See chapter 3, sections 3.2 and 3.3.

18. See chapter 3, section 3.6.

19. "Technology and Science as 'Ideology,'" pp. 91ff.

20. See, for example, R. D. Luce and H. Raiffa; *Games and Decisions* (New York, 1957). A brief discussion of the concept of rationality along these lines can be found in C. Hempel; *Aspects of Scientific Explanation* (New York, 1965), pp. 463ff. I shall leave aside the question of the adequacy of decision-theoretic models for an analysis of rational choice.

21. Max Weber; *Economy and Society* (New York, 1968), p. 4.

22. Ibid., p. 24.

23. For instance, in *Legitimation Crisis,* pp. 86–89. In Habermas's view the central sphere of this type is the economic; and this might explain his conflation of "rational decision" and "strategic action." In mathematical economics strategic action is idealized as rational choice; the theory of economic behavior takes the form of a theory of rational choice that abstracts from questions concerning the technical appropriateness of means (in the narrower sense). In any case, this confusion, as well as that between moments and types of action in general, is cleared up in Habermas's most recent writings on the theory of action. See for example *Communication and the Evolution of Society* (Boston, 1979), pp. 117ff.

24. For instance, in "Technology and Science as 'Ideology,'"

25. Erich Hahn; "Die theoretischen Grundlagen der Soziologie von Jürgen Habermas" in *Die "Frankfurter Schule" im Lichte des Marxismus* (Frankfurt, 1970), pp. 70ff.; A. Lorenzer; *Psychoanalyse als Sozialwissenschaft* (Frankfurt, 1971), esp. pp. 47ff.; G. Therborn; "Jürgen Habermas: A New Eclecticism," in *New Left Review* 67 (1971): 69–83.

26. "A Postscript to *Knowledge and Human Interests,*" *Philosophy of the Social Sciences* 3 (1973): 186, n. 27.

27. "Labor and Interaction: Remarks on Hegel's Jena Philosophy of Mind," in *Theory and Practice,* pp. 158–159.

28. This confusion is avoided in Habermas's most recent writings. Cf. for example the introduction mentioned in note 23 above, where he explicates his distinction in basically the same way as I have here.

29. *Economy and Society,* p. 22; but see note 31 below.

30. Ibid., p. 24

31. It could be argued that Weber's "orientation solely to the behavior of inanimate (*sachlicher*) objects" is also to be taken in this broader sense. After

giving this general characterization, he goes on to say: "not every type of contact between men has a social character, but only behavior that is meaningfully oriented to the behavior of others" (p. 23). Although the example he gives of nonsocial human contact—the collision of two cyclists— does not lend itself to this interpretation (it is, as he says, "merely a happening, like a natural event"), the distinguishing feature (not meaningfully oriented to the behavior of others) might be interpreted to include purely instrumental action toward others. But for our comparative purposes, the "literal" interpretation is more useful; no claims to an adequate exegesis of Weber are intended.

32. For example, in Rationalism Divided in Two," *Positivism and Sociology,* ed. A. Giddens (London, 1974), p. 195, and in *Zur Logik der Sozialwissenschaften* (Frankfurt, 1970), pp. 128ff.

33. See for example *Communication and the Evolution of Society,* pp. 66–67. The definition of instrumental action in "Technology and Science as 'Ideology,'" pp. 91–92, is "Instrumental action is governed by technical rules based on empirical knowledge. In every case they imply empirical predictions about observable events, *physical or social*" (my emphasis).

34. Habermas uses the term monologic in several different contexts and in several different senses. In addition to the "objectification" of others, he uses it when characterizing strategic action (for example, in *Theory and Practice,* p. 151) and empirical-analytic science (for example, in *Knowledge and Human Interests,* pp. 191–192.).

35. cf. *Legitimation Crisis,* pp. 9ff., 117ff.

36. "Labor and Interaction," pp. 156–157.

37. Ibid., p. 148. It should be kept in mind that the quotations (and terminology) in this discussion are from Habermas, not Hegel. Habermas uses his interpretation to make a number of systematic points, which are fully developed only later in his theory of communication (cf. chapter 4).

38. Ibid., p. 148.

39. Ibid.

40. Ibid.

41. Ibid.

42. Ibid., p. 149.

43. Ibid., p. 154. In a series of lectures delivered at Boston University in the fall of 1974 and soon to be published in revised and expanded form, Marx Wartofsky takes a similar characterization of the generality embedded in tools as the point of departure for his "historical epistemology."

44. Ibid., p. 158.

45. Ibid.

46. Ibid., p. 159.

47. Ibid.

48. Ibid., p. 161. Compare the master-slave dialectic in Hegel's *Phenomenology of Mind.*

49. *Knowledge and Human Interests,* pp. 57–58.

50. Ibid., p. 52

51. Ibid., p. 55.

52. "Labor and Interaction," pp. 168ff.

53. Ibid., p. 151.

54. "Classical Doctrine of Politics," p. 42.

55. "Labor and Interaction," pp. 150ff.

56. Ibid., p. 151.

57. Ibid., p. 297, nn. 7, 11, where Habermas invokes Durkheim and Mead in support of this view of socialization. Compare his "Stichworte zur Theorie der Sozialisation" in *Kultur und Kritik* (Frankfurt, 1973), pp. 118–194.

58. Ibid., p. 151.

59. "Technology and Science as 'Ideology,'" pp. 93–94. In elaborating this distinction, Habermas does not entirely avoid the terminological confusion of moments and aspects of wholes with independently existing wholes. Rather than repeating the points made above, I shall simply incorporate them into the presentation of his argument.

60. Ibid., pp. 95–96.

61. Ibid., p. 96. This insight is attributed to Marx and Schumpeter.

62. Ibid., p. 98.

63. Ibid., p. 99.

64. Ibid., p. 97.

65. Ibid.

66. Ibid., p. 101. This point is argued at greater length in *Legitimation Crisis;* cf. chapter 5.

67. Ibid., p. 105.

68. Ibid., p. 111.

69. Ibid., p. 112.

70. Ibid., p. 113.

Section 1.3

1. *Knowledge and Human Interests*, p. 67 (hereafter cited as KHI).

2. Ibid., p. 67.

3. Ibid., p. 5.

4. "Postscript," p. 159. In Habermas's view this critique is already well under-way: "In 1967, I had planned to write three books, one of which, *Knowledge and Human Interests,* was to have the function of a prolegomenon, as I noted in the

preface. I decided not to carry out the idea of writing the two companion volumes, which were to have contained a critical reconstruction of the development of analytic philosophy. There are good reasons for this decision, not the least important among them being the fact that today the criticism and self-criticism of scientistic assumptions is already well under way." Ibid. He mentions explicitly the work of Apel, Geigel, Kambartel, Schnädelbach, Tugendhat, and Wellmer in Germany; the constructive philosophy of the Erlangen school (Paul Lorenzen and others); the recent discussion of the rational reconstruction of the history of science by Popper, Kuhn, Feyerabend, Lakatos, and Toulmin, among others; and the development of linguistic philosophy from Wittgenstein through Austin to the work of Searle and others on a pragmatic theory of language.

5. KHI, pp. vii, 4. This reconstruction is a central aim of the book.

6. A second line of argument, that running through the work of Wittgenstein, will be touched upon in chapter 3; the pragmatic theory of language will be dealt with in chapter 4.

7. KHI, pp. 87–88.

8. For an elucidation of this idea see K. O. Apel: "The A Priori of Communication and the Foundation of the Humanities," *Man and World,* no. 5 (February 1972): 3–37. Apel directs his critical remarks at Carnap and later logical positivists; their applicability to Mach's phenomenalism is obvious.

9. Ibid., p. 5.

10. Although there is no detailed analysis of the Popper-Kuhn controversy in Habermas's writings, it seemed appropriate to include a few remarks here, since their debate provides the Anglo-American reader with a natural bridge to his "quasi-transcendental" approach. Moreover I have been able to rely, especially for the criticism of Popper, on remarks scattered throughout Habermas's writings. See in particular his contributions to *The Positivist Dispute in German Sociology* (New York, 1976): "The Analytical Theory of Science and Dialectics," pp. 131–162, and "A Positivistically Bisected Rationalism," pp. 198–225. Cf. also Albrecht Wellmer; *Methodologie als Erkenntnistheorie. Zur Wissenschaftslehre Karl R. Poppers* (Frankfurt, 1967). Although Kuhn's book was translated into German for a series that Habermas edits, his references to it are few. My guess is that he was uncomfortable with the relativistic leanings of Kuhn's original statement.

11. "The Bucket and the Searchlight: Two Theories of Knowledge," in Popper; *Objective Knowledge* (Oxford, 1972), p. 342.

12. Ibid., p. 345.

13. Ibid., pp. 346–347.

14. Ibid., p. 346.

15. Ibid., pp. 347–348.

16. KHI, pp. 94–95.

17. Cf. Karl Popper: "Epistemology Without a Knowing Subject," in *Objective Knowledge,* pp. 106–152.

18. Habermas criticizes Popper on these points in "A Positivistically Bisected Rationalism."

19. Popper; "Epistemology Without a Knowing Subject," p. 112.

20. Cf. ibid., pp. 106ff.

21. Cf. *Criticism and the Growth of Knowledge,* ed. Imre Lakatos and Alan Musgrave, (Cambridge, 1970).

22. Thomas Kuhn, "Postscript—1969," in *The Structure of Scientific Revolution,* 2d ed. (Chicago, 1970), p. 185.

23. Ibid., pp. 205–206.

24. This is not to deny the very real differences that separate them, such as, the different weight given to "falsifications" and Kuhn's insistence, against Popper, that the progress of science cannot be described as an increasing approximation to the truth in a realistic sense.

NOTES TO CHAPTER 2

Section 2.1

1. *Knowledge and Human Interests* (Boston, 1971), p. 24 (hereafter cited as KHI).

2. Published under the title "Erkenntnis and Interesse" in *Technik und Wissenschaft als Ideologie* (Frankfurt, 1968), pp. 146–168; English translation by Jeremy Shapiro as an appendix to KHI, p. 303.

3. Ibid.

4. Ibid., p. 304.

5. Ibid., p. 307.

6. Ibid., p. 308.

7. Introduction to *Theory and Practice* (Boston, 1973), pp. 8–9.

8. Appendix to KHI, p. 311.

9. Ibid., p. 313.

10. Introduction to *Theory and Practice,* p. 14.

Section 2.2

1. See especially his contributions (1963, 1964) to *The Positivist Dispute in German Sociology* (New York, 1976); cf. also A. Wellmer, *Methodologie als Erkenntnistheorie. Zur Wissenschaftslehre Karl. R. Poppers* (Frankfurt, 1967).

2. Cf. J. Habermas and N. Luhmann, *Theorie de Gesellschaft oder Socizltechnologie-Was leistet die Systemforschung?* (Frankfurt, 1971), pp. 202ff. Some of these suggestions are touched upon in section 4.2.

3. Kuhn's *The Structure of Scientific Revolutions,* is mentioned in a footnote of KHI (p. 336 n. 30), but here as elsewhere the remarks are brief and tentative.

4. Cf. "A Positivistically Bisected Rationalism," in *The Positivist Dispute in German Sociology,* pp. 207–208; compare also the remarks on social evolution in section 3.6.

5. For instance, in his summary of the differences between empirical-analytic and hermeneutic inquiry on pp. 161–162 and 191ff. of KHI.

6. KHI, p. 35. A second, non-Kantian component of synthesis through social labor is also basic to Marx's position; cf. ibid., pp. 37ff., and Alfred Schmidt; *The Concept of Nature in Marx* (London, 1971). In addition to the fixed framework rooted in the abstract structure of labor, the materialist theory of knowledge takes account of historically changeable forms of synthesis grounded in the level of development of the forces and relations of production. Labor is not a "fixed essence" but a mechanism of human development. See section 2.4.

7. Quoted in KHI, p. 120 from C. S. Peirce, *Collected Papers,* ed. C. Hartshorne and P. Weiss, (Cambridge, Mass., 1931–35), 5:27, 398.

8. KHI, p. 124.

9. KHI, appendix, p. 308.

10. Ibid.

11. Ibid., p. 192.

12. H. Albert, "The Myth of Total Reason," in *The Positivist Dispute in German Sociology,* pp. 163–197.

13. This is, more or less, the view of Albert.

14. Cf. T. Adorno and M. Horkheimer, *Dialectic of Enlightenment* (New York, 1972); Horkheimer, *Eclipse of Reason* (New York, 1947); and Marcuse, *One-Dimensional Man* (Boston, 1964). Compare the discussion of William Leiss in *The Domination of Nature* (New York, 1972).

15. "Technology and Science as 'Ideology,' " in *Toward a Rational Society* (Boston, 1970), p. 87.

16. Ibid., p. 90.

17. Ibid., p. 88.

Section 2.3

1. KHI, p. 176.

2. Introduction to *Theory and Practice,* p. 21.

3. The same could be said of Habermas's interpretations of Hegel, Marx, Peirce, and Freud. In response to criticisms of an exegetical nature, he points out that his intentions were not purely exegetical but critical and systematic: "If one keeps in mind that I analyzed the prehistory of modern scientism be-

cause I realized that it would converge on a new concept of transcendental philosophy, it becomes easy to understand why many of the objections brought against my interpretations of individual theorists leave me rather dumbfounded." "A Postscript to KHI," *Philosophy of the Social Sciences* 3(1973): 165–166.

4. KHI, p. 148.

5. Ibid., p. 155.

6. Ibid., p. 156.

7. Ibid., p. 158.

8. Ibid., p. 168.

9. Compare the discussions of "indexicality" by Garfinkel and other ethnomentodologists.

10. Ibid., p. 168.

11. Ibid., p. 175.

12. Ibid., pp. 176–177. Cf. the discussion of hermeneutics in section 3.3.

13. Ibid., p. 195.

14. Ibid., p. 193.

Section 2.4

1. KHI, appendix, p. 310.

2. Ibid., pp. 306.

3. Paul Thiry d'Holbach; *Nature and Her Laws by Mirabaud* (London, 1816), pp. 5–6, cited by Habermas in *Theory and Practice,* p. 257.

4. "What Is Enlightenment?" in *Kant on History,* ed. L. W. Beck (New York, 1963), p. 3.

5. *Mündigkeit,* literally "majority" (from *mündig*: "of age"), is a central concept of classical German philosophy. The word translated as "tutelage" in the preceding quote from Kant is, for example, *Unmündigkeit.* Following Jeremy Shapiro in his translation of *Knowledge and Human Interests,* I have rendered it here as "autonomy and responsibility." As will become evident below, the *Mündigkeit* of an individual or group is conceived as the *telos* of a developmental or formative process (*Bildungsprozess*).

6. Kant; *Foundations of the Metaphysics of Morals,* trans. L. W. Beck (New York, 1959), p. 80, quoted in KHI, p. 200.

7. Ibid., p. 80, quoted in KHI, p. 201.

8. Fichte; "Erste Einleitung in die Wissenschaftslehre," *Ausgewählte Werke,* ed. Fritz Medicus, (Hamburg, 1962), 3: 17, quoted in KHI, p. 205.

9. KHI, p. 208.

10. Fichte, "Erste Einleitung," quoted in KHI, p. 206.

11. KHI, p. 209.

12. *Bildung,* generally "formation," can also be used more narrowly to connote processes of overall spiritual development or their completion (as "education" or "cultivation"). *Bildungsprozess* is used by Habermas in this latter sense. Cf. ibid., p. 320, translator's N. 6.

13. Ibid., pp. 17–18.

14. Ibid., p. 18.

15. Ibid., p. 10.

16. Ibid., p. 20.

17. Ibid., p. 22.

18. Ibid., p. 28.

19. Quoted in ibid. p. 29, from Marx and Engels, *Gesamtausgabe,* I, 3 (Berlin, 1932): 162.

20. KHI, pp. 39–40.

21. Ibid., p. 42.

22. A striking example of this can be found in Marx's discussion of the relation of production to distribution in *A Contribution to the Critique of Political Economy,* ed. Maurice Dobb (New York, 1970). Compare Habermas's remarks in KHI, pp. 326–329, n. 14.

23. KHI, p. 46.

24. My discussion of Habermas's methodological adaptation of psychoanalysis will be put off to chapter 3.

25. "Introductory Lectures on Psychoanalysis," in *The Standard Edition of the Complete Psychological Works of Sigmund Freud,* ed. James Strachey (London, 1953–64), V 16: 312, quoted in KHI, p. 275.

26. Ibid.

27. "The Future of an Illusion," in *Standard Edition,* 21: 6, quoted in KHI, p. 278.

28. Ibid., p. 12; in KHI, p. 281.

29. Ibid., p. 10; in KHI, p. 278.

30. KHI, p. 280.

31. Freud, *Standard Edition,* 21: 40ff; in KHI, pp. 283–284.

32. KHI, p. 284.

33. Ibid., pp. 283–284.

34. Ibid., p. 55.

35. Ibid., p. 287.

36. *Theory and Practice,* pp. 22–23.

37. KHI, appendix, p. 314.

38. Ibid., pp. 312–313.

39. This thesis is developed in the theory of communicative competence; see section 4.2.

40. KHI, p. 211.

Section 2.5

1. KHI, p. 194.

2. Ibid., pp. 94–95.

3. Ibid., pp. 194–196.

4. For example, in the appendix to KHI, p. 313, and in *Zur Logik der Socialwissenschaften,* p. 289. In *Knowledge and Human Interests* itself, this characterization is applied explicitly only to work and interaction; but the discussion of "power" in chap. 12 (pp. 281ff.) seems to imply that it has the same status.

5. For example, in the critical pages 194–197 of KHI.

6. *Theory and Practice,* p. 9.

7. Ibid., p. 22.

8. "Postscript," p. 176.

9. KHI, appendix, p. 314.

10. *Theory and Practice,* p. 17.

11. KHI, appendix, p. 315.

12. *Theory and Practice,* p. 22.

13. KHI, p. 228.

14. Ibid., p. 197.

15. Chapter 1, "Hegel's Critique of Kant," introduces the discussion of Marx in chapters 2 and 3; in chapter 2 Marx's concept of "synthesis through social labor" is broken down into Kantian and Fichtean "moments." Chapter 9 on Kant and Fichte introduces the discussion of Freud in chapters 10, 11, and 12.

16. KHI, p. 208.

17. Ibid., p. 210.

18. Ibid., pp. 210–211.

19. "Wissenschaft als Emanzipation? Eine Kritische Würdigung der Wissenschaftskonzeption der 'Kritischen Theorie,'" in *Zeitschrift für allgemeine Wissenschaftstheorie* 1 (1970): 173–195, reprinted in *Materialien zu Habermas' 'Erkenntnis und Interesse,'* ed. W. Dallmayr (Frankfurt, 1974), pp. 341–342. Cf. Dallmayr; "Critical Theory Criticized: Habermas' *Knowledge and Human Interests* and Its Aftermath," in *Philosophy of the Social Sciences* 2(1972): 211–229.

20. Ibid., pp. 341–342.

21. "Zum Problem des emanzipatorischen Interesses and seiner gesellschaftlichen Wahrnehmung," *Man and World* 3 (1970), reprinted in revised form as "Zur Geltung des emanzipatorischen Interesses," in *Materialien zu Habermas' 'Erkenntnis and Interesse,'* p. 351.

22. Ibid., p. 351.

23. Ibid., p. 358.

24. Ibid., pp. 359–360.

25. Ibid., p. 361.

26. The same lack is evident in his discussion of "the only tangible example of a science incorporating methodical self-reflection," that is, Freudian psychoanalysis (KHI, chaps. 10–11). Habermas's interpretation of the therapeutic process tends to overemphasize its cognitive side (understanding and insight) and to underplay its emotional-affective-interactional side. Although he mentions transference, working-through, and so forth, he sometimes writes as if insight were equivalent to emancipation.

27. Habermas later acknowledges this problem; cf. "Über das Subjekt der Geschichte," in *Kultur and Kritik* (Frankfurt, 1973), pp. 389ff. I take it up briefly in section 3.1.

28. Cf. for instance the introduction to *Theory and Practice* and the "Postscript" to KHI.

29. "Postscript," p. 182; cf. *Theory and Practice*, pp. 22ff.

30. "Analytic insights intervene in life, if I may borrow this dramatic phrase from Wittgenstein. . . . But [rational reconstruction] has no practical consequences. By learning logic or linguistics I do not thereby change my previous practice of reasoning or speaking." *Theory and Practice*, p. 23.

31. Ibid., p. 24. As we shall see in chapters 3 and 4, Habermas's current position is that rational reconstructions provide the normative-theoretical basis for reflection in the other (critical) sense: "The critical sciences such as psychoanalysis and social theory also depend on being able to reconstruct successfully general rules of competence. To give an example, a universal pragmatics capable of understanding the conditions that make linguistic communication at all possible has to be the theoretical basis for explaining systematically distorted communication and deviant processes of socialization." "Postscript," p. 184.

32. Because rational reconstruction provides the normative-theoretical basis for critique, Habermas assigns to it "an indirect relation to the emancipatory interest of knowledge." But it still remains that this interest "enters directly only into the power of [critical] self-reflection." *Theory and Practice*, p. 24.

33. See in particular the discussion of truth in section 4.2.

34. KHI, pp. 62–63. Habermas refers here (n. 18) to Adorno's *Negative Dialectics* (New York, 1973).

35. Ibid., p. 19.

36. Ibid., p. 52.

37. Ibid., p. 62.

38. Ibid., p. 60.

39. Ibid., p. 55.

40. "Die Rolle der Philosophie im Marxismus," remarks made at the tenth annual summer school of the Yugoslavian *Praxis* philosophers, Korcula, August 1973; subsequently printed in *Die Zukunft der Philosophie*, ed. M. Gerhardt, (Munich, 1975), pp. 191–204; an English translation, "The Place of Philosophy in Marxism," appeared in *Insurgent Sociologist* V 5, no. 2 (Winter 1975): 41–48.

41. "Wozu noch Philosophie?" *Philosophisch-politische Profile* (Frankfurt, 1971), pp. 11–36; an English translation, "Why More Philosophy?" appeared in *Social Research*, 38 (1974): 643–645.

42. "Why More Philosophy?" pp. 646– 649.

43. Ibid., p. 649.

44. Ibid., p. 643.

45. T. W. Adorno; *Eingriffe* (Frankfurt, 1963), p. 14, quoted in "Why More Philosophy?" p. 633.

46. KHI, appendix, pp. 314–315.

47. Ibid., p. 317.

48. Alasdair MacIntyre; "Ideology, Social Science, and Revolution," *Comparative Politics* 5 (1973): 322.

49. *Dialectic of Enlightenment* (New York, 1972), pp. xi–xii.

50. Ibid., p. xii.

51. "Urgeschichte der Subjektivität und verwilderte Selbstebehauptung," in *Philosophisch-politische Profile*, p. 188; compare "Ein philosophierender Intellektueller" in the same volume, pp. 176–183.

52. Generally his charge of ideological distortion is by no means as total as theirs. This is clearly implied by his criticism of their views on science and technology. See sections 1.2 and 2.2.

53. KHI, appendix, p. 314.

54. *Theory and Practice*, p. 13.

55. In *Knowledge and Human Interests* the most specific indications of how this is to be done appear in the discussion of Freud's "systematic generalization of self-reflection" in chapters 10 and 11. This will be taken up in section 3.4. Habermas's adaptation of certain methodological features of psychoanalysis does provide a clarification of, and to some extent an answer to, the questions raised here but in the end the same problems remain.

56. Ibid., p. 311; the term *Unüberschreitbarkeit* appears in the original "Erkenntnis und Interesse," in *Technik und Wissenschaft als "Ideolgie"* (Frankfurt, 1969), p. 160. Böhler, "Zur Geltung des emanzipatorischen Interesses," uses *nicht hintergehbar* to characterize the interests of knowledge; p. 350.

57. KHI, appendix, p. 311.

58. Ibid., pp. 312, 314.

59.They are "philosophy," however, not in the sense of a mode of thought opposed to "science" but in the sense of a new type of "reconstructive" science. As we shall see in chapter 4, Habermas feels that transcendental philosophy, like philosophical cosmology before it, will increasingly become less "philosopical " and more "scientific." But "reconstructive" sciences, because of their reflexive character, will be in important respects methodologically different from science in the received sense. See n. 117 below.

60. Ibid., p. vii; cf. "Postscript," pp. 158ff.

61. Ibid., p. 35.

62. Ibid., p. 36.

63. Ibid., p. 30.

64. Ibid., p. 39.

65. Ibid., p. 35.

66. Ibid., p. 135.

67. Michael Theunissen; *Gesellschaft und Geschichte: Zur Kritik der kritischen Theorie* (Berlin, 1969).

68. Ibid., pp. 4,5.

69. Section 2.1; cf. the appendix to KHI.

70. Theunissen, *Gesellschaft*, p. 13.

71. Ibid., p. 14.

72. KHI, Chap. 2.

73. C. F. von Weizäcker; Die *Einheit der Natur* (Munich, 1971), pp. 140–141, cited by Habermas in "Postscript," p. 163.

74. KHI, chap. 2. In his approach to Marx's epistemology, Habermas is indebted to Alfred Schmidt; *The Concept of Nature in Marx* (London, 1971).

75. KHI, p. 26.

76. Ibid., p. 34.

77. Ibid.

78. Ibid., p. 41.

79. Ibid., p. 27.

80. Ibid., p. 26.

81. Ibid., p. 28.

82. Ibid., p. 34.

83. Ibid., p. 28.

84. Ibid., p. 33.

85. Ibid., p. 27.

86. Ibid., p. 34.

87. Ibid., p. 41.

88. Ibid., p. 100. Since my concern here is with Habermas's own position, I will ignore problems arising from the different stages of development in Peirce's thought.

89. Ibid., p. 98.

90. Ibid., p. 101.

91. Ibid., p. 102; his criticism of this approach follows on pp. 102–107.

92. Ibid., pp. 107ff.

93. Ibid., p. 102; his discussion of this approach is the burden of chapter 6.

94. Ibid., p. 130.

95. Ibid., p. 131.

96. Ibid., p. 27.

97. Cf. *Theory and Practice,* p. 9: "expressions capable of truth refer to a reality that is objectivated (i.e. *simultaneously* disclosed *(freigelegt)* and constituted) as such in two different contexts of action and experience." Questions of truth, objectivity, and reality are reexamined in Habermas's later writings on the theory of communication. See, for example, "Wahrheitstheorien" in *Wirklichkeit und Reflexion: Festschrift für Walter Schulz* (Pfullingen, 1973), pp. 211–265; there is a brief discussion in English in "Postscript," pp. 166–172. "I shall return to these problems in chapter 4.

98. KHI, p. 101.

99. Ibid.

100. Ibid., p. 34.

101. Ibid., p. 282.

102. Ibid.

103. Ibid., p. 196.

104. Ibid., p. 211.

105. Ibid., appendix, pp. 313–314.

106. *Theory and Practice,* p. 21.

107. "Postscript," p. 185. Habermas's emphasis there is different from mine.

108. Ibid., p. 27.

109. Ibid., p. 41.

110. Ibid., p. 286.

111. Ibid., p. 35.

112. Ibid., p. 41.

113. Ibid., pp. 133–134.

114. Ibid., p. 285. Compare the contemporary discussion concerning the implicit anthropomorphism of concept formation in ethology.

115. *Theory and Practice,* pp. 21–22. In his lectures at Frankfurt University on "Probleme einer philosophischen Anthropologie" (Winter Semester, 1966/ 67—a transcript was published in a "pirate edition"), Habermas pursued just such a "reflection on the prehistory of culture" in the context of contemporary evolutionary, ethological, and anthropological research. Apparently, what he has in mind is a nonidealist reworking of certain centeral themes from the philosophy of nature of German Idealism, themes that he previously examined in his dissertation on Schelling. See note 118.

116. KHI, p. 286.

117. This seems to be implied by his remarks in "Die Rolle der Philosophie im Marxismus," p. 201: "The unity of nature and history cannot be comprehended philosophically so long as progress in physics and social theory has not led to a general theory of nature or a general theory of social development. . . . Philosophy is the—until now irreplaceable—regent [*Statthalter*] of a claim to unity and generalization, a claim that will of course be redeemed scientifically or not at all." As Habermas made clear in conversation, the term *Statthalter* (literally: "place-holder") is deliberate; it is meant to convey the provisory status of philosophy in relation to science. Just as natural philosophy, for example, gave way to natural science, so too will the tasks remaining to philosophy eventually be assumed by science. Of course the "science" capable of assuming these tasks will not be the science of today. See note 59.

118. *Theory and Practice,* p. 285, n. 38. Habermas's evident wariness in regard to "the traditional problem of ultimate foundations" does not spring from any easy scepticism. His doctoral dissertation, *Das Absolute und die Geschichte. Von der Zwiespältigkeit in Schellings Denken* (University of Bonn, 1954), dealt historically and systematically with the repeated attempts of Schelling and his contemporaries to resolve it. He is quite clear there about the failure of transcendental idealism, *Naturphilosophie,* and *Identitätsphilosophie,* as well as of more traditional approaches, to do so. In his published works, Habermas has since been reluctant to treat the problem explicitly; his remarks are typically confined to critical allusions to "First Philosophy." But as I hope to have shown in the preceding pages, the spectre of ultimate foundations still haunts the theory of cognitive interests; Habermas is not unaware of the problem but seems to feel that it can be remedied (if at all) only to the extent that the future progress of "science" leads to a unified theory of nature and society. See note 117.

NOTES TO CHAPTER 3

Section 3.1

1. The "Literaturbericht" first appeared in *Philosophische Rundschau* 5, nos. 3/4, (1957): 165ff., and was subsequently reprinted in *Theorie und Praxis* (Neuwied, 1963), pp. 261–335.

2. The former exchange is documented in T. Adorno et al.; *Der Positivismusstreit in der deutschen Soziologie* (Neuwied, 1969); the English translation is *The Positivist Dispute in German Sociology* (New York 1976). The latter exchange

is documented in K.-O. Apel et al.; *Hermeneutik und Ideologiekritik* (Frankfurt, 1971).

The first important restatement of Habermas's views on methodology that systematically incorporates ideas from these traditions is the "Literaturbericht zur Logik der Sozialwissenschaften," which first appeared in *Philosophische Rundschau,* Beiheft 5 (Tübingen, 1967) and was subsequently reprinted in *Zur Logik der Sozialwissenschaften* (Frankfurt, 1970), pp. 71–310.

In the first edition of *Theorie und Praxis* (1963), the 1957 review of Marxist literature was reprinted without explicit reservations. In the preface to the second edition (1967), Habermas noted that he would no longer use the same formulations and referred the reader to his (1967) review of literature on the logic of the social sciences, indicating that he regarded the latter as an advance over his earlier statements. The same indication is conveyed in his remarks on the essay "Zwischen Philosophie und Wissenschaft: Marxismus als Kritik," which first appeared in *Theorie und Praxis* (1963); in the most recent edition of this work (Frankfurt, 1971), a footnote is added (p. 287, n. 19) referring the reader to his "changed conception" in *Zur Logik der Sozialwissenschaften* (1967) and *Erkenntnis und Interesse* (1968); in the English translation, *Theory and Practice* (Boston, 1973), see p. 301; n. 19. Thus the appearance of these two works may be taken as the first watershed in the development of Habermas's views on methodology. This development was, to be sure, gradual; a comparison of his 1957 review with his contributions to the Positivismusstreit (1963, 1964) already reveals differences in formulation and emphasis. See note 3 for a remark on subsequent developments.

3. Cf. Habermas and Luhmann: *Theorie der Gesellschaft oder Sozialtechnologie-Was leistet die Systemforschung?* (Frankfurt, 1971); "Was heisst Universal-pragmatik?" in K.-O. Apel, ed; *Sprachpragmatik und Philosophie* (Frankfurt, 1976), pp. 174–272; and *Zur Rekonstruktion des Historischen Materialismus* (Frankfurt, 1976); English translation, *Communication and the Evolution of Society* (Boston, 1979).

Again Habermas himself regards these developments as a further improvement on his previous views. This is evident from his remarks in the introduction to *Theory and Practice* and in the postscript to *Knowledge and Human Interests*. The preface to the 1970 edition of *Zur Logik der Sozialwissenschaften* already expressed dissatisfaction with the treatment of methodology presented there.

While freely admitting the roughness of the divisions, it will be convenient for us to view Habermas's writings on the logic of social inquiry in three stages: (1) the early formulations extending from the *Literaturbericht* of 1957 through the contributions to the *Positivismusstreit* (1963, 1964); (2) the first attempts at systematization in the 1967 review of methodological literature and the 1968 examination of the relations of knowledge to interest; and (3), beginning roughly in 1970, the recent attempts to construct a theory of social evolution on the foundations of a theory of communication.

4. As will become evident in the course of this chapter, Habermas's understanding of these ideas shifts significantly. The general direction of this development will be discussed toward the close of the chapter in section 3.6.

5. *Theory and Practice* p. 79.

6. "Literaturbericht zur philosophischen Diskussion um Marx und den Marxismus" in *Theorie und Praxis,* 3d ed. (Neuwied, 1969), pp. 261ff.; on this point see pp. 278ff. (hereafter cited as "Marxismus").

7. Cf. "Between Philosophy and Science: Marxism as Critique" in *Theory and Practice,* pp. 195–252; (hereafter cited as "Critique").

8. "Marxismus," p. 289.

9. Ibid., p. 310.

10. Cf. Habermas, "Analytische Wissenschaftstheorie und Dialektik," first published in 1963, later reprinted in *Der Positivismusstreit in der deutschen Soziologie* (Neuwied, 1969), pp. 155–192; the English translation is "The Analytical Theory of Science and Dialectics," in *The Positivist Dispute in German Sociology* (London, 1976), pp. 131–162.

11. Cf. Habermas, "Kritische und konservative Aufgaben der Soziologie," in *Theorie und Praxis,* pp. 215–230.

12. *Theory and Practice,* pp. 303–304,

13. Ibid., p. 13.

14. "Über das Subjekt der Geschichte," in *Kultur und Kritik* (Frankfurt, 1973), p. 398.

15. *Communication and the Evolution of Society,* p. 140.

16. "Über das Subject der Geschichte," pp. 394ff.

17. "Critique," pp. 249ff.

18. *Ibid.,* pp. 250–251.

19. "Über das Verhältnis von Politik und Moral," in *Arbeit, Erkenntnis, Fortschritt: Aufsätze 1954—1970* (Amsterdam, 1970), p. 238.

20. "*Critique,*" pp. 236ff.

21. The first extended discussion appears in "Analytische Wissenschaftstheorie und Dialektik," where he draws a distinction among the objectivating procedures of empirical-analytic inquiry, the interpretive procedures of a hermeneutics of subjective meaning, and the simultaneously interpretive and causal-explanatory procedures of a critical theory concerned with "objective" meaning. In discussing hermeneutic *Sinnverständnis* he refers to the ideas of Dilthey, Husserl, and Schutz (n.5, p. 160; English edition, p. 135) and not, as in later writings, to those of Gadamer; hence the identification of the object of hermeneutic understanding with *subjectively* intended meaning. Cf. sections 3.2 and 3.3.

22. "Analytische Wissenschaftstheorie und Dialektik," p. 160; English edition, pp. 135ff. The phrase, "the formal language of a hypothetico-deductive framework," suggests an additional source of difficulty in Habermas' notion of "empirical": the inadequate model of empirical-analytic science that he uses as a standard of comparision. It appears to be the model of a theory as an

uninterpreted calculus with only subsequent and external relations to the observational data that interpret it. This model, stemming from the work of Carnap, Hempel, and others, seems to be behind much of what Habermas has to say in his early writings about the limitations of strict empirical science. Even after he has incorporated the very different ideas of Popper and Peirce, the shadows of the logicist conception are often visible.

23. "Marximus," p. 299.

24. "Analytische Wissenschaftstheorie und Dialektik," p. 155; English edition, p. 131. Cf. "Marxismus," pp. 321ff.

25. Ibid., pp. 159ff.; English edition, pp. 135ff. Cf. *Theory and Practice*, pp. 1–2.

26. "Marxismus," p. 303.

27. Ibid., pp. 321–322, n. 2. These lines were dropped from the 1971 edition.

28. "Analytische Wissenschaftstheorie und Dialektik," p. 191; English edition, p. 162.

29. "The Classical Doctrine of Politics in Relation to Social Philosophy," in *Theory and Practice*, p. 81.

Section 3.2

1. C. G. Hempel, "Logical Positivism and the Social Sciences," in P. Achinstein and S. Barker, eds *The Legacy of Logical Positivism* (Baltimore, 1969), p. 163.

2. The sketch that follows ignores the controversies that have developed within neopositivism around most of the tenets mentioned; as well as the refinements and revisions that have resulted from them. But the position presented here has served as the point of reference for these controversies and is no less influential for having been the subject of extended discussion.

3. See the bibliographies in F. Dallmayr and T. McCarthy, eds. *Understanding and Social Inquiry* (Notre Dame, 1977). For a stimulating account of these controversies and of Habermas's response to them, see R. J. Bernstein, *The Restructuring of Social and Political Theory* (New York, 1976).

4. *Zur Logik der Sozialwissenschaften*, Beiheft 5 of *Philosophische Rundschau* (Tübingen, 1967); reprinted by the Suhrkamp Verlag (Frankfurt, 1970). I will cite the latter edition, hereafter referred to as LSW. The lines in the text appear on p. 73.

5. This was already explicit in his contributions to the *Positivismusstreit*. In his reply to Albert, for example, he wrote:
It has quite escaped Albert's notice that a critique of empirical-analytic inquiry itself is far from being my intention. He imagines that I desired to play off the methods of understanding against those of explanation. On the contrary, I regard as abortive, even reactionary, the attempts which characterized the old methodological dispute, namely, attempts to set up barriers from the outset in order to remove certain sectors altogether from the clutches of certain types of research. It would be a bad dialectician who immunized himself in this way. ("Rationalism Divided in Two: a Reply to Albert," pp. 218–219.)

6. T. Parsons, ed. *The Theory of Social and Economic Organization* (New York, 1947), introduction, pp. 10–11. See also his "Value-freedom and Objectivity" in Otto Stammer, ed. *Max Weber and Sociology Today* (New York, 1971), pp. 27–50 and Habermas's critique of Parsons's Weber interpretation on pp. 59–65.

7. LSW, pp. 83ff.; see also the critique of Parsons mentioned in n. 6.

8. Parsons, ed., *Theory of Social and Economic Organization,* p. 88.

9. Ibid., p. 88.

10. Ibid., p. 90.

11. Ibid., pp. 96–97.

12. Ibid., pp. 99–100.

13. Ibid., p. 94.

14. "Objectivity in Social Science and Social Policy" in Edward A. Shils and Henry A. Finch, eds., *The Methodology of the Social Sciences* (New York, 1949), pp. 75–76.

15. Ibid., p. 76.

16. Ibid., p. 84

17. Ibid., pp. 105–106.

18. Runciman; *Social Science and Political Theory* (Cambridge, 1963), p. 59 quoted in LSW p. 89. See also Runciman's *A Critique of Max Weber's Philosophy of Social Science* (Cambridge, 1972).

19. "The Operation Called *Verstehen*" in the *American Journal of Sociology* 54 (1968), reprinted in H. Feigl and M. Brodbeck, eds. *Readings in the Philosophy of Science* (New York, 1953). Page references are to this anthology, here p. 684. Although Abel is himself neither by background nor conviction a logical positivist, his article has become a *locus classicus* for the position presented here. It is essentially the same position defended by Hempel, Nagel, and Rudner, among others.

20. Ibid., pp. 684–687.

21. LSW, pp. 143–144.

22. Ibid., p. 142. Cf. the related arguments of Charles Taylor, "Interpretation and the Sciences of Man," *The Review of Metaphysics,* 25, no. 1 (September 1971): 3–51, and T. McCarthy, "On Misunderstanding Understanding," *Theory and Decision* 3 (1973): 351–370.

23. The neopositivist analysis of *Verstehen* may be relevant to some of the versions in which the theory was historically propounded—for instance, to the psychologically oriented conceptions of Schleiermacher and the early Dilthey, and to certain aspects of Weber's position. Its relevance to other versions is less evident—for instance, to the neo-Kantian approaches derived from a transcendental conception of culture as constituted by certain *Wertbeziehungen* or value-relations (Rickert, early Weber); to approaches incor-

porating Hegel's notion of objective spirit (later Dilthey); or to approaches based on a theory of "language games" (Winch) or on a hermeneutics of language (Heidegger, Gadamer).

24. This does not mean that *Verstehen* is necessary only when there is a marked cultural or historical distance to be overcome. Even when the investigator can safely assume that he and his subject "speak the same language," the logical issue involved remains unaffected. The relative difficulty or ease of understanding the intersubjective meanings that provide the matrix for action does not alter the fact that it is a necessary presupposition of motivational explanation. On the other hand, as cultural distance increases and the difficulties of interpretation move into the foreground, there is a greater need for explicitly working out appropriate procedures and techniques of *Sinnverstehen*.

25. LSW, p. 188.

26. Cf. ibid., pp. 148–164.

27. N. Chomsky, "A Review of B. F. Skinner's Verbal Behavior," in J. A. Fodor and J. J. Katz, eds., *The Structure of Language* (Englewood Cliffs, 1964), pp. 547ff.

28. LSW, pp. 163–164.

29. Ibid., pp. 162 f.

30. A more detailed critique of the Skinnerian approach to human behavior would have to include an analysis of specific categories and procedures. It can be shown, I think, that the central category of an "operant" (a class of functionally equivalent behavioral responses) can be applied to actions only on the basis of a preunderstanding of the specific life-worlds in which they are located. The assignment of "topographically" (physically) different responses to the same operant is possible only in the light of such preunderstandings. The same type of argument can be made for other key behaviorist concepts in their application to human behavior. The point of this line of argument would be that the preunderstanding on which behavioral research at the human level relies extends far beyond that operative in animal studies. Of course, given this (unacknowledged) preunderstanding, behavioral techniques can, within certain limits, be successfully applied to "behavior-shaping," therapy, and the like. The validity of its self-understanding as a general theory of human behavior, however, is another matter.

31. Ibid., p. 84.

32. Cf. M. Friedman, "The Methodology of Positive Economics," in May Brodbeck, ed., *Readings in the Philosophy of the Social Sciences* (New York, 1968), pp. 508–528.

33. Cf. Hans Albert, "Modellplatonismus, Der neoklassische Stil des ökonomischen Denkens" in E. Topitsch ed., *Logik der Sozialwissenschaften* (Köln, 1965), pp. 406ff.

34. LSW, p. 135.

35. Ibid., p. 188. The nature of "communicative experience" in social inquiry was discussed in the first of Habermas's six lectures; "Thoughts on the Foundation of Sociology in the Philosophy of Language," delivered at Princeton University in 1971. These lectures, translated by Jeremy Shapiro, have remained unpublished primarily because Habermas has since revised and developed his ideas on the theory of communication. He is working on a manuscript (scheduled to appear in 1981) in which the foundations of social inquiry in a theory of language are discussed at length and in detail.

36. Compare the account of Lazarsfeld and Barton, "Qualitative Measurement in the Social Sciences: Classification, Typologies and Indices," in D. Lerner and H. D. Lasswell, eds., *The Policy Sciences* (Stanford, 1951).

37. Habermas is here adapting arguments of A. V. Cicourel; *Method and Measurement in Sociology* (Glencoe, 1964). He also refers to the work of C. Coombs; *A Theory of Data* (New York, 1964), and W. Torgerson; *Theory and Method of Scaling* (New York, 1958). On pp. 21–22. Torgerson writes:

We might call this measurement by fiat. Ordinarily it depends on the presumed relationships between observations and the concept of interest. Included in this category are the indices and indicants so often used in the social and behavioral sciences. This sort of measurement is likely to occur whenever we have a prescientific or common sense concept that on a priori grounds seems to be important but which we do not know how to measure directly. Hence we measure some other variable or weighted average of other variables presumed to be related to it. As examples, we might mention the measurement of socio-economic status, or emotion through the use of GSR.

38. LSW, p. 197. The term *protophysics* is a reference to the work of P. Lorenzen and other members of the Erlangen school. Following in the tradition of Hugo Dingler, they have argued that geometry and physics are ultimately based on idealizations of measurement operations (for space, time, and mass) performed in everyday life. Cf. G. Böhme, ed., *Protophysik* (Frankfurt, 1976). Habermas is arguing that there is no corresponding "protosociology," for the rules relevant to the construction of social life-worlds do not involve "ideal measurement requirements."

39. For bibliography, see G. Psathas, (ed.,) *Phenomenological Sociology* (New York 1973). The line of argument leading from problems of measurement to the need for a theory of the life-world is developed by Cicourel, *Method and Measurement*. On pp. 14–15, he writes:

The precise measurement of social process requires first the study of the problem of meaning in everyday life. Social inquiry begins with reference to the common-sense world of everyday life. The meanings communicated by the use of ordinary day-today language categories and the non-linguistic shared cultural experiences inform every social act and mediate (in a way which can be conceptually designated and empirically observed) the correspondence required for precise measurement. The literal measurement of social acts . . . requires the use of linguistic and nonlinguistic meanings that cannot be taken for granted but must be viewed as objects of study. In other words, measurement presupposes a bounded network of shared meanings, i.e. a theory of culture.

40. Cf. the first and second Princeton lectures, "Thoughts on the Foundation of Sociology."

41. *Theorie der Gesellschaft oder Sozialtechnologie—Was leistet die Systemforschung?* (Frankfurt, 1971), p. 177.

42. Schutz, "Concept and Theory Formation in the Social Sciences," in *Collected Papers I: The Problem of Social Reality*, ed. M. Natanson (The Hague, 1962), p. 62.

43. Compare W. M. Mayrl, "Ethnomethodology: Sociology without Society?" *Catalyst*, no. 7 (Winter 1973): 15–28, as well as the "Comment" by Beng-Huat Chua and "Reply" by Mayrl in the following issue.

44. J. Coulter, "Decontextualized Meanings: Current Approaches to Verstehende Investigations," in M. Truzzi, ed., *Verstehen: Subjective Understanding in the Social Sciences* (Reading, Mass., 1974), pp. 151ff.

45. Habermas's discussion of ethnomethodology in LSW is rather undifferentiated; he tends to overemphasize its similarities to Schutz's phenomenology. This is no doubt because at the time (1967) very little had been published by Garfinkel and his coworkers. (*Studies in Ethnomethodology* also appeared in 1967.) In fact, the footnotes refer only to Garfinkel's dissertation (1952) and to an unpublished manuscript from 1957, as well as to the work of Cicourel, which, from the perspective of the present, represents only one—and not the principal—strand of development.

Habermas has recently readdressed these problems in an unpublished manuscript on "Intention, Konvention und sprachliche Interaktion" (1976), which contains a discussion of later developments in ethnomethodology. Parts of this discussion were incorporated in "On Communicative Action," a paper delivered to the Boston Colloquium for the Philosophy of Science in December 1976.

Since the argument developed in these writings draws heavily on the theory of communicative competence, I shall not introduce it into the present context; an indication of its general tenor will be given in chapter 4. It might be noted here that his evaluation of the relative merits of Wittgensteinian and ethnomethodological approaches (see below in text) has altered somewhat. He now regards the notion of rule-governed behavior characteristic of the former as too closely modeled on the example of "meaning-constitutive rules" (for example, grammatical or mathematical rules) and consequently "too poor" to enable us to grasp the complexities of social action; the concepts of meaning, intention, and (social) norm are not adequately differentiated. Ethnomethodology is now classed with hermeneutics as providing an "interpretive" model of social action, one that avoids the complementary extremes (and weaknesses) of both individualistic models of intentional action—which do not give the intersubjective matrix of norms, roles, institutions, cultural traditions, its due—and holistic models of normatively guided behavior (for

example, conventional role theory)—which tend to obliterate the independence and activity of the social actor. Nevertheless he still wants to argue that
the ethnomethodological program is beset by new forms of the inadequacies
attaching to previous "phenomenological" approaches: subjectivism and spec-
tatorism.

As to the first, it overemphasizes the exploratory and creative moments of
social interaction and underplays its objective context: "For ethnomethodology
. . . the situation-transcending generality and stability of social structures is a
veil spread by the acting parties themselves over the fleeting and accidental
situations of their highly diffuse, fragile, continually revised and only
momentarily successful communications. According to this extremely
nominalistic conception, the intersubjectively shared normative reality of
society disintegrates into the punctual multiplicity of individual, context-
dependent and context-shaping interpretive accomplishments." "On Communicative Action," p. 9.

Stressing the "indexicality" or context-dependence of communication,
ethnomethodologists have argued forcefully that the social scientist as interpreter must enter, at least as a virtual participant, into the context in which
the action to be interpreted is embedded. (On this point compare the discussion
of hermeneutics in section 3.3). The methodological implications of this thesis
are far-reaching: "If a context of action can be opened up only from within,
that is through (at least virtual) participation in a communication that is set
within, and at the same time further develops, this context, the sociologist must
in principle assume the same position as the lay member. He has no privileged
access to the object domain." Ibid., p. 10. This, of course, raises the question of
what ethnomethodologists conceive themselves to be doing. Some (among
them, Blum, and McHugh) have accepted the radically relativistic implications
of applying this insight to their own work: "Interpretive sciences must give up
the claim to produce theoretical knowledge. . . If the insight into the unavoidable self-referential character of research practice cannot open a way to
context-independent knowledge, then social research can exist only as one
particular form of life alongside others. . . . It cannot dissolve its situational
ties." Ibid., p. 11. Others (Cicourel, for example), have seen in it a challenge to
reform "social research in such a way that it can fulfill its own ideals of
objectivity better than previously," that is, "by taking into methodological
consideration the . . . [interpreter's] participation in the context he wants to
understand" so that "everyday theories no longer flow unreflected into measurements." Ibid., p. 11. But neither a "self-destructive relativism" nor the
surrender of ethnomethodology's "claim to replace conventional action
theories with a new paradigm" accords with Garfinkel's original intention. His
more orthodox followers (such as Zimmerman) have attempted to analyze
formally the invariant properties of the "practices" through which "members"
produce the objective appearance of a stable order: "To the extent that
ethnomethodology no longer presents itself only as a critique of method, but as
a theory in its own right, there become visible the outlines of a program aimed

at the presuppositions of everyday communications." Ibid., p. 12. But this immediately raises the question; "How can this type of research into universals be carried through if social-scientific interpretations are context-dependent in the same way as everyday interpretations?" Ibid., p. 13. According to Habermas, the ethnomethodologist is here confronted with a dilemma from which he cannot escape without altering his basic self-understanding. Either he claims a privileged access to his object domain—an analogue of Husserl's epoche—and thus betrays his original methodological insight or he remains true to that insight and surrenders the claim to theory (to reconstruct the general presuppositions of communication). The only way out of this dilemma of either a "Husserlian absolutism" or a "confessed relativism" is, Habermas argues, to show "how social-scientific analysis must unavoidably fasten onto the everyday interpretations it examines, and how it can nevertheless refectively penetrate them and transcend the given context." Ibid., p. 13. To do this, he goes on, requires that one acknowledge the "binding force of general structures of rationality" rather than regarding them as mere phenomena: "Garfinkel treats standards of rationality, like all other conventions, as the result of a contingent interpretive practice that can be described, but not systematically reconstructed and evaluated. . . . He regards unconditional and universal validity claims merely as something that the participants take to be unconditional and universal. . . . Garfinkel thus once again reserves for the ethnomethodologist the position of the neutral observer. . . . But then the ethnomethodologist has to claim for his own statements standards of validity which *a fortiori* lie outside the domain of those claimed by the participants; to the extent that he does not credit himself with such an extramundane position, he cannot claim a theoretical status for his statements." Ibid., p. 14.

The full force of this criticism as well as the sense of the suggested alternative—taking validity claims seriously and attempting systematically to reconstruct and evaluate them—can be appreciated only in the context of Habermas' theory of communication; see chapter 4.

46. LSW, pp. 218–219.

47. Compare Habermas's discussion of socialization theory, "Stichworte zur Theorie der Sozialisation," in *Kultur und Kritik*, pp. 118–194; see also section 4.4. It is in this context that his considerable debt to Mead and the social-interactionist tradition becomes evident.

Section 3.3

1. E. Stenius; *Wittgenstein's Tractatus* (Oxford, 1960); K.-O. Apel; *Analytic Philosophy of Language and the Geisteswissenschaften* (Dordrecht Holland, 1967); David Pears; *Wittgenstein* (London, 1971). Habermas draws heavily upon Apel in his interpretation of Wittgenstein.

2. Habermas uses the characterizations "transcendental" and "sociolinguistic" in LSW; there is a more recent discussion of Wittgenstein in the third Princeton lecture.

3. Wittgenstein; *Philosophical Investigations* (New York, 1955); references are to paragraph number; here paragraphs 5 and 6.

4. LSW, pp. 231–232.

5. Wittgenstein, *Philosophical Investigations,* para. 206.

6. Ibid., para. 241.

7. Ibid., para. 77.

8. LSW, p. 242.

9. Peter Winch; *The Idea of a Social Science and Its Relation to Philosophy.* (London, 1958), pp. 42–43.

10. Ibid., p. 52.

11. Ibid., p. 63.

12. Ibid., pp. 86–87.

13. Ibid., pp. 87–88.

14. See, for example, Richard Rudner; *Philosophy of Social Science* (Englewood Cliffs, 1966), chap. 4.

15. Winch, *Idea of a Social Science,* p. 133.

16. Ibid., p. 121.

17. LSW, pp. 244–245. These criticisms apply only to the position advanced in Winch's book. In a later article, "Understanding a Primitive Society," (*American Philosophical Quarterly* 1, no. 4 (1964)), Winch takes up the questions that were left unposed in his book. The position he develops there is much closer to that of Gadamer. (Cf. my discussion in "On Misunderstanding Understanding," *Theory and Decisions* 3 (1963): 351–370.) The criticisms applicable to this later version would be similar to those Habermas raises against hermeneutics.

18. For background on hermeneutics, see K.-O. Apel, "Das Verstehen," in *Archiv für Begriffsgeschichte* (Bonn, 1955) vol. 1; R. Palmer; *Hermeneutics* (Evanston, Illinois, 1969); and G. Radnitzky; *Contemporary Schools of Metascience,* (Göteborg, Sweden, 1968), vol. 2.

19. Gadamer; *Wahrheit und Methode* (Tübingen, 1965); English translation, *Truth and Method* (New York, 1975).

20. LSW, pp. 251–290. An English translation of these pages appeared as "A Review of Gadamer's *Truth and Method*" in F. Dallmayr and T. McCarthy, eds., *Understanding and Social Inquiry* (Notre Dame, 1977), pp. 335–363. (With the possible exception of the third, these contrasts no longer apply to Winch's later position.)

21. "Review of Gadamer," pp. 335–336.

22. Gadamer, *Truth and Method,* pp. 346–347.

23. The translation of *Vorurteile* as "prejudices" is somewhat misleading, since the English term now has an almost exclusively perjorative connotation, whereas Gadamer—while allowing for the similar connotation of the German

term—attempts to elaborate a positive sense. A *Vor-Urteil* is literally a prejudg-ment; as Gadamer uses the term, its meaning corresponds more closely to the etymological meaning of "prejudice" (Latin: *prae-* + *judicum*) than to current usuage. The accent here, as in the case of the other key hermeneutical concepts compounded from *vor*, is on this prefix (for example, *Vorverständnis:* "prior understanding"; *Vorgriff:* "anticipation"; *Vorbegriffe:* "preconceptions"). This is meant to bring out the fact that the interpreter's own language, practice, form of life, and so forth are pre-conditions for understanding. They belong to the initial situation (*Ausgangssituation*) from which interpretation proceeds. Cf. *Truth and Method,* p. 240, for Gadamer's elucidation of *Vorurteil.*

24. Ibid., pp. 263–264.

25. See, for example, the criticisms of Alasdair MacIntyre in "Is Understanding a Religion Compatible with Believing?" read to the Sesquicentennial Seminar of the Princeton Theological Seminar in 1962 and published in *Faith and the Philosophers,* ed. John Hick (London, 1964).

26. "Review of Gadamer," pp. 339–340.

27. Gadamer, *Truth and Method,* p. 261.

28. Ibid., pp. 263–264.

29. "Review of Gadamer," p. 345.

30. A. C. Danto; *Analytical Philosophy of History* (Cambridge, England, 1968), chap. 8.

31. Ibid., pp. 17–18; cited in "Review of Gadamer," p. 349.

32. Ibid., p. 142; cited in "Review of Gadamer," p. 349.

33. LSW, p. 93.

34. Ibid., pp. 121–122.

35. "Review of Gadamer," p. 351.

36. Gadamer, *Truth and Method,* p. 274.

37. Ibid., p. 275.

38. Paul Ricoeur, "Ethics and Culture: Habermas and Gadamer in Dialogue," *Philosophy Today* 17 (1973): 157.

39. For Gadamer the force of this argument is not normative but tran-scendental. That is, he is not saying that we ought to relate the meaning to be understood to our own situation, but that we cannot understand without doing so; —this relation belongs to the very structure of *Verstehen.* Thus in a "Reply" to critics in *Hermeneutik und Ideologiekritik* (Frankfurt, 1971), pp. 283–317, he writes: "Philosophical hermeneutics is certainly 'normative' in the sense that it attempts to replace a worse philosophy with a better one. But it does not propagate a new practice, and it does not conceive hermeneutic practice as if it were guided by a consciousness of application and an intention of application." The same idea is expressed more aphoristically in *Truth and Method*: "Not what we do, not what we ought to do, but what happens with us beyond our wanting and doing is in question," foreword, p. xvi.

40. Winch, "Understanding a Primitive Society," p. 317.

41. "Review of Gadamer," pp. 356–357.

42. Ibid., p. 358.

43. Ibid., p. 359.

44. Ibid., p. 360.

45. LSW, p. 305.

46. "Review of Gadamer," p. 361.

47. Ibid.

48. Ibid., p. 350; (my emphasis).

49. Ibid., p. 351.

50. *Hermeneutik und Ideologiekritik* (Frankfurt, 1971) contains Gadamer's reply to Habermas's critique in LSW: "Rhetorik, Hermeneutik und Ideologiekritik" (English translation, "On the Scope and Function of Hermeneutical Reflection," in H.-G. Gadamer, *Philosophical Hermeneutics* (Berkeley, 1976), pp. 18–43); Habermas's answer: "Der Universalitätsanspruch der Hermeneutik" (partly translated in "On Systematically Distorted Communication," *Inquiry* 13 (1970): 205–218); and a further "Replik" by Gadamer. Portions of this exchange were translated in *Continuum* 8 (1970).

51. Gadamer, "Scope and function," p. 38.

52. Ibid., p. 34.

53. "Replik," p. 289.

54. "Scope and function," p. 31.

55. Ibid.

56. Ibid., p. 34.

57. Ibid., p. 32.

58. "Replik," pp. 315–316.

59. Ibid., p. 316.

60. "Der Universalitätsanspruch der Hermeneutik," pp. 130ff.

61. "Replik," p. 302.

62. Ricoeur, "Ethics and Culture," pp. 164–165. Compare the editor's Epilogue to *Materialien zu Habermas' Erkenntnis und Interesse*, ed. Fred Dallmayr (Frankfurt, 1974), pp. 418–432. See also D. Misgeld, "Critical Theory and Hermeneutics," in *On Critical Theory*, ed. John O'Neill (New York, 1976), pp. 164–183.

63. Recall that the interest in emancipation is grounded in the interest in communication; the critique of ideology is an effort to remove barriers to unconstrained dialogue. And this effort draws on tradition: "The ideas of the Enlightenment stem from the store of historically transmitted illusions. Hence we must comprehend the actions of the Enlightenment as the attempt to test the limit of the realizability of the utopian content of cultural tradition under given conditions." KHI, p. 284.

Section 3.4

1. Cf. P. Robinson, *The Freudian Left* (New York, 1969); M. Jay, *The Dialectical Imagination* (Boston, 1973), chap. 3; R. Jacoby, *Social Amnesia* (Boston, 1975).

2. Horkheimer, "Geschichte und Psychologie," *Zeitschrift für Sozialforschung* I, 1/2 (1932).

3. KHI, p. 285. Cf. also p. 256 where he writes: "Impulse potential, whether incorporated in social systems of collective self-preservation or suppressed instead of absorbed, clearly reveals libidinal and aggressive tendencies. This is why an instinct theory is necessary. But the latter must preserve itself from false objectivism. Even the concept of instinct that is applied to animal behavior is derived privatively from the pre-understanding of a linguistically interpreted, albeit reduced human world."

4. Ibid.

5. See section 4.4.

6. KHI, p. 214.

7. Cf. A. Lorenzer, *Sprachzerstörung und Rekonstruktion* (Frankfurt, 1970), and *Kritik des psychoanalytischen Symbolbegriffs* (Frankfurt, 1970).

8. KHI, p. 253.

9. Ibid., p. 252.

10. Ibid., p. 217.

11. Ibid., p. 219.

12. "Der Universalitätsanspruch der Hermeneutik" in *Hermeneutik und Ideologiekritik* (Frankfurt, 1971), pp. 138–139. An English translation of parts of this essay can be found in "On Systematically Distorted Communication," *Inquiry* 13 (1970): 205–218. The term *scenic understanding* refers to Lorenzer's interpretation of the analyst's task; he seeks to make the meaning of the "symptomatic scenes" comprehensible by relating them to analogous "scenes" in the transference situation; this provides the clue to the "original scenes" from early childhood that are at the root of the disturbance.

13. Ibid., p. 149

14. As Jeremy Shapiro pointed out in his translation of KHI: "The official translation of Freud's concepts *das Ich* and *das Es* as the ego and the id was a serious mistake that both reflects and has contributed to the scientistic self-misunderstanding of metapsychology. *Das Ich* means the I and *das Es* the it. . . . Freud's famous statement of the goal of psychoanalysis: 'Wo Es war, soll Ich werden' should read in English: 'Where it was, I shall become' " (p. 344, n. 31).

15. KHI, p. 240.

16. Ibid., p. 243.

17. "Der Universalitätsanspruch der Hermeneutik," pp. 137–138.

18. LSW, p. 297.

19. Ibid., p. 304.

20. KHI, p. 254.

21. Ibid., p. 255.

22. Ibid., p. 258.

23. Ibid., pp. 261–262.

24. Ibid., p. 264.

25. Ibid., p. 269. This is not to deny that "individual hypotheses can be detached from the metapsychological framework of interpretation and independently tested. For this purpose, it is necessary to translate them into the theoretical framework of strict empirical sciences. Of course, this translation eliminates that specific context in which covariances between observable events do not signify a natural-law nexus, but a relation that can be dissolved in reflection, a nature-like (*naturwüchsigen*) nexus." LSW, p. 302.

26. "Replik," pp. 294–295.

27. "Scope and function," p. 42.

28. "Replik," pp. 316–317.

29. Reflexion and Emanzipation," in *Hermeneutik und Ideologiekritik*, p. 247.

30. Ibid., pp. 278–279.

31. *Theory and Practice*, pp. 25ff. Within the Marxist tradition his specific target is Lukács's theory of the party, which, in Habermas's view, subordinates both theoretical discussion and proletarian enlightenment to the exigencies of party organization.

32. Ibid., p. 32.

33. Ibid.

34 One can, of course, designate certain groups as "objectively" oppressed, but in the absence of actual possibilities of enlightenment, this judgment cannot be confirmed. Cf. Habermas's remarks on Marx's designation of the proletariat as a revolutionary class and on the specific conditions Marx adduced to make this plausible (conditions that, according to Habermas, are no longer present): "Science and Technology as Ideology," in *Toward a Rational Society* (Boston, 1970); "Über einige Bedingungen der Revolutionierung spätkapitalistischer Gesellschaften" in *Kultur und Kritik;* and *Legitimation Crisis* (Boston, 1975).

35. *Theory and Practice*, p. 37. In an interview with Boris Frankel published in *Theory and Society* 1 (1974): 37–58, Habermas expressed the opinion that the most promising strategy *within present-day Western Germany* is the "radical reformism" pursued by the Jusos (Young Social Democrats): an attempt to use the institutions of present-day capitalism to challenge basic institutions of this system (for example, by pushing the Social Democratic party in the direction of reforms incompatible with the present economic system).

36. Ibid., pp. 33–34.

37. Ibid., p. 34.

38. Ibid., p. 40.

39. KHI, p. 237.

Section 3.5

1. "Review of Gadamer," p. 361.

2. Supplement I, *Encyclopaedia Britannica* (Chicago, 1926), pp. 132–133.

3. Alfred R. Radcliffe-Brown, *Structure and Function in Primitive Societies* (London, 1952), pp. 179–180.

4. Cf. R. K. Merton, *Social Theory and Social Structure* (Glencoe, 1949).

5. Cf. T. Parsons, *The Social System* (Glencoe, 1951); Parsons and Shils, eds., *Toward a General Theory of Action* (New York, 1951).

6. LSW, p. 170.

7. T. Parsons, "An Approach to Psychological Theory in Terms of the Theory of Action," in S. Koch, ed., *Psychology: A Study of a Science* (New York, 1959), 3: 631.

8. Cf. C. G. Hempel, "The Logic of Functional Analysis," in L. Gross, ed., *Symposium on Sociological Theory* (New York, 1959), pp. 271ff.; E. Nagel, *The Structure of Science* (New York, 1969), pp. 521ff.

9. Nagel, *Structure*, p. 530.

10. LSW, p. 176.

11. More recently, in *Legitimation Crisis* and in *Communication and the Evolution of Society*, Habermas suggests that these difficulties might be overcome within the framework of a theory of social evolution. See section 3.6.

12. LSW, pp. 176–177.

13. Ibid., pp. 179–180.

14. Cf. T. Parsons: "Pattern Variables Revisited," *American Sociological Review* 25 (1960): 457ff.

15. Habermas, *Toward a Rational Society*, p. 91.

16. LSW, pp. 181–182.

17. Ibid., pp. 306–308. Habermas has revised this conception of critical theory in his more recent writings on social evolution. See section 3.6.

18. Ibid., p. 301.

19. The debate is documented in Habermas and Luhmann, *Theorie der Gesellschaft oder Sozialtechnologie—Was leistet die Systemforschung?* (Frankfurt, 1971). In addition to Habermas's critique, this volume includes three essays by Luhmann: "Moderne Systemtheorie als Form gesamtgesellschaftlicher Analyse" (pp. 7–24); "Sinn als Grundbegriff der Soziologie" (pp. 25–100); and "Systemtheoretische Argumentationen—Eine Entgegnung auf Jürgen Habermas" (pp. 291–405). Cf. also N. Luhmann, *Zweckbegriff und System-*

rationalität (Tübingen, 1968; Frankfurt, 1973) and *Soziologische Aufklärung* (Köln, 1970).

20. Habermas's critique, "Theorie der Gesellschaft oder Sozialtechnologie? Eine Auseinandersetzung mit Niklas Luhmann," appears on pp. 142–290 of the discussion volume referred to in note 19 (hereafter cited as "Sozialtechnologie"). The debate initiated by Habermas and Luhmann has been continued by others; to date three supplementary volumes have appeared in the *Theorie-Diskussion* series published by the Suhrkamp Verlag.

In the remarks that follow, I shall be concerned only with Habermas's critique of Luhmann; I will discuss neither Luhmann's response nor the subsequent course of the controversy. Moreover I shall be dealing only with certain aspects of this critique. Many of Habermas's central objections are based on a preliminary sketch of his theory of communication (especially in part II on the question of "meaning," in part III on the relation between experience and communication, and in part IV on the notion of truth). This theory will be examined in chapter 4. For the present I shall confine myself to objections that can be formulated somewhat independently of his views on communication; the final issue considered will point directly ahead to that complex of problems.

21. "Sozialtechnologie," pp. 147–148. The reference is to W. R. Ashby, *An Introduction to Cybernetics* (London, 1961).

22. Ibid., pp. 153–155.

23. Ibid., p. 151. As Luhmann himself points out: "No jackass can become a snake, even if such a development were necessary for survival. A social order can, by contrast, undergo profound structural alteration without sacrificing its identity and its continuous existence. An agrarian society can develop into an industrial society . . . without our being able to decide when a new system is present." Cited in ibid., p. 150.

24. Ibid., p. 164.

25. Ibid., p. 157.

26. Ibid., pp. 162–163.

27. Ibid., p. 143.

28. Ibid., p. 170.

29. Quoted in *Legitimation Crisis*, p. 133; cf. Habermas's reply in ibid., pp. 130ff

30. Quoted in *Legitimation Crisis*, p. 98.

31. "*Sozialtechnologie*," pp. 243–244.

32. He agrees that the notion of truth is linked to that of consensus; but the consensus in question is normatively conceived and not merely factual. "The concept of truth evidently cannot be divorced from certain idealizations. Not every factually attained, or to be attained, consensus can be a sufficient criterion for truth. . . . We attribute truth only to statements to which (we counterfactually assume) every responsible subject would agree if only he

could examine his opinions at sufficient length in unrestricted and unconstrained communication." What is in question is a "rational" or "grounded" consensus.

33. "Sozialtechnologie," p. 237. This criticism should make it clear that Habermas does not understand his own theory of interests as an immediate identification of theory with practice. Its claims are, rather, transcendental claims about the different frameworks within which reality is known. The statements about the different object domains, however, remain subject to the appropriate criteria of argumentative validation. The underlying interests account for the fact that, when valid, they have an intrinsic relation to certain kinds of practice. This will become clearer in chapter 4

34. Ibid., p. 259.

Section 3.6

1. A number of the important essays are collected in *Zur Rekonstruktion des Historischen Materialismus* (Frankfurt, 1976), hereafter cited as RHM. I shall be dealing primarily with the following: "Einleitung: Historischer Materialismus und die Entwicklung normitiver Strukturen," pp. 9–48 (English translation: "Historical Materialism and the Development of Normative Structures," in *Communication and the Evolution of Society* (Boston, 1979), pp. 95–129), "Zur Rekonstruktion des historischen Materialismus," pp. 144–199 (English: "Toward a Reconstruction of Historical Materialism," in *Communication and the Evolution of Society*, pp. 130–177), and "Geschichte und Evolution," pp. 200–259. Cf. also J. Habermas and N. Luhmann, *Theorie der Gesellschaft oder Sozialtechnologie*, pp. 171–175, 270–290, and *Legitimation Crisis*, pt. I and passim.

2. "Zum Theorienvergleich in der Soziologie: am Beispiel der Evolutionstheorie," in RHM, p. 129.

3. "Development of Normative Structures," pp. 124–125. Habermas credits Lucien Goldmann with having seen the significance of Piaget's work for Marxist theory earlier than most.

4. Ibid., p. 95.

5. Ibid., p. 96.

6. Ibid., pp. 97–98.

7. *Legitimation Crisis*, p. 7.

8. Compare the argument in pt. II of *Legitimation Crisis*.

9. "Development of Normative Structures," pp. 127–128.

10. "Thesen zur Rekonstruktion des Historischen Materialismus," paper delivered at the Hegel Conference in Stuttgart (May 1976), p. 1.

11. "Development of Normative Structures," pp. 126–127.

12. "Toward a Reconstruction of Historical Materialism," p. 130.

13. The discussion that follows is based primarily on the essay "Toward a

Reconstruction of Historical Materialism." A summary of the main points appeared earlier in *Theory and Society* 2 (1975): 287–300.

14. "Reconstruction of Historical Materialism," p. 132.

15. "Reconstruction of Historical Materialism," pp. 134–135.

16. "Reconstruction of Historical Materialism," pp. 137–138. Similar theses were already advanced in Habermas's lectures on philosophical anthropology (Frankfurt University, 1966–67).

17. Ibid., p. 139.

18. Ibid., p. 149.

19. Cf. ibid., pp. 150–152. The relevant literature is mentioned in the notes.

20. Cf., for example, M. Finley, "Between Slavery and Freedom," *Comparative Studies in Society and History* 6, no. 3 (April 1964).

21. "Reconstruction of Historical Materialism," p. 153.

22. Ibid., pp. 153–154. Compare *Legitimation Crisis,* pp. 7–8, and pt. I, chap. 3.

23. In *Legitimation Crisis* he admitted the for-want-of-a-theory inadequacy of his inductive approach on pp. 17–18. As he points out in "Reconstruction of Historical Materialism," the problem is that "the formal components of these fundamental institutions lie in so many different directions that they can hardly be brought into a developmental-logical series" (p. 154).

24. "Reconstruction of Historical Materialism," p. 143.

25. Ibid., p. 144. Cf. the discussion of *Legitimation Crisis,* pt. I, chap. 1.

26. Ibid., pp. 145–146.

27. Ibid., p. 147. The citation is from Marx's preface to his "Contribution to the Critique of Political Economy."

28. Ibid., pp. 147–148.

29. "Geschichte," p. 232.

30. Cf. J. H. Flavell and J. F. Wohlwill, "Formal and Functional Aspects of Cognitive Development," and A. Pinard and M. Laurendeau, "'Stage' in Piaget's Cognitive-Developmental Theory: Exegesis of a Concept," both in D. Elkind and J. H. Flavell, eds., *Studies in Cognitive Development* (Oxford, 1969), pp. 67–120, 121–170; J. H. Flavell: "An Analysis of Cognitive Developmental Sequences," *Genetic Psychology Monographs* 86 (1972): 279–350.

31. Although he feels that Piaget's approach to cognitive development has stood up well and that it is the most promising research strategy available today, Habermas is aware of the need for clarifying and revising some of its basic concepts and assumptions. Thus in an unpublished manuscript, "Zur Entwicklung der Interaktionskompetenz," the third section, "The Structure of Developmental Theories," is marked "still to be worked out."

32. Cf. "Development of Normative Structures," pp. 102–103, 110–111, for a mention of some of the other restrictions.

33. "Reconstruction of Historical Materialism," p. 154.

34. "Development of Normative Structures," p. 121.

35. "Zum Theorienvergleich in der Soziologie," p. 133. Cf. *Legitimation Crisis,* pt. I, chap. 2.

36. "Development of Normative Structures," p. 120.

37. Cf. A. Gehlen, "Anthropologische Ansicht der Technik," in H. Freyer et al., eds., *Technik im technischen Zeitalter* (Düsseldorf, 1965).

38. Cf. S. Moscovici, *L'histoire humaine de la nature* (Paris, 1968).

39. For a summary of Piaget's work and an extensive bibliography of primary and secondary sources, see J. H. Flavell, *The Developmental Psychology of Jean Piaget* (Princeton, 1963). Cf. also H. G. Furth, *Piaget and Knowledge* (Englewood Cliffs, 1969).

40. "Reconstruction of Historical Materialism," p. 169.

41. Habermas has taken some tentative steps in this direction; cf. section 4.4.

42. Cf. "Development of Normative Structures," pp. 98ff. Within the Institute, R. Dobert has been working on the evolution of world views, with particular emphasis on religion. Cf. his *Systemtheorie und die Entwicklung religiöser Deutungssysteme* (Frankfurt, 1973), and "Zur Logik des Übergangs vom archaischen zu hochkulturellen Religionssystemen," in K. Eder, ed. *Entstchung von Klassengesellschaften* (Frankfurt, 1973), pp. 330–364. Habermas makes some very general observations on the "homologies" between ego identity and social identity in "Development of Normative Structures" and in "Können komplexe Gesellschaften eine vernünftige Identität ausbilden?" RHM, pp. 92–128, part of which is translated in *Telos* 19 (1974): 91–103.

43. This schema, taken from Kohlberg's "From Is to Ought," in T. Mishel, ed., *Cognitive Development and Epistemology* (New York, 1971), pp. 151–236, appears on pp. 72–73 of RHM. Kohlberg's investigations focus on the "cognitive" side of moral consciousness, that is, on the ability to make moral judgments. A general theory of moral development would have to take account of other dimensions as well (the motivational, for example). In "Moralentwicklung und Ich-Identität," RHM, pp. 63–91, Habermas reformulates Kohlberg's stages in a more general framework intended to capture the multidimensionality of identity formation. See section 4.4 below.

44. "Reconstruction of Historical Materialism," p. 156. Actually a more complete developmental analysis of this dimension would require reference to ontogenetic structures other than those researched by Kohlberg. See n. 43.

45. Ibid., 157–158.

46. For a general characterization of the "rationality" of modern law, see "Überlegungen zum evolutionären Stellenwert des modernen Rechts," RHM, pp. 260–270.

47. "Development of Normative Structures," p. 98.

48. "Reconstruction of Historical Materialism," pp. 171–172. He mentions other differences as well.

49. "Development of Normative Structures," p. 125. While agreeing with Marx's emphasis on class struggle as a motor of social evolution, Habermas finds his account of its connection with the development of productive forces to be "confusing, in any case insufficiently analyzed." Ibid., p. 118.

50. "Geschichte," p. 235. The "functionalist analysis" in question must, of course, connect problems of system integration with problems of social integration in such a way that it becomes possible to specify nonarbitrarily system boundaries and goal values (cf. section 3.5; *Legitimation Crisis*, pt. I, chap. 1; "Geschichte," pp. 222ff.). One step in this direction is Habermas's shift of emphasis from the institutionalization of specific cultural values (which makes certain orientations binding for action) to the institutionalization of general rationality structures (which opens up structural possibilities for the rationalization of action). Cf. "Development of Normative Structures," p. 122. Habermas suggests that in this framework it might be possible to resolve some of the difficulties with orthodox functionalist analysis—for example, by constructing a correlate for the biological notion of death in terms of a fallback to an earlier, or an advance to a new, structurally defined level of learning. Cf. "Geschichte," pp. 231ff.

51. This sketch appears in "Reconstruction of Historical Materialism," pp. 161–163; it is based on Eder's study, Die *Entstehung staatlich organisierter Gesellschaften* (Frankfurt, 1976). Habermas and other members of the institute are now working out a similar explanation sketch for the rise of capitalism. In "Geschichte," pp. 234ff., he advances some preliminary suggestions in the context of a comparison of the Marxian and Weberian approaches.

52. "Reconstruction of Historical Materialism," p. 174.

53. Ibid., p. 163.

54. Ibid., pp. 164–165. In conversation Habermas has stressed the need to trace the "dialectic of enlightenment" backward to discover what we have lost in the course of social evolution. For this task, a hermeneutic approach—an effort to understand other cultures as partners in dialogue about the common problems of human existence—is necessary. Thus although the evolutionary approach necessarily involves a hierarchical classification of cultures (as more or less developed, at higher or lower stages of rationality, and so on), it does not obviate the necessity of learning from societies at all different levels.

55. "Development of Normative Structures," p. 123. As the last sentence suggests, Habermas's approach does represent a materialist reformulation of the idea that reason informs human history.

56. A glance at Kohlberg's schema for moral development (above in text) will immediately suggest why this last problem should be taken seriously.

57. LSW, pp. 306–308.

58. "Geschichte," p. 246.

59. Ibid., pp. 248–249. The reference is to Marx's suggestive methodological observations in the preface to his *Contribution to a Critique of Political Economy*.

60. Ibid., p. 217.

61. Ibid., p. 250.

62. This is certainly not to say that it is an easy task. Within Habermas's framework, the problems familiar in the literature on social change remain. Thus, for example, an explanation of the rise of capitalism still has to face the well-known difficulties in identifying and weighing the different (economic, political, social, cultural) problems that contributed to the breakdown of the feudal order, in estimating the relative importance of different social movements (in the cities and in the country), and so on. The theory of social evolution does not claim to dispense from these problems or to render the vast literature on them obsolete. The claim is rather that it provides a fruitful theoretical framework for pursuing them.

63. *Legitimation Crisis*, pp. 113–114.

64. "Geschichte," pp. 244–245.

65. Ibid., p. 249.

66. As Hempel, Popper, and others have pointed out, even strictly causal explanations can be restructured in narrative form (for example, the temperature dropped below freezing, the water in the pipes froze, expanded, burst the pipes). Habermas understands "narrative," however, in a more restricted sense, as essentially involving reference to actors. "In the framework of developmental theory, these transitions must be conceived as abstract transitions to new levels of learning. . . . They cannot be translated into the achievements of actors . . . without endangering the categorial framework and thus the explanatory force of the theory." Ibid., p. 245. But, as Habermas himself points out in ibid., pp. 204ff., historians—especially those who draw on the systematic social sciences—typically refer to factors other than actors and their actions (such as institutions, economic, political and legal systems, cultural traditions). And Habermas's schema does look to social groups as the "carriers" of new ideas and practices, as the "agents" of transformation. The fact that evolutionary transitions are structurally described as developments from one to another level of learning does not mean that they come to pass with an internal logical necessity, that is, without the agency of social actors.

67. Concretely this means such transitions as those from Neolithic societies to archaic civilizations, from the latter to high civilizations, from these to early modern societies, and from liberal to organized capitalism. Historical changes that take place *at* a given level of learning (for example, within Neolithic, traditional, or liberal capitalist societies) would have to be handled otherwise, perhaps by a historiography enriched with a variety of concepts and assumptions taken over from the systematic social sciences, including the theory of social evolution. In any case, Habermas's evolutionary schema does not bring us much further in this regard. Even if we accept his schema, most of the

familiar historiographical problems remain. In explaining the transition to capitalism, for example, he focuses on the institutionalization (roughly in the sixteenth century) of the "universalistic potential [contained in] world views that arose . . . between 800–300 B.C. "Geschichte," p. 241 (where he is discussing Weber's account of the role of religion in the rise of capitalism). That is, part of the explanation would refer to the institutionalization and stabilization of rationality structures that arose some 2,000 years earlier. Even if we grant the structural description of what is involved, the two millennia of development preceding the actual transition, as well as the factors involved in it, seem to require the usual types of investigation.

68. KHI, pp. 56ff. and appendix, p. 315.

69. The problems concerning the relation of theory to practice that we have raised in a general way here will reemerge there in a more concrete form. See the concluding pages of chapter 5.

NOTES TO CHAPTER 4

Section 4.1

1. *Knowledge and Human Interests* (Boston, 1971), p. 317.

2. *Zur Logik der Sozialwissenschaften* (Frankfurt, 1970), p. 220.

3. "Was heisst Universalpragmatik?" in *Sprachpragmatik und Philosophie*, ed. K. O. Apel (Frankfurt, 1976), pp. 174–272; English translation: "What is Universal Pragmatics?" in *Communication and the Evolution of Society* (Boston, 1979), pp. 1–68, here pp. 5–6; hereafter cited as UP.

4. N. Chomsky, *Aspects of the Theory of Syntax* (Cambridge, Mass., 1965), pp. 3–4.

5. UP, p. 26. This entails, of course, a revision of the concepts of competence and performance. While those aspects of the meaning of concrete utterances that are determined by contingent boundary conditions, the personality structures of the speaker/hearer, the role system in force, and so forth belong to the sphere of performance (and hence of empirical pragmatics), the invariable elements of speech situations belong to the sphere of competence (and hence of universal pragmatics). In "Vorbereitende Bemerkungen zu einer Theorie der Kommunikativen Kompetenz," *Theorie der Gesellschaft oder Sozialtechnologie?* (Frankfurt, 1971), pp. 101–141, the case is made as follows: the usual distinction between competence and performance "does not take account of the fact that the general structures of possible speech situations are themselves produced through speech acts." They do not belong "to the extralinguistic boundary conditions under which linguistic competence is merely applied, for they are language-dependent." That is, "under standard conditions there recur in every possible speech situation general elements that are produced anew by the performances of a specific class of linguistic expressions." The classes of linguistic expressions whose employment serves to produce these general elements (such as performatives, personal pronouns, deictic ex-

pressions, intentional verbs) are "pragmatic" or "dialogue-constitutive" universals.

6. Cf. ibid., pp. 6ff. The relevant literature is indicated in the footnotes.

7. J. R. Searle, *Speech Acts* (Cambridge, 1969), p. 16.

8. For example, in different situations the utterance of p may amount to "I assert that p," "I promise that p," "I request that p," In general the pragmatic features constitutive of speech situations need not be expressly verbalized, but they can be rendered explicit by employing certain classes of progmatic universals: "If this is the case, however, we should assume that these elements do not serve as a subsequent verbalization of a previously coordinated speech situation; on the contrary, they must be the very factors which enable us to generate the structures of potential speech. It is the dialogue-constitutive universals . . . that establish in the first place the form of intersubjectivity between any competent speakers capable of mutual understanding." "Towards a Theory of Communicative Competence," *Inquiry* 13 (1970): 369.

9. "Vorbereitende Bemerkungen," p. 102. See also the fourth Princeton Lecture.

10. Habermas refers to this mastery as the "rule-consciousness" of a competent subject. Given the contrast between implicit and explicit knowledge that underlies the idea of rational reconstruction, this terminology is somewhat misleading. Typically the mastery of generative rules is intuitive and in this sense preconscious.

11. UP, p. 14.

12. Chomsky, *Theory of Syntax,* pp. 18–21.

13. UP, p. 19. Habermas is not unaware of the objections that have been raised against this type of approach by Levelt and others, but he feels that they can be met. See ibid., pp. 17ff.

14. Ibid., p. 16. This is of course a controversial claim.

15. Ibid., p. 20.

16. Ibid., pp. 21ff.

17. Ibid., pp. 24–25.

18. Ibid., p. 27.

19. Habermas's choice of this terminology seems to derive from Austin's distinction between the ways in which illocutionary acts can be "in order" or "not in order" and the ways in which they can be "right" or "wrong." Cf. *How To Do Things with Words* (Oxford, 1962). On Habermas's interpretation, the first form of appraisal relates to typical context restrictions, while the second relates to the basic type of claim raised. Since the ways in which speech acts can be right or wrong are not all reducible simply to the true/false distinction, there is a need for a more general term. On p. 237 of "Was heisst Universalpragmatik?" Habermas introduces the term *Rechtsansprüche* ("claims to be right"), for which he immediately substitutes *Geltungsansprüche* ("validity claims").

20. The propositional content is not actually asserted in every speech act. In nonconstative speech acts, it is merely "mentioned"; but the "unasserted proposition" implies "existential presuppositions" that have to be satisfied for the speech act to have a point. In general, an unasserted (mentioned) proposition can be transformed into an asserted proposition by making it the propositional content of a constative speech act.

21. Other remarks by Habermas imply that even the claim to comprehensibility takes us beyond the sphere of theoretical linguistics as usually conceived, because "semantic theory cannot be completely carried out in the attitude of the linguist, under an abstraction from pragmatic aspects." UP, p. 32. Cf. ibid., pp. 30–31, where he argues that an account of the meaning of linguistic expressions requires a consideration of their employment. Of course universal pragmatics (unlike, for instance, the philosophical semantics stemming from Wittgenstein) is not interested in the determination of meaning through typical (not to mention accidental) situations of use but only through "the formal characteristics of speech situations in general." See also Habermas's earlier argument that semantic theory cannot be adequately developed on the "monological, aprioristic and elementaristic" presuppositions of Chomsky and his followers, in "Towards a Theory of Communicative Competence."

22. UP, p. 29.

23. The logic underlying the use of deictic expressions would, according to Habermas, have to be worked out within the framework of a theory of experience. He makes some preliminary suggestions in this regard in *Theorie der Gesellschaft oder Sozialtechnologie?* (Frankfurt, 1971), pp. 202–220. With a fundamental revision of the Kantian "constitution theory" of experience in view, he argues there that "the construction of a world of objects of possible experience is based on a systematic interplay of sense reception, action and linguistic representation" (p. 206). In particular the ability to identify objects through the use of deictic expressions rests on the mastery of certain "basic operations" that underlie the "cognitive schemata" used to organize experience.

24. According to Habermas, this aspect of universal pragmatics would have to be worked out within the framework of a theory of intersubjectivity. For some suggestions along this line see ibid., pp. 186–195. Drawing on Mead, he argues there that the identity of meaning peculiar to communication in language must be traced back to the "reciprocal reflexivity of expectations," which in turn presupposes a "reciprocal recognition of subjects."

25. "Was heisst Universal pragmatik?" p. 225; slightly altered in UP, p. 42.

26. In Habermas's view, this methodologically fruitful narrowing of focus does not restrict the generality of the analysis, since he assumes a weaker version of Searle's "principle of expressibility" (Searle, *Speech Acts*, pp. 19ff.) to the effect that "in a given language, for every interpersonal relation that a speaker wants explicitly to take up with another member of his language community, either a suitable performative expression is available or, if necessary, can be acquired or introduced through a specification of available expressions" (UP, p. 40).

27. UP, p. 59. Compare Chomsky's contrast between acceptable/ grammatical following from his performance/competence distinction. Chomsky, *Theory of Syntax*, pp. 10ff. Although Habermas does not mention Chomsky in this connection, the counterpoint seems intentional.

28. Habermas concedes that this criterion does not always lead to unambiguous classifications: "There can be commands wherever relations of authority are institutionalized; appointments presuppose special, viz. bureaucratically articulated organizations of official positions; and marriages require a single institution (which, on the other hand, is universally disseminated). But this does not detract from the usefulness of the analytical viewpoint." UP, p. 39.

29. Cf. Searle, *Speech Acts*, pp. 54ff.

30. UP, p. 61.

31. Ibid., p. 63. Cf. ibid., pp. 53ff., where Habermas distinguishes three different "uses of language" or "modes of communication" according to which validity claim is thematically stressed; the results of his analysis are summarized in a table on p. 58. As he points out in "Some Distinctions in Universal Pragmatics," *Theory and Society* 3 (1976): 155–167, "the modes of language can only be paradigmatically bounded"; "given speech act sequences" cannot always be "unambiguously classified from this viewpoint"; but a competent speaker has in principle the possibility of choosing "to state a propositional content as such, to stress an interpersonal relationship as such, or to express an intention as such." Of course even when one validity claim is emphasized in this way, the others come into play; the four validity claims are "universal, that is, they must always be raised *simultaneously*, even if they cannot all be thematized at the same time."

32. UP, pp. 63–64. Cf. section 4.2.

33. Ibid., p. 64. Cf. section 4.3.

34. Ibid.

35. Ibid., p. 65.

36. KHI, appendix, p. 314.

37. UP, p. 1. The discussion of communication (like that of hermeneutics in section 3.3) turns on the meaning of *Verständigung* and cognate terms. Like their English counterparts, but more so, the German terms referring to understanding can typically be used in stronger and weaker senses, running the gamut from mere intelligibility to complete agreement. Thus we speak of understanding a word, sentence, argument; understanding what someone means with a given utterance; understanding a person's intentions, feelings, desires; coming to an understanding with someone; having reached an understanding with someone; and so on. In translating the German terms, I shall attempt to use English terms that cover the same range of meaning.

38. From an unpublished reply to Ernst Tugendhat, "Zu Tugendhats kritischen Bemerkungen" (spring 1976). For purposes of social analysis, however, Habermas takes *verständigungsoreitntiertes Handeln* as central. This is connected

with his rejection of the consensualistic assumptions of mainstream role theory. In this respect he accepts the arguments of those critics (among them, Goffman and Garfinkel) who stress the actors' interpretive response to established norms (role taking, negotiation of situation definitions). Cf. "On Communicative Action," paper delivered to the Boston University Colloquium for the Philosophy of Science in December 1976, and section 4.4.

39. UP, p. 1.

40. Ibid., pp. 2–3.

41. Ibid., p. 3.

42. "Vorbereitende Bemerkungen," p. 120.

Section 4.2

1. *Theory and Practice* (Boston, 1973), pp. 25ff.

2. Ibid., pp. 19–21. The related terms *Gründe, begründen* and *begründet* appear again and again in Habermas's discussion of discourse. It is sometimes difficult to find appropriate terms in English whose relations are so transparent. *Gründe* refers to the reasons or arguments offered in support of a position. The English term "ground" (as in "On what grounds does he hold that?") is close enough. *Begründen* is what one does when one gives reasons or provides grounds in this way—thus to substantiate, to justify, or, less usually, to ground a statement, theory, and so on. A statement is then *begründet* if this has been done (if it is well founded, substantiated, supported by reasons and arguments, or rather unusually, grounded). Where I think it important to preserve the manifest relations I shall use "grounds," "to ground," "(well)grounded." Otherwise I shall use such less jarring equivalents as "reasons" and "arguments"; "provide reasons and arguments for," "justify"; "substantiated," "justified." To bring out the connections to Dewey's theory of truth as "warranted assertability" (to which Habermas sometimes refers) I shall also use "warrant," "to warrant," "warranted." In any case, it is important to keep in mind that Habermas views these as pragmatic and not syntactic notions. He is not in general referring to that justification qua deductive proof that Popper and others have roundly criticized as an unattainable ideal for the sciences.

3. Cf. "Postscript to *Knowledge and Human Interests," Philosophy of Social Sciences* 3 (1973): 157–189, esp. 161ff.

4. *Critique of Pure Reason,* trans. N. Kemp Smith (New York, 1961), pp. 191ff.

5. "Postscript," p. 180. This point is argued at length by K.-O. Apel in *Der Denkweg von Charles S. Peirce* (Frankfurt, 1975); *Transformation der Philosophie* (Frankfurt, 1973) vols. 1–2; and "Sprechakttheorie und transzendentale Sprachpragmatik: zur Frage ethischer Normen," in *Sprachpragmatick und Philosophie* (Frankfurt, 1976), pp. 10–173.

6. *Theorie der Gesellschaft oder Sozialtechnologie?* pp. 206–207.

7. Cf. UP, pp. 21ff.

8. "Postscript," p. 173. In *Theorie der Gesellschaft oder Sozialtechnologie?* pp.

207ff., he elaborates on this a bit, explaining that the category of causality has a different status than the others: "the linguistic representatives of the causal relation do not belong to the class of deictic expressions." Cf. A. Wellmer; *Erklärung und Kausalität* (Habilitationsschrift, 1970).

9. "Der Universalitätsanspruch der Hermeneutik," in Apel et al. *Hermeneutik und Ideologiekritik* (Frankfurt, 1971), p. 142. Cf. "On Systematically Distorted Communication," *Inquiry* 13 (1970): 212. In *Theorie der Gesellschaft oder Sozialtechnologie?* pp. 210–211, he elaborates on this for the category of time, distinguishing between "physically measured time . . . an abstract continuum of temporal points," and "biographical and historical temporal horizons."

10. "Some Distinctions in Universal Pragmatics," *Theory and Society* 3 (1976): 161.

11. "Postscript," p. 174. Habermas feels that the "protophysics" of Dingler, Lorenzen and others is the most promising attempt to work out a substantive theory of measurement capable of elucidating the connection of theory construction in the natural sciences with the prior action-related constitution of the domain of physical objects. Cf. G. Böhme, ed., *Protophysik* (Frankfurt, 1975). He maintains that a corresponding "protosociology" must have the form of a theory of communication (see section 3.2).

12. "Postscript," pp. 171–172. This view of the logic of inquiry—as determined by both the "a priori of experience" and the "a priori of argumentative reason"—allows for the critical rationalists' (Popper et al.) insistence on the universal features of criticism without confusing the unity of argumentative reasoning with the unity of scientific method.

13. Cf. C. S. Peirce, "How to Make Our Ideas Clear" (1878).

14. "Wahrheitstheorien," in *Wirklichkeit und Reflexion: Festschrift für Walter Schulz* (Pfullingen, 1973), p. 219.

15. Cf. G. Pitcher, ed.; *Truth* (Englewood Cliffs, N.J., 1964). Habermas's most extensive discussion of the problem is in "Wahrheitstheorien." Cf. Also "Vorbereitende Bemerkungen zu einer Theorie der kommunikativen Kompetenz" and the fifth Princeton lecture.

16. P. F. Strawson; "Truth," in Pitcher, *Truth,* p. 33. Habermas does not agree with Ramsey's view that in all statements of the form "*p* is true" the expression "is true" is redundant, or with Strawson's refinement of it. He insists on the difference between a first-order assertion about objects or events in the world and second-order assertions to the effect that the truth claim made in the former is justified. He argues that it is precisely in discourse, in which truth claims that have been called into question are thematized, that statements about the truth of statements are not redundant. At the level of communicative interaction an explicit expression would be redundant.

17. "Wahrheitstheorien," p. 219.

18. Ibid., p. 223.

19. "Postscript," p. 170. Despite this close affinity, Habermas explicitly rejects

singular observation statements as the paradigm from which to develop a theory of truth. Instead he takes as paradigmatic the general and modal (for example, hypothetical, counterfactual) statements characteristic of science, since "they bring to expression what is specific to knowledge, namely the conceptual organization of experiential material." "Wahrheitstheorien," p. 233.

20. "Wahrheitstheorien," p. 218 .

21. "Postscript," p. 169. A basic function of measurement is precisely to provide for the systematic transformation of experiences into data that can function in a warranting process.

22. K. Popper, *Objective Knowledge* (Oxford, 1974), p. 348.

23. Wahrheitstheorien," p. 216.

24. Strawson, "Truth," p. 38.

25. Cf. Pitcher, *Truth*, pp. lff.

26. "Wahrheitstheorien," p. 218.

27. At one point Habermas considered dropping the designation "consensus theory of truth" in favor of "discourse theory of truth," to avoid unnecessary misunderstandings of his own position ("Wahrheitstheorien," p. 264, n. 33); but he has not done so.

28. Ibid., p. 219.

29. Ibid., p. 239.

30. He furnishes examples on p. 239 of ibid. Cf. my criticism in "A Theory of Communicative Competence," *Philosophy of the Social Sciences* 3 (1973): 149, and his response in "Postscript," pp. 169–170.

31. Cf. St. Toulmin; *The Uses of Argument* (Cambridge, England, 1964).

32. As might be expected from the discussion of the theory of social evolution in section 3.6, Habermas holds that it is not only possible but necessary to arrange conceptual shifts in a developmental logic. Viewing cognitive development on the social level as a learning process is essential to the critique of knowledge if this is to provide us with standards that are not merely language- or culture-relative. Moreover it is only from this point of view, Habermas argues, that the problem of induction—of justifying the (nondeductive) step from "backing" to "warrant"—can be profitably approached.

Although there are no deductive relations between the statements occurring in warrant and backing, an argument draws its consensus-producing power from the justification of going from B to W. . . . If we conceive of the language system employed in argumentation, i.e. the grounding language which in a certain way precedes experience, as at the same time a product of learning processes dependent upon experience, we can explain why induction is possible. . . . The basic predicates of well-tested grounding languages express cognitive schemata . . . [which] are the results of an active encounter between personality- and social-systems and nature. . . . If now the fundamental predicates of the grounding language express such cognitive schemata, induction means something rather trivial, namely the exemplary repetition of exactly that type of experience on the basis of which the cognitive schemata that have entered into the basic predicates of the language were previously formed. . . . This is what guarantees the 'appropriateness' of a grounding language to a determinate object domain. "Wahrheitstheorien," pp. 245–246.

33. Ibid., p. 232

34. Ibid., p. 239.

35. In ibid., Habermas argues that the universal pragmatic features of the ideal speech situation themselves guarantee the freedom of movement from level to level of discourse. As I have argued in "A Theory of Communicative Competence," pp. 150ff., this implication does not seem plausible.

36. It would be interesting to compare Habermas's argument with Popper's move from "the logic of inquiry" to the conception of an "open society." The differences would be as instructive as the similarities.

37. "Wahrheitstheorien," pp. 258–259.

Section 4.3

1. 'Wahrheitstheorien," pp. 226–227.

2. Ibid., p. 242. The motivation behind this dual paradigm of right/wrong and good/bad is evidently a desire to accommodate both deontological and teleological modes of argument.

3. Thus in practical discourse it is not the rightness claim implicit in the original action that is subject to argumentative examination but the rightness of the norms that the action is taken to fulfill. The rightness of the action is "borrowed" from that of the underlying norms. Thus the claim that has to be discursively grounded is that attached to the "recommendation" that a norm or standard be adopted. By contrast, in theoretical discourse it is the truth claim of the original assertion that is subject to argumentative redemption or rejection. Cf. (ibid., pp. 226ff., and UP, pp. 239ff.

4. "Wahrheitstheorien," p. 251.

5. Ibid., p. 251.

6. "Postscript," pp. 170–171.

7. "Wahreitstheorien," pp. 251–252. Thus the rationality of practical discourse is more directly tied to "truthfulness"—the absence of deception and self-deception—than is the case with theoretical discourse. Compare also n. 32 to section 4.2; as might be expected from the discussion of social evolution in section 3.6; Habermas holds that moral-practical language must also be viewed developmentally "as a product of learning processes dependent upon experience." Here too the relation of the warranting language to the domain of reality under discussion is determined "by an independent learning and developmental process." But here the process in question is the development of world views and moral-political systems. Just as the possibility of induction has to be clarified in the light of cognitive development, the feasibility of universalization is based on a development of moral-political consciousness.

8. "Wahrheitstheorien," p. 254.

9. P. Winch; "Understanding a Primitive Society," *American Philosophical Quarterly* (1964): 307–324, reprinted in Bryan Wilson, ed., *Rationality* (New York, 1970), pp. 78–79.

10. See, for instance, the essays collected in Wilson, *Rationality*.

11. Winch, "Understanding a Primitive Society," p. 99. Winch's position in this essay is close to Gadamer's in many respects. Cf. T. McCarthy; "The Operation Called *Verstehen*: Towards a Redefinition of the Problem," in Schaffner and R. Cohen, eds., *PSA 1972* (Dordrecht, Holland, 1974), pp. 167–193.

12. T. McCarthy; "The Problem of Rationality in Social Anthropology," *Stony Brook Studies in Philosophy* (1974): 1–21.

13. R. Horton; "African Traditional Thought and Western Science," in Wilson, *Rationality*, pp. 258–166.

14. Cf. Winch, "Understanding a Primitive Society," pp. 107ff.

15. Cf. K. -O. Apel; "Das Apriori der Kommunikationsgemeinschaft und die Grundlagen der Ethik," in *Transformation der Philosophie* (Frankfurt, 1973), 358–436, and "Sprechakttheorie und transzendetale Sprachpragmatik: zur Frage ethischer Normen," in *Sprachpragmatik und Philosophie* (Frankfurt, 1976), pp. 10–173.

16. Cf. Legitimation Crisis (Boston, 1975) pp. 109–110, 158–159, n. 16. Compare his earlier criticism of Popper on the same point in "A Positivistically Bisected Rationalism."

17. "Towards a Theory of Communicative Competence," p. 372.

18. "Zwei Bemerkungen zum praktischen Diskurs," in *Zur Rekonstruktion des Historischen Materialismus* (Frankfurt, 1976), pp. 339–340.

19. "Wahrheitstheorien," p. 265, n. 45. Cf. Also the introduction to *Theory and Practice*, pp. 25ff. As I pointed out in the discussion of Habermas's theory of social evolution (section 3.6), he holds that it is only at "post-conventional" stages of moral development that the ability to participate in discourse is presupposed.

20. Cf., for example, "Zwei Bemerkungen," p. 341.

21. In one passage Habermas points out that these principles are necessary but not sufficient for the foundations of ethics: "Wahrheitstheorien," p. 226, n. 18.

22. "Labor and Interaction: Remarks on Hegel's Jena *Philosophy of Mind*," in *Theory and Practice*, pp. 150–151.

23. This shift in emphasis stands out most clearly if one interprets Kant from a procedural point of view. Cf. John Silber; "Procedural Formalism in Kant's Ethics," *Review of Metaphysics* 28 (1974): 197–236. Silber interprets the categorical imperative as a statement of the procedure that moral judgment must follow if it is to be sound. The second of Kant's general rules for judgment is "to put oneself in thought in the place or point of view of another," "to imagine oneself in the place of every other person," "to think from the standpoint of

everyone else." As Silber points out, Kant is concerned here with "universal communicability"; but (and this is Habermas's point) this communicability is secured monologically. Thinking from a "universal standpoint" is, in Silber's terms, a "kind of thought experiment": "If in the decision regarding the treatment of others, one has placed himself in thought in the place of others, and followed the other principles of judgment too, we must *presume* that the treatment of another might be mistaken but hardly arbitrary, since the affected parties would *presumably* concur." (p. 217, my emphasis). The contrast between my presumption that others would concur with the results of my deliberation and the achievement of consensus in dialogue, brings out very nicely the differences between the two procedures.

24. "Postscript," p. 177.

25. The consequences of this exclusion become evident in the "Dialectic" of the Second Critique. Having divorced virtue from happiness, Kant must place the realization of "the highest good"—the union of virtue and happiness—beyond this world. Their union, a necessary object of the will, requires the postulates of the existence of God and the immortality of the soul. For Habermas this split does not arise since the content of the consensus sought for in discourse directly concerns happiness.

26. *Legitimation Crisis*, p. 89.

27. "The assumption of basic *material* norms capable of being justified leads to the difficulty that certain normative contents must be singled out theoretically. Hitherto, philosophical efforts to rehabilitate traditional . . . or modern natural law, in whatever version, have proved as unavailing as attempts to found a material value ethics. . . . Moreover, there is no need to accept such a burden of proof in order to demonstrate the criticizability of claims." Ibid., p. 100.

28. *Foundations of the Metaphysics of Morals*, trans. L. W. Beck (New York, 1959), pp. 54-55.

29. Ibid., p. 56. My remarks here are based on the negative formulations of the *Foundations*. They would have to be qualified somewhat if applied to the concept of "ends which are at the same time duties" developed by Kant in the "Doctrine of Virtue" of the *Metaphysics of Morals*.

30. Ibid., p. 46.

31. "Perpetual Peace," in L. W. Beck, ed., *Kant on History* (New York, 1963), p. 112.

32. *Legitimation Crisis*, p. 87.

33. Ibid., p. 89.

34. "Legitimationsprobleme in modernen Staat," *Zur Rekonstruktion des Historischen Materialismus*, p. 279. Basically the same distinction was already drawn in Habermas's discussion of "political participation" in *Student und Politik* (Neuwied, 1961) pp. 13–17. Rousseau is a central figure in Habermas's reading of modern political theory. Although contract theorists (Hobbes and Locke, for example) had previously developed the themes of self-determination and

rational agreement, it was with Rousseau that the formal conditions of rational agreement themselves became the principle of justification. For Habermas this represents the final step on the long journey from mythological, through cosmological, religious, and ontological types of legitimation to the "procedural type" in which free agreement among equals is decisive. See also the key role assigned Rousseau in Habermas's discussion of "Natural Law and Revolution," *Theory and Practice*, pp. 82–120.

35. Cf. "Die Utopie des guten Herrschers," in *Kultur und Kritik* (Frankfurt, 1973), p. 380 and "Stichworte zum Legitimationsbegriff—eine Replik," *Zur Rekonstruktion des Historischen Materialismus*, p. 333.

36. "Die Utopie des guten Herrschers," pp. 384–386.

37. *Legitimation Crisis*, p. 113.

38. Ibid., p. 117. On pp. 114ff. Habermas reiterates for this model some of the restrictions he pointed out in connection with the psychoanalytic model for the "organization of enlightenment" discussed in Section 3.4. The results of such simulated discourse remain hypothetical—"indeed a direct confirmation of this hypothesis would be possible only in the form of a practical discourse among the very individuals or groups involved," p. 114. But short of this there are, he maintains, empirical indicators that lend a degree of indirect confirmation to such reconstructions.

Section 4.4

1. "Moralentwicklung und Ich-Identität," paper delivered at the Institut für Sozialforschung in Frankfurt on the occasion of its fiftieth anniversary, July 1974; subsequently printed in *Zur Rekonstruktion des Historischen Materialismus* (Frankfurt, 1976), pp. 63–91; English translation, "Moral Development and Ego Identity," in *Communication and the Evolution of Society* (Beacon, 1979), pp. 69–94; here pp. 70–71.

2. Cf. H. Marcuse, *Five Lectures* (Boston, 1970); and T. Adorno, "Sociology and Psychology," *New Left Review* 46 (1967): 67–80 and 47 (1968): 79–97.

3. "Moral Development," p. 72. It seems likely that Habermas's less pessimistic diagnosis was stimulated to some extent by the student movement of the 1960s. This was a frequent topic of his early writings—cf. the essays collected in *Protestbewegung und Hochschulreform* (Frankfurt, 1969)— and he pointed to it as an indication that Marcuse's analysis of the family and socialization was inadequate in certain important respects: "Stichworte zur Theorie der Sozialisation" (1968), in *Kultur und Kritik* (Frankfurt, 1973), pp. 184–185.

4. *Theorie der Gesellschaft oder Sozialtechnologie* pp. 217–18.

5. Cf. "Stichworte zur Theorie der Sozialisation," pp. 124ff. for details and bibliography.

6. "Zur Entwicklung der Interaktionskompetenz," unpublished manuscript (1974), p. 4.

7. "Zur Einführung," in R. Döbert, J. Habermas and C. Nunner-Winkler, eds., *Die Entwicklung des Ichs* (Köln, 1977) p. 27.

8. UP, pp. 66–67.

9. "Interaktionskompetenz," p. 10. In part 4, of this manuscript (pp. 58–123) Habermas discusses various "interdependencies" among the three dimensions.

10. Ibid., pp. 11–12. Habermas also discusses ego development in terms of a system of "ego demarcations" [Ich-Abgrenzungen]: the acquisition of cognitive, linguistic, and interactive competence means that "complementary relations of the subjectivity of the ego to the objectivity of outer nature, to the normativity of society and to the intersubjectivity of language are established." "Subjectivity" is the way in which the subject encounters his own inner nature. He experiences himself in his subjectivity through "demarcations" in relation to "perceptions that are objective because every other person would perceive the same thing 'in my place'; normative structures whose validity every other person would acknowledge or reject 'in my situation'; and comprehensible utterances that are intersubjective because everyone that shares my language would understand them." In so demarcating and thus "constituting" itself, the ego knows itself not only as subjectivity but as "something that at the same time always transcends the bounds of subjectivity in cognition, language and interaction. The ego can identify with itself precisely in the distinction of the merely subjective from the nonsubjective. From Hegel through Freud to Piaget, the idea was developed that subject and object are reciprocally constituted, that the subject can secure itself only in relation to and by way of the construction of an objective world." Finally, it is the subject himself that demarcates his subjectivity; the boundaries with outer nature, language, and society are "drawn and maintained in his distinguishing the subjectivity of inner-related experiences (*Erlebnisse*) from the objectivity of experiences (*Erfahrungen*), from the normativity of precepts and values, and . . . from the intersubjectivity of meanings. These distinctions are expressed in the differentiation of validity claims that are connected with corresponding classes of utterances"—for example, with assertions, precepts, and evaluations as opposed to opinions, inclinations, and feelings. Insofar as these validity claims are acknowledged and transmitted, they can be incorporated into the "objective spirit" of a society (as elements of world views or institutions, for example).

11. Compare the model advanced in "Notizen zum Begriff der Rollenkompetenz" written in 1972 (in *Kultur und Kritik*, pp. 195–231) with that advanced in "Interaktionskompetenz" and "Moral Development," both written in 1974.

12. "Development of Normative Structures," pp. 100–101.

13. Ibid., p. 101.

14. Ibid.

15. Ibid., pp. 102ff. On pp. 16ff., Habermas suggests certain "homologies" between this pattern of ego development and the evolution of world views.

16. "Einführung," p. 10. In developing this concept of identity, Habermas draws mainly on three traditions: analytic ego psychology, symbolic interactionism, and cognitive developmental psychology. For relevant bibliography see "Moral Development," n. 7, p. 220.

17. "Development of Normative Structures," p. 109.

18. "Einführung," pp. 10–11.

19. Ibid., p. 16.

20. Ibid., p. 14

21. Ibid., p. 15.

22. Cf. "Stichworte zur Theorie der Sozialisation," pp. 132ff.

23. Cf. "Notizen zum Begriff de Rollenkompetenz," pp. 222ff.; "Development of Normative Structures," pp. 106ff; and "Können komplexe Gesellschaften eine vernünftige Identität ausbilden?" in *Zur Rekonstruktion*, pp. 92–128. The bulk of this last essay appeared in English as "On Social Identity," *Telos* 19 (1974).

24. Adapted from schema 4 of "Moral Development," p. 89. For a brief description of Kohlberg's six stages, see above, pp. 250–251.

25. "Einführung," p. 21. Compare Mead's concept of the "generalized other."

26. This point is developed in an unpublished manuscript; "Notizen zu Auwärter/Kirsch" (1977), pp. 4 ff.

27. "Einführung," pp. 23–24.

28. Cf. ibid., pp. 24–25.

29. Ibid., p. 25. Thus Habermas agrees with the emphasis placed on the subject's interpretive activity by Goffman and Garfinkel, among others; for points of disagreement, see section 3.2. The use of the term *communicative action* in this narrower sense (as opposed to *role behavior* in its conventional understanding) is relatively recent with Habermas. Formerly he used *interactive competence* and *role competence* interchangeably and spoke of the acquisition of interactive competence in terms of acquiring the "qualifications for role behavior." Cf. for example "Moralentwicklung," p. 76.

30. "Notizen zu Auwärter/Kirsch," pp. 10–11.

31. "Einführung," p. 25.

32. "Moral Development," p. 88.

33. Ibid., p. 90.

34. Ibid., p. 93.

35. Ibid., pp. 91–92. Habermas's most extensive discussion of the psychodynamics of the formative process can be found in the earlier (1968) "Stichworte zur Theorie der Sozialisation"; cf. also "Die kommunikative Organisation der inneren Natur," unpublished manuscript (1974).

36. *Legitimation Crisis* p. 14.

37. Ibid.

38. "Über sozialwissenschaftlichen Objektivismus," unpublished manuscript (1977), pp. 6–7.

39. Ibid., pp. 3ff. Cf. "Das Konzept des regelgeleiteten Verhaltens," unpublished manuscript (1975), for an analysis of the different strata of social action.

40. "On Communicative Action," paper delivered to the Boston Colloquium for the Philosophy of Science, December 1976, pp. 20–21. Compare the discussion of the "applicative" moment of *Verstehen* in section 3.3.

41. Ibid., pp. 14–15; cf. also "Intention, Konvention und sprachliche Interaktion," unpublished manuscript (1976). In "Über sozialwissenschaftlichen Objektivismus," pp. 43–46, Habermas suggests that he intends his "reconstructive" approach to transcend hermeneutics in a more strongly theoretical direction than I have indicated here. The pretheoretical foreknowledge on which the hermeneuticist relies is now to be systematically reconstructed. This move, he seems to suggest, would make it possible to formulate interpretations in a universalistic language, such that they could claim and be tested for "objectivity" (not to be confused with objectivism). But I am not certain just how far he means to push this. Taken in the strongest sense, the success of such a program would seem to require a universal semantics of language and something equivalent for action—and Habermas himself has furnished grounds for doubting that this is possible. As long as the reconstructive enterprise is restricted to formal structures, I cannot see how the hermeneutic problem in regard to the interpretation and critique of concrete utterances or actions can be avoided. Of course, even the success of the more modest reconstructive program outlined in this chapter would increase the objectivity of interpretations.—for instance; a structural description of a given moral system or world view would permit us to locate it in a developmental hierarchy in a nonarbitrary way.

NOTES TO CHAPTER 5

1. *Legitimation Crisis* (Boston, 1975), pp. 45ff.

2. Ibid., p. 49.

3. Ibid., p. 40.

4. Ibid.

5. Ibid., p. 93.

6. Cf. ibid., p. 117, pp. 141–142.

7. Ibid., p. 92.

8. Preface to ibid.

9. Ibid., p. 143. Cf. p. 33, where he writes: "It is not easy to determine empirically the probability of boundary conditions under which the *possible* crisis

tendencies *actually* set in and prevail. The empirical indicators we have at our disposal are as yet inadequate. . . It goes without saying that an argumentation sketch cannot replace empirical investigations, but can be best guide them."

10. Ibid., p. 2.

11. Ibid. Throughout the book Habermas makes rather free use of systems-theoretic terminology. On the other hand, he argues explicitly that the systems-theoretic approach is inadequate, that it must be integrated with the "life-world" perspective. "Both paradigms, life-world and system, are important. The problem is to demonstrate their interconnection" (p. 4). Although Habermas provides a number of suggestions as to how this might be done (cf. pp. 8–17), he has not (nor does he claim to have) yet worked out an integrated general theory. Nevertheless the argument in *Legitimation Crisis* is constructed with such a theory in view; aspects of both self-regulation and symbolic interaction figure essentially in it. One could argue, however, that the life-world perspective predominates, since the crisis argument depends on action-theoretic assumptions developed in the theory of communication.

12. Ibid., p. 4.

13. What follows is Habermas's interpretation, in his terminology.

14. Ibid., p. 22. This is not to say that the bourgeois ideology of the inherent justice of the market was effective in all social classes: "The loyalty and subordination of the members of the new urban proletariat, recruited mainly from the ranks of peasants, were certainly maintained more through a mixture of traditionalistic ties, fatalistic willingness to follow, lack of perspective, and naked repression than through the convincing force of bourgeois ideologies" (p. 22).

15. Ibid., p. 26.

16. Ibid., p. 29.

17. Ibid., pp. 56–57.

18. Ibid., p. 57.

19. Ibid., p. 62.

20. Ibid., p. 64.

21. Ibid., p. 36.

22. Ibid., p. 37.

23. Ibid., p. 75.

24. Ibid., pp. 47–48. As he puts it in "Legitimation Problems in the Modern State," *Communication and the Evolution of Society*, pp. 178–204, the state is perceived as generally responsible for shortcomings and for their removal (pp. 194–195).

25. Ibid., p. 72.

26. Ibid., p. 72.

27. Ibid., p. 70.

28. Ibid., p. 69.

29. Ibid., pp. 74–75.

30. Ibid., p. 93.

31. Ibid., 43–44. Habermas does not deny that "whether legitimations are believed certainly depends on empirical motives"; he wants to insist, however, that the latter "are not shaped independently of the reasons that can be mobilized." "Legitimation Problems," p. 183.

32. Ibid., p. 77.

33. Ibid., p. 85.

34. Ibid., p. 12. In "Legitimation Problems" he makes a related point in terms of a hierarchy of "levels of justification," that is, of "formal conditions for the acceptability of reasons that lend to legitimations their effectiveness, their power to produce consensus and shape motives." p. 184. The *kind* of reason effective at one level loses its power to convince at the next; at present he wants to argue, only the "procedural type of legitimation," that is, the appeal to free agreement among equals, is effective.

35. Ibid., pp. 12–13.

36. Ibid., p. 43. The qualifying phrase "as long as we have to do with" is an allusion to the "end of the individual" thesis discussed in part III of ibid.

37. Cf. ibid., pp. 90ff.

38. Ibid., p. 90.

39. Habermas admits as much on p. 129 of ibid.

40. An alternative reading is suggested below. Of course, in Habermas's view the objectivity of empirically ascertainable crisis tendencies is a necessary part of any crisis argument—hence the usefulness of the systems-theoretic perspective. But critical social theory is also supposed to provide insight into the *practical* necessity for social change, to assist in the formation of what Marx referred to as class consciousness and Habermas refers to as action-orienting self-understanding.

41. *Theorie und Praxis* (Neuwied, 1963) p. 311.

42. *Zur Logik der Sozialwissenschaften* (Frankfurt), 1970, pp. 251ff.

43. Cf. "Perpetual Peace" in *Kant on History,* trans. L. W. Beck (New York, 1963).

44. *Legitimation Crisis*, p. 113.

45. Ibid., 113.

46. Ibid., p. 114.

47. "The Public Sphere," *New German Critique* 3 (1974): 54.

48. *Toward a Rational Society* (Boston, 1970), p. 111.

49. Ibid., p. 112.

50. Ibid., p. 113.

51. Ibid., pp. 107–109. Cf. also "Über einige Bedingungen der Revolutionierung spätkapitalistischer Gesellschaften," in *Kultur und Kritik* (Frankfurt, 1973) pp. 70ff., and *Legitimation Crisis*, pp. 37ff. Habermas credits Clause Offe for this analysis; cf. Offe's "Political Authority and Class Structure," *International Journal of Sociology* (Spring 1972): 73–108.

52. *Toward a Rational Society*, pp. 109–110.

53. *Theory and Practice*, pp. 6–7. In the same passage he raises a series of open questions concerning the potential for political action within the working class.

54. The terminology in quotation marks appears in "Technology and Science as 'Ideology,'" *Toward a Rational Society* (Boston, 1970), p. 120. For Habermas's views on the student movement, see *Protestbewegung und Hochschulreform* (Frankfurt, 1969), parts of which were translated in chapters 1 to 3 of *Toward a Rational Society*. In general his position is that (a) the situation of organized capitalism is not "revolutionary,"; (b) "radical reformism" is at present the only way to bring about conscious structural change; (c) for this a repoliticization of the public sphere is necessary; and (d) student protest can and did serve this end. Apart from this active role in politicizing the public sphere, student protest is important as a symptom of fundamental changes in the socialization process that are undermining the orientations to achievement and possessive individualism and eroding formal-democratic and technocratic legitimations. While Habermas developed both of these perspectives in his writings of the late sixties, his more recent writings stress the social-psychological potential rather than the active political role of youth.

A Bibliography of Works by Habermas, with Translations and Reviews
prepared by René Görtzen and Frederik van Gelder

Publications are arranged chronologically, by year, from 1952 onward; reprints, new editions, translations, and reviews are also indicated. For reprints, a superscript has been used; thus 1976⁵ is to be read as reprinted for the fifth time in 1976. When an English translation exists, the entry number appears in square brackets and indication is given in the text of where the translation may be found. An earlier version of this bibliography appeared in *Human Studies*, volume 2, number 4, October 1979.

ABBREVIATIONS

AEF *Arbeit-Erkenntnis-Fortschritt* (Work, knowledge, progress) Amsterdam 1970. (70k)

AFK *Arbeit-Freizeit-Konsum* (Knowledge, leisure, consumption) 's-Gravenhage, The Netherlands 1973. (73a)

KuK *Kultur und Kritik* (Culture and critique) Frankfurt/Main 1973. (73b)

LSW *Zur Logik der Sozialwissenschaften* (Towards a logic of the social sciences) Frankfurt/Main 1970. (70a)

PKR *Politik, Kunst, Religion* (Politics, art, religion) Stuttgart: Reclam 1978. (78d)

PPP *Philosophisch-politische Profile* (Philosophical-political profiles) Frankfurt/Main 1971. (71b)

PuH *Protestbewegung und Hochschulreform* (Protest movement and university reform) Frankfurt/Main 1969. (69a)

RHM *Zur Rekonstruktion des Historischen Materialismus* (Towards a reconstruction of historical materialism) Frankfurt/Main 1976. (76a)

TuP *Theorie und Praxis* Frankfurt/Main 1963, 1971. (63a, 71d) Translated as:

TaP *Theory and Practice* London 1974. (74c)

TWI *Technik und Wissenschaft als 'Ideologie'* (Technology and science as 'ideology') Frankfurt/Main 1968. (68a) Translated, in part, as:

TRS *Towards a Rational Society* London 1971. (71e)

1952

52a "Gottfried Benns neue Stimme" (Gottfried Benn strikes a new note) *Frankfurter Allegemeine Zeitung* 19 July.

52b "Wider den moral-pädagogischen Hochmut der Kulturkritik" (Against the moral-pedagogic arrogance of kulturkritik) *Die Literatur* September (No. 13), p.6.

1953

[53a] "Mit Heidegger gegen Heidegger denken. Zur Veröffentlichung von Vorlesungen aus dem Jahre 1935" (Thinking with Heidegger against Heidegger: On the occasion of the publication of lectures dating from 1935) *Frankfurter Allgemeine Zeitung* 25 July. c.f. PPP, pp. 67–75. In English: "Martin Heidegger, on the publication of lectures from the year 1935," *Graduate Faculty Philosophy Journal*, 1977, 6 (No. 2), pp. 155–180. (includes entries 59a, 59b; c.f.)

1954

54a *Das Absolute und die Geschichte. Von der Zwiespältigkeit in Schellings Denken* (The Absolute and History; concerning the internal conflict within Schelling's Thought), Ph.D. dissertation, Bonn University. 424 pages. (c.f. 54 h)

54b "Die Dialektik der Rationalisierung. Vom Pauperismus im Produktion und Konsum." (The dialectics of rationalisation: Concerning alienation in production and consumption) *Merkur* 8 (No. 78), pp. 701–724; AEF, pp. 7–31; AKE, pp. 3–27.

54c "Der Moloch und die Künste. Zur Legende von der technischen Zwechmässigkeit" (Moloch and the arts: On the illusion of technical efficacy) *Jahresring* (Stuttgart) I, pp. 258–263.

54d "Neun Jahre unter die Lupe. Deutschlands geistige Entwicklung seit 1945. Der Versuch einer Bilanz" (Nine years under scrutiny: Germany's intellectual development since 1945. Towards an assessment) *Handelsblatt* (Düsseldorf) 9 (No. 135), p. 4.

54e "Die Masse—das sind wir" (The masses: That's us) *Handelsblatt* (Düsseldorf) 9 (No. 126), p. 4.

54f "Beamte müssen Phantasie haben. Gibt es ein Heilmittel gegen die Schwächen der Bürokratie?—Für eine Kontrolle 'von innen'" (Officials should have imagination. Is there a cure for the weaknesses of bureaucracy? The case for 'internal control') *Handelsblatt* (Düsseldorf) 25 July.

54g "Sie gehören zum 'Staat' oder zum 'Betrieb.' Die unpersönliche Macht der modernen Bürokratie—Ihre Herkunft und ihre Gefahr" (One belongs either to the 'state' or to the 'organisation.' The impersonal power of the modern bureaucracy: Its origins and danger) *Handelsblatt* (Düsseldorf) 11 July.

54h "Schelling und die 'Submission' unter das Höhere. Zum 100 Todestag des Philosophen—nicht nur ein Memoriam" (Schelling and the 'submission' to the transcendental. On the centenary of the philosopher's death: More than a commemoration) *Frankfurter Allgemeine Zeitung* 21 August.

1955

55a "'Stil' auch für den Alltag: Die 'Industrieformung' nutzt und hilft dem Konsumenten" ('Industrial design' benefits and helps the Consumer) *Handelsblatt* (Düsseldorf) 23 September, p. 4.

55b "'Ohne mich' auf dem Index" (The 'without me' attitude in disfavour) *Deutsche Studentenzeitung* (Hamburg) 5 (No. 5), pp. 1–2.

55c "Marx in Perspektiven" (Marx in perspective) *Merkur* 9 (No. 94), pp. 1180–1183; AEF, pp. 75–81.

55d "Jeder Mensch ist unbezahlbar" (Everyone is priceless) *Merkur* 9 (No. 83), pp. 994–999.

55e "Der Pfahl im Fleische . . . Eine verlegene Bemerkung zu Kierkegaards 100 Todestag" (A thorn in the flesh . . . An embarrassed comment on the centenary of Kierkegaard's death) *Frankfurter Allgemeine Zeitung* 12 November.

1956

56a "Karl Jaspers über Schelling" (Karl Jaspers on Schelling) *Frankfurter Allgemeine Zeitung* 14 January. PPP, pp. 93–99.

56b "Der Zeitgeist und die Pädagogik" (The spirit of the times and education) *Merkur* 10 (No. 96), pp. 189–193.

56c "Notizen zum Missverhältnis von Kultur and Konsum" (Incongruities between culture and consumption: Some notes) *Merkur* 10 (No. 97), pp. 212–228; AEF, pp. 31–47; AFK, pp. 27–43.

56d "Illusionen auf dem Heiratsmarkt" (Illusions on the marriage-market) *Merkur* 10 (No. 104), pp. 996–1004; AEF, pp. 81–92; AFK, pp. 43–54.

56e "Der Verrat und die Masstäbe" (The betrayal and its criteria) *Deutsche Universitäts-zeitung* (Göttingen) 11 (No. 19), pp. 8–11.

56f Man Möchte Sich Mitreissen Lassen Feste und Feiern in dieser Zeit" (Feasts and celebrations in these times) *Handelsblatt* (Düsseldorf) 11 (No. 21), p. 4.

1957

57a "Das chronische Leiden der Hochschulreform" (The chronic malaise of university reform) *Merkur* 11 (No. 109), pp. 265–284; PuH, pp. 51–82.

57b "Literaturbericht zur philosophischen Diskussion um Marx und den Marxismus" (Overview of the literature: The philosophical debates about Marx and Marxism) *Philosophische Rundschau* 5 (No. 3–4), pp. 165–235; TuP, pp. 387–463 (1st edition: pp. 261–335).

57c "Konsumkritik—eigens zum Konsumieren" (Konsumkritik—especially with regard to consumption) *Frankfurter Hefte* 12 (No. 9), pp. 641–645; AEF, pp. 47–56; AFK, pp. 54–63.

57d "Der biografische Schleier. Bei Gelegenheit des Stresemann-Filmes notiert" (Biographical obfuscation: Some notes on the Stresemann-film) *Frankfurter Hefte* 12 (No. 5), pp. 357–361.

1958

58a "Der befremdliche Mythos: Reduktion oder Evokation?" Book review of E. Topitsch, *Vom Ursprung und Ende der Metaphysik* (Vienna 1958); W. Bröckner, *Dialektik, Positivismus, Mythologie* (Frankfurt/Main 1958); and B. Liebrucks, *Sprache und Mythos* in G. Funke (Ed.), *Konkrete Vernunft. Festschrift für E. Rothacker* (Bonn 1958), pp. 253–281; and in *Philosophische Rundschau* 6 (No. 3–4), pp. 215–228; AEF, pp. 149–164.

58b "Jaspers und die Gestalten der Wahrheit" (Jaspers and the Forms of Truth) *Frankfurter Allgemeine Zeitung* 22 Feb. Reprinted in PPP, pp. 99–109; H. Saner (Ed.), *Karl Jaspers in der Diskussion* (Munich 1973), pp. 309–316.

58c "Philosophische Anthropologie. Ein Lexikonartikel" (Philosophical Anthropology. An encyclopaedia article), Fischer Lexicon series, *Philosophie* (Frankfurt/Main), pp. 18–35; AEF, pp. 164–181; KuK, pp. 89–111.

58d "Soziologische Notizen zum Verhältnis von Arbeit und Freizeit" (Sociological notes on the relationship of work and leisure) G. Funke (Ed.), *Konkrete Vernunft: Festschrift für E. Rothacker* (Bonn), pp. 219–231. Reprinted in AEF, pp. 56–75; AFK, pp. 63–81; H. Plessner, H. Boch, D. Grupe (Eds.), *Sport und Leibeserziehung* (Munich 1967), pp. 28–46.

58e "Der verschleierte Schrecken. Bemerkungen zu C. F. von Weizsäckers 'Mit der Bombe leben'" (The hidden horror. Review of C. F. von Weizsäcker's 'Living with the Bomb') *Frankfurter Hefte* 13 (No. 8) pp. 530–532; AEF, pp. 92–97.

1959

[59a] "Die grosse Wirkung. Eine chronistische Anmerkung zu Martin Heideggers 70 Geburtstag" (The great fascination. Some remarks on Martin Heidegger's 70th birthday) *Frankfurter Allgemeine Zeitung* 26 Sept.; PPP, pp. 76–85. In English: c.f. 53a.

[59b] "Ein anderer Mythos des zwanzigsten Jahrhunderts" (A new mythology for the twentieth century). Review of W. Bröcker, *Dialektik, Positivismus, Mythologie* and P. Füstenau, *Heidegger, das Gefüge seines Denkens* (Frank-

furt/Main 1958) in *Frankfurter Hefte* 14 (No. 3) pp. 206–209. Reprinted in AEF, pp. 97–103; PPP, pp. 85–92. In English: c.f. 53a.

59c "Die Grenze in uns. Helmuth Plessner: Die verspätete Nation" (Our internal schisms: Review of Helmuth Plessner: *Die verspätete Nation*) *Frankfurter Hefte* 14 (No. 11), pp. 826–831; AEF, pp. 103–112; PPP, pp. 222–234.

59d "Zum Einfluss von Schule und Hochschulbildung auf das politische Bewusstsein der Studenten" (The influence of school and university education on the political awareness of students) *Verhandlungen des Deutschen Soziologentages* (Tübingen) 14, p. 217ff. Reprinted in *Gesellschaft, Staat, Erziehung* 4 (No. 8), pp. 348–355. (c.f. 65c).

59e "Konservativen Geist und die modernistischen Folgen. Zum Reformplan für die deutsche Schule" (The conservative spirit and its modernistic consequences. On the reform proposals for German schools) *Der Monat* (Berlin) 12 (No. 133), pp. 41–50.

59f "Brief an H. Mörchen" (Letter to H. Mörchen) *Frankfurter Hefte* 14 (No. 7), p. 537.

1960

[60a] "Ein marxistischer Schelling. Zu Ernst Blochs spekulativem Materialismus" *Merkur* 14 (No. 153) pp. 1078–1091. Reprinted in M. Walser, I. Wenzer et al. (Eds.), *Über Ernst Bloch* (Frankfurt/Main 1968), pp. 61–82; TuP (1st. edition), pp. 336–351; PPP, pp. 147–167; PKR, pp. 11–32. In English: "A speculative materialist," *Telos*, Fall 1977, 33; and "A marxist romantic," *Salmagundi*, 1969/1970, 10/11, pp. 633–654.

60b "Verrufener Fortschritt—verkanntes Jahrhundert. Zur Kritik an der Geschichtsphilosophie. Replik R. Koselleck und H. Kesting" (Discredited progress-underrated century. A critique of the philosophy of history. Reply R. Koselleck and H. Kesting) *Merkur* 14 (No. 147), pp. 468–477; AEF, pp. 112–122; KuK, pp. 355–365.

1961

61a "Der deutsche Idealismus der judische Philosophen" (The German Idealism of the Jewish Philosophers) T. Koch (Ed.), *Porträts deutsch-jüdischer Geistesgeschichte* (Cologne), pp. 99–125. Reprinted in PPP, pp. 37–66.

61b *Student und Politik. Eine soziologische Untersuchung zum politischen Bewusstsein Frankfurter Studenten* (co-authors: L. von Friedeburg, C. Oehler, F. Weltz) (Berlin 1967², 1969³). Papers by Habermas: "Uber den Begriff der politischen Beteiligung" (The concept of political activism). Reprinted in AEF, pp. 258–304; KuK, pp. 9–60. "Der politische Habitus" (Political attitudes); "Das Gesellschaftsbild" (Conception of society).

61c "Pädagogischer Optimismus vor Gericht einer pessimistischen Anthropologie. Schelskys Bedenken zur Schulreform" (Educational optimism in the face of a pessimistic anthropology. Schelsky's reservations about educational reform) *Neue Sammlung* (Göttingen) 1, pp. 252–278; also in AEF, pp. 181–219.

61d "Die Bundesrepublik-Eine Wahlmonarchie?" *Magnum* (Cologne) Sonderheft: *Woher-Wohin. Bilanz der Bundesrepublik,* pp. 26–29.

1962

62a *Strukturwandel der Öffentlichkeit. Untersuchungen zu einer Kategorie der bürgerlichen Gesellschaft* (Structural change of the 'public sphere.' Investigating a category of bourgeois society) Berlin (Luchterhand) second edition 1965, 1968³, 1969⁴, 1971⁵, 1974⁶, 1976⁷. Translated into Norwegian, Italian, Hungarian, Serbocroatian, French. (c.f. also entry 66f). Reviews: M. Rassem, *Philosophische Rundschau,* 1964, 12, pp. 116–122; W. F. Haug, *Das Argument,* 1963, 25, pp. 55ff.; W. Steinbeck, *Philosophische Literaturanzeiger,* 1964, 17, pp. 145–149; R. Dahrendorf, *Frankfurter Hefte,* November 1962, pp. 781–783; M. Brentano, *Spandauer Volksblatt,* 6 October 1964; G. Bohring, *Deutsche Zeitschrift für Philosophie,* 1965, 14 (11), pp. 1421–1427; P. Häberle, *Zeitschrift für Politikologie,* 1969, 1, pp. 273–287; T. Ellwein, *Neue Politische Literatur,* 1965, 1, pp. 74–78; R. Mayntz, *American Journal of Sociology,* 1965, No. 71, pp. 350ff.; H. S. Arndt, *Der Staat* (Berlin), 1964, 3 (No. 3), pp. 335–345.

62b "Kritische und konservative Aufgabe der Soziologie" (Critical and conservative mandates for sociology). A lecture delivered at the University of Berlin, January 1962. *Universitätstage* Wissenschaft und Verantwortung. Freie Universität, Berlin, pp. 157–172. Reprinted in TuP, pp. 290–307.

62c "Diskutieren—was sonst?" (Debate—What else?) *Daten* (Dortmund) 2, p. 47ff. Reprinted in PuH, pp. 83–89.

62d "Über das Verhältnis von Politik und Moral" (The relationship between politics and morality), H. Kuhn, Fr. Wiedmann (Eds.), *Das Problem der Ordnung.*(Munich 1960). H. D. Wendland (Ed.), *Politik und Ethik* (Darmstadt 1969), pp. 61–91. Reprinted in AEF, pp. 219–243.

1963

[63a] *Theorie und Praxis. Sozialphilosophische Studien* (Neuwied-Berlin) 1967², 1968³, 1971: second edition. (c.f. entry 71d). Translated into English, Japanese, French. Contents: 63b, 63c, 63d, 63e, 63f, 62b, 63g, 57b, 60a, 63h.)

Reviews: A. Künzli, *Frankfurter Rundschau,* 6 February 1965; W. Steinbeck, *Philosophische Literaturanzeiger,* 1964, 17, pp. 272–280; O. Pöggeler, *Bibliographie de la Philosophie,* 1964, 11, pp. 286–287; W. Jopke, *Deutsche Zeitschrift für Philosophie,* 1965, 13, pp. 1375–1381; P. C. Kuiper, *Psyche* (Heidelberg), 1965, 19, pp. 852–857; M. Kangrga, *Praxis* (Zagreb), 1965, 1, pp. 392–398; W. Dallmayr, *Archiv für Rechts- und Sozialphilosophie* (Main/Wiesbaden), 1968, 54, pp. 435–445; F. Ronneberg, *Universitas* (Stuttgart), 1969, 24, pp. 90–91; S. D. Berger; *Social Research,* 1966 (33), p. 137.

[63b] "Die klassische Lehre von der Politik in ihrem Verhältnis zur Sozialphilosophie." Revised version of Habermas's inaugural lecture, Marburg, December 1961, in TuP, pp. 48–89; TaP, pp. 41–81.

[63c] "Naturrecht und Revolution." Revised version of paper delivered to "VII Deutschen Kongress für Philosophie" and to the "Internationalen Vereinigung für Rechts- und Sozialphilosophie," October 1962. Reprinted in TuP, pp. 89–128; H. Kuhn, F. Wiedmann (Eds.), *Die Philosophie und die Frage nach dem Fortschritt* (Munich 1964), pp. 160–179; TaP, pp. 82–120.

[63d] "Hegels Kritik der franszösischen Revolution." Revised version of inaugural lecture, Heidelberg, July 1962, in TuP, pp. 128–148; TaP, pp. 121–141.

63e "Dialectischer Idealismus im Übergang zum Materialismus. Geschichtsphilosophische Folgerungen aus Schellings Idee einer Contraction Gottes" (Dialectical Idealism in its transition to Materialism. The implications, for a philosophy of history, of Schelling's concept of a contract with God). Revised version of a lecture at Heidelberg University, July 1961, in TuP, pp. 172–228.

[63f] "Zwischen Philosophie und Wissenschaft. Marxismus als Kritik." Lecture before the "Züricher Philosophischen Gesellschaft" in TuP, pp. 228–290. In English: TaP, pp. 195–252.

[63g] "Dogmatismus, Vernunft und Entscheidung. Zu Theorie und Praxis in der verwissenschaftlichten Zivilisation," TuP, pp. 307–336. In English: TaP, pp. 253–282.

63h "Karl Löwiths stoischer Rückzug vom historischen Bewusstsein" (Karl Löwith's stoical retreat from a consciousness of history), TuP (1st edition only), pp. 331–370; *Merkur* 17 (No. 184), pp. 576–590; PPP, pp. 116–240.

[63j] "Analytische Wissenschaftstheorie und Dialektik. Ein Nachtrag zur Kontroverse zwischen Popper und Adorno," M. Horkeimer (Ed.), *Zeugnisse. Theodor W. Adorno zum sechzigsten Geburtstag* (Frankfurt/Main), pp. 473–503. Reprinted in: LSW, pp. 9–39; T. W. Adorno et al., *Der Positivismusstreit in der deutschen Soziologie* (Berlin 1969), pp. 155–192; in E. Topitsch (Ed.) *Logik derr Sozialwissenschaften* (Cologne/Berlin 1971) pp. 291–311. In English: T. W. Adorno et al., *The Positivist Dispute in German Sociology* (London 1976), pp. 131–163.

63k "Ein philosophierender Intellektueller. Zum 60 Geburtstag von Theodor W. Adorno" (A philosophising intellectual: On the occasion of Theodor W. Adorno's 60th birthday) *Frankfurter Allgemeine Zeitung*, 11 Sept. Reprinted in: K. Oppens, H. Kudszus et al., *Über Theodor W. Adorno* (Frankfurt/Main 1968), pp. 35–44; PPP, pp. 176–184.

63m "Parteirügen an Schriftsteller—hüben und drüben" (Attacks by political parties on writers—over here and over there) (i.e. West and East Germany) *Merkur* 17 (No. 180), pp. 210–212; AEF, pp. 127–131.

63n "Auf und Abrüstung, moralisch und militärisch" (Re- and disarmament, moral and military) *Merkur* 17 (No. 185), pp. 714–717; AEF, pp. 131–135.

63p "Vom sozialen Wandel akademischer Bildung" (The social change of academic education) Lecture at Berlin University, January 1963. Reprinted in: *Merkur* 17 (No. 183), pp. 413–427; *Universitätstage:* Freie Universität, Berlin, pp. 165–180; TuP, pp. 359–376; S. von Leibfried (Ed.), *Wider die Untertanen-Fabrik; Handbuch zur Demokratisierung der Hochschule* (Cologne 1967), pp. 10–24, 384; AEF, pp. 243–258.

63q "Eine psychoanalytische Konstruktion des Fortschritts. (Alexander Mitscherlich)" (A psychoanalytic interpretation of progress: Alexander Mitscherlich) *Merkur* 17 (No. 189), pp. 1105–1109; AEF, pp. 122–127; KuK, pp. 112–117.

1964

[64a] "Verwissenschaftlichte Politik und öffentliche Meinung." Revised version of Habermas's contribution to R. Reich (Ed.), *Humanität und politische Verantwortung; Festschrift für Hans Barth* (Zürich), pp. 54–73; TWI, pp. 120–145. In English: TRS, pp. 62–81.

[64b] "Öffentlichkeit. (Ein Lexikonartikel)" Fischer Lexikon (Frankfurt/Main), pp. 220–226. Reprinted in: KuK, pp. 61–69. In English: "The Public Sphere: An encyclopaedia Article," *New German Critique,* 1974 (No. 3).

64c "Von der Schwierigkeit nein zu sagen. (Klaus Heinrich)" (The difficulties of saying No re Klaus Heinrich) *Merkur* 18 (No. 201), pp. 1184–1189. Reprinted in: LSW, pp. 322–329; AEF, pp. 135–141.

64d "Wissenschaft und Politik" (Science and Politics) *Offene Welt* (Cologne), 86, pp. 413–423.

[64e] "Gegen einen positivistisch halbierten Rationalismus. Erwiderung eines Pamphlets," *Kölner Zeitschrift für Soziologie und Sozialpsychologie,* 16 (No. 4), pp. 636–659. Reprinted in: T. W. Adorno et al., *Der Positivismusstreit in der deutschen Soziologie* (Berlin 1969), pp. 235–260; LSW, pp. 39–71. In English: "Rationalism divided in two," A. Giddens (Ed.), *Positivism and Sociology* (London: Heinemann, 1974), pp. 195–223; and "A positivistically bisected Rationalism," T. W. Adorno et al., *The Positivist Dispute in German Sociology* (London 1976), pp. 131–163.

64f Diskussion über 'Revolution' (c.f. entry 63c). Panel discussion: Werner Conze, Helmut Kuhn, Eric Weil, J. Habermas. Reprinted in: H. Kuhn, F. Wiedman (Eds.), *Die Philosophie und die Frage nach dem Fortschritt* (Munich: Pustet), pp. 317–325.

64g "Wissenschaftliche Politberatung—staatliche Forschungspolitik," *Süddeutsche Zeitung,* 26 June (No. 153).

64h "Vom Ende der Politik," *Frankfurter Allgemeine Zeitung,* 17 October. Reprinted in: J. Schickel (Ed.), *Über Hans Magnus Enzensberger* (Frankfurt am Main: Suhrkamp, 1970), pp. 154–160.

64j "Ein Verdrängungsprozess wird enthüllt," *Die Zeit,* 12 June. Reprinted in: V. Canaris (Ed.): *Über Peter Weiss* (Frankfurt am Main: Suhrkamp, 1970), pp. 64–68.

1965

65a "Gesellschaft und Demokratie in Deutschland. Die verzögerte Moderne" (Society and democracy in Germany; Retarded modernisation) *Der Spiegel* 29 (No. 53); PPP, pp. 234–239.

65b "Wittgensteins Rückkehr. Zum zweiten Band der 'Schriften': 'Philosophische Bemerkungen' (Wittgenstein's return. Notes on the second volume of the collected works: *Philosophical Investigations*), *Frankfurter Allgemeine Zeitung,* 20 Feb.; PPP, pp. 141–146.

65c "Zum Einfluss von Schul—und Hochschulbildung auf das politische Bewusstsein von Studenten" (c.f. entry 59d), L. von Friedeburg (Ed.), *Jugend in der modernen Gesellschaft* (Cologne), pp. 424–431.

65d "Vorwort" zu: W. Nitsch, U. Gerhardt, C. Offe, U. K. Preuss, *Hochschule in der Demokratie* (Berlin), pp. V–VI. (Preface to Nitsch et al., Universities in a democracy). Reprinted in: PuH, pp. 90–91.

[65e] "Wertfreiheit und Objektivität. Eine Diskussionsbemerking," O. Stammer (Ed.), *Max Weber und die Soziologie heute* (Tübingen), pp. 74–81. Reprinted in: LSW, pp. 313–321; AEF, pp. 304–312. In English: "Value-freedom and Objectivity," O. Stammer (Ed.), *Max Weber and Sociology Today* (New York 1971), and F. Dallmayr, T. McCarthy (Eds.), *Understanding and Social Enquiry* (Indiana, USA).

65f "Resumé" (der Starnberger Gespräche 1964: Aspekte der Angst), H. von Ditfurth, *Aspekte der Angst* (Stuttgart), pp. 124–129; 1974², pp. 150–156.

[65g] "Erkenntnis und Interesse." Inaugural lecture, Frankfurt, 28 June. Reprinted in: *Merkur* 19 (No. 213), pp. 1139–1153; TWI, pp. 146–168; *Inquiry* (Norway) 1966, 9 (No. 4), pp. 285–300; D. Emmet, A. MacIntyre (Eds.), *Sociological Theory and Philosophical Analysis* (London 1970), pp. 36–55; *Knowledge and Human Interests,* pp. 301–317. (c.f. entry 71a).

1966

66a "Deutschland wohin? Ansichten und Einsichten: Karl Japsers über den moralischen Notstand in der Bundesrepublik" (Whither Germany? perspectives and insights: Karl Jaspers and the moral plight of the Bundesrepublik) *Die Zeit* 20, 13 May; PPP, pp. 109–115.

[66b] "Technischer Fortschritt und soziale Lebenswelt" *Praxis* (Zagreb), 2 (No. 1–2), pp. 217–228; TWI, pp. 104–119; H. Kreuzer (Ed.), *Literarische und Naturwissenschaftliche Intelligenz* (Stuttgart 1969), pp. 238–253. In English, TRS, pp. 50–61.

66c "Die Geschichte von den zwei Revolutionen" (The history of the two revolutions, on Hannah Arendt) *Merkur* 20 (No. 218), pp. 479–483; KuK, pp. 365–370; AEF, pp. 141–146.

66d "Zwangsjacke für die Studienreform. Die befristete Immatrikulation und der falsche Pragmatismus der Wissenschaftrates" (Straight-jacket for university reform. The time-limit on matriculation and the false pragmatism of the Science Council) *Der Monat* 18 (No. 218); pp. 7–13; S. von Leibfried (Ed.), *Wider die Untertanen-Fabrik* (Cologne 1967), pp. 86–96, 384; PuH, pp. 92–107.

[66e] "Zu Hegels politische Schriften, Nachwort," Hegel, *Politischen Schriften* (Frankfurt/Main 1966), pp. 343–370; TuP, 1971, pp. 148–172; AEF, pp. 312–335. In English: TaP, pp. 170–194.

66f "Strukturwandel der Öffentlichkeit." Abridged version of *Strukturwandel der Öffentlichkeit* (c.f. entry 62a) H. U. Wehler (Ed.), *Moderne deutsche Sozialgeschichte* (Cologne), pp. 197–223, 496–503.

66g "Verwissenschaftlichte Politik in demokratischer Gesellschaft," H. Krauch, W. Kunz, H. Rittel (Ed.), *Forschungsplanung. Eine Studie über Ziele und Strukturen amerikanischer Forschungsinstitute* (Munich-Vienna), pp. 130–144.

66h "Soziologie," H. Von Kunst, S. Grundmann (Eds.), *Evangelisches Staatslexikon,* (Kreuz-Verlag, Stuttgart), pp. 2108–2113.

66j "Partisanenprofessor im Lande der Mitläufer. Der Marburger Ordinarius Wolfgang Abendroth wird am 2 Mai sechzig Jahre alt," *Die Zeit* 29 April, p. 24.

66k "Thesen gegen die Koalition der Mutlosen mit den Machthabern," *Diskus* (Frankfurter Studentenzeitung), December, p. 2.

1967

67a *Zur Logik der Sozialwissenschaften* (The logic of the social sciences) *Philosophische Rundschau* 14, Beiheft 5, 1966–1967 (Tübingen). Reprinted in: LSW, pp. 71–310. (c.f. entry 70a).

Reviews: Y. Gauthier, *Dialogue* 1967/1968, 6, pp. 604–609; C. Menze, *Vierteljahrschrift für wissenschaftliche Pädagogik,* 1968, 44 (No. 4), pp. 343–349; H. Albert, *Kölner Zeitschrift für Soziologie und Sozialpsychologie,* 1968, 20 (No. 2), pp. 341–345; O. F. Bollnow, *Zeitschrift für Pädagogik,* 1968, 14 (No. 1), pp. 69–78; G. Floeistad, *Inquiry,* 1970, 13, pp. 175–198; A. Geuss, *Soziale Welt,* 1969, 20 (No. 2), pp. 213–220.

[67b] "Arbeit und Interaktion. Bemerkungen zu Hegels Jenenser Philosophie des Geistes," H. Braun, M. Riedel (Eds.), *Natur und Geschichte. Karl Löwith zum 70. Geburtstag*, Stuttgart, pp. 132–156; TWI, pp. 9–47. In English: TaP, pp. 142–169, as "Labor and Interaction: Remarks on Hegel's Jena 'Philosophy of Mind'."

[67c] "Universität in der Demokratie—Demokratisierung der Universität." Address delivered at the Berliner Universitätstage, 20 Jan. 1967. Reprinted in *Merkur* 21 (No. 230), pp. 416–433; *Universitätstage* (Freie Universität, Berlin, 1967), pp. 67–79; PuH, pp. 108–133. In English: TRS, pp. 1–12.

67d "Offener Brief an den AStA der Freien Universität Berlin" (Open letter to the Student Government, Free University of Berlin) (Co-author: L. von Friedeburg), April 1967. Reprinted in: PuH, pp. 134–136.

67e "Rede über die politische Rolle der Studentenschaft in der Bundesrepublik" (The political role of student organisations in West Germany). Address delivered at the congress "Hochschule und Demokratie" in Hannover, 9 June 1967. Reprinted in: *Der Politologe* (Berliner Zeitschrift für Wissenschaft) 23, pp. 2, 6ff.; *Stimme der Gemeinde zum Kirchlichen Leben, zur Politik, Wirtschaft und Kultur* (Frankfurt/Main) 19 (No. 15–16), pp. 469–474; *Voltaire-Flugschrift* (Berlin), 12, pp. 42–49; PuH, pp. 137–146.

67f "Diskussionsbeiträge" (Contributions to the debate) *Voltaire-Flugschrift* (Berlin), 12: *Bedingungen und Organisation des Widerstandes. Der Kongress in Hannover*, pp. 75–77, 100–103; PuH, pp. 146–149.

67g "Brief an Erich Fried" (Letter to Erich Fried) PuH, pp. 149–151.

[67h] "Studentenprotest in der Bundesrepublik." Address delivered at the Goethe-Haus in New York. PuH, pp. 153–177. In English: TRS, pp. 13–30.

67j "Nachwort," H. Plessner, H. Boch, D. Grupe (Eds.), *Sport und Leibeserziehung*, (Munich: Piper), p. 121. (c.f. 58d).

1968

[68a] *Technik und Wissenschaft als 'Ideologie'* (Technology and science as "ideology") (Frankfurt/Main 1969^{2+3}, 1970^4, 1971^5, 1973^6, 1976^8). Translated into English, French, Italian, Norwegian, Dutch, Japanese. Contents: 67b, 68c, 66b, 64a, 65g. Reviews: O. Pöggeler, *Bibliographie de la Philosophie*, 1970, 16, p. 290; D. Misgeld, *Dialogue*, 1972, 11, pp. 155–159; W. Steinbeck, *Zeitschrift für philosophische Forschung*, 1972, 26, pp. 469–470. English translation: item 67b in *Theory and Practice*; 68c-66b-64a are translated in *Towards a Rational Society*; item 65g in *Knowledge and Human Interests*.

[68b] *Erkenntnis und Interesse*, with a new postscript (Frankfurt/Main 1973^4) (c.f. entry 73h). Translated into English, Italian, French, Serbocroatian (for English version, c.f. entry 71a). Reviews: R. Bubner, *Philosophische Rundschau*, 1969, 16, pp. 229–249; N. Lobkowicz, *Philosophische Rundschau*, 1969, 16, pp. 249–273; J. de Vries, *Stimmen der Zeit*, 1970, 186, pp. 214–215; U. Anacker,

"Erkenntnis und Interesse; Ein Diskussionsbeitrag zu Jürgen Habermas' . . . ," *Philosophisches Jahrbuch* (Freiburg i. Br.), 1971, 78, pp. 394–401; K. Lorenz, *Bibliographie de la Philosophie*, 1971, 18, pp. 308–309; K. Priester, *Marxistische Blätter*, Sept./Oct. 1973, pp. 112–114.

[68c] "Technik und Wissenschaft als 'Ideologie'," *Merkur* 22 (No. 243), pp. 591–610 and (No. 244), pp. 682–693. The paper is reprinted in the book of the same title: TWI, pp. 48–103; also in *Man and World* 1 (No. 4), pp. 483–523; D. Ulich (Ed.), *Theorie und Methode der Erziehungswissenschaft* (Basle 1972), pp. 342–378. In English: TRS, pp. 81–122.

68d "Einleitung einer Podiumsdiskussion" (Introducing a panel-discussion) PuH, pp. 178–184.

68e "Zu Nietzsches Erkenntnistheorie. Ein Nachwort" (Nietzsche's epistemology: a postscript). Postscript to Fr. Nietzsche, *Erkenntnistheoretische Schriften*, H. Holz (Ed.), (Frankfurt/Main), pp. 237–262; KuK, pp. 239–263; AEF, pp. 356–376.

68f "Thesen zur Theorie der Sozialisation" (Theses on socialisation-theory. Lecture notes: Summer semester 1968) KuK, pp. 118–194; AEF, pp. 376–430.

68g "Einleitung zu einer Antifestschrift. Zum 70. Geburtstag von Herbert Marcuse. Zum Geleit" (Introduction to an anti-festschrift: on the occasion of Herbert Marcuse's 70th Birthday. By way of a preface) J. Habermas (Ed.), *Antworten auf Herbert Marcuse* (Frankfurt/Main), pp. 9–16; PPP, pp. 168–175.

68h "Brief an C. Grossner" (Letter to Cl. Grossner) PuH, pp. 151–152.

68j "Minister Stoltenberg diffamiert bedenkenlos" (Minister Stoltenberg defames thoughtlessly) (Co-authors: Fetscher, von Friedeburg, Mitscherlich) *Frankfurter Rundschau* 9 May; PuH, pp. 185–187.

68k "Die Scheinrevolution und ihre Kinder. 6 Thesen über Taktik, Ziele und Situationsanalyse der oppositionellen Jugend" (The phoney revolution and its children. Six theses on the tactics, aims and political conceptions of the rebellious youth) *Frankfurter Rundschau* 5 June; O. Negt (Ed.), *Die Linke antwortet Jürgen Habermas* (Frankfurt/Main 1968), pp. 5–15; *Pädagogische Beiträge* 20 (No. 10), pp. 551–556; PuH, pp. 188–201; H. Baier (Ed.), *Studenten in Opposition. Beiträge zur Soziologie der deutschen Hochschule* (Bielefeld 1968), pp. 151–160.

68m "Grundsätze für ein neues Hochschulrecht" (Foundations for a new university code) (Co-authors: Denninger, von Friedeburg, Wiethölter) *Frankfurter Allgemeine Zeitung* 23 July; PuH, pp. 202–216.

68n "Heilige Kühe der Hochschulreform" (The holy cows of university reform) *Die Zeit* 23 (No. 39), p. 17; PuH, pp. 216–223.

68p "Ein Beitrag zur Diskussion des Hessischen Hochschulgesetzentwurfs" (A contribution to the discussion about new university legislation proposals in Hessen) (Co-authors: Denninger, von Friedeburg, Wiethölter) *Der Spiegel* 2 December; PuH, pp. 223–234.

68q "Gegen Wissenschaftsstürmerei" (Against anti-intellectualism) PuH, pp. 244–248.

68r "Praktische Folgen der wissenschaftlich-technischen Fortschritts" (The practical effects of technical-scientific progress) H. Maus (Ed.), *Gesellschaft, Recht und Politik. Festschrift für W. Abendroth* (Niewied Berlin), pp. 121–146; TuP, 1971, pp. 336–359; AEF, pp. 335–356.

68t "Scheinrevolution unter Handlungszwang. Über Fehldenken und Fehlverhalten der linken Studentenbewegung" (Pseudo-revolution and the compulsion to "do something." Concerning errors of judgment and errors of behavior on the part of the left-wing student movement) *Der Spiegel* 22 (No. 24), pp. 57–59.

68u "Werden wir richtig informiert?" (Are we being correctly informed?) *Die Zeit* 31 May; AEF, pp. 146–149.

1969

69a *Protestbewegung und Hochschulreform* (Protest movement and university reform) (Frankfurt/Main 1969², 1970³). Contents: 69c, 57a, 62c, 65d, 66d, 67c, 67d, 67e, 67f, 67g, 68h, 67h, 68d, 68j, 68k, 68m, 68n, 68p, 69d, 68q.

Reviews: G. Kloss, *Minerva*, 1972, 10 (No. 3), pp. 495–498; H. Beth, *Liberal* (Bonn), 1969, 11 (No. 8–9), pp. 709–715; K. Horn in *Frankfurter Allgemeine Zeitung* 14 July 1969.

69b "Odyssee der Vernunft in der Natur. Theodor W. Adorno wäre am 11 September 66 Jahre alt geworden" (Odyssey of reason in nature. Theodor W. Adorno would have turned 66 on 11 September) *Die Zeit* 12 Sept. Reprinted in: H. Schweppenhäuser (Ed.), *Theodor W. Adorno zum Gedächtnis* (Frankfurt/Main 1971), pp. 26–39; PPP, pp. 184–199 (under the new title of "Urgeschichte der Subjektivität und verwilderte Selbstbehauptung"); PKR, pp. 33–47.

[69c] "Einleitung" (introduction to PuH), PuH, pp. 9–50. In English: TRS, pp. 31–49 (abridged version)

69d "Empfehlungen zur technokratischen Hochschulreform?" (Recommendations for a technocratic university reform?) H. W. Nicklas (Ed.), *Politik, Wissenschaft, Erziehung. Festschrift für E. Schutte* (Frankfurt/Main), pp. 77–82; PuH, pp. 234–243.

69e "Bedingungen für eine Revolutionierung spätkapitalistischer Gesellschaftssysteme" (Preconditions for revolutionary change within late capital societies) *Praxis* (Zagreb) 5 (No. 1–2), pp. 212–223; E. Bloch, H. Marcuse et al., *Marx und die Revolution* (Frankfurt/Main 1970), pp. 24–44; KuK, pp. 70–87.

69f "Demokratisierung und Hochschule. Politisierung der Wissenschaft" (Democratisation and the universities. Politicization of science). Address to the "Westdeutschen Rektoren Konferenz," May. *Merkur* 23 (No. 255), pp. 597–604; TuP, 1971, pp. 376–387; AEF, pp. 430–439.

69g "Die wissenschaftstheoretischen Begründungen der Teilnahme der Mitglieder der Universität an den Entscheidungsprozessen und der Universitätsorganisation" (A science-theoretical justification for the participation of members of a university in its decisionmaking processes and its organisation) *Dokumentationsabteilung der Westdeutschen Rektorenkonferenz,* 1969 (Bad Godesberg), 50 pages.

69h "Für eine handlungsfähige Hochschule. Von einer bevorstehenden 'Herrschaft der Räte' an den Universitäten kann keine Rede sein," *Frankfurter Rundschau* 10 December.

1970

70a *Zur Logik der Sozialwissenschaften* (Towards a logic of the social sciences) (Frankfurt/Main 1971², 1973³), 329 pages. Translated into Italian. Reviews: c.f. entry 67a. Contents: 63j, 64e, 67a, 65e, 64c. English translation in part, as follows: 63j, 64e, 65e. The main text (67a) remains untranslated. For reviews: c.f. entry 67a; pp. 251–290 are "A Review of Gadamer's 'Truth and Method'," Dallmayr, McCarthy, op. cit. (c.f. entry 71h).

70b "Nachgeahmte Substantialität. Eine Auseinandersetzung mit Arnold Gehlens Ethik" (Counterfeit substantiality. Arnold Gehlen's ethics disputed) *Merkur* 24 (No. 4), pp. 313–327; PPP, pp. 200–221.

70c "Der Universalitätsanspruch der Hermeneutik" (Hermeneutics' claim to universality) R. Bubner, K. Cramer, R. Wiehl (Eds.), *Hermeneutik und Dialektik. Festschrift für H. G. Gadamer* (Tübingen), Part 1, pp. 73–104; K. O. Apel, C. Bormann et al. (Eds.), *Hermeneutik und Ideologiekritik* (Frankfurt/Main 1971), pp. 120–160; H. Holzer, K. Steinbacher (Eds.), *Sprache und Gesellschaft* (Hamburg 1972), pp. 86–105; KuK, pp. 264–301; AEF, pp. 439–467.

70d "Machtkampf und Humanität. Eine Erwiderung auf Ernst Topitsch," *Frankfurter Allgemeine Zeitung* 12 December; KuK, pp. 371–377.

[70e] "On Systematically Distorted Communication," *Inquiry* 13 (No. 3), pp. 205–218. Reprinted in: H. P. Dreitzel (Ed.), *Recent Sociology,* No. 2 (New York 1970), pp. 114–130; P. Connerton (Ed.), *Critical Sociology; Selected Readings* (abridged version, Penguin 1976), pp. 348–362.

[70f] "Towards a Theory of Communicative Competence," *Inquiry* 13 (No. 4), pp. 360–376. Reprinted in: H. P. Dreitzel (Ed.), *Recent Sociology,* No. 2 (New York 1970), pp. 130–148.

[70g] "Summation and Response" (of and to a colloquium, reprinted in same issue), *Continuum* (Chicago) 8 (No. 1).

70h "Über Sprachtheorie. Einführende Bemerkungen zu einer Theorie der kommunikativen Kompetenz" (Concerning linguistic theory. Introductory remarks about a theory of communicative competence). Reprinted (c.f. entry 71c), Vienna. Pirate edition.

70j "Gedanken zu einer sprachtheoretischer Grundlegung der Soziologie" (Sechs Gastvorlesungen, Berlin). Mimeograph, unpublished, c.f. entry 75c.

70k *Arbeit-Erkenntnis-Fortschritt. Aufsätze 1954–1970* (Work, knowledge, progress. Essays. . . .), unauthorized "pirate" edition, published without the author's consent (Amsterdam). Contents: 54b, 56c, 57c, 58d, 55c, 56d, 58e, 59b, 59c, 60b, 63q, 63m, 63n, 64c, 66c, 68u, 58a, 58c, 61c, 62d, 63p, 61b, 65e, 66e, 68r, 68e, 68f, 69f, 70c.

1971

[71a] *Knowledge and Human Interests* (Translator: Jeremy Shapiro), (London). Translation of 68b (without the postscript) and 65g. For the postscript of 68b, c.f. 73h.

Reviews: H. L. Parsons, *Philosophy and Phenomenological Research* (Buffalo), 1972, 33, pp. 281–282; R. E. Innis, *International Philosophical Quarterly* (New York), 1972, 13, pp. 555–563; B. Riesterer, *Thought,* 1972, 7, pp. 207–210; D. Misgeld, *Dialogue,* 1972, 11, pp. 639–643; S. Lukes, *The British Journal of Sociology,* 1972, 23, pp. 499–500; S. Ruddick, *Canadian Journal of Philosophy* (Alberta), 1973, 2, pp. 545–569; J. A. Bradley, *The Heythrop Journal* (London), 1973, 14, pp. 441–443; E. J. DeLattre, *The Journal of Value Inquiry* New York), 1974, 8, pp. 237–240; E. Vallance, *The Philosophical Quarterly* (S. Andrews), 1973, 23, pp. 170–172; G. Hawthorn, *Science Studies* (London), 1973, 13 (3), pp. 78–87; R. Ginsberg, *The Philosophy Forum* (Dekalb), 1973, 13, pp. 125–129; R. W. Miller, *The Philosophy Review,* 1975, 84, pp. 261–267; M. Kohl, *Philosophy and Phenomenological Research,* 1972, 33 (2), pp. 281–283; K. L. Deutsch, *American Political Science Review,* March 1975. For a reader on secondary literature, c.f. W. Dallmayr (Ed.), *Materialien zu Habermas' 'Erkenntnis und Interesse'* (Frankfurt/Main 1974). English-language references quoted therein: G. Fløistad, *Inquiry* 13, 1970, pp. 175–198; G. Therborn, *New Left Review,* May/June 1971, 67; C. Nichols, *Philosophy of the Social Sciences,* 1972, 2, pp. 261–270. A. Giddens, *Sociology,* 1977, 83, pp. 198–212.

71b *Philosophisch-politisch Profile* (Philosophical-political sketches), (Frankfurt/Main 1973²). Translated into French. Contents: 71g, 61a, 53a, 59a, 59b, 56a, 58b, 66a, 63h, 65b, 60a, 68g, 63k, 69b, 70b, 59c, 65a, 71f. In English: c.f. entries 60a, 71f.

Reviews: O. Spear, *Universitas* (Stuttgart), 1972, 27, pp. 1002–1003; O. Spear, *Philosophy and History* (Tübingen), 1972, 5, pp. 140–142.

71c *Theorie der Gesellschaft oder Sozialtechnologie. Was leistet die Systemforschung?* (Theory of Society or Social Technology. What Does Systemstheory Provide?), (Co-author: Niklas Luhmann), (Frankfurt/Main 1976⁵). Translated into Italian. By Habermas: "Vorbereitende Bemerkungen zu einer Theorie der kommunikativen Kompetenz," pp. 101–141; and "Theorie der Gesellschaft oder Sozialtechnologie? Eine Auseinandersetzung mit Niklas Luhmann," pp. 142–290. Reviews: J. H. Kaufmann, *Dialogue*, 1973, 12, pp. 184–189; K. H. Tjaden, *Das Argument*, 1972, 14, pp. 153–160. In book form: *Beiträge zur Habermas-Luhmann Diskussion*, Supplement I, II, and III.

Supplement I: F. Maciejewski (Ed.), *Theorie der Gesellschaft oder Sozialtechnologie* (Frankfurt/Main 1973).

Supplement II: F. Maciejewski (Ed.), *Theorie der Gesellschaft oder Sozialtechnologie* (Frankfurt/Main 1974).

Supplement III: H. J. Giegel, *System und Krise* (Frankfurt/Main 1975).

[71d] *Theorie und Praxis* (c.f. entry 63a), fourth edition, revised, expanded, with new introduction (Frankfurt/Main). Contents: 71j, 63b, 63c, 63d, 66e, 63e, 63f, 62b, 63g, 68r, 63p, 69f, 57b. English translation: c.f. entry 74c & 71j.

[71e] *Towards a Rational Society: Student protest, science and politics.* (Translator: Jeremy J. Shapiro), (London). Contents: 67c, 67h, 69c, 66b, 64a, 68c. A. Giddens, *Sociology*, 1977, 83, pp. 198–212.

Reviews: D. A. Kelly, *Philosophy and Phenomenological Research* (Buffalo), 1971, 32, pp. 281–283; D. Misgeld, *Dialogue*, 1972, 11, pp. 155–159; G. Hawthorn, *Science Studies* (London), 1973, 3, pp. 78–87.

[71f] "Die deutsche Mandarine." A review of F. K. Ringer, *The Decline of the German Mandarins. The German Academic Community 1890–1933* (Cambridge, Mass.), 1969, 528 pages. PPP, pp. 239–251. In English: *Minerva* (London), 9 (No. 3), pp. 422–428.

[71g] "Wozu noch Philosophie?" Radio broadcast, Hessischer Rundfunk, 4 January 1971. Reprinted: PPP, pp. 11–36. In English: "Why More Philosopy," *Social Research* (Albany), 38 (No. 4), pp. 633–654.

[71h] "Zu Gadamers 'Wahrheit und Methode'," K. O. Apel et al., *Hermeneutik und Ideologiekritik* (Frankfurt/Main), pp. 45–57; this is a reprint of LSW, 1967, pp. 172–179 and of LSW, 1970, pp. 251–290. In English: "A Review of Gadamer's 'Truth and Method'," F. Dallmayr, T. McCarthy (Eds.), *Understanding and Society Enquiry* (Indiana, USA, 1977), pp. 335–363.

[71j] "Einige Schwierigkeiten beim Versuch, Theorie und Praxis zu vermitteln. Einleitung zur Neuausgabe 'Theorie und Praxis'," TuP, 1971, pp. 9–48; P. Hucklenbroich et al. (Eds.), *Wissenschaftskritik. Struktur und Strategie des Wissenschaftsbetriebs* (Kronberg, 1974), pp. 27–73. In English: TaP, pp. 1–40.

1972

72a "Die Utopie des guten Herrschers. Eine Antwort an Robert Spaemann (The Pipe-dream of the benevolent dictatorship; an answer to Robert Spaemann) *Merkur* 26 (No. 296), pp. 1266–1273; KuK, pp. 378–388.

72b "Notizen zum Begriff der Rollenkompetenz" (Notes on the concept of role competence) KuK, pp. 195–231.

458

A Bibliography of Works by Habermas

72c "Aus einem Brief an Helmuth Plessner" (Extracts from a letter to Helmuth Plessner) *Merkur* 26 (No. 293), pp. 944–946; KuK, pp. 232–235.

72d "Bewusstmachende oder rettende Kritik. Die Aktualität Walter Benjamins. (Critique which brings awareness and rescues: The Contemporary relevance of Walter Benjamin) S. Unseld (Ed.), *Zur Aktualität Walter Benjamins* (Frankfurt/Main), pp. 175–223; KuK, pp. 302–344; PKR, pp. 48–95.

72e "Zwischen Kunst und Politik. Eine Auseinandersetzung mit Walter Benjamin" (Between art and politics: A critique of . . .) *Merkur* 26 (No. 293), pp. 856–869.

72f "Einige Bemerkungen zum Problem der Bergründung von Werturteilen" (Some comments on the problem of justifying value judgments) L. Landgrebe (Ed.), *Philosophie und Wissenschaft. 9. Deutscher Kongress für Philosophie* (Düsseldorf 1969), pp. 89–100.

72g "Diskussion: Autorität und Revolution" (A panel discussion; participants: Benseler, v. Friedeburg, Adorno, Lenk, Hofmann, Krahl, Wolff, Habermas, Holz, Strecker). Reprinted in: *Autorität-Organisation-Revolutiin* (s' Gravenhage, The Netherlands), Adorno, Agartz et al. (Eds.). Also reprinted in: *Politbuchvertrieb: Rotdruck* 24 (Giessen).

1973

73a *Arbeit-Freizeit-Konsum. Frühe Aufsätze.* (Work, leisure, consumption: Early essays). Unauthorized "pirate" edition. Contents: 54b, 56c, 56d, 57c, 58d (s' Gravenhage, The Netherlands).

73b *Kultur und Kritik. Verstreute Aufsätze.* (Culture and critique: Scattered essays), Frankfurt/Main. Contents: 61b, 64b, 69e, 58c, 63q, 68f, 72b, 72c, 68e, 70c, 72d, 73d, 60b, 66c, 70d, 72a, 73j.

[73c] *Legitimationsprobleme im Spätkapitalismus* (Frankfurt/Main 1977⁴). Translated into English, French, Spanish.

Reviews: S. Gassert, K. Meyer, *Frankfurter Rundschau*, 1974, 46, p. 4; J. Rieder, N. Wiley, *Contemporary Sociology*, 1977, 6, (No. 4), pp. 411–424; M. Theunissen, *Frankfurter Allgemeine Zeitung*, 9 Oct. 1973; G. Höhn, "Habermas et le matérialisme historique," *La Quinzaine Littéraire*, 1975, No. 210, pp. 23–24. In English: *Legitimation Crisis* (Boston 1975), (Translator: T. McCarthy); A. Giddens, *Sociology*, 1977, 83, pp. 198–212; D. Held, *The Sociological Review* (new series) 1978, 26, pp. 183–194; J. Rex, *Sociology* (London), pp. 561–566.

Reviews: D. Held, L. Simon: "Towards understanding Habermas. Review essay of Legitimation Crisis," *New German Critique*, Winter 1976, No. 7; J. Miller, "Jürgen Habermas; Legitimation Crisis," *Telos*, Fall 1975, No. 25, pp. 210–220; J. J. Shapiro, "Reply to Miller's Review of Habermas's Legitimation Crisis," *Telos*, Spring 1976, No. 27, pp. 170–177; R. Lowenthal, "Social Transformation and Democratic Legitimacy," *Social Research* 43 (No. 2), Summer 1976, pp. 246–275.

73d "Herbert Marcuse über Kunst und Revolution" (Herbert Marcuse on Art and Revolution) *Frankfurter Allgemeine Zeitung* 9 June; KuK, pp. 345–351; PKR, pp 96–102.

73e "Wahrheitstheorien" (Theories of truth) H. Fahrenbach (Ed.), *Wirklichkeit und Reflexion. Festschrift für W. Schulz* (Pfüllingen), pp. 211–265. (c.f. G. Skirbekk: *Wahrheitstheorien*, Frankfurt/Main, 1977).

73f "Was heisst heute Krise? Legitimationsprobleme im Spätkapitalismus." Address to the Goethe Institute, Rome. Reprinted in: *Merkur* 27 (No. 4–5), p. 345–364; RHM, pp. 304–328; W. Oelmüller (Ed.), *Weiterentwicklung des Marxismus* (Darmstadt 1977), pp. 408–435. In English: "What Does a Crisis Mean Today? Legitimation problems in Late Capitalism," *Social Research*, 1973, 40 (No. 4), pp. 643–667; P. Connerton (Ed.), *Critical Sociology. Selected Readings* (abridged version, Penguin 1976), pp. 363–387.

73g "Demokratie und Planung" (Democracy and planning) *Neues Forum* (Vienna) 20 (No. 223), pp. 34–36.

[73h] "Nachwort." A new 'postscript' to *Erkenntnis und Interesse* (c.f. entry 68b). In English "A Postscript to 'Knowledge and Human Interests'," *Philosophy and the Social Sciences* (Aberdeen), 3 (No. 2), pp. 157–185.

73j "Über das Subjekt der Geschichte. Diskussionsbemerkung zu falsch gestellten Alternativen" (Concerning the "historical subject." Some comments on falsely posed alternatives) R. Koselleck, W. D. Stempel (Eds.), *Geschichte und Erzählung* (Munich), pp. 470–477; KuK, pp. 389–398.

1974

[74a] "Können komplexe Gesellschaften eine vernünftige Identität ausbilden?" Paper delivered on the occasion of the award, by the City of Stuttgart, of the Hegel Prize to Habermas, 19 Jan. 1974. Reprinted in: *Zwei Reden* (Coauthor: D. Henrich), (Frankfurt/Main), pp. 23–84; RHM, pp. 92–126. English version (abridged): "On Social Identity," *Telos*, Spring (No. 19), pp. 91–103.

Reviews: M. J. Rudolph, "Wo finden wir unsere Identität? Der Hegel-Preis für Habermas und Habermas' Rede," *Frankfurter Allgemeine Zeitung*, 21 January 1974, p. 2; K. Podak, "Auf der Suche nach Identität. Jürgen Habermas erhielt Hegel-Preis der Stadt Stuttgart," *Süddeutsche Zeitung* (Munich), 21 January 1974, p. 8; F. Weigend, "Wider eine schlechte Wirklichkeit. Die Hoffnung d. Hegel-Preisträgers Jürgen Habermas," *Stuttgarter Zeitung*, 21 January 1974, p. 12; R. Vollmann, "Wie an einem Ende. Hegel-Preis für Habermas," *Die Zeit*, 25 January 1974, p. 18; A. Gethmann-Siefert, *Hegel-Studien*, 1975, 10, pp. 355–357.

[74b] "Die Rolle der Philosophie im Marxismus," *Praxis* 10 (No. 1–2), pp. 45–52; M. Gerhardt (Ed.), *Die Zukunft der Philosophie* (Munich 1975), pp. 191–205; RHM, pp. 49–59. In English: "The Place of Philosophy in Marxism," *Insurgent Sociologist* (USA) 5 (No. 2), pp. 41–48.

[74c] *Theory and Practice* (London), (Translator: John Viertel). Contents: 71j, 63b, 63c, 63d, 67b, 66e, 63f, 63g. (c.f. entries 63a & 71d.).

Reviews: R. E. Innis, *Social Praxis,* 1974, 2 (No. 1-2), pp. 145–156; D. MacRae, Jr., *American Journal of Sociology,* Jan. 1975, pp. 1078–1079; O. Blanchette, *Studies in Soviet Thought,* 1975, 15, pp. 341–351; L. Feuer, *Contemporary Sociology,* July 1974 (c.f. next two issues of same journal for controversy); A. Giddens *Sociology,* 1977, 83, pp. 198–212; N. J. Smelser, *Social Forces,* 1975, p. 650.

74d "Beitrag zur Podiumdiskussion" (Contribution to a panel-discussion) M. Baumgarten, O. Höffe, C. Wild (Eds.), *Philosophie, Gesellschaft, Planung* (Munich), (Bayerische Hochschulforschung, Sonderband), pp. 186–188.

[74e] "Habermas Talking: An Interview" (Interviewer: Boris Frankel), *Theory and Society* 1 (1974), pp. 37–58.

74f "Sie werden nicht schweigen können." Ein Briefwechsel zwischen Jürgen Habermas und W. R. Beyer (Ein Satyrspiel um Philosophie, Politik und Vereinsmeierei: Wie man Jürgen Habermas vom Moskauer Hegel-Kongress fernhielt), *Die Zeit,* 23 September (No. 38), p. 22.

1975

75a "Ein biedermeierlicher Weg zum Sozialismus?" (Co-authors: S. Skarpelis-Sperk, Peter Kalmbach, Claus Offe), *Der Spiegel,* 1975 (No. 9), p. 44.

[75b] *Zur Entwicklung der Interaktionskompetenz* (Frankfurt/Main). Unauthorized pirate edition of unpublished Starnberg paper. A fragment of this has subsequently been published as "Universalpragmatische Hinweise auf das System der Ich-Abgrenzungen" in M. Auwärter, E Kirsch, M. Schröter (Eds.), *Kommunikation, Interaktion, Identität* (Frankfurt/Main 1976), pp. 332–347. In English: "Some Distinctions in Universal Pragmatics; a working Paper," *Theory and Society,* Summer 1976, 3 (No. 2).

75c "Sprachspiel, Intention und Bedeutung. Zu Motiven bei Sellars und Wittgenstein" (Language-game, intention and meaning; on the question of motives in Sellars and Wittgenstein). Lecture series delivered within the ambit of the Christian Gauss Lectures, Princeton University, 1971. Reprinted in: R. Wiggershaus, (Ed.), *Sprachanalyse und Soziologie* (Frankfurt/Main), pp. 319–341. (This is lecture 3 of a 6-lecture series; the others are unpublished. c.f. 70j, which is the German original.)

[75d] "Zur Rekonstruktion des Historischen Materialismus," Hegel Congress, May 1975. Reprinted in: RHM, pp. 144–200. In English: "Towards a Reconstruction of Historical Materialism," *Theory and Society* 2 (No. 3), pp. 287–300 (abridged version). Also in: *Arena* (No. 38), p. 69ff, as "Historical Materialism Reconsidered"; and *Communications and the Evolution of Society* (Boston 1979), c.f. entry 76a.

75e "Kontroverse über 'Herrschaft und Legitimität'." Reply to W. Fach. (Controversy over "Domination and legitimacy") *Soziale Welt* 26 (No. 1), pp. 112–117, 120–121; RHM, pp. 329–337.

[75f] "Moralentwicklung und Ich-Identität." Lecture delivered at the Institut für Sozialforschung in Frankfurt, July 1974. Reprinted in: RHM, pp. 63–91. English version: "Moral Development and Ego Identity," *Telos* 24 (Summer), pp. 41–56; and *Communication and the Evolution of Society* (c.f. 76a).

[75g] "A Reply to Müller and Neusüss," *Telos*, No. 25 (Fall), pp. 91–99. This is an extract from *Legitimation Crisis* (entry 73c), pp. 50–60, and is a reply to an article of above authors in *Sozialistische Politik*, 1970, 6–7, pp. 4–67.

75h "Legitimationsprobleme der Religion—Gesprächsauszüge Arbeitskreis Theologie und Politik." Discussion between Habermas, Sölle, Bahr et al. in Sölle, Habermas, Bahr et al., *Religiongespräche: zur Gesellschaftliche Rolle der Religion* (Luchterhand) Darmstadt, pp. 9–31.

1976

[76a] *Zur Rekonstruktion des Historischen Materialismus* (Frankfurt/Main 1976²). Contents: 76b, 74b, 75f, 74a, 76c, 75d, 76d, 76f, 76e, 73f, 75e, 76g.

Reviews: A. I. Ignatov, *Philosophische Literaturanzeiger*, 1977, 30, pp. 65–68; E..Bornemann, *Betrifft: Erziehung* (Weinheim), 1977, 10 (Nr. 6), pp. 74–75; A. Schneeberger *Wiener Jahrbuch für Philosophie*, 1977, 10, pp. 334–339; J. P. Aranson, *Telos*, No. 39, Spring 1979. In English: *Communication and the Evolution of Society* (Boston 1979), (Translator: T. A. McCarthy). Contents: 76j, 75f, 76b, 75d, 76e. Translated separately: c.f. 76d.

[76b] "Einleitung: Historischen Materialismus und die Entwicklung normativer Strukturen," RHM, pp. 9–49. In English: "Historical Materialism and the Development of Normative Structures," *Communication and the Evolution of Society* (c.f. entry 76a).

76c "Zum Theorienvergleich in der Soziologie: am Beispiel der Evolutionstheorie," (Co-author: K. Eder). Congress paper in *Verhandlungen des Soziologentages* (Stuttgart), RHM, pp. 129–144. Original title: "Zur Struktur Einer Theorie der Sozialen Evolution."

[76d] "Geschichte und Evolution." A reply to N. Luhmann's article, "Evolution und Geschichte;" both in *Geschichte und Gesellschaft* (Göttingen) 2 (No. 3), pp. 310–357; RHM, pp. 200–260. In English: "History and Evolution" *Telos* 39, Spring 1979.

[76e] "Legitimationsprobleme im modernen Staat." Congress paper, Deutsche Vereinigung für politische Wissenschaft, 1975. Reprinted in: *Merkur* 30 (No. 332), pp. 37–57 (abridged version); RHM, pp. 271–304. In English: "Legitimation Problems in the Modern State," *Communication and the Evolution of Society* (c.f. entry 76a).

76f "Überlegungen zum evolutionären Stellenwert des modernen Rechts," RHM, pp. 260–268.

76g "Zwei Bemerkungen zum praktischen Diskurs: Paul Lorenzen zum 60. Geburtstag" (Two comments on practical discourse. Paul Lorenzen's 60th Birthday) RHM, pp. 338–346.

76h "Wissenschafts- und Bildungssprache Beim Empfang des Sigmund-Freud-Preises" (c.f. entry 77c), *Süddeutsche Zeitung*, 23–24 October (No. 247). Reprinted in: *Jahrbuch der Deutsche Akademie für Sprache und Dichtung* (Heidelberg 1976), pp. 83–88.

[76j] "Was heisst Universalpragmatik?" in K. O. Apel (Ed.), *Sprachpragmatik und Philosophie* (Frankfurt/Main), pp. 174–273. In English: "What is Universal Pragmatics?" *Communication and the Evolution of Society* (c.f. entry 76a).

[76k] "Hannah Arendts Begriff der Macht," *Merkur* 30 (No. 341), pp. 946–961. In English: "Hannah Arendt's Communications Concept of Power," *Social Research* 44 (No. 1), 1977, pp. 3–24; PKR, pp. 103–127.

1977

77a "Antwort." Response to critical remarks of H. Girndt, E. Simons in P. Kielmansegg (Ed.), *Legitimationsprobleme politischer Systeme*, Sonderheft 7, *Politische Vierteljahresschrift*, 1976, pp. 76–80.

77b *Entwicklung des Ichs* (Ego-development), (Co-editors: R. Döbert, G. Nunner-Winkler), (Cologne). The introduction is by the editors: pp. 19–31.

77c "Umgangssprache, Wissenschaftssprache, Bildungssprache." Paper delivered at the Max Planck Institut, Bielefeld. *Max-Planck-Gesellschaft*, Jahrbuch 1977, pp. 36–51 (Göttingen). Radio broadcast, May 1977. Reprinted in *Merkur*, 1978, 32 (No. 4), pp. 327–342.

[77d] "Probe für Volksjustiz. Zu den Anklage gegen die Intellektuellen," *Der Spiegel* 10 October, p. 32. In English: "A Test for Popular Justice: The Accusations Against the Intellectuals," *New German Critique*, Fall 1977 (No. 12), pp. 11–13.

77e "Die Bühne des Terrors. Ein Brief an Kurt Sontheimer," *Merkur* 31 (No. 10), pp. 944–959. Reprinted under the new title of "Stumpf gewordene Waffen aus dem Arsenal der Gegenaufklärung. An Prof. Kurt Sontheimer," F. Duve, H. Böll, K. Staeck (Eds.), *Briefe zur Verteidigung der Republik* (Hamburg: Rowohlt), pp. 54–73. French version: *Esprit* 12 (Paris 1977), pp. 13–27. c.f. next entry.

77f "Linke, Terroristen, Sympathisanten; Ein Briefwechsel mit Kurt Sontheimer," *Süddeutsche Zeitung* 26/27 November. Abridged version reprinted in H. Glaser (Ed.), *Bundesrepublikanisches Lesebuch. Drei Jahrzehnte geistiger Auseinandersetzung*. Munich (Hanser), 1978, pp. 699–713.

77g "Der Demoralisierung widerstehen. Die jugoslawische Gruppe 'Praxis' stand immer zwischen den Feuern," *Die Zeit*, 2 December (No. 50).

1978

78a "Der Ansatz von Habermas." Protocolls from a congress in Paderborn, in Willi Oelmüller (Ed.), *Transzendentalphilosophische Normenbegründung* (Paderborn 1978).

78b "Wo bleiben die Liberalen? Wenn die Gesinnungsschutzbehörden Nebel verbreiten, brauchen wir vielleicht doch ein Russel-Tribunal," *Die Zeit*, 5 May 1978 (No. 19). Reprinted under the new title of "Das ernstlich Fatale an diesem Tribunal ist, dass wir es brauchen," F. Duve, H. Böll, K. Staeck (Eds.), *Briefe zur Verteidigung der bürgerliche Freiheit* (Hamburg: Rowohlt, 1978) (together with reply by the editor of *Die Zeit*), pp. 100–111.

[78c] "Theorie und Politik." Conversations with Marcuse: together with Heinz Lubasz, Tilman Spengler, in *Jürgen Habermas, Silvia Bovenschen u.a.: Gespräche mit Herbert Marcuse* (Frankfurt/Main 1978), pp. 9–64. *Merkur* 32 (No. 361), pp. 579–592. In English: "Theory and Politics: A Discussion with Herbert Marcuse, Jürgen Habermas, Heinz Lubasz and Telman [sic] Spengler," *Telos* 38, Winter 1978–1979, pp. 124–153. Also reprinted in: *New Political Science* (New York: Suhrkamp, 1979), pp. 19–29, under the title of "A Discussion on Democracy and Critical Theory."

[78d] *Politik, Kunst, Religion* (Politics, art, religion), (Stuttgart: Reclam). Contents: Vorwort, 60a, 69b, 72d, 73d, 76k, 78e. In English: c.f. 60a, 76k.

78e "Die verkleidete Tora. Rede zum 80. Geburtstag von Gershom Scholem" *Merkur* 1 (1978), pp. 96–104; PKR, pp. 127–144.

78f "Arzt und Intellektueller. Alexander Mitscherlich zum 70. Geburtstag" (Physician and intellectual: on Alexander Mitscherlich's 70th Birthday) *Die Zeit*, 22 September 1978 (No. 39).

[78g] "Response to the Commentary of Bernstein and Dove," D. P. Verene (Ed.), *Hegel's Social and Political Thought: The Philosophy of Objective Spirit* (New York: Humanities Press, 1978).

[78h] "Intervista con Jürgen Habermas. I potenziali critici nella societa" and "Crisi e democrazia" (Interviewer: A. Bolaffi) *Rinascita* (Italy), two parts: 28 July (No. 30), pp. 16–17 and 4 August (No. 31), pp. 16–17. In English: "Conservatism and Capitalist Crisis," *New Left Review* (No. 115), pp. 73–85. The *same* interview is titled "The Crisis of Late Capitalism and the Future Democracy," in *Telos*, Spring 1979 (No. 39).

1979

79a "Urbanisierung der Heideggerschen Provinz. Laudatio auf Hans-Georg Gadamer" in H. G. Gadamer, J. Habermas, *Das Erbe Hegels. Zwei Reden aus Anlass des Hegel-Preises* (Frankfurt am Main: Suhrkamp), pp. 9–31.

79b "Kolonialisierung der Lebenswelt? Bemerkungen zur intellektuellen Szene in der Bundesrepublik." This is Habermas's introduction to J. Habermas (Ed.), *Stichworte zur "Geistige Situation der Zeit"* (Frankfurt: Suhrkamp), two volumes. French translation: "La Colonisation du quotien. Sur la situation intellectuelle en Allemagne Féderale," *Esprit* (Paris), December 1979.

[79c] "Comments on papers by Ekman and Goffman," M. Von Cranach, F. Foppa, W. Lepenies, and D. Ploog (Eds.), *Human Ethology. Claims and Limits of a new Discipline.* Maison des Sciences de l'Homme and Cambridge University Press, pp. 241–245.

79d Interview with Gad Freudenthal (in Hebrew), *Machschavot* (Jerusalem), 48, pp. 70–79.

[79e] "Interview with Jürgen Habermas" (Interviewers: Detlev Horster, Willem van Reijen) *New German Critique,* Fall (No. 18), pp. 29–43. In Dutch: "Jürgen Habermas als burgerlijk intellektueel," *Intermediair* (Amsterdam), 26 June, pp. 1–7.

79f "Handlung und System—Bemerkungen zu Parsons' Medientheorie" W. Schluchter (Ed.), *Verhalten, Handeln und System. Talcott Parsons' Beitrag zur Entwicklung der Sozialwissenschaften* (Frankfurt: Suhrkamp), pp. 68–105.

1980

80a "Die Frankfurter Schule in New York—Max Horkheimer und die 'Zeitschrift für Sozialforschung,'" *Süddeutsche Zeitung* 2/3 August (No. 177).

80b "Die Moderne—ein unvollendetes Projekt. Rede aus Anlass des Adorno-Preises," *Die Zeit* 26 September (No. 39).

80c "On the German-Jewish Heritage," commencement address delivered at the New School for Social Research, June 4, 1980; published in *Telos* 44 (1980), pp. 127–131.

1981

81a "Talcott Parsons: Konstruktionsprobleme der Gesellschaftstheorie," *Verhandlungen des 20. Deutschen Soziologentages.*

81b *Theorie des Kommunikativen Handelns* (Frankfurt: Suhrkamp).

Index

Abel, Theodor, 145–146
Achievement ideology, 373
Action. *See also* Instrumental action
  communicative, 23, 290–291, 295, 435n29 (*see also* Speech acts)
  consensual, 289–290
  purposive-rational, 22, 24–25, 26, 28, 63
Action theory, 390n23
  as communication theory, 233
  framework of, 220–222
  in social inquiry, 354
  sociological, 335
Adaptation, in social evolution, 255. *See also* Social evolution
Administrative systems. *See also* Political systems
  bureaucratization of, 19
  and legitimation crisis, 368
  and rationality crisis, 366, 367
  and social organization, 6
  and social sciences, 9
Adolescent
  crisis, 343, 376, 385
  ego development of, 340
  identity formation of, 341–342
Adorno, Theodor W., 193, 333, 334
  on historical materialism, 20, 21, 22
  methodological views of, 135
  negative dialectic of, 105, 107, 108
  on technical interests, 66
Agreement. *See also* Consensus
  in communication theory, 290
  in language, 310
  rational consensus, 305, 328
Albert, Hans, 65
Anthropology
  of conceptual systems, 164
  criteria of rationality in, 318
  English cultural, 214
  functionalism in, 149

and human interests, 55
of knowledge, 122
and natural sciences, 138
of self-reflection, 92
in social evolution theory, 236
Apel, Karl-Otto, 96, 171, 320–321
Arendt, Hannah, 387n4
Argumentation, theoretical vs. practical, 313–314
Argumentative discourse, 292, 325. *See also* Discourse
Argumentative reasoning, 298, 308, 320–321
  in traditional societies, 320–321
  unity of, 298
Aristotle, 2, 35, 76
Art
  and capitalist society, 374
  Freudian view of, 86
Austin, J. L., 275, 300
Austin-Strawson debate, 299
Authority, vs. reason, 381
Autonomy. *See also Mündigkeit*
  and emancipatory interests, 78–79
  in formalist ethics, 352
  meaning and conditions of, 327–328
  and moral consciousness, 251
  of reason, 88, 90

Base, theory of, 243
Begründen, 427n2
Behavior, animal, 151
Behavior, human, 4. *See also* Socialization
  control of, 7
  deviant, 24
  incompetent, 24
  objectifying, 70
  and social inquiry, 145–146
  socialization of, 84

Critical reflection (*continued*)
Self-reflection
anthropological status of, 93
and emancipatory interests, 88,
101–102
Critical sciences, 58, 60, 386, 399n31
Critical sociology, 205
Critical theory
as advocacy, 332
aims of, 265, 269–270
and autonomous self, 333, 334
basis of, 101
and class interests, 383
development of, 126, 272
emancipatory interest of, 75
empirical aspects of, 134
foundations of, 381
of Frankfurt school, 386
and functionalism, 220
goal of, 273
Habermas's earlier formulations of,
177
and hermeneutics, 181–182,
187–193
and history, 267–268, 422n66
institutionalization of discourse, 293
methodology of, 261
moral-practical foundations for,
307 (*see also* Morality)
and political struggle, 209
and practice, 136, 207, 264–267,
378
psychology in, 195
self-application of, 210
social-psychological framework for,
334
vs. traditional theory, 112
Critique. *See also* Critical theory
identification with rigorous science,
107
legitimating grounds of, 108
Cultural sciences, 73. *See also* Science
hermeneutic goal of, 73
knowledge-constitutive interest of,
69–70
logic of inquiry in, 74
self-reflection of, 94
Cultural tradition, and societal
learning, 255. *See also*
Socialization; Tradition
Culture

bourgeois, 372, 374
and criteria of rationality, 318
Marx's view of, 68
prehistory, 122
Weber's concept of, 143
Cybernetics
and social organizations, 10–11
in systems theory, 223–224

Dallmayr, Fred, 398n19, 406n3,
415n62
Danto, A. C., 263, 379
on interpretation of historical
events, 176–177
on philosophy of history, 185–186
Darwin, Charles, 113
Decisionism, 105
Decisionistic models
for organization of society, 9
of political practice, 11
Decision making, democratic form
of, 39
Decision theory, 8
Defense mechanisms, formation of,
339. *See also* Psychoanalysis
Democracy, 15. *See also* Political
systems
discussion of, 331–332
formal, 368
Luhmann on, 228
Descriptions, reference system for,
297
Development
cognitive, 249, 338–339
dynamics of, 260
ego, 338–341, 434n10
interactive, 338–339, 344–353
linguistic, 338–339
of moral consciousness, 250,
350–353, 420
motivational, 339
Developmental logic, 246–247, 253,
269
and cognitive psychology, 246–247
and communicative competence,
321
conceptual shifts in, 429n32
of moral systems, 252, 376
Developmental studies, 336–337
Deviance, 24, 84
Dewey, John, 12

Peirce's view vs., 61
and science, 40
and social inquiry, 16
value-neutrality of, 7
Power
anthropological status of, 93
institutionalization of, 86
and relations of production, 38
in theory of knowledge, 59
Practical discourse, 210, 430nn2,3,7
logic of, 310–333
and norms, 312–313
rationally motivated consensus, 316
Practical interests, 56, 68–75
Practice
connection of language with, 163
critical theory and, 263, 264–267
ordinary language as, 166
and political theory, 378
Pragmatics
semantics and, 427n21
universal, 274
and critical theory, 399n31
goal of, 276
initial task of, 288
and sociocultural symbols, 356
and speech functions, 281–282
Preconceptions, and interpretive
understanding, 173
Predictions, in scientific method,
50–51
Preference systems, determinants of,
373
Prejudgments, 173, 175, 413n23
Prejudice, 79
Presuppositions, implicit, 101
"Primitive" societies, 215
discursive argumentation in, 324
and productive forces, 245
relations of production in, 243
taboos in, 320
transition from, 236
Privatism, civil, 369, 370, 371, 374,
385. See also Public sphere
Production
forces and relations of, 34, 237, 244
forces of, 238–239, 240
development of, 258
Marxist view of, 83
and kinship system, 238
modes of

anthropological status of, 240–241
"asiatic," 241
types of, 239
relations of, 17, 239, 244
defined, 243
and power, 38
repoliticization of, 364, 368
socialized, 366
Progress, 132
dialectic of, 259–260
scientific, 51
Propositional content
asserted, 300
in constative speech acts, 299
nature of, 424n20
of speech acts, 283
of utterances, 275
Protest syndromes, 376, 384–385
Protophysics, 409n38, 428n11
Psychoanalysis
and causal explanation, 201, 205
as depth hermeneutics, 197–198
development studies in, 336–337
and distorted communication,
197–198
Freudian, 75, 94
and general interpretations,
202–203
instinct theory in, 194, 416n3
interpretation of, 399n26
logic of, 204–205
metapsychology, 198
methodological features of, 400n55
and social critique, 205, 211
and social theory, 193–213
superego formation in, 339
theoretically generalized history
and, 221–222
theoretical structure of, 202
transference in, 212
Psycholinguistics, development
studies in, 336. See also Linguistics
"Public sphere," 11–12, 15
bourgeois, 388n22
depoliticization of, 368, 381–382
and hermeneutics, 15
refeudalization of, 382
repoliticization of, 385, 439n54
Purposive-rational action, 28
Marxist concept of, 22
moments of, 24–25

and class consciousness, 87
and class struggle, 384
Rickert, Heinrich, 140
Ricoeur, Paul, 180, 192
Rightness, discourse models of, 314, 323
Roles
  concept of, 162
  and ego formation, 342
  in functionalist theory, 221
  in identity formation, 341
  and legitimacy, 257
  phenomenological perspective on, 161
Role theory, and socialization, 334–335. *See also* Socialization
Romanticism, tradition in, 187
Rousseau, Jean Jacques
  on just political rule, 331
  on rational agreement, 432n34
Rules
  concept of, 162
  for identifying, 297
  of interpretation, 74, 161
  and meaningful expressions, 277
  in speech actions, 283, 284
Runciman, W. G., 144
Ryle, Gilbert, 276

Saint-Simon, Comte de, 137
Sanctions, 23–24
Schelling, F. W. J., 403n118
Schutz, Alfred, 140, 157, 158, 159, 162, 168
Science
  authority of, 374
  critically oriented, 58, 60, 386, 399n31
  cultural, 69, 70, 73, 74, 94
  empirical-analytic, 74
  expanded role of, 133
  hermeneutic, 73
  historical-hermeneutic, 58, 68–75
  history of, 301
    and consensus theory of truth, 305
    rational reconstruction of, 393n4
    validity claims, 301
  instrumentalist theory of, 64
  measurement operations in, 156
  metalanguage of, 69
  natural, 94, 154, 195

normative-analytic, 154
objectivity of, 58
vs. philosophy, 136
philosophy as, 102
philosophy of, 61, 129
political, 126
psychology of, 41
reconstructive, 276–279, 355–356, 401n59, 436n41
social, 1, 4, 5, 6, 138, 178
and technology
  and legitimization of power, 39
  progress of, 26
Scientific community, 43–44, 47, 66, 69
Scientific discourse, 208
Scientific inquiry
  goals of, 138–139
  and purposive-rational action, 63
Scientific method. *See also* Methodology
  critical attitude of, 47
  Popper's view of, 44–51
  predictions in, 50–51
Scientific theory, 4, 65
"Scientism," 41, 395
Scientistic assumptions, criticism of, 393n4
Searle, J. R., 283
Self-assertion, 31
Self-formative processes
  (*Bildungsprozesse*), 54, 79, 80, 397n12
  Hegel on, 32–33
  Marx's view of, 81, 83
  and subjective nature, 119
Self-knowledge, 230
Self-preservation, interest in, 90
Self-reflection. *See also* Reflection
  ambiguities in concept of, 94
  and emancipation, 88, 96
  emancipatory power of, 79
  and interests, 120 (*see also* Interests)
  phenomenological, 95
  and psychoanalysis, 200
Semantics, and pragmatics, 425n21. *See also* Linguistics; Pragmatics
Sensations, and reality, 116. *See also* Reality
Sensuous human activity, 22, 114
Sentences, in pragmatics, 274–275.

Values (*continued*)
in functionalist theory, 231–232
Gadamer's view of, 181
generalized, 315
"goal," 217
vs. interests, 380
phenomenological approach to, 161
and social classes, 104
Value systems
and decision theory, 8
Freudian view of, 86
irrationality in, 9
Parsonian view of, 220
suitability of, 10
and techniques, 12
universalistic, 376
Value theory, 364, 365
Verständigung, meaning of, 426n37
Verstehen (understanding)
Abel's reflections on, 147
and application of text, 179–180
Dilthey's approach to, 170
as heuristic device, 148
and history, 174–175
in logic of social sciences, 139, 145
neopositivist analysis of, 407n23
and participation, 180
and translation, 172
Winch's conception of, 167
Vico, Giovanni Battista, 1
Vienna circle, 137, 138, 162–163
Vorentwurf (preliminary projection), 172

Wage-labor relationship, Marxist view of, 38
Wages, "political," 364
Wahrheit und Methode, 170
Wartofsky, Marx, 391n43
Weber, Max, 4
classification of action, 28
concept of rationalization, 36
on modern man, 18–19
on political practice, 9
on purposive-rational action, 153
on revolution, 19
on social action, 25, 391n31
on social sciences, 140–145
social theory of, 221
on value judgments in social inquiry, 4

Welfare state, 370–371
Will-formation, discursive, 380
Winch, Peter, 166, 167, 168
criteria of rationality of, 318, 320
on logic of social inquiry, 317–318
Wittgenstein, Ludvig, 72, 140, 148, 197, 353
later philosophy of, 162–165
on understanding language, 171
Work, 30, 112. *See also* Labor
and human interests, 92, 93
vs. interaction, 36
as purposive-rational action, 28
in theory of knowledge, 59
World view
in archaic civilizations, 252
components of, 375
in functionalist theory, 231–232
legitimacy in, 229
restructuring of, 184
and social action, 147
and social evolution, 250
traditional, 373, 374
Wrong, Dennis, 334

Young Hegelians, 16, 17
Youth, in advanced capitalism, 385. *See also* Adolescent

Zur Logik der Sozialwissenschaften, 261
Zur Rekonstruktion des Historischen Materialismus, 242
Zweckrational (means-end rationality), 7